CORRECTIONS TODAY

CORRECTIONS TODAY

THIRD EDITION

LARRY SIEGEL
University of Massachusetts, Lowell

CLEMENS BARTOLLAS
University of Northern Iowa

Australia • Brazil • Japan • Korea • Mexico • Singapore • Spain • United Kingdom • United States

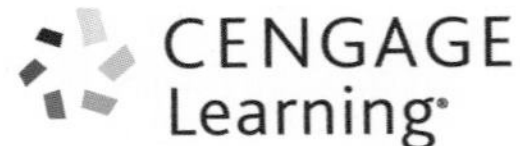

***Corrections Today*, Third Edition**
Larry Siegel and Clemens Bartollas

Product Director: Marta Lee-Perriard

Senior Product Manager: Carolyn Henderson Meier

Senior Content Developer: Shelley Murphy

Product Assistant: Stephen Lagos

Media Developer: Ting Jian Yap

Senior Marketing Manager: Kara Kindstrom

Senior Content Project Manager: Christy Frame

Art Director: Brenda Carmichael, Lumina Datamatics

Senior Manufacturing Planner: Judy Inouye

Production Service: Margaret McConnell, Integra

Photo Development: Kim Adams Fox

Photo Researcher: Veerabhagu Nagarajan, Lumina Datamatics

Text Researcher: Nandhini Srinivasagopalan, Lumina Datamatics

Copy Editor: Lunaea Weatherstone

Text and Cover Designer: Brenda Carmichael, Lumina Datamatics

Cover Images: left: Michael Beiriger/Alamy; right: Caro/Alamy

Interior Design Element:
© T33kid/Shutterstock.com;
© GlebStock/Shutterstock.com;
© GlebStock/Shutterstock.com

Composition: Integra

Library of Congress Control Number: 2014950538

ISBN: 978-1-305-26108-2

Cengage Learning
20 Channel Center Street
Boston, MA 02210
USA

Printed in China
2 3 4 5 6 18 17 16 15

This book is dedicated to my children, Eric, Andrew, Julie, and Rachel, and to my grandchildren, Jack, Kayla, and Brooke. It is also dedicated to Jason Macy (thanks for marrying Rachel) and Therese J. Libby (thanks for marrying me).

—LJS

To my wife, Linda, and my children, Kristin, Mya, and Kristen, and my grandchildren, Jake, Jordan, Rayne, Starley, Khosi, and Irie Sky.

—CB

LIST OF **CONTRIBUTORS**

Our thanks to the following corrections professionals who share their experience and expertise in these pages:

Shirley Addison
Judy Anderson
Allen Ault
Steven Ayers
Diane Bailey
Jennifer Wyatt Bourgeois
Alvin J. Bronstein
James H. Bruton
Mary Leftridge Byrd
Barbara Casey
Gina Curcio
James Dare
Derek DuFresne
Christopher E. Epps
Michael Fogel
Cathy Fontenot
Julie Fox
Arnot Gaston
Kent Grandlienard
James M. Higgins
Manny Jaquiss
Paul A. Magnuson
Carol Higgins O'Brien
Kay Pranis
Jim Redmond
Jennifer Reynoldson
Charles Samuels
Kelly Culshaw Schneider
Ray Stanelle
Jean Tomlinson
James Young

BRIEF CONTENTS

CONTENTS

PART THREE

How Do We Correct in the Community?

4 Intermediate Sanctions 89

PART FOUR

Where Do We Punish?

5 Jails and Houses of Correction 117

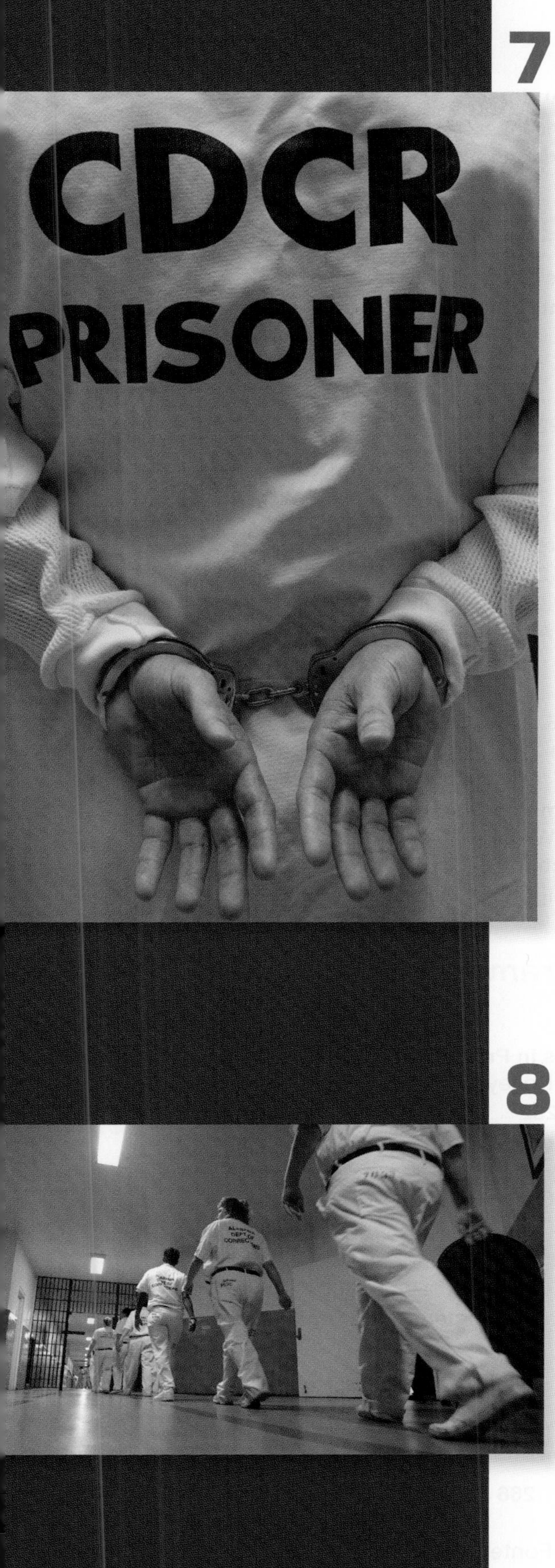

7 The Prison Experience: Males 173

8 The Prison Experience: Females 201

PART FIVE
How Do We Rehabilitate?

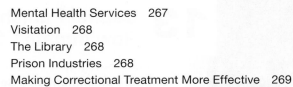

11 Parole and Release to the Community 275

PART SIX

What Are Special Needs Populations?

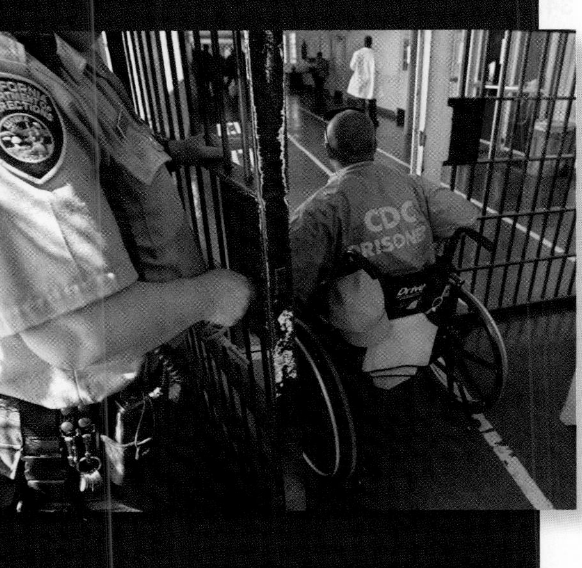

12 Special Prison Populations 299

13 Capital Punishment and the Death Row Inmate 319

14 The Juvenile Offender 343

PART SEVEN

What Is the Future of Corrections?

PREFACE

In 1999, Clayton Lockett and two other men drove to the Perry, Oklahoma, home of Bobby Lee Bornt, 23, who owed Lockett money. Bornt was tied up and beaten. During the assault, two young women happened to show up to see their friend, Bobby. They were pulled into the house, beaten, and bound. One of the women was raped by all three men, and then all three were driven to rural Kay County, where Lockett told the captives he was going to kill them all. He told one of the women, Stephanie Neiman, to get out of the pickup, and then shot her twice when she failed to give him her keys. The men dug a grave for Neiman and buried her while she was still alive. The other two women were left alive.

Lockett was arrested, convicted, and sentenced to death. He remained an anonymous death row inmate until April 29, 2014, when he was put to death. It was his bungled execution that brought attention to the case. His drug cocktail did not work, and he gasped and struggled in full view of observers as the lethal injection entered his veins; authorities quickly closed the curtains on the death chamber. Though he was unconscious 10 minutes after receiving the drug cocktail, Lockett's death via a heart attack happened 43 minutes after the drugs began flowing. A few days later Oklahoma's attorney general agreed to a six-month stay on new executions as the death process was evaluated.

The Lockett case illustrates why corrections is such a salient and important topic in contemporary criminal justice. While Lockett was hardly a sympathetic character, a rapist and career criminal who callously killed a young woman merely because she did not give him her car keys, his cruel execution brought outrage to those who oppose the death penalty. Who is correct? Those who seek legal vengeance for an unthinkable crime, or those who believe that the death penalty is both archaic and cruel? Should Lockett have spent the rest of his life in prison? And could someone like him ever be successfully rehabilitated? What is the proper course to take? After all, thousands of people are convicted of murder each year, but only a handful are executed. How can we fairly decide who is to live and who is to die? These are some of the dilemmas facing the contemporary correctional system.

GOALS AND OBJECTIVES

Despite sharing the same sense of horror and frustration felt by many Americans over how people are treated in the correctional system, we believe in this "new corrections" so much so that we wanted to create a textbook specifically designed to help train the "new corrections professional." We have had the opportunity to channel our interests in punishment and corrections into careers as professors of criminal justice, between us spending more than 50 years teaching, working within the corrections system, and consulting with correctional personnel. We have incorporated this lifetime of knowledge and service into *Corrections Today*, which describes, probes, and analyzes the new ideology, priorities, and programs found in corrections. The text is designed to be informative and scholarly, while at the same time being practical and career oriented. We examine the field of corrections through the lens of students who are giving serious thought to careers in corrections or are now working in corrections. Our text aims to be highly readable, engaging, and authoritative, without losing sight of its goal and target audience. So while the topics covered include historical and theoretical perspectives in corrections, we strive to provide the type of context and concrete illustration that makes such material meaningful and relevant to the career-minded student.

Corrections Today has at its core a number of unique attributes:

- **It is realistic.** We conducted a "reality check" by conducting interviews with "spokespersons" for corrections: probationers, inmates, parolees, correctional personnel, and correctional administrators. We constantly asked them: Is this the way it is? Is this a fair assessment? Do we have it right?
- **It is research oriented.** We include the most recent studies of corrections and have tried to explain findings in a user-friendly way aimed at increasing student interest—resulting in a book that is briefer but no less academically sound than more encyclopedic texts.
- **It emphasizes evidence-based research findings.** In nearly every chapter, we include studies of evidence-based research findings. For example, in Chapter 9 we explore the existing evidence on wrongful convictions in order to help students understand how often miscarriages of justice actually occur and how many people are wrongfully convicted each year.
- **It also emphasizes the expanding role of technology in the field.** Unique "TechnoCorrections" boxes spotlight the use of cutting-edge technology to supervise offenders in the community and in correctional institutions—providing an essential and compelling look at a major emphasis in corrections today.
- **It does not pull punches.** In nearly every chapter, there is an evaluation of what is taking place in the correctional system today, where the problems lie, and what can be done to correct them.
- **It focuses on how to become a corrections professional.** Our goal is to help students with career choices and explore what careers are out there in the correctional system. We feature numerous interviews with practicing professionals as well as interviews with correctional clients to get their take on what works and what does not. And for the Third Edition we have added a comprehensive new chapter on careers and professionalism in corrections.
- **It is hopeful.** Time after time in this text, those who work in the field remind students that corrections has been a very positive and fulfilling career for them, that they feel they have made a difference, and they invite students to join them on this exciting journey.

ORGANIZATION OF THE TEXT

This text has 15 chapters. Parts I and II of the text set out to address the key questions of why and how we punish. Part III introduces students to the increasingly important world of community corrections. Part IV addresses institutional corrections. Rehabilitation in corrections is the focus of Part V of the text. Part VI addresses special populations in corrections. Finally, Part VII looks at careers in corrections.

CHAPTER 1, THE CORRECTIONAL SYSTEM, covers the goals and philosophy of punishment as well as the history of punishment from the Code of Hammurabi through the Enlightenment through the origins of American corrections up to the twentieth century, and concludes with a discussion of the corrections system today, including the extent and consequences of prison overcrowding, the cost of corrections, and what it means to be a professional in corrections.

CHAPTER 2, SENTENCING AND THE CORRECTIONAL PROCESS, focuses on *how* we punish—discussing the basic goals and philosophy of sentencing, the various types of sentencing and sentencing guidelines, three-strikes laws, and truth-in-sentencing.

CHAPTER 3, COMMUNITY CORRECTIONS: DIVERSION AND PROBATION, begins by explaining diversion and diversionary programs, considers community corrections legislation, and then focuses on probation services.

CHAPTER 4, INTERMEDIATE SANCTIONS, identifies and discusses the continuum of intermediate sanctions, including fines, forfeiture, house arrest, and electronic monitoring, and places a major emphasis on restorative justice.

CHAPTER 5, JAILS AND HOUSES OF CORRECTION, offers comprehensive coverage of the jail from its origins through the various generations of jail supervision, as well as issues concerning jail confinement, such as overcrowding, violence, and suicide.

CHAPTER 6, PRISONS, covers the main types of federal, state, and private prisons, including an examination of the levels of security from minimum to supermax, architectural design innovations, and prison administration.

CHAPTER 7, THE PRISON EXPERIENCE: MALES, focuses on the changing social structure of men's prisons, including gangs, racial tensions, contraband, violence, and sex in prison.

CHAPTER 8, THE PRISON EXPERIENCE: FEMALES, identifies the differences between men's and women's prisons when it comes to social structure, focuses on issues such as motherhood, health concerns, and sexual abuse, and discusses professionalism among workers in women's prisons.

CHAPTER 9, PRISONERS' RIGHTS, identifies what First, Fourth, Eighth, and Fourteenth Amendments substantive rights have been awarded to inmates and addresses the consequences of the Prison Litigation Reform Act on prisoners' rights.

CHAPTER 10, CORRECTIONAL PROGRAMS AND SERVICES, looks at the role of treatment and services in prisons today, discussing the classification for treatment, individual-level treatment programs, group programs, and inmate self-help programs.

CHAPTER 11, PAROLE AND RELEASE TO THE COMMUNITY, examines parole practices today, how the parole board functions, the various roles of parole officers, the legal rights of parolees, and the problems faced by ex-offenders returning to the community.

CHAPTER 12, SPECIAL PRISON POPULATIONS, reviews three categories of inmates who pose particular challenges to correctional administrators and who face challenges themselves in adjusting to prison environments: **special offense inmates**—inmates with substance abuse histories, sex offenders, and terrorists; **special needs inmates**—HIV inmates and inmates with chronic mental health issues; and **special population inmates**—elderly inmates and inmates who are illegal immigrants.

CHAPTER 13, CAPITAL PUNISHMENT AND THE DEATH ROW INMATE, examines the status of the death penalty today, its legality and role in contemporary society both nationally and internationally, and describes the positions and responsibilities of those working on death row.

CHAPTER 14, THE JUVENILE OFFENDER, looks at the juvenile offender as he or she is processed through the juvenile justice system and then considers the transfer of juveniles to adult court and the placement of juveniles in boot camps and adult prisons.

CHAPTER 15, PROFESSIONALISM AND CAREERS IN CORRECTIONS, considers how far professionalism has brought corrections, the various corrections careers, the advantages of a corrections career, the challenges it presents, and the reasons why internships make sense to those considering working in corrections.

WHAT IS NEW IN THE THIRD EDITION

NEW CAPSTONE CHAPTER ON PROFESSIONALISM AND CAREERS IN CORRECTIONS. Chapter 15 is an entirely new chapter in which we inform students of the many career opportunities available in the field of corrections. We define professionalism and the need for it, and discuss how far professionalism has brought corrections today. We describe the various career paths and why corrections is a promising career. We provide detailed information about requirements and qualifications, what it's like to work in corrections, earning potential, benefits, hiring, and training, as well as the challenges of a career in corrections. Finally, we explain why an internship in corrections would benefit the student who is interested in a corrections career.

Web Apps have been added throughout each section of the text to provide students with links to relevant websites, with discussion questions and activities, all tied to the chapter learning objectives.

Marginal **For Group Discussion** activities have been added to each section of the text to facilitate critical thinking and group discussion. All are keyed to the chapter's learning objectives.

Marginal **Critical Thinking** activities have been added throughout the text for further reinforcement of critical thinking about corrections today, all tied to the chapter's learning objectives. And **For Critical Thinking and Writing** assignments have been added to the all of the boxed features in the text, as well.

CHAPTER-BY-CHAPTER CHANGES IN THE THIRD EDITION

CHAPTER 1 begins with a new opener on the Boston Marathon bombing in 2013. There is a new Careers in Corrections feature provided by Christopher B. Epps, commissioner of the Louisiana Department of Corrections. The chapter has been reorganized, beginning with expanded coverage of history at the beginning of the chapter, followed with the philosophies and goals of punishment, and concluding with the overview of corrections within the criminal justice system. There is expanded text on the Code of Hammurabi and a new exhibit on the theoretical constructs of the classical school of criminology, as well as a new exhibit on the positivist school. Moreover, the history section has been expanded to include more on the development of twentieth century corrections, including the rise of modern management, increased use of technology, turning increasingly to privatization, and the industrial era. Beginning in this chapter and extending throughout the manuscript, all the figures have been updated, whenever possible, and the most recent citations have been used.

CHAPTER 2 begins with a new opener featuring former New England Patriots tight end Aaron Hernandez. The Voices Across the Professions feature is new, contributed by federal Judge Paul A. Magnuson. Bail and pretrial, which had previously been in the jail chapter, have been moved to this chapter. The section on three-strikes laws has been expanded. A brief discussion has been included indicating how state legislatures can further dilute sentencing in the process of relieving prison overcrowding. A new exhibit has been included comparing determinate and indeterminate sentencing. And a new Careers in Corrections box on the pretrial officer has been included, featuring Jennifer Wyatt Bourgeois.

CHAPTER 3 has an updated timeline, and an exhibit has been added outlining the categories and duties of probation officers. Another new exhibit shows the differences between probation and parole. A new Careers in Corrections box contributed by Manny Jaquiss, probation supervisor in Tampa, Florida.

CHAPTER 4 now more clearly defines the concept of intermediate sentencing. The section on drug courts has been expanded. Discussions of other types of specialized courts have been added. An exhibit featuring Curt's Café is new to the chapter. This nonprofit restaurant is an example of a successful restorative justice program, hiring at-risk young adults, particularly those with criminal records, and providing them with job training and work experience. A new Voices Across the Professions box, with James M. Higgins, features substance abuse counseling and Julie Fox adds a Careers in Corrections box on substance abuse counseling.

CHAPTER 5 has been thoroughly revised and expanded from the previous edition. It has a new chapter opener showing how Tavon White, a leader of the Black Guerilla Family, spearheaded jail corruption in Baltimore, Maryland. The chapter has expanded coverage on the functions of jails, it discusses the diversity of jails, and has an expanded section on the types of inmates in jail. A new exhibit on the four generations of jails compares the types of supervision in each. The sections on jail programs, jail suicides, and mental health issues in jails have been expanded, with new exhibits on mental health issues at the Cook County Jail, and suicide prevention in local jails. A new Careers in Corrections box on the jail officer has been added, which features Gina Curcio, who worked at the House of Corrections in Middleton, Massachusetts.

CHAPTER 6 has a new opener on the closing of the notorious Tamms Correctional Center, a supermax prison in Illinois. The chapter also has a new Voices Across the Profession box featuring Kent Grandlienard, warden of the Oak Park Heights Supermax prison in Minnesota. A new exhibit showing the differences between men's and women's prisons is included in this chapter.

CHAPTER 7 is another chapter that is greatly revised. It includes a new case study of an offender going through the inmate classification process, including the indicators and characteristics that affect how a new inmate is housed and treated. The discussion of mental health services in prison is expanded. In the section on women officers in men's prisons, a brief mention of several court cases is included. There is also a Correctional Life quote from an inmate who was sexually victimized. The Voices Across the Profession and Careers in Corrections boxes in this chapter are contributed by Barbara Casey, who tells of the particular challenges presented to women working as correctional officers in a men's prison.

CHAPTER 8 has a new discussion of the gender differences in classification, and has expanded coverage of programs and services in women's prisons, including court cases challenging gender differences in prison programs. There is an expanded discussion of sexual abuse in women's prisons, especially by other female inmates. The section on prison health care for women has been further expanded as well.

CHAPTER 9 has a new Voices Across the Professions contributed by Dr. Allen Ault, former commissioner of corrections in Colorado, Georgia, and Mississippi. It also now includes a brief discussion of the least eligibility principle. Several cases are updated, and a new exhibit explains Section 1983 of the federal code.

CHAPTER 10 has an expanded section on inmate self-development programs, and also includes an expanded section on prison industries, including federal laws related to prison industry. There is a new Careers in Corrections box contributed by Cathy Fontenot, assistant warden for programming at the Louisiana State Penitentiary, Angola.

CHAPTER 11 includes a new exhibit on the Irish mark system, updated parole statistics, and a more thorough discussion of the parole board role in contemporary corrections. We have expanded our comparison of standard and special conditions of parole. A Correctional Life box tells a parolee's success story. Technical violations and parole revocations are further given greater attention.

CHAPTER 12 has a new discussion of the impact of Megan's Law. The section on chronic mentally ill inmates has been revised and expanded. And there is a new Careers in Corrections box on the forensic psychologist, contributed by Michael H. Fogel.

CHAPTER 13 has a new opener that discusses the case of Anthony Sowell, a serial murderer from Cleveland, Ohio. There is a brief discussion of the impact of capital punishment on non–death row inmates, an exhibit comparing the death penalty policies by state has been updated, and there is a new section on death penalty and female offenders, including an exhibit on women who have been executed since the death penalty was reinstated in 1976.

CHAPTER 14 updates the discussion of sentencing practices in juvenile court, including determinate sentencing, mandatory sentencing, and blended sentencing. There is a new Careers in Corrections box provided by Jim Redmond, a therapist in a juvenile residential facility in Minnesota.

CHAPTER 15 is an entirely new chapter on professionalism and careers in corrections. The opener tells of a woman prisoner who became a dog handler in prison and went on to become a corrections professional, training service dogs to help inmates and people with disabilities. We wrote a new Evidence-Based Corrections feature for this chapter that reviews the application and success of a structured training program for probation officers. There are discussions on why a career in corrections is beneficial, the variety of career paths in corrections, what is it like to work in corrections, and the challenges of working in corrections. The importance of internships in corrections is also discussed in this new chapter.

LEARNING TOOLS

In keeping with our desire to create the most student-centric text available, we have created a complete learning system. Each chapter begins with a set of learning objectives, which are also integrated in the chapter where each learning objective is addressed, and keyed to the summary at the end of the chapter for optimum reinforcement. Key concepts and terms are previewed in the chapter opener, boldfaced in the text where they are introduced and defined, and are repeated in the running marginal glossary. Additionally, we have included the following boxes and features to help students get the most out of the course:

VOICES ACROSS THE PROFESSION Each chapter has at least one Voices Across the Profession feature in which real-world professionals share their first-hand experiences and give students a concrete view of what it's like to work in a variety of corrections careers.

CAREERS IN CORRECTIONS Throughout the book, we highlight a variety of careers in corrections by giving students "snapshots" of individuals who work in corrections. In their own words, corrections professionals talk about the challenges and rewards of a career in corrections.

CORRECTIONAL LIFE This feature looks at the experiences of probationers, inmates, and parolees in their own words, describing life inside correctional institutions. The purpose is to bring the reader as close as possible to what life is like behind the walls: What are the problems? How do they cope? What is it really like living on death row? How do parolees/probationers make it in the community? For this edition we have expanded these perspectives to include more insider perspectives from a variety of individuals involved in the correctional system, from offenders to victims, staff, and families of offenders.

EVIDENCE-BASED CORRECTIONS This box focuses on policies and practices that are supported by research, a key driver in the field today, as underscored by several of the professionals interviewed for our Voices feature when they comment that they are expected to use evidence-based practices to justify the efficacy of the programs they implement. We include critical thinking and writing activities, which are new to this edition.

TECHNOCORRECTIONS These boxes spotlight the use of cutting-edge technology to supervise offenders in the community and in correctional institutions. In Chapter 4, a TECHNOCORRECTIONS feature entitled "EM and GPS Systems in the Community" discusses the use of electronic monitoring systems, including a program at Bryan Adams High School in East Dallas, Texas, that monitors students who have been chronically truant. New to this edition, we now include critical thinking and writing activities in each of our boxed features.

THINKING LIKE A CORRECTIONS PROFESSIONAL These boxes give students an opportunity to make a decision on how they think a corrections professional would handle a particular situation. Many of these features represent actual situations that have taken place, while others are possible scenarios.

MYTH/FACT BOXES Each chapter contains Myth/Fact boxes designed to separate myth from reality and thereby inform students of the incorrect notions, perceptions, and biases they bring to class as a result of what they see on television or read in fiction and on the Internet.

END-OF-CHAPTER REVIEW Includes a chapter summary linked back to the chapter-opening learning objectives and a set of critical thinking questions designed to help students think critically about the material.

ANCILLARY MATERIALS

A number of supplements are provided by Cengage Learning to help instructors use *Corrections Today* in their courses and to aid students in preparing for exams. Supplements are available to qualified adopters. Please consult your local sales representative for details.

To access additional course materials, please visit **www.cengagebrain.com**. At the CengageBrain.com home page, search for the ISBN of your title (from the back cover of your book), using the search box at the top of the page. This will take you to the product page where these resources can be found.

To get access, visit CengageBrain.com.

MINDTAP CRIMINAL JUSTICE from Cengage Learning represents a new approach to a highly personalized, online learning platform. A fully online learning solution, MindTap combines all of a student's learning tools—readings, multimedia, activities, and assessments—into a singular Learning Path that guides the student through the curriculum. Instructors personalize the experience by customizing the presentation of these learning tools for their students, allowing instructors to seamlessly introduce their own content into the Learning Path via "apps" that integrate into the MindTap platform. Additionally, MindTap provides interoperability with major Learning Management Systems (LMS) via support for open industry standards and fosters partnerships with third-party educational application providers to provide a highly collaborative, engaging, and personalized learning experience.

INSTRUCTOR'S RESOURCE MANUAL WITH LESSON PLANS AND TEST BANK includes learning objectives, key terms, a detailed chapter outline, a chapter summary, lesson plans, discussion topics, student activities, "What If" scenarios, media tools, a sample syllabus, and an expanded test bank with 30 percent more questions than the prior edition. The learning objectives are correlated with the discussion topics, student activities, and media tools.

Each chapter of the test bank contains questions in multiple-choice, true/false, completion, essay, and new critical thinking formats, with a full answer key. The test bank is coded to the learning objectives that appear in the main text and includes the section in the main text where the answers can be found. Finally, each question in the test bank has been carefully reviewed by experienced criminal justice instructors for quality, accuracy, and content coverage so instructors can be sure they are working with an assessment and grading resource of the highest caliber.

CENGAGE LEARNING TESTING POWERED BY COGNERO This assessment software is a flexible, online system that allows you to import, edit, and manipulate test bank content from the *Corrections Today* test bank or elsewhere, including your own favorite test questions; create multiple test versions in an instant; and deliver tests from your LMS, your classroom, or wherever you want.

ONLINE POWERPOINT® LECTURES Helping you make your lectures more engaging while effectively reaching your visually oriented students, these handy Microsoft PowerPoint® slides outline the chapters of the main text in a classroom-ready presentation. The PowerPoint® slides are updated to reflect the content and organization of the new edition of the text, are tagged by chapter learning objective, and feature some additional examples and real-world cases for application and discussion.

ACKNOWLEDGMENTS

We would like to give thanks to our terrific and supportive product manager, Carolyn Henderson Meier, and our wonderful and fantastic content developer, Shelley Murphy. This text would not have been possible to complete without their assistance and TLC.

The preparation of this text would not have been possible without the aid of our colleagues who helped by reviewing the Second Edition and making valuable suggestions for the Third Edition:

Troy Hove, Minnesota State Southeast Technical College

Michelle D. Lee, Hinds Community College

Cathy A. Levey, University of Massachusetts, Lowell

Louis F. Shepard, West Georgia Technical College

SaRita Stewart, Dallas County Community College District

Bethany K. Teeter, Missouri State University

John Sieminski, Manchester Community College

Marcy L. Hehnly, Chattahoochee Technical College

Kenneth Sissom, Johnson County Community College

We are also grateful to the individuals who were willing to be interviewed and become our Voices Across the Profession, and to Karen Hess for her significant contribution to the careers chapter. Further, we express our appreciation to those who helped us in various ways during the preparation of the manuscript: Brannon Carter, Gloria Hadachek, Austin Howard, Allison Sorg, and James Wertz.

Many thanks to all.

Josh Haner/The New York Times/Redux

Two explosions went off near the finish line of the Boston Marathon on April 15, 2013. Three deaths and more than 260 injuries were reported.

Jeff Bauman, who lost his lower legs in the Boston Marathon bombings, rests between occupational therapy sessions at Spaulding Rehabilitation Hospital in Boston. Bauman went to the marathon to see his girlfriend run, but now his supporters are watching his efforts to walk again. How should we punish terrorists who cause havoc and seriously injure and kill multitudes of innocent people? Should they be housed in a prison and subject to the same conditions as someone convicted of selling marijuana?

WHO CAN EVER FORGET THE EVENTS OF APRIL 15, 2013, when two men, Dzhokhar and Tamerlan Tsarnaev, set off bombs at the finish line of the Boston Marathon, killing three people, and maiming and injuring many more? The two had conspired for many months to use improvised explosive devices (IEDs) to harm and kill people in the crowds of spectators who were cheering the runners on toward the marathon finish line. The IEDs were constructed from pressure cookers, explosive powder, shrapnel, adhesives, and other items and were designed to shred skin, shatter bone, and cause extreme pain and suffering as well as death.[1]

After carefully poring over footage from surveillance cameras and other sources, on April 18, 2013, the FBI released photographs to the media of the Tsarnaev brothers, identifying them as suspects in the marathon bombings. These photographs were widely disseminated on television and elsewhere, and the brothers must have realized their identification and arrest were imminent. Soon after, the Tsarnaevs, armed with five IEDs, a Ruger P95 semi-automatic handgun, ammunition, a machete, and a hunting knife, drove to the MIT campus, where they shot Police Officer Sean Collier and attempted to steal his service weapon. After killing Officer Collier, the brothers carjacked a Mercedes, and kidnapped the driver and forced him to drive to a gas station, robbing him of $800 along the way. After the driver managed to escape, the brothers drove the carjacked vehicle to Watertown, Massachusetts. A shootout occurred when city police officers located the pair, during which Tamerlan was injured. To make his escape, Dzhokhar Tsarnaev reentered the carjacked vehicle, drove it directly at the officers, and ran over and killed his injured brother. He then hid in a dry-docked boat in a Watertown backyard until he was spotted by the owner, who called the police. Gravely wounded, he is currently being held pending trial.

Who were these killers? Tamerlan Tsarnaev was born in the Kalmyk Autonomous Soviet Socialist Republic, North Caucasus; Dzhokhar in Kyrgyzstan. Because their father was a Chechen they identified themselves as being of Chechen descent. Though the family prospered in the United States and Dzhokhar attended a state university, they held radical Islamic views and blamed the U.S. government for conducting a war against Islam in Iraq and Afghanistan. Their actions were quickly disavowed by Islamic, Chechen, and other groups that distanced themselves from the atrocity. A prominent Boston mosque condemned the violence and distanced itself from the suspects, refusing to give Tamerlan a Muslim burial (he was later buried in Virginia).

1

The Correctional System

LEARNING OBJECTIVES

 Identify the ideas found within Enlightenment thinking and how they influenced corrections

 Define the early prison reformers and what they contributed

 Articulate how the Pennsylvania and Auburn models differ from one another

 Explain how reformatories contributed to the rehabilitation model

 Discuss the purpose of corrections

LO6 Summarize the reasons why we punish

 Discuss the theories of punishment

 Explain the relationship between corrections and the criminal justice system

 Describe the extent and consequences of prison overcrowding

LO10 Discuss the financial costs of corrections

LO11 Explain the importance of professionalism in corrections

PREVIEW OF KEY CONCEPTS

corrections
Code of Hammurabi
monastic confinement
bridewells
houses of corrections
Charles-Louis de Secondat, Baron de Montesquieu
Cesare Bonesana Beccaria
Jeremy Bentham
John Howard
Alexander Maconochie
Walter Crofton
Irish mark system
penitentiary
Eastern State Penitentiary
Pennsylvania model
Auburn cellblock
Auburn silent system
First Correctional Congress
Zebulon Brockway
reformatory model
medical model
Howard B. Gill
blameworthy
just deserts
retribution
general deterrent effect
specific deterrence
incapacitation
selective incapacitation
rehabilitation
evidence-based programs
restorative justice
equity goal of punishment
nolle prosequi
mass incarceration
prison-industrial complex
professionalism

Josh Raab/Redux

What should be done with the surviving Tsarnaev brother? He is old enough to face the death penalty for his crimes. But the law frowns upon executing the young, and the Supreme Court has prohibited the execution of teenagers under 18; Tzarnaev was 19 at the time of the bombing.[2] Some reports portrayed him as being led astray by his older brother. Others pointed to a note he penned while he was surrounded by police, saying, "The [Boston] bombings were in retribution for the U.S. crimes in places like Iraq and Afghanistan [and] that the victims of the Boston bombing were collateral damage, in the same way innocent victims have been collateral damage in U.S. wars around the world. . . . When you attack one Muslim, you attack all Muslims."[3] Should this young killer be spared death? Is that fair to those he killed and those he maimed for life? Should a message be sent that all terrorists, even teenagers, must face the ultimate penalty for their crimes?

It is the responsibility of federal, state, and county government, established by both law and practice, to protect us from evildoers, treat them, and reduce their potential for social harm. A key part of this mission is to prevent those convicted of both serious felonies and petty misdemeanors from repeating their criminal activities. To accomplish this goal, a correctional system has developed to confine, manage, and provide rehabilitative programs for those convicted of crime, all within a safe, secure, and humane environment. To carry out this task, the correctional system utilizes the services of trained professionals who are committed to public safety, the rehabilitation of inmates, and, after completion of their sentence, the reentry of offenders into society.

While the contemporary correctional system is functionally independent, it is also a subsystem of a broader *criminal justice system*—those agencies of social control: police, courts, and corrections—that are responsible for investigating criminal conduct, gathering evidence, identifying suspects, making arrests, bringing charges, conducting trials, deciding sentencing, and treating criminal offenders. **Corrections** also takes place in particular social contexts—environments and situations that influence people's response to events and shape their beliefs about crime and punishment. Because of its place in the social context of society, all the participants in the correctional process are important: victims, criminals, employees, professionals, and the general public that pays for the correctional system and is concerned about its effectiveness and efficiency. In Voices Across the Profession, corrections professional James Bruton discusses his view of the association between corrections and punishment.

corrections The institutions and methods that society uses to correct, control, and change the behavior of convicted offenders.

THE HISTORY OF CORRECTIONS: FROM VENGEANCE TO REFORM

Identify the ideas found within Enlightenment thinking and how they influenced corrections

To understand the present, it is necessary to examine the past of corrections. In this section, we present a brief review of the development of corrections and show its evolution from the first formal punishments employed in early societies to development of modern corrections in Europe and the United States.

In this chapter, the role of punishment is examined. Throughout history, people have struggled to determine the proper punishment for crime, hoping to find a formula that is neither too harsh nor too lenient. In nearly every age, some people cry out for draconian punishments against criminals while others urge the humane treatment of those who violate the law. The history of punishment and corrections is examined, beginning with the Middle Ages and ending with the development of the correctional system in the United States. Finally, an overview of the correctional system is presented, including critical issues of corrections, and the development of professionalism in the field of correctional service.

© James H. Bruton

VOICES ACROSS THE PROFESSION

The most important message I can give to anyone working in the field of corrections is to have an internal belief that every day you have the opportunity to make a difference in people's lives.

James Bruton
Corrections Professional

James Bruton has worked in corrections for more than 35 years, including 14 in correctional facilities, and served as the warden at the Minnesota Correctional Facility, Oak Park Heights, from 1996 to 2001. He is the author of *The Big House: Life Inside a Supermax Security Prison* (Osceola, WI: Voyageur Press, 2004). Here is what he has to say about the field of corrections:

"The most important message I can give to anyone working in the field of corrections is to have an internal belief that every day you have the opportunity to make a difference in people's lives. In order to be successful in this difficult business, you have to have a dedicated and committed desire to look forward to going to work, keeping in mind the philosophical belief of making a difference. In conjunction with this mindset, whether you are working in a correctional facility or individually with a client, you must find a way to create an environment conducive to rehabilitation for those offenders who want to make a change in their lives. Your job, along with all of the inherent duties and responsibilities that come with it, is to provide a catalyst for the change in people's behavior to take place.

"It is important to recognize that the courts administer the punishment to the client. It is not the job of the corrections official to extend the punishment beyond the court's disposition. With respect to the administration of prisons, this conceptual philosophy is often misunderstood. The public often is confused and wants standards set both ways. For example, they may want the prison system to expand the punishment with substandard conditions and limited resources for the inmates, and then want the offender to be completely rehabilitated upon release. It quite simply cannot work like that. Keeping in mind that 95 percent of offenders sent to prison will at some point be released, we must find ways for the environment to be filled with incentive-based programming. We must find ways for each inmate to get up every day and look forward to doing something positive and productive. Good behavior will bring about rewards, and negative behavior will result in consequences. This philosophy is effective and it does work."

James Bruton is saying that the purpose in corrections is not to punish offenders—the courts have already done that—but to suggest that we resolve to go to work each day believing that offenders can change and that we can have an impact on their lives. Bruton is espousing the goal of reform, but, as documented throughout this chapter, the goal of repression has also been a constant theme of corrections.

Development of Formal Corrections

As states, kingdoms, and empires superseded clan and tribal societies, the state assumed the role of punishing violators of societal norms. For the state to take over private vengeance, it was necessary to formalize the system of government, and written laws accomplished this purpose. The importance of the early codes, or written laws, is that they embodied the customs by which organized societies dealt with violators of the norms of conduct. See the Timeline for the development of corrections from ancient times to the nineteenth century.

The first formal legal code was the **Code of Hammurabi**, created by the king of Babylonia (the region which is now Iraq) in about 1780 BCE. Hammurabi's code is especially memorable because it was carved on stone rather than clay and it is believed that we have it nearly in its entirety. When discovered by French archaeologists in 1901, the slab on which the code was inscribed was taken to the Louvre in Paris, where it remains.

Code of Hammurabi Law code issued during the reign of Hammurabi of Babylon. The law of *lex talionis* makes its appearance in this code, one of the first comprehensive views of the law.

TIMELINE

DEVELOPMENT OF **CORRECTIONS**

FROM THE MIDDLE AGES TO THE TWENTIETH CENTURY

SSPL/Getty Images

1500'S The English lock up their poor in institutions known as workhouses and hold their criminals in bridewells.

1558–1603 During the rule of Elizabeth I, roughly a dozen English common-law crimes are punishable by execution.

1593 Protestants of Amsterdam build a house of corrections for women.

1603 Protestants of Amsterdam build a house of corrections for men.

1656 The French create the largest and most complex web of penal institutions when Louis XIV establishes the Hospital General hospital-prison complex.

1703 In Rome, Pope Clement XI builds the famous Hospice of San Michele Prison as a house of correction for younger offenders.

Mondadori/Hulton Fine Art Collection/Getty Images

1718 England begins transporting all felons serving sentences of three years or more to New South Wales (Australia).

1748 Montesquieu writes *The Spirit of the Laws.*

Dea/G. Dagli Orti/De Agostini Picture Library/Getty Images

The Code of Hammurabi, preserved on black balsalt rock, set out crimes and punishments in ancient Sumeria. It was based on the concept of *lex talionis*, "an eye for an eye." Are there elements in the American legal system that seem similar to Hammurabi's code? For example, the civil law mandates that you have to pay an amount equal to the damage you caused another.

Hammurabi's code consists of 282 clauses, most of them having to do with matters that modern jurisprudence assigns to the civil laws. The principle of *lex talionis* ("law of talion," from the Latin *talio*, as in retaliation) or "an eye for an eye" makes its appearance through the sections on the punishment of criminals. While people were punished commensurate for the harm they caused (a thief's hand was cut off, for example), the code also rewarded compensation in the event that the perpetrator could not be identified. Take for instance the crime of robbery. If the thief was not caught, the code called for compensation to the victim of a robbery by the authorities of the city in which the robbery occurred. By making the state directly responsible for restitution, Babylonian law reduced intergenerational feuds and blood vengeance between families, a practice that has stood the test of time.[4]

Punishment During the Middle Ages

A number of punishments were used for criminals in medieval Europe. The most widely used were flogging and branding, torture, servitude as galley slaves, the gallows or other forms of execution, and banishment and transportation. The medieval punishment of flagellation was the act of whipping (Latin *flagellum*, "whip") or flogging the human body with implements such as rods, switches,

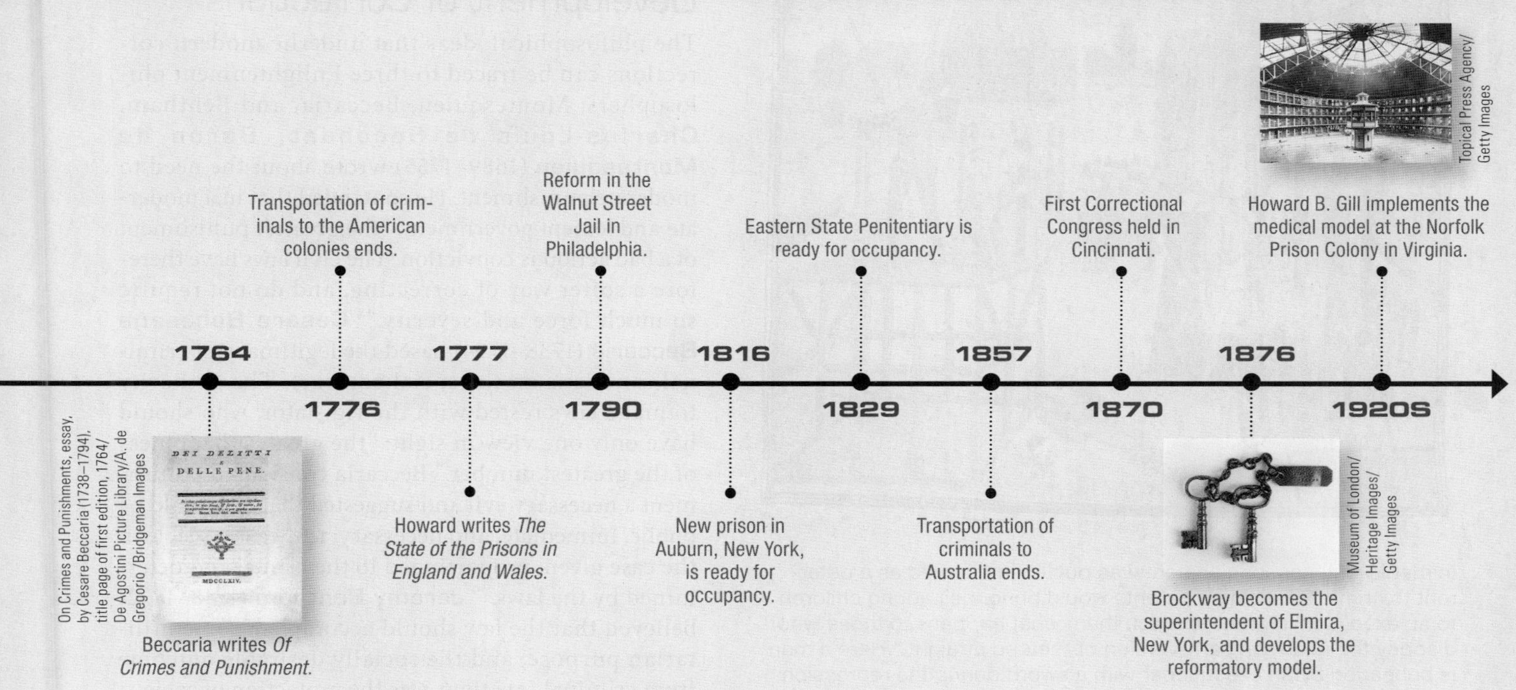
Transportation of criminals to the American colonies ends.
Reform in the Walnut Street Jail in Philadelphia.
Eastern State Penitentiary is ready for occupancy.
First Correctional Congress held in Cincinnati.
Howard B. Gill implements the medical model at the Norfolk Prison Colony in Virginia.
1764
1776
1777
1790
1816
1829
1857
1870
1876
1920s
DEI DELITTI E DELLE PENE
MDCCLXIV
Howard writes *The State of the Prisons in England and Wales.*
New prison in Auburn, New York, is ready for occupancy.
Transportation of criminals to Australia ends.
Brockway becomes the superintendent of Elmira, New York, and develops the reformatory model.

Beccaria writes *Of Crimes and Punishment.*

On Crimes and Punishments, essay, by Cesare Beccaria (1738–1794), title page of first edition, 1764/ De Agostini Picture Library/A. de Gregorio/Bridgeman Images

Topical Press Agency/ Getty Images

Museum of London/ Heritage Images/ Getty Images

and the cat-o'-nine-tails, nine knotted cords fastened to a wooden handle. The "cat" got its name from marks it left on the body, which resembled the scratches of a cat. Flagellation likely originated in the Near East but quickly spread throughout the ancient world.

It was believed that criminals deserved severe punishments, and most of the punishments provided for torture as well. Executions were public, with large throngs gathered to enjoy the proceedings. At Mons, a city in what is now Belgium, the citizens actually bought a brigand for the pleasure of seeing him quartered—that is, pulled apart by horses drawing on his arms and legs, "at which the people rejoiced more than if a new holy body had risen from the dead."[5] Criminals were seen as menaces to the community and as insults to God. Punishments of appalling cruelty were administered to make certain that the contrast between the riches of the few and the miseries of the many did not diminish.

Some of the first correctional institutions were developed during the medieval period and were still used in the seventeenth and eighteenth centuries. These included **monastic confinement** for violations of penal law; jails, which were used for the temporary detention of debtors and those who had committed minor offenses; **bridewells** or poor-houses, almshouses, and hospitals intended primarily for those incapable of looking after themselves; and **houses of corrections** or workhouses, where vagrants, beggars, and delinquents would be forced to work by way of discipline and punishment.[6] As a general rule, incarceration was not used as a means of correction but as a secure detention of suspected wrongdoers until they could be punished by execution, corporal punishment, or exile. Incarceration was also used to temporarily constrain the liberty of high-status persons who had fallen out of favor because they were political opponents of the ruling regime.[7] While minor offenders might receive corporal punishment such as whipping or branding, criminals who committed more serious offenses received sentences to the galleys and gallows or were transported to one of the penal colonies.

CRITICAL THINKING

How do different forms of discipline used in the past help us to understand the historical evolution of the criminal justice system? LO1

monastic confinement Prisons established by the Church in the Middle Ages for those laity involved in offensive acts, such as incest and magic.

bridewells Houses of corrections run by local authorities to teach habits of industry to vagrants and idlers.

houses of corrections Workhouses where vagrants were forced to work to achieve the purposes of discipline and punishment.

In medieval times, punishment was public and served as a deterrent to crime. Sometimes parents would bring their young children to an execution in order to teach them what happens to those who disobey the ruler—an early version of "scared straight." Here a man is beheaded by an executioner with a sword during the repression of the Jacquerie, a popular revolt in France in 1358, at the time of the Hundred Years' War.

Enlightenment Thinkers and the Development of Corrections

The philosophical ideas that underlie modern corrections can be traced to three Enlightenment philosophers: Montesquieu, Beccaria, and Bentham. **Charles-Louis de Secondat, Baron de Montesquieu** (1689–1755) wrote about the need to moderate punishment. He contended that in a moderate and lenient government, "the greatest punishment of a bad action is conviction. The civil laws have therefore a softer way of correcting, and do not require so much force and severity."[8] **Cesare Bonesana Beccaria** (1738–1794) based the legitimacy of criminal sanctions on the social contract. The authority to make laws rested with the legislator, who should have only one view in sight: "the greatest happiness of the greatest number." Beccaria considered punishment a necessary evil and suggested that "it should be public, immediate, and necessary; the least possible in the case given; proportioned to the crime; and determined by the laws."[9] **Jeremy Bentham** (1748–1832) believed that the law should accomplish some utilitarian purpose, and the socially desirable outcome from criminal sanctions was the protection of society. He contended that punishment would deter criminal behavior if it was made appropriate to the crime. Beccaria and Bentham believed that offenders are responsible for their behavior and should be punished, but they also believed that the goal of the state should be deterrence, not revenge. See Exhibit 1.1 for the main beliefs of what is now known as the classical school of criminology.

Charles-Louis de Secondat, Baron de Montesquieu One of the founders of the classical school of criminology, who advocated the moderation of punishment.

Cesare Bonesana Beccaria One of the founders of the classical school of criminology, who advocated that punishment should be public, immediate, and necessary.

Jeremy Bentham One of the founders of the classical school of criminology, who believed that the law should accomplish the utilitarian purpose of the protection of society.

EXHIBIT 1.1

Theoretical Constructs of the Classical School

- Human beings are seen as rational creatures, who being free to choose their actions, could be held responsible for their behavior. This doctrine of free will was substituted for what had been previously the widely accepted concept of theological determinism, which saw humans as predestined to certain actions.
- Punishment is justified because of its practical usefulness or ability. No longer was punishment acceptable for purposes of vengeful retaliation or as expiation on the basis of superstitious theories of guilt and repayment. According to utilitarianism, the aim of punishment is the protection of society, and the dominant theme is deterrence.
- The classical school sees the human being as a creature governed by a felicific calculus—an orientation toward obtaining a favorable balance of pleasure and pain.
- There should be a rational scale of punishment painful enough to deter the criminal from further offenses and to prevent others from following his or her negative example.
- Sanctions should be proclaimed in advance of their use; these sanctions should be proportionate to the offense and should outweigh the rewards of crime.
- Equal justice should be available to everyone.
- Individuals should be judged by the law solely for their acts, not for their beliefs.

THE POSITIVIST SCHOOL AND THE DEVELOPMENT OF CORRECTIONS

The treatment and rehabilitation model can be traced to the development of positivism. Instead of viewing crime as arising from free will, positivists argue that the social world operates according to laws or rules like the physical world. Hence, according to positivism, offenders are affected by biological or psychological factors that (1) impair or alter their decision-making abilities and (2) can be identified through the use of social scientific techniques.

Armed with a positivistic approach, social reformers of the early twentieth century set out to deal with the problem of crime, confident that they knew how to find its cause. Some progressives looked first to environmental factors, pinpointing poverty as a major cause of delinquency. Other positivists were attracted to the doctrine of eugenics and believed that certain biological features drove offenders to crime. The psychological origins of crime became widely accepted. Eventually, in the twenty-first century, the sociological origins of crime gained the widest acceptance among scholars in the field. The positivist approach to crime is based on three basic assumptions, set out in Exhibit 1.2.[10]

FOR GROUP DISCUSSION Identify the main concepts of Montesquieu, Beccaria, and Bentham and discuss examples of these concepts that you find in today's corrections system. What has changed since the days of Enlightenment thinking? What hasn't changed? **LO1**

The Early Prison Reformers

LO2 Define the early prison reformers and what they contributed

Early prisons were harsh environments. The worst felons were cut off from all contact with other prisoners; they had no hope of pardon to relieve their solitude or isolation. They were forced to remain alone and silent during the entire day, and breaking rules resulted in brutal punishments. This practice, which led to mental breakdowns, suicides, and self-mutilations, and the harsh and demeaning conditions of confinement in the eighteenth century inspired some leaders to call for prison reform. **John Howard** (1726–1790) was the first English prison reformer. Appointed high sheriff of Bedfordshire in 1773, Howard inspected the county prison and was shocked by the squalor in which inmates lived. He went on to inspect prisons throughout England and was particularly concerned about prisoners who were held indefinitely because they could not pay the jailer's fee—money paid to the owner or keeper of the prison for upkeep. In addition, terrible living conditions and poor hygiene produced plagues and other illnesses. Indeed, jail fever or typhus was endemic in most jails, and Howard himself died of typhus following his inspection of a jail in Russia. Before his death, Howard provided the English government with detailed proposals for improving the physical and mental health of prisoners, including where prisons should be located, the provision of clean water, proper diet, and adequate hygiene, and guidelines for hiring qualified prison personnel. He also advocated an independent inspection process to make sure reforms were being implemented.[11]

John Howard English sheriff who advocated jail reform.

EXHIBIT 1.2

Assumptions of the Positivist School

- The character and personal backgrounds of individuals explain criminal behavior. Positivism, relegating the law and its administration to a secondary role, looks for the cause of deviance in the actor.
- The existence of determinism is a critical assumption of positivism. Crime and deviance, like any other phenomenon, are seen as determined by prior causes (personality issues, poverty, family conflict); they do not just happen. Because of this deterministic position, positivism rejects the view that the individual exercises freedom, possesses reason, and is capable of choice.
- Criminals have personal characteristics that make them fundamentally different from noncriminals. These characteristics can be identified and measured. In attempting to explain these differences, positivists conclude that wayward youths and criminal adults are driven into crime by something in their physical makeup, by aberrant psychological impulses, or by a dysfunctional and damaging social environment.

Alexander Maconochie Served as director of the prison colony in Australia and set up the "mark" system.

Alexander Maconochie (1786–1860) served as director of the prison colony on Norfolk Island in Australia. There, inmates were "doubly convicted," having been convicted of a crime after being transported from Britain for a previous crime. Norfolk Island was considered the end of the line for both inmates and prison administrators. Instead of continuing the previous brutal treatment of prisoners, when Maconochie took up duties as commandant of the penal settlement in 1840, he set up a system where newly arriving convicts were awarded marks to encourage effort and thrift. Sentences were served in stages, each increasing in responsibility. Cruel punishments and degrading conditions were reduced, and convicts' sense of dignity was respected. In many ways, Maconochie succeeded far better than could be anticipated, but the political unpopularity of what he was doing eventually resulted in his recall to England. Maconochie left his post certainly feeling that his experiment had not worked the way he had hoped.

Walter Crofton Prison reformer who developed the Irish mark system, which eventually spread to the United States and influenced the development of parole.

Irish mark system A system in which prisoners received "marks of commendation" for completing assigned tasks. They could use the marks to buy food and clothing. Prisoners who accumulated enough marks received a ticket-of-leave.

Walter Crofton (1815–1897), a retired army officer, developed what became known as the **Irish mark system**, an innovation that made him a celebrity in international penology circles. Crofton believed in reformation, and inmates could earn early release or "tickets-of-leave" if they demonstrated achievement and positive attitude change. The system applied to convicts serving terms of three years or more. It was separated into three stages. The first stage lasted eight or nine months, depending on the man's conduct. The second stage included four classes, and in each class, a prisoner had to earn marks for a maximum of nine per month. The third stage was spent at Lusk Commons, where convicts were housed in dormitories and given vocational training to fit them for employment when finally released. Crofton argued that the Irish mark system induced the convict to cooperate in his own "amendment" or rehabilitation:

> He cannot ignore the conviction ... that the system, however penal in its development is intended for his benefit, and that, moreover, it has by its stringent regulations and arrangements after the liberties of the convict ... made the volition of crime very unprofitable and hazardous to follow.[12]

Aided by widespread foreign interest, the Irish or Crofton's system became the standard in England. It was adopted at the Elmira Reformatory in the 1870s in the United States, and parole, as it was called in America, soon spread across the nation.[13] There is more discussion of the Irish mark system in Chapter 11.

MPI/Archive Photos/Getty Images

The use of severe punishment in the United States can be traced back to the early settlers who routinely used strict correctional punishments, including mutilations, hangings, burnings, and brandings, to enforce their strict legal codes. They viewed the deviant as willful, a sinner, and a captive of the devil so they did not hesitate to resort to tough punishments, such as this 1676 public hanging. Punishments were often public and served the dual purpose of punishing the wicked and deterring those who might be planning to commit crime.

The Origins of American Corrections

The American experience of corrections was shaped from a particular context, both from the culture that existed in this nation and from what had taken place in Europe. For the most part, punishments were derived from European methods, which featured harsh criminal codes and often sadistic punishments. But the idealism and social activism upon which the American colonies were founded led to the development of distinctly American legal practices, such as the penitentiary.[14]

THE QUAKERS AND CRIMINAL LAW After the adoption of the Declaration of Independence, the

Pennsylvania legislature repealed the British laws that the colonies had enacted. A series of statutes abolished capital punishment for all crimes other than first-degree murder.[15] For the major felonies, terms of imprisonment were provided. Fines or jail terms replaced the whipping post, the pillory, and the stocks. A system of state prisons was established to accommodate felons avoiding the gallows under the terms of the new laws. It has been argued that "a more thorough transformation in the character of a penal code, by peaceful legislation, is not recorded in the world's history than that which took place in Pennsylvania during the eighteen years immediately following the Declaration of Independence."[16] Inmates began to be held in the city jails, including a new one located on Walnut Street in Philadelphia.

PENNSYLVANIA PRISON SOCIETY AND THE WALNUT STREET JAIL While the new laws were considered humane, public reaction against the display of convicts on the streets of the city, and the disgraceful conditions in city jails led to the formation in 1787 of the Philadelphia Society for Alleviating the Miseries of Public Prisons (renamed the Pennsylvania Prison Society in that same year).[17] Members of the society were appalled by the overcrowded, unsanitary, and corrupt conditions of the Walnut Street Jail and appealed to the legislature for reform. In 1790, an act was passed that brought about sweeping reforms. The act authorized a penitentiary house with 16 cells to be built in the yard of the jail to carry out solitary confinement with labor for "hardened atrocious offenders," thus removing them from the general inmate population.[18]

LO3 Articulate how the Pennsylvania and Auburn models differ from one another

DEVELOPMENT OF THE PENITENTIARY Pennsylvania's major innovation in penal reform, the **penitentiary**, had actually a long process of development.[19] The word *penitentiary* was first used in the English Penitentiary Act of 1779, which authorized the building of national penitentiaries in which convicts would be kept in order with strict discipline and hard labor. But the buildings were never actually constructed. Not until 1818 did the legislature authorize construction of two new penitentiaries, one near Pittsburgh and the Eastern State Penitentiary in Philadelphia.[20] The American version of the penitentiary was designed to isolate people found guilty of a felony from normal society. It was believed that penitence, pastoral counseling, and reasonable discipline would correct antisocial behavior.

penitentiary A prison in which persons found guilty of a felony are isolated from normal society.

The **Eastern State Penitentiary** was finished in 1829 and became a model for prisons in several European countries. It had a radial design, with seven wings, each containing 76 cells, radiating from a central hub, where control personnel were stationed (see Figure 1.1). Each cell was 12 feet long, 8 feet wide, and 10 feet high, designed for single occupancy.[21] A separate exercise yard, in which the prisoner was allowed to be in the open air for an hour a day, was provided adjacent to the cell. Cells were separated by stone partitions 18 inches thick, which effectively prevented communication from prisoner to prisoner. Solitude was the goal, and prisoners spent their days alone. Even at compulsory chapel services they could not see one another, because they were seated in chairs that looked like upended coffins. The building was a massive fortress, resembling a medieval castle, intended to deter would-be offenders.

Eastern State Penitentiary A fortress-like prison in Philadelphia consisting of seven wings radiating from a control hub. Prisoners were kept in solitary confinement. It became a model for prisoners in several European countries.

The **Pennsylvania model** was a penal system based on the belief that most prisoners would benefit from the experience of incarceration.[22] However, within a few years, when crowding became a problem, prisoners were doubled up in cells and solitude was no longer possible. It was not long before the conditions of imprisonment at the Eastern State Penitentiary were investigated, and charges of brutality were launched and substantiated against it at hearings that took place in 1834.[23] By the end of the Civil War, the penitentiary's population had reached 1,117 prisoners.[24] Eastern underwent many renovations over the years, new wings were built, and many famous inmates became residents, including Chicago's mob boss Al Capone, who spent eight months at Eastern State in 1929–1930. Arrested for carrying a concealed deadly weapon, this was Capone's first prison sentence. His time in Eastern State

Pennsylvania model A penal system based on the belief that most prisoners would benefit from the experience of incarceration.

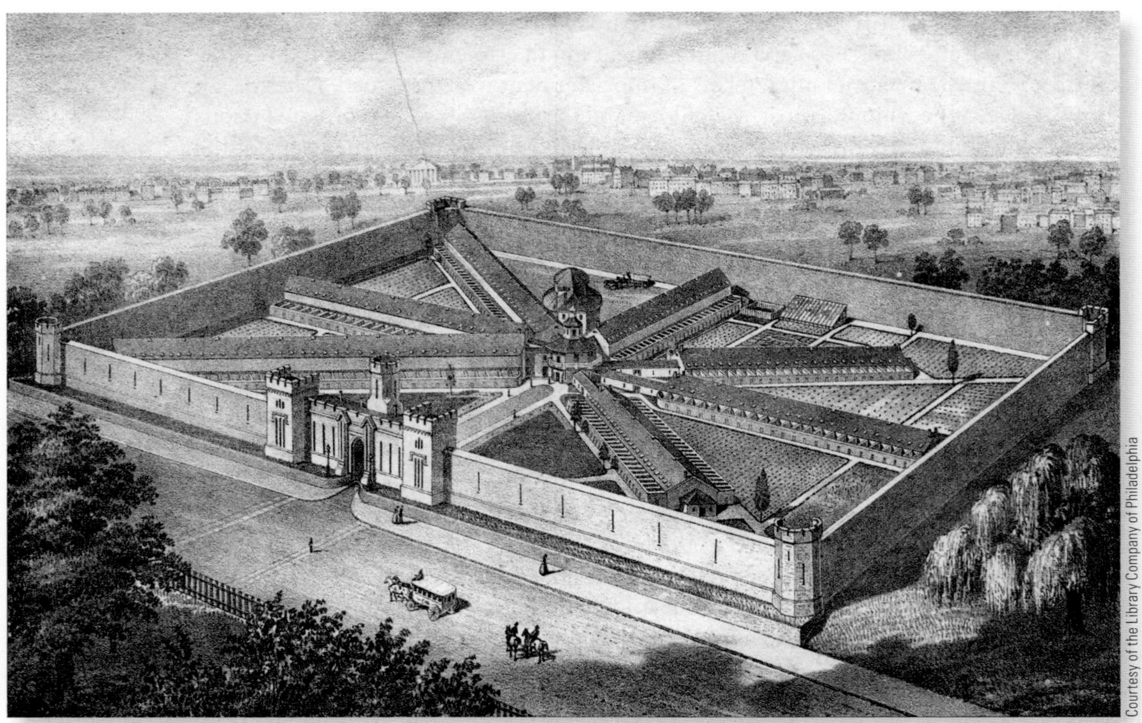

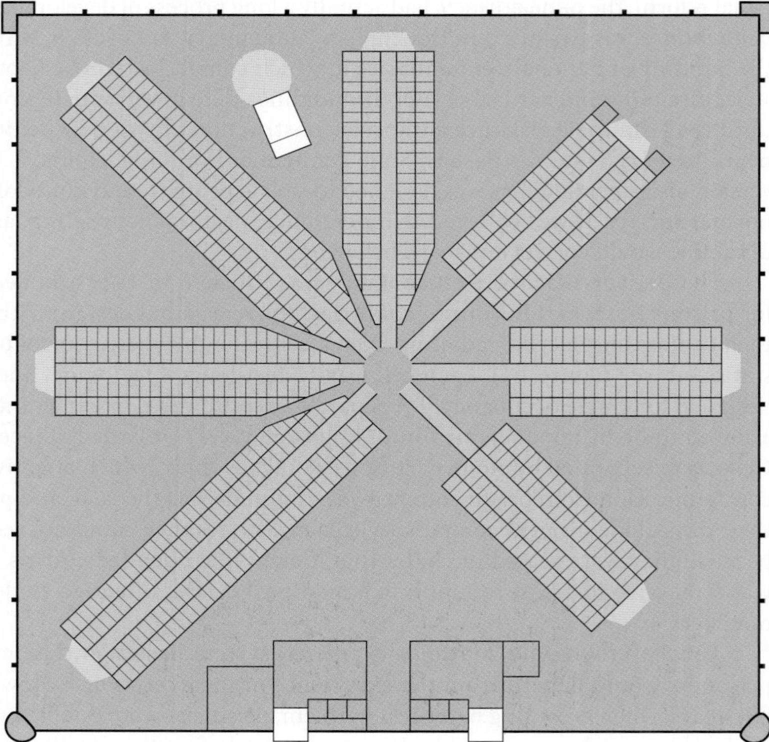

FIGURE 1.1

The Layout of Eastern State Penitentiary in Philadelphia

An early print showing the "hub and spoke" model of prison design. In this model, guards could patrol the penitentiary from a central location.

A floor plan of Eastern State Prison, created in 1836. The prison would see additions over the next century.

Source: Norman Bruce Johnston, Kenneth Finkel, Jeffrey A. Cohen, and Norman Johnson, *Eastern State Penitentiary: Crucible of Good Intentions* (Philadelphia: Philadelphia Museum of Art, 1994).

Auburn cellblock An austere prison setting in Auburn, New York, in which inmates were made to endure great suffering.

Auburn silent system A system first used in the prison in Auburn, New York, that demanded silence from all prisoners at all times, even when they were eating or working together.

was spent in relative luxury. His cell on what is called the Park Avenue Block had fine furniture, oriental rugs, and a cabinet radio, all of which remain in the cell to this day. By the 1960s, the prison was in need of costly repairs. The Commonwealth closed the facility in 1971, 142 years after it admitted Charles Williams, prisoner number one.[25]

THE NEW YORK PENAL SYSTEM In 1796, New York enacted legislation abolishing capital punishment for all offenses other than first-degree murder and treason. To accommodate felons who now would do time rather than be subjected to flogging or the gallows, Newgate Prison was built in 1797 in what is now Greenwich Village in Manhattan. A crime wave at the end of the War of 1812 led to overcrowding at Newgate Prison, and in 1816 the legislature authorized a new prison in the western New York town of Auburn. It became a model for maximum-security prisons. When Auburn filled up in 1825, the legislature authorized the building of Sing Sing Prison at Ossining on the Hudson River. Sing Sing was built in three years by convict labor, except for three civilians—a master carpenter, a blacksmith, and a mason.[26]

Two years after the completion of the prison at Auburn, a new wing was built that became famous as the **Auburn cellblock**.[27] Prisoners assigned to this block, first occupied Christmas Day in 1821, were not allowed to work nor were they permitted to sit or lie down during daylight hours.[28] The rationale for this austere program was to make incarceration so unpleasant that inmates would never dare reoffend.[29] Suicides, attempted murders, and various mental and physical infirmities attributed to the requirement that men be on their feet all day became so prevalent that this regimen was ended in 1825.

Auburn officials were committed to the idea that solitude is essential to prison discipline. The challenge was to maintain solitude while large numbers of prisoners were eating, working, and moving together through the prison. An ingenious deputy warden, John D. Cray, found a solution that became known as the **Auburn silent system**. It was the successful alternative to the Pennsylvania model, and, like the Auburn cellblock, was the basis of practical penology until the mid-twentieth century. This system demanded silence from all convicts at all times. They marched in lockstep from the cellblock to the mess hall and to the factory. With right hand on the right shoulder of the person immediately ahead, face turned toward the watching guards, each convict in the platoon of silent offenders was watched for any attempt to communicate.[30] The prison was renamed the Auburn Correctional Facility in the 1970s and is still in use today.

Bob Krist/Encyclopedia/Corbis

A cell at Eastern State Penitentiary, located in Philadelphia, Pennsylvania. Opened on October 25, 1829, Eastern State was the world's first penitentiary. It used solitary confinement as a form of rehabilitation. The term penitentiary, which comes from the word "penance," hinted at the institution's original goal: prisoners were expected to open up to God and seek salvation as a method of reform. As this contemporary photo shows, the cells were concrete and many of them contained a single glass skylight, designed to make the prisoners believe that God was always watching them. Outside the cell, there was an individual area for exercise, enclosed by high walls so prisoners couldn't communicate.

Thom Lang/Latitude/Corbis

Al Capone was one of the most famous residents of the Eastern State Penitentiary. His cell is still furnished as it was when he served time. You can visit it today if you take a tour of the penitentiary, a fascinating experience.

MYTH The first large prisons to hold convicted criminals can be traced back to European dungeons of the Middle Ages.

FACT Before their creation in the United States, penal institutions were used mostly to house criminal defendants before their trial, while they arranged to pay back a debt, or while they were awaiting execution. The use of prison for reform is an American invention.

Both the Pennsylvania and Auburn systems must be seen as an attempt to meet the urgent requirements of justice. The Pennsylvania system had the merit of adopting Bentham's goals of the reformation and deterrence of the offender. The Auburn system, in contrast, was a pragmatic effort to administer the processes of punishment as thriftily as possible. The pragmatics of the times called for measures that we would now see as unacceptably brutal but that were tolerable in an age when criminals were thought to be uniformly defective in mind and morals.

THE REHABILITATION MOVEMENT BEGINS In 1870, a group of reformers, including wardens and politicians, unhappy with the Auburn system, convened the leading figures in penology to hear proposals for change in the management of prisons. The **First Correctional Congress**, held in Cincinnati in 1870, was carefully planned and chaired by Ohio's Governor Rutherford B. Hayes, who was later to become the nineteenth president. Speakers from the United States and abroad were invited to present new and progressive ideas, such as giving prisoners educational opportunities and religious instruction. Practical prison men from 22 states, Canada, and Latin American nations enthusiastically "rose above the monotony of four gray walls, men in stripes shuffling in lockstep, sullen faces staring through the bars, coarse mush and coffee made of bread crusts, armed sentries stalking the walls. They forgot it all and voted their remarkable Declaration of Principles."[31]

First Correctional Congress A congress held in Cincinnati in 1870 to present progressive ideas about corrections, which resulted in the formulation of the Declaration of Principles.

The Declaration of Principles passed by this correctional congress emphasized that the reformation of prisoners should be the goal of corrections. To achieve it, prisoners should be classified on the basis of a marks system, rewards should be provided for good behavior, and indeterminate sentences should be substituted for fixed sentences. The prison's aim should be to create industrious free men, rather than orderly and obedient prisoners. Prisons should be small, and separate institutions should exist for different types of offenders.[32]

CRITICAL THINKING

List the primary features of the Pennsylvania and Auburn systems of imprisonment. What are the pros and cons of these system models? What features from the Pennsylvania and Auburn systems have carried forth into today's prison systems? LO3

Explain how reformatories contributed to the rehabilitation model LO4

THE REFORMATORY MODEL AT ELMIRA **Zebulon Brockway**, warden of the Detroit House of Correction, attended the First Congressional Congress and presented a paper entitled "The Ideal Prison System for a State." In this paper, he urged that the very word "prison" be stricken from the statutes: "The true attitude of government is that of guardian; its true function to shelter, shield, help, heal."[33] In 1876, Brockway became superintendent of the Elmira Reformatory in New York, where his proposals for a model reformatory were to have free rein.

Zebulon Brockway Superintendent of the Elmira Reformatory in New York.

reformatory model A penal system for youthful offenders featuring indeterminate sentencing and parole, classification of prisoners, educational and vocational training, and increased privileges for positive behavior.

Brockway felt strongly about the merits of what has been called the **reformatory model**. He advocated indeterminate sentencing as "quite indispensable to the ideal of a true prison system" and an essential part of his rehabilitative model.[34] Admission was restricted to first offenders between the ages of 16 and 30. All inmates received an indeterminate sentence—no minimum sentence but a statutory maximum. The program was aimed at changing the prisoner's character, and the superintendent would then decide when the change in the convict's character justified release. All releases were conditional, and discharge depended on conduct while under supervision in the community over a period of six months.

Elmira was the first correctional institution to pay wages to prisoners as a reward for diligence and productivity. From their wages, inmates paid for room and board, clothing and other necessities, and medical care. The economics of the system were arranged so that at the time of discharge there would be some money to the prisoner's credit. The Elmira program was emulated in 12 other states by the turn of the twentieth century and in 11 more by 1933, despite growing doubts about the success of the system.[35]

The reformatory model, as established in Elmira and other prisons, made some lasting contributions to corrections—the system of indeterminate sentencing, the payment of inmates for work, the supervision of inmates in the community, a system of behavior modification, and the development of what later came to be parole.

THE MEDICAL MODEL OF REHABILITATION By the 1920s, the **medical model** was implemented in correctional institutions throughout the United States. Many correctional authorities looked forward to a time when the diagnosis and treatment of criminals would match the successes of modern medicine. The prison would become an analogue to the hospital. Cures would be found for most if not all forms of criminal behavior.

One of the earliest advocates of the treatment prison was **Howard B. Gill** (1889–1989), who proposed that the Norfolk Prison Colony in Virginia rehabilitate offenders by curing criminals of the "disease of crime." He carried the hospital metaphor even further. Hospitals had to diagnose before treatment could be initiated, so he devised a classification system for sorting out the "mental diseases" from which his inmates suffered. This was a "scamp" system, an acronym for five categories of convicts: situational offender, custodial (old and senile), asocial cases, medical (handicapped, deformed, tubercular), and personality (psychotics, neurotics, and those with personality difficulties). However, in the aftermath of an escape attempt by a team of inmates, a successful escape by two inmates, and increasing institutional disorders, Gill was dismissed.[36]

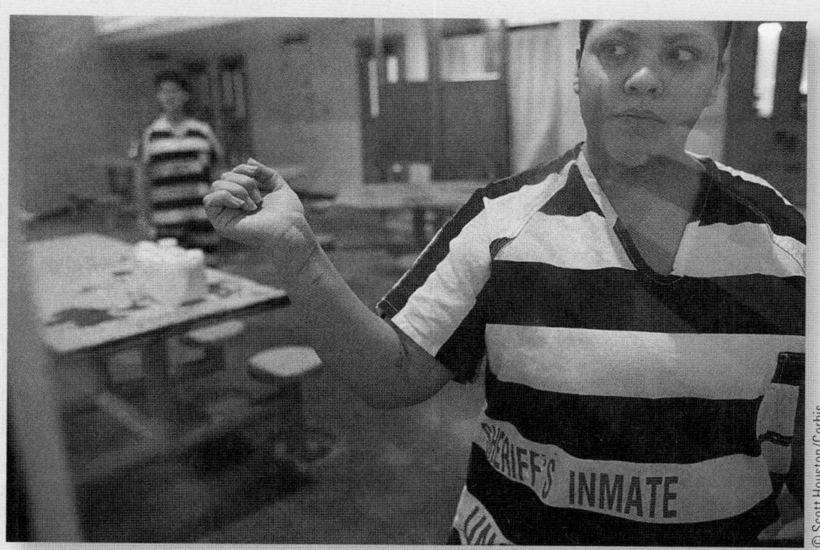

© Scott Houston/Corbis

An inmate shows the cuts on her wrist from a failed suicide attempt at Estrella Jail in Phoenix, Arizona. The Estrella Jail was built in 1991, is podular/dormitory in design, and holds approximately 1,000 inmates, predominantly female. The jail has a fully staffed and equipped medical clinic, a nondenominational chapel area for religious services, and three classrooms where inmates can attend educational, drug rehabilitation, or life-skills classes. It is also home to the only female chain gang in America. Inmates stay in their tiny 8-foot by 12-foot cells 23 hours of the day during lockdown, unless they are out on assigned chain gang duty. The inmates must memorize 10 rules of conduct, addressing grooming, behavior, and attitude. Chain gang and other privileged duties can be suspended for infractions such as swearing. The chain gangs work six days a week contributing thousands of hours of free labor to the community. The tough regimen is viewed by jail administrators as a means of rehabilitating the inmates through hard work.

While attempts were being made to introduce treatment in institutions housing men, women did not fare as well. Typical women's prisons during the nineteenth century were harsh and disciplinary institutions in which the reformatory tradition was ignored and little concern was shown for the incarcerated women.[37] In the twentieth century, growing numbers of African Americans and descendants of immigrants from southern and eastern Europe filled women's institutions.[38] Chapter 8 discusses women in prison in the twentieth and twenty-first centuries.

medical model The idea that criminality is a sickness that can be cured through psychological intervention.

Howard B. Gill Developed the "scamp" system at the Norfolk Prison colony in Virginia.

CRITICAL THINKING 

What are the pros and cons of the reformatory model and the medical model? What were some of the lasting contributions of these approaches? **LO4**

CORRECTIONS IN THE TWENTIETH CENTURY

By the twentieth century, community-based corrections had sprouted in nearly every state and included pretrial release and diversion, probation, residential and reentry programs, and parole. Some reformers actually believed that it might even be possible to phase out correctional institutions and to place all offenders in community-based programs.

That dream has never been achieved, and during the beginning of the twentieth century prisons remained harsh and brutal, many ruled with an iron hand by wardens who practiced control rather than treatment and rehabilitation. Specialized prisons designed to treat particular types of offenders were developed. In New York, the prisons at Clinton and Auburn were viewed as industrial facilities for hard-core inmates, Great Meadow was an agricultural center for nondangerous offenders, and Dannemora was a facility for the criminally insane. In California, San Quentin housed inmates considered salvageable by correctional authorities, and Folsom was reserved for hard-core offenders.

Until the 1960s, U.S. prisoners were deemed to have no rights and were regarded as slaves of the state. Then the courts became extensively involved in rulings on prisoners' rights. Though recently there has been more emphasis on crime control by the courts, much reform has still been accomplished, and courageous judges and public officials have changed the nature and quality of corrections for the future. Beginning in the 1970s, the adult prison population began to increase, and since 1980 there has been nearly a fivefold increase in this population. As a later section documents, prison crowding has resulted in many problems, resulting in an increase in tensions and violence within the prison, double and sometimes triple celling, the inability to provide sufficient programs and jobs for those inmates who desire them, and the demoralization of staff as well as their increased risks.

Rise of Modern Management

The Federal Bureau of Prisons was created in 1930, and the bureaucratization of corrections took place after World War II, when governors and state legislatures demanded the creation of management systems that would ensure the control of prisons through accountability. Departments of corrections were now headed by directors or commissioners who were appointed by the governor and who, in turn, would supervise wardens or superintendents of correctional institutions. The types of prisons increased to include minimum-security, medium-security, maximum-security, and supermax.

Increased Use of Technology

Today, technology is called upon to control offenders in both prisons and community-based corrections. For example, electronic monitoring (EM) is increasingly seen as a means of punishing high-risk offenders. In addition to the traditional methods of security and control, the correctional system is entering a new phase of technocorrections, which involves using technology rather than personnel to monitor prison populations.

Turning Increasingly to Privatization

Private operations were involved in community-based programs long before the twentieth century, but it was in the twentieth century that private corporations began to operate correctional facilities. Companies such as the Corrections Corporation of America, the GEO Group (formerly Wackenhut Corrections), and Cornell Companies presently operate more than 260 correctional facilities that house nearly 100,000 adult offenders.

THE PURPOSE AND FUNCTION OF THE CORRECTIONS SYSTEM TODAY

Discuss the purpose of corrections **LO5**

After this long history, the contemporary correctional system has emerged as an institution that serves to provide sufficient consequences to individuals convicted by the courts for violating the law so that the public will be protected, fear of crime will be reduced, and offenders are given a chance to reform. Over the centuries, these goals have taken on various meanings and emphasis. Consequently, the tactics used to achieve correctional goals have shifted from one generation to the next.

The general public's reaction to crime has a major influence on the types of punishable behavior and the punishments that are acceptable at a given time. Today, the public's reaction to crime, intensified by the fear of terrorist attacks, has encouraged a conservative, hard-line approach to corrections even though the actual crime rate has been in decline. This approach affects the number of offenders sent to correctional institutions and the duration and severity of their punishments. In this climate of fear, we should not expect a great deal of public sympathy for those who commit violent crimes.

While the correctional system may be used for punishment, it is also a venue for treatment and rehabilitation. In the midst of the sanctions given offenders because they have harmed society, there are those individuals who work with offenders to help them become productive, law-abiding citizens. It is important to examine their roles and how they do their jobs. There are, of course, sad stories of corruption, abuse, and incompetence, but there are also thrilling stories of those who pursue integrity in everything they do.

WHY DO WE PUNISH?

LO6 Summarize the reasons why we punish

The purpose of punishment—or what rulers, legislatures, and judges claimed was the purpose—has changed over time. Depending on the era and the culture, offenders were subject to extremely harsh physical punishments; they were hanged, decapitated, tortured, mutilated, incarcerated, ostracized, publicly humiliated, or otherwise restrained from the enjoyment of life and freedom. While today the cruel and public punishments of years past are usually no longer found, incarceration for life and execution are still routinely used for those committing the most serious crimes.

What are the justifications for punishment in contemporary society? What purpose is served when a fellow human being suffers punishment? After all, punishment involves applying pain, often long after the evil deed has been committed. At its core, criminal punishments result in harm to another human being—something that is in opposition to the moral values of modern society. Nonetheless, criminal punishment is considered justified because it is applied by (a) a duly authorized governmental body on (b) somebody who has violated the laws of society. Yet, how can a practice that results in the loss of personal liberty and freedom be justified in a nation such as ours? Punishment is considered justified in modern society for the following reasons:

- *Punishing law violators provides beneficial consequences.* Although it can be harsh and demeaning, punishing law violators is believed to create benefits for law-abiding citizens. Both the threat and application of criminal punishment are cost-effective means to an end: protecting the public, preventing disorder, and reducing social harm. Some might argue that while punishing people to improve society may be effective it sometimes presents a moral dilemma: would it be just and fair to execute a mentally ill criminal even if his execution helped lower crime rates? Those who believe that punishment is justified by its consequences counter that it is aimed at controlling harmful behavior. To paraphrase Mr. Spock (in *Star Trek II: The Wrath of Khan*), "The needs of the many outweigh the pain of the few." According to this view, even a morally unjust punishment—isolating and torturing terrorists in a harsh prison—is justified if it produces beneficial consequences: locating a deadly bomb they had planted. Critics might retort that it is unlikely that people willing to apply immoral and draconian punishments such as torture could be trusted to do so in a just and fair manner.
- *Punishment is deserved.* Criminal sanctions are justified because those who voluntarily break the law forfeit some of the rights claimed by citizens. They are **blameworthy**: their wrongdoing justifies treatment that under other circumstances would be considered coercive and/or a violation of civil rights, such as imprisonment or confiscation of wealth. According to the **just deserts** philosophy, punishment is justified only when it conforms to what the guilty deserve, no

blameworthy The law defines that a person is criminally liable for his or her behavior.

just deserts Punishment that is commensurate with the seriousness of the offense or the harm done.

more and no less. Because law violations involve taking an unfair advantage over those who obey the law, the purpose of punishment is to remove or neutralize any benefit gained through illegal activity. For example, a person who does not pay his proper share of taxes gains an unfair advantage over another who meets this civic burden. The tax cheat can use his excess wealth to invest and make even more money. It would be fair not only to demand the taxes he owed originally but to penalize him further to recover his ill-gotten gains from having use of the funds denied to the upstanding and law-abiding taxpayer.

- *Punishment expresses public outrage.* Criminal punishment is a method of expressing public outrage over the commission of a heinous crime. Because such wrongdoing provokes anger and sorrow, the public demands that the perpetrator suffer to "pay for their sins." While a private citizen may seek *revenge* for the pain they feel, the public demands **retribution** for its collective grief by forcing those who caused it to suffer in turn. In this sense, punishment embodies and expresses the public's moral indignation aroused by crime and the anger toward its perpetrator. State-sponsored punishment justifies their anger. By taking responsibility for retribution, the state eliminates the need for personal vengeance and the social chaos that follows in its wake.
- *Punishment teaches a lesson.* By punishing wrongdoers, the state demonstrates its disapproval of their behavior and in so doing teaches them not to repeat their misdeeds. Just as a parent punishes a misbehaving child so she won't repeat her behavior, so too does the government punish a citizen who violates its rules. The educative effect of punishment is not lost on the general population, which learns from the mistakes of others. Corrections serves as a substitute for language, and its important message is that society condemns the behavior committed.
- *Punishment helps maintain the government, the social structure, and society.* A state cannot survive unless it maintains a set of rules that create, support, and protect its structure and process. As the government becomes more structured, these rules are formalized into laws designed to control behaviors that threaten state security and well-being. The law provides that people may be corrected or punished if they engage in socially proscribed wrongs—conduct that is condemned as wrong and threatens the social norm. The American economic system, based on capitalism and free enterprise, could not exist unless there were laws protecting private property and protecting businesspeople from fraud and embezzlement. Because criminal laws are designed to protect the social fabric, the defendant must answer not just to the individual victim but to the whole polity through its criminal courts.

retribution Something given or demanded as repayment for wrongdoing; "getting even" for violating the social contract on which the law is based.

Web App 1.1
Conduct a case study by finding articles about Michael Fay, who in 1994 pleaded guilty to several acts of vandalism in Singapore. What happened to him? Do you agree with the punishment? Could you ever see a punishment like this used in the United States? Why or why not? LO6

Discuss the theories of punishment LO7

GOALS AND PHILOSOPHY OF PUNISHMENT

While criminal punishments are ideally designed to maintain the social order, there is no single vision of who should be punished, how the sanctions should be administered, and the ultimate goals that justify the application of punishment. Concepts are constantly shifting, reflecting the social, economic, and political realities of the time. Today, the objectives of criminal punishment can be grouped into seven distinct areas: general deterrence, specific deterrence, incapacitation, rehabilitation, retribution/just deserts, restoration, and equity/restitution. Each is discussed below in some detail.

FOR GROUP **DISCUSSION**
In your group, discuss what you believe the goals of punishing criminal offenders should be. Identify the "values" you think are contained in those goals. LO6

General Deterrence

Deterrence is a goal of punishment designed to prevent others from committing similar crimes. The public application of punishment produces a **general deterrent effect**, designed to signal the community at large that crime does not pay. The logic

general deterrent effect The idea that punishing one person for his or her criminal acts will discourage others from committing similar acts.

is quite simple: By severely punishing those people convicted of crime, others who are contemplating criminality will be frightened, deterred, and discouraged from their planned actions.[39] Anyone, the argument goes, would be foolish to commit crime if they see another person languishing in prison or actually being executed for the same offense. The state's need to deter criminals, however, must be balanced against the mandate to dispense fair and equal justice to all citizens. In addition, if sentences are too lenient, they may encourage criminal conduct, but if sentences are too severe, they may also provoke anger, revenge, and disrespect for the law. A good example of this would be if the crime of rape were punished by the death penalty. Though some potential rapists might be deterred, others might be encouraged to kill their victims to avoid identification since a conviction for either murder or rape produced the same consequences.

Work together in small groups to (1) create a definition for deterrence and (2) consider how you would go about measuring deterrence (in communities and individuals). LO7

The effectiveness of general deterrence is compromised by the ability of the criminal justice system to effectively identify, apprehend, and punish criminals. To be an effective deterrent, punishment must be certain: people must believe if they violate the law they will almost certainly be caught, convicted, and punished. But typically only 20 percent of all recorded criminal acts result in arrest, and only about 20 percent of arrestees wind up in prison, so the ability of punishment to deter crime is undermined by lack of system effectiveness and efficiency.[40] Most offenders are never arrested, and many who are arrested have their cases dropped. Still other offenders are given community-based sanctions rather than prison sentences. For some crimes, such as larceny, relatively few offenders are ever caught or punished.

If the chances of getting caught and punished are relatively small, and punishment does not deter crime per se, why have crime rates been dropping? Some criminal justice experts reason that the recent decline in crime rates is due to the fact that criminal penalties have been toughened for many criminal offenses. They find that once individuals are arrested, they have a greater chance of being convicted than in the past, which is referred to as *expected punishment*; this can be defined as the number of days in prison that a typical offender can expect to serve for each crime committed.[41] It stands to reason that the likelihood of being apprehended and convicted, as well as the length of sentences, influences offenders' expected punishments. Crime rates have fallen significantly during the past two decades while expected punishments rose.

The percentage of convicted offenders who receive a prison sentence has been declining recently.[42] Cost cutting and budget deficits may consciously or unconsciously encourage some judges to rely more on community sentences such as probation that are significantly less expensive than jail or prison. It is possible that if this trend continues, expected punishment will decrease and, therefore, crime rates may increase.

MYTH **The fear of punishment can deter crime. The more harshly we punish crimes, the less likely people will risk committing criminal acts.**

FACT **The association between crime and punishment is less than clear cut. Many criminals are not apprehended, neutralizing the effect of punishment. For some crimes, relatively few offenders are ever caught or punished. If expected punishments could increase, crime rates might go down.**

Specific Deterrence

The philosophy of **specific deterrence** focuses on the fact that individual offenders should learn firsthand that crime does not pay when they experience harsh criminal penalties. What this position suggests is that the suffering caused by punishment should inhibit future criminal activities. Historically, physical punishments were designed to inflict so much pain that only the bravest or most demented criminal would risk reoffending. In our society, a stay in a violent and dangerous prison should be enough to convince people that crime does not pay. But does it work?

specific deterrence The idea that an individual offender will decide against repeating an offense after experiencing the painfulness of punishment for that offense.

Although a few research efforts have found that punishment can have significant specific deterrence on future criminal behavior, these studies are balanced by research that has failed to uncover specific deterrence effects. Most prisoners (more than 80 percent) who are released from prison have had prior convictions, and the great majority (68 percent) will reoffend soon after they are released.[43] The fact that

FOR GROUP **DISCUSSION** Discuss with your group the philosophies of general deterrence and specific deterrence, and have each person provide an example with an explanation for both. Present your examples to the class. LO7

most convicted criminals reoffend weakens the argument that experiencing punishment produces a specific deterrent effect.

The effectiveness of specific deterrence may be crime specific. For example, parking offenses that have a rapidly increasing scale of punishment and a high rate of ticketing will affect parking behaviors.

Incapacitation

incapacitation Isolating offenders to protect society.

Another goal of punishment is to incapacitate dangerous people so they do not have the opportunity to harm others. Offenders are sentenced to prison to restrain them physically so during the time they are confined society is protected, a concept known as **incapacitation**. Sentencing for the purpose of incapacitation is embraced by both liberals and conservatives. According to liberals, prison was to be reserved for especially dangerous repeat offenders who require incapacitation to protect society while they are being treated and reformed. Conservatives may be less concerned about treatment but view incapacitation as a crime-prevention strategy that can reduce crime rates by imprisoning significant numbers of felons.

Although considerable research has been done on the effects of incapacitation in reducing crime, the results are inconclusive.[44] While it is true that the current prison population is extremely high and the crime rate has been in decline, the prison population also jumped in the decade between 1980 and 1990, while the crime rate increased substantially. It is possible that crime rates have little relationship to incarceration trends and that the reductions in crime are related to such factors as the economy, police effectiveness, and declining drug use.[45] An incapacitation strategy to reduce crime is also terribly expensive, costing taxpayers billions each year. And there are diminishing returns. Many people are kept in prison well past the age when they would stop committing crime spontaneously. The number of elderly inmates is skyrocketing, despite the fact that the elderly are expensive to maintain and are not really a danger to society.

selective incapacitation Identifying high-rate offenders and providing for their long-term incarceration.

SELECTIVE INCAPACITATION According to the policy of **selective incapacitation**, because only a small number of offenders commit a significant portion of all crimes, it is more effective to sentence repeat offenders to long prison terms while granting first-time and nonviolent offenders shorter and more lenient sentences.[46] As a result, "career offenders" are locked up for long periods, while one-time or occasional criminals are given probation or other community sentences.[47] While enticing, selective incapacitation is not without its drawbacks. It relies on predicting who will commit future crimes, something that has proven quite elusive to calculate. It also produces false positives—some people are severely punished who may never commit another crime. Is it ethical to punish people whom we believe may be dangerous in the future based on what they have done in the past?

Rehabilitation

rehabilitation Changing an offender's character, attitudes, or behavior patterns so as to diminish his or her criminal propensities.

The **rehabilitation** aspect of sentencing suggests that people who violate the law are "society's victims." They have been maltreated by their family, forced to live in poverty, or suffered some life trauma which through no fault of their own has forced them into a life of crime. They will refrain from further criminal activity if they can be successfully helped and treated rather than condemned and punished.

Rehabilitation is also based on being able to predict the future needs of the offender, not on the gravity of the current offense. For example, if a judge sentences a person convicted of a felony to a community-based program, the judge's actions reflect his or her belief that the offender can be successfully treated and presents no future threat to society.

During the twentieth century, the concept of rehabilitation dominated sentencing and corrections. People were placed behind bars until they were thought to be "cured" and then released. The parole board took control of determining when an offender was rehabilitated and thus ready to return to the community. Sentence length shifted from the control of the judge to the correctional system.

Support for rehabilitation-based sentencing practices began to erode when reformers raised questions about the ethics of the rehabilitation model. The erosion accelerated in the early 1970s when criminal justice researcher Robert Martinson and his associates failed to find any systematic evidence that indeterminate sentencing actually worked and prison programs rehabilitated inmates.[48] It was also charged at the time that parole boards were unable to determine when inmates eligible for release had been cured of their criminal propensities. The combined evidence made a mockery of the term "correctional institution." It also raised fundamental questions about the wisdom of maintaining a sentencing policy that was not only failing to achieve its primary objective but doing so in a manner that lacked fairness and consistency.

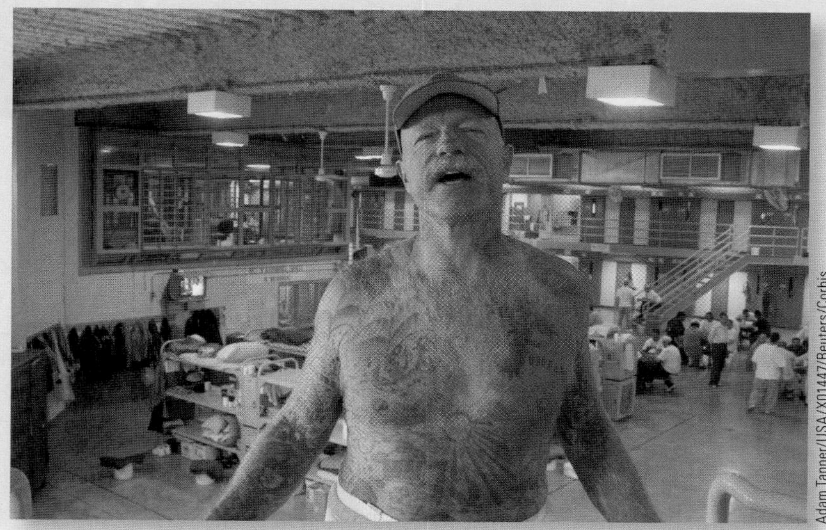

Adam Tanner/USA/X01447/Reuters/Corbis

Prison conditions are a significant concern for correctional administrators. Inmate Dennis Howie, 53, a three-strike offender, is pictured at the Mule Creek State Prison in Ione, California. The prison, which houses murderers, child molesters, thieves, and other criminals, is one of the most overcrowded in California. Some inmates have to share triple bunk beds in large public areas, including gyms, because of a shortage of prison cells. The Supreme Court has ordered California to release more than 30,000 inmates or take other steps to ease overcrowding in its prisons to prevent "needless suffering and death." California's 33 adult prisons were designed to hold about 80,000 inmates and now have about 135,000. The United States has more than 2 million people in state and local prisons. It has long had the highest incarceration rate in the world.

After more than 40 years, rehabilitation has made a comeback. Many private, community, and even institutional corrections are rehabilitative focused, and many are readopting the principles of rehabilitation. Also, a number of comprehensive reviews of research on the effectiveness of correctional treatment have found that some treatment programs do have positive outcomes in improving the attitudes of offenders and in reducing recidivism.[49] The challenge is to identify which program will work with what offenders in what setting.[50]

EVIDENCE-BASED PROGRAMS The norm for planners and correctional administrators in many jurisdictions today is to use the research on evidence-based programs to design programs that work with offenders. **Evidence-based programs** rely on careful analysis of program outcomes using scientifically approved methods, and are designed to discover which programs work with which offenders, in what types of settings, and in what frequency of treatment. One of the tenets of evidence-based practices is "targeted interventions." This principle essentially states that a jurisdiction's most expensive and intensive resources should be directed to those offenders who pose the highest risk to reoffend. Throughout this text, we will focus on some of the most effective evidence-based programs. See the accompanying Evidence-Based Corrections feature.

evidence-based programs This approach is an analysis of programs with scientifically approved methods to discover what works with which offenders.

Retribution/Just Deserts

A retributionist position is that punishment is justified if and only if it is deserved because of a past crime. Similarly, the theory of just deserts holds that it is unfair to deprive a person of liberty as a consequence of committing a criminal act for any other reason than the act they engaged in *deserves* to be punished. One should be punished

EVIDENCE-BASED CORRECTIONS

Successful Reentry: What Differentiates Successful and Unsuccessful Parolees?

In a recent study, sociologists Stephen Bahr, Lish Harris, James Fisher, and Anita Harker Armstrong sought to identify what differentiates successful parolees from those who fail on parole. Their goal was to achieve a better understanding of the reentry process in order to enable professionals, friends, and family members to help former inmates adjust to life outside of prison and successfully complete their parole.

To achieve their research objective, they followed 51 parolees during the three years that followed their release from parole. They found that at the end of the three-year period, 55 percent (28) of the parolees had successfully completed their parole and were formally discharged, 25 percent (13) remained on parole, and 20 percent (10) were back in prison.

What differentiated the successes from the failures? One big reason for parole failure, as might be expected, is continued trouble with the law. Successes committed fewer crimes and were arrested less than failures: the mean number of arrests for those who successfully completed parole was 0.28—only 5 of the 28 successful parolees had been arrested. By contrast, those who returned to prison had been arrested at least twice within the three years after release.

Another factor that shaped parole outcome was participation in a prison-based treatment program. Those who succeeded on parole were more likely to have taken a substance abuse class while in prison, an experience that helped some parolees succeed in their attempt to stay off drugs after release and change their identity. The class may have provided the skills, motivation, and support useful in learning to remain substance free.

A number of other economic, personal, and social factors contributed to successful reentry into society. Those who worked at least 40 hours a week were more likely to have completed parole successfully. Work may be important in establishing routines that reduce opportunities and time for associations with deviant peers. Full-time work may also help parolees establish a conventional identity.

Nurturing family ties and friendship networks were also important for parole success. Conventional family and friendship networks insulated the successful parolees from the influence of friends who used drugs. Those without social supports drifted back into crime because they were less connected and more alone.

In sum, success on parole was a multifaceted construct, involving support from family and friends as well as institutional support from employees and the correctional system.

FOR CRITICAL THINKING AND WRITING

Considering the factors that make for successful reentry into society, what would you require inmates to do before they are released back into the community? Is it possible to help them create nurturing family ties and friendship networks while still behind bars?

Source: Stephen J. Bahr, Lish Harris, James K. Fisher, and Anita Harker Armstrong, "Successful Reentry: What Differentiates Successful and Unsuccessful Parolees?" *International Journal of Offender Therapy and Comparative Criminology* 54 (October 2010): 667–692.

because they deserve it and not to deter others or reduce future criminality. These views of sentencing are retrospective rather than prospective; those who administer punishment need not be concerned with future outcomes, only with providing appropriate punishment for a given harm.[51]

The task of just deserts is to assess the magnitude of the harm and to devise a punishment that is proportionate in severity. The assessment of the magnitude of the harm is typically defined by the type of crime (e.g., petty theft would be seen as less serious than felonious assault) and the offender's prior record. A one-time offender might be treated more leniently than a chronic criminal. Motivation might also be considered. A person who embezzles to maintain a lavish lifestyle would be judged more harshly than one who embezzles the same amount for the more noble purpose of subsidizing the company's underpaid and exploited overseas workers.[52]

Restorative Justice

The **restorative justice** goal of sentencing is designed to reintegrate the criminal offender back into the community. Restorative justice has roots in the concept of reparation, something done or paid to make amends for harm or loss. In victim-oriented reparation, the offender returns to the rightful owner either what has been taken away or its equivalent, usually in money or service. In community-oriented reparation, the offender either pays a fine or renders community service; the community thus functions as a substitute victim. By helping the victim and the community, the offender begins to understand the harm caused by their actions. Rather than being cast out of society, they are given the opportunity to be restored in good standing.[53]

Jim Wilson/The New York Times/Redux Pictures

Principal Betsye Steele speaks with a student in a restorative justice talking circle at Ralph J. Bunche High School in Oakland, California. Restorative justice, which encourages young people to develop empathy for one another, is increasingly offered in schools seeking an alternative to "zero tolerance" policies that feature punishment rather than reconciliation.

Restorative justice is grounded in the concept that the government should surrender its control over responses to crime to those who are most directly affected—the victim, the offender, and the community. This expression of punishment is based on the premise that communities will be strengthened if local citizens participate in the response to crime, and this response is tailored to the needs and preferences of victims, communities, and offenders. The discussion of restorative justice will be expanded in Chapter 4 on intermediate sanctions.

restorative justice Making amends to the victim or to society for the harm resulting from a criminal offense.

Equity/Restitution

The **equity goal of punishment** means that convicted offenders must pay back their victims for their loss, the justice system for costs related to processing their cases, and society for the disruptions caused because of their crimes. In drug trafficking, the social costs may include expenses involved with drug enforcement efforts, day treatment centers, and care for infants born to drug-addicted mothers. In predatory crimes, the costs may include services of emergency room physicians, lost workdays and productivity, and therapy for long-term psychological problems. To help meet these costs, convicted defendants might be required to pay fines, do community service, make financial restitution to victims, forfeit the property they acquired through illegal activities, and reimburse the state for costs related to the criminal process. Thus, the demands of justice require that offenders who have profited from their crimes lose privileges and rights to restore the social balance.

equity goal of punishment That offenders usually gain from criminal violations makes it seem just and right that they repay society and victims for losses, expenses, and damages that result from their crimes.

Web App 1.2
Go to Restorative Justice Online to view the video "Victim Story: Restorative Justice," where a crime victim tells about her "restorative encounter with her father's killer." http://www.restorativejustice.org/press-room/02personal/videos-relating-stories-of-restorative-justice/victim-story-restorative-justice LO7

The Criminal Justice System and Corrections

Corrections today is an important cog in the contemporary criminal justice system. These agencies, located at the federal, state, and local levels of government, serve as society's instruments of social control. They are designed to regulate behaviors considered so dangerous that they cannot be tolerated within the confines of society. The justice system is therefore designed to maintain and control people considered so destructive that they must be monitored and/or confined. The agencies of justice—law enforcement, the courts, and corrections—control these outlawed behaviors by apprehending, adjudicating, and sanctioning lawbreakers. Society maintains other forms of informal social control, such as religious institutions, but these deal with moral—not

LO8 Explain the relationship between corrections and the criminal justice system

FIGURE 1.2

Components of the Criminal Justice System

Police

Police departments are those public agencies created to maintain order, enforce the criminal law, provide emergency services, keep traffic on streets and highways moving freely, and develop a sense of community safety. Police officers work actively with the community to prevent criminal behavior; they help divert members of special needs populations, such as juveniles, alcoholics, and drug addicts, from the criminal justice system; they participate in specialized units such as a drug prevention task force or antirape unit; they cooperate with public prosecutors to initiate investigations into organized crime and drug trafficking; they resolve neighborhood and family conflicts; and they provide emergency services, such as preserving civil order during strikes and political demonstrations.

Courts

The criminal courthouse is the scene of the trial process. Here the criminal responsibility of defendants accused of violating the law is determined. Ideally, the court is expected to convict and sentence those found guilty of crimes, while ensuring that the innocent are freed without any consequence or burden. The court system is formally required to seek the truth, to obtain justice for the individual brought before its tribunals, and to maintain the integrity of the government's rule of law. The main actors in the court process are the judge, whose responsibilities include overseeing the legality of the trial process, and the prosecutor and the defense attorney, who are the opponents in what is known as the adversary system. These two parties oppose each other in a hotly disputed contest—the criminal trial—in accordance with rules of law and procedure.

Corrections

In the broadest sense, correctional agencies include community supervision or probation, various types of incarceration (including jails, houses of correction, and state prisons), and parole programs for both juvenile and adult offenders. These programs range from the lowest security, such as probation in the community with minimum supervision, to the highest security, such as 23-hour lockdown in an ultra-maximum-security prison. Corrections ordinarily represent the postadjudicatory care given to offenders when a sentence is imposed by the court and the offender is placed in the hands of the correctional agency.

legal—misbehavior. Only the criminal justice system maintains the power to control crime and punish behavior in its role as the operational arm of criminal law.

Criminal justice agencies are political entities lodged within the legislative, judicial, and executive branches of the government.

- The legislature creates law, defines its content, and establishes criminal penalties. The legislative branch of government also appropriates funds for criminal justice agencies, thereby shaping their structure and mission.
- The judiciary interprets the existing law and determines whether it meets constitutional requirements. It provides oversight on criminal justice practices and has the power to insist that they meet legal obligations. The courts have the right to overturn or ban policies that are in conflict with constitutional rights.
- The executive branch helps set justice policy and appoints key leaders within the justice system, such as the head of the prison system and judges.

Agencies of the Criminal Justice System

Because of its varied and complex mission, the contemporary criminal justice system in the United States is monumental in size. It now costs federal, state, and local governments about $230 billion per year for civil and criminal justice, up more than 300 percent since 1982.

One reason the justice system is so expensive to run is because it employs more than 2.4 million people. The nation has almost 18,000 law enforcement agencies, nearly 17,000 courts, more than 8,000 prosecutorial agencies employing more than

80,000 people, about 1,200 correctional institutions such as jails and prisons, and more than 3,500 probation and parole departments.

The system is massive because it must process, treat, and care for millions of people. Although the crime rate has been in decline for most of the past decade, more than 12 million people are still being arrested each year, including about 1.5 million for serious felony offenses.[54] In addition, about 1 million juveniles are handled by the juvenile courts. When traffic and local ordinance violations are included with felony and misdemeanor cases, the nation's courts handle over 100 million cases per year.[55] Figure 1.3 shows how offenders are handled by the criminal justice process.

More than 7 million people are under some form of correctional supervision, including 2.2 million men and women in the nation's jails and prisons and about

FIGURE 1.3

Criminal Justice Funnel

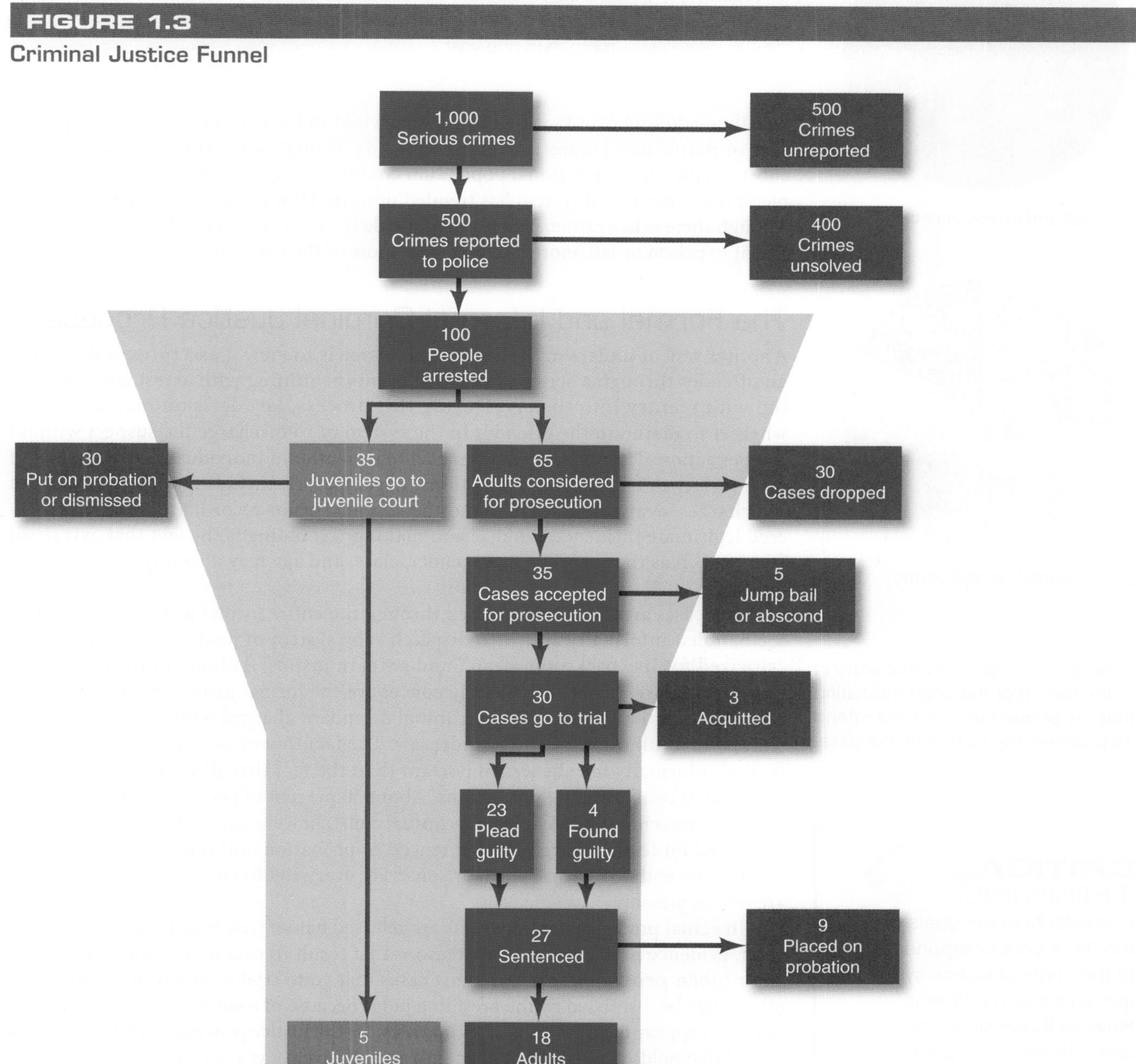

FIGURE 1.4

Populations of Community-Based and Institutional Corrections

Source: Lauren E. Glaze and Erinn J. Herberman, *Correctional Populations in the United States, 2012* (Washington, DC: Bureau of Justice Statistics, December 2013), p. 3.

Jail and prison inmates

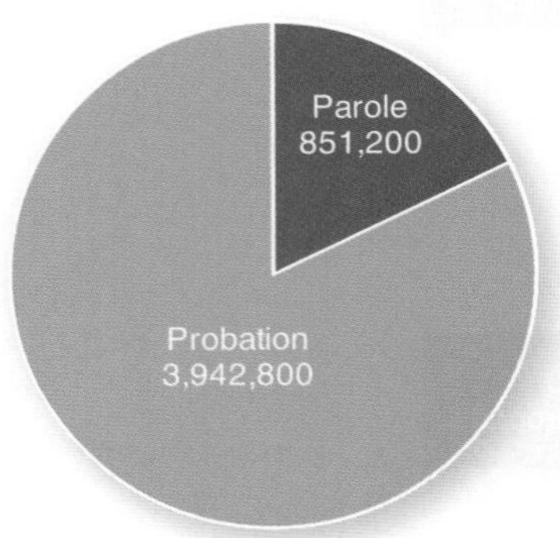

Probation and parole

nolle prosequi A formal entry in the record of the court indicating that the prosecutor does not intend to proceed any further in this case.

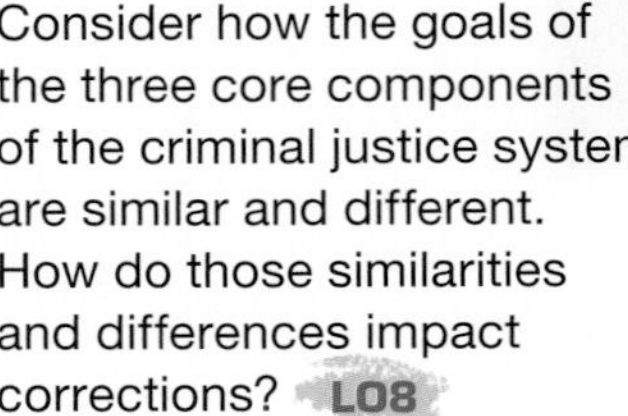

CRITICAL THINKING

Consider how the goals of the three core components of the criminal justice system are similar and different. How do those similarities and differences impact corrections? LO8

EXHIBIT 1.3

Elements of the Correctional System

Probation	Court-ordered community supervision of convicted offenders by a probation agency. Offenders on probation are required to obey specific rules of conduct while in the community.
Parole	Community supervision after a period of incarceration.
Jail	A county correctional facility that holds people pending trial, awaiting sentencing, serving a sentence that is usually less than one year, or awaiting transfer to other facilities after conviction.
Prison	A state or federal correctional facility that houses convicted criminals sentenced to a period of confinement that is typically more than one year.

5 million adult men and women being supervised in the community while on probation or parole (see Figure 1.4 and Exhibit 1.3). Though the crime rate has declined substantially, this correctional population continues to grow, and the number of people in the correctional system has trended upward. How can this trend be explained? Though there is less crime, people are more likely to be convicted than in the past and, if sent to prison or jail, more likely to serve more of their sentence.

The Formal and Informal Criminal Justice Process

Another way of understanding criminal justice is to view it as a process that takes an offender through a series of decision points beginning with arrest and concluding with reentry into society. During this process, key decision makers resolve whether to maintain the offender in the system or to discharge the suspect without further action. This decision making is often a matter of individual discretion, based on a variety of factors and perceptions. Legal factors, including the seriousness of the charges, available evidence, and the suspect's prior record, are usually considered legitimate influences on decision making. Troubling is the fact that extralegal factors such as the suspect's race, gender, class, and age may also influence decision outcomes.

Few cases are actually processed through the entire formal justice system. Most are handled informally and with dispatch. The system of justice has been roundly criticized for its "backroom deals" and bargain justice. Although informality and deal making are in fact the rule, the concept of the formal justice process is important because it implies that every criminal defendant charged with a serious crime is entitled to a full range of rights under law. The fact that most criminal suspects are treated informally may be less important than the fact that all criminal defendants are granted constitutional protections. About 30 percent of people arrested on felony charges are eventually convicted in criminal court; however, almost one-third of those convicted on felony charges are sentenced to probation and released back into the community without doing time in prison.[56] For every 1,000 crimes, less than 20 people are sent to prison.

In actual practice, many suspects are released before trial because of a procedural error, evidence problems, or other reasons that result in case dismissal by the prosecutor (***nolle prosequi***). Though most cases that go to trial wind up in a conviction, others may be dismissed by the presiding judge because of a witness or a complainant's failure to appear or procedural irregularities. So the justice process can be viewed as a funnel that holds many cases at its mouth and relatively few at its end. Figure 1.5 shows the interrelationship of the component agencies of the criminal justice system and the criminal justice process.

FIGURE 1.5

Criminal Justice process

The Interrelationship of the Criminal Justice System and the Criminal Justice Process

THE CRIMINAL JUSTICE SYSTEM	THE CRIMINAL JUSTICE PROCESS
POLICE 	1. Contact 2. Investigation 3. Arrest 4. Custody
PROSECUTION AND DEFENSE 	5. Complaint/charging 6. Grand jury/preliminary hearing 7. Arraignment 8. Bail/detention 9. Plea negotiations
COURTS 	10. Adjudication 11. Disposition 12. Appeal/postconviction remedies
CORRECTIONS 	13. Correction 14. Release 15. Postrelease

Corrections in the Criminal Justice System

LO9 Describe the extent and consequences of prison overcrowding

While corrections is an element within a complex set of criminal justice organizations and processes, it is functionally independent from the other agencies, with a unique set of values, procedures, and policies. It also faces problems and issues unknown in other agencies such as the police and court system. What are some of these challenges?

SYSTEM OVERLOAD One of the major challenges affecting the ability of corrections to function as a system is overload. The past four decades can be defined as a period of **mass incarceration**. There are now 2.2 million men and women who are serving time in jails and prisons in the United States. What this means is that nearly one in every fifty people in the United States, excluding the elderly and juveniles, is in prison. The U.S. prison population has increased nearly fivefold since 1980 (see Figure 1.6). Significantly, a larger proportion of the U.S. adult population is in prison than anywhere else in the world. With 5 percent of the world's population, the United States has nearly a quarter of its prisoners. The U.S. incarceration rate of more than 724 per 100,000 is five to twelve times the rate of western European countries and Japan.[57] There is evidence that the massive increase and the inmate population has finally stabilized.

mass incarceration A term given to the high rates of incarceration in the United States.

Since 1995 there has been nearly a 40 percent increase in the inmate population with a 33 percent increase in male prisoners and a 51 percent increase in female prisoners.[58] A closer examination of prison overcrowding reveals that the rate varies significantly

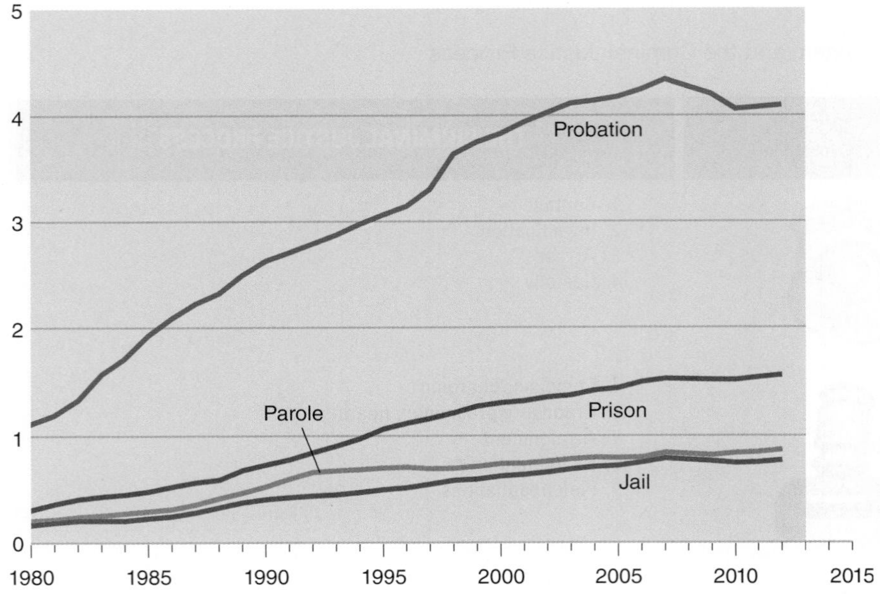

FIGURE 1.6

Adult Correctional Populations

Source: Lauren E. Glaze and Erinn J. Herberman, *Correctional Populations in the United States*, 2012 (Washington, D.C.: Bureau of Justice Statistics, December 2013), p. 3.

from one region to another and from one state to another. The South has the highest rate of imprisonment, followed by the West, Northeast, and Midwest.[59] The Federal Bureau of Prisons has the largest number of inmates, followed closely by California and Texas; these three jurisdictions have nearly 34 percent of the U.S. prison population. See Table 1.1 for the number of state and federal prisoners in the seven largest jurisdictions.

Prison crowding leads to increased inmate defiance and makes prisons (especially maximum-security and supermax prisons) more dangerous places to work. In 2011, for example, the California prison system was beset by prolonged hunger strikes by inmates who were protesting degrading conditions in isolation cells and gang-security measures that unfairly punish prisoners. In July of that year, thousands of inmates staged a three-week hunger strike at prisons across the state.[60]

The federal courts have intervened to mandate strict population ceilings for individual prisons and, in some cases, for entire state systems. Ironically, efforts to reduce prison crowding have led to the overcrowding of county jails, where convicted felons wait for vacant cells in a state prison.

THE BUSINESS OF CORRECTIONS Another difference between corrections and the other agencies of justice is the shift in public perception about its role and value. While police and courts are perceived as a drain on local budgets, prisons are now viewed as an economic savior for local economies. At one time few wanted to see a prison or jail built in their community.

CORRECTIONAL LIFE

TIM: An Ex-Offender Speaks Out

One time I was placed in jail and was still a little intoxicated. You never want to cause problems in jail in the middle of the night. I said something to one of them, and they took me in a side room. They beat me until I s— on myself. Then they took me into a tiny cell, hog-tied me, and gave me mace, probably two inches from my face. I was not giving up, and I told them that they were punks and cowards. They gave me mace a couple more times. I laid in there all night long. They knew what they were doing and didn't leave bruises or anything. In the morning, one of the shift supervisors got me out of there and cleaned me up. I thought this was extreme punishment for lipping off a bit.

Then there was the experience I had with this civilian who worked in the prison. She did not like me. One day, while I was working the chow line, she humiliated me in front of other inmates. She tried to make me look like an idiot. I simply turned to her and said, "You can't tell me s—." She went into the office and called the goon squad. I did about 10 days in the "hole" as punishment, or administrative segregation. And if this wasn't enough, I was taken to a special needs, or mental health, ward. In prison, if you have a mental health disorder, you are called a "bug." You are not down there with the status of child molesters, but you don't have much higher status. This was the special section of the correctional facility where I would spend the rest of my time. The warden came and talked with me and told me that he was making an example of me.

TABLE 1.1

Six Largest Jurisdictions of Prisoners Under the Jurisdiction of State or Federal Correctional Authorities

	Number of Prisoners 12/31/10	Percent Change 2010–2011
Federal Bureau of Prisons	145,416	3.1
California	149,560	–9.4
Texas	172,204	–0.8
Florida	103,005	–1.2
Michigan	42,940	–2.8
New York	55,435	–2.2

Source: E. Ann Carson and William J Sabol, Prisoners in 2010–2011 (Washington, D.C.,: U.S. Department of Justice, 2012).

THINKING LIKE A CORRECTIONS PROFESSIONAL

The governor has appointed you chairman of a task force to bring reform to your state's correctional efforts. She is particularly concerned that you find ways to reduce the prison population, without compromising public safety. Whom will you appoint to your committee? What is your strategy for developing this plan of reform? What is your plan to disseminate the results of your report?

Today, this "not in my backyard" philosophy has been replaced with welcome mats. Take for instance Canon City, Colorado, which now calls itself the "Corrections Capital of the World." In Leavenworth, Kansas—a community that recently added a private facility to its already well-known corrections stockade—a billboard reads, "How about doin' some TIME in Leavenworth?" A prison has become a quick way to fix the economic struggles of small counties. Towns that are economically strapped know that if they can induce jail and prison construction, they will receive jobs and attract other businesses such as fast food chains, department stores, and motels—all of which contribute to their tax base. As a result, they are more than willing to offer land, cash incentives, and cut-rate deals on utilities.[61] Today, correctional systems are involved in prison-building booms. Prisons are developing economically profitable relationships among politicians, corporations, and the private sector, and even becoming a commodity on the stock market. This configuration is why the term **prison-industrial complex** is sometimes used to describe correctional systems in the United States.

Web App 1.3

Research and identify the prison facilities located in your state. What are the names of the facilities? Where are they located? Which facility has the largest inmate population? Has the inmate population increased or decreased in recent years? LO9

THE SOCIAL COST OF CORRECTIONS Another problem that is unique to corrections is the social costs that the policy of mass confinement has had on the American public. While law enforcement and the courts have a relatively short-term impact on people's lives, correctional confinement is a long, drawn-out process that affects both people and the communities in which they reside.

Corrections has had a significant impact on urban neighborhoods in the United States. Most immediate is the effect on the families of prisoners. There are now about 1.5 million children who have a parent in prison. For African American children, one of every fourteen has a parent behind bars on any given day. For these children, shame, stigma, and loss of financial and psychological support are profound aspects of their life experience.

MYTH **No one wants a prison in their backyard, and most areas fight prison construction tooth and nail in order to preserve their communities.**

FACT **Many rural communities see prison construction as an economic boon and fight to have state governments build institutions in their community. Prisons provide jobs and bolster the local economy. Prison construction is especially welcome during tough economic times.**

The toll of corrections is often borne by minority group members. According to Marc Mauer, the effect on these communities is compounded by the fact that imprisonment has become a commonplace experience of growing up as an African American male in the United States. Government figures show that an African American male born today has a one in three chance of spending at least a year in prison at some point in his life. While children in well-off communities grow up with the expectations that they will go to college, many in low-income communities grow up with the prospect of doing time in prison.[62]

prison-industrial complex A term given to describe the multimillion-dollar prison-building boom in which powerful corporate interest groups, large businesses, and politicians join together to profit from the burgeoning corrections industry.

AP Images/Eric Risberg

There are many hidden costs of the correctional system. Here is a photo of the fortress-like San Quentin prison in San Quentin, California, taken on May 20, 2009. San Quentin, with 5,300 inmates, is located in upscale Marin County not too far from San Francisco. Rather than being tucked away in the woods, it sits on some of the most prized waterfront land in the country. Facing billion-dollar budget deficits, every few years someone proposes shutting down the prison and selling off the land at market rate. Some Californians suggest that it be torn down and sold to developers. It would be more valuable as a condo complex than as a prison.

Discuss the financial costs of corrections **LO10**

FIGURE 1.7

Direct Expenditure by Criminal Justice function

Source: Bureau of Justice Statistics, *Employment and Statistics in the U.S., 2007* (Washington, DC: U.S. Department of Justice, 2011).

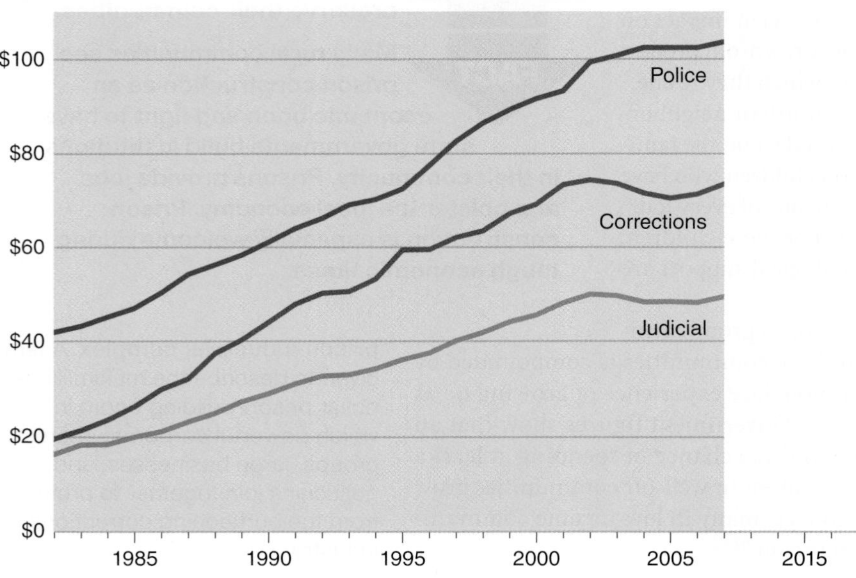

FINANCIAL COST OF CORRECTIONS The economic problems of the past decade have impacted all the agencies of justice, including corrections (see Figure 1.7). With virtually every state in the United States facing huge deficits, most have begun cutting prison budgets and closing institutions, especially prison camps and minimum-security prisons, to help balance the budget. This process is found not only in the United States, but also in other countries such as Canada, the United Kingdom, and Australia.[63]

States have recently responded to this crisis in a variety of different ways:

- North Carolina closed seven prisons and nine others had major changes. This eliminated 516 positions for a $22.3 million annual savings.
- Washington State closed nine institutions. Three hundred employees statewide stood to lose their jobs.
- Texas eliminated one prison, three Texas Youth Commission lockups, and 2,000 private prison beds. About 1,560 prison jobs were also chopped. Probation programs saw funding cut by 20 percent, parole supervision cut by almost 9 percent, and the agency construction and maintenance cut, along with 90 jobs. The victims services division was also eliminated.
- Oregon shut down a minimum-security prison, marking the first prison closure in Oregon history. This was part of a $2.5 billion budget cut that included laying off 63 prison employees.
- Michigan closed three prisons and five prison camps in hopes of narrowing a $1.4 billion budget gap.[64]

PROFESSIONALISM IN CORRECTIONS All agencies of justice have strived for **professionalism**, requiring education, training, and innovation in order to improve the effectiveness of services. The corrections system has also confronted the need for professionalism, though its mission sometimes makes this goal difficult to achieve. For those who have been in a maximum-security prison or a supermax prison, with their tall walls or razor-wire fences, tiny cells, foreboding segregation units, and ever-present dangers, concepts such as valued career or professionalism may seem totally foreign, unrealistic, and idealistic. Certainly, corrections is not an easy job. Corrections is a complex field riddled with critical issues and deeply disturbing realities, focused on human tragedy and failure. It is a field so shaped by its social context that political and economic realities at times make it seem impossible either to maintain or to change.

One corrections professional, Norman C. Carlson, who served as director of the Federal Bureau of Prisons from 1970 to 1987, was an individual who did as much as anyone to introduce professionalism into correctional service. Carlson's vision of corrections as a profession was one of the earliest themes he articulated once he became director. At that time, corrections was considered anything but a profession. In state departments of corrections, horror stories were commonplace—the inmate trusties in Arkansas who carried weapons and brutalized inmates, the backbreaking work of stoop, or field, labor in the fields of Texas, and the staff brutality that was an ever-present feature in American corrections. Even in the federal system, there were incidents of staff brutality, and Carlson wanted the bureau's staff to know what would be tolerated and what would not be tolerated.

It was not long before signs of professionalism began to appear in state correctional systems. State correctional training academies were established across the nation. Accreditation, spearheaded by the American Correctional Association, was developed and spread throughout community-based agencies and correctional institutions. Affirmative action policies were developed and implemented throughout corrections. The abuse of inmates began to be replaced by the belief that inmates were to be treated with dignity and respect. Some states moved more quickly than others, but this spirit of professionalism is now found throughout the nation. The characteristics and attitudes of what it means to be a corrections professional can be summarized as follows:

- To see yourself as a person of integrity and to live at integrity level. A definition of integrity is to do the right thing even when no one else is around.
- To treat offenders with dignity and respect. As one corrections professional puts it, treat inmates as you would want your father or brother to be treated in a correctional setting.[65]
- To model positive behaviors. One way this can be done is to adhere to the ethical principles set forth by the American Correctional Association.[66]
- To be a person committed to a learning model and to be open to new ways of doing things. Such a person seeks to learn throughout his or her career and is always willing to pursue all the training opportunities available.
- To believe that it is possible to make a difference. Believe that you can have an impact and are not limited by what others have done.
- To keep your personal stuff from getting in the way. Do not let your personal problems or issues keep you from doing an effective job.[67]
- To refuse to accept unethical behavior from fellow staff members.
- To stay positive and do what is possible to create a workplace that is safe, healthy, and free of harassment in any form.[68]

Throughout this book, we highlight a number of careers in corrections. In this chapter, we examine the director of corrections, who can also be referred to as the commissioner of corrections or the secretary of corrections. One of the hopeful signs of corrections is the increase in professionalism among these top corrections officials.

We discuss in detail a variety of careers in corrections, including pretrial officer, probation officer, substance abuse counselor, jail officer, warden, correctional officer, corrections ombudsman, parole officer, correctional supervisor, social worker, and more, in Chapter 15, where you will learn about preparation for the job, nature of the work, qualifications and required education, job outlook, and earnings and benefits.

In addition to these careers, it is possible to obtain employment in corrections in a number of other jobs, including accountant, office manager, secretary, business manager, building-grounds maintenance staff, dental hygienist, dentist, food service worker, registered nurse, physician, storekeeper, programmer/analyst, boiler operator, and treatment plant operator.

CRITICAL THINKING

What are some ways in which correctional agencies can reduce their operating costs or raise their revenues to help address the financial costs of corrections? LO10

LO11 Explain the importance of professionalism in corrections

professionalism The conduct, aims, or qualities that characterize or make a profession or professional person.

Web App 1.4
Visit the American Correctional Association (ACA) website at http://www.aca.org/ and identify indications of professionalism in corrections. LO11

Courtesy of Clem Bartollas

CAREERS IN CORRECTIONS

Christopher B. Epps

Mississippi Commissioner of Corrections

"This August will mark my 12th year as corrections commissioner in my native and great state of Mississippi. I am the state's longest serving commissioner because I'm just as passionate about corrections today as I was when I started my career as a correctional officer more than 30 years at the Mississippi State Penitentiary at Parchman, the state's oldest prison.

"As head of the American Correctional Association, I am focusing especially on increasing the number of accredited agencies and reentry programs. Accreditation not only leads to more uniformity in standards but also ultimately better working conditions for staff and more humane treatment for the care, custody, and control of inmates. This organization has provided me with the professional network to learn about what is working in other states and various member nations. It is an invaluable resource for professional and personal development.

"Mississippi currently has the second-highest incarceration rate in the country (Louisiana's prison rate per 100,000 residents is first). But I believe we can do better, not only in Mississippi but also nationwide. We can be smarter and more efficient with taxpayers' money without appearing soft on crime. We need to decide whom we are mad at and what we are afraid of. There will always be a need for prisons, and there will always be inmates too dangerous to be with the general population. But mass incarceration, especially for low-level property and drug offenses, and indiscriminate use of restricted housing, mislabeled as solitary confinement, are not the solutions.

"Mississippi has led the way with administrative segregation reform in housing and the use of a managed access system to counter illegal cell phone usage. I am extremely concerned about the proliferation of cell phones in prisons. Keeping out contraband is one of our greatest challenges today in Mississippi and elsewhere. Traditional ways of smuggling items in prison has been replaced by nontraditional ways, such as throwing things over security fences, sometimes hidden in basketballs. Therefore, we need to be just as creative defensively and offensively. We are the front-runner for the use of netting to keep people from throwing knives, cell phones, chargers, tobacco, and other contraband over secure perimeter fences.

"Low wages and staff turnover, which are directly related, also are other critical areas of concern in Mississippi. I am also placing greater attention on reentry because more people will be returned to society than those who remain behind bars. Therefore, we need to help ex-offenders get back on their feet by ensuring they have something as simple as an identification card. Fewer inmates returning to prison, of course, improve the recidivism rate. Mississippi's current recidivism rate of 32.09 percent for a three-year period is lower than the national average.

"I am still in corrections for the simple belief that has guided me my whole life: I believe I can make a difference."

See Chapter 15 for more detailed information on careers in corrections.

SUMMARY

LO1 Identify the ideas found within Enlightenment thinking and how they influenced corrections

During the Enlightenment, Montesquieu, Beccaria, and Bentham wrote about the need to moderate punishment. The most important of these ideas were that punishment should be swift and certain as well as moderate, that the purpose of punishment was to prevent and deter the commission of crime, and that the reform of punishment meant the rejection of torture and the end of the indiscriminate application of capital punishment to hundreds of crimes.

LO2 Define the early prison reformers and what they contributed

John Howard, Alexander Maconochie, and Walter Crofton were widely hailed for the reforms they attempted to bring to corrections during the eighteenth and nineteenth centuries. Howard attacked the abuses in jails in England and on the European continent. Maconochie attempted to improve the treatment of convicts in Australia by installing the mark system on Norfolk Island, and Crofton adapted the mark system to a prison setting in Ireland.

LO3 Articulate how the Pennsylvania and Auburn models differ from one another

The Pennsylvania penitentiary, with its solitary confinement and penitence model, was widely hailed both in the United States and Europe. The Auburn silent system demanded silence from convicts at all times. They marched in lockstep from the cellblock to the mess hall and to the factory.

LO4 Explain how reformatories contributed to the rehabilitation model

The reformatory model contributed to the rehabilitation model because of its system of indeterminate sentencing, the payment of inmates for work, the supervision of inmates in the community, and a system of behavior modification.

LO5 Discuss the purpose of corrections

The purpose of corrections is to provide sufficient consequences to individuals convicted by the courts so that the public will be protected, crime will be reduced, and offenders will learn that crime does not pay.

LO6 Summarize the reasons why we punish

The justifications for punishment are that it provides beneficial consequences, it is deserved, it expresses public outrage, it teaches a lesson, and it helps maintain the government.

LO7 Discuss the theories of punishment

The objectives of criminal punishment can be grouped into seven distinct areas: general deterrence, specific deterrence, incapacitation, rehabilitation, retribution/just deserts, restoration and justice, and equity/restitution.

LO8 Explain the relationship between corrections and the criminal justice system

Corrections in the United States has developed as part of the larger criminal justice system, of which the police, the court system, and corrections are the three components or subsystems.

LO9 Describe the extent and consequences of prison overcrowding

One of the major issues in corrections today is prison overcrowding. There are currently more than 2.2 million inmates in U.S. prisons and jails. The consequences of prison overcrowding are that it leads to increased inmate defiance and makes prisons more dangerous places to work.

LO10 Discuss the financial costs of corrections

Corrections today is extremely expensive. Costs run in the billions, an expense that has become prohibitive for cash-starved state governments. States are seeking ways to cut correctional costs, including the recent closing of prisons and the release of inmates before the completion of their sentence.

LO11 Explain the importance of professionalism in corrections

One of the most hopeful signs of corrections today is the increased emphasis on professional behavior expected of staff. Professionalism includes a number of positive attributes, including treating inmates with dignity and respect, modeling positive behaviors, and being a person of integrity.

CRITICAL THINKING QUESTIONS

1. Which of the reasons why we punish has the greatest influence on the public and its policy makers today?
2. Do you think retribution will continue to be as popular as it has been in recent years? Will the costs of corrections affect this desire to incarcerate so many, for so long, and in long-term institutions?
3. With the rise of professionalism in corrections, what can be done about those who continue to demonstrate a retributive spirit and express brutality toward inmates?
4. In *Voices Across the Profession*, James Bruton, who has been a correctional professional throughout his career, claims that we can make a difference. Do you agree that it is possible to make a difference in corrections?

5. What were the advantages and disadvantages of public executions of offenders? Would you favor televised public executions? If not, why not?
6. Alexander Maconochie thought that prison governors or wardens should belong to a profession. If so, how would the warden qualify as a professional? What experience and talents are needed?
7. What can corrections today learn from the correctional systems found at the Eastern State and Auburn penitentiaries? It can be argued that the reforms proposed in the First Correctional Congress, held in 1870, still have not been fully implemented in contemporary corrections? Why is that? Why did the reformatory model fall short of its hopeful goals? Is the medical model of rehabilitation an appropriate model for a prison setting?

NOTES

1. U.S. Department of Justice, "Federal Grand Jury Returns 30-Count Indictment Related to Boston Marathon Explosions and Murder of MIT Police Officer Sean Collier," June 27, 2013, http://www.fbi.gov/boston/press-releases/2013/federal-grand-jury-returns-30-count-indictment-related-to-boston-marathon-explosions-and-murder-of-mit-police-officer-sean-collier (accessed May 2014).
2. *Roper v. Simmons*, 543 U.S. 551 (2005).
3. Andres Jauregui, "Boston Marathon Bombing Suspect's Note: 'You Kill One of Us, You Hurt Us All,'" *Huffington Post*, April 17, 2014, http://www.huffingtonpost.com/2014/04/17/dzhokhar-tsarnaev-note_n_5168357.html (accessed May 2014); CBS News, "Boston Bombings Suspect Dzhokhar Tsarnaev Left Note in Boat He Hid In, Sources Say," http://www.cbsnews.com/news/boston-bombings-suspect-dzhokhar-tsarnaev-left-note-in-boat-he-hid-in-sources-say/ (accessed May 2014).
4. C. H. Johns, *The Oldest Code of Laws in the World* (Edinburgh: T & T Clark, 1905). See also Peter Watson, *Ideas: A History of Thought and Invention* (New York: Harper Perennial, 2005), pp. 93–95.
5. John Huizinga, *The Warning of the Middle Ages* (London: Edward Arnold, 1924), p. 15.
6. Norman Johnston, *Forms of Constraint: A History of Prison Architecture* (Urbana and Chicago: University of Illinois Press, 2000), p. 5. See also P. Spierenburg, *The Prison Experience: Disciplinary Institutions and Their Inmates in Early Modern Europe* (New Brunswick, 1991), p. 1–11.
7. Johnston, *Forms of Constraint*, pp. 40–41.
8. Cesare Bonesana Beccaria, *On Crimes and Punishments*, trans. Kenelm Foster and Jane Grigson (New York: Oxford University, 1964), p. 13; originally published as *Dei delitti e delle pene* (1764).
9. Ibid.
10. This section on the influence of positivism is adapted from David J. Rothman, *Conscience and Convenience: The Asylum and Its Alternatives in Progressive America* (Boston: Little, Brown, 1980), p. 32.
11. Marie Gottschalk, *The Prison and the Gallows: The Politics of Mass Incarceration in America* (London: Cambridge University Press, 2006), p. 80.
12. Mary Carpenter, *Reformatory Prison Discipline, as Developed by the Hon. Sir Walter Crofton* (London: Longman, Green, Reader and Dyer, 1872), pp. 5–11.
13. Gottschalk, *The Prison and the Gallows*.
14. Ibid., p. 18.
15. One reformer, Dr. Benjamin Rush, the leading physician of Philadelphia, argued vigorously but unsuccessfully against the death penalty even in the case of murder.
16. Harry Elmer Barnes, *The Evolution of Penology in Pennsylvania* (Whitefish, MT: Literary Licensing, 2011), p. 73, quoting from Pennsylvania Prison Society, *A Sketch of the Principal Transactions of the Philadelphia Society for Alleviating the Miseries of Public Prisons* (Philadelphia: Merrihew and Thompson, 1859), p. 5.
17. Norman Johnston, *Prison Reform in Pennsylvania*, http://www.prisonsociety.org/about/history.shtml (accessed May 2014).
18. Ibid.
19. Adam Jay Hirsch, *The Rise of the Penitentiary: Prisons and Punishment in Early America* (New Haven: Yale University Press, 1992), p. 32.
20. Ibid., p. 83.
21. Note that, at 96 square feet, these cells far exceeded the 60 square feet called for in the present Standards of Accreditation of the American Correctional Association.
22. Barnes, *Evolution of Penology in Pennsylvania*, pp. 159–160.
23. Norman Johnston, "The World's Most Influential Prison: Success or Failure?" *Prison Journal* 84 (2004).
24. For an expansive treatment of this prison, see Negley K. Teeters and John D. Shearer, *The Prison at Philadelphia: Cherry Hill* (New York: Columbia University Press, 1957).
25. Eastern Penitentiary website, http://www.easternstate.org/learn/research-library/history (accessed May 2014).
26. Ibid.
27. W. David Lewis, *From Newgate to Dannemora: The Rise of the Penitentiary in New York, 1796–1848* (Ithaca, NY: Cornell University Press, 1965).
28. Ibid. The Auburn officials were an unsentimental lot.
29. Ibid., p. 68. Lewis is quoting from the *Journal of the State Assembly* (1822), p. 218.
30. Blake McKelvey, *American Prisons: A Study in American Society* (Montclair, NJ: Patterson Smith, 1977).
31. For a condensed version of this landmark speech, see Zebulon Brockway, *Fifty Years of Prison Service* (Ithaca, NY: Cornell University Library, 2009).
32. Ibid.
33. McKelvey, *American Prisons*.
34. Ibid.
35. Ibid.
36. Ibid.
37. Lewis, *From Newgate to Dannemora*, p. 159.
38. Mark Colvin, *Penitentiaries, Reformatories, and Chain Gangs: Social Theory and History of Punishment in Nineteenth-Century America* (New York: St. Martin's Press, 2000), p. 181.
39. Steven N. Durlauf and Daniel S. Nagin, "Imprisonment and Crime: Can Both Be Reduced," *Criminology and Public Policy* 10 (2011): 13–54.
40. Steven N. Durlauf and Daniel S. Nagin, "The Deterrent Effect of Imprisonment," in *Controlling Crime: Strategies and Tradeoffs*, ed. Philip J. Cook, Jens Ludwig, and Justin McCrary (Chicago: University of Chicago Press, 2011).
41. See Bruce A. Jacobs, "Deterrence and Deterrability," *Criminology* 48 (2010): 417–441.
42. Matthew R. Durose, Donald J. Farole, and Sean P. Rosenmerkel, *Felony Sentences in State Courts, 2006* (Washington, DC: Bureau of Justice Statistics, 2009).
43. David M. Kennedy, *Deterrence and Crime Prevention: Reconsidering the Prospect of Sanction* (New York: Routledge, 2009).
44. Durlauf and Nagin, "The Deterrent Effect of Imprisonment."
45. Tomislav Kovandzic and Lynne Vieraitis, "The Effect of County-Level Prison Population Growth on Crime Rates," *Criminology and Public Policy* 5 (2006): 213–244.
46. Peter Greenwood did the research that brought selective incapacitation to the attention of others. See Peter W. Greenwood, with Alan Abrahamse, *Selective Incapacitation* (Santa Monica, CA: Rand, 1982).

47. Kathleen Auerhahn, *Selective Incapacitation and Public Policy: Evaluating California's Imprisonment Crisis* (Albany, NY: SUNY Editions, 2003).
48. Robert Martinson, "What Works? Questions and Answers about Prison Reform," *Public Interest* 35 (Spring 1974): 22–54.
49. See Chapter 10 for these various studies suggesting that some treatment programs have had positive outcomes.
50. For examination of the revival of rehabilitation as a penal strategy, see Gwen Robinson, "Late-Modern Rehabilitation: The Evolution of a Penal Strategy," *Punishment and Society* 10 (2008): 429–445; Tony Ward and Shadd Maruna, *Rehabilitation: Beyond the Risk Principle* (London: Routledge, 2007); Mark W. Lipsey and Francis T. Cullen, "The Effectiveness of Correctional Rehabilitation: A Review of Systematic Reviews," *Annual Review of Law and Social Science* 3 (2007): 297–320.
51. Matthew Haist, "Deterrence in a Sea of 'Just Deserts': Are Utilitarian Goals Achievable in a World of 'Limiting Retributivism'?" *Journal of Criminal Law and Criminology* 99 (2009): 789–822.
52. Ibid.
53. Mark S. Umbreit, Robert B. Coates, and Betty Vos, "Restorative Justice Dialogue: A Multi-Dimensional, Evidence-Based Practice Theory," *Contemporary Justice Review* 1 (2007): 25–41.
54. Federal Bureau of Investigation, *Crime in the United States, 2012*, http://www.fbi.gov/about-us/cjis/ucr/crime-in-the-u.s/2012/crime-in-the-u.s.-2012/persons-arrested/persons-arrested (accessed May 2014).
55. Bureau of Justice Statistics, State Court Caseload Statistics, http://www.bjs.gov/index.cfm?ty=tp&tid=30 (accessed May 2014).
56. Brian A. Reaves, *Felony Defendants in Large Urban Counties, 2009 – Statistical Tables* (Washington, DC: Bureau of Justice Statistics, 2013), http://www.bjs.gov/content/pub/pdf/fdluc09.pdf (accessed May 2014).
57. Gottschalk, *The Prison and the Gallows*, p. 1. See also Marie Gottschalk, "The Past, Present, and Future of Mass Incarceration in the United States," *Criminology and Public Policy* 10 (2011): 483–504.
58. *Prison and Jail Inmates at Midyear 2009* (Washington, DC: Bureau of Justice Statistics, 2010).
59. Ibid.
60. Robert Lopez, "State Prison Officials Vow to Crack Down on Inmate Hunger Strikes," *Los Angeles Times*, September 9, 2011, http://latimesblogs.latimes.com/lanow/2011/09/california-prison-hunger-strikes.html (accessed May 2014).
61. Michael Welch, "Force and Fraud: A Radically Coherent Criticism of Corrections as Industry," *Contemporary Justice Review* 6 (2003): 234. See also Marc Mauer, "Addressing the Political Environment Shaping Mass Incarceration," *Criminology and Public Policy* 10 (2011): 699–705.
62. Marc Mauer, "Don't Throw Away the Key: Lessons from the 'Get Tough on Crime' Initiates," *Resist Newsletter* (March–April 2006).
63. Randall G. Shelden, "Imprisonment Binge Comes Home to Roost," http://www.sheldensays.com/imprisonmentbinge.htm (accessed May 2014).
64. Ibid.
65. Clemens Bartollas, *Becoming a Model Warden: Striving for Excellence* (Landham, MD: American Correctional Association, 2004), p. 26.
66. The Code of Ethics for the American Correctional Association can be found online at http://www.aca.org/pastpresentfuture/ethics.asp (accessed May 2014).
67. Bartollas, *Becoming a Model Warden*, p. 83.
68. Code of Ethics for the American Correctional Association.

AP Images/Josh Reynolds

New England Patriots NFL football player Aaron Hernandez is shown being led into court in Attleboro, Massachusetts. Hernandez was accused of shooting former friend Odin Lloyd, whose body was found in an industrial park area less than a mile from Hernandez's home. Police speculate that Lloyd had witnessed Hernandez's involvement in a drive-by shooting in 2012 in which two men were killed, and his murder was an effort to remove a witness who might have gone to the authorities.

IN JUNE 2013, Aaron Hernandez, the New England Patriots star tight end, was charged with murder. Hours after the arrest, the Patriots—a team that once gave him a $40 million contract—dropped him from its roster. Hernandez was accused of shooting Odin Lloyd, whose body was found in an industrial park area less than a mile from his home. First Assistant District Attorney Bill McCauley said in court that Hernandez "drove the victim to the remote spot and then he orchestrated his execution. He orchestrated the crime from the beginning, he took steps to conceal and destroy evidence, and he took steps to prevent the police from speaking to ... an important witness."[1] The reason for the shooting: to remove a witness who saw Hernandez kill two other men, Daniel Abreu and Safiro Furtado, in a 2012 drive-by shooting motivated by a mild altercation at a local club.

Hernandez has been incarcerated at the Bristol County Jail since his June 2012 arrest. On February 24, 2013, having been kept away from other inmates because of his celebrity status, he was allowed to walk along a hallway and got into a scuffle with another inmate who had been harassing him. Hernandez appeared to snap and pummeled his antagonist. He has been placed in a higher-level security unit and is allowed out of his cell for one hour a day.[2]

If it was not bad enough for Hernandez, on February 27, he was sued by families of 2012 fatal shooting victims. The $6 million lawsuits filed on behalf of the families of Daniel Abreu and Safiro Furtado claimed that Hernandez "recklessly" and "maliciously" shot a firearm from his vehicle into a vehicle that carried Abreu and Furtado resulting in their deaths.[3] And then on May 15, 2014, Hernandez was indicted criminally for the double murder by Suffolk County prosecutors in Boston.[4]

2

Sentencing and the Correctional Process

LEARNING OBJECTIVES

 Explain the roles of the court team in the sentencing process

 Summarize the bail process, pretrial release, and preventive detention

 Explain what is meant by indeterminate sentencing

 Identify the various forms of determinate sentencing

 Describe the role of sentencing guidelines

 Discuss what is meant by truth-in-sentencing

 Identify the most serious issues in sentencing

PREVIEW OF **KEY CONCEPTS**

pretrial release
bail bond
bail bondsman
release on own recognizance (ROR)
unsecured bail
percentage bail
third-party custody
signature bond
supervised release
Manhattan Bail Project
Bail Reform Act of 1966
Bail Reform Act of 1984
preventive detention
concurrent sentence
consecutive sentence
good time
sentencing sanctions
indeterminate sentence
determinate sentence
sentencing guidelines
presumptive sentencing
federal sentencing guidelines
mandatory minimum sentences
three-strikes laws
truth-in-sentencing
nonlegal factors in sentencing
racial disparity in sentencing

AP Images/Kalamazoo Gazette-MLive Media Group, Mark Bugnaski

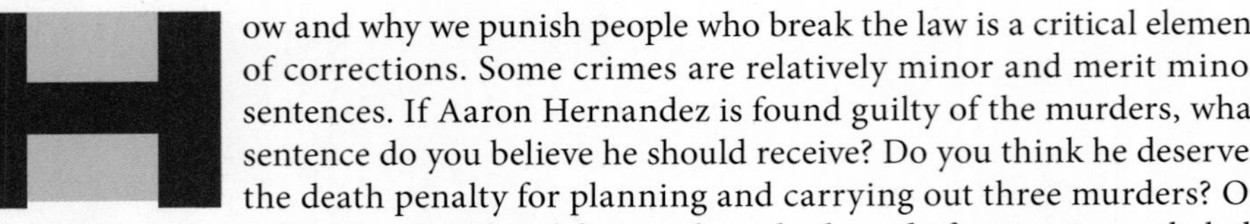

How and why we punish people who break the law is a critical element of corrections. Some crimes are relatively minor and merit minor sentences. If Aaron Hernandez is found guilty of the murders, what sentence do you believe he should receive? Do you think he deserves the death penalty for planning and carrying out three murders? Or should convicted killers be considered for parole and released after serving only half their sentence? In 2012, Mississippi Governor Haley Barbour made headlines when he pardoned more than 200 convicted criminals, including 17 convicted of murder, 10 convicted of manslaughter, 8 convicted of aggravated assault, and 5 convicted of drunken-driving incidents that caused deaths.[5] Barbour told the press that he was "very comfortable" with his decision to grant pardons or clemency to more than 200 people, some of whom are convicted murderers, in his final days in office. His reason: while he recognizes the strong feelings of the victims and their families, and respects them, the state does not carry out vengeance on their behalf; "Christianity teaches us forgiveness and second chances. I believe in second chances, and I try hard to be forgiving."[6] The victims' families were outraged—are you? And as the TechnoCorrections feature shows, once incarcerated many inmates use technology to continue their criminal careers. Should their punishment also include removing such personal items as cell phones and access to other electronic devices?

In this chapter, we will explore the intersection of punishment and corrections in the contemporary criminal justice system. We begin by looking at the role of court personnel in making sentencing decisions, then turn to the different type of sentences now being used in the United States. Finally, we will review the social and economic forces that impact on the sentencing process.

Explain the roles of the court team in the sentencing process

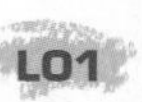

ACTORS IN THE SENTENCING PROCESS

While sentence type and length are typically created by some legislative body, the sentencing process rests in the hands of a number of actors, nested within the court system, who use their power and discretion to shape the administration of criminal punishments. Choosing the "correct" sentence is a complex decision. Why we punish, how we punish, and whom we punish are concepts that are constantly shifting, reflecting the social, economic, and political realities of the time. Who makes these decisions and what guides their judgments?

The Prosecutor

A member of the practicing bar, the prosecutor is typically an appointed or elected official who is responsible for bringing the state's case against the accused. He or she focuses the power of the state on those who disobey the law by charging them with a crime and eventually bringing them to trial or, conversely, releasing them after deciding that the evidence at hand does not constitute proof of a crime.

Although the prosecutor's primary duty is to enforce the criminal law, his or her fundamental obligation as an attorney is to seek justice as well as convict those who are guilty. If, for example, the prosecutor discovers facts suggesting that the accused is innocent, he or she must bring this information to the attention of the court. In recent years, prosecutors have gained greater leverage to extract guilty pleas from defendants and, as a result, reduce the number of cases that go to trial. New laws have resulted in giving prosecutors more power in the courtroom. With the advent of mandatory sentences and other harsher penalties, it is now possible for prosecutors to use the threat of more serious charges to get criminal defendants to accept pleas and cooperate in other ways.[7]

Defendants can choose to have their day in court, but they risk facing a judge and jury who may place them in prison for more years, sometimes far more years, than the plea bargain they were offered. In some courtrooms, the increased use of the plea bargain has nearly put the trial system out of business. One study of nine states found that

Cell Phones in Prison

What can be a technological innovation to some can be an instrument of crime to another. An inmate escaped from a Kansas prison with the aid of a phone smuggled in by an accomplice. In Texas, a death row inmate charged with killing four persons, including two teenage girls, used a cell phone from within the prison to threaten a prominent state senator and his family. These incidents serve as just two examples where individuals used cell phones to facilitate criminal acts from within a correctional institution.

Because of incidents such as these, correctional administrators have sought to place restrictions that not only limit the number of persons an inmate may call but dictate that none of the individuals called have a criminal record. As a general matter, correctional staff may monitor inmate calls when "pursuant to a policy statement" and when prisoners receive "reasonable notice that monitoring of telephone conversations might occur." Authorities may also impose restrictions on telephone use based on the security level in which an inmate is housed. While prisoners may use their cell phones for benign purposes, such as maintaining contact with family and friends, the devices also can provide inmates with an avenue for conducting criminal activity without concerns about the restrictions imposed on landline telephone use. Prisoners have used them to, for example, intimidate and threaten witnesses; transmit photographs, including offensive pictures sent to victims; orchestrate crimes, such as gang activity; coordinate escapes; bribe prison officers; order retaliation against other inmates; text other prisoners; gain access to the Internet; and create security breaches. Hoping to stop federal inmates from directing crimes from behind bars, the federal government passed a law in 2010 prohibiting cell phone use by prisoners. The law prohibits the use or possession of mobile phones and wireless devices, and calls for up to a year in prison for anyone found guilty of trying to smuggle one to an inmate.

DETECTION BY AUTHORITIES

Despite bans, illegal cell phones are still smuggled into prisons. As a result of the influx of cell phones within facilities, officials have taken aggressive measures to detect and confiscate illegal devices. Authorities have implemented not only random cell inspections but perimeter searches. Some institutions have used traditional security measures to detect cell phones, such as metal detectors, X-ray technology, and routine searches of staff, visitors, and contractors. Officials also have used body orifice security scanner (BOSS) systems to detect cell phones and parts concealed in body cavities.

An innovative proactive approach to detection is the use of dogs. For instance, as part of their crackdown on cell phone possession by inmates, the Maryland Department of Public Safety and Correctional Services uses canines trained specifically to detect wireless devices, including even the small SIM cards, which is important because prisoners often store them separately, "minimizing the

AP Images/Rich Pedroncelli, File

loss in case a phone is seized." The use of dogs to sniff out cell phones has proved quite successful. Some agencies have begun to use electronic cell phone detection systems, which can indicate to security staff when a device is in use in a facility. Some such systems rely on wireless sensors to detect phone signals. Others may be hardwired within a facility. Although effective, use of these technologies requires startup costs.

Another approach is jamming using radio frequency (RF) technology in order to disrupt cell phone signals. While this may seem like an attractive possibility, it is illegal unless done pursuant to specific authorization by a court authority. Congress is examining the possibility of permitting the proactive use of jamming to prevent inmates' use of cell phones in correctional institutions. One bill under consideration would allow state governors or the director of the Federal Bureau of Prisons to petition the FCC to permit mobile jamming in prisons. But so far that has not been implemented. Other methods have been tried. Mississippi became the first state to implement a managed cellular access system at its state penitentiary at Parchman. This means installing a dedicated cellular base station in the prison that passes calls along to carriers. Authorized

(*continued*)

phones are listed on the system and all others are blocked or redirected. Both the number of intercepted transmissions and the number of confiscated phones has dropped inside the walls of Parchman since the system was implemented in 2010.

All these efforts have their downsides, both legal and practical. But there is little doubt that correctional authorities will continue to devise innovative methods to control inmate use of this technology within prison walls.

FOR CRITICAL THINKING AND WRITING

While at first glance the control of cell phones and communication seems like a good idea, cutting inmates off from the outside world can help lock them into an inmate lifestyle and make the transition to the outside more difficult. Do you believe all cell phones should be blocked or confiscated or does merely increase prison isolation? Would you distribute cell phone privileges for good behavior? How might that put pressure on inmates who have earned the right to have a cell phone?

Source: Tod W. Burke and Stephen S. Owen, "Cell Phones as Prison Contraband," FBI Law Enforcement Bulletin, July 2010, http://www.fbi.gov/stats-services/publications/law-enforcement-bulletin/july-2010/cell-phones-as-prison-contraband (accessed May 2014).

FOR GROUP DISCUSSION

Think about a current newsworthy criminal case and imagine you are the prosecutor. In a group discussion, each person should explain what punishment/sentence they would seek and justify their position. LO1

in 1970, about one in 12 cases made it to trial; today, fewer than one in 40 felony cases are tried in court. The decline has been steeper in federal courts.[8]

The *Florida v. Shane Guthrie* case illustrates why plea bargaining has become the norm. In this case, Guthrie, 24, was arrested in 2010, accused of beating his girlfriend and threatening her with a knife. He was offered a deal by the prosecutor of two years in prison plus probation. Guthrie rejected this and a later offer of five years, because he believed he was not guilty. The prosecutor's response was severe. He filed a more serious change that would mean life imprisonment if Guthrie were convicted, and the sentence would be mandatory.[9]

What has taken place is that there has been a transfer of power to prosecutors from judges that has undercut the formal court process with a more informal system shaped by backroom deals and agreements.[10]

AP Images/The Florida Times/Union/Will Dickey/Pool

In most jurisdictions it is the presiding judge who decides on criminal punishments. Here, Circuit Judge Don Lester speaks to Jarred Harrell, February 3, 2012, in the Clay County Courthouse in Green Cove Springs, Florida. Harrell, an unemployed restaurant worker, pleaded guilty in the abduction, sexual battery, and slaying of Somer Thompson, a 7-year-old Florida girl who was found in a landfill. Dozens of her family and friends packed a crowded courtroom wearing shades of purple, the little girl's favorite color, and saw Harrell admit that he raped and murdered Somer in October 2009. Judge Lester then sentenced him to six life sentences without the possibility of parole.

The Judge

The senior officer in a court of criminal law, a judge's duties are quite varied and are far more extensive than the average citizen might suspect. During trials, the judge rules on the appropriateness of conduct, settles questions of evidence and procedure, and guides the questioning of witnesses. When a jury trial occurs, the judge must instruct jury members on which evidence can be examined and which should be ignored. The judge also formally charges the jury by instructing its members on what points of law and evidence they must consider before reaching a decision of guilty or innocent. When a jury trial is waived, the judge must decide whether the defendant is guilty. Finally, and most importantly for our purposes, upon a guilty finding, the judge decides on the sentence. This duty includes choosing the type of sentence, its length, and—in the case of probation—the conditions under which it may be revoked. Even where sentences are legislatively determined, the judge can sometimes use his or

Courtesy of Clem Bartollas

VOICES ACROSS THE PROFESSION

I would like for every defendant I sentence to live a productive, fulfilling, and crime-free life once he or she is released from prison. I know that will not always be the case, but I believe that the sentencing system currently in place makes it more likely, because I am able to sentence the person, not a data point.

Judge Paul A. Magnuson
Federal Judge

In 2005, the United States Supreme Court ushered in a new era in federal court sentencing in *United States v. Booker*, 543 U.S. 220. Before that, federal courts were bound to follow the United States Sentencing Guidelines, which effectively mandated a sentencing range based on the defendant's criminal history and the nature of his or her crime. Federal judges could depart from the established range, either above or below, only in extraordinary circumstances. This framework effectively stripped federal judges of their discretion and judgment in sentencing. It felt more like a mathematical undertaking than a considered decision based on the individual before me.

The Sentencing Guidelines were designed this way for a reason, however. In the decades leading up Congress's creation of the Sentencing Guidelines, there were wide disparities in the federal sentencing system, which depended, almost solely, on each judge's discretion.

We now have the best of both systems. In *Booker*, the Supreme Court determined that the Sentencing Guidelines are not mandatory, but rather are merely advisory. This new framework provides a principled basis for a sentence range that can be adjusted more freely by the court to fit the case and, more importantly, each individual defendant. A judge's determination to sentence outside of the guidelines range will be overturned only if deemed unreasonable by the court of appeals.

I find that this system allows me to impose individualized and humane sentences for each and every defendant that comes before me. Before *Booker*, for example, I would have been unable to impose a sentence below the guideline range based on factors such as post-arrest rehabilitation, family support, age, or family responsibilities. In my view, these and other factors can be strong indicators of success following imprisonment. I would like for every defendant I sentence to live a productive, fulfilling, and crime-free life once he or she is released from prison. I know that will not always be the case, but I believe that the sentencing system currently in place makes it more likely, because I am able to sentence the person, not a data point.

I should note that while the Sentencing Guidelines have changed dramatically in recent years, mandatory minimum sentences have not. Congress has placed required minimum sentences on certain crimes, most notably drug trafficking. When sentencing for such crimes, federal judges have no independent discretion to sentence below the required minimum. I no longer preside over mandatory minimum cases because I do not believe a person can be sentenced fairly without fully considering their background and circumstances. Unfortunately, I think it is unlikely that Congress will revisit the wisdom of minimum sentences because politicians do not want to be accused of being soft on crime. But hope springs eternal.

her discretion to lighten the defendant's burden. Obviously, this decision has a significant effect on an offender's future.

The public's expectations of the judge's role contain several erroneous assumptions. It is often assumed that the judge is in isolation from the political and social pressures that appear to dominate other public officials; that the judge is always a neutral arbitrator; that he or she carefully follows the statutory and legal prescriptions applicable to the case and is not swayed by personal opinion; and that the judge dominates the criminal justice system, from arrest through sentencing.[11] Judges' actual behavior represents a blend of the duties they are expected to perform, the public's expectations and influence, tradition, political pressure, and the realities and pressures of their jobs. These and other issues are addressed in the Voices Across the Profession box featuring Federal Judge Paul A. Magnuson.

Sentences are given by judges, who because they are only human often share the public's sentiments and reactions to crime. Those who are elected officials are aware that unpopular sentences may result in their being voted out of office. Some may have a particular value or bias that shapes their approach to punishment.[12] For example, a judge may have little regard for people who drink and be especially harsh on alcoholics who commit crime. Others may have greater sympathy for the mentally handicapped and feel compelled to grant them more lenient sentences.

Probation Staff

Before sentencing takes place in felony cases, it is common for the court's probation staff to conduct a presentence investigation. An inquiry, performed by a probation

CAREERS IN CORRECTIONS

PRETRIAL OFFICER

Jennifer Wyatt Bourgeois
Criminal Justice Instructor and Criminalist (Forensic Scientist)

"Pretrial officers have both investigation and supervision responsibilities. The investigative responsibilities of pretrial officers consist of gathering information regarding the individual in order to compile a presentence investigation (PSI) report that will include information regarding their family, education, employment, finances, physical and mental health, and alcohol or drug usage. The PSI report also contains a recommendation on behalf of the pretrial officer as to whether or not the individual should remain detained, be released, is a good candidate for probation, etc. The supervisory responsibilities of pretrial officers consist of monitoring the individual via face-to-face office visits or in the field at the individual's residence or place of employment depending upon their risk level.

"Pretrial officers also appear in court to testify about their office visits with individuals and prepare PSI reports. Appearing in court and attending hearings are important because pretrial officers serve as the liaison between the individual on bond and the court. Pretrial officers update the court about the individual's progress regarding their compliance with their conditions of bond and their rehabilitation.

"Average day-to-day duties consist of supervision of individuals by office visits, preparing reports, and appearing in court. Office visits are the most effective way for pretrial officers and probation officers to ensure that individuals abide by the conditions required by the courts. Pretrial officers also are required to recommend services and programs that can help the individual, such as substance abuse/anger management counseling, educational and work services, and GED programs. Court duties consist of appearing in court in order to present PSI reports or to discuss bond conditions imposed by a judge.

"Even though the day-to-day working environment for pretrial officers can be stressful, there are still satisfying moments. Through office visits, pretrial officers are able to determine the needs of individuals in order to help them improve various areas of their lives and become productive law-abiding citizens who can be of value to the community. Stressful aspects include long days in court and individuals who reoffend, but for every failure there are also success stories. The success stories outweigh the negative stories; the success stories are the moments when pretrial officers remember why they enjoy their jobs and why they continue to do what they do each day."

See Chapter 15 for more detailed information on careers in corrections.

officer attached to a trial court, contains information about the defendant's background, prior criminal record, education, previous employment, and family. The defendant may be interviewed, and interviews also may be conducted with neighbors, acquaintances, and employers. Treatment staff may be asked to evaluate the defendant's mental and/or physical condition. The report may contain information that would be inadmissible as evidence at a trial but is influential and important at the sentencing stage.

This presentence investigation serves as the basis for sentencing and has a significant influence on whether the convicted defendant will be granted community release or sentenced to secure confinement. In the event that the offender is placed on probation, the investigation becomes useful as a tool to shape treatment and supervision efforts.

The pretrial officer is related to probation services, but serves the primary purpose of recommending defendants who are eligible to be released to pretrial release.

LO2 Summarize the bail process, pretrial release, and preventive detention

BAIL, PRETRIAL, RELEASE, AND PREVENTIVE DETENTION

Half of the detainees in jail are misdemeanants who could not make bail. The defendants who receive bail or **pretrial release** will be given an opportunity to post bail and be released from jail. Those who are unable to post bond or receive pretrial diversion must remain in jail until their trial. The average delay between arrest and trial is more than six months.[13]

pretrial release Release from jail or a pretrial detention center pending adjudication of the case.

The following sections discuss what bail bonds and pretrial release are and how they are administered.

Bail

Bail is generally considered at a hearing conducted shortly after a defendant has been taken into custody. At this hearing, the judge considers such issues as whether the defendant is a flight risk or is dangerous before setting bail. Some jurisdictions have developed bail schedules to make certain that the amounts are uniform based on criminal history and on crime. **Bail bonds** are generally cash deposits but may also consist of property or other valuables. Indigent defendants who are unable to make bail may turn to a **bail bondsman**.

bail bond The means, financial or property, used to release a defendant from jail.

bail bondsman Bonding agents lend money for a fee to people who cannot make bail. They normally charge a percentage of the bail amount.

Pretrial Release

For those defendants unable to make cash bail, pretrial alternatives to jail include **release on own recognizance (ROR)**, unsecured bail, percentage bail, third-party custody, signature bail, and supervised release.

- Defendants who are released on their own recognizance (ROR) must appear at trial when scheduled. An ROR staff member interviews arrestees and then verifies data about each defendant. A defendant who scores the required number of verified points, as determined by established criteria, is recommended for ROR.
- **Unsecured bail** allows release without a deposit or bail arranged through a bondsman. It differs from ROR in that the defendant is obligated to pay an established fee upon default. But because the full bond amount is rarely collected, this program is basically the same as ROR.
- In **percentage bail**, the defendant deposits a portion of the bail amount, usually 10 percent, with the court clerk.
- **Third-party custody** occurs when the court assigns custody of the defendant to an individual or agency that promises to ensure his or her later appearance in court.
- A **signature bond** is usually given for minor offenses, such as minor traffic offenses, and is based on the defendant's written promise to appear in court.

release on own recognizance (ROR) The release without bail of defendants who appear to have stable ties in the community and are a good risk to appear for trial.

unsecured bail Allows defendants' release without a deposit or bail arranged through a bondsman.

percentage bail Defendants deposit about 10 percent of the bail amount with the court clerk.

third-party custody Takes place when the court assigns custody of the defendant to an individual or agency that promises to ensure his or her appearance in court.

signature bond Generally given for minor offenses and based on the defendant's written promise to appear in court.

supervised release Requires more frequent contact with pretrial officers, phone calls, and officer interviews.

- **Supervised release** programs require more frequent contact with a pretrial officer, phone calls, and office interviews. Although the purpose of supervision is to enforce the conditions imposed, the defendants also receive assistance with housing, finances, health problems, employment, and alcohol- or drug-related problems. Percentage bond, cash bail, or unsecured bail may be part of supervised release; in high-risk cases, intensive supervision may be used, requiring several contacts a week with a pretrial release officer.

BAIL REFORM Until the early 1960s, money bonds were relied upon as the basic form of pretrial release. However, a great deal of research found that the bail system was not applied in a fair and equal manner. One study examining the racial and ethnic differences in the processing of felony defendants in large urban courts found that Hispanic defendants were less likely to receive pretrial release than African American and white defendants. Hispanic defendants experienced a triple burden at the pretrial release stage. As a group, they:

- Were most likely to be required to pay bail to gain release
- Received the highest bail amounts
- Were least able to pay bail

These racial/ethnic differences were most pronounced in drug cases and are consistent with the perspective that suggests Hispanics are a newly immigrated group especially prone to harsher treatment in the criminal justice process.[14] Clearly reforms were needed.

Manhattan Bail Project A Vera Institute of Justice program that provided ROR release for eligible defendants, which influenced later bail reform movements.

Bail Reform Act of 1966 Federal legislation that further spurred the bail reform movement by urging pretrial release for all noncapital cases unless the defendant appeared unlikely to return to court.

Bail Reform Act of 1984 This federal act formalized preventive detention provisions for those considered dangerous or unlikely to return to court.

preventive detention Retaining in jail defendants who are deemed dangerous or likely to commit crimes while awaiting trial.

The bail reform movement is most closely linked with the **Manhattan Bail Project**, a program pioneered by the Vera Institute of Justice in New York. The early success of the ROR program resulted in bail reform that culminated with the enactment of the federal **Bail Reform Act of 1966**. The intent of this legislation was to ensure that release would be granted in all noncapital cases in which sufficient reason existed that the defendant would return to court. During the 1970s and early 1980s, public pressure over increases in crime hampered the pretrial release movement and, as a result, the more recent federal legislation, the **Bail Reform Act of 1984**, required that no defendant be kept in pretrial detention simply because they could not afford financial bail. Yet, it established the presumption for ROR in all cases in which a defendant can be bailed and formalized restrictive preventive detention provisions, which are explained in the next section.

Preventive Detention

Those defendants who are charged with serious crimes or are thought likely to escape are generally held in jail until trial. Public concern about crimes committed by those who have been granted pretrial release has given rise to the preventive detention movement. The objective of **preventive detention** is to retain in jail defendants who are deemed dangerous or likely to commit crimes while awaiting trial. This concern for public safety became so strong that by the mid-1980s well over half of the states had enacted preventive detention laws. Despite efforts of reform, millions of people either do not make bail or are denied bail and find themselves in jail awaiting trial while others who have committed misdemeanors are given a jail sentence.

IMPOSING THE SENTENCE

The sentence is usually imposed by the judge, but sentencing may also be exercised by a jury or may be mandated by statute, such as mandatory prison sentences for certain crimes.[15] In the majority of felony cases, excluding required mandatory prison terms, sentencing is generally based on the information available to a judge. Some jurisdictions permit victims to make impact statements that receive consideration at the sentencing hearing. Most judges also consider a presentence investigation report prepared by a probation officer in making the sentencing decision. The report is based on a social and

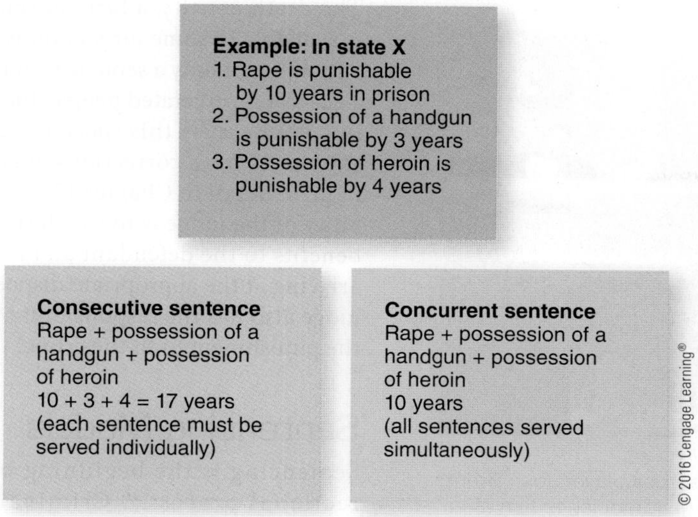

Example: In state X
1. Rape is punishable by 10 years in prison
2. Possession of a handgun is punishable by 3 years
3. Possession of heroin is punishable by 4 years

Consecutive sentence
Rape + possession of a handgun + possession of heroin
10 + 3 + 4 = 17 years
(each sentence must be served individually)

Concurrent sentence
Rape + possession of a handgun + possession of heroin
10 years
(all sentences served simultaneously)

FIGURE 2.1

Consecutive versus Concurrent Sentences

A man is arrested for rape and is found to have an illegal handgun and a quantity of heroin of his person at the time of arrest.

personal history of the defendant, including the defendant's prognosis of successful integration into the community. Some judges give this report greater weight than others.

Concurrent versus Consecutive Sentences

The person who is convicted of two or more charges must receive a sentence on each charge. **Concurrent sentence** means that multiple sentences begin on the same day and are completed when the longest term has been served.

In contrast, **consecutive sentence** means that on completing the sentence for one crime, the offender begins serving time for the second of what may be multiple crimes. Concurrent sentences are usually the norm, but consecutive sentences are requested for the most serious offenders and for those who refuse to cooperate with authorities. Figure 2.1 shows the difference between consecutive and concurrent sentences.

concurrent sentence Two or more sentences imposed at the same time and served simultaneously.

consecutive sentence Two or more sentences imposed at the same time and served one after the other.

The Effect of Good Time

Judges sentencing defendants to prison know and take into account the fact that the amount of time spent in confinement is reduced by the implementation of "time off for good behavior." This was first used in 1817 in New York and was quickly adopted in other jurisdictions. **Good time** is still found in prisons today but not in all jurisdictions. In some states, prisoners can accrue as much as 10 days per month of good time. Some correctional authorities also grant *earned* sentence reductions to inmates who participate in educational and vocational programs, treatment groups, or who volunteer for experimental medical testing programs. Accordingly, in some correctional systems, it has been possible to earn up to half of a sentence by accumulating both standard and earned good time.

A major advantage of good time is that it permits prisoners to calculate their release date at the time they enter prison by subtracting the anticipated good time from their sentence. However, if prisoners become involved in serious disciplinary offenses or attempt to escape, they can lose their good time. Some jurisdictions even return former prisoners to prison to serve the balance of their unexpired sentence when their good time is revoked for failing to comply with conditions set down for their release, such as abusing drugs or failing to report to postrelease supervision.

CRITICAL THINKING

Which type of sentencing encourages the most deterrence? Retribution? Potential for rehabilitation? LO1

good time A deduction of time awarded to inmates for good behavior.

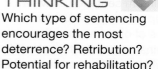

Web App 2.1
Go to the National Conference of State Legislatures website at http://www.ncsl.org/Portals/1/Documents/cj/Earned_time_report.pdf to see how much good time each state offers. LO1

Sentencing Sanctions

The forms of **sentencing sanctions** available to judges vary from jurisdiction to jurisdiction, but generally include diversionary programs, fines, probation, intermediate sanctions, confinement in jail, incarceration in a state or federal prison, and the death penalty. These sanctions will be examined in some detail in later chapters.

sentencing sanctions The various types of sentences that can be awarded by the courts.

AP Images/Pool/LM Otero

On January 24, 2014, former Dallas Cowboys NFL football player Josh Brent, left, stands with his lawyers as Judge Robert Burns III admonishes him after the sentencing for his intoxication manslaughter conviction was read in court. Brent was sentenced to 180 days in jail and 10 years of probation for a drunken car crash that killed his friend and teammate Jerry Brown. Is 180 days in jail sufficient punishment for a drunk driver whose careless and selfish behavior resulted in the death of a friend?

The death penalty, a form of sanction that is available in some jurisdictions across the nation, is not only a sentence but has created a class of incarcerated people: the death row inmate. Because this special population is so important to corrections, it is discussed in great detail in Chapter 13. The responsibility of the judge is to weigh the costs and benefits to the defendant and to society in arriving at the appropriate disposition. The judge also has the responsibility to escalate the punishment to fit the crime.

Sentencing Models

Sentencing is the beginning of the correctional process.[16] Criminal sentencing and sanctions imposed by it represent society's most powerful means to discourage repeated unlawful behavior. Society expects sentences that are appropriate to the seriousness of the criminal act, that incarcerate violent criminals, and that prevent innocent people from becoming victims of crime. The sentencing of convicted offenders is being transformed in a number of ways today. The discretion available to judges has decreased over the past decade, as many states have experimented with one or more types of sentencing reform—sentencing guidelines, determinate sentencing, mandatory sentences, and alternative forms of punishment. The purposes of sentencing have shifted from an emphasis on utilitarian aims, especially rehabilitation, toward a greater focus on appropriate punishment proportionate to the harm done.

FOR GROUP DISCUSSION

Indeterminate sentences usually allow inmates to serve a minimum amount of their sentence by providing them with opportunities to prove they can be productive members of society, then releasing them before they have served their maximum sentence. Have a group discussion about what types of opportunities the criminal justice system should provide in order to assist inmates with their goals. LO3

Explain what is meant by indeterminate sentencing LO3

indeterminate sentence Sentence that permits early release from a correctional institution after the offender has served a required minimum portion of his or her sentence.

Indeterminate Sentences

The **indeterminate sentence** first appeared in the late nineteenth century. Prison reformers, such as Enoch Wines and Zebulon Brockway, called for the creation of indeterminate sentences that could be tailored to fit individual needs. Offenders, it was argued, should be placed in confinement until they were rehabilitated and then they should be released on parole. As previously discussed, criminals were presumed to be sick, not bad, and could be successfully treated in prison. Rather than holding that "the punishment should fit the crime," reformers believed that "the treatment should fit the offender." This meant the establishment of a low minimum sentence that had to be served and a much longer maximum sentence that defined the outer boundary of the punishment. For example, a sentence of 1 to 15 might be given for a burglary. After a year, in this case, the average burglar would be eligible for parole (i.e., serve the remaining part of his sentence in the community) providing this person had entered treatment programs, cooperated with authorities, and otherwise proven he had been rehabilitated. On the other hand, if the inmate refused treatment, got into scrapes, or tried to escape, he could be forced to serve the entire 15-year sentence behind bars. Under this model, the amount of time to be served in prison was at the discretion of the parole board rather than the judge.

The law never allowed an indeterminate sentence to be completely indefinite. For minor felonies—auto theft, for example—a minimum sentence of at least a year would be prescribed in a typical penal code. More serious felonies would carry a longer minimum sentence, at least 3 or more years, and sometimes would allow a maximum sentence of life imprisonment. For first-degree murder, if the convicted person was not to be executed, the sentence would always be for life.

The indeterminate sentence has been subjected to considerable criticism. Some critics complain that it creates sentencing disparity (offenders with similar crimes receive diverse sentences from one jurisdiction to another). Others charge that it takes sentencing discretion out of the hands of judges and gives it to parole boards who determine when an offender is released even if he or she has served only a small portion of the sentence behind bars. Another argument is that because it is impossible to tell what the future holds, sentencing should not be based on predictions of future outcomes but rather on what people did in the past (i.e., based on their crimes). Today the primary purpose of indeterminate sentences remains an effort to individualize each sentence in the interest of rehabilitating offenders. Yet, no one can accurately determine who can be rehabilitated and who are poor candidates for treatment. Should sentencing be based on guesswork? In *Tapia v. United States* (2011), the U.S. Supreme Court found that federal law does not allow rehabilitation to be used as a factor when handing down a sentence. Tapia was given a longer sentence than usual so that she would have sufficient time behind bars for her to participate in the Bureau of Prisons' Residential Drug Abuse Program (RDAP); she felt this was unfair and filed suit. The Supreme Court found in her favor and acknowledged that prison has no rehabilitative properties and that a judge cannot extend a sentence that would have typically been handed down in the interest of rehabilitation.[17]

One advantage of indeterminate sentencing is that it permits flexibility both in the type of sentences that are imposed and in the length of time that has to be served. Jurisdictions using indeterminate sentencing often employ statutes that specify minimum and maximum terms but permit judicial discretion to fix the actual sentence given within these limits. Typically, minimum sentences are at least one year; a few state jurisdictions require a two-year minimum sentence be given to felons.

Even though rehabilitation and parole have been under heavy attack by critics who argue that criminals should be punished and not coddled, the indeterminate sentence is still the most widely used type of sentence. Today, more than 30 states retain some form of indeterminate sentencing.[18]

State legislatures can further dilute sentencing in the process of releasing prison overcrowding. For example, in Missouri, the legislature changed the sentencing law to help ease prison overcrowding. Under the new law, an inmate had to serve only one-third of the minimum before they were eligible for parole. A murderer who got 15 years to life could get parole after only serving 5 years.

Determinate Sentences

Determinate sentences give the defendant a fixed term of years, the maximum set in law by the legislature, which is to be served by the offender sentenced to prison for a particular crime. For example, if the law provides for a sentence of up to 20 years for robbery, the judge might sentence a repeat offender to a 15-year term. Yet, another robber with few violations might receive a more lenient sentence of 5 years.

determinate sentences Sentencing that imposes a sentence for a definite term. Its main forms are flat-time sentences, mandatory sentences, and presumptive sentences.

Determinate sentences were the ones used early in the nation's history but gave way to the indeterminate model in the 1870s when reformers began to stress treatment and rehabilitation of inmates. However, 100 years later a rising crime rate created dissatisfaction with the indeterminate sentence and the treatment model. Conservatives disliked the apparent leniency of parole and early release, which seemed to link short sentences to good grades in school and satisfactory reports from work supervisors. Liberals were critical of the charade of coerced rehabilitation performed by prisoners in order to gain parole. Both sides of the political spectrum agreed that sweeping changes in the penal code were in order. What was difficult to decide was the direction of change—toward a harder line or toward shorter but better-defined sentences. Nevertheless, in 1977, liberals and conservatives combined their usually incompatible forces to produce a federal Determinate Sentencing Law (DSL), referred to as Senate Bill (SB) 42. Under SB 42, judges were required to fix, within a very narrow range of choice, sentences at the time of the offender's conviction. The DSL allowed judges to give much harsher sentences, a provision that subsequently increased prison overcrowding.

Determinate sentencing reform has been implemented in a dozen states: Alaska, Arizona, California, Connecticut, Colorado, Illinois, Indiana, Maine, Minnesota, North Carolina, Pennsylvania, and Washington. A number of other legislatures are considering determinate sentencing acts. Moreover, parole practices and policies have undergone significant reform in Oregon, Minnesota, and the federal government, to cite several jurisdictions. See Exhibit 2.1 for the differences between indeterminate and determinate sentencing.

Identify the various forms of determinate sentencing 

sentencing guidelines Federal and state guidelines were created to limit judicial discretion so that persons committing similar crimes received similar terms of incarceration. They created structured punishments: the more severe the crime, the longer the sentence.

presumptive sentencing Sentencing in which the legislature sets penalties for criminal acts.

Structured Sentences

In order to regulate sentence length and curb judicial discretion, most determinate sentencing jurisdictions have developed methods to structure and control the sentencing process and make it more rational. To accomplish this task, **sentencing guidelines** have been implemented by determinate sentencing states and the federal government. Guidelines give judges a recommended sentence based on the seriousness of a crime and the background of an offender. The more serious the crime and the more extensive the offender's criminal background, the longer the prison term recommended by the guidelines. For example, guidelines might recommend a sentence of five years for robbery if the offender had no prior offense record and did not use excessive force or violence. For a second offense, the recommended sentence would increase to seven years; those who used force and had a prior record would have three years added to their sentence, and so on. By eliminating judicial discretion, guidelines are designed to reduce racial and gender disparity.[19]

The first four states to develop **presumptive sentencing** guidelines—a form of sentencing determination in which the legislature sets the penalties for criminal acts—were Minnesota (1980), Washington (1981), Pennsylvania (1982), and Florida (1983). In 1994, Ohio switched to presumptive guidelines.[20] About twenty states and the federal government established sentencing guidelines in the final two decades of the twentieth century. Eighteen of these guidelines are still in effect. Sentencing guidelines have been particularly well received in Delaware, Minnesota, Oregon, Pennsylvania, and Washington.[21] A good many other states have rejected guidelines because they perceive them as an improper interference with the role of the judiciary or because respected judges have been vocal in their opposition.

EXHIBIT 2.1

Differences Between Indeterminate Sentencing and Determinate Sentencing

Indeterminate Sentencing	Determinate Sentencing
Sentence is imposed for a crime but the criminal is not given a definite sentence.	The judge imposes a fixed term of incarceration.
The criminal will serve a range of years so determined by the judge.	Inmates can be released early due to good time credits or because of overcrowding.
The parole board makes the decision when to release the inmate on parole.	The judge is denied any discretion over the length of the sentence and also rules out any possibility of probation alternative to parole.
The parole board is influenced by such factors as the original recommendation of the judge, the offender's criminal history, participation in or refusal to become involved in rehabilitation programs, and evidence that the inmate presents a danger to the community if released.	Eliminates the parole board.
Indeterminate sentencing is designed to encourage inmates to profit from incarceration.	The participation in programs will not affect the length of incarceration.
Has been criticized for allowing too much control to members of the parole board, which has led to inequitable sentences.	Has been criticized as a factor leading to increases in prison population.

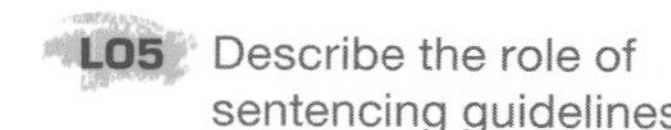
Describe the role of sentencing guidelines

federal sentencing guidelines These guidelines were adopted by Congress and until the U.S. Supreme Court ruled otherwise were to be binding on federal judges.

FEDERAL SENTENCING GUIDELINES **Federal sentencing guidelines** had their beginning in October 1984, when Congress passed the Comprehensive Crime Control Act, which among other things abolished parole as of November 1987.[22] The United States Sentencing Commission was created in a companion Sentencing Reform Act of 1984.

Forty-three levels of offenses were specified, and most federal crimes were assigned to a defined level. Departures by the sentencing judges from the guidelines were discouraged. If a judge believed he or she has to depart from the guidelines, the judge was expected to justify that departure in writing and expect that it would be appealed. For example, on October 12, 2011, a 11-year prison term was handed down to Raj Rajaratnam, founder of the Galleon Group hedge fund; this was the latest example of an inside trader receiving a lighter sentence than suggested by federal guidelines. U.S. District Judge Richard Holwell said that under the federal guidelines, Rajaratnam faced a minimum of 19.5 years in prison. In opting for a substantially lighter sentence, Holwell took both Rajaratnam's charitable works and health issues into consideration.[23]

EVALUATIONS OF FEDERAL GUIDELINES As originally constituted, the federal sentencing guidelines were criticized on several fronts:

- Judges complained about their complexity and difficulty of use along with the fact that they limited the exercise of judicial discretion.
- Defense counselors had little use for them because of their harshness and because they shifted sentencing authority from judges to prosecutors and were based on prior record and offense elements rather than on conviction charges.
- Many federal officials also disliked the guidelines because of their dissimilarity to the prior system of sentencing and because of the disruption they brought to a system that was working well enough before the change. Some complained the guidelines were developed with insufficient attention paid to either ethical considerations of basic justice or basic concerns about their effects on prison populations.
- Some experts argued that they were biased against African Americans and Hispanics, despite the stated goal of removing discrimination from the sentencing process.[24] Most troubling was the rule that possession of crack cocaine was to be punished far more severely than the possession of powdered cocaine. Critics rightly claimed that this amounts to racial bias because African Americans are much more likely to possess crack cocaine, while whites are more likely to use powdered cocaine.[25] In response to these criticisms, Congress eventually passed the Fair Sentencing Act in August 2010, changing the 100-to-1 disparity between minimum sentences for crack and powder cocaine to 18 to 1. The U.S. Sentencing Commission voted to make the reduced crack penalties retroactive, so that more than 12,000 inmates became immediately eligible to request reduced sentences.
- Some defense attorneys opposed the use of guidelines because they believed that they result in longer prison terms and prevent judges from considering mitigating circumstances. Some jurisdictions gave longer sentences if defendants had prior juvenile convictions or if they were on juvenile probation or aftercare (parole) at the time of their arrest.

LEGALITY OF SENTENCING GUIDELINES Because of these and other criticisms, there were challenges to the guidelines in federal and state courts resulting in a revision of their use. Two U.S. Supreme Court cases ended the mandatory use of presumptive guidelines. In *Blakely v. Washington* (2004), the Court found that Washington State's sentencing guidelines violated a defendant's Sixth Amendment rights because they permitted a judge to consider aggravating factors that would increase the sentence. The Court held that no criminal sentence in state courts can be enhanced beyond the allowable maximum guideline for an offender, unless the defendant waives the right to a jury or admits the facts in his or her guilty plea.[26]

Then, in *United States v. Booker* (2005), the Court ruled on two questions of whether the federal guidelines were unconstitutional and whether the federal guidelines violate the Sixth Amendment right to trial by jury. On the first question, the Court found that a sentence cannot be increased based on facts that were determined solely by a judge and were not found by a jury or admitted by the defendant. On the second question, rather than striking down the federal guidelines, the Court held that the guidelines could be taken into consideration by federal judges but that they no longer had to be regarded as mandatory, they were now merely advisory.[27]

These two cases did not in fact outlaw guidelines but ruled that changes must take place in how they are administered, particularly if they involve sentencing enhancement. A 2006 report by the Federal Sentencing Commission found that even though federal courts interpreted the *Booker* decision in different ways, the majority of cases continue to be sentenced within the range of existing sentencing guidelines. The guidelines may now be advisory, rather than mandatory, but they still have considerable impact on sentencing decisions.[28] Sentencing guidelines are also still being used in this advisory fashion in Minnesota as well as other states.[29]

Mandatory Minimum Sentences

mandatory minimum sentences The imposition of sentences required by statute for those convicted of a particular crime with specific circumstances, such as selling drugs to a minor close to a school or robbery with a firearm.

A further attempt to limit judicial discretion while at the same time getting tough on crime has been the development of **mandatory minimum sentences.**[30] A mandatory minimum sentence specifies a certain required number of years of incarceration for specific crimes.[31] It can take a number of different forms; two of the most prominent are:

- The legislature may prohibit defendants convicted of certain violent crimes, drug offenses, or other crimes from being placed on probation.
- The legislature may require that certain offenses, such as drug sales and/or gun possession, carry a mandatory term of imprisonment.

AP Images/Illinois Department of Corrections, File

Kamil Krzaczynski/Landov

Police officers surround an apartment building in Arlington Heights, Illinois, as they search for Robert Maday, 39, a federal bank robbery suspect. Maday had escaped from custody and went on a day-long crime spree in suburban Chicago. After his capture, Maday was convicted on multiple charges, including escape and bank robbery. He was already sentenced to more than 40 years in prison, but the judge tacked on another 30 for his post-escape crimes.

The purpose of mandatory minimum sentences is to provide equal treatment for all offenders who commit the same crime, regardless of sex, age, race/ethnicity, or other personal characteristics. More than 35 states have replaced various forms of discretionary sentencing with fixed-term mandatory sentences for such crimes as violent offenses, kidnapping, gun possession, arson, and sale of hard drugs.

Mandatory sentencing carries its own set of baggage. It has helped increase the size of prison populations to record levels, because many offenders who would formerly have been placed on probation are now being incarcerated. An example of this is women offenders who are minimally involved in drug crime but are punished disparately by the existing criminal justice system. These women became involved in crime because of their financial dependence on, romantic attachment to, or fear of a male drug trafficker. These "women of circumstance" find themselves imprisoned and subject to draconian sentences because the men in their lives persuaded, forced, or tricked them into carrying drugs.[32]

Three-Strikes Laws

During the 1990s, 25 states and Congress passed **three-strikes laws** for those who are repeat offenders.[33] Popularly known as "three strikes and you're out" (3×) laws or habitual offender statutes, these rules require long sentences without parole for those convicted of a third or higher-order felony. California and Washington's three-strikes laws are well known, and the Federal Crime Act of 1994 requires a mandatory life sentence for any offender convicted of three felony offenses. The legality of the three-strikes concept has been challenged in two critical cases, *Andrade* and *Ewing*, and these are set out in Exhibit 2.2.

three-strikes laws Rules for repeat offenders that require long sentences without parole for conviction of a third or higher-order felony.

EXHIBIT 2.2

Three-Strikes Laws

California's controversial three-strikes law sends repeat offenders to prison for 25 years to life for violent and even nonviolent crimes. The three-strikes movement continues the trend toward determinate sentencing that began in the 1980s. California's law is the harshest of the states that have recently adopted similar laws. In California, Leandro Andrade was given a 50-years-to-life sentence for shoplifting videotapes from Kmart, and Gary Ewing was given 25-years-to-life for attempting to steal three golf clubs from a country club pro shop. He slipped them down the leg of his pants, and a shop employee called the police when he noticed Ewing was limping from the shop.

Andrade and Ewing were given stiff sentences because on the third offense California's three-strikes law considers some misdemeanors, including shoplifting, as felonies. California approved the law overwhelmingly in 1994, largely because of the kidnapping-murder of 12-year-old Polly Klaas by a repeat offender out on parole.

There have been efforts to repeal these laws which have led to court action. The Ninth U.S. Circuit Court of Appeals in San Francisco threw out Andrade's sentence; the court said that it was "grossly disproportionate" to the crime of stealing $153 worth of videotapes. It was appealed to the U.S. Supreme Court, and in April 2002, the Court decided to review whether the law forces judges to mete out "cruel and unusual punishment."

On March 7, 2003, a divided Supreme Court upheld California's three-strikes law, rejecting constitutional challenges to sentences for the two men convicted of petty theft. The rulings in *Ewing v. California* and *Lockyer v. Andrade* were 5 to 4. The Court could not agree on the precise reasoning for upholding the sentence. Nevertheless, with the decisions in the two cases, the Court effectively foreclosed criminal defendants from arguing that their non-capital sentences were disproportional to the crime they had committed.

Justice Sandra Day O'Connor wrote an opinion for herself, Chief Justice William H. Rehnquist, and Justice Anthony M. Kennedy. She observed that the three-strikes law represented a new trend in criminal sentencing: "These laws respond to widespread public concerns about crime by targeting the class of offenders who pose the greatest threat to public safety: career criminals." Such laws were a "deliberate policy choice" on the part of legislatures to isolate those who "repeatedly engaged in serious or violent criminal behavior." Although California's three-strikes law, O'Connor reasoned, may have generated some controversy, "we do not sit as a superlegislature to second guess" the policy choices made by particular states. "It is enough," she concludes, "that the State of California has a reasonable basis for believing that dramatically enhanced sentences for habitual felons advances the goals of its criminal justice system in any substantial way."

Source: *Ewing v. California*, 538 U.S. 11 (2003); Patrick Marshall, "Three-Strikes Laws," *CQ Researcher*, May 10, 2002.

TIMELINE

CHRONOLOGY OF **SENTENCING** IN THE UNITED STATES

1950–PRESENT Congress and the states adopt get-tough sentencing policies.

1956 Narcotic Control Act establishes minimum sentences for drug crimes.

© iStock.com/enckic

1970 Congress repeals mandatory sentences for drug violations.

1972 The first clear call for sentencing guidelines comes from Federal District Court Judge Marvin Frankel in his groundbreaking book, *Criminal Sentences: Law Without Order.*

1973 New York State's Rockefeller laws require lengthy sentences for drug crimes.

Stephen Chernin/Getty Images

1980 U.S. Supreme Court issues key ruling applying the Eighth Amendment's ban on cruel and unusual punishment. In *Rummel v. Estelle*, it upholds a life sentence for a man convicted of obtaining $120 under false pretenses after two prior credit card forgery convictions. Defendant is eligible for parole after 12 years.

1983 In another key Eighth Amendment ruling, the Supreme Court in *Solem v. Helm* overturns a mandatory life-without-parole sentence for a defendant convicted of passing a $100 bad check.

1984 Sentencing Reform Act of 1984 creates the U.S. Sentencing Commission. The act also reintroduces mandatory-minimum sentences for drug and firearms offenses.

USE IT TO PROTECT FIREARMS FREEDOM.

MPI/Archive Photos/Getty Images

The various three-strikes laws differ among the states, but typically the first two strikes must be serious felonies. In California, the crime that triggers the life sentence can be any felony; this may include grand theft, attempted burglary, and even possession of a controlled substance. Most states require a serious felony as the third strike. The law typically doubles for a second strike and that requires the extended sentence to be served in prison instead of in jail or on probation. The law also cuts back on good time, limiting it to 20 percent of the sentence rather than the 50 percent that is earned in most states. What this means is that inmates would not be up for parole until they had served at least 80 percent of their term.

Discuss what is meant by truth-in-sentencing 

Truth-in-Sentencing

truth-in-sentencing A close connection between the imposed sentence and the actual time served in prison. The time that offenders actually serve on their sentence.

From the time that indeterminate sentencing was first imposed in the 1870s until late in the twentieth century, the amount of time offenders served in prison was almost always shorter than the time they were sentenced to serve by the court. Prisoners released in 1996 served an average of 30 months in prison and jail, or 44 percent of their sentence. Some states then enacted **truth-in-sentencing** laws that require offenders to serve a substantial portion of their sentence and to reduce the discrepancy between the sentence imposed and the actual time served in prison.[34]

To ensure that convicted offenders serve a large portion of their sentence, the U.S. Congress authorized funding for additional state prisons and jails through the Violent Crime Control and Law Enforcement Act of 1994. In 1998, incentive grants were awarded to 27 states and the District of Columbia that met the eligibility criteria for the truth-in-sentencing program (requiring offenders to serve 85 percent of their sentence). Parole eligibility and good time credits are greatly restricted or eliminated under truth-in-sentencing legislation. In all, more than 35 states and the District of Columbia eventually met the federal Truth-in-Sentencing Incentive Grant Program

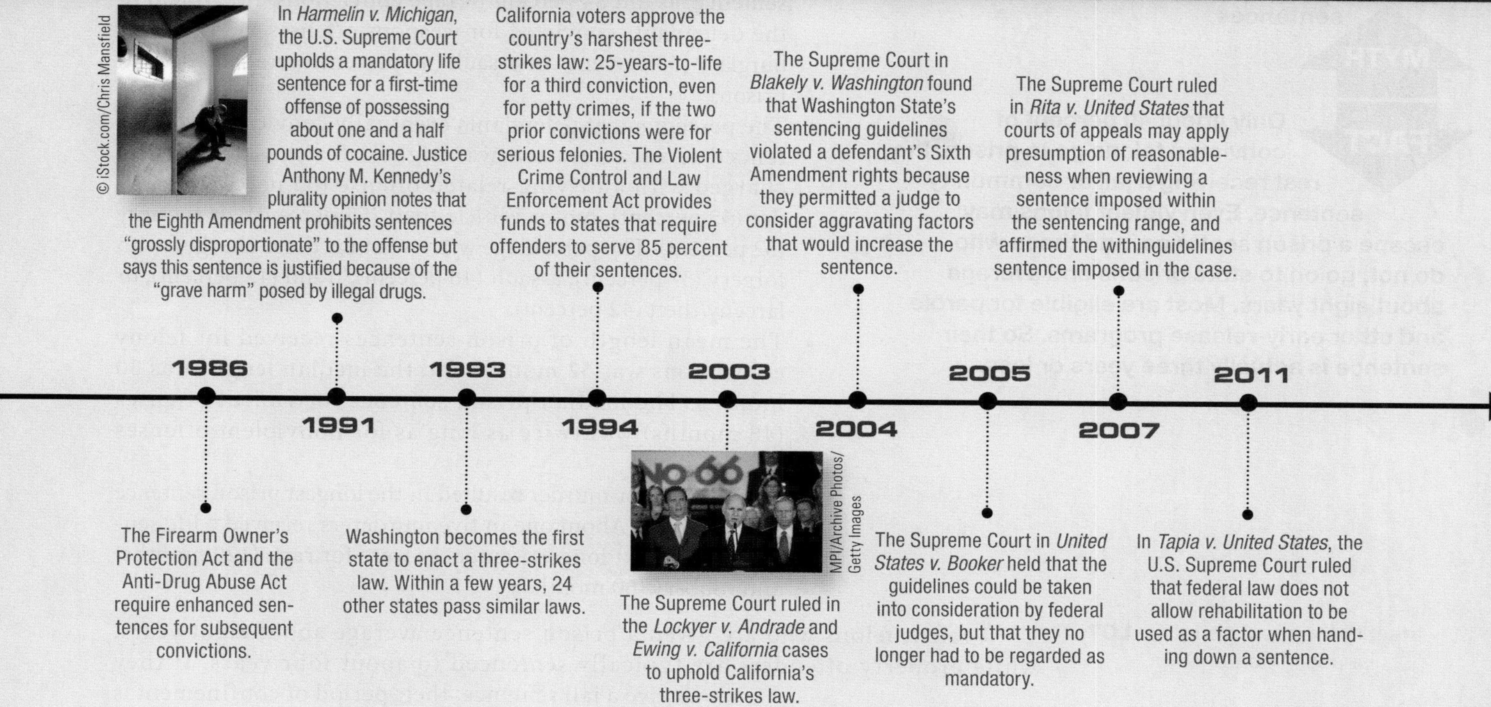

eligibility criteria.[35] Evaluations of the program found that it only had a modest effect on state sentencing policy and was one of many factors that produced a costly expansion of the inmate population.[36] The funding portion of this program was discontinued in 2004; truth-in-sentencing laws still remain in place in a few jurisdictions around the United States.

© iStock.com/Chris Mansfield
In *Harmelin v. Michigan*, the U.S. Supreme Court upholds a mandatory life sentence for a first-time offense of possessing about one and a half pounds of cocaine. Justice Anthony M. Kennedy's plurality opinion notes that the Eighth Amendment prohibits sentences "grossly disproportionate" to the offense but says this sentence is justified because of the "grave harm" posed by illegal drugs.
California voters approve the country's harshest three-strikes law: 25-years-to-life for a third conviction, even for petty crimes, if the two prior convictions were for serious felonies. The Violent Crime Control and Law Enforcement Act provides funds to states that require offenders to serve 85 percent of their sentences.
The Supreme Court in *Blakely v. Washington* found that Washington State's sentencing guidelines violated a defendant's Sixth Amendment rights because they permitted a judge to consider aggravating factors that would increase the sentence.
The Supreme Court ruled in *Rita v. United States* that courts of appeals may apply presumption of reasonableness when reviewing a sentence imposed within the sentencing range, and affirmed the withinguidelines sentence imposed in the case.
1986
1991
1993
1994
2003
2004
2005
2007
2011
The Firearm Owner's Protection Act and the Anti-Drug Abuse Act require enhanced sentences for subsequent convictions.
Washington becomes the first state to enact a three-strikes law. Within a few years, 24 other states pass similar laws.
MPI/Archive Photos/Getty Images
The Supreme Court ruled in the *Lockyer v. Andrade* and *Ewing v. California* cases to uphold California's three-strikes law.
The Supreme Court in *United States v. Booker* held that the guidelines could be taken into consideration by federal judges, but that they no longer had to be regarded as mandatory.
In *Tapia v. United States*, the U.S. Supreme Court ruled that federal law does not allow rehabilitation to be used as a factor when handing down a sentence.

For the sentencing changes in the past 50 years, see the Timeline.

HOW PEOPLE ARE SENTENCED

The federal government conducts surveys on sentencing practices in state and federal courts.[37]

- About 75 percent of the defendants convicted of a felony were sentenced to incarceration in a state prison or local jail, compared to 56 percent of those convicted of a misdemeanor. Nonetheless, about one in four felony convictions and one in three misdemeanor convictions resulted in a probation sentence.
- Convictions for murder (100 percent), rape (89 percent), and robbery (89 percent) were the most likely to result in a sentence to some form of incarceration. Felony convictions were least likely to result in an incarceration sentence when they were for forgery (64 percent) or a nontrafficking drug offense (64 percent).
- Overall, incarceration sentences were almost evenly divided between prison (36 percent) and jail (37 percent). Felony convictions were more likely to result in a sentence to prison (42 percent) than jail (33 percent). Nearly all incarceration sentences for misdemeanor convictions were to jail (53 percent) rather than prison (3 percent).

MYTH Violent felons receive very long prison sentences.

FACT Only about 40 percent of convicted felons go to prison, the rest receiving a jail or community sentence. Even violent felons may escape a prison sentence, and those who do not, go on to state prisons and average about eight years. Most are eligible for parole and other early-release programs. So their sentence is actually three years or less.

- Nearly all (98 percent) murder convictions resulted in a prison sentence, as did 84 percent of rape convictions. About half of the defendants convicted for weapons offenses (53 percent), burglary (53 percent), or assault (47 percent) were sentenced to prison.
- The percentage of defendants eventually convicted and sentenced to incarceration was highest for those originally charged with a driving-related offense (65 percent), murder (55 percent), motor vehicle theft (55 percent), or robbery (52 percent). The percentage was lowest for those charged with forgery (37 percent), assault (40 percent), fraud (42 percent), or larceny/theft (42 percent).
- The mean length of prison sentences received for felony convictions was 52 months and the median length was 30 months. The median prison sentence for violent offenses (48 months) was twice as long as for nonviolent offenses (24 months).
- Convictions for murder resulted in the longest prison sentence (360 months). About one in five murderers received a life sentence. The next longest sentences were for rape (120 months) and robbery (60 months).

LO7 Identify the most serious issues in sentencing

Violent felons who are given a prison sentence average about eight years, while property offenders are typically sentenced to about four years. If they receive a jail sentence, their period of confinement is considerably less.

There is a large difference between the number of crimes reported and the number of offenders convicted and facing a specific criminal sanction. There is a very small percentage of cases sentenced to federal or state confinement.

CORRECTIONAL LIFE

My Son Never Had a Chance

My son never had a chance in life. I have been married a number of times, and he just never had a father. He is not a bad person; he just made a mistake. I am afraid that they are going to put him in prison for the rest of his life. With a daughter to support, I won't have money to go see him in prison on a regular basis. This whole thing just breaks my heart.

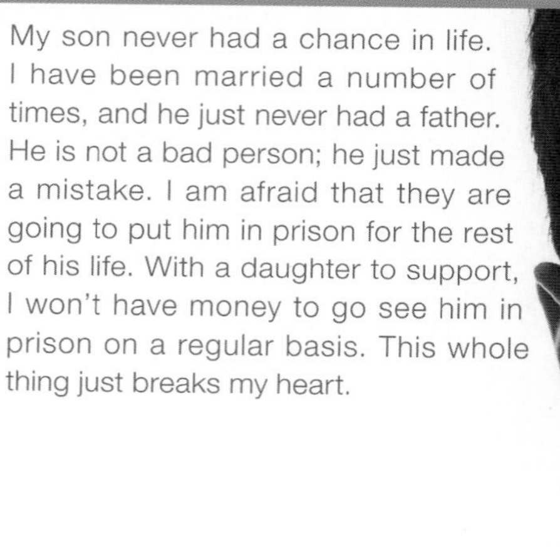

Excessive Length of Sentences

Sentences given by state and federal courts have traditionally been long in the United States. The late Norval Morris, well-known student of corrections and professor of law at the University of Chicago Law School, posed throughout his career the questions: "Why should America for identical nonviolent crimes with identical nonviolent crime rate hand out punishments in bucketfuls when Western Europe hands out punishments in spoonfuls? Why are we so excessive in our punishment?"[38] Of course, critics would retort that European crime rates have skyrocketed while those in the United States are in sharp decline.

The answer to why the United States has been so punitive in its sentencing practices is tied up in the social and political factors of our history. Yet, as much as the indeterminate sentence was faulted, it did serve to reduce the length of sentences. Inmates were usually paroled after they had served a fraction of their original sentence. However, with the rise of determinate sentences, sentencing guidelines, and

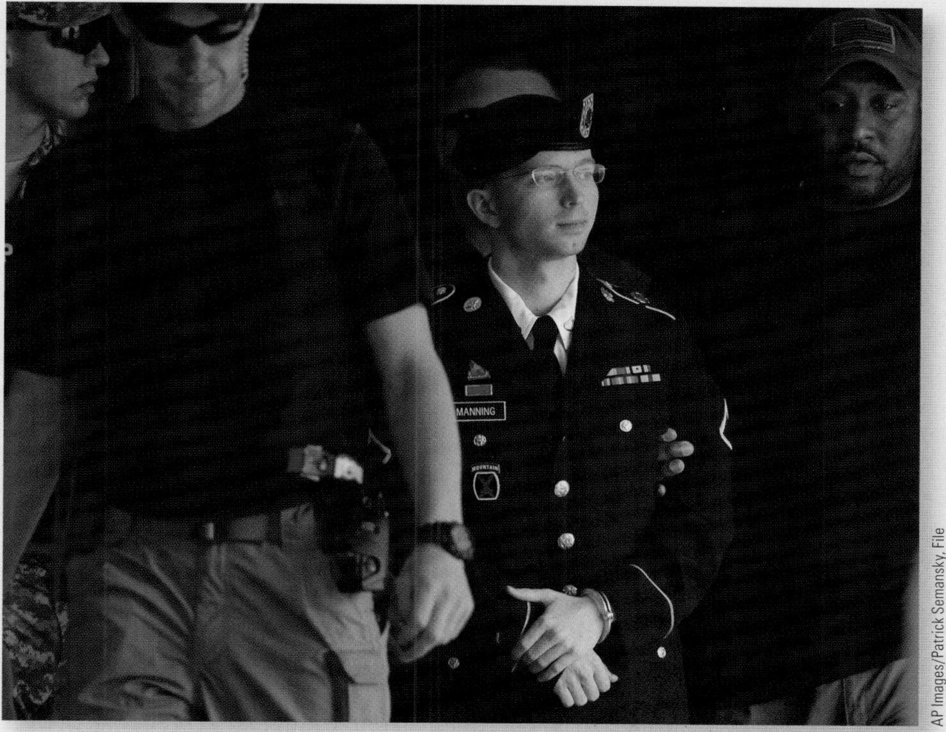

AP Images/Patrick Semansky, File

Army Pfc. Bradley Manning is escorted out of a courthouse in Fort Meade, Maryland, on July 30, 2013, after receiving a verdict in his court martial. Manning was acquitted of aiding the enemy—the most serious charge he faced—but was convicted of espionage, theft, and other charges, more than three years after he revealed secrets to WikiLeaks. He received a 35-year prison sentence. Is this excessive? His lawyers think so and filed an appeal. Manning, who changed his name to Chelsea Elizabeth Manning, is seeking hormone treatment therapy and the right to live as a woman while confined. Such treatment is not available in military prisons, but the Pentagon is considering a transfer to a civilian institution where such treatment is now available.

mandatory sentences, inmates began serving a longer part of their original sentence. The three-strikes laws were draconian for inmates with three felony convictions in states that implemented this sentencing structure. This sentencing legislation still applied to a small percentage of inmates. But with the rise of truth-in-sentencing laws, supported financially by the federal government, more and more inmates were sentenced to prison and required to serve 85 percent of their sentence.[39]

It is the length of prison sentences that really distinguishes American prison policy. American prisoners stays are much longer than found in other industrial nations. For example, burglars in the United States stay an average of 16 months in prison, compared with five months in Canada and seven months in England.[40] In addition, the U.S. is the only advanced nation to incarcerate individuals from minor property crimes, such as passing bad checks. In most European countries today, sentences over a year are uncommon and human rights norms make sentences longer than 12 to 14 years unconstitutional.

Nonlegal Factors Affecting Sentencing

There are a number of legal factors in sentencing that can legitimately influence the length of prison sentences, including:

- The severity of the offense
- The offender's prior criminal record
- Whether the offender used weapons
- Whether the offender was involved in violence
- Whether the crime was committed for money

Research does reveal a strong correlation between these legal variables and the type and length of sentence received. Beyond these legally appropriate factors, however, some critics believe that extralegal and therefore inappropriate factors influence judges when they make sentencing decisions. In other words, while it is appropriate for judges to consider a defendant's prior record in making their decision, age, race, and income cannot and should not influence the color of justice. What are some of the suspected **nonlegal factors in sentencing** factors?

nonlegal factors in sentencing These include contextual factors, social class, gender, race, age, and victim characteristics.

racial disparity in sentencing An actual pattern of racial discrimination in sentencing.

CONTEXTUAL FACTORS Judges in courts with smaller caseloads appear to sentence more severely than judges in larger courts. Similarly, counties that have larger jail capacities seem to send more defendants to jail.

SOCIAL CLASS Some evidence lends support to an association between social class and sentencing decisions. Lower-class offenders have typically expected to receive longer prison sentences than higher-class defendants, and they find that this frequently is true. One reason for this is that lower-class defendants often are less able to obtain quality legal representation than more affluent defendants or are unable to make bail, both factors influencing sentencing decisions.[41]

GENDER Most research reveals that women receive more favorable outcomes the further they are processed in the criminal justice system.[42] They are more likely to receive preferential treatment from a judge at sentencing than is accorded them by a police officer making the arrest or the prosecutor seeking the indictment.[43] This preferential treatment from judges seems especially to be true if women have dependent children; they are the ones who are more likely to receive leniency, no doubt because judges are reluctant to incarcerate a child's basic caregiver.[44]

AGE Judges may further be influenced by the extra-legal factor of age. The elderly may receive greater leniency, while younger defendants receive more punitive sentences.[45] Yet, judges may wish to protect some younger defendants from a prison sentence, fearing they will be attacked and brutalized in prison.[46]

VICTIM CHARACTERISTICS The characteristics of victims may also affect sentencing outcomes. This is especially true when it comes to victim impact statements before the sentencing judge. In victim impact statements, victims tell of their experiences and ordeals stemming from the crime, or in the case of a murder trial, surviving family members can tell of the effect that the murder has had on their lives.[47] But other studies have found that the impact of victim and witness statements is insignificant.[48]

© Becky Stein

The rising population of elderly inmates is an offshoot of the excessive criminal sentences routinely used in the nation's court system. Shown here is a "perm inmate," who is permanently housed at the maximum-security Georgia Diagnostic and Classification Prison, taking a midday stroll. The routine use of excessively long sentences accompanied by reduction in parole eligibility has produced an aging inmate population. The older inmate must be housed and treated for serious problems ranging from heart disease to liver failure. Many have long histories of drug abuse that substantially increase the risk of health problems and add to correctional costs. Would you keep people in prison past age 65?

Racial Disparities of Sentencing

There has been a long history of **racial disparity in sentencing**.[49] Yet, some recent research indicates that the association is far from linear: in some instances research shows a distinct pattern of discrimination, while other efforts indicate that sentencing may be more racially neutral than previously believed.[50]

Research supportive of racial discrimination in sentencing generally shows that for some categories of criminals—those convicted of drug offenses, those who accumulate more serious prior criminal records, those who refuse to plead guilty, and those unable to secure pretrial release—minorities are singled out for harsher treatment.[51] Minority defendants receive harsher sanctions if their victims are white than if their victims are fellow minority group members. Those minorities who murder whites are more likely to receive the death penalty than those who kill other minorities. In addition, minority defendants are more likely to be prosecuted under habitual offender statutes where the likelihood increases that there will be a white victim (burglary and larceny) than if they commit violent crimes that are largely interracial.[52]

Social status may influence sentencing because judges see the lower income and higher unemployment percentage of minorities and therefore view them as "social dynamite"—individuals more dangerous and more likely to be repeat offenders than white offenders.[53] Minority defendants who earn less on average than white defendants are less likely to afford bail and, as a result, are more likely to receive more severe sentences than those who have received pretrial detention. Finally, minorities are less likely than whites to be able to afford a private attorney who can put on a vigorous legal defense with the use of highly paid expert witnesses. All of these factors contribute to minorities being placed at a disadvantage during the sentencing process and contribute to sentencing disparity.

The issue of racial disparity in sentencing is explored more fully in the Evidence-Based Corrections feature.

THINKING LIKE A CORRECTIONS PROFESSIONAL

You are a district court judge, and a 30-year-old public school teacher is appearing before you on a bench trial. She is charged with having sex with two male high school students, both of whom are juniors. She has pleaded guilty and is awaiting your sentence. The teacher is six months pregnant and has been divorced for a number of years.

What will be your sentence? What are the most important factors leading you to your sentence? Is it important that you make an example of her so that other similar cases will not take place in nearby school districts?

EVIDENCE-BASED CORRECTIONS

Does Race Influence Criminal Sentencing?

It is commonly believed that race influences sentencing, and that because of racial bias African Americans routinely receive harsher sentences than whites. When Ojmarrh Mitchell and Doris MacKenzie conducted a thorough empirical review of the existing evidence on the effects of race on sentencing, they found that after taking into account a defendant's criminal history and current offense seriousness, African Americans and Latinos were generally sentenced more harshly than whites. The greatest disparity was found in crimes involving drug offenses and in decisions involving incarceration versus community sentencing. In addition, they found evidence to suggest that sentencing guidelines were associated with smaller sentencing disparities. Overall, their findings suggest that policy makers need to reevaluate sentencing practices, especially in regard to drug offenses and the decision to incarcerate.

The association between race and criminal court sentencing outcome is quite complex. While some evidence shows that racial bias in sentencing exists, other studies are not so clear cut, finding little evidence that judges are racially biased. Why does the critical issue of racial disparity in sentencing remain so murky? One reason may be that the conditions that produce sentencing disparity may actually occur before the trial takes place. This would suggest that system disparity rather than judicial bias is the true cause of any differences in sentencing outcomes. Research efforts show that because

(continued)

of economic disparity minorities are less likely than whites to make bail and therefore more likely to be detained in jail before trial; pretrial detention significantly increases the chance of an incarceration sentence upon conviction. When Tracy Nobiling, Cassia Spohn, and Miriam DeLone, as well as Pauline Brennan, examined race and sentencing, they found that racial status influences sentencing partially because minority group members have a lower income than whites and are more likely to be unemployed, rendering them less likely to make bail, afford high-priced private lawyers, or pay for expert witnesses. Each of these factors impacts on sentencing.

There is also evidence that racial bias in sentencing flows through the victim's status and not the criminal's. Minority defendants are sanctioned more severely if their victim is white than if their target is a fellow minority group member; minorities who kill whites are more likely to get the death penalty than those who kill other minorities. In their research, Charles Crawford, Ted Chiricos, and Gary Kleck found evidence that African American defendants are more likely to be prosecuted under habitual offender statutes if they commit crimes where there is a greater likelihood that their victim will be white (larceny and burglary) than if they commit violent crimes that are largely intraracial. In other words, judges may base sentencing decisions on the race of the victim and not the race of the defendant.

FOR CRITICAL THINKING AND WRITING

While clear-cut evidence of bias is insufficient to cast a shadow over judicial decision making, the empirical evidence clearly shows that race does play a role in sentencing outcomes Do you find this result unacceptable in our democratic society?

Sources: Pauline Brennan, "Sentencing Female Misdemeanants: An Examination of the Direct and Indirect Effects of Race/Ethnicity," *Justice Quarterly* 23 (2006): 60–95; Ojmarrh Mitchell and Doris MacKenzie, "The Relationship Between Race, Ethnicity, and Sentencing Outcomes: A Meta-Analysis of Sentencing Research," report to the United States Department of Justice, 2004, http://www.ncjrs.gov/pdffiles1/nij/grants/208129.pdf (accessed May 2014); Tracy Nobiling, Cassia Spohn, and Miriam DeLone, "A Tale of Two Counties: Unemployment and Sentence Severity," *Justice Quarterly* 15 (1998): 459–486; Charles Crawford, Ted Chiricos, and Gary Kleck, "Race, Racial Threat, and Sentencing of Habitual Offenders," *Criminology* 36 (1998): 481–511.

SUMMARY

LO1 Explain the roles of the court team in the sentencing process

The sentencing process rests in the hands of a number of actors—the prosecutor, the judge, and the probation staff. A major change in recent years is the increased power of the prosecutors in affecting sentencing decisions.

LO2 Summarize the bail process, pretrial release, and preventive detention

Defendants, of course, wish to receive bail, which means they are released from jail until their trial takes place. If they cannot raise the money for bail or are ineligible for pretrial release, it is necessary for them to stay in jail until their trial. Preventive detention is a recent movement with an objective to retain in jail defendants who are deemed dangerous or likely to commit crimes while awaiting trial.

LO3 Explain what is meant by indeterminate sentencing

More than 30 states still retain some form of indeterminate sentencing. This is a sentence that permits early release from a correctional institution after the offender has served a required portion of his or her sentence.

LO4 Identify the various forms of determinate sentencing

The variations of determinate sentencing discussed in this chapter include sentencing guidelines, mandatory minimum sentences, three-strikes laws, and truth-in-sentencing. Determinate sentencing remains popular in nearly one-third of the states.

LO5 Describe the role of sentencing guidelines

Beginning with the federal sentencing guidelines, about 20 states have adopted sentencing guidelines. Their purpose is to provide direction to judges when they impose sentences.

LO6 Discuss what is meant by truth-in-sentencing

Many states have enacted truth-in-sentencing laws that require a close connection between the imposed sentence and the actual time served in prison. The goal of these laws is to require offenders to serve a substantial portion of their imposed sentence in prison.

LO7 Identify the most serious issues in sentencing

The three most serious issues in sentencing are excessive length of today's sentence; the nonlegal factors, including age and gender, that influence sentencing; and the racial disparities that are present in sentencing outcomes.

CRITICAL THINKING QUESTIONS

1. Tomorrow you will appear before the judge. Are you hoping for an indeterminate or a determinate sentence? Why? Compare the two types of sentencing.
2. Of the various goals of sentencing, which one do you favor? Why? Explain the disposition suitable to your choice.
3. Do you believe the punishment should fit the crime or the needs of the offender? Explain your reasoning.
4. Do you think a just system of sentencing is possible? Why or why not?
5. Attend a criminal trial and describe the difficulties you would have in imposing a just and reasonable sentence.

NOTES

1. Rick Hall, Susan Candiotti, and Catherine E. Shoichet, "Former New England Patriot Hernandez Charged with Murder," *CNN Justice*, June 27, 2013.
2. Sasha Goldstein, "Aaron Hernandez Beats Down Fellow Inmate at Bristol County Jail: Report," New York Daily News, February 25, 2014, http://www.nydailynews.com/news/crime/aaron-hernandez-beats-fellow-inmate-bristol-county-jail-report-article-1.1701678 (accessed May 2014).
3. Halimy Assafa and Chris Boyette, "Aaron Hernandez Sued by Families of 2012 Fatal Shooting Victims," CNN U.S., February 27, 2014.
4. Tom Winter and Tracy Connor, "Aaron Hernandez Indicted for Double Murder in Boston," NBC News, May 15, 2014, http://www.nbcnews.com/storyline/aaron-hernandez/aaron-hernandez-indicted-double-murder-boston-n106211 (accessed June 2014).
5. Holbrook Mohr, "Haley Barbour Pardons: Former Mississippi Gov. 'Very Comfortable' with Decision," *Huffington Post*, January 15, 2012, http://www.huffingtonpost.com/2012/01/13/haley-barbour-pardons-mississippi-governor_n_1205450.html (accessed May 2014).
6. Maggy Patrick, "Haley Barbour Defends Decision to Grant Pardons, Says He Believes in 'Second Chances,'" ABC News, January 13, 2012, http://abcnews.go.com/blogs/politics/2012/01/haley-barbour-defends-decision-to-grant-pardons-says-he-believes-in-second-chances/ (accessed June 2014).
7. Richard A. Oppel, Jr., "Sentencing Shift Gives New Leverage to Prosecutors," *New York Times*, September 25, 2011.
8. Ibid.
9. Ibid.
10. Ibid.
11. John Wooldredge, "Judges' Unequal Contributions to Extralegal Disparities in Imprisonment," *Criminology* (May 2010): 539–567.
12. Ibid.
13. Todd D. Minton, *Jail Inmates at Midyear 2010—Statistical Tables* (Washington, DC: U.S. Department of Justice, 2011).
14. Stephen Demuth, "Racial and Ethnic Differences in Pretrial Release Decisions and Outcomes: A Comparison of Hispanic, Black, and White Felony Arrestees," *Criminology* 41 (August 2003): 873–907.
15. For an overview of sentencing in the United States, see Nicole D. Porter, *The State of Sentencing 2010* (Washington, DC: The Sentencing Project, 2011).
16. For a current statement on the status of sentencing in the United States, see Ryan S. King, *The State of Sentencing: Developments in Policy and Practice* (Washington, DC: The Sentencing Project, 2009).
17. *Tapia v. United States*, 18 U.S.C. AS 3582(a), 2011.
18. Don Steman and Andres F. Rengifo, "Policies and Imprisonment: The Impact of Structured and Determinate Sentencing on State Incarceration Rates, 1978–2004," *Justice Quarterly* 28 (2011): 174–201; Michael Tonry, "Reconsidering Indeterminate and Structured Sentencing," *Sentencing and Corrections: Issues for the 21st Century* (Washington, DC: U.S. Department of Justice, 1999), p. 1.
19. Wooldredge, "Judges' Unequal Contributions to Extralegal Disparities in Imprisonment."
20. John Wooldredge, "State Versus Long-Term Effects of Ohio's Switch to More Structured Sentencing on Extralegal Disparities in Prison Sentences in an Urban Court," *Criminology and Public Policy* 8 (2009): 285–312.
21. John H. Kramer and Jeffrey T. Ulmer, *Sentencing Guidelines: Lessons from Pennsylvania* (Boulder, CO: Lynne Rienner Publishers, 2008); Michael Tonry, "Sentencing Commissions and Their Guidelines," in *Crime and Justice: A Review of Research* 17 (Chicago: University of Chicago Press, 1993), p. 138.
22. For an overview of the federal sentencing guidelines, see Paul J. Hofer and Mark H. Allenbaugh, "The Reason Behind the Rules: Finding and Using the Philosophy of the Federal Sentencing Guidelines," *Criminal Law Review* (Winter 2003): 19–56; and Marc Mauer, *The Impact of Mandatory Minimum Penalties in Federal Sentencing* (Washington, DC: The Sentencing Project, 2010).
23. Andrew Longstreth, "Rajaratnam Prison Term Follows Sentencing Trends," Reuters, http://www.reuters.com/article/2011/10/13/us-galleon-rajaratnam-guidelines-idUSTRE79C7DG20111013 (accessed May 2014).
24. Lisa Pasko, "Villain or Victim: Regional Variation and Ethnic Disparity in Federal Drug Offense Sentencing," *Criminal Justice Policy Review* 13 (2002): 307–328; Wooldredge, "Judges' Unequal Contributions to Extralegal Disparities in Imprisonment."
25. Michael Tonry, "Racial Policies, Racial Disparities, and the War on Crime," *Crime and Delinquency* (1994): 475–494.
26. *Blakely v. Washington*, 124 S.Ct. 2531 (2004).
27. *United States v. Booker*, No. 04-104, decided January 12, 2005.
28. United States Sentencing Commission, *Final Report on the Impact of the* United States v. Booker *on Federal Sentencing*, March 2006.
29. See Brian D. Johnson, Jeffrey T. Ulmer, and John H. Kramer, "The Social Context of Guidelines Circumvention: The Case of Federal District Courts," *Criminology* 46 (2008): 737–745. To evaluate racial disparity in the light of these decisions, see Jeffrey T. Ulmer, Michael T. Light, and John H. Kramer, "Racial Disparity in the Wake of the *Booker/Fanfin* Decision: An Alternative Analysis of the USSC's 2010 Report," *Criminology and Public Policy* 10 (2011): 1077–1118.
30. For a discussion of mandatory minimum sentencing, see Natasha A. Frost, "Mandatory Minimum Sentencing," *Criminology and Public Policy* (February 2006): 1–4.
31. To further examine mandatory minimum sentences, see Jeffrey T. Ulmer, Megan C. Kurlychek, and John H. Kramer, "Prosecutorial Discretion and the Imposition of Mandatory Minimum Sentences," *Journal of Research in Crime and Delinquency* 44 (2007): 427–432; and Kirk J. Henderson, "Mandatory-Minimum Sentences and the

Jury: Time Again to Revisit Their Relationship," *Dayton Law Review* 33 (2007): 37–57.

32. Shimica Gaskins, "'Women of Circumstance': The Effects of Mandatory Minimum Sentencing on Women Minimally Involved in Drug Crimes," *American Criminal Law Review* (Fall 2004): 1533.
33. Tomislav V. Kovandzic, John J. Sloan III, and Lynne M. Vieraitis, "'Striking Out' as Crime Reduction Policy: The Impact of 'Three Strikes' Laws on Crime Rates in U.S. Cities," *Justice Quarterly* 21 (2004): 207.
34. Paula M. Ditton, *Truth in Sentencing in State Prisons* (Washington, DC: Bureau of Justice Statistics, 1999), p. 1.
35. Ditton and Wilson, *Truth in Sentencing in State Prisons*.
36. William Sabol, Katherine J. Rosich, Kamala Mallik Kane, David Kirk, and Glenn Dubin, *Influences of Truth-in-Sentencing Reforms on Changes in States' Sentencing Practices and Prison Populations* (Washington, DC: Urban Institute, Justice Policy Center, 2002), https://www.ncjrs.gov/pdffiles1/nij/grants/195161.pdf (accessed June 2014).
37. Matthew R. Durose and Patrick A. Langan, *Felony Sentences in State Courts* (Washington, DC: Bureau of Justice Statistics, 2007).
38. Personal correspondence with Bartollas.
39. Ditton, *Truth in Sentencing in State Prisons*, pp. 3–4.
40. Adam Liptak, "U.S. Prison Population Dwarfs That of Other Nations," *New York Times*, April 23, 2008.
41. Susan Welch, Cassia Spohn, and John Gruhl, "Convicting and Sentencing Differences Among Black, Hispanic, and White Males in Six Localities," *Justice Quarterly* 2 (1985): 67–80.
42. Fernando Rodriguez, Theodore Curry, and Gang Lee, "Gender Differences in Criminal Sentencing: Do Effects Vary Across Violent, Property, and Drug Offenses?" *Social Science Quarterly* 87 (2006): 318–339.
43. See Janet Johnston, Thomas Kennedy, and I. Gayle Shuman, "Gender Differences in the Sentencing of Felony Offenders," *Federal Probation* 87 (1987): 49–56; Cassia Spohn and Susan Welch, "The Effect of Prior Record in Sentencing Research: An Examination of the Assumption That Any Measure Is Adequate," *Justice Quarterly* 4 (1987): 286–302.
44. Barbara Koons-Witt, "The Effect of Gender on the Decision to Incarcerate Before and After the Introduction of Sentencing Guidelines," *Criminology* 40 (2002): 417–432.
45. Dean Champion, "Elderly Felons and Sentencing Severity: Interregional Variations in Leniency and Sentencing Trends," *Criminal Justice Review* 12 (1987): 7–15.
46. Darrell Steffensmeier, Jeffery Ulmer, and John Kramer, "The Interaction of Race, Gender and Age in Criminal Sentencing: The Punishment Cost of Being Young, Black, and Male," *Criminology* 36 (1998): 763–798.
47. *Payne v. Tennessee*, 111 S.Ct. 2597, 115 L.Ed.2d 720 (1991).
48. Robert Davis and Barbara Smith, "The Effects of Victim Impact Statements on Sentencing Decisions: A Text in an Urban Setting," *Justice Quarterly* 11 (1994): 453–469.
49. Michael Tonry, *Malign Neglect: Race, Crime and Punishment in America* (New York: Oxford University Press, 1995), p. 68.
50. J. D. Unnever and L. A. Hembroff, "The Prediction of Racial/Ethnic Sentencing Disparities: An Expectation States Approach," *Journal of Research in Crime and Delinquency* 25 (1987): 69–92.
51. Cassia C. Spohn, "Thirty Years of Sentencing Reform: The Quest for a Racially Neutral Sentencing Process," in *Policies, Processes, and Decisions of the Criminal Justice System*, Vol. 3, ed. J. Horney (Washington, DC: U.S. Government Printing Office, 2000), p. 428.
52. Charles Crawford, Ted Chiricos, and Gary Kleck, "Race, Racial Threat, and Sentencing of Habitual Offenders," *Criminology* 36 (1998): 481–511.
53. Tracy Nobiling, Cassia Spohn, and Miriam DeLone, "A Tale of Two Counties: Unemployment and Sentence Severity," *Justice Quarterly* 15 (1998): 459–486.

© Photo by Citrus County Sheriff's Department via Getty Images

This family photo shows 9-year-old Jessica Marie Lunsford of Homosassa, Florida, before she was kidnapped, raped, and killed by John Evander Couey, 46. He was on community release despite a long list of convictions, including burglary, carrying a concealed weapon, disorderly intoxication, indecent exposure, and larceny. Before he died of natural causes in 2009, he was on death row. Should dangerous offenders such as Couey be maintained in the community? Research indicates they are actually good candidates for rehabilitation.

ON FEBRUARY 24, 2005, 9-year-old Jessica Lunsford was reported missing from her home. Police checked up on known sex offenders living in the area, which included John Evander Couey, 46. He had a long list of convictions, including burglary, carrying a concealed weapon, disorderly intoxication, driving under the influence, indecent exposure, disorderly conduct, fraud, insufficient funds, and larceny. He was on unsupervised county probation at the time. A habitual drug abuser, in 1991 he had been arrested and charged with "fondling a child under the age of 16." Nineteen days after Jessica Lunsford was first reported missing, detectives returned to Couey's home, and this time found blood, but Couey had fled and was later arrested in Georgia. While in police custody, Couey admitted that he had entered the Lunsford home at around 3 A.M. on February 24 and found Jessica asleep in her bed. He woke her, ordered her to be quiet ("Don't yell or nothing"), and told her to follow him back to his sister's house where he raped her repeatedly and kept her in a closet for three days. Couey showed investigators the shallow grave where they found Jessica's body inside two tied plastic garbage bags. Her wrists were bound, but she had managed to poke two fingers through the plastic in an attempt to free herself; she had tried to escape but failed.[1] Couey had an IQ of 78, which is slightly above the level usually considered mentally disabled, but the judge rejected an argument by his lawyer that he could not be legally executed. Couey was found guilty of murder on March 7, 2007, and on August 24, 2007, was sentenced to death.[2]

On September 30, 2009, Covey, 51, died of natural causes at a Jacksonville hospital where he had been since August 12. Couey died just over a month before the Florida Supreme Court was scheduled to hear his automatic appeal.[3]

3

Community Corrections:
Diversion and Probation

Joel Gordon

LEARNING OBJECTIVES

 Explain what is meant by the term *community corrections act*

 Compare the main types of diversion programs and identify their advantages and disadvantages

 Discuss the advantages of being placed on probation

 Explain the risk assessment models and their current emphasis

 Describe the various ways probation is administered

 Clarify the legal rights of probationers

 Evaluate the effectiveness of probation and identify some of the promising programs in probation services

PREVIEW OF KEY CONCEPTS

judicial reprieve
recognizance
sureties
reintegrative philosophy
community corrections act (CCA)
true diversion
minimization of system penetration
deferred prosecution programs
Treatment Alternatives to Street Crime (TASC)
probation
financial restitution
community service
risk management system
new penology
presentence investigation (PSI)
revocation of probation
technical violation
deferred sentence
shock probation
bench, or unsupervised, probation
split sentence
intensive probation

It is hard to imagine a repeat sex offender on community release, and yet this is not uncommon. The majority of people convicted of sex offenses are placed on probation, and many never set foot in jail or prison.[4] Should these offenders be given a second chance? Understandably, the public and its officials have reacted to shocking sex crimes and murders by adopting tough laws and regulations that limit what sex offenders on probation can do and where they can live.[5] Sometimes things don't work out as planned: the most current research indicates that the overwhelming majority of sex offenders were not rearrested for a future sex crime, despite the fact that sex registration and notification laws have become the norm. In fact, committing other crimes such as robbery seems to be a better predictor of future sex offending than is past sex offending.[6] The Evidence-Based Corrections feature covers this topic in some depth.

EVIDENCE-BASED CORRECTIONS

Registering Sex Offenders on the Internet

In 1994, Megan Kanka, a 7-year-old New Jersey girl, was raped and murdered by Jesse Timmendequas, a sex offender who had moved into her neighborhood after being released from prison. Because Megan's family had no prior knowledge of his presence, they did not warn her to stay away from the new neighbor. Outraged because the Kankas had been left in the dark, community members successfully lobbied for the enactment of a law that requires sex offender registration and notification to the public that a sex offender is living and working in the community. Their crusade was so successful that by the mid-1990s, all 50 states and the District of Columbia had passed similar "Megan's Laws." Now many states are using the Internet to post information about sex offenders so residents can search for them by name or address.

In New Jersey, for example, sex offenders are grouped into three tiers based on their dangerousness: low (1), medium (2), and high (3). The Internet registry excludes low-risk offenders but includes the following information about moderate and high-risk sex offenders: the offender's name and address; any aliases used by the offender; any Megan's Law sex offenses committed by the offender, including a brief description and the date and location of disposition of any such offense; a general description of the offender's modus operandi, if any; the determination of whether the risk of reoffense by the offender is moderate or high; the offender's age, race, sex, date of birth, height, weight, hair, eye color, and any distinguishing scars or tattoos; a photograph of the offender and the date on which the photograph was entered into the registry; and the make, model, color, year, and license plate number of any vehicle operated by the offender. The Internet registry is continually updated with information about additional

AP Images/Jeff Zelevansky

Jesse Timmendequas, right, convicted murderer of 7-year-old Megan Kanka, is escorted out of the Mercer County Courthouse and back to prison after Judge Andrew Smithson sentenced him to two consecutive life sentences for felony murder, kidnapping, and aggravated sexual assault, July 30, 1997. His crimes prompted states to get tough on sex offenders, requiring sex offender registration under what is now referred to as "Megan's Law."

registrants added as court orders are issued authorizing Internet disclosure about those individuals.

DOES IT REALLY WORK?

In 2009, Kristen Zgoba and Karen Bachar conducted an in-depth study of the effectiveness of the New Jersey registration and found that the system was expensive to maintain and did not produce effective results. Sex offense rates in New Jersey were in a steep decline before the system was installed and the rate of decline actually slowed after 1995. Their data show that the greatest rate of decline in sex offending occurred prior to the passage and implementation of Megan's Law. They also found that passage and implementation of Megan's Law did not reduce the number of rearrests for sex offenses, nor did it have any demonstrable effect on the time between when sex offenders were released from prison and the time they were rearrested for any new offense, such as a drug, theft, or sex offense.

So while using technology such as Internet registrations may seem like a panacea to some, innovations must be thoroughly tested before they can be reasonably relied upon.

FOR CRITICAL THINKING AND WRITING

If sex offenders are registered, do you think other types of criminals should be also—for example, white-collar criminals? After all, you would not want to be getting stock tips from your next-door neighbor who, unbeknownst to you, just got out of prison for insider trading! Why one and not the other?

Source: Kristen Zgoba and Karen Bachar, "Sex Offender Registration and Notification: Research Finds Limited Effects in New Jersey," National Institute of Justice, April 2009, http://www.ncjrs.gov/pdffiles1/nij/225402.pdf (accessed June 2014).

© James Dare

VOICES ACROSS THE PROFESSION

Locking offenders up is easy, but providing services in the community takes work and creativity. What works for one client won't work for the next one. In probation, "one size does not fit all."

James Dare

Deputy Court Administrator, Montgomery County Common Pleas Court, Division of Criminal Justice Services, Dayton, Ohio

Ensuring public safety is a huge responsibility [of the probation officer] besides performing the following duties: office visits, field work, jail visits, treatment visits, court appointments, conducting investigation, transports, urine collections, arrests, ensuring victims are compensated, providing meaningful interventions, ensuring compliance with court-ordered sanctions, developing case plans with clients, completing statistics, and making recommendations for or against probation. You need to be organized, flexible, and a team player.

Other challenges of being a probation officer are balancing power, understanding diversity, and imposing sanctions proportionate to the violation. Locking offenders up is easy, but providing services in the community takes work and creativity. What works for one client won't work for the next one. In probation, "one size does not fit all."

Probation officers should be encouraged to join professional organizations in order to network with other professionals, attend training, and learn about the newest technology. You may be required to be proficient with weapons, handcuffs, and other equipment, but it's your ability to assess situations and use common sense that will ensure your safety and the safety of your coworkers.

Probation continues to be held to a high standard. The next generation of officers will bring new ideas, tackle new challenges, and expand the use of technology. Probation officers will bring a new level of hope to provide the best service to the court, the client, and the community.

MYTH Sex offenders are almost always sent to prison, where they are victimized by other inmates.

FACT The majority of convicted sex offenders are placed on probation and monitored in the community.

Community-based programs are alternatives to institutional placements and keep offenders out of jails and federal, state, and private prisons. They are known to be more humane than overcrowded, violent, and anti-therapeutic prisons and, at the same time, can help the offender maintain family and community ties. They are more economical than costly institutionalization and are able to curtail the number of new prisons that must be built for the ever-increasing correctional population. And some evidence exists that they are more effective in reducing recidivism than short- and long-term institutionalization.[7] These are the reasons why community placements are at an all-time high; it simply makes more sense, whenever possible, to keep offenders in the community under the supervision of trained court officers than to send offenders to prison.

The agencies of community-based corrections consist of diversion programs, probation, intermediate sanctions, reentry programs, parole, and supervision of ex-offenders. This chapter focuses on diversion and probation, the next chapter examines intermediate sanctions and restorative justice, and Chapter 11 considers parole and supervision of ex-offenders.

AP Images/Nicholas K. Geranios

On August 29, 2013, teacher Michael Hunley, left, works with inmate Jose Flores in an aerospace composites class at the Airway Heights Corrections Center, in Washington. About a dozen inmates there are training for jobs in the state's huge aerospace industry as certified aerospace composite technicians. Their goal is a post-prison chance to land jobs at companies like Boeing and its suppliers. Would offenders like Jose Flores be better served with a probation sentence than a stay in prison?

THE DEVELOPMENT OF COMMUNITY-BASED CORRECTIONS

Treating offenders in the community is not a new idea and is actually a tradition that can be traced back to the English common law. During the Middle Ages, judges willing to spare deserving offenders from the harsh punishments of the day used their power to grant clemency and stays of execution. This practice of **judicial reprieve** allowed judges to suspend punishment so that convicted offenders could seek a pardon or gather new evidence that they were now reformed. **Recognizance** was a practice that permitted convicted offenders to remain free if they agreed to take care of their debt obligation with the state, and **sureties** were occasionally required—individuals who made themselves responsible for the behavior of offenders who had been released.

judicial reprieve Permitted judges to suspend judgment until offenders could seek a pardon or gather new evidence.

recognizance Permitted offenders to remain free if they promised to pay their debts to the state.

sureties Individuals who would agree to make themselves responsible for offenders who had been released from custody.

Community-based corrections programs can also be found early in the history of the United States. The Puritans in New England attempted to punish deviants in the community, as a means to enforce their strict Puritan codes. Informal community pressures, such as gossip, ridicule, and ostracism, were found to be effective in keeping most citizens in line. Offenders might be confined in the stocks and the public cage, or for the most the serious crimes, they might be whipped, branded, banished, or hanged.

The community nature of corrections receded in importance with the rise of the American version of the penitentiary. Yet, in the middle of the nineteenth century, probation began with the volunteer services of John Augustus in Massachusetts. Born in Woburn, Massachusetts, in 1785, Augustus moved to Boston in 1829 where he started a successful boot-making business. He joined the Washington Total Abstinence Society, a group whose members abstained from alcohol themselves and were convinced that abusers of alcohol could be rehabilitated through understanding and kindness rather than punishment. As a society member, Augustus was drawn to the Boston courtroom in an effort to save people whose drinking had gotten them in trouble with the law. In 1841, he accepted his first probation client, whose offense was "yielding to his appetite for strong drink." He provided bail for this person, subject to the man appearing in court three weeks later. Beginning with this first client, he was to devote himself to the cause of probation as he became convinced that many lawbreakers only needed the interest and concern of another to be able to straighten out their lives. Augustus worked with women and children as well as with adult male offenders and in fact was willing to work with all types of offenders—drunkards, petty thieves, prostitutes, and felons—as long as he was met with a contrite heart. Over an 18-year period, Augustus bailed out and supervised approximately 2,000 probationers, helping them get jobs and establishing themselves in the community. Augustus instigated such services as investigation and screening, supervision of probationers, interviewing, and arranging for relief, employment, and education—all of which are still used today. He had a remarkably high success rate, as few of his probationers became involved in crime again. Recognizing Augustus's achievements, Massachusetts formalized probation in 1859, a year after his death, creating the nation's first paid probation officers.[8]

Following its beginnings as a voluntary movement in the late nineteenth century, probation experienced rapid growth in the first decades of the twentieth century and in the 1960s. It spread to every state and was administered by both state and local authorities and became the most common form of criminal sanction during the twentieth century. The use of volunteers had disappeared by the turn of the century, only to return in the 1950s. Probation became more treatment oriented, and early in the century, the medical treatment model was used. Later in the 1960s and 1970s, probation officers became brokers who delivered services to clients. The upgrading of standards and training was also emphasized in the 1960s and 1970s. The significant events in the development of probation in the United States are set out in the Timeline.

The Community Corrections Revolution

The social context of the 1960s was such that widespread support was given to the rehabilitative ideal, spurring the development of new forms of community-based corrections programs. Several commissions recommended the establishment of alternatives to the juvenile justice system and the development of various types of diversion programs for adults. The main rationale of diversion was to keep juvenile and adult offenders out of the justice system and avoid the stigma of criminal/juvenile delinquent labels.

The new challenge of corrections was seen as keeping offenders in the community and reintegrating them into community living. It was believed that because prisons dehumanize people and prepare inmates for lives of criminality, every effort

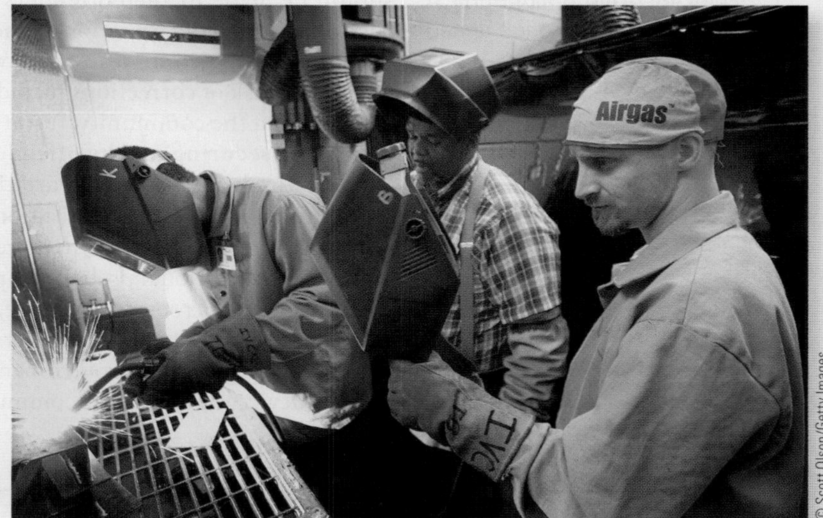

By teaching inmates usable skills, correctional treatment programs can help reintegrate them back into the community. Welding instructor Harry Bell (center) guides inmates Richard Johnson (left) and Tony Bailey in the weld shop at the Sheridan Correctional Center in Sheridan, Illinois, a dedicated center for the treatment of inmates with drug and alcohol abuse problems. A majority of inmates in the Illinois prison system have histories of substance abuse and/or have committed drug and alcohol-related crimes. The state opened Sheridan in January 2004 to combat a recidivism rate of 54 percent in its penal system. The recidivism rate for prisoners who have served time at Sheridan is only about 8 percent.

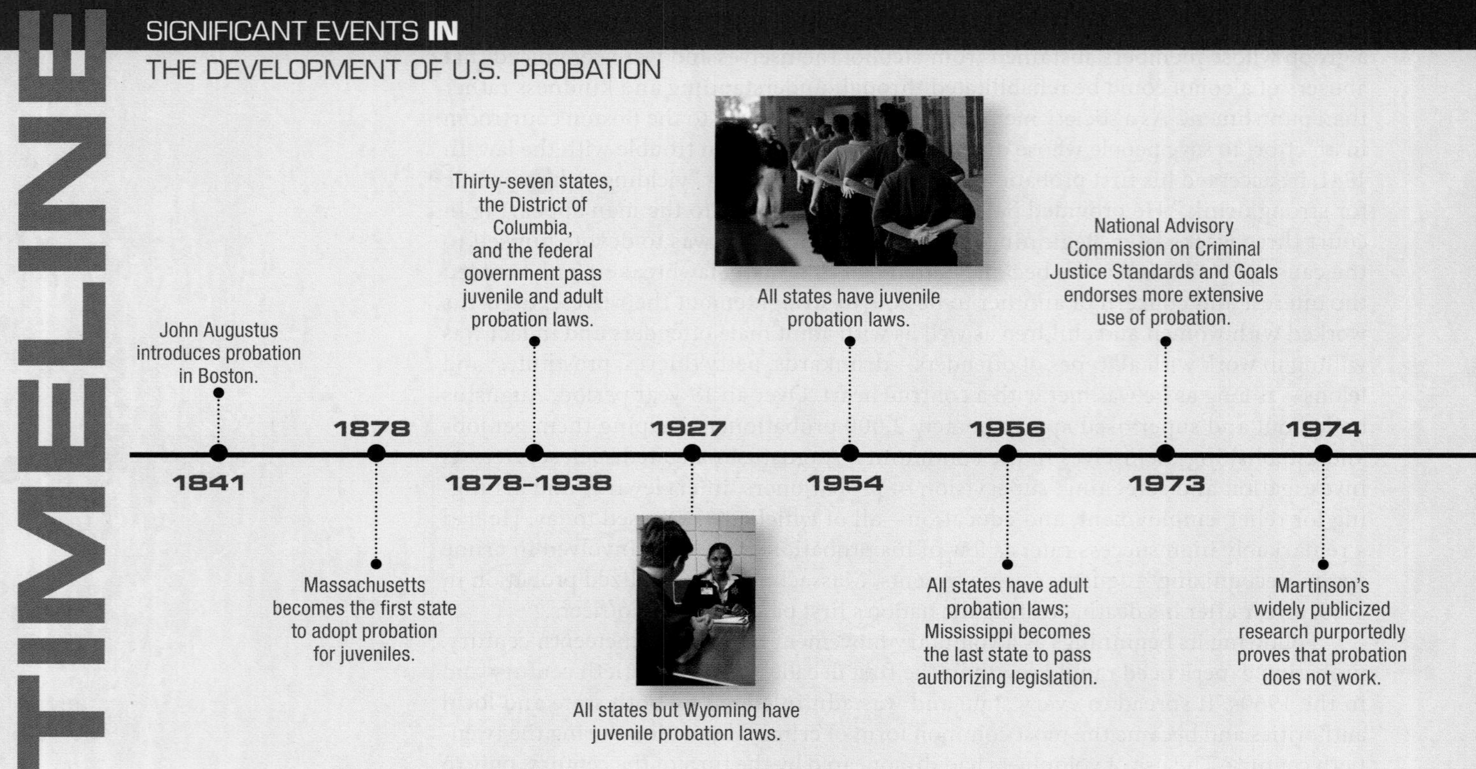
TIMELINE
SIGNIFICANT EVENTS IN
THE DEVELOPMENT OF U.S. PROBATION
1841
John Augustus introduces probation in Boston.
1878
Massachusetts becomes the first state to adopt probation for juveniles.
1878–1938
Thirty-seven states, the District of Columbia, and the federal government pass juvenile and adult probation laws.
1927
All states but Wyoming have juvenile probation laws.
1954
All states have juvenile probation laws.
1956
All states have adult probation laws; Mississippi becomes the last state to pass authorizing legislation.
1973
National Advisory Commission on Criminal Justice Standards and Goals endorses more extensive use of probation.
1974
Martinson's widely publicized research purportedly proves that probation does not work.

reintegrative philosophy A correctional approach aimed at returning offenders to the community as soon as possible.

should be made to keep offenders out of long-term institutions. The **reintegrative philosophy** of corrections—the idea that every effort should be made to return offenders to the community as law-abiding citizens—was also developed at this time. This task of corrections included building or rebuilding social ties between the offender and the community, restoring family ties, obtaining education and employment, and securing for the offender a place in the normal functioning of society. This required efforts both toward the rehabilitation of offenders and toward change of the community and its institutions. As part of the expansion of community-based corrections, residential facilities were designed to house probationers having difficulties with traditional probation and high-risk parolees being released from prison.

Because it was so cost effective, probation gained the favor of judges and politicians, and the numbers of offenders on probation soared. The increasing probation population inspired state governments to reorganize and support probation initiatives, and the device they used was community corrections acts.

Explain what is meant by the term *community corrections act* **LO1**

Community Corrections Acts

community corrections act (CCA) State-based acts through which local governments that participate receive subsidies for diverting minor offenders from state prisons.

A **community corrections act (CCA)** is a law passed by a state legislature in which a state grants funds to local units of government to plan, develop, and deliver correctional services and sanctions. CCAs are found in the philosophy of community-oriented corrections. One of the major purposes of community corrections acts is to encourage local sentencing options in lieu of state imprisonment.

Since the first and most developed community corrections act took place in Minnesota, about 25 states have implemented CCAs for adults. These statutes have a number of characteristics in common:

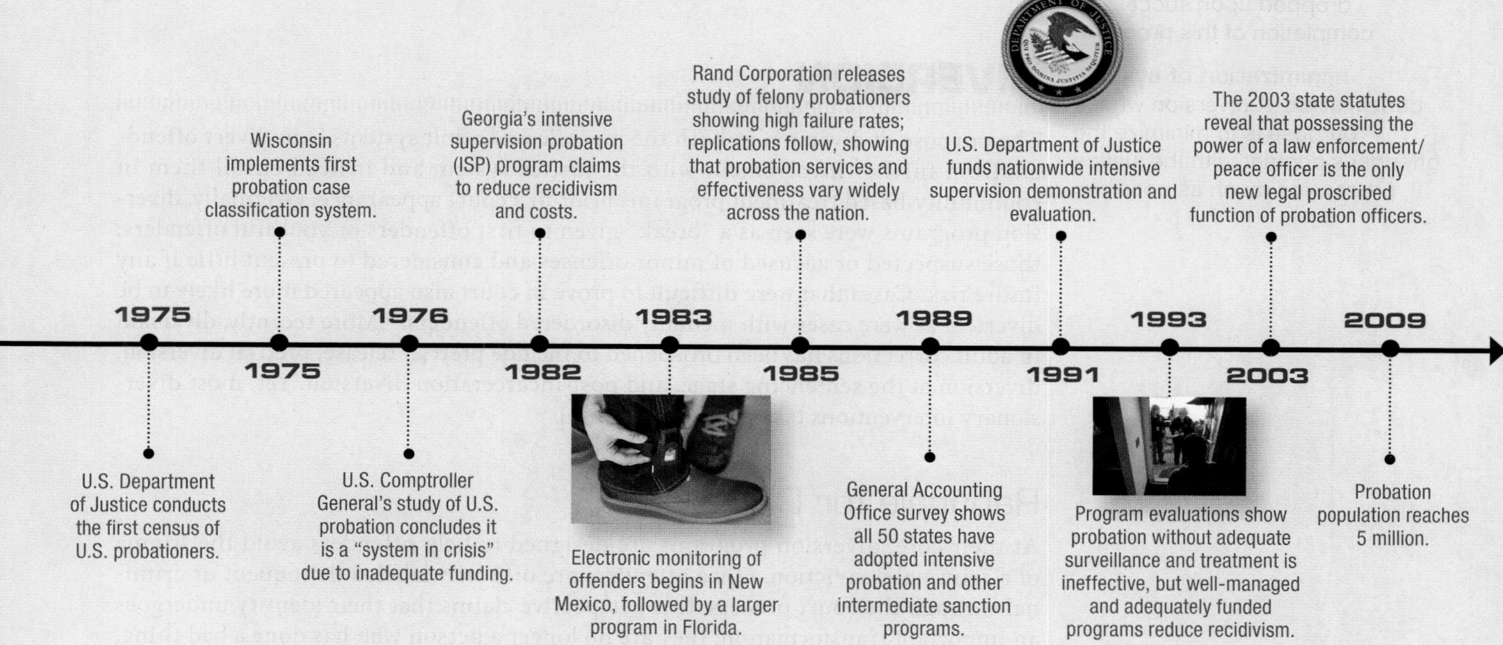
Wisconsin implements first probation case classification system.
Georgia's intensive supervision probation (ISP) program claims to reduce recidivism and costs.
Rand Corporation releases study of felony probationers showing high failure rates; replications follow, showing that probation services and effectiveness vary widely across the nation.
U.S. Department of Justice funds nationwide intensive supervision demonstration and evaluation.
The 2003 state statutes reveal that possessing the power of a law enforcement/peace officer is the only new legal proscribed function of probation officers.
1975
1976
1983
1989
1993
2009
1975
1982
1985
1991
2003
U.S. Department of Justice conducts the first census of U.S. probationers.
U.S. Comptroller General's study of U.S. probation concludes it is a "system in crisis" due to inadequate funding.
Electronic monitoring of offenders begins in New Mexico, followed by a larger program in Florida.
General Accounting Office survey shows all 50 states have adopted intensive probation and other intermediate sanction programs.
Program evaluations show probation without adequate surveillance and treatment is ineffective, but well-managed and adequately funded programs reduce recidivism.
Probation population reaches 5 million.

- CCAs are legislatively authorized. Statutes provide the framework and authority for the other defining features of CCAs.
- CCAs call for decentralized program design and delivery. They provide for local control of the processes employed to serve as the basis for the development, implementation, and modification of local correctional sanctions and services.
- CCAs are authorized statewide. They mandate or authorize all localities, individually or in combination, to take advantage of the funds and authority granted.
- CCAs provide for citizen involvement and specify roles that citizens may play.
- CCAs define an intergovernmental structure. They delineate the roles to be performed and the power and authority to be exercised by involved state and local agencies or units of government.
- CCAs require local planning. They provide that local planning will serve as the basis for the development, implementation, and modification of local correctional sanctions and services.
- CCAs provide for state subsidies to support local correctional programs and services.
- CCAs process employees, assess local needs, establish local priorities, and plan local programs.
- CCAs endorse locally determined sanctions and services. They provide resources and authority for sanctions and services to be developed and delivered at the local level.[9]

Community corrections acts have spread rapidly since Minnesota's effort. Counties have found them an effective means to control offenders and to coordinate

true diversion A diversion program where the offender has his or her criminal prosecution dropped upon successful completion of this program.

minimization of system penetration A diversion whose purpose is to minimize the offender's contact with the justice process as much as possible.

correctional efforts, and most states feel that CCAs are reducing prison populations in a promising way. In the following sections, the major forms of community corrections are laid out in some detail.

DIVERSION

The purpose of diversion in both the juvenile and adult systems is to divert offenders from further involvement with the justice system and instead enroll them in community-based treatment programs prior to a court appearance. Originally, diversion programs were seen as a "break" given to first offenders or youthful offenders, those suspected or accused of minor offenses and considered to present little if any future risk. Cases that were difficult to prove in court also appeared more likely to be diverted, as were cases with mentally disordered offenders.[10] More recently, diversion in adult corrections has been broadened to include pretrial release, pretrial diversion, diversion at the sentencing stage, and post-incarceration diversion. Yet, most diversionary interventions take place prior to trial.

Rationale for Diversion

At their core, diversion programs are designed to help offenders avoid the stigma of a criminal conviction. Once offenders are officially labeled delinquent or criminal through the court process, this perspective claims that their identity undergoes an important transformation: they are no longer a person who has done a bad thing, they are now a bad person. People suspect and fear them and their life chances are undermined. Their label shadows them for the remainder of their lives. Because they are now outcasts, they may join other similarly labeled people in deviant cliques and gangs, escalating the likelihood they will repeat their illegal behaviors. To break this cycle and to keep them out of a life of crime, something must be done to help offenders avoid the stigma of an official criminal label.

Early proponents of diversion programs for juveniles also claimed that these interventions offered numerous other advantages that would lead to a more effective and humane justice process. These included the reduction of caseloads, a more efficient administration of the juvenile justice system, and provision of therapeutic environments in which children and parents could resolve family conflicts.

Other analysts, in applying diversion to the adult system, have added to or elaborated on these goals. They have also pointed to the objectives to reverse the uneven imposition of serious sanctions onto those who are already socially disadvantaged. In this sense, diversion can accomplish a variety of goals:

- Avoiding the harsh and criminogenic impacts of incarceration in prison
- Informing and providing a range of alternatives for decision makers to choose from
- Providing a "more justifying justice" for victims and communities
- Dealing with the economic, social, and personal factors associated with crime, rather than the punitively oriented alternative[11]

CRITICAL THINKING

If you were a victim of crime, do you feel that diverting the perpetrator would be "justifying justice"? How? LO1

Compare the main types of diversion programs and identify their advantages and disadvantages LO2

Diversion Programs

Diversion programs can be divided into those providing true diversion and those seeking minimization of system penetration. **True diversion** takes place when an offender is referred to a program and the completion of this program will enable him or her to avoid criminal prosecution. For example, if an offender is referred to a deferred prosecution program and he or she is willing to participate in the program, the court will be asked to defer formal charging. In contrast, those aiming for **minimization of system penetration** focus on reducing the offender's interface with the justice system. In this model, the convicted drug defendant may be given a choice of either going to prison or becoming part of a therapeutic community for drug offenders.

Diversion's attractiveness has increased with the awareness of the importance of keeping minor offenders, the mentally ill, and drug offenders, whenever possible, out of the justice system.[12] Deferred prosecution, deferred judgment, and Treatment Alternatives to Street Crime (TASC) are three main types of adult pretrial diversion programs.

DEFERRED PROSECUTION AND DEFERRED JUDGMENT For those who have made a mistake resulting in a criminal charge, there are programs, like deferred prosecution and deferred judgment, that make it possible for defendants to avoid criminal penalties and have an opportunity to clear their record if they stay out of further trouble with the law. The programs, though slightly different, are both designed to give offenders accused of a crime a second chance. Many are administered through special courts, including drug courts, DUI courts, or juvenile courts for youthful offenders.[13]

There are some major differences between the two: deferred judgment occurs after offenders admit to all or part of the charges against them but before the plea is entered on the record. Defendants then serve a period of informal probation, in a sense deferring judgment. In some states, such as Maryland, this is called probation before judgment (PBJ). In contrast, deferred prosecution does not require a guilty plea or the admission of facts. Offenders voluntarily serve a period of probation in lieu of court appearances and formal charges.[14]

Deferred prosecution programs have traditionally operated in one of two ways. In the first model, when an offender is arrested, he or she may be screened according to a number of pre-established criteria to determine if the problem can be handled through a formal diversion program. If so, project staff will explain the program to the accused offender, and if the offender is willing to participate in the program, the court will be asked to defer formal charging. Prosecutors are usually willing to dismiss the criminal charges for those offenders who successfully complete their diversion programs.

deferred prosecution programs Those referred to these programs benefit from having their charges dropped upon their successful completion.

Under the second model, formal charges are lodged before defendants are screened for their eligibility for diversion programs. If the court and the offender agree, criminal proceedings are suspended pending the outcome of the findings and conclusions of the programs. A successful solution through the program ensures that formal charges are dropped; failure results in formal criminal charges. The length of the probation term is generally up to the prosecutor, with approval from the judge. Because this is considered a plea agreement, offenders generally will know the length of time before they agree to the program.

The Manhattan Court Employment Project, the District of Columbia's Project Crosswords, and the Flint (Michigan) Citizens Probation Authority were the pilot deferred programs. Pretrial intervention, as it is commonly termed, has included about 150 programs in 37 states. Programs have been formalized according to court rules in 2 states, and 7 states have statewide authorizing legislation.[15]

Deferred prosecution programs have focused on persons suffering from alcohol, drug, or mental health problems who can ask permission of the court to go through an intensive treatment program in lieu of being prosecuted. Successful completion of the treatment, as well as continued lawful conduct, will result in the dismissal of the charge and perhaps also avoid suspension of the person's driver's license.

TREATMENT ALTERNATIVES TO STREET CRIME (TASC) The **Treatment Alternatives to Street Crime (TASC)** program is the most widespread of the various national programs that have been designed to divert drug abusers away from the criminal justice system and into the jurisdiction of agencies offering specialized support services. TASC is centered around a screening unit, an intake unit, and a tracking unit. The screening unit attempts to identify drug users entering the criminal

Treatment Alternatives to Street Crime (TASC) A treatment program designed to divert minor drug abusers away from the criminal justice system.

justice system and to offer the program to those offenders who are eligible under locally determined criteria. The intake unit diagnoses each offender referred to it and recommends the appropriate treatment program. The tracking unit constantly monitors the progress of TASC clients. Those violating the locally determined success/failure criteria are returned to the criminal justice system for appropriate action.

TASC programs are a cost-effective way of delivering treatment because of their ability to identify and link appropriate services to drug-involved individuals. By focusing on reducing the stigma associated with incarceration, drug abuse, and mental illness, TASC eases the transition to the community for clients. Supporters firmly believe that TASC's programs and the high quality of their treatment, monitoring, case management, and referrals offer a far better chance of breaking the cycles of addiction, crime, and incarceration than other programs. Yet, in the midst of extremely high risk of recidivism for drug offenders, it is not surprising that the findings on criminal recidivism for TASC programs are mixed.[16]

In sum, the outstanding feature of informal, voluntary, reconciliation-focused, community-based programs is their usefulness in keeping offenders in the community. Deferred prosecution programs appear to be a good option for most first offenders because they avoid the stigma of a criminal record and reduce the volume of persons going through the criminal justice process. The major limitations, especially of deferred prosecution and TASC programs, are that not all offenders will choose to benefit from these diversionary efforts and, more importantly, these programs may increase the numbers of those who otherwise would have been ignored by the criminal justice system in the past.

probation A form of punishment that permits a convicted offender to remain in the community, under the supervision of a probation officer and subject to certain conditions set by the court.

Discuss the advantages of being placed on probation 

PROBATION

Probation is a correctional service allowing an offender to remain in the community for the duration of a sentence under supervision by an officer of the court and requiring the offender to comply with whatever conditions the court imposes. Probation is the most widely used correctional option. The basic goals of probation are to promote law-abiding behavior by the offender; to keep the adjudicated individual in the community and out of prison and, thereby, avoid the stigma of incarceration; to provide a less expensive sanction than institutionalization; and to provide a sanction that is as effective as confinement in reducing recidivism. While originally conceived as an alternative to prison, it is possible to require probationers to serve a portion of their sentence behind bars. This jail time may be served on weekends or at night, or a specified term in jail may be followed by a period of probation.

Brian L. Frank/Redux

If the rules of probation are violated, probationers can have their probation revoked and be sent to a secure institution. Here, Detectives Felipe Lucero and Miguel Alvarez of the Multi-Agency Gang Enforcement Consortium (MAGEC) question Bulldog gang member "Droopy" before taking him to jail for violating his probation by possessing weapons in his home.

Probation generally involves suspension of the offender's sentence in return for the promise of good behavior in the community under the supervision of a probation officer. As practiced by the federal government and all 50 states, probation implies a contract between the court and the offender in which the former promises to hold or suspend a prison term while the latter promises to follow a set of rules or conditions that are mandated by the court. If the rules are violated or the probationer commits another offense, probation may be revoked, which means that the contract is terminated and the original sentence is enforced. If an offender on probation commits a second offense that is more serious than the first, this person may be indicted, tried, and sentenced on the second offense. However, probation also may be revoked if the offender has failed to meet rules and conditions of probation (called "technical violations of probation").

Each probationary sentence is for a fixed period of time, and it depends on the seriousness of the offense and the statutory law of the jurisdiction. Probationers must report to a probation officer as often as required. The court sets down certain conditions or rules that must be followed by the offender. Some rules are standard and are applied in every probation case. Typically, probationers cannot leave the jurisdiction and must keep their officer informed of changes in their circumstances, especially as to contacts with the police, employment, address, marital status, and income or indebtedness.

Special rules of probation vary from jurisdiction to jurisdiction and may also vary to meet the personal situation of particular offenders. The payment of fines, restitution to victims, community service assignments, random or regular urine and alcohol testing, and regular employment are common requirements. **Financial restitution** and **community service** are two conditions often placed on probationers by many courts. The use of restitution actually predates both incarceration and modern forms of community treatment; the current trend is toward a more purposeful and imaginative use of restitution. At times, the victim is even involved with the offender in the development of restitution agreements. (See Chapter 4 for a more extensive discussion of fines, restitution, and community service as well as involvement of the victim as part of restorative justice in the adult criminal justice process.)

financial restitution Payment of a sum of money by an offender either to the victim or to a public fund for victims of crime.

community service Requires an offender to perform a certain number of work hours at a private nonprofit or government agency.

Probation Populations

Today, there are about 4 million adults on probation in the United States.[17] And while the crime rate has decreased significantly, the probation population rose continuously for more than 20 years but began to decline in 2010 (see Figure 3.1). Most probationers are concentrated in a few large states: Georgia, Texas, California, Ohio, Florida, Michigan, and Pennsylvania account for more than a third of all probationers. Probationers account for more than half the growth in the correctional population since 1990.[18]

Most probationers are white males who have committed felony offenses. While many people believe probation is used only with petty offenders, more than half of all probationers have been convicted of a felony, including drug law violations, property offenses public order offenses and violent offenses.

Probation supervision is made more difficult by the variety of offenders that must be supervised. The supervision of violent offenders on probation status represents a serious concern and can represent safety issues. Nearly 20 percent, or over 800,000, of

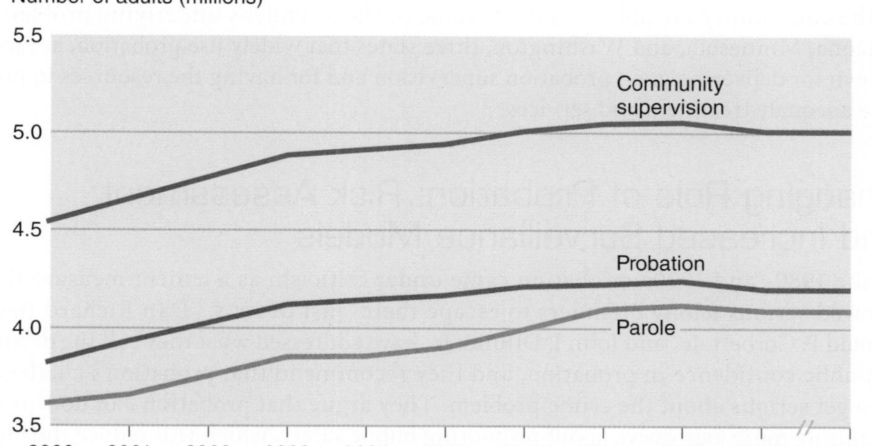

FIGURE 3.1

Annual Probation Population and Entries to Probation

Source: Laura M. Maruschak and Erika Parks, *Probation and Parole in the United States, 2012* (Washington, D.C.: Bureau of Justice Statistics, 2013), p. 1.

all probationers have been convicted of a violent offense, such as assault, sexual assault, and domestic violence. Many probationers have substance abuse problems, and while the rate of substance dependence or abuse among probationers has declined in recent years, illegal drug use among people on probation remains a persistent challenge. Surveys find rates of drug abuse and dependence among probationers are two to three times higher than rates among nonprobationers. Similarly, rates of any physical illness, serious mental illness, serious psychological distress, and depression are two to three times higher among probationers than the general population. Probationers are more likely than others to have received some mental health services and are also more likely to report an unmet need for mental health services.[19] The community corrections population now serves over 700,000 individuals with an identified mental illness.[20] In view of the fact that these offenders have a difficult time adjusting to jail and prison, imprisonment is frequently an inadequate placement, especially for those mentally ill offenders deemed not dangerous or likely to create societal problems. Furthermore, about twice as many HIV-risk offenders are under community supervision as are incarcerated at a given time.[21] With high rates of injection drug use and prevalence of risky sexual behavior, it is not surprising that so many probationers are HIV positive.

Web App 3.1
Go online and search for articles about the privacy case of Dharun Ravi. What sanctions did he receive? Do you think they were appropriate? LO3

Granting Probation

Probationary sentences are granted by federal and state district court judges and state superior (felony) courts. In some states, juries may also recommend probation if the case meets legally regulated criteria (for instance, it falls within a certain class of offenses as determined by statute). Yet, even in those jurisdictions that permit juries to recommend probation, judges still have the final say in the matter at their discretion. In nonjury trials, probation is granted entirely by judicial mandate. Some states have created guidelines for granting probation in an attempt to shape judicial discretion.

MYTH Probation is used for minor or petty offenders who pose little threat to the community and can be easily managed.

FACT About half of all probationers are felons. Many have severe social problems such as drug use and mental illness and may be HIV positive. Dealing with probationers in an effective manner is a challenge for the correctional system.

HOW COMMON IS THE USE OF PROBATION? Wide variability exists in the use of probation across the nation. One study of 32 jurisdictions found that the numbers receiving probation varied from 30 percent in New York County (Manhattan) to 75 percent in Hennepin County (Minneapolis). Some of the variation is due to the sentencing laws under which these jurisdictions function. Courts in states with determinate sentencing (without a parole board) typically use probation more frequently than do courts in states with indeterminate sentencing (with a parole board). Judges may be less willing to sentence to prison when lengths of sentences are fixed.[22]

Studies also reveal that judges seem to be more willing to place felons on probation when they perceive that the probation department is able to monitor the offender closely and that the resources of the community are able to address some of the offender's underlying problems. Arizona, Minnesota, and Washington, three states that widely use probation, are well known for delivering good probation supervision and for having the resources to provide adequate treatment and services.[23]

Web App 3.2
Go to your state's Division of Parole and Probation website and look at the characteristics of the offenders. LO3

Explain the risk assessment models and their current emphasis LO4

Changing Role of Probation: Risk Assessment and Increased Surveillance Models

In the 1980s and 1990s, probation came under criticism as a lenient measure that allowed serious felony offenders to escape their "just deserts." Dan Richard Beto, Ronald P. Corbett, Jr., and John J. DiIulio, Jr., have addressed what they call the decline in public confidence in probation, and they recommend that probation's challenge is to get serious about the crime problem. They argue that probation can do this by becoming more aggressive about promoting public safety, which will reduce the high rates of recidivism and expand the resources given to probation services.[24]

The political backlash against rehabilitation or "being soft on crime" that occurred in the 1980s and 1990s, coupled with the decline of resources provided for probation agencies, led many large correctional and community supervision agencies to adopt new mandates involving risk management and avoidance. Their institutional focus shifted from concerns about rehabilitating or reforming probationers to minimizing the risks that these offenders posed to public order.[25] Thus, in an attempt to convince the public, as well as policy makers, that probation could be tougher on criminals, probation administrators attempted to enter into a bureaucratic-managerial stage characterized by stricter controls of probationers.[26] In shifting away from counseling and program interventions, agencies' strategies moved toward actuarial calculation and controls via offender-based data systems; drug-testing technologies, such as urinalysis, antabuse, and methadone; and classification systems.[27]

The emerging bureaucratic-managerial stage of probation began to emphasize strategies that would better ensure public protection.[28] The most widely used of these strategies have been the combination of probation and incarceration, intensive probation, and electronic monitoring and house arrest, which (excluding intensive probation) are examined in Chapter 4.

This movement in probation and parole toward a **risk management system** is what Malcolm Feeley and Jonathan Simon have called "the **new penology**." They argue that the old penology goal of normalizing individual offenders has been replaced by a new penology focused on goals aimed at regulating groups of offenders.[29] Feeley and Simon have identified three features of the new penology.

risk management system A correctional system that is focused more on regulating and controlling offenders than on providing treatment or services for them.

new penology A new approach in probation and other community-based corrections that focuses more on administrative control and regulation than on treatment and offering services.

First, the language of the new penology is anchored in the discourse of system analysis and operations research. It conceives of crime as a systemic phenomenon and crime policy as a problem of actuarial risk management. Second, in contrast to previous efforts of transforming individuals, the new penology embraces a new objective, that of risk management and the management of the system itself.

Third, the administrative techniques are adapted from the world of insurance, financial management, and even retailing. These techniques (profiling, auditing, and screening) were introduced as ways of improving administrative knowledge of and control over penal agents and subjects. The new penology, its proponents contend, provides a useful analytic grid on which to interpret the emergent set of practices, discourses, and objectives in the criminal process.[30]

The use of these techniques has filtered into the provision of treatment services. The risk-need-responsivity (RNR) model, now being used in a number of jurisdictions, including Maine, Illinois, and Oregon, uses risk assessment tools to classify each probationer and match him or her to the right treatment program. Typically, treatment efforts are behavioral (relying on a system of rewards and punishments), and higher-risk offenders receive the most services. Cognitive behavioral and "social learning" techniques—ranging from anger management training to sessions devoted to reducing negative and antisocial attitudes—are emphasized. RNR programs rely on peers and family members to reinforce their messages. Several research efforts have found that they can cut the recidivism of high-risk offenders by as much as 20 percent.[31]

Administration of Probation

LO5 Describe the various ways probation is administered

The United States has approximately 2,000 adult probation agencies. More than half are associated with a state-level agency; in about one-fourth of the states, probation is primarily a local responsibility. About 30 states combine probation and parole supervision into a single agency. A number of states have also permitted the private sector to administer probation supervision, especially for minor offenders. The federal courts also administer probation services.

LOCALLY ADMINISTERED PROBATION DEPARTMENTS In those states in which probation is a local responsibility, the state is accountable only for providing financial support, setting standards, and arranging training courses. This locally based approach accounts for about two-thirds of all probationers supervised in the United States.

One of the most persuasive arguments for local administration of probation is that citizens and agencies of the community more readily support programs that are open to their participation and are responsive to local needs and problems. Another supporting argument is that small operations are more flexible, adjust more quickly to change, and are less encumbered by bureaucratic rigidity. Yet, three arguments against local administration have won the support of many policy makers: (1) A state-administered probation system can set standards of service, thereby ensuring uniformity of procedures, policies, and services. (2) A larger agency can make more effective use of funds and personnel. (3) Greater efficiency in the disposition of resources is possible when all probation officers are state employees.

STATE OR EXECUTIVE ADMINISTERED PROBATION DEPARTMENTS Assignment of probation to the executive branch on a statewide basis allows uniform standards of policy making, recruitment, training, and personnel management. Coordination with the state department of corrections and with the parole service is also facilitated. The most significant disadvantage is the development of a large probation bureaucracy with echelons of decision makers shuffling memoranda from out-basket to in-basket with little contact with the real world of the streets. Firm leadership with a grasp of sound management procedures can prevent this dismal prospect.

COMBINED PROBATION AND PAROLE DEPARTMENTS Critics of the 30 states providing both probation and parole services argue that probationers, especially first-time offenders, should be kept separate from parolees, and that probation is a service to judges and should be under their control. However, it is argued that a combined system conserves scarce resources and has greater public acceptance. A combined system requires only one office, one set of directives, and one supervisory hierarchy. In both probation and parole, the same goals are sought and the same skills are required for supervision of offenders (see Exhibit 3.1.)

FEDERAL PROBATION The U.S. Probation and Pretrial Services carries out probation and pretrial services functions in the U.S. District Courts. District judges of the U.S. courts control federal probation services, but the probation division's administrative offices administer recruitment and training of personnel.

PRIVATIZING PROBATION The private sector and the supervision of misdemeanant probationers were widely implemented in Florida in the 1970s. At its peak, the Salvation Army Misdemeanant Program (SAMP) in Florida employed 200 counselors in 37 counties

EXHIBIT 3.1

Differences Between Probation and Parole

Probation	Parole
Often given to defendants often instead of jail or prison time	Is an early release from prison
Sentence set by the court and a probation officer provides supervision	The parole board makes the decision when inmates are placed on parole
Persons revoked from probation can be sentenced to prison	Persons revoked from parole can have their parole revoked and be returned to prison
Probationers are supervised by a probation officer	Parolees may be supervised either by a parole officer or a probation officer
Some probation officers are armed with a weapon and some are not	Nearly all parole officers are armed with a weapon
Under the jurisdiction of federal, state, and local governments	Under the jurisdiction of state agencies
Probation officers are not paid as well as parole officers	Parole officers are usually paid better than probation officers
The purpose of probation is to use the supervision of probation officers to achieve prosocial behavior from clients	The function of parole is to try to reintegrate ex-offenders into society
The conditions of probation are usually the result of a court order	Parole conditions are generally set by the parole board

© Derek Dufresne

VOICES ACROSS THE PROFESSION

"The best thing is when your effort with an offender takes hold and contributes to their success."

Derek Dufresne
U.S. Probation Officer

In the U.S. Probation offices, we have three major components or tasks: pretrial investigation, presentence investigation, and postconviction. I am involved in the supervision unit of postconviction.

Probation is a delicate balance between law enforcement and social work. One thing I like about my job is that my caseloads are manageable. I have 80 probationers on my caseload and that allows me to intensely supervise those on release. In contrast, state probation officers may have 150 to 200 on their caseloads. Another thing I like about federal probation is that we have had adequate resources allotted to us. However, with recent budget cuts, we have had to use networking to be able to find volunteers because we cannot pay for resources.

and supervised 14,000 clients a month. Today probation agencies in 15 states use privatized probation services for low-risk offenders. Connecticut and Colorado are two states that have widely used the private sector for the supervision of low-risk probationers.

In sum, the management of probation and parole can be organized in several ways. On the whole, the executive control of probation probably utilizes more effectively the scarce resources available to probation systems. Yet, decentralized services make sense in counties with a tradition of effective probation programming. In addition, statewide

CAREERS IN CORRECTIONS

Manny Jaquiss
Probation Supervisor

A. Ramey/PhotoEdit Inc.

"As senior supervisor of the Department of Corrections pretrial office in Tampa, Florida, with approximately 1,650 offenders assigned to 14 probation officers, my job is to oversee the office operations and ensure that the assigned officers are seeing their cases, as required.

"During a typical day on the job, I am reading and approving the various reports that are submitted, fielding calls from concerned offenders and others as to specific cases questions, mentoring staff, and performing tasks required from my superiors, as well as maintaining the relationships with the other officials in the criminal justice community.

"I am involved in all aspects of running the office, conducting internal case reviews to ensure cases are being supervised as required, and mentoring less tenured staff."

See Chapter 15 for more detailed information on careers in corrections.

EXHIBIT 3.2

Comparing the Administration of Probation Services

Responsibility	Size	Advantages
Locally administered	Two-thirds of all U.S. probationers	Citizens and agencies of the community respond to local needs and problems
State or executive	Over half the states	Allows uniform standards of policy making, recruitment, training, and personnel management
Combining probation and parole	About 30 states	Requires only one office, one set of directives, and one supervisory hierarchy
U.S. federal probation	94 U.S. district courts	Restricted to those sentenced by district courts
Privatizing	A few states	Efficient use of resources for low-risk probationers

organization of combined probation and parole services seems to offer the best assurance of accountability and economy, given firm leadership by an administrator who knows what has to be done and how to do it. See Exhibit 3.2.

Basic Functions of a Probation Officer

The probation department is situated in a single court district, such as a juvenile district, superior, or municipal court. The relationship between the department and court personnel, particularly the judge, is extremely close. In a typical department, the chief probation officer (CPO) supervises hiring, sets policy, determines training needs, and may be involved with the sentencing decision with the judge. In state-controlled departments, some of the CPO's duties, such as training guidelines, are mandated at the state level. In locally controlled probation departments, the CPO has great discretion in his or her management, as long as there is judicial approval.

The three basic functions of an adult probation officer are to manage a caseload, to supervise adult probationers, and to make presentence investigation and other reports to the courts (see Exhibit 3.3).

EXHIBIT 3.3

Categories and Duties of Probation Officers

Categories	Duties
Casework management	Maintains a file on each probationer
	Meets with the probationer periodically as assigned by the court
	Ensures that the requirements of the court are met
	Is part of a team to monitor and manage the offender
	Maintains relationships with public and private nonprofit agencies to help refer probationers to these programs as needed
	Refers probationer to the courts when stricter or looser requirements are warranted
Supervision, investigation, and surveillance	Becomes familiar with the history and background of probationers
	Checks with employers and others to confirm what probationer has told the officer
	Visits the probationer at home and at work
Presentence investigation	Conducts presentence investigation on probationers
	Examines the offense, prior criminal record, and personal and family data
	Compiles and reports to the court information contained during the presentence investigation
	Develops appropriate sentencing and community alternatives
	Formulates specific recommendations to the court

CAREERS IN CORRECTIONS

Derek Dufresne
U.S. Probation Officer

"I enjoy the fact that every day is different. One day I can do financial investigations in my office; the next day I am in the community verifying employments, community service, and education. On a daily basis, I begin the day by contacting offenders who are having problems. I complete financial reports, review monthly background checks, look at documents of offenders' progress, contact judges on progress or lack thereof, write letters to offenders, and review drug testing of those on my caseload."

See Chapter 15 for more detailed information on careers in corrections.

CASEWORK MANAGEMENT AND OTHER ADMINISTRATIVE DUTIES The probation officer maintains a file on each probationer for whom he or she is responsible. Within this file are the court documents that spell out the requirements of probation, chronological entries of contacts between the officer and the probationer and others whose relationship with the probationer might be significant, items of correspondence, and periodic reports made to the courts or to officials of the agency. Probation officers' caseloads vary in size, ranging from 50 to 300.

Commonly, probation departments divide probationers into several categories, based on their needs or on the risk they pose to the community. Some offenders are placed on minimum supervision status and are required only to mail in a report once a month or even less frequently. Offenders on medium supervision status must visit their probation officers at least once a month. Offenders on maximum or intensive supervision status must see their officers several times a month. About 90 percent of probationers in the United States are supervised on regular caseload levels, about 4 or 5 percent are placed on intensive supervision, and from 1 to 5 percent constitute specialized caseloads of individuals subject to electronic monitoring, under house arrest, or sent to boot camps.[32]

Studies seeking to link caseload size and recidivism in probation go back 40 years, and a number have found evidence that smaller caseloads were related to lower recidivism rates. More recently, John Worrall and colleagues' macro-level analysis of the relationship between probation caseloads and property crime rates in California counties found over a nine-year period that as probation loads increased, so did property crime.[33]

SUPERVISION, INVESTIGATION, AND SURVEILLANCE The officer is required to determine as much as possible whether a client is obeying the law and complying with the terms of probation, and if not, to follow up on the violation. In some jurisdictions, probation officers are now authorized to carry handguns because the department began to require officers to spend more time visiting their clients in their neighborhoods and homes.[34]

Even though personal involvement in the supervision of offenders is no longer emphasized, officers still must establish a relationship with the probationer, establish supervision goals to comply with the conditions of probation, and decide how and when to terminate probation. The investigation and surveillance aspects of supervision call for at least periodic checks on probationers' employment, the status of their restitution payments, whether they are clean on their urine "drops," and whether they are participating in required programs.

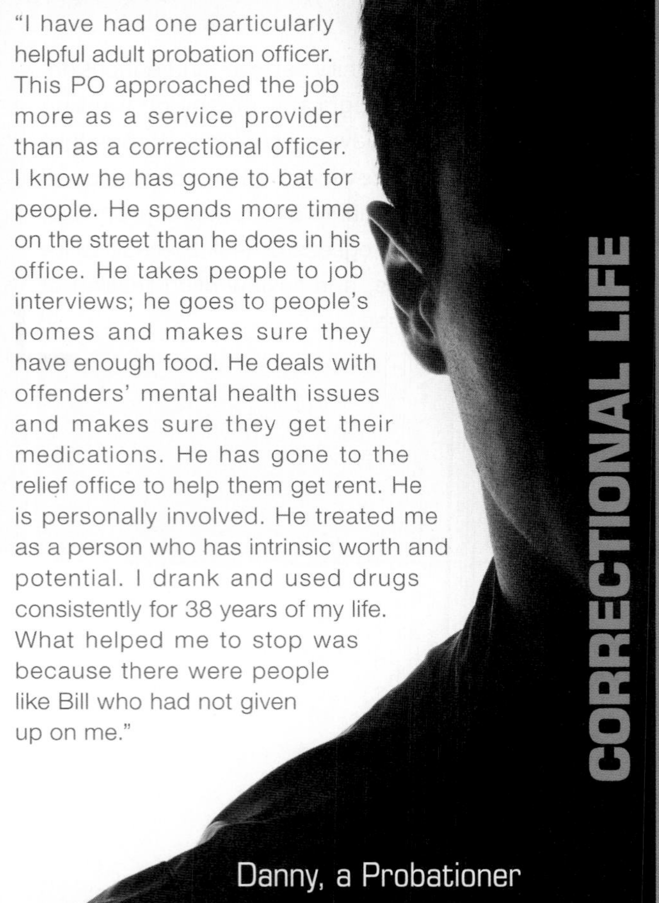

"I have had one particularly helpful adult probation officer. This PO approached the job more as a service provider than as a correctional officer. I know he has gone to bat for people. He spends more time on the street than he does in his office. He takes people to job interviews; he goes to people's homes and makes sure they have enough food. He deals with offenders' mental health issues and makes sure they get their medications. He has gone to the relief office to help them get rent. He is personally involved. He treated me as a person who has intrinsic worth and potential. I drank and used drugs consistently for 38 years of my life. What helped me to stop was because there were people like Bill who had not given up on me."
CORRECTIONAL LIFE
Danny, a Probationer

Effective officers enjoy the respect of colleagues in the justice system and maintain good relationships within the office. Whether they are promoted or not (promotions are impossible in a one-person office and are difficult to obtain in small offices with a few officers), they are rewarded by an awareness of their reputations for fairness, genuineness, and commitment to their jobs. In short, their efforts do pay off, and they do make a difference in the lives of probationers.

Effective supervision is also critical because it protects the probation department from civil liability. The failure to supervise probationers adequately and to determine whether they are obeying the rules of probation can result in both the officer and the department being held legally responsible for civil damages. For example, if a probationer has a history of child molestation and attacks a child while working as a school custodian, the probationer's case supervisor can be held legally responsible for failing to check on the probationer's employment activities.

PRESENTENCE INVESTIGATION REPORTS The **presentence investigation (PSI)** report is the major report required of a probation officer and is used at the time of the sentencing hearing. The main purposes of the PSI report are to help the court decide whether to grant probation, determine the conditions of probation, determine the length of the sentences, and decide on community-based or institutional placement for the defendants.

PSI reports vary somewhat in form but usually have six categories:

presentence investigation (PSI) An investigation whose main purposes are to help the court decide whether to grant probation, to determine the conditions of probation, to determine the length of the sentence, and to decide on community-based or institutional placement for the defendant.

1. Information about the offense and a description of its exact nature
2. The defendant's prior record, including juvenile adjudications
3. Background information on the defendant's upbringing, educational background, employment, marital situation, physical and emotional health, military service, financial situation
4. A statement by the prosecution about what the appropriate disposition should be
5. A summary of the foregoing information along with sentencing alternatives available to the court
6. The probation officer's recommendation on the most appropriate sentence, based on the information in the report

In most states, a PSI report must be prepared regardless of whether the offender is eligible for probation. If he or she is sent to prison, the report will accompany the commitment document for the information of the prison authorities. The PSI may be less important in states with sentencing guidelines and not at all important for offenders sentenced using mandatory and presumptive sentencing.[35] The long form of a PSI report may take up to 20 hours to complete, but it is not uniform from one jurisdiction to another. Probations must first interview the defendant, preferably more than once, in order to verify information. Officers then review the defendant's arrest record, reports concerning the current offense, previous presentence reports, and any available psychiatric psychological reports. Occasionally they must interview the arresting officer and the defendant's employer, and they often talk with the defendant's family.

CRITICAL THINKING

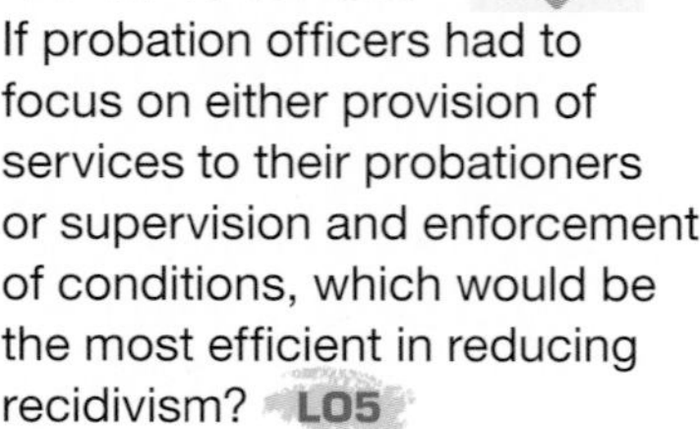

If probation officers had to focus on either provision of services to their probationers or supervision and enforcement of conditions, which would be the most efficient in reducing recidivism? LO5

Probation officers have the authority to file a notice of violation with the court when a probationer commits a violation of the conditions of probation or is arrested again. The prosecutor may decide to prosecute the new offense, especially if the penalty exceeds revocation and he or she has a solid case. If the prosecutor decides not to prosecute, the case is placed on the court calendar, and the probationer is directed to appear in court for a preliminary hearing. If a revocation hearing is scheduled after the preliminary, the probation officer is charged before the hearing to present the judge a full violation-of-probation report documenting the charges and summarizing the probationer's degree of adjustment of probation.

What Are Probationers' Legal Rights?

LO6 Clarify the legal rights of probationers

The most important cases concerning probation that have been litigated by the courts have involved disclosure of PSI reports, civil rights of probationers, and the rights of probationers during probation revocation.

DISCLOSURE OF PSI REPORTS Defense attorneys prefer disclosure of the information on the PSI compiled by the probation officer because they seek the opportunity to challenge any disputable statements in the report. The question of disclosure of the PSI report to defense counsel was first raised in three cases: *Williams v. New York* (1949),[36] *Gardner v. Florida* (1977),[37] and *Booth v. Maryland* (1987).[38] Both in the *Gardner* and *Booth* cases, the U.S. Supreme Court decided that in death penalty cases the PSI must be available to the defense and could not contain victim impact statements that would inflame the jury.[39]

CIVIL RIGHTS The U.S. Supreme Court has ruled that probationers constitute a unique state and, as a result, are entitled to fewer constitutional protections than other citizens. In *Minnesota v. Murphy* (1984), the Court ruled that the probation officer–client relationship is not confidential, as attorney–client or physician–patient relationships are.[40] In *Griffin v. Wisconsin* (1987), the Court held that a probationer's home may be searched without a warrant on the grounds that the probation departments "have in mind the welfare of the probationer" and must "respond quickly to evidence of misconduct."[41] In *United States v. Knights* (2001), the Court upheld the legality of a warrantless search of a probationer's home for the purposes of gathering criminal evidence. The Court reasoned that the state's interest in preventing crime, along with Knights's diminished expectation of privacy, required only a *reasonable suspicion* to make the search fit within the protections found in the Fourth Amendment.[42]

REVOCATION OF PROBATION A violation of the rules or terms of probation or the commitment of a new crime can result in the **revocation of probation**, at which time the offender may be placed in an institution. Revocation because of a rule violation is referred to as a **technical violation**.

revocation of probation A violation of the rules or terms of probation or the commitment of a new crime, which may result in the offender being placed in an institution.

technical violation A probationer violates one of the rules of probation, such as leaving the district without permission, drinking in a tavern, or losing employment.

Technical violations have become a hotly debated item because of the numbers of probationers who are incarcerated in state or local facilities due to rule violations, and this, of course, has contributed to the increasing costs of corrections. For example, a Department of Justice report noted that 9 percent of all offenders who exited probation supervision were incarcerated in state or local facilities due to rule violations.[43] As the next chapter on intermediate sentencing reveals, a number of states are using intermediate sanctions as an alternative to incarceration for technical violations.[44]

Revocation is not an easy decision, but when it takes place, the officer is notified and a formal hearing is scheduled. If the charges against the probationer are upheld, the offender can be placed in a prison setting to serve the remainder of the sentence. The probationer has been given certain procedural due process at this stage of the criminal process. In four significant cases, the U.S. Supreme Court provided procedural safeguards to apply at proceedings to revoke probation (and parole):[45]

- The Court ruled in *Mempa v. Rhay* (1967) that because Mempa did not have counsel at his revocation hearings, the decision of the lower courts was reversed and Mempa was to be released from prison.[46]
- In *Gagnon v. Scarpelli* (1973), the Court held that both probationers and parolees have a constitutionally limited right to counsel in revocation proceedings. This means that during a probation revocation hearing, the probationer must be given

counsel if he or she requires it for an effective defense.[47] On appeal in the *Gagnon* decision, the Supreme Court ruled that if a state determines a fine or restitution to be appropriate and an adequate penalty for the crime, it may not thereafter imprison a defendant solely because he or she lacks the resources to pay, because this would be a violation of a probationer's right to equal protection.[48]

- In *Bearden v. Georgia* (1983), the Court ruled that a judge cannot revoke a defendant's probation for failure to pay a fine and make restitution, unless the probation is somehow responsible for the failure or the alternative forms of punishment are inadequate to meet the state's interest in punishment and deterrence. The trial court revoked probation, and the defendant was sent to prison.[49]
- The Court helped clarify in the *United States v. Granderson* (1994) decision what can happen to a probationer whose community sentence is revoked. Granderson was eligible for a six-month prison sentence; instead, he was given 60 months of probation. When he tested positive for drugs, his probation was revoked. Since the statute he was sentenced under required that he serve one-third of his original sentence in prison, the trial court sentenced him to 20 months. He appealed. The Court ruled that it would be unfair to force a probationer to serve more time in prison than he would have if originally incarcerated and, as a result, his proper term should have been one-third of the six months, or two months.[50]

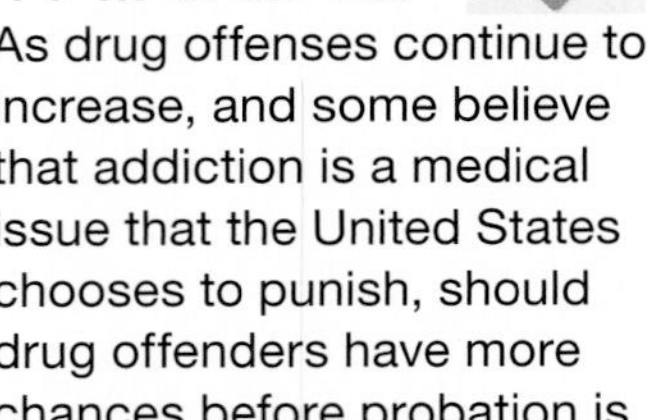

As drug offenses continue to increase, and some believe that addiction is a medical issue that the United States chooses to punish, should drug offenders have more chances before probation is revoked? LO10

Evaluate the effectiveness of probation and identify some of the promising programs in probation services LO7

Is Probation Effective?

The effectiveness of probation varies by the offense behavior of offenders. Recidivism rates are low among those placed on probation for a misdemeanor: data suggest that upwards of three-fourths of offenders placed on probation for a misdemeanor successfully complete their supervision.[51] In addition, adult probation is having increased success with drug offenders. Research at UCLA and elsewhere has found that drug abuse treatment is effective and that individuals coerced into treatment derive benefits similar to the benefits of those who enter voluntarily.[52] Another study followed a sample of probationers for the first eight months of their probation term and found that a significant reduction in criminal activity occurred after being placed on probation. The study did find that carrying guns or using alcohol predicted the likelihood of new criminal behavior.[53] However, in a classic study Joan Petersilia and Susan Turner found that 65 percent of those who had committed felonies and were on probation were rearrested.[54] The increased numbers of felony probationers sentenced to probation, as well as the "get tough on crime" mood in the wider society, led to the development of increased surveillance models.

Gender also appears to affect probation's effectiveness. One study found that women were more likely to be sentenced to probation for drug or property offenses, while men were sentenced to probation more for crimes of violence and for driving under the influence. Women also were less likely to be assessed court costs, fines, and probation supervision fees, largely because they were more likely to be unemployed or earned less than men. Women did perform better on probation with respect to technical violations and new arrests.[55]

IMPROVING PROBATION EFFECTIVENESS To improve probation effectiveness, several steps appear to be necessary.[56] More financial resources must be provided to implement quality programming for appropriate probation target groups. The credibility of probation with the public and the judiciary must be improved. Support is needed from a public that views the probation sanction as sufficiently punitive to make up for the harm of criminal behavior and from a judiciary that is convinced offenders will be held accountable for their behavior. More innovative programs in probation across the nation need to be implemented. In addition, probation must be made a priority research topic, such as in implementing evidence-based practice (EBP) in community programs; this will identify proven methods of reducing offender recidivism. Exhibit 3.4 illustrates some of the probation practices that have proven to be successful in improving probation effectiveness.

Derek Dufresne
U.S. Probation Officer

In terms of supervision, we like to push education. We encourage them to get either a GED or high school diploma. We know if we can make offenders' supervision a positive experience, there is a higher chance of success. The best thing is when your effort with an offender takes hold and contributes to their success.

Contemporary Probation Services

With an expanding caseload and greater responsibility to treat and care for nontraditional clients, probation departments have or are now developing a variety of new programs to amplify the effectiveness of community corrections. Some of the ongoing programs include:

- Some jurisdictions allow a **deferred sentence**. This variation delays conviction on a guilty plea until the completion of a term of probation, at which time the offender withdraws the guilty plea. The court dismisses the charge, thereby clearing the offender's record of a conviction. This procedure is not the same as pretrial diversion, because a probation officer supervises the offender when the deferred sentence is imposed by a judge; in pretrial diversion the offender is diverted from the system.
- **Shock probation** calls for the shock of a few weeks in prison for a first-time offender followed by a standard term of probation.
- Some jurisdictions permit **bench, or unsupervised, probation**, especially with misdemeanants (persons convicted of a misdemeanor).
- The **split sentence**, or intermittent sentence, is also used by some jurisdictions. Offenders spend a period of time in jail before being placed on probation in the

deferred sentence A sentence that delays conviction on a guilty plea until the sentenced offender has successfully served his or her probation term.

shock probation The offender, his or her attorney, or the sentencing judge can submit a motion to suspend the remainder of a sentence after a felon has served a period of time in prison.

bench, or unsupervised, probation A type of probation in which probationers are not subject to supervision.

split sentence A sentence requiring an offender to spend a period of time in jail before being placed on probation in the community.

EXHIBIT 3.4

Successful Probation Practices

- *The use of risk and needs assessment.* Corrections research supports the use of risk and needs assessment when offenders are first placed on probation and periodically thereafter. These assessments also provide probation departments with limited resources to be able to prioritize intensive rehabilitation services.
- *Referral to community-based programs to reduce recidivism.* Offenders are more likely to be successful while on probation provided effective treatment and assistance programs are made available. This includes drug treatment and mental health counseling, employment assistance, and anger management. In the current fiscal austerity experienced in the United States, with its high rates of unemployment, employment is particularly needed.
- *Manageable supervision caseloads.* No national standard is available for how many probationers should be on a probation officer's caseload. Supervision generally is only effective at reducing recidivism when coupled with treatment-oriented programs.
- *System of graduated sanctions.* One of the key strategies for effectively intervening and interrupting the cycle of reoffending is to establish a system of graduated sanctions.
- *Program reviews and evaluations.* Implementing certain programs and practices have been found to result in better outcomes and reduced recidivism. Several states, such as Oregon, utilize assessment tools to measure programs' fidelity, a measurement of how well the program or practice is implemented. In addition to measuring programs' fidelity, it is important to collect data on probationer outcome that can indicate which programs are most effective in rehabilitating offenders.

Source: Mac Davis, *Achieving Better Outcomes for Adult Probation: Executive Summary*, California Legislative Analyst's Office, 2009, http://www.lao.ca.gov/2009/crim/probation/probation_052909.pdf (accessed June 2014).

community, or they are sentenced to a number of weekends in jail while remaining in the community on probation status during the week.

intensive probation Supervision that is far stricter than standard probationary supervision.

- Under **intensive probation**, a probationer is supervised far more strictly than under standard services. Intensive probation is discussed more fully in Exhibit 3.5.[57]

Future of Probation Services

A number of characteristics of probation widely used in the present will likely continue. In addition, several recent innovations promise to affect probation in the future. The following is a list of some of these current trends and probable developments:

- Attention will continue to be paid to substance abusers, because of the close relationship between drugs and crime.

EXHIBIT 3.5

Intensive Supervised Probation

Initiated in Georgia in 1982, intensive supervised probation (ISP) permits probationers to live at home but under relatively strict restrictions. ISP offenders usually are required to perform community service, work, attend school or treatment programs, meet with a probation officer or a team of two officers as often as five times a week, and submit to tests for drug and alcohol use, curfews, and employment checks. This widely used program seems especially useful with high-risk probationers. Currently, about 5 percent of those on probation or parole are assigned to ISP.

ISP programs provide several services to the justice system. Without intensive supervision, high-risk offenders would ordinarily be sent to already crowded jails or prisons. ISP lets high-risk probationers be maintained in the community, helping them maintain community ties and avoid the pains of imprisonment.

ISP programs are used in several different ways in the justice system. ISP can be a:

- Direct sentence imposed by a judge
- Postsentencing alternative used to divert offenders from prison
- Case management tool that provides local probation staff flexibility in dealing with probationers, especially those who appear to be high risk
- Method to deal with probation violators, bringing them halfway back into the community without sending them to prison

Some jurisdictions use ISP in all of these ways. For example, New Jersey's ISP program emphasizes a law enforcement approach, but it also contains a rehabilitation component: most program participants attend peer support sessions led by probation/parole officers and receive substance abuse counseling. Moreover, senior supervisors and policy makers further encourage the rehabilitation components of the ISP program.

Evaluation of ISP Programs

Because felons sentenced to probation have high recidivism rates, ISP programs should be an effective method of controlling these more serious offenders. In a well-known study, Joan Petersilia and Susan Turner evaluated ISP programs in three counties in California (Contra Costa, Ventura, and Los Angeles) and found that 25 percent of the ISP offenders in each site had no new incidents (technical violations or new arrests), about 40 percent had only technical violations (violations of probation conditions), and about 33 percent had new arrests during a one-year period. Evaluation of the ISP project revealed that ISP participants had more technical violations than traditional probationers simply because of the increased supervision of intensive probation. Thus, ISP may cut down on criminal offending while increasing technical violations.

There has also been criticism that ISP programs sacrifice treatment services for surveillance and control. In one review, Paul Gendreau and colleagues found "that only 18 percent of ISPs surveyed in their meta-analysis offered even a modicum of treatment services, and even among those, all were of unknown quality." Gendreau and colleagues found that without the provision of treatment services, ISP programs will have marginal effects on recidivism.

It is not surprising that the failure rate in ISP caseloads is high, given that caseloads are made up of more serious offenders who might otherwise have been incarcerated and who are receiving close supervision, which can detect technical violations. Probation officers are more willing to revoke their ISP clients for fairly minor technical violations because they believe that they are a risk to the community. Evidence so far indicates that ISP appears to work better for offenders with good employment records than it does for those who are unemployed. Younger offenders who commit petty crimes are also the most likely to be failures on ISP.

Sources: "An Intensive Supervision Program that Worked: Service Delivery, Professional Orientation, and Organizational Supportiveness," *Prison Journal* 85 (2005): 445–466; Joan Petersilia and Susan Turner, "Evaluating Intensive Supervision Probation and Parole," in *Intermediate Sanctions in Overcrowded Times*, eds. Michael Tonry and Kate Hamilton (Boston: Northeastern University Press, 1995); Paul Gendreau, C. Goggin, F. Cullen, and D. A. Andrews, "The Effects of Community Sanctions and Incarceration on Recidivism," *Forum on Corrections Research* 12 (2000): 10–13.

- Screening and classification systems will continue to guide the level of probation supervision.
- Efficiency and accountability will continue to be demanded of probation departments.
- At least 25 states now impose some form of fee on probationers to defray the cost of probation and other community programs. Massachusetts started the day fees, which are based on a probationer's wages (the typical fee is between one and three days' wages each month). Texas requires judges to impose supervision fees unless the offender is totally unable to pay, and fees make up more than half of each probation department's annual budget. It is likely this practice will increase in other states.
- Another recent innovation is the use of performance indicators that reveal whether probation is doing its job. These indicators include probationers' days free of drug use, employment rates, amount of restitution collected, and the days of community service served.
- Community partnerships will be used more frequently. These bring together community service teams to work jointly on providing treatment. Maryland's HotSpot probation initiative involves probation officers, police officers, social service professionals, and neighbors to form community probation teams. Using a team approach, they provide increased monitoring of offenders through drug testing, home visits, and regular meetings.[58] Whether this will expand to other states or not, this approach seems to have a great deal of utility for probation and community corrections.
- In a number of jurisdictions, probation automated management (PAM) permits low-risk probationers to report in 24 hours a day, seven days a week, using their fingerprints as biometric identifiers.[59] This is such a cost-effective measure that it is likely to spread throughout probation departments across the nation.
- Philadelphia has developed a high-tech program that may be helpful in predicting murders and intervening before they occur. In the Strategic Anti-Violence Unit (SAV-U), which was implemented in January 2007, this program gives special attention to probationers considered high risk. Using software tools and research covering thousands of past crimes, Richard Berk, professor of criminology and statistics at the University of Pennsylvania, developed a computer model for the Philadelphia probation department that identifies these high-risk probationers.[60]
- Innovative treatment approaches will continue to be developed. For example, the Good Lives Model (GLM), a framework used for sex offender treatment programs, is now being applied successfully in a case management setting. The GLM is a strengths-based approach to offender rehabilitation, premised on the idea that the capabilities and strengths of probationers must be built up, in order to reduce their risk of reoffending. According to the GLM, people offend because they are attempting to secure some kind of valued outcome in their life. As such, offending is essentially the product of a desire for something that is inherently human and normal. All too often, this desire or goal manifests itself in harmful and antisocial behavior, due to a range of deficits and weaknesses within the offender and his/her environment. Essentially, these deficits prevent offenders from securing their desired ends in prosocial and sustainable ways, thus requiring that they resort to inappropriate and damaging means—that is, offending behavior. Rather than threaten punishment, GLM focuses on developing strengths.[61]

THINKING LIKE A CORRECTIONS PROFESSIONAL

You accepted a position in the Dodge County Probation Department. You lack experience and you want to be effective in your new job. Your supervisor hands you a casebook and tells you to do the best you can. She says she is swamped with reports to write and court appearances and cannot spend much time with you. What should you do first, second, and third?

During your first hours after settling into the job, six young men barge into your office. They are very belligerent. They want to know whether you are going to continue the racist actions of your predecessor, filing violations against members of their gang for wearing gang colors. What is the best way to respond to this confrontation?

Some of the other officers decide to carry a weapon, which is optional in your office. What will you do? What would be the decisive factors in your decision making?

AP images/The Salt Lake Tribune/Rick Egan

Dean Zabriskie, left, appears with his client, Joseph Berg, for his sentencing hearing at the 4th District Court, in Provo, Utah, Monday, April 23, 2012. Berg, who last year kidnapped and assaulted his longtime girlfriend, was sentenced to 180 days in jail followed by 36 months of **probation**, including anger management and **substance abuse** treatment.

SUMMARY

LO1 Explain what is meant by the term *community corrections act*

A community corrections act is a law passed by the state legislature in which a state grants funds to local units of government to plan, develop, and deliver correctional services and sanctions. Twenty-five states have passed community corrections acts and have made the establishment of strong community-based programs a priority.

LO2 Compare the main types of diversion programs and identify their advantages and disadvantages

The three major types of adult diversion programs are deferred prosecution, deferred judgment, and Treatment Alternatives to Street Crime (TASC). Deferred judgment and deferred prosecution permit some minor offenders who complete a deferred program to have their formal charges dropped, and TASC is designed to divert drug abusers from the justice system and into specialized support services. The major advantage of diversion programs is avoiding justice system processing. The disadvantage is they may increase the number of those who otherwise would have been ignored by the justice system in the past.

LO3 Discuss the advantages of being placed on probation

The major advantage of being placed on probation is that probationers are permitted to remain in the community as long as they comply with the conditions of the court under supervision of a probation officer.

LO4 Explain the risk assessment models and their current emphasis

In the 1980s and 1990s, probation was widely criticized by those who wanted to get tough on crime. As a result, probation has gotten tougher. Probation's institutional focus shifted from concern about rehabilitating probationers to minimizing the risks that these offenders posed to public order. The risk assessment models that developed began to emphasize strategies that would better ensure public protection. The most widely used of these strategies have been the combination of probation and incarceration, intensive probation, and electronic monitoring and house arrests.

LO5 Describe the various ways probation is administered

Probation can be administered in a variety of ways (local executive or local judicial, state executive or state judicial, or a combination), but combining probation and parole departments seems to be gaining public acceptance and is used in about 30 states. Probation can also be administered by the federal government.

LO6 Clarify the legal rights of probationers

The most important cases dealing with probationers' legal rights have involved disclosure of PSI reports, civil rights of probationers, and the rights of probationers during probation revocation.

LO7 Evaluate the effectiveness of probation and identify some of the promising programs in probation services

Today, adult probation is the most widely used correctional option. Probation continues to demonstrate that it is as effective, if not more so, than other forms of correctional intervention. In addition to intensive probation, new approaches to probation in the present and future may include fees for probation services, performance indicators to measure probation effectiveness, and more attention to drug abusers.

CRITICAL THINKING QUESTIONS

1. "I sentence you to 18 months of probation," the judge says. What benefits do you expect from serving out your sentence in the community?
2. Why is probation considered a second chance?
3. Probationers enjoy many of the same rights as unconvicted citizens. But a probationer's right to know on what information his or her sentence is based is a hotly debated issue. Why do many probation officers object to making PSI reports public?
4. How do you feel about placing on probation those who have committed felonies? How about placing sex offenders on probation?
5. How would one develop the attributes described as needed to be an effective probation officer?

NOTES

1. Anthony Bruno, "Jessica Lunsford, Death of a 9-Year-Old," http://www.crimelibrary.com/serial_killers/predators/jessica_lunsford/1_index.html (accessed June 2014).
2. Curt Anderson, "Death Sentence Endorsed in Lunsford Case," *Washington Post*, March 15, 2007, http://www.washingtonpost.com/wp-dyn/content/article/2007/03/15/AR2007031500518.html (accessed June 2014).
3. CNN, "Convicted Child Killer Couey Dies in Prison, Florida Officials Say," September 20, 2009, http://www.cnn.com/2009/CRIME/09/30/florida.couey.dead/ (accessed June 2014).
4. David Ballingrud, "Probation and Sex Offenders," *St. Petersburg Times Online*, January 15, 2006.

5. David Ballingrud, "Judgment Calls," *St. Petersburg Times Online*, January 15, 2006.
6. Lisa L. Sample and Timothy M. Bray, "Are Sex Offenders Dangerous?" *Criminology and Public Policy* 3 (2003): 9–82; Franklin Zimring, Alex Piquero, Wesley Jennings, and Stephanie Hays, "The Predictive Power of Juvenile Sex Offending: Evidence from the Second Philadelphia Birth Cohort Study," June 21, 2007, Social Science Research Network, http://papers.ssrn.com/sol3/papers.cfm?abstract_id=995918 (accessed June 2014).
7. See the final section of this chapter on whether probation is effective.
8. John Augustus, *First Probation Officer* (Montclair, NJ: Patterson Smith, 1972), pp. 4–5.
9. M. Kay Harris, "Key Differences Among Community Corrections Acts in the United States: An Overview," *Prison Journal* 76 (June 1996): 202.
10. Joan Nuffield, *Diversion Programs for Adults 1997–2005*, Public Safety and Emergency Preparedness Canada website, http://www.getprepared.gc.ca (accessed June 2014).
11. Ibid.
12. K. Michael Reynolds, Sophia F. Dzigieleski, and Chris Sharp, "Serving Mentally Ill Offenders Through Community Corrections: Joining Two Disciplines," *Journal of Offender Rehabilitation* 40 (2004): 185–198.
13. "Deferred Prosecution and Deferred Judgment," http://www.experiencedcriminallawyers.com/articles/deferred-prosecution-deferred-judgment (accessed June 2014).
14. Ibid.
15. New Jersey and Pennsylvania have had supreme court rulings authorizing intervention on a statewide basis; Arkansas, Colorado, Connecticut, Florida, Massachusetts, Tennessee, and Washington have had statewide enabling legislation.
16. M. Douglas Anglin, Douglas Longshore, and Susan Turner, "Treatment Alternatives to Street Crime," *Criminal Justice and Behavior* 26 (1999): 168–195.
17. Thomas P. Bonczar and Laura M. Maruschak, *Probation and Parole in the United States, 2012* (Washington, DC: Bureau of Justice Statistics, 2013), p. 1.
18. Ibid.
19. Thomas E. Feucht and Joseph Gfroerer, "Mental and Substance Use Disorders Among Adult Men on Probation or Parole: Some Success Against a Persistent Challenge," Substance Abuse and Mental Health Services Administration, Department of Health and Human Services, 2011, http://oas.samhsa.gov/2k11/NIJ_Data_Review/MentalDisorders.htm (accessed June 2014).
20. Reynolds, Dzigieleski, and Sharp, "Serving Mentally Ill Offenders Through Community Corrections," p. 185.
21. Steven Belenko, Sandra Langley, Susan Crimmings, and Michael Chaple, "HIV Risk Behaviors, Knowledge, and Prevention Education Among Offenders Under Community Supervision: A Hidden Risk Group," *AIDS Education and Prevention* 16 (2004): 367–385.
22. Joan Petersilia, "Probation in the United States," in *Crime and Justice: A Review of Research* vol. 22, ed. Michael Tonry (Chicago: University of Chicago Press, 1997).
23. Statements given by individuals who work in community-based corrections in the states of Arizona, Minnesota, and Washington.
24. Dan Richard Beto, Ronald P. Corbett, Jr., and John J. DiIulio, Jr., "Getting Serious About Probation and the Crime Problem," *Corrections Management Quarterly* 4 (Spring 2000): 1–5.
25. Michael Jacobson, *Downsizing Prisons: How to Reduce Crime and End Mass Incarceration* (New York: New York University Press, 2005), p. 151.
26. Fergus McNeil, "Developing Effectiveness: Frontline Perspectives," *Social Work Education* 20 (2001): 671–675.
27. Jacobson, *Downsizing Prisons*, p. 151.
28. Risk assessment research has begun in terms of prediction and explanation; see Daniel A. Krauss, Bruce D. Sales, Judith V. Becker, and A. J. Figueredo, "Beyond Prediction to Explanation in Risk Assessment Research," *International Journal of Law and Psychiatry* 23 (2000): 91–112.
29. Jonathan Simon and Malcolm M. Feeley, "The Forms and Limits of the New Penology," in *Punishment and Social Control*, 2nd ed., eds. Thomas G. Blomberg and Stanley Cohen (New York: Aldine De Gruyter, 2003), pp. 75–116.
30. Ibid.
31. Joan Petersilia, "Beyond the Prison Bubble," *NIJ Journal 268* (October 2011), http://www.nij.gov/nij/journals/268/prison-bubble.htm (accessed June 2014).
32. See Richard P. Seiter and Angela D. West, "Supervision Styles in Probation and Parole: An Analysis of Activities," *Journal of Offender Rehabilitation* 38 (2003): 57–75.
33. John L. Worrall, Pamela Schram, Eric Hays, and Matthew Newman, "An Analysis of the Relationship Between Probation Caseloads and Property Crime Rates in California Counties," *Journal of Criminal Justice* 32 (2004): 231–241.
34. Paul Von Zielbauer, "Probation Dept. Is Now Arming Officers Supervising Criminals," *New York Times*, August 7, 2003, p. 5. Two other articles that address the risk of probation officers are Maria O'Beirne, David Denney, and Jonathan Gabe, "Fear of Violence as an Indicator of Risk in Probation Work: Its Impact on Staff Who Work with Known Violent Offenders," *British Journal of Criminology* 44 (2004): 113–126; and Hazel Kemshall, "Conflicting Knowledge on Risk: The Case of Risk Knowledge in the Probation Service," *Health, Risk, and Society* 2 (2000): 143–157.
35. Current sentencing structures permit judges much less discretion than in the past and, as a result, the PSI is not as helpful to judges.
36. *Williams v. New York State*, 337 U.S. 241, 69 S.Ct. (1949).
37. *Gardner v. Florida*, 430 U.S. 349 (1977).
38. *Booth v. Maryland*, 482 U.S. 496 (1987).
39. *Williams v. New York State*, 337 U.S. 241, 69 S.Ct. (1949).
40. *Minnesota v. Murphy*, 465, U.S. 420, 104 S.Ct. 1136, 79 L.Ed.2d 409 (1984).
41. *Griffin v. Wisconsin*, 483 U.S. 868, 107 S.Ct. 3164, 97 L.Ed.2d 709 (1987).
42. *United States v. Knights*, 122 S.Ct. 587 (2001).
43. Alison Lawrence, *Probation and Parole Violations: State Responses* (Washington, DC: National Conference of State Legislatures, 2008), p. 1.
44. Ibid., for how a number of states are using intermediate sanctions in view of incarceration for technical violations,
45. *Morrissey v. Brewer* (1972) is an important case relating to the revocation of parole, but this will be discussed in Chapter 11.
46. *Mempa v. Rhay*, 359 U.S. 128 (1967).
47. *Gagnon v. Scarpelli*, 411 U.S. 778, 93 S.Ct. 1756, 36 L.Ed.2d 656 (1973).
48. Ibid.
49. *Bearden v. Georgia*, 33 CrL 3101 (1983).
50. *United States v. Granderson*, 114 Ct. 1259, 12 L.Ed.2d 656 (1994).
51. Petersilia, "Probation in the United States," pp. 180–181.
52. See the studies cited in Chapter 10 regarding the effectiveness of coercive treatment among drug offenders.
53. Doris Layton-MacKenzie and Spencer De Li, "The Impact of Formal and Informal Social Controls on the Criminal Activities of Probationers," *Journal of Research on Crime and Delinquency* 39 (August 2002): 243–276.
54. Petersilia, "Probation in the United States," pp. 180–181. For a more recent discussion of felony probation in California, see Kathleen Auerhahn, "Do You Know Who Your Probationers Are? Using Simulation Modeling to Estimate the Composition of California's Felony Probation Population, 1980–2000," *Justice Quarterly* 234 (March 2007): 28–47.
55. D. E. Olson, A. J. Lurigio, and M. Seng, "A Comparison of Female and Male Probationers: Characteristics and Case Outcomes," *Women and Criminal Justice* 11 (2000): 47.
56. Petersilia, "Probation in the United States," p. 185.
57. M. A. Paparozzi and P. Gendreau, "An Intensive Supervision Program that Worked: Service Delivery, Professional Orientation, and Organizational Supportiveness," *Prison Journal* 85 (2005): 445–466.
58. Nicole Leeper Piquero, "A Recidivism Analysis of Maryland's Community Probation Program," *Journal of Criminal Justice* 31 (2003): 295–308.
59. Thomas G. Ogden, "Pagers, Digital Audio, and Kiosk: Office Assistants," *Federal Probation* 65 (2001): 35–37. See also Leanne Fiftal Alarid and Rolando V. Del Carmen, *Community-Based Corrections*, 8th ed. (Belmont, CA: Wadsworth, 2011).
60. David Ho, "Philadelphia Using Computers to Help Predict Murders," *Cox News Service*, January 5, 2007. See also Lawrence W. Sherman, "Use Probation to Prevent Murder," *Criminology and Public Policy* 6 (2007): 843.
61. The Good Lives Model, http://www.goodlivesmodel.com (accessed June 2014).

AP Images/Steve Helber

Philadelphia Eagles quarterback Michael Vick is shown leaving a Newport News, Virginia, federal court after a bankruptcy hearing. Once reviled for his involvement in a dogfighting ring, Vick has emerged from the ashes (and prison) to become an NFL star. Was it necessary to put someone like Vick in prison, or would he have been a good candidate for community treatment? Was he really a threat to society?

2011 WAS A GREAT YEAR FOR MICHAEL VICK. He signed a $100 million contract to play football for the Philadelphia Eagles. However, things were not always so rosy. On July 18, 2007, a federal grand jury in Richmond indicted Vick and three other men on charges related to their alleged operation of a dogfighting ring based at a property that Vick owns in southeastern Virginia. According to the indictment, Vick decided in his rookie season of 2001 to start a dogfighting operation with two other defendants, Quanis Phillips and Tony Taylor. The indictment went on to say that this property was used as the main staging area for housing and training the pit bulls involved in the dogfighting and housing dogfights.[1] The indictment also stated that in April 2007, Purnell Peace, Phillips, and Vick "executed approximately eight dogs that did not perform well in testing sessions by various methods, including hanging, drowning, and/or slamming at least one dog's body to the ground."[2] On December 11, 2007, Vick was sentenced up to 23 months in prison for running a dogfighting operation. Because he lied in court about his involvement, his sentence was longer than his two codefendants. On February 8, 2008, a federal judge ruled that Vick could keep all but $3.75 million of the nearly $20 million in bonus money he received from the Atlanta Falcons.[3]

On November 26, 2008, Vick pleaded guilty to a state dogfighting charge and received a three-year suspended prison sentence and a $2,500 fine on a charge of attending, sponsoring, and participating in dogfights. He also received four years of probation, and a fine that was dismissed when Vick paid his court costs and kept to his probation terms.[4] Vick was released from Leavenworth Penitentiary on May 21, 2009, and arrived home in Hampton, Virginia, that same day. He was released from home confinement in July 2009 and signed a contract to play for the Philadelphia Eagles.[5]

On December 29, 2010, President Obama called Jeffrey Lurie, the owner of the Philadelphia Eagles. Reports are that Obama praised him for taking a chance on Vick and lamented that, even after paying their debt to society, ex-cons rarely get such a second chance.[6] While on probation, Vick lectured all over the country on the horrors of dogfighting and fulfilled the terms of his probation.[7] He played five years with the Eagles without further incident and is now a member of the New York Jets football team.

4

Intermediate Sanctions

CALISTA CONDO/South Jersey Times/Landov

Michael Vick is one of the most promising athletes to come into the professional ranks in recent years. As quarterback for the Atlanta Falcons, beginning in the 2001 season, he had exciting moments on the football field. Then he was arrested, charged, convicted of dog-fighting and housing dogfights, and sentenced to federal prison. l a person like Vick have been incarcerated? Does he present a danger to society? uld his punishment serve a symbolic purpose, letting people know that no one is the law? Is his case similar to style guru Martha Stewart, who was convicted in a narket scheme and sent to prison? Though no threat to society, some say she was erated to set an example for others contemplating white-collar crimes. Is it fair ish celebrities like Vick and Stewart in order to send other people "a message"?

lany of those who have difficulty adjusting to probation or other sanctions pose hreat to society. It seems questionable to incarcerate them in an overcrowded ten violent prison system. It appears to make more sense, in terms of being more ve in reducing recidivism and less costly to society, to have them remain in the unity in more intensive relationships than is true in traditional probation super-. The public is concerned about the high recidivism rates of probationers and yet illing to place young, inexperienced offenders in forbidding and dangerous pris-s a consequence, local, state, and federal governments have developed a series of ıediate sanctions that enable offenders to avoid the harsh reality of prison life.

termediate sanctions are alternative forms of punishment imposed by iminal justice system that fall between fines and boot camp. These sanctions ;ed during the 1980s as a result of three trends:

- he belief that prisons were being overused for offenders who really did not need cure confinement, especially drug offenders
- rison crowding that forced states to consider lower-cost, community-based alterna-ves that would impose "tough time" in the community without endangering the public
- Vide public support for "just desert" sentencing structures, sparking interest in reating community sanctions geared toward the seriousness of crime

ather than placing everyone on probation, the most serious offenders could e the most severe community sanctions. The resulting intermediate sanctions le a number of benefits:

- hey are a cost-saving alternative to jails and prisons. Prisons, especially, are ostly, ineffective, and damaging to inmates.
- hey help reduce prison crowding and result in lower rates of recidivism.
- hey can serve the needs of certain offenders who would ordinarily be sent to rison but are a low risk for recidivism and pose little danger to society.
- hey can be used as a halfway-back strategy for probation and parole violators.

Vhile these alleged advantages have been debated, what is most clear is that inter-te sanctions help fill the void between routine probation and prison. This may be e defensible and obtainable goal than the reduction of prison crowding, cost, and ler recidivism.

ay Pranis served as the restorative justice planner for the Minnesota Department rrections from 1994 to 2003 and is now a nationally respected consultant for ative justice. In Voices Across the Profession, she tells why she feels sanctions in mmunity have the possibility of healing and restoration.

E CONTINUUM OF INTERMEDIATE NCTIONS

cates for more effective sentencing are increasingly calling for a range of punish-options, providing graduated levels of supervision in the community. Judges are exercise discretion by selecting from a range of sentencing options, choosing the

© Kay Pranis

VOICES ACROSS THE PROFESSION

When I came to this work, I did not think that my work was about crime. It was more about community and to see crime as an opportunity to bring people together.

Kay Pranis
Restorative Justice Planner

When I came to this work, I did not think that my work was about crime. It was more about community and to see crime as an opportunity to bring people together. We know that crime is negative energy because crime is harm, but the restorative approach gave us opportunities to transform that negative energy into positive energy. The peacemaking circles were the most obvious example of transforming negative community-level energy around crime into positive community-building energy and of moving toward a more healthy community.

I am continually humbled by human capacities for openness, heart-centered connecting, humility, compassion, understanding, and love. I find that restorative justice in general and peacemaking circles in particular help us connect with our deepest and best selves and bring these dimensions of ourselves to some of the hardest challenges we face.

punishment that best fits the circumstances of the crime and the offender. Intermediate sanctions are said to allow judges to match the severity of punishment with the severity of the crime. Prisons, then, are treated as backstops, rather than backbones, of the corrections systems.[8]

Providing justice through a continuum of sanctions, ranging from being forced to pay a small fine to being placed in a community correctional facility, is now a routine element of corrections. The basic assumption behind intermediate sanctions, or alternative sanctions as they are sometimes called, is to escalate punishments to fit the crime. These sanctions are typically administered by probation departments. They involve such sanctions as intensive probation (which was examined in Chapter 3), financial restitution, community service, house arrest, and electronic monitoring. But they also involve sentences that are administered independently of probation, such as fines and forfeiture, day treatment programs, drug courts, and residential care. See Figure 4.1 for some of the range of intermediate sanctions now available.

Intermediate sanctions fall along a continuum ranging from the least intrusive (fines and community service) to the most intrusive

AP Images/Steve Helber

Tappahannock Children's Center administrator, Ina Minter, is shown in 2012 removing coats of paint from the front of a mural painted by rapper Chris Brown as part of his community service at the center in Tappahannock, Virginia. Brown logged more than 1,400 hours of community service for the 2009 beating of former girlfriend Rihanna before completing his sentence. About one-third of those hours were recorded at this rural daycare center where the singer spent time as a child and his mother once served as director. Do you believe community service helped Chris Brown? Unfortunately for him, he has been in and out of trouble with the law since 2012, entering and leaving rehab on a regular basis.

FIGURE 4.1

The Ladder of Intermediate Sanctions

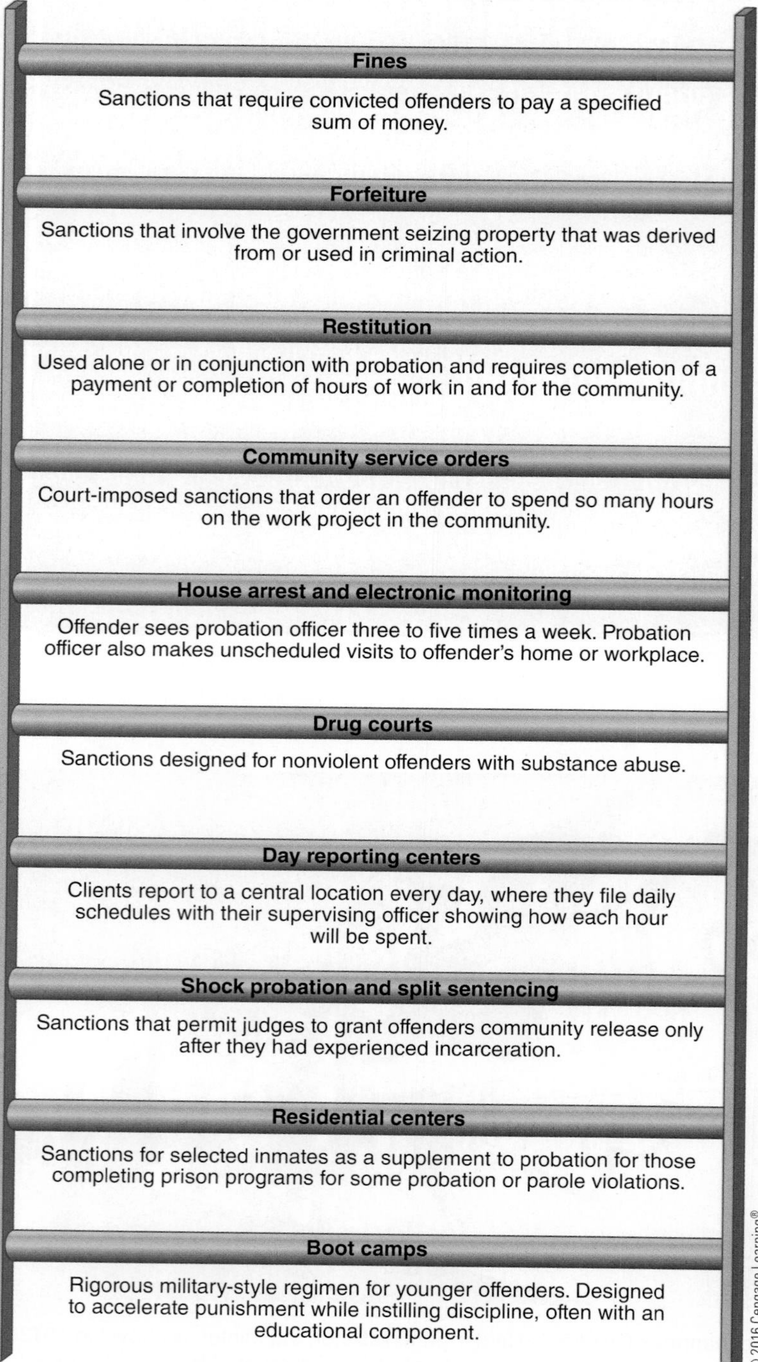
Fines
Sanctions that require convicted offenders to pay a specified sum of money.
Forfeiture
Sanctions that involve the government seizing property that was derived from or used in criminal action.
Restitution
Used alone or in conjunction with probation and requires completion of a payment or completion of hours of work in and for the community.
Community service orders
Court-imposed sanctions that order an offender to spend so many hours on the work project in the community.
House arrest and electronic monitoring
Offender sees probation officer three to five times a week. Probation officer also makes unscheduled visits to offender's home or workplace.
Drug courts
Sanctions designed for nonviolent offenders with substance abuse.
Day reporting centers
Clients report to a central location every day, where they file daily schedules with their supervising officer showing how each hour will be spent.
Shock probation and split sentencing
Sanctions that permit judges to grant offenders community release only after they had experienced incarceration.
Residential centers
Sanctions for selected inmates as a supplement to probation for those completing prison programs for some probation or parole violations.
Boot camps
Rigorous military-style regimen for younger offenders. Designed to accelerate punishment while instilling discipline, often with an educational component.

(house arrest, electronic monitoring, placement in a residential community-based facility). It is also possible to combine a variety of intermediate sanctions into a single sentence. Clients in an intensive probation may also be assigned to house arrest and be placed on electronic monitoring. Other offenders may be sentenced to a period of confinement, such as split sentencing and shock probation. Residential confinement is a confinement that takes place prior to (halfway-in) or following imprisonment (halfway-back), and boot camps are also perceived as intermediate sanctions. See Exhibit 4.1, which compares the various intermediate sanctions. Each of these sanctions will be discussed independently below.

Fines

Monetary sanctions, better known as **fines** (from the Latin term *finis*, "end," as in to end the criminal matter), can be traced to the early common-law practice of requiring that compensation be paid to the victim and the state for criminal acts. Fines are more commonly used in Europe, where they are frequently the sole punishment, even in cases involving chronic offenders who commit fairly serious offenses. Nonetheless, over $1 billion in fines are collected each year in the United States.

The purpose of fines is to equalize the financial impact of sentences on offenders. They are more frequently used in cases involving misdemeanors and lesser offenses, but they are also used in felony cases when the offender benefited financially from wrongful behavior. Fines may be used as a sole sanction or they may be combined with probation or a time in jail.

Judges sometimes claim that the reason they do not make greater use of the fine is the difficulty of collecting from offenders, who frequently are poor and who may use additional illegal acts as a means to pay their fines. Other judges contend that relying on fines may end up permitting affluent offenders to buy their way out of other punishment. While recognizing that incarcerating a person who is financially unable to pay a fine discriminates against the poor, many judges continue to incarcerate offenders for noncompliance with court orders.[9]

Prevailing evidence seems to support that judges use fines in a rational and reasonable way. Low-risk offenders are the ones most likely to receive fines instead of jail confinement: the more serious the crime, the higher the fine. Yet there has been little research finding that fines reduce recidivism rates.

Identify the sanctions that stand alone and what they contribute to intermediate sanctions **LO3**

fine A sanction that requires convicted offenders to pay a specified sum of money.

DAY FINES Day fines, which are also used more frequently in Europe than in the United States, are designed to equalize the financial impact of sentences on offenders. The **day fine** addresses the concern that fines are unduly harsh on poor offenders but permit affluent offenders to buy their way out of more punitive sanctions. This concept

EXHIBIT 4.1

Comparison of the Various Intermediate Sanctions

Sanctions That Stand Alone	
Fines	The court requires convicted offenders to pay a specified sum of money.
Forfeiture	The government seizes property that was derived from or used in criminal action.
Drug courts	The court assigns nonviolent offenders with substance abuse problems to these courts.
Day reporting centers	Clients report to a central location every day, where they file daily schedules with their supervising officer showing how each hour will be spent.
Sanctions as an Add-On to Probation	
Restitution	Used alone or in conjunction with probation and requires completing of a payment.
Community service orders	Court-imposed sanction that orders an offender to spend so many hours on the work project in the community.
Intensive probation	Offender sees probation officer three to five times a week. Probation officer also makes unscheduled visits to offender's home or workplace.
House arrest and electronic monitoring	Offender is confined to the house or required to wear electronic monitoring device, usually around the ankle, when he or she leaves the house.
Sanctions That Include Incarceration	
Residential centers	Used as a supplement to probation for some probation or parole violators.
Shock probation and split sentencing	Sanctions that permit judges to grant offenders community release only after they have experienced incarceration.
Work release centers	Offenders are released to these centers following incarceration as a form of gradual integration into the community.
Boot camps	Rigorous military-style regimen for younger offenders. Designed to accelerate punishment while instilling discipline, often with an education component.

originated in Europe, and the first day fines pilot program in the United States was designed and conducted by the Vera Institute of Justice in Staten Island, New York, between 1987 and 1989.

Day fines are catching on in the United States, and programs have been initiated in Arizona, Connecticut, Iowa, New York, and Oregon, among other states.[10] Judges in Phoenix experimented with a form of day fine called FARE (Financial Assessment Related to Employability) probation. Under a FARE probation sentence, a certain number of units are assigned to a particular offense based on its seriousness—for example, 30 units for credit card forgery and 160 units for a burglary. Each unit was given a dollar value based on the offender's income. The penalty amount ranged widely, from $180 for a laborer with six children who was convicted of making a false statement in an unemployment claim, to $22,000 for a restaurant owner who was convicted of money laundering.[11]

day fine A fine that represents one day of income for the defendant.

MYTH Fines are only used in minor cases such as traffic offenses.

FACT Fines are probably the most widely used sanction in the United States and are commonly employed in serious felony offenses. In some white-collar crimes, fines can be in the hundreds of millions of dollars.

The day fine has the promise of becoming an equitable solution to the problem of setting fines for varying offenders. However, problems remain—such as discrimination against the poor who do not have sufficient funds to pay fines, the difficulty of collecting fines, and the perception that day fines are a weak punishment. Another problem is that there is little or no evidence concerning the effectiveness of fines in terms of reducing recidivism.[12] In fact, one of the largest studies of fines (as a deterrent) was conducted in Australia with 70,000 people who received a court-imposed fine for a driving offense between 1998 and 2000. Researchers then followed each offender for a period of five years to see whether they committed another driving offense. The conclusion: higher fines do not reduce the risk of reoffending.[13] After controlling for a wide range of factors likely to influence reoffending, the study found no relationship between the magnitude of the fine imposed and the likelihood of a further driving offense. The Australian study indicates that fines do not carry with them strong deterrent values.

Forfeiture

forfeiture Involves the government seizing property that was derived from or used in criminal activity.

Forfeiture involves the government seizing property that was derived from or used in criminal activity. It goes back to the Middle Ages, in which "forfeiture of estate" was a mandatory result of most felony convictions; the king could seize the property of someone convicted of a crime against the state. The modern application of forfeiture is related to the passage of the Racketeer Influenced and Corrupt Organization (RICO) Act and the Continuing Criminal Enterprise (CCE) Act, both of which permit the seizure of any property derived from illegal conspiracies or enterprises. These acts initially were designed to apply to criminal conspiracies, but they are now being applied to an extensive series of criminal acts, including white-collar crimes. In fact, more than 100 federal statutes currently use forfeiture of property as a punishment.[14] There are two forms of forfeiture—civil and criminal.[15]

civil forfeiture To confiscate property used in law violations and remove the illegally gained profits from violators.

CIVIL FORFEITURE The purpose of **civil forfeiture** is to confiscate property used in violation of the law and to remove the illegally gained profits from violators. Civil forfeitures are *in rem*, which means that the legal action is directly and solely against the property based on a legal finding that the property itself was used in an illegal manner. An *in rem* proceeding is not an action against a violator but against the property involved, and is a separate legal action from any criminal actions taken against the violator.

Civil forfeiture can be accomplished through administrative and/or judicial means. Administrative proceedings are conducted by the seizing agencies, while judicial proceedings are conducted in a court before a judge. The value and type of seized property and whether the forfeiture is contested determine the proceeding used.

criminal forfeiture Following conviction, offenders must relinquish assets related to the offense.

CRIMINAL FORFEITURE Under criminal law, forfeiture takes place following conviction and requires that offenders relinquish assets related to the crime. **Criminal forfeiture** takes place as part of the criminal process, while civil forfeiture does not involve a criminal action taken against the violator. The purpose of a criminal forfeiture is to punish the violator, and it is imposed as part of that punishment following conviction. Upon completion of a criminal trial, if the defendant is found guilty, criminal forfeiture proceedings are conducted in the court before a judge. The proceedings may result in a verdict forfeiting property used in the crime or obtained with proceedings from the crime. For instance, under federal law, after arresting drug traffickers, the government can seize the boats they used to import the narcotics, the vehicles they used to carry the drugs overland, the warehouses in which the drugs were stored, and the homes they paid for with drug profits.

Since the attacks of September 11, 2001, forfeiture has been used to disrupt terrorist activities. Terrorist organizations, it can be argued, are a species of organized crime, motivated by ideological or political ends. They are usually quite clever in finding ways of money laundering, which is a process designed to give illegally obtained property the appearance of having been legally obtained. Terrorists may use the same laundering methods that organized crime groups adopt, such as shell companies and trusts. The challenge for federal officials is the seizure, detention, and forfeiture of terrorist cash.[16]

However, the use of forfeiture has met with considerable criticism. There are those who claim that the government has been overzealous in the use of forfeiture. For example, million-dollar yachts have been seized because someone aboard had a small amount of marijuana. This confiscatory practice is known as *zero tolerance*. It is also claimed that forfeiture unfairly targets a narrow range of offenders. Government employees, for instance, involved in corruption commonly forfeit their pensions, but employees of public companies are exempt from such punishments. It is further charged that the Civil Asset Forfeiture Reform Act (CAFRA) of 2000 is not responsible for significant change in the practice of civil asset forfeiture because it fails to address problems associated with assets' forfeiture and has a questionable standard of proof.[17] Finally, critics note that law enforcement is involved in a conflict of interest. Law enforcement agencies can use forfeited assets to supplement their budgets and, therefore, they may focus on cases that promise the greatest payoff rather than ones that have the highest law enforcement priority.[18]

financial restitution The purposes of financial restitution are to compensate victims for their losses and to teach offenders financial responsibility.

community service order A court order that requires an offender to perform a certain number of work hours at a private nonprofit or government agency.

LO4 Identify the sanctions as an add-on to probation and what they contribute to intermediate sanctions

Financial Restitution

Financial restitution (from the Latin term *restitutionem*, restoring) is payment of a sum of money by the offender either to the victim or to a public fund for victims of crime. This payment for the victim or victim's family is how financial restitution differs from fines. The amount is usually based on the crime and, in some instances, on the offender's ability to pay. Judges will sometimes order a wealthy offender's compensation be paid out of income that is derived from performing public works or a low-paid social service job, in order to avoid the situation in which a wealthy offender can easily fill a restitution order by merely writing a check.

The twin purposes of financial restitution are to compensate victims for their losses and to teach offenders financial responsibility. Offenders who do not have the resources to make their restitution payments may be confined to a correctional facility at night while they are employed elsewhere during the day to earn money for their payments.

About 30 states now operate restitution centers. Some evidence indicates that restitution may make an important contribution to the effectiveness of community sanctions. R. B. Rubeck and colleagues found from their study of financial restitution in four Pennsylvania counties that the likelihood of arrest went down as the proportion of restitution paid increased.[19]

Financial restitution offers several positive outcomes to the justice process. It can offer offenders a chance to avoid a jail or prison sentence. It can help victims regain lost property and income, and it can return something to the community without asking the community to foot the bill for an incarceration stay.

AP Images/L.G. Patterson

On June 29, 2011, Jimmy Tebeau sings with his Grateful Dead cover band, Schwag, at a concert at the Blue Note in Columbia, Missouri. Tebeau owns an Ozarks "campitheater" that hosts national touring acts and thousands of fans at weekend festivals. Federal prosecutors charged him with one count of maintaining a drug premises. That follows a civil lawsuit seeking forfeiture of the 350-acre property and nearly $200,000 in fines. Under forfeiture statutes, to seize the property the prosecution does not need to convict Tebeau of a crime but merely show a "preponderance of evidence" that the property was part of criminal activity. The case is still ongoing.

Community Service

A **community service order** is a court order that requires an offender to work a certain number of hours at a private nonprofit or government agency. Two general patterns have emerged for structuring community obligations: (1) referring offenders to community agencies that handle the work placement and supervise completion of the community service obligation and (2) assigning a group of offenders to provide a community service. The number of hours of community service to be completed is generally determined by the court or sometimes by program staff. Commonly assigned public service projects include cleanup work on the local streets or in city parks, volunteer service in hospitals or in nursing homes, and repair jobs in rundown housing.

At first, community service sentencing was used to permit misdemeanants, traffic defendants, minor property offenders, and other offenders who could not pay their fines to work off their obligations by working without pay for the community. Community service sentences were considered a rehabilitative alternative to jail sentences.

Today, some form of community service is used in all 50 states. Georgia, Texas, and Washington are three states that widely use community service. About one-third of Washington's convicted felons are sentenced to community service, substituting eight hours of community service for one day of incarceration. Offenders in Georgia work 1.6 million hours of community service.[20] In Texas, two-thirds of the state's corrections departments operate a specialized community service restitution unit, which is used two-thirds of the time as a supplement to probation supervision.[21]

Community service has many advocates because it can relieve jail and prison crowding by diverting certain kinds of offenders. Nevertheless, community service programs are difficult to design, implement, and manage. A program must appear punitive enough to satisfy the public that justice is being served. A sizeable staff is also needed to keep track of convicted offenders doing community service.

House Arrest

house arrest A court-imposed sentence that orders an offender to remain confined in his or her residence for the duration or remainder of the sentence.

House arrest is a court-imposed sentence ordering that an offender remain confined to his or her own residence for a specific amount of time. Home confinement ranges from evening curfew to detention during all nonworking hours to continuous confinement at home. House arrest can last from several days to several years. For example, a person convicted of a drunk-driving charge might be sentenced to spend from 6 P.M. Friday to 8 A.M. Monday and every weekday after 5:30 P.M. in their home for a number of months. Current estimates reveal that more than 10,000 people are under house arrest.

The concept of house arrest, or home confinement, tends to vary from one jurisdiction to another. Some programs are administered by probation departments and others are merely judicial sentences that are monitored by surveillance officers. The Florida Community Control Program checks clients 20 or more times a month, but others only do a few curfew checks. Varying programs also produce varying degrees of offender control. Some use 24-hour confinements, while others permit offenders to attend work or school.

The most severe form of home confinement, or house arrest, requires offenders to remain in their homes, other than when they have permission to leave for employment, religious services, and medical reasons. The sanctions of house arrest can stand alone or be coupled with electronic monitoring, fines, community service, and other obligations. Monitoring techniques, a sanction widely used with home confinement, range from periodic visits or telephone calls to continuous monitoring using electronic equipment.

home confinement program The federal courts use this program with both postsentence offenders and with pretrial defenders.

In the federal courts, the **home confinement program** is used with both postsentence offenders (to punish) and with pretrial defendants (to ensure their appearance in court and to protect the community). Home confinement is also used as an intermediate sanction for supervision violators and by the Bureau of Prisons for inmates in prerelease status serving the last 10 percent of their imprisonment term under the direction of probation officers. One study of the federal home confinement program found that house arrest can serve as an effective crime deterrent and that it lowers the recidivism rate. However, defendants with drug charges appeared to have a higher risk of flight and to pose more of a danger to the community than defendants charged with crimes against property.[22]

Another study found that offenders most likely to complete the period of supervision are older, are sentenced for multiple charges, serve longer sentences, accrue fewer violations, come from less crime ridden neighborhoods, and are serving a sentence for a DIU-related offense. Significant predictors of rearrest include being sentenced for multiple charges and being younger, African American, and male.[23]

In sum, the advantages of house arrest in reducing costs and overcrowding in the correctional system clearly make further experimentation desirable. There may also be some unanticipated advantages of house arrest. For example, house arrest keeps offenders' family relations intact, and those with health problems can maintain better access to health care in the community than in prison.[24] Yet home confinement is a labor-intensive and time-consuming form of community supervision and can be dangerous. Officers provide round-the-clock coverage and respond to electronic monitoring alerts 24 hours a day. Home confinement also requires officers to make more frequent home and community visits, often in response to alerts signaling that participants may have violated program rules.[25]

Electronic Monitoring (EM)

For house arrest to be effective, supervising officers must be certain that arrestees are actually at home when they are supposed to be there. Although random calls and visits are one way to check on compliance, **electronic monitoring (EM)** adds another way to determine whether offenders are complying with their home confinement orders.

electronic monitoring (EM) The use of electronic equipment to verify that an offender is at home or in a community correctional center during specified hours.

Electronic monitoring can be traced back to 1964 when an electronic telemetry system based on a triangulation process using radio signals was adapted for possible criminal justice applications. During the mid-1960s, electronic monitoring systems were used in Boston to determine the location of mental patients, research volunteers, and parolees. The initial systems used multiple receivers to trace movement throughout specified areas. The number of receivers used and transmission characteristics of the environment depended on the size of the monitored area.

Electronic monitoring is usually applied in one of two ways. It can be a sanction in and of itself, or it can be used in conjunction with other sanctions—for example, offenders receive a prison or jail sanction and then are placed on electronic monitoring when they are released to the community.[26] In addition to probationers, EM can also be used with bailees and with parolees. Offenders who are electronically monitored wear devices around their wrists, ankles, or necks that send signals to a control office. There are four basic types of systems that are used: active phone line systems, passive phone line systems, remote location monitoring, and global positioning systems (GPS).

ACTIVE PHONE LINE SYSTEMS This type of EM employs a transmitter that is attached to an offender's ankle; the receiver is inside the offender's home. The active system continually monitors offenders as the transmitter sends a signal to the central office. If offenders leave their home at an unauthorized time, this breaks the signal. A computer sends a report of the violation to a central computer, and the failure is recorded. In some cases the control officer is immediately notified by pager.

PASSIVE PHONE LINE SYSTEMS Passive systems lack a continuous signal from a transmitter to a receiver. They generally involve random phone calls generated by computers, to which offenders must respond within a certain time frame such as 30 seconds. The offender verifies his or her presence at home by placing the transmitter on the verifier box. More recent methods of confirmation permit offenders to provide voice verification or visual verification by still-picture video phone.

AP Images/Kirsty Wigglesworth

The United States is not the only nation to employ electronic monitoring and house arrest. Here, WikiLeaks founder Julian Assange is seen with his ankle security tag at the house where he is required to stay, near Bungay, England, on June 15, 2011. Assange says his house arrest over sex allegations is hampering the work of the secret-spilling site, and his supporters accuse Britain of spying on him. The 39-year-old Australian has spent six months at a supporter's rural estate as he fights extradition to Sweden, where he is accused of the rape and sexual assault of two women. The case is still being considered in the British court system.

REMOTE LOCATION MONITORING This type of EM monitors an offender periodically or continuously throughout the day and night by means of a pager number that only the probation officer knows. The offender is instructed to call the probation officer when the pager beeps. The computer is able to determine whether or not the offender's voice matches the voice sample associated with the phone number where the call originated. Voice verification is able to determine a positive match between the voice sample and the voice on the phone.[27]

global positioning system (GPS) technology This has affected EM technology by the transmitter making continuous calls to a reporting station that updates the offender's location.

GLOBAL POSITIONING SYSTEMS EM technology has been altered dramatically by the introduction of **global positioning system (GPS) technology**. The Satellite Monitoring and Remote Tracking (SMART) program monitors offenders equipped with a GPS receiver with a microprocessor and an ankle transmitter device. The offender must remain within 100 feet of the portable receiver. The transmitter makes continuous calls to a reporting station that updates the offender's location, which is tracked by a computer.[28] The TechnoCorrections feature focuses on some of the various technology-aided services provided by EM systems.

MYTH While electronic monitoring of criminals sounds good, it is rarely used, expensive, and ineffective.

FACT EM is actually a widely used intermediate sanction for the justice system and is a cost-effective way of keeping offenders out of prison. There is growing evidence that it can reduce recidivism.

EM TODAY More than 150,000 offenders, or approximately 20 percent of community-based supervision in the United States, are monitored at home.[29] Electronic monitoring equipment is being provided by some 20 private companies. Internationally, about 20 percent of 50,000 offenders in England and Wales who started pre- or postrelease supervision receive electronic monitoring. In Sweden, about 25 percent of all inmates are placed on electronic monitoring.[30]

Electronic monitoring advocates see many advantages to this intermediate sanction. It has relatively low cost and high security; it helps offenders avoid overcrowded and often dangerous prison environments. EM also is cost effective because offenders are monitored by computers, and an initial investment in technology can help avoid the cost of hiring more supervising officers to handle larger numbers of offenders. Most importantly, there is evidence that EM can be highly effective with probationers, reducing the likelihood of recidivism.[31]

The public, as would be expected, supports EM, in that it provides greater security for offenders. Offenders, at least according to some surveys, prefer EM to incarceration.[32] Furthermore, EM can be used in a pretrial diversionary program, to enhance probation, or as a post-prison release sanction.[33]

However, EM does have its critics. It is claimed that this sanction is not really an alternative to incarceration but simply a new sentencing alternative that widens the net of criminal justice control. There are those who hold that offenders sentenced to EM are actually offenders who in the past would have been informally diverted from the justice system.[34] It is also held that EM has privacy issues and erodes privacy and liberty. It is further questioned whether citizens should be watched over by a computer and whether it will be employed with inappropriate offenders, such as mental patients, suicidal adolescents, or even

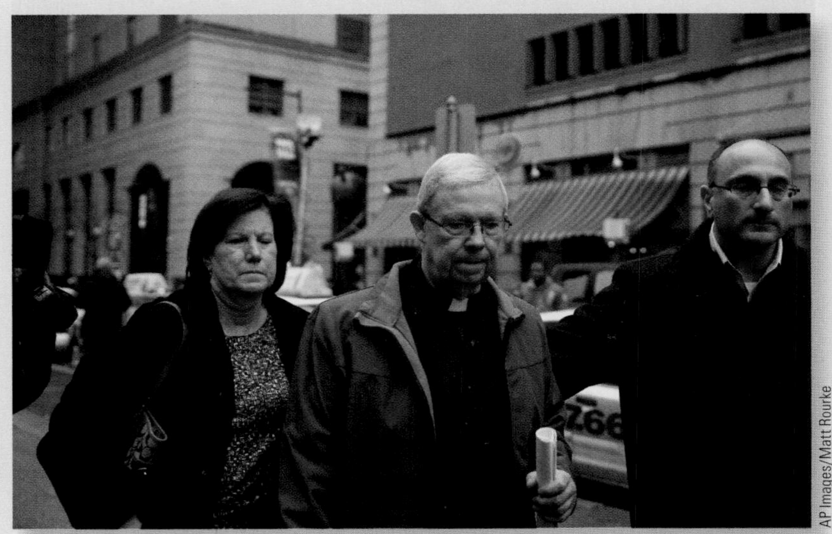

AP Images/Matt Rourke

Thousands of defendants who are released before final disposition of their case are monitored electronically. Here, Monsignor William Lynn walks from the criminal justice center after a bail hearing on January 6, 2014, in Philadelphia. Lynn, a Roman Catholic priest who recently won an appeal of his landmark conviction in the priest-abuse scandal, was released from prison but ordered to be electronically monitored while prosecutors asked the state Supreme Court to restore the conviction.

EM and GPS Systems in the Community

People usually think of electronic systems as a technological method to keep tabs on offenders in the community. However, use of the technology is expanding into a variety of applications. For example, at Bryan Adams High School in East Dallas, Texas, students who have been chronically truant are now being monitored with a global positioning system, which tracks their whereabouts 24/7 in a court-ordered attempt to keep truants in school. Across the state, in Midland, county officials started using electronic ankle monitors to track the most chronically truant students.

The use of EM to track criminal offenders who are granted community release should also expand as systems become more sophisticated. Some of the services provided by EM systems include the following:

- *Programmed contact systems* are used to contact and verify the location of offenders in their homes or elsewhere.
- *Identity verification devices* can recognize different parts of the body to ensure that the reporting person is the offender.
- *Remote alcohol detention devices* require users to blow into the device to measure blood alcohol content. Another type is Tattle Tale, which can detect alcohol or drug use by the offender. It senses these substances through the pores and perspiration.
- *Ignition interlock devices* are linked to the electrical systems of automobiles. The driver expels deep lung air into the device, and the vehicle will not start if the driver's blood alcohol content is registered above a level deemed unsafe for driving.
- *Victim notification systems* alert the victim when the offender is approaching his or her residence. A transmitter is worn by both the offender and the victim, and a receiver is placed at both residences.
- *Field monitoring devices*, or drive-by units, are used by probation or parole officers or other authorities. They are portable devices that can be handheld or used in a vehicle with a roof-mounted antenna. When within 200 to 800 feet of an offender's ankle or wrist transmitter, the portable device can detect the transmitter's radio signals.
- *Group monitoring units* permit supervisors to monitor several offenders in the same location, in order to verify attendance of multiple offenders in a day-reporting program or to monitor offenders confined in a residential group setting.
- *GPS (global positioning system) location tracking systems* have receivers that detect satellite signals relating the exact time the signal is sent and the identity of the satellite sending the signal. This technology, which is generally used for high-risk offenders, can determine when an offender leaves an area where he or she is supposed to be (inclusion zone) or enters an area where he or she is not allowed to be (exclusion zone) as ordered by a judge. For example, Massachusetts Probation Services has implemented GPS to track sex offenders being supervised by probation who have been deemed appropriate for this type of supervision. If an offender enters an area from which they have been restricted, an alert goes off. A probation employee contacts the offender on a specialized GPS cell phone to find out why they entered the area and instruct them to leave. If the offender does not comply, the employee contacts a probation officer and an arrest warrant may be issued.

These and other EM systems should revolutionize community supervision, allowing more people to be placed in intermediate sanction programs without compromising community safety.

FOR CRITICAL THINKING AND WRITING

Would you advocate installing an ignition interlock system on all cars? After all, what is to prevent someone who is forced to have such a device installed as part of their probation order from borrowing or stealing another vehicle? Considering that 35,000 people are killed each year in traffic accidents, wouldn't that be a prudent thing to do? Or does it reduce personal freedom?

Sources: Sam Merten, "For Whom the Bell Tolls," *Dallas Observer*, June 26, 2008, http://www.dallasobserver.com/2008-06-26/news/for-whom (accessed June 2014); iSecureTrac Systems, Omaha, Nebraska, http://www.isecuretrac.com/Services.aspx?p=EMManagement (accessed June 2014).

high-risk future offenders.[35] Moreover, it does provide a false sense of security, because knowing where someone is does not substitute for knowing what they are doing.

IS ELECTRONIC MONITORING EFFECTIVE? The issue of the ability of EM to reduce recidivism is an important one. The effectiveness of EM is still open for debate, but several recent studies have produced positive results.[36] For example, Kathy G. Padgett and her colleagues found that the EM program for public intoxication saved money and avoided new construction costs, without widening the net of social control. This study examined 75,661 offenders placed on home confinement in Florida and found that both radio frequency and global positioning system monitoring significantly reduced the likelihood of technical violations, reoffending, and absconding for this population of offenders. In addition, Padgett found that those placed on home confinement with EM had original charges that were significantly more serious than those placed on home confinement without EM, which challenges the net-widening charge that is sometimes made of this intermediate sanction. It appears that electronic monitoring of offenders in the community can prove to be an effective public safety alternative to prison.[37]

Specialized Courts

The advent of specialized courts has increased the scope of intermediate sentencing. Examples of specialized courts include drug courts, mental health courts, reentry courts, domestic violence courts, and veterans courts.[38]

Specialized courts differ from traditional courts in that they usually focus on one type of offenders or offense. The judge generally plays an intensive supervisory role. Probation officers and social service agencies (i.e., drug treatment) are involved and collaborate in case processing.[39] These specialized courts programs are motivated by two sets of goals:

- Case management to expedite case processing and reduce caseload and increase trial capacity for more serious crimes
- Therapeutic interaction to reduce criminal offending through treatment and interdisciplinary approaches that address addiction and other underlying issues without endangering public safety and other processes[40]

Drug Courts

About 80 percent of offenders in the United States were under the influence of drugs or alcohol at the time of their arrest or had a serious history of substance abuse.[41] It is not surprising therefore that intermediate sanctions have been aimed at treating the drug-involved offender.

This problem was particularly vexing when judges were left with prison as their only sentencing option for nonviolent offenders who had substance abuse problems. In 1989, at the request of presiding Judge Gerald Wetherington in Miami's Eleventh Judicial Circuit, Judge Herbert Klein proposed a strategy for dealing with the large number of drug offenders. Judge Klein's recommendation was simple: "We could help them."[42] And he proposed using **drug courts** as the means to treat drug offenders within the community.

drug courts Courts designed for nonviolent offenders with substance abuse problems who require integrated sanctions and services such as mandatory drug testing, substance abuse treatment, supervised release, and parole.

Drug courts are designed for nonviolent offenders with substance abuse problems who require integrated sanctions and services, including (a) mandatory periodic testing for the use of controlled substances; (b) substance abuse treatment; (c) diversion, probation, or other supervised release; and (d) aftercare services such as relapse prevention, health care, education, vocational training, job placement, housing placement, and child care. In the Voices Across the Profession feature, a drug abuse counselor discusses the elements of this critical profession.

© James M. Higgins

VOICES ACROSS THE PROFESSION

The job of a substance abuse correctional counselor requires a cool head, positive attitude, patience, and, above all, compassion and a desire to help inmates put their lives together again after having spent time in prison.

James M. Higgins
Clinical Director, Community Corrections Center, Salisbury, Massachusetts

I've been working as a substance abuse counselor for the last 22 years. For 10 of those years, I managed a substance abuse residential treatment program where 60 percent of the clients were referred by the criminal justice system. The job of a substance abuse correctional counselor requires a cool head, positive attitude, patience, and, above all, compassion and a desire to help inmates put their lives together again after having spent time in prison. In my experience the most important aspect of the job is to develop rapport, the degree to which trust and openness are present in the relationship between the counselor and client—it's an essential element of the therapeutic relationship. Having a good grasp of motivational interviewing techniques will go a long way toward developing this trust, which is a lot easier said than done. Being fair and consistent, and having concrete, swift consequences for noncompliance issues, are required to keep the therapeutic relationship on course.

A multidimensional assessment—not based on the single condition of addiction but identifying the multiple conditions of the client's life adjustment problems—is always the starting point for the change process to begin. It is important to remember that individuals go through stages when making changes in their lives. Typically it takes two to three months before trust and openness can be established with a client. Clients need a thorough education of the disease concept of addiction and the principles of recovery; they also need be introduced to self-help options in the community, such as AA and NA.

Using cognitive behavioral therapy to help restructure criminal thinking and self-destructive behavior is a key approach to implementing change. In my experience the majority of clients have difficulty thinking about the consequences of their actions. These clients have developed habits of thinking that allow them to not focus on the truth of their past actions and the consequences of future actions. A focus on cognitive restructuring and coping with social skills training are vitally important to these clients.

Finally, developing a concrete relapse prevention plan, an aftercare plan to include mental health counseling when indicated and identifying family and community supports, is essential for continued success.

In the larger court community, Judge Klein's recommendation was initially met with an uncomfortable silence, but his leadership helped drug courts become popular in Florida. Other drug courts began in Oakland, California, and the drug court movement received considerable federal support. The First National Drug Court Conference was held in Miami in December 1993. The term *drug court*, as well as the components of the drug court model, soon became common in the everyday language of criminal justice, and the ideas that underlie drug courts began to be applied in other contexts. The development of the drug courts model certainly was helped by the fact that Janet Reno, the attorney general during the Clinton administration, was one of its early proponents and supported funding for drug courts, including the 1994 Crime Act. Drug courts began to be used experimentally in Australia, Britain, and Iceland.[43] Drug courts rapidly proliferated in the United States in the 1990s and the early years of the twenty-first century. As seen in Table 4.1, drug courts number more than 2,600, made up of a variety of courts. Drug courts are operating or

THINKING LIKE A CORRECTIONS PROFESSIONAL

You are a drug court judge and a drug user is appearing before you for the fourth time. This offender has more potential than you have seen in a long time. She has finished three years of college, earning high grades, but simply does not seem to successfully complete drug rehabilitative programs. What will be your approach with this offender? What sanction will you give her?

being planned in 50 states, 3 U.S. territories, 62 Native American tribal courts, and 8 countries. Several states, including New York, California, Arizona, and Florida, have implemented statewide drug diversion initiatives for all nonviolent, nonrecidivist drug offenders.[44] The key elements of drug courts are set out in Exhibit 4.2.

ARE DRUG COURTS EFFECTIVE? Adele Harrell, a drug court specialist, has argued: "The development of drug courts is a paradigm shift from court practices designed for fast and efficient delivery of penalties to court practices designed for crime prevention."[45] Still, Harrell cautions that while drug courts may be effective for some offenders, they are not a magic bullet, as many offenders involved in these courts fail.[46] There is every reason to believe that as less treatable groups participate, rates of compliance and graduation will decline and recidivism will increase.[47] Nonetheless, the success and acceptance of drug courts have prompted the creation of other specialized courts, including domestic violence courts, gun courts, and mental health courts, which employ similar principles.[48] The effectiveness of drug courts is set out more fully in the Evidence-Based Corrections feature.

MYTH Drug courts are a fad that looks good on paper but does not work in practice.

FACT Drug courts represent a major improvement in how drug offenders are treated by the criminal justice system. Though program and recidivism rates remain high for graduates from these programs, drug courts are a far more effective and more rehabilitative way of handling drug offenders than costly and often dangerous prison settings.

TABLE 4.1

Number and Types of Drug Courts

Type of Drug Court	Number
Adult drug courts	1,435
Juvenile drug courts	458
Family drug courts	329
Tribal drug courts	79
Designated DUI courts	192
Campus drug courts	5
Reentry drug courts	31
Federal reentry drug courts	46
Veterans drug courts	95
Co-occurring disorder courts	20

Source: National Drug Court Institute, http://www.ndci.org/ (accessed June 2014).

EXHIBIT 4.2

Elements of Drug Courts

The National Association of Drug Court Professionals (NADCP) in Alexandria, Virginia, works closely with the U.S. Department of Justice, coordinating and implementing standardized training and linkages among the various programs and community policing partnerships. Federal discretionary grants are available under the Violent Control and Law Enforcement Act of 1994, Title V. The NADCP and the U.S. Department of Justice identify that a drug court has the following key elements:

- Integration of substance abuse treatment with justice system case processing
- Use of the nonadversarial approach, in which prosecution and defense promote public safety while protecting the right of the accused to due process
- Early identification and prompt placement of eligible participants
- Access to a continuum of treatment, rehabilitation, and related services
- Frequent testing for alcohol and illicit drugs
- Coordinated strategy among judge, prosecution, defense, and treatment providers to govern offender compliance
- Ongoing judicial interaction with each participant
- Monitoring and evaluation to measure achievement of program goals and to gauge effectiveness
- Continuing interdisciplinary education to promote effective planning, implementation, and operation
- Partnerships with public agencies and community-based organizations to generate local support and enhance drug court effectiveness

Source: Richard S. Gebelein, "The Rebirth of Rehabilitation: Promise and Perils of Drug Courts," National Institute of Justice, http://www.ncjrs.gov/pdffiles1/nij/181412.pdf (accessed June 2014).

EVIDENCE-BASED CORRECTIONS

Are Drug Courts Effective?

Drug courts are currently being established throughout the nation, and the initial evaluations have been favorable. A number of evidence-based evaluations conducted in Miami, Philadelphia, and Las Vegas reveal that drug courts can produce comparatively lower rates of recidivism. Using a nationally representative sample (including all drug courts that had been in operation for at least one year and had at least 40 program graduates), the National Institute of Justice and the Drug Court Program Office found that within one year 16 percent of drug court graduates had been arrested and charged with a serious offense (84 percent success rate), and within two years, 28 percent had been arrested and charged with a serious offense (73 percent success rate). The programs seem to work best for high-risk offenders who might normally have been sent to prison.

An analysis of the Multnomah Drug Court Program in Oregon also found the program was a success. The analysis looked at the overall impact of the drug court on the target population over time, variations over time on that impact, and external and internal conditions that influenced outcomes. A cost analysis was also conducted to assess the overall investment of taxpayer money in the court compared to its benefits. During the study period of 1991 through 2001, the entire population of offenders identified as eligible for drug court by the Multnomah County District Attorney's Office was identified and tracked through a variety of administrative data systems. Approximately 11,000 cases were identified; 6,500 participated in the drug court program during that period, and 4,600 had their case processed outside the drug court model. Data on outcomes were gathered including criminal recidivism, investment costs, outcome costs, and total costs per participant.

The researchers found that rearrests were lower five years or more later compared to rearrests for similar drug offenders within the same county. They also found, however, that the drug courts' impact on recidivism varied by year as a result of changes in programming and judge assignments over time. Reductions in recidivism ranged from 17 to 26 percent.

Compared to traditional criminal justice system processing, treatment and other investment costs averaged $1,392 lower per drug court participant. Reduced recidivism and other long-term program outcomes resulted in public savings of $6,744 on average ($12,218 if victimization costs are included), or an estimated $79 million over 10 years.

Although general research findings are that drug courts can reduce recidivism and promote other positive outcomes such as cost savings, several factors affect a drug court program's success:

- Proper assessment and treatment
- The role assumed by the judge and the nature of offender interactions with the judge
- Other variable influences such as drug use trends, staff turnover, and resource allocation

FOR CRITICAL THINKING AND WRITING

What other specialized courts do you believe would be effective? Courts for former military personnel? Courts for the mentally ill? Courts for hate crimes? Is there a danger for a court to become too specialized or do you see this as an efficient approach to dispense justice?

Sources: Douglas B. Marlowe, "Evidence-Based Policies and Practices for Drug-Involved Offenders," *Prison Journal* 9 (2011): 27–47; Michael W. Finigan, Shannon M. Carey, and Anton Cox, "Impact of a Mature Drug Court over 10 Years of Operation: Recidivism and Costs," NPC Research, 2007; National Institute of Justice, "Do Drug Courts Work? Findings from Drug Court Research," http://nij.gov/nij/topics/courts/drug-courts/work.htm (accessed June 2014).

Day Reporting Centers

Day reporting is another form of intermediate sanction. The offender is assigned to a facility where he or she must report at a specific time every day to participate in activities such as counseling, social skills training, and employment training. The goals of the **day reporting center (DRC)** are to provide a punishment in a cost-effective way, to ensure community safety, and to rehabilitate the offender through intensive programming. The number of contacts per week is normally greater than offenders would receive through normal community supervision, and the programs provide or refer offenders to services that are not available to offenders outside the DRC or are not available in as focused or intensive a manner.[49]

day reporting center (DRC) A facility where an offender, usually on probation, must report every day to participate in counseling, social skills training, and other rehabilitative activities.

Julie Fox

CAREERS IN CORRECTIONS

Julie Fox
Substance Abuse Counselor

Substance abuse counselors are key participants in drug courts. They are also needed in therapeutic communities, detoxification units, short-term residential programs, and outpatient treatment—such as antabuse, drug education classes, relapse prevention, and methadone or naltrexone maintenance.

"I am the clinical manager for outpatient services at a nonprofit behavioral health organization. We focus primarily on substance abuse treatment and problem gambling treatment and prevention. I provide clinical oversight for our outpatient services, including direct supervision of 13 staff members (counselors and prevention specialists). Basically, I ensure that our staff is well trained in the treatment of addictions, and that we continually provide high quality services to all who enter our facilities.

"In a substance abuse treatment facility, we often see people at one of the worst times of their lives. Clients are frequently worn out physically, mentally, and emotionally, and my day includes showing kindness, compassion, and understanding to all people. Most of our clients do not have insurance, are unemployed/underemployed, and often do not have the resources to pay for our services. We welcome them without judgment, believing that all people have the capacity for change. We strive to show people a way to live without drugs and alcohol, and live in recovery. I also spend my days working with my staff to get through difficult issues with our clients. As the leader of the outpatient team, my job is to be available to staff and clients, to answer questions and discuss options for care. I track counselor productivity and client outcomes, and manage committal client issues with the court system. I am also responsible for reporting to funding sources about how their funding was used.

"I have found that working in the human services field feeds my soul as a human being. I am able to use my education and experience to literally help other human beings survive addiction. At times, our clients die from their addiction, which is an incredibly hard reality to face. We continue to do this type of work knowing that we have helped thousands of people make better decisions with their lives, and ultimately for the lives of their family and their community. It's very rewarding to be a part of the healing process."

See Chapter 15 for more detailed information on careers in corrections.

Web App 4.1
Go to the website for Harlem Children's Zone at http://www.hcz.org/ to learn about the services, schools, and programs provided to both parents and children who live in the area. Write an essay discussing the potential of decriminalizing day reporting centers in favor of providing these services to all people, not just offenders. LO4

Day reporting centers can trace their origins to the British experience with probation day centers in the 1970s and the 1980s. The purpose of these probation centers was to divert offenders whose problems seemed to be linked to personal inadequacies. Several communities in the United States created day treatment programs to deliver therapeutic services to at-risk youth and deinstitutionalized mental patients. Over a 10-year period, beginning in the mid-1980s, the number of day reporting centers grew from a handful clustered in a few states to 114 programs in 22 states.[50]

Little evidence supports that DRCs contribute to lower rates of recidivism. A North Carolina study compared the outcome of probationers sentenced to day reporting centers along with intensive supervision to those sentenced to intensive probation alone, and it found that the addition of the day reporting center component did not reduce the rearrest rates.[51] A Cook County, Illinois, study did find that the day reporting center clients who remained in the program for at least 70 days had not been rearrested compared to one-quarter of the control group (those in the program less than 10 days). Also, two-thirds of the DRC clients remaining in the program for at least 70 days had not been reincarcerated compared with less than one-half of the control group.[52] On balance, day reporting centers remain a promising intervention, although they may require another intermediate sanction, such as intensive probation, to increase the rates of those who finish the program.

Shock Probation and Split Sentencing

LO5 Identify the sanctions that include incarceration and what they contribute to intermediate sanctions

Shock probation and split sentencing are intermediate sanctions that permit judges to grant offenders community release only after they have experienced incarceration. In recent years, shock probation has been largely replaced by shock incarceration, or boot camps, which will be discussed later in this chapter. The major difference between shock probation and shock incarceration programs relates to the required participation in drills and physical training in boot camp prison settings that are components of the recent shock incarceration programs.

Shock probation had its beginnings in Ohio in 1965 and has been used in Kentucky, North Carolina, Texas, Indiana, Idaho, and Maine. Ordinarily, a felon is sent to prison (usually at least for 30 days but less than 60 days) in states that have shock probation, and his or her attorney can submit a motion to suspend the remainder of the sentence and to release him or her on probation. Until the court acts on the petition, the institutionalized inmate remains uncertain about how much more time he or she will spend in prison. This sanction is based on the premise that if offenders are given a taste of incarceration, this will be sufficient to shock them into law-abiding behavior, and they will be reluctant to violate probation or commit another crime.[53]

Split sentencing is also a standard feature in many states with intensive supervision programs. The split sentence had its beginning in the federal system and requires the probationer to serve a period of confinement. Intermittent confinement means weekend, night, or vacation confinement in jail during the time a person is on probation. More than 10 percent of probationers are now given split sentences. Split sentencing, like shock probation, is based on the premise that a short jail stay or an intermittent jail stay will shock the person into law-abiding behavior.

Both shock probation and split sentencing have received praise as ways to limit prison time, maintain family ties, reintegrate the offender into the community, reduce the costs of corrections, and reduce prison populations. It is argued that even a short jail or prison sentence will make offenders more receptive to the conditions of probation because it is a warning of what awaits them if probation is violated. However, there are those who argue that shock probation and split sentencing interfere with the purpose of probation, which is to provide offenders with a nonstigmatizing, community-based treatment. These critics argue that even a short-term institutional confinement subjects a person to the stigmatizing and destructive effects of confinement.

Residential Community Corrections Centers

The role of reentry to the community was traditionally supplied by the nonsecure **halfway house**. Its purpose was to be a point of reentry for paroled or soon-to-be paroled prison inmates. Inmates would spend the last few months of their confinement in these facilities, as they were given an opportunity to learn such skills as interviewing and acquiring suitable jobs, obtaining a place to live, and managing a checking account.

Halfway houses continue to serve as prerelease centers for inmates soon to be paroled, but they also serve as intermediate sanctions. The main types of halfway houses for probationers are called probation centers, restitution centers, county work-release centers, and therapeutic communities. These programs usually are reserved for probationers who are having problems adjusting to community supervision.

Residential community corrections centers have further served as residential pretrial release centers for offenders who require immediate need of social services before their trial and as halfway-back alternatives for probation and parole violators who get a last chance before being sentenced to a correctional institution. These

halfway house Prerelease centers for inmates and intermediate sanctions for probationers, they include probation centers, restitution centers, county work-release centers, and therapeutic communities.

residential community corrections centers Residential centers for offenders that frequently offer a last chance before an offender is sent to prison or a last chance for parole violators.

programs are sometimes used as a base from which offenders can be placed in drug and alcohol treatment programs, job training, and outpatient psychiatric facilities.

There are more than 1,800 state and federal community-based facilities in use today. In addition, more than 400 private programs operate in the United States. About half are used as halfway-back facilities for ex-offenders who have been released from prison, and the other half are true intermediate sanctions. Community-based residential treatment programs for drug users have also been increasingly developed.[54]

Some counties have established work-release facilities to provide more intensive services for offenders who need more than probation but less than prison. Finally, some therapeutic communities, particularly those in Minnesota, are reserved for offenders who have committed serious crimes. They are characterized by almost total reliance on in-house resources and confrontation groups (encounter groups and intensive attack therapies).

There has been a significant increase in the number and types of services purchased from private vendors operating group homes, halfway houses, and work-release programs. In addition to residential services for probationers and parolees, they sometimes offer programs to assist drug abusers, ex-offenders, and victims. Private agencies profit from being smaller operations and thus escaping some of the bureaucratic red tape that affects state residential programs. These programs depend on a variety of funding sources, including federal, state, local, and private foundations. Among these, Talbert House is well known for the high-quality services they offer to offenders.

Founded in 1965 in Cincinnati, Ohio, by a group of citizens who wanted to develop a better way of returning individuals to the community, Talbert House has expanded its services through the years. It now operates multiple service sites throughout Cincinnati for clients struggling with criminal victimization, chemical dependency, personal crisis, mental illness, and criminal justice issues. The services include prevention services, adolescent treatment, outpatient services for adult substance abuse, residential treatment for drug abuse, mental health services, a community corrections center, and residential programs for women offenders. Funding is typically a problem for private programs, but Talbert House receives support from agencies such as the Hamilton County Community Mental Health Board, Hamilton County Alcohol and Drug Addiction Services Board, Ohio Department of Rehabilitation and Corrections, Hamilton County Commissioners and Courts, United Way–Community Chest, and the city of Cincinnati–Neighborhood Services Division.

Lucy Nicholson/Reuters/Landov

Residential programs can offer a cost-saving alternative to prison. And some produce excellent results. Here, Tammy Fah, 48, is hugged by her son Matthew Stenger, 13, as she sits with Kathy Jamieson, 43, at the Prototypes residential treatment program in Pomona, California. Prototypes is part of the Second Chance Women's Reentry Court program, one of the first in the United States to focus on women. It offers an alternative to prison for women who plead guilty to nonviolent crimes and volunteer for treatment.

Delancey Street is another of the leading residential organizations for former substance abusers, ex-convicts, the homeless, and others who have hit bottom. Beginning in 1971 in San Francisco, it now also has centers in Los Angeles, New Mexico, North Carolina, New York, and Massachusetts. The minimum stay is two years, but the average resident remains for nearly four years—drug, alcohol, and crime free.

It has been difficult to obtain reliable evaluation data on residential facilities due to their varying programs, target populations, and treatment alternatives and goals. Some critics question their overall effectiveness, but the fact is that these programs appear to work for some types of offenders, and the approaches of some centers seem more effective than other settings. What may contribute to greater effectiveness with these programs is that instead of being used as a last resort before sentencing to incarceration in a jail or prison, residential community center placements might work more effectively with first-time offenders who have little experience with the criminal justice process; who are not users or addicted to drugs, especially crack cocaine; and who have a history of employment.[55]

Boot Camps

Boot camps began in adult corrections but in recent years have been more frequently used in juvenile corrections. When boot camps are used in adult corrections, they are usually first-time offenders in their late teens or early twenties who undergo rigorous physical and behavioral training for three to six months. Boot camps are designed to give offenders a sense of responsibility and accomplishments while improving self-discipline.[56] In a survey of boot camp programs, it was found that the typical pattern was the use of strict discipline, physical training, drill and ceremony, military bearing and courtesy, physical labor, and summary punishment for minor violations of rules. Boot camps originated in Georgia and Oklahoma in 1983 and at one time were offered by more than 30 states.

boot camp A military-style facility used as an alternative to prison in order to deal with prison crowding and public demands for severe treatment.

Critics are quick to say that boot camps present a number of disturbing issues:

- Journalistic accounts of boot camp celebrate a popular image of a dehumanizing experience marked by hard, often meaningless, physical labor. The inmate is portrayed as deficient and requiring something akin to being clubbed over the head to become "a man." This imagery is particularly troubling when it is remembered that the inmates are disproportionately minorities and underclass members.
- Why would a facility developed to prepare people to go into war be considered to have much potential in deterring or rehabilitating offenders?
- How do the aggressive treatment of residents and the insistence on unquestioning obedience to authority foster prosocial behavior?[57]

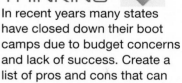

MYTH Boot camps work wonders because their military atmosphere and training help whip undisciplined offenders into shape and give them a sense of achievement and responsibility.

FACT There is growing disenchantment with boot camps. They don't seem to work and recidivism is quite high.

To some, boot camps are a failed panacea, and as a result of the growing pessimism about them, a number of states and the federal government have ended their boot camp programs. Nor have the studies of recidivism rates of boot camp graduates been encouraging—the rearrest rates of boot camp graduates are similar to those of prison inmates. Some corrections experts argue that the boot camp experience does not have a lasting impact because boot camps do not do enough to meet the needs of offenders.

While the future of boot camps is in doubt, there has been some interest in developing aftercare services for boot camp graduates to reduce the recidivism rates.[58] One boot camp in New York combines a military regimen with substance abuse counseling, community services, and high school equivalency classes. Upon release, the men and women in this program are required to participate in an intensive six-month aftercare program that provides them with a job and helps them stay employed. Nonetheless, the trend is for boot camps to be closed rather than opened or expanded.

CRITICAL THINKING 

In recent years many states have closed down their boot camps due to budget concerns and lack of success. Create a list of pros and cons that can be related to their success and failure. LO5

RESTORATIVE JUSTICE

LO6 Examine the relationship between restorative justice and intermediate sanctions

Restorative justice has recently been coupled with intermediate sanctions. Humanistic in its treatment of offenders, **restorative justice** has as its focus the welfare of victims in the aftermath of crime. In bringing criminal and victim together to heal the wounds of violation, the campaign for restorative justice advocates alternatives to incarceration, such as intensive community supervision. The most popular of the restorative strategies are victim–offender conferencing and community restitution. In many states, representatives of the victims' rights movement have been instrumental in setting up programs

restorative justice Focuses on the welfare of victims in the aftermath of crime.

VOICES ACROSS THE PROFESSION

To me, restorative justice is like ground water. You can't always see it, but it is always moving. And it will always find its way through because this work appeals to who we want to be in our best self.

Kay Pranis
Restorative Justice Planner

I am incredibly hopeful about this movement, and I do see it as a movement. It is not in isolation; there are movements happening in many fields that are along the same path and are congruent with restorative justice. I know that programs come and go, but the people who are involved in restorative justice make a shift in how they look at their work. And the people I see who make that shift do not go back. They take that way of thinking about how we relate with one another and how we respond to harm into whatever work they do.

To me, restorative justice is like ground water. You can't always see it, but it is always moving. And it will always find its way through because this work appeals to who we want to be in our best self. When you create space for people to be in touch with who they want to be in their best selves and you give them permission to bring that forward, that is a place where people want to stay.

in which victims/survivors confront their violators. Every state has a crime victim compensation commission or some agency with a similar name to perform this function.[59] In Voices Across the Profession, Kay Pranis tells why she feels sanctions in the community have the possibility of healing and restoration.

There are more than 1,000 restorative justice programs operating throughout North America and Europe, according to the international survey done by the Center for Restorative Justice and Peacemaking.[60] Included in this number are many programs operating inside U.S. prisons. On the international stage, the thrust for a restorative vision has been embraced through the role of the United Nations, which has created formal standards of guidelines for countries to use in restorative justice programming.[61] They encourage the use of restorative justice programming by member states at all stages of the criminal justice process.

Over the past 20 years, restorative justice has emerged as a different way for communities to respond to the harm caused by crime. Several definitions of restorative justice can be found, but at the heart of most of these definitions is the conviction that those most directly involved in a crime (individual victims, offenders, families of victims and offenders, and victimized communities) are those who should be central in responding to the harm caused by crime. The focus is more on repairing the harm that was done to victims by holding offenders directly accountable for their behavior than on the law that was broken.[62]

Restorative justice processes pay attention not only to the harm inflicted on the victims of a crime, but also to the ways the crime has harmed the offender and the community. The focus then is on victim healing, offender reintegration, and community restoration. This emphasis on victim healing has persuaded some to consider restorative justice to be a victim-centered approach. Yet the emphasis on providing offenders an opportunity to make amends and to increase their awareness of the consequences of their actions has persuaded others to regard restorative justice as offender-focused. It is the third emphasis, community restoration, that puts victim healing and offender reparation into perspective.

With its roots in the rituals of indigenous populations and traditional religious practices, restorative justice represents a growing international movement with a relatively clear set of values, principles, and guidelines for practice. Its purpose is to restore the torn fabric of community and wholeness to all those affected by crime, to repair the harm that was done to the victim and the community, and to make the offender accountable to all.[63] See Exhibit 4.3 for a success story of restorative justice.

Courtesy of Curt's Café

Curt's Café employs young adults in a training program that includes work, an hour of independent study, and a daily circle where they sit together and revisit their personal development. The program's success shows that restorative justice can work.

Restorative Justice Programs

While stressing accountability for offenses committed, restorative strategies operate with the goal of repairing injuries to victims and to communities in which crimes have taken place. Ross London, a former judge, prosecutor, and public defender, proposes that restoration, and particularly the restoration of trust, be viewed as the overarching goal of all criminal justice policies and practices. It is his opinion that punishment—far from contradicting the goal of restoration—is both essential to the victim and the community, and a necessary component for offenders' reintegration.[64]

Community conferencing and circle sentencing are vital parts of restorative justice programming. Whether these conferences occur

EXHIBIT 4.3

A Second Chance at Curt's Café

Curt's Café in Evanston, Illinois, is an unlikely crossroads for restorative justice to take place. Owner Susan Trieschmann hires at-risk young adults, particularly those with criminal records, providing them with hard-to-find job training and work experience. The nonprofit restaurant is one of the only adult ex-offender reentry programs in a city that focuses most of its reentry resources on at-risk youths.

Trieschmann says the road to opening the experimental business was far from smooth, with some neighbors concerned about the business drawing former criminals to the area. Still, it's an experiment that restorative justice advocates and even Evanston Mayor Elizabeth Tisdahl says is worth a shot.

"I've learned that our children have really hard lives, and I've learned that we don't handle it very well and that no child should have to go through what these kids go through," Trieschmann says. "And I don't know why it is. I don't know if it's the parents or the community, but their lives are not fair. I can only speak for myself, but I'm glad I stepped up when I did."

Curt's Café employs five to six young adults at a time for three-month training programs. Employees work eight-hour shifts, which include an hour of independent study and a daily circle in which they sit together and revisit their personal development and reentry experience.

Trieschmann says in addition to making the personal transition from a for-profit to nonprofit mindset, she faced challenges of training at-risk students and warming up her Central Street neighbors to the idea of a restorative justice restaurant. When Curt's Café was first proposed, she received some reports that a neighborhood group was concerned about the restaurant's concentration of ex-offenders. Only after meeting with Evanston police was Trieschmann able to explain her ambitions for the café and settle neighbors' qualms.

Still going strong, the menu features such specialties as Italian flatbread (prosciutto, fresh mozzarella, pesto, and arugula on pressed basil Tuscan bread) and the Mediterranean wrap (a tortilla filled with hummus, garbanzo salad, feta cheese, and spinach). The café's story has attracted a faithful clientele that swarms the counter during lunch hour. The employees' improvement has been significant, considering they struggled to make coffee at the end of the first week and were often late for work, Trieschmann says.

Northwestern sociology professor Mary Pattillo says the list of things ex-offenders need to successfully reintegrate into society is extensive, and the reentry process is made increasingly difficult when ex-offenders in many parts of the country are ineligible to live in public housing, receive many public sector benefits, or cast votes. Coupled with the stigma associated with having a criminal record, it can be difficult for ex-offenders to get jobs and become financially independent, she said.

"Those various forms of exclusion make it very difficult for people to get back on their feet," Pattillo says. "These are places that we need to make headway in actually reintegrating people rather than continuing their exclusion and stigma."

Sources: Susan Du, *The Daily Northwestern*, June 5, 2012, http://dailynorthwestern.com/2012/05/13/archive-manual/in-focus-a-second-chance-at-curts-cafe/ (accessed June 2014); Curt's Café, http://curtscafe.org/.

before, during, or after adjudication, they promote education and transformation within a context of respect and healing. These models are neither mutually exclusive nor complete in and of themselves. They can be combined or adapted depending on the special situation at hand.[65] Some of the most important initiatives are described in the sections that follow.

COMMUNITY CONFERENCING AND CIRCLE SENTENCING Community conferences make it possible for victims, offenders, and community members to meet one another to resolve issues raised by the offender's trespass.[66] A particularly promising form of community conferences is called circle sentencing. Historically, sentencing circles have their roots in U.S. native and Canadian aboriginal cultures. These circles were adopted by the criminal justice system in the 1980s as First Nations peoples of the Yukon and local criminal justice officials endeavored to build more constructive ties between the criminal justice system and the grassroots community. In 1991, Judge Barry Stuart of the Yukon Territorial Court introduced circle sentencing in order to empower the community to participate in the justice process.

One of the most promising developments in sentencing circles is the Hollow Water First Nation Community Holistic Healing Circle, which simultaneously addresses harm created by the offender, healing the victim, and restoring community goodwill. Circles have been developed most extensively in the western provinces of Canada. They have also experienced a resurgence in modern times among American Indian tribes, for example, in the Navajo courts. Today circles increasingly may be found in most mainstream criminal justice settings. In Minnesota, circles are used in many kinds of ways for a variety of crimes and in different types of settings.[67] A Hawaii minimum-security prison has a reentry restorative circles program that began in 2005.[68]

Participants in healing or sentencing circles typically speak out while passing around a "talking piece" (such as a feather or stone). Separate healing circles are initially held for the victim and offender. After the healing circles meet, a sentencing circle (with feedback from family, community, and the justice system) determines a course of action. Other circles then follow up to monitor compliance, which may involve restitution or community service.[69]

FAMILY GROUP CONFERENCES Growing out of both aboriginal and feminist approaches, family group conferences (FGCs) use a group decision-making model in order to try to stop family violence. The FGC made its mainstream criminal justice debut in New Zealand in 1989. It has been tested in Newfoundland and Labrador, as well as in communities in New Zealand, Austria, England and Wales, Canada, and the United States.[70] FGCs are used in many countries as a preferred sentencing and restorative justice forum for youthful offenders. Despite differences among jurisdictions, one common theme is overriding: family group conferences are more likely than traditional forms of dispute resolution to give effective voice to those who are traditionally disadvantaged.[71]

REPARATION AND RESTITUTION Often referred to as the "Vermont model" of reparative probation, this form of restorative justice can be implemented more quickly within existing structures and processes of the criminal justice system.[72] It involves a reparation programs track designed for offenders who commit nonviolent offenses and who are considered at low risk for reoffense. The reparative programs track mandates that the offender make reparations to both the victims(s) and the community. A reparative probation program, moreover, directly engages the community in sentencing and monitoring offenders, and depends heavily on small-scale community-based committees to deal with minor crimes. Reparative agreements are made between perpetrators and these community representatives, while citizen volunteers furnish social support in order to facilitate victim and community reparation.

RESTITUTION PROGRAMS Restitution is the most popular model of restorative justice. It enables in-kind or actual return of what has been lost to the victim. Restitution is best viewed within the larger context of "making amends." This includes the provision that the offender offers a sincere apology and promises to change the behavior that caused the initial injury. Ideally, restitution also encourages a move toward "balancing the scales" with a true spirit of generosity and forgiveness on both sides.[73] Victims identify and then seek redress for their losses, whether identified as material (damage to property), personal (bodily or psychological harm), or communal (injury to the quality of life of an entire community).

In many cases, offenders can offer individuals, families, or communities compensation for losses. Using a community justice focus, Ventura County, California, juvenile justice officials have implemented a successful program that emphasizes restitution as the key element of the reparative process. To compensate for material losses, youthful offenders in the South Oxnard Challenge Project offer various innovative types of financial or in-kind restitution to victims. The latter have included needed projects for victims, whether individuals or neighborhoods, such as painting a victim's garage, cleaning up graffiti, or working in an office reception area.[74]

VICTIM–OFFENDER CONFERENCING Introduced formally into the criminal justice arena in the 1980s, victim–offender conferencing encourages one-on-one victim–offender reconciliation facilitated through a mediator. Key issues include the utilization of co-mediators; the nature and duration of follow-up victim–offender meetings; the use of victim–offender mediation for more serious and violent offenses; and the implementation of victim–offender mediation in multicultural and prison settings. A growing body of empirical research worldwide reveals that successful victim–offender programs have been implemented in British Columbia and Ontario, Canada; Valparaiso, Indiana; Minneapolis, Minnesota; Quincy, Massachusetts; and Batavia, New York, as well as in Kettering, England, and Glasgow, Scotland.[75] Outcome research does indicate considerable satisfaction among both victims and offenders, although the question of recidivism looms. It remains to be seen how such programs can begin to be viewed with utmost seriousness by attorneys and judges as a viable alternative to traditional retributive justice procedures.

In evaluating the effectiveness of restorative justice practices using meta-analysis techniques, Jeff Latimer, Craig Dowden, and Danielle Muise compared restorative justice programs to traditional approaches to criminal behavior. They found that restorative justice programs were significantly more effective in terms of offender and victim satisfaction, restitution compliance, and recidivism. However, the authors noted that these findings must be tempered by an important self-selection bias inherent in restorative justice programs.[76]

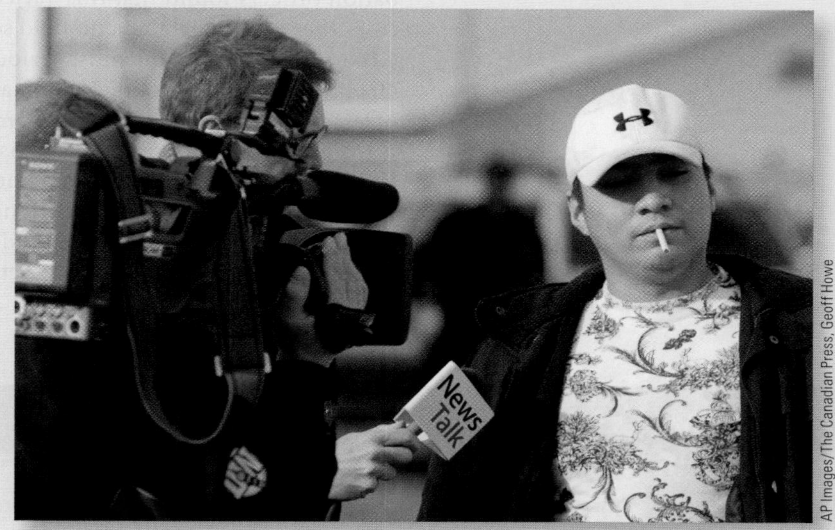

AP Images/The Canadian Press, Geoff Howe

Sentencing circles are a key program in restorative justice. They are used extensively in native Canadian communities. However, the recommendations are advisory and not binding. Here, Christopher Pauchay, the father of two toddlers found frozen to death in Yellow Quill reserve, leaves the Rose Valley, Saskatchewan, courthouse after pleading guilty to criminal negligence because he was drunk at the time the girls were left in the open. Saskatchewan Provincial Court Judge Barry Morgan heard recommendations from an aboriginal sentencing circle that suggested Pauchay should not go to prison but should be reunited with his wife and their other child. The group also recommended Pauchay receive drug and alcohol treatment, and assist elders with cultural and spiritual activities. Pauchay's wife made a passionate plea for the judge not to send her husband to jail. However, the judge decided against the sentencing circle recommendation in this case, saying that Pauchay lacked insight into his behavior and wasn't willing to accept responsibility for what happened.

Evaluate the effectiveness and future of intermediate sanctions **LO7**

Future of Intermediate Sanctions

Agreement is widespread that graduated sanctions hold the promise for increasing compliance to the conditions of the courts and for providing cost-effective crime control measures, usually without widening the net of the criminal justice system. In addition, they reduce the overreliance on incarceration, with its rising corrections costs. Moreover, the experiences of drug courts have revealed that this approach reduces rates of substance abuse.[77] A number of benefits have been attributed to graduated sanctions:

- *Certainty* because infractions of the behavioral contract are quickly discovered and sanctioned
- *Celerity* because the response to violations is swift
- *Proportionality* because the structured sanctions menu is designed to ensure that the level of punishment is commensurate with the severity of the criminal behavior
- *Progressiveness* because the structured sanctions menu is designed to result in increasingly stringent responses to continued violations[78]

In the midst of the wide praise that intermediate sanctions is receiving today, there has been criticism. Some experts are concerned that intermediate sanctions are expanding the net of the criminal justice system. Instead of reducing the number of those sentenced to prison, it is argued that intermediate sanctions are resulting in an expansion of the overall system. One study of sentencing recommendations of probation officers found that this varied by probation officers, but in two-thirds of the cases the intermediate sanction did serve a net widening (or net repairing) function.[79] Others contend that the most serious problems with intermediate sanctions are the 40 to 50 percent rates of revocation and subsequent incarceration, and the assignment of less serious offenders than program developers anticipated to these programs.[80]

The "net widening" criticism is particularly disturbing and must be addressed by the courts and policy makers. Enough research on the reduction of recidivism has been done on intermediate sanctions indicating what is needed to improve the quality of these programs. The needs and safety of victims are a further consideration. The future efficacy of intermediate sanctions certainly depends on these criticisms being taken seriously.

SUMMARY

LO1 Discuss the benefits of intermediate sanctions

Intermediate sanctions are a cost-saving alternative to jails and prisons; they help reduce prison crowding; they help serve the needs of offenders who are a low risk of recidivism and pose little danger to society; they can be used as a halfway-back strategy for probation and parole violators; and they help fill the void between routine probation and prison.

LO2 Describe the continuum of intermediate sanctions

The types of intermediate sanctions include intensive supervision of probation, restitution and fines, community service orders, day reporting centers, house arrest, electronic monitoring, halfway houses, drug courts, and boot camps. They can be divided into sanctions without incarceration (fines, forfeiture, and drug courts), sanctions as part of being placed on probation (community service orders, restitution, and intensive probation), and sanctions that include incarceration (shock probation and split sentencing).

LO3 Identify the sanctions that stand alone and what they contribute to intermediate sanctions

The sanctions that stand alone are fines, forfeiture, drug courts, and day reporting centers. They are widely used, especially drug courts and day reporting centers. They are not as restrictive as some of the other sanctions, but they provide opportunities to make changes and to become more law abiding.

LO4 Identify the sanctions as an add-on to probation and what they contribute to intermediate sanctions

These sanctions include restitution, community service orders, intensive probation, house arrest and electronic monitoring, and residential centers. These sanctions are added to probation because it is felt that these offenders need more restrictions. The hope is that offenders will become responsive and will not need to be sent or returned to prison.

LO5 Identify the sanctions that include incarceration and what they contribute to intermediate sanctions

These sanctions include shock probation and split sentencing, work release centers, and boot camps. All three of them involve incarceration: shock probation requires a prison sentence before being released on parole; work release centers' placements usually follow a term of incarceration; and boot camps involve high-stress physical training as a means to build self-discipline.

LO6 Examine the relationship between restorative justice and intermediate sanctions

The focus of restorative justice is to bring criminal and victim together to heal the wounds of violation and to advocate alternative methods of incarceration.

LO7 Evaluate the effectiveness and future of intermediate sanctions

The reviews of sanctions are mixed, but there seems to be general agreement that they are preferable to returning offenders to prison for technical violations of probation and that some offenders, especially drug offenders, appear to profit from these programs. The future appears to be promising for the increased use of intermediate sanctions.

CRITICAL THINKING QUESTIONS

1. Why are intermediate sanctions one form of punishment about which individuals with competing views can reach some agreement?
2. Of the various types of intermediate punishments, which one makes the most sense to you? How would you recommend expanding it?
3. Of the various types of intermediate punishments, which makes the least sense to you? What do you feel is needed to make it more acceptable?

NOTES

1. Mark Manke, "Falcons' Vick Indicted in Dogfighting Case," *Washington Post*, July 18, 2007.
2. Ibid.
3. "Federal Judge Rules Vick Can Keep More than $16 Million in Bonus Money," ESPN.com, February 5, 2008.
4. Orlando Ledbetter, "Vick Enters Guilty Plea, Gets Suspended Sentence," *Atlanta Journal Constitution*, November 28, 2008.
5. Bob Kent, "Mornhinweg Says Vick Will Play," PhiladelphiaEagles.com, September 24, 2009.
6. Anthony L. Hall, "Rehabilitation (and Vindication?) of Michael Vick," *IPINIONS Journal*, December 29, 2010.
7. Ibid.
8. Patricia M. Harris, Rebecca D. Petersen, and Samantha Rapoza, "Between Probation and Revocation: A Study of Intermediate Sanctions Decision-Making," *Journal of Criminal Justice* 29 (2001): 308.
9. *Tate v. Short*, 401 U.S. 395, 91 S.Ct. 668, 28 L.Ed.2d 130 (1971).
10. Pennsylvania Department of Corrections, "Day Fines, 2003."
11. William M. DiMascio, *Seeking Justice: Crime and Punishment in America* (New York: Edna McConnell Clark Foundation, 1995), p. 36.
12. Doris Layton MacKenzie, "Evidence-Based Corrections: Identifying What Works," *Crime and Delinquency* 46 (2000): 457–472; Census of State and Federal Correctional Facilities 2005 (Washington, DC: U.S. Department of Justice).
13. Steve Moffatt and Suzanne Poynton, "The Deterrent Effect of Higher Fines on Recidivism: Driving Offences," NSW Bureau of Crime Statistics and Research, New South Wales, Australia, 2007, http://www.bocsar.nsw.gov.au/agdbasev7wr/bocsar/documents/pdf/cjb106.pdf (accessed June 2014).
14. U.S. Treasury Department, "About Forfeiture."
15. John L. Worrall, "The Civil Asset Forfeiture Reform Act of 2000: A Sheep in Wolf's Clothing," *Policing* (2004): 220–240.
16. R. E. Bell, "The Confiscation, Forfeiture, and Disruption of Terrorist Finances," *Journal of Money Laundering Control* 7 (2003): 105–125.
17. John L. Worrall, "Addicted to the Drug War: The Role of Asset Forfeiture as a Budgetary Necessity in Contemporary Law Enforcement," *Journal of Criminal Justice* 29 (2001): 171–187.
18. Ibid.
19. R. B. Rubeck, J. N. Schaffer, and M. A. Logue, "The Imposition and the Effects of Restitution in Four Pennsylvania Counties: Effects of Size of County and Specialized Collection Units," *Crime and Delinquency* 50 (2004): 168–188.
20. *2001 Annual Report* (Atlanta: Georgia Department of Corrections, 2002).
21. Gail A. Caputo, "Community Service in Texas: Results of a Probation Survey," *Corrections Compendium* 39 (March/April 2005): 8–9.
22. Darren Gowen, "Overview of the Federal Home Confinement Program 1988–1996," *Federal Probation* 64 (December 2000): 11–18.
23. Robert Stanz and Richard Tewksbury, "Predictors of Success and Recidivism in a Home Incarceration Program," *Prison Journal* 80 (2000): 326–344.
24. Brian Payne and Randy Gainey, "The Influence of Demographic Factors on the Experience of House Arrest," *Federal Probation* 66 (2002): 64–70.
25. Gowen, "Overview of the Federal Home Confinement Program."
26. Brian K. Payne and Randy R. Gainey, "The Electronic Monitoring of Offenders Released from Jail or Prison: Safety, Control,

and Comparisons to the Incarceration Experience," *Prison Journal* 84 (December 2004): 413–435.
27. D. Gowen, "Remote Location Monitoring—A Supervision Strategy to Enhance Risk Control," *Federal Probation* 65 (2001): 38–41.
28. Ibid.
29. Jennifer Lee, "Some States Track Parolees by Satellite," *New York Times*, January 31, 2002, p. A3.
30. Ralph Gable and Robert Gable, "Electronic Monitoring: Positive Intervention Strategies," *Federal Probation* 69 (2005): 21–25.
31. Sudipto Roy, "Exit Status of Probationers and Prison-Bound Offenders in an Electronic Monitoring Home Detention Program: A Comparative Study," *Federal Probation*, December 2013, http://www.uscourts.gov/viewer.aspx?doc=/uscourts/FederalCourts/PPS/Fedprob/2013-12/index.html (accessed June 2014).
32. Payne and Gainey, "The Electronic Monitoring of Offenders Released from Jail or Prison: Safety, Control, and Comparisons to the Incarceration Experience."
33. Ibid., p. 415.
34. Ibid., p. 414; and J. Bonta, S. Wallace-Capretta, and J. Rooney, "Can Electronic Monitoring Make a Difference?" *Crime and Delinquency* 46 (2000): 61–75.
35. J. Robert Lilly, "Issues Beyond Empirical EM Reports," *Criminology and Public Policy* (February 2006): 93–101.
36. George Mair, "Electronic Monitoring: Effectiveness and Public Policy," *Criminology and Public Policy* (February 2006): 57–60.
37. Kathy G. Padgett, William D. Bales, and Thomas G. Blomberg, "Under Surveillance: An Empirical Test of the Effectiveness and Consequences of Electronic Monitoring," *Criminology and Public Policy* (February 2006): 61–91.
38. National Institute of Justice, *Specialized Courts* (Washington, DC: U.S. Department of Justice, 2013), http://www.nij.gov/topics/courts/pages/specialized-courts.aspx (accessed June 2014).
39. Ibid.
40. Ibid.
41. National Center on Addiction and Substance Abuse, *Behind Bars II: Substance Abuse and America's Prison Population* (New York: National Center, 2010).
42. John S. Goldkamp, "The Impact of Drug Courts," *Criminology and Public Policy* (March 2003): 198.
43. Candace McCoy, "The Politics of Problem-Solving: An Overview of the Origins and Development of Therapeutic Courts," *American Criminal Law Review* (Fall 2003): 1513–1534.
44. "In the Spotlight," *Drug Courts: Facts and Figures* (Washington, DC: National Criminal Justice Reference Service, 2011); Douglas B. Marlowe, David S. Festinger, Patricia A. Lee, Maria M. Schepise, Julie E. R. Hazzard, Jeffrey C. Merrill, Francis D. Mulvaney, and A. Thomas McLellan, "Are Judicial Status Hearings a Key Component of Drug Courts? During-Treatment Data from a Randomized Trial," *Criminal Justice and Behavior* 30 (April 2003): 142.
45. Adele Harrell, "Judging Drug Courts: Balancing the Evidence," *Criminology and Public Policy* (March 2003): 207–212.
46. Ibid.
47. Richard S. Gebelein, "The Rebirth of Rehabilitation: Promise and Perils of Drug Courts," National Institute of Justice, http://www.ncjrs.gov/pdffiles1/nij/181412.pdf (accessed June 2014).
48. For evidence of effectiveness of drug courts, see "GAO Highlights," *Adult Drug Courts: Studies Show Courts Reduce Recidivism but DOJ Could Enhance Future Performance Measure Revision Efforts* (Washington, DC: United States Government Accountability Office, December 2011).
49. Amy Craddock, "Estimating Criminal Justice System Costs and Cost-Savings Benefits of Day Reporting Centers," *Journal of Offender Rehabilitation* 39 (2004): 70–71.
50. James R. Brunet, "Day Reporting Centers in North Carolina: Implementation Lessons for Policymakers," *Justice System Journal* 23 (2002): 135–156.
51. Roy Sudipto, "Adult Offenders in a Day Reporting Center: A Preliminary Study," *Federal Probation* 66 (June 2002): 44–51; Roy Sudipto, "Factors Related to Success and Recidivism in a Day Reporting Center," *Criminal Justice Studies* (2004): 3–17. For a study with similar findings, see Liz Marie Marciniak, "Addition of Day Reporting to Intensive Supervision Probation: A Comparison of Recidivism Rates," *Federal Probation* 64 (June 2000): 34–39.
52. Christine Martin, Arthur J. Lurigio, and David E. Olson, "An Examination of Rearrests and Reincarcerations Among Discharged Day Reporting Center Clients," *Federal Probation* 67 (June 2003): 24–31.
53. The Ohio Department of Rehabilitation and Corrections evaluated shock probation for over two decades.
54. Michelle A. Lang and Steven Belenko, "Predicting Retention in a Residential Drug Treatment Alternative to Prison Program," *Journal of Substance Abuse Treatment* 19 (2000): 145–160; Eric J. Workowski, "Criminal Violence and Drug Use: An Exploratory Study Among Substance Abusers in Residential Treatment," in *Treating Substance Abusers in Correctional Contexts: New Understandings, New Modalities*, ed. Nathaniel J. Pallone (New York: Routledge, 2003), pp. 109–121.
55. Hung-En Sung and Steven Belenko, "Failure After Success: Correlates of Recidivism Among Individuals Who Successfully Completed Coerced Drug Treatment," *Journal of Offender Rehabilitation* 42 (2005): 75–97.
56. Faithe E. Lutze and Corney A. Bell, "Boot Camp Prisons as Masculine Organizations: Rethinking Recidivism and Program Design," *Rehabilitative Issues: Problems and Prospects in Boot Camp* (2005): 133–152; Edwin W. Zedlewski, "Alternatives to Custodial Supervision," National Institute of Justice, 2010, https://www.ncjrs.gov/pdffiles1/nij/grants/230401.pdf (accessed June 2014).
57. Merry Morash and Lisa Rucker, "A Critical Look at the Idea of Boot Camp as a Correctional Reform," *Crime and Delinquency* 36 (April 1990): 206.
58. Ojmarrh Mitchell, Doris L. MacKenzie, and Deanna M. Perez, "A Randomized Evaluation of the Maryland Correctional Boot Camp for Adults: Effects on Offender Antisocial Attitudes and Cognitions," *Rehabilitative Issues: Problems and Prospects in Boot Camp* (2005): 71–80; Brent B. Benda, Nancy J. Harm, and Nancy J. Toombs, "Survival Analysis of Recidivism of Male and Female Boot Camp Graduates Using Life-Course Theory," *Rehabilitative Issues: Problems and Prospects in Boot Camp* (2005): 88–96.
59. See Ross London, *Crime, Punishment, and Restorative Justice: From the Margins to the Mainstream* (Boulder, CO: Lynne Rienner, 2011); and John P. J. Dussich and Jill Schellenberg, eds., *The Promise of Restorative Justice: New Approaches for Criminal Justice and Beyond* (Boulder, CO: Lynne Rienner, 2011).
60. Mark Umbreit, *National Survey of Victim–Offender Mediation Programs in the United States* (St. Paul, MN: Center for Restorative Justice and Peacemaking, 2000). For a more updated international review, see Prison Fellowship International, http://www.pfi.org (accessed June 2014).
61. D. Van Ness, "UN Expert Meeting Recommends Declaration of Basic Principles on Restorative Justice," http://www.restorativejustice.org/articlesdb/articles/519 (accessed June 2014).
62. Mark S. Umbreit, Betty Vos, Robert B. Coates, and Katherine A. Brown, *Facing Violence: The Path of Restorative Justice and Dialogue* (Monsey, NY: Criminal Justice Press, 2003), p. 7. Also see articles at Prison Fellowship International, http://www.pfi.org (accessed June 2014).
63. Katherine Stuart van Wormer and Clemens Bartollas, *Women and the Criminal Justice System*, 3rd ed. (Upper Saddle River, NJ: Prentice Hall, 2011), pp. 165–186.
64. London, *Crime, Punishment, and Restorative Justice*.
65. Van Wormer and Bartollas, *Women and the Criminal Justice System*, p. 181.
66. Mark Umbreit, Sheryl Wilson, and Annie Roberts, "Restorative Justice for Victims, Offenders and Community," Center for Restorative Justice and Peacemaking, University of Minnesota, School of Social Work, January 2006.
67. G. Bazemore and M. Umbreit, *A Comparison of Four Restorative Conferencing Models*, U.S. Department of Justice, Office of Juvenile Justice and Delinquency Prevention (Washington, DC: U.S. Department of Justice, National Institute of Corrections, 2001).
68. Lorenn Walker, Ted Sakai, and Kat Brady, "Restorative Circles—A Reentry Process for Hawaii Inmates," *Federal Probation* 70 (2006): 33–37, 86.
69. Ibid.

70. J. Hudson, B. Galaway, A. Morris, and G. Maxwell, "Introduction," in J. Hudson et al., *Family Group Conferences: Perspectives on Policy and Practice* (Monsey, NY: Criminal Justice Press, 1996), pp. 1–16.
71. Van Wormer and Bartollas, *Women and the Criminal Justice System*, p. 181.
72. D. Karp and L. Walther, "Community Reparative Boards in Vermont: Theory and Practice," in *Restorative Community Justice: Repairing Harm and Transforming Communities*, ed. G. Bazemore and M. Schiff (Cincinnati: Anderson, 2001), pp. 199–217.
73. D. Van Ness and K. H. Strong, *Restoring Justice*, 2nd ed. (Cincinnati: Anderson, 2002).
74. Karp and Walther, "Community Reparative Boards in Vermont: Theory and Practice."
75. Umbreit, Vos, Coates, and Brown, *Facing Violence: The Path of Restorative Justice and Dialogue*.
76. Jeff Latimer, Craig Dowden, and Danielle Muise, "The Effectiveness of Restorative Justice Practices: A Meta-Analysis," *Prison Journal* (June 2005): 127–144.
77. Faye S. Taxman and Adam Geib, "Graduated Sanctions: Stepping into Accountable Systems and Offenders," *Prison Journal* 79 (1999): 182–204.
78. Ibid.
79. Robert J. Homant and Mark A. DeMercurio, "Intermediate Sanctions in Probation Officers' Sentencing Recommendations: Consistency, Net Widening, and Net Repairing," *Prison Journal* 89 (December 2009): 426–439.
80. Michael Tonry and Mary Lynch, "Intermediate Sanctions" in *Crime and Justice: A Review of Research*, ed. Michael Tonry (Chicago: University of Chicago Press, 1999), pp. 99–144.

Robert K. Hamilton/Baltimore Sun/MCT/Getty Images

Tavon White ran a drug-dealing gang in the Baltimore jail, aided by female correctional officers who helped him import drugs until the ring was discovered and indictments handed down. What would motivate a female correctional officer to get involved with a jailed gang leader and bear his child?

TAVON WHITE, AN INMATE IN THE BALTIMORE JAIL, had at least four women correctional officers who brought him anything he wanted—drugs, the latest cell phones, money, tobacco, and food. Over a period of four years, these four women allegedly bore him five children. One correctional officer had "Tavon" tattooed on her neck; another one had "Tavon" on her wrist.[1] White was a Baltimore member of the Black Guerilla Family (BGF) prison gang, and indictments released in April 2013 alleged that 14 Baltimore corrections officers assisted White and his gang in running a lucrative drug operation behind bars.[2] According to the indictment, BGF members were taught to target female correctional officers and recruit them into gang operations.[3] It is not surprising to Lt. Col. Kim Spadaro, president of the American Jail association and head of the Broward County (Florida) Department of Detention, that some female correctional officers get involved with make inmates. As she says: "In general, when the men do these things, [they] do it to make the money; the women do it because they've fallen in love."

While this story is disturbing, the great majority of female correctional officers working in jails and houses of correction approach the job as professionals involved in treatment and rehabilitation efforts and not gang activity. Nationwide, the number of women corrections officers is rapidly approaching parity with male officers. According to the American Correctional Association, more than a third of all jail officers are women.[4]

5

Jails and Houses of Correction

Erica Brough/Gainesville Sun/Landov

LEARNING OBJECTIVES

 LO1 Describe the history and development of the jail

 LO2 Identify the makeup of the jail population

 LO3 Discuss jail administration and structure

 LO4 Compare the new-generation jail with more traditional jails

 LO5 Describe jail-based treatment programs

 LO6 Recognize the legal and administrative issues of jail confinement

 LO7 Discuss the future trends of the jail

PREVIEW OF KEY CONCEPTS

jail
booking
first-generation jails
second-generation jails
new-generation jail
direct-supervision jails
OmniView Total Supervision (OVTS)
Prison Rape Elimination Act (PREA)

Describe the history and development of the jail LO1

ORIGINS OF THE JAIL

The local correctional center had its origin in medieval England. Although initially conceived as a place for detaining suspected offenders until they could be tried, jails gradually came to serve the dual purposes of detention and punishment. The English jail became an expression of the dominant authority of the county, which maintained control over the jails because the state had not developed its own institutions. The concept of the English jail was brought to Britain's colonies in North America soon after the settlers arrived from the Old World. The jail was used to detain individuals awaiting trial and those awaiting punishment. The stocks and pillory, and sometimes the whipping post, were usually located nearby. Instead of cells, the early colonial jails consisted of small rooms that housed up to 30 prisoners. An example of these early colonial facilities is the jail (gaol) at Williamsburg, Virginia, built in 1703–1704 (see Figure 5.1).

Prisoners in each county were placed under the jurisdiction of the sheriff, who fed and lodged them. A fee system was also used in the colonies in which inmates were required to pay for their own food and services, including wood and coal for heat; those who could not pay were fed scraps until they starved to death.[5] Jail conditions were deplorable because jailers ran them for personal gain. The fewer the services provided, the greater their profit. Early jails were catchall institutions that held not only criminal offenders awaiting trial but also vagabonds, debtors, the mentally ill, and assorted others. In fact, the most common reason for locking people in jails was unpaid debts, a practice that guaranteed the poor could never earn the money they owed. The New York legislature said in 1732 that "many poor persons may be imprisoned a long time for very small sums of money ... to the ruin of their families, great damage to the public who are in Christian charity obliged to provide for them and their families ... and without any real benefit to their creditors." Yet only in the 1830s did the United States begin to abolish debtors' prisons.[6]

Virginia established the first colonial jail, but it was the Pennsylvania jails established by reformer William Penn in the seventeenth century that later became the model for other states. Penn advocated that torture and mutilation as punishment for crimes be replaced with hard labor in houses of correction. Though not implemented in his lifetime, Penn's efforts left a mark on the laws of Pennsylvania. In 1773, the Walnut Street Jail was constructed in Philadelphia in which prisoners were employed in hard labor in the institution and released during the day to repair and clean streets and highways. The assumption was that hard work would build discipline and aid reform.

FIGURE 5.1

Jail (Gaol) at Williamsburg, Virginia, Built 1703–1704

Source: Marcus Whiffen, *The Public Buildings of Williamsburg* (Williamsburg, VA: Colonial Williamsburg Foundation, 1958).

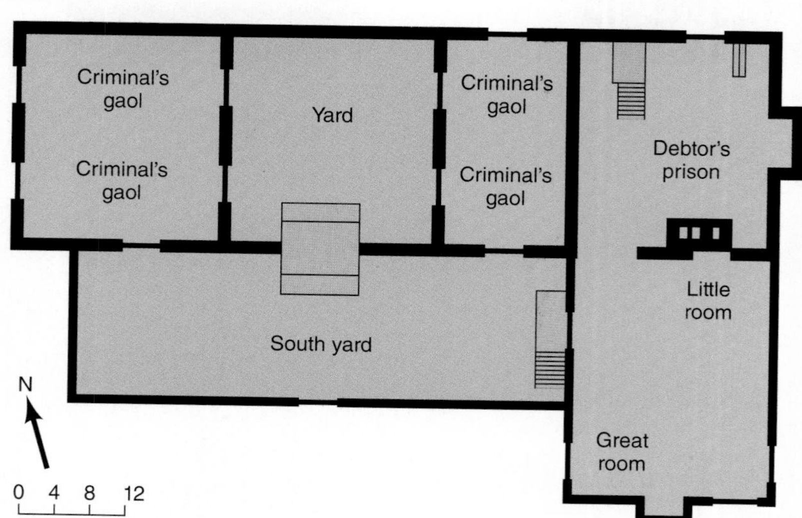

At the beginning of the nineteenth century, children, debtors, slaves, the mentally ill, and the physically ill were housed in jails, but as the century progressed, children and the mentally ill were more often sent to other institutions. Jails began to house both pretrial and posttrial prisoners; some jails also held felons as well as misdemeanants.

Walnut Street Jail in Philadelphia in 1799. The Walnut Street Jail was the first to use individual cells and to employ inmate work details.

MPI/Getty Images

CONTEMPORARY JAILS

From its early beginnings, the contemporary jail has been a social institution. It is generally located in the community, under the authority of a sheriff who must be politically elected, and is dependent on local funding.

Types of Local Correctional Institutions

The local or county level correctional center is a pivotal institution that touches the lives of more people than any other penal institution. The **jail** has a long reputation of being a problem, and there will continue to be charges of corruption and brutality. But fortunately, the culture of the jail is changing in a positive way. The Voices Across the Profession feature includes an interview with Dr. Arnett Gaston, who reflects on the new culture of the jail—one built on up-to-date facilities, able jail administrators, professionalism, and training of jail staff.

jail A facility that is authorized to hold pretrial detainees and sentenced misdemeanants for periods longer than 48 hours.

Each year millions of people enter local institutions, stay there for short periods of time, and then are replaced by more people who commit petty crimes and misdemeanors. Jails typically are used to detain people before trial who cannot make or afford bail. In addition to being intake centers for the entire criminal justice system, local correctional centers also serve as a place of first or last resort for individuals who belong in public health, welfare, and social service agencies.

There are three types of local correctional institutions:

- *Jails* have the authority to detain individuals for periods of 48 hours or longer; they also hold convicted inmates sentenced to short terms (generally a year or less) for petty offenses. Jails are usually administered by the county sheriff but are sometimes managed on a regional basis or, in a few cases, by the state or federal government.
- *Lockups*, sometimes called temporary holding facilities or police lockups, are

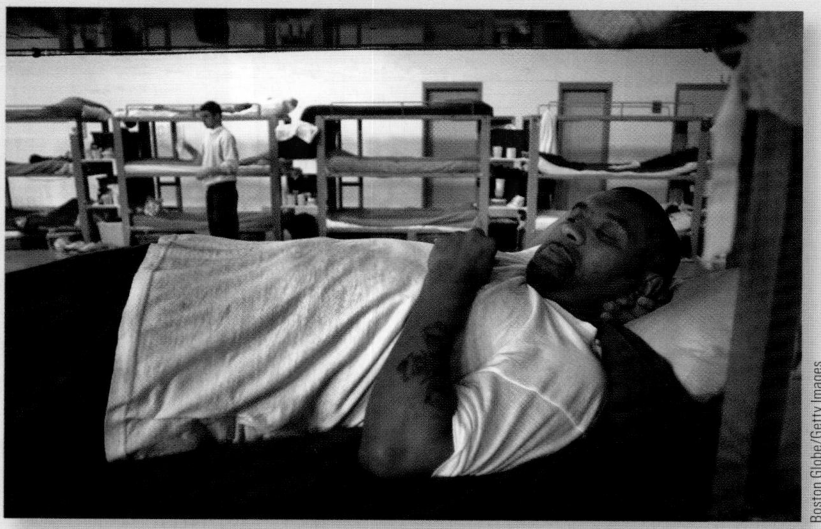

At the Norfolk House of Corrections in Massachusetts, inmate Zeferino Fortes is shown in his middle bed on a triple bunk. Like many other houses of correction, Norfolk is overcrowded, a condition that inhibits programs and rehabilitation efforts.

Boston Globe/Getty Images

© Arnett Gaston

VOICES ACROSS THE PROFESSION

We wound up reducing 78 percent of the violence through our facilities on and off the island.

Arnett Gaston
Former Commanding Officer, Rikers Island

Arnett Gaston worked in corrections for 38 years. He began as a uniformed officer in the old Tombs Prison in New York City, and has worked throughout the department. He served as a deputy commissioner and as a warden in two jails, one holding a population of 2,500 inmates and another facility having a population of 2,000 inmates. He then became chief of management planning. Gaston ended his career as commanding officer at Rikers Island, where he had 10 facilities under his command. Rikers Island is an extremely large institution, holding 18,000 prisoners and employing 11,000 staff.

"I was part of the restructuring of the Rikers Island jail complex. I was very much involved with what ultimately became known as the reformation of the policies and practices that led to the reduction of violence. First of all, we decided that the approach we were taking was out of date. We were reacting to violence in many instances with violence, and that really did not work. We determined to take a more preemptive and analytical approach where we would analyze the problem, try to look at certain strategies, develop operational plans and put them into operations, and evaluate their success or failure.

"We started analyzing how the events occurred, who were the victims, and who were the perpetrators or predators. We classified them into various categories. In essence, we developed a violence mapping strategy. Once we began to recognize that there were certain times of the day when certain instances began to happen in certain locations, we developed operational plans to correct that. We kept doing that everywhere we found the problem. As we were able to combat the violence, we put systems in place to minimize recurrence. We did this initially in one pilot facility and eventually extended it to all the island facilities. We wound up reducing 78 percent of the violence through our facilities on and off the island."

Arnett Gaston reminds us that competent jail administration is what is needed to improve the quality of what takes place in the jail, that a preemptive or proactive model can do much to reduce violence and other problems of the jail, and that many contemporary administrators are operating jails in a much more professional and humane fashion that serves to diminish the ghastly reputations for violence and the sordid conditions of jails, though much work still needs to be done. Inmate health care needs are often neglected, drug use commonplace, and violence an everyday event.

generally found in city police stations or precinct houses, and they hold persons for periods of less than 48 hours. Lockups have been traditionally used for those who are arrested for alcohol possession or intoxication. The inebriated are allowed to sober up before being released with a court date, a fine, or both.

- *Workhouses and houses of corrections*—operated by cities and counties and sometimes known as county prisons—hold convicted inmates sentenced to short terms. In New Hampshire and Massachusetts, a house of corrections holds convicted misdemeanants and a county jail holds pretrial detainees.

How correctional institutions arose, how they are structured today, and what services they provide are discussed in the following sections.

Characteristics

Contemporary jails have a number of characteristics:

- Most jails are small. Today there are about 1,500 jails with 1 to 49 beds, 1,300 jails with 50 to 249 beds, 500 jails with 250 to 999 beds, and fewer than 200 jails with more than 1,000 beds.[7] The physical size of the small rural jail may be a fraction of the size of the large urban jail, holding several thousand inmates.

- Jails are quite diverse. Jails vary according to the size of their operations, the problems they face, and the jail programs that are in place. The small rural jail with fewer than 50 inmates typically provides few programs. Because they are unable to provide mental health services for those in need and lack meaningful treatment programs, they often have problems with supervision of inmates. Jail operations in an urban setting such as Rikers Island or the Los Angeles County Jail are dramatically different from those found in a small suburban jail and even more different from a rural jail. But jails also differ in various parts of the United States and even within a single state. A metropolitan county jail holding 1,200 inmates and using the latest security technology may abut a rural jail built in the 1940s that only holds 65 inmates.
- The challenges they face vary from one jail to another. Urban jails sometimes must deal with overcrowding, violence among inmates and occasionally directed toward staff, the possibility of collective violence on the part of inmates, sexual victimization on the part of inmates, contraband being brought into the jail, and even corruption on the part of staff. Rural jails, on the other hand, generally lack programming for inmates, sometimes do not have adequate staffing, may have inadequate facilities, and are likely to have less than satisfactory suicide prevention policies in place. Accordingly, an inmate may be admitted to a rural jail who is clearly a suicide risk and still may be able to commit suicide because the lack of staffing prevents adequate supervision (frequent cell checks).

Lucas Jackson/Reuters /Landov

Inmates of Rikers Island Correctional Facility hug each other during a service held the day before Christmas in 2013. Things are not always as tranquil among the 12,000 inmates being held in the facility. Correctional officers have been accused of maintaining a "fight-club culture," deputizing experienced thugs and allowing them to beat and rob overmatched, weaker teens. It's the way they maintain order without having to use force and endanger their careers. The system, called the Program, first came to light in 2009, after the beating death a year earlier of 18-year-old Christopher Robinson, who was being held on a parole violation.

Functions

Contemporary jails have a number of functions and hold a variety of different types of offenders, including the following:

- Pretrial detainees who cannot afford or were denied bail or prerelease and who are held until their trial or disposition of their case. Some of these offenders may be accused of committing serious or vicious crimes in the community and may be high-profile cases.
- Convicted offenders who are housed in jail for periods of less than one year. These offenders may be gang related, sexual predators, or vulnerable to more aggressive inmates. A culture may develop that can generate racial conflict, gang domination, conflict among gangs, drugs in the institution, or corruption among staff, especially in large urban jails.
- Convicted offenders awaiting sentences; these offenders may be federal, state, or local prisoners.
- Misdemeanants, drunks, and the mentally ill. It is this group that seems to have more difficulty adjusting to the jail. The mentally ill especially may have considerable difficulty with jail adjustment.

- Mandatory arrests for drunken driving, known across the nation as DWI (driving while intoxicated), DUI (driving under the influence), or OMVI (operating motor vehicle while intoxicated). This group does much better in a police lockup than in a regular jail setting.
- Inmates being held on retainer warrants from other states.
- Probation, parole, and bail-bond violators and absconders.
- Temporarily detained juveniles pending transfer to juvenile authorities. Historically, this was the group vulnerable to sexual exploitation by adult jail inmates, but as juvenile jail populations have declined they are better able to be separated from the adults and, as a result, better protected than in the past.
- Witnesses who are in protective custody or being held prior to trial. These individuals must be carefully protected, both in terms of their identity and in terms of being assaulted or killed by inmates who are informed from the streets "to take them out."
- Those held for contempt of court.
- Inmates about to be released after completing their prison sentence.
- Jails may be used by the military for military police detainees until it is possible to transfer the convicted to a military correctional facility.
- The courts sometimes place individuals in jail who are found in contempt of court.[8]

booking The process of admitting an arrestee or sentenced misdemeanant to jail.

Taken together, the criminal justice system would have difficulty, perhaps an impossibility, of functioning without the contemporary jail. The jail is needed for so many functions that the system would come to a standstill and be thrown into chaos without the jail.

CRITICAL THINKING

Does the United States arrest and detain too many people? Should we build more jails to handle different populations such as juvenile offenders and drug offenders who have not committed other crimes? What should they look like, how should they be run?

Initial Booking and Classification

Jails usually have a central area for **booking**, admitting, and releasing inmates. Deputy sheriffs or police officers bring arrested offenders to the jail, where they are identified and fingerprinted, and their property is inventoried and stored. If they are there for a misdemeanant offense, they may be quickly released on bond. These offenders sit in an unsecured part of the jail booking area until someone comes to post their bond. But if arrested for a felony, they will have to wait until an initial appearance before a magistrate to see if they are granted bail. They are placed in a general holding area within the jail, where they are housed with other offenders.

MYTH: All people, even dangerous felons, are entitled to pretrial release on bail.

FACT: Preventive detention statutes have been created that deny bail to dangerous defendants who are charged with serious crimes or are thought likely to escape. These defendants are generally held in jail until trial.

Those not released on bond or personal recognizance are first placed in a secure housing unit until they can be interviewed, and some preliminary information is collected regarding their crime and past criminal history. The purpose of this classification process is to identify the dangerousness and risk of the offenders and to determine whether they should be separated from other offenders. Furthermore, such major problems as a need for detoxification or potential for suicide are identified and considered in their assignment of housing. Once they are classified, they are moved to the most suitable housing area.

The jail has developed into a complex correctional institution serving various kinds of inmate populations.

Identify the makeup of the jail population

JAIL POPULATIONS

About 785,000 inmates are held in jails today, mostly pretrial detainees being held in the nation's largest counties. After decades of steep increases in the nation's jail populations, inmate levels have begun to stabilize and even decline in some jurisdictions. Nonetheless, there are still about 230 per 100,000 U.S. residents incarcerated in county jails.[9] (See Figure 5.2.)

FIGURE 5.2

Persons Held in Jail

Source: Minton Jail Statistics 2011 (Washington, D.C.: U.S. Department of Justice, 2012).

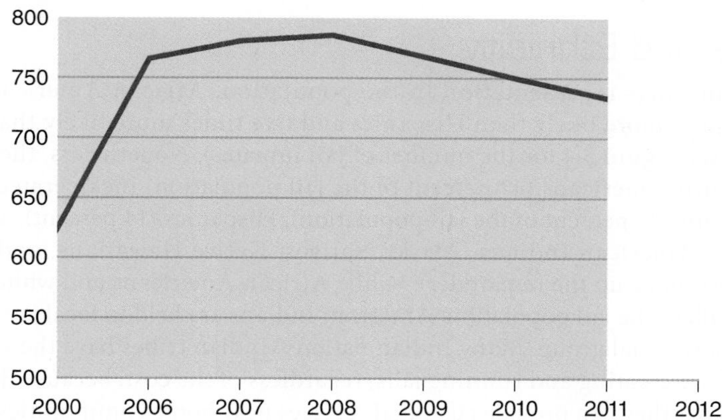

Considering reform efforts and the declining crime rate, why did jail populations increase in this period? There are a number of reasons for this phenomenon. As prisons become more overcrowded, correctional officials use local jails to house inmates for whom there is no room in state prisons. Jail populations also respond to the efforts being made to reduce or control particular crime problems, including substance abuse, spousal abuse, and driving while intoxicated (DWI). Some jurisdictions have passed legislation requiring that people arrested on suspicion of domestic violence be held in confinement for a number of hours to "cool off" before becoming eligible for bail. Other jurisdictions have attempted to deter drunk driving by passing mandatory jail sentences for people convicted of DWI; such legislation can quickly result in overcrowded jails. The recent decline in the actual number of jail inmates may signal an end to growth in the inmate population. Perhaps the decade-long downturn in the crime rate has begun to impact the number of people in jail.

Age

The number of juveniles held in jail peaked at about 10,000 in 1999 and then began a decade-long decline; today there are about 4,600 kids being held in adult jails. The number of juveniles held in jails has declined primarily because of the Juvenile Justice and Delinquency Prevention Act (JJDPA), which grants federal money to cities and states that agree not to confine juveniles in jail. In contrast, the population of elderly jail inmates has more than doubled in size during the past decade. Elderly inmates bring with them their own set of problems, such as the economic challenge of providing health care at a time when state and local budgets are being squeezed.[10]

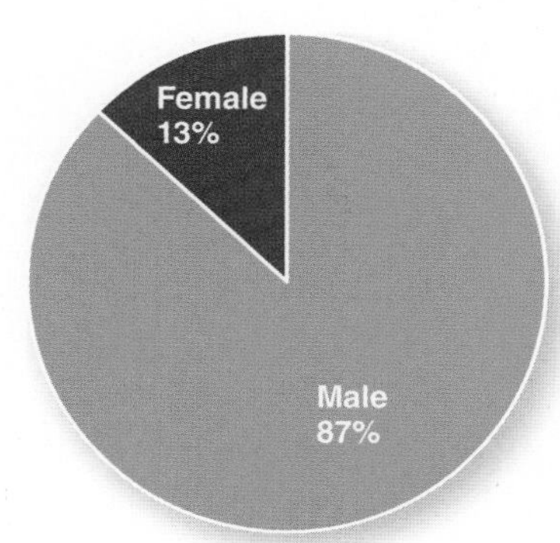

FIGURE 5.3

Percent of Jail Population by Gender

Source: Minton Jail Statistics 2011 (Washington, D.C.: U.S. Department of Justice, 2012).

Gender

Male inmates far outnumber females, though the disparity is narrowing somewhat. In 2000, about 90 percent of jail inmates were male; today, males make up about 87 percent of the jail population (see Figure 5.3). More than 100,000 women are now incarcerated in jails. There are also racial disparities in the female jail populations: African American and Hispanic females are more likely to receive jail sentences than are white female inmates.[11]

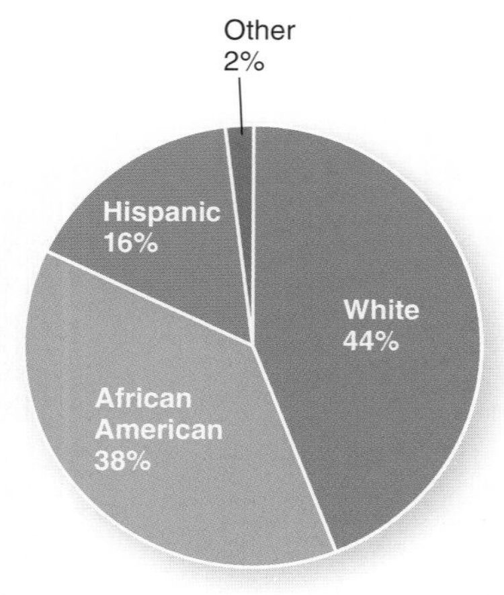

FIGURE 5.4

Jail Population by Race and Ethnicity

Source: Minton Jail Statistics 2011 (Washington, D.C.: U.S. Department of Justice, 2012).

Female jail inmates face many challenges. The majority of them have children who are dependent on them, and housing is frequently an issue when they are released from jail confinement. Most come from significantly disadvantaged backgrounds. Many have suffered abuse and severe economic disadvantage. One study of 100 female inmates found extremely high rates of lifetime trauma exposure (98 percent), current mental disorders (36 percent), and drug/alcohol problems (74 percent).[12]

Race and Ethnicity

Based on their representation in the population, African Americans are almost three times more likely than Hispanics and five times more likely than whites to be in jail (see Figure 5.4 for the number of jail inmates). Nonetheless, there are actually more Euro-Americans (47 percent of the jail population) incarcerated than African Americans (35 percent of the jail population), Hispanics (14 percent), and other races (Asians, American Indians, Alaska Natives, Native Hawaiians, and other Pacific Islanders make up the remainder). While African Americans and whites make up the great bulk of the jail population, American Indians are held in local jails at the highest rate of any racial group. Many Indian nations (Indian tribes have the sovereignty of a nation) are creating and running jails, regardless of the cost, because they have determined that they can provide custodial services near home communities.

Social Class

Despite bail reform efforts, the poor are still the group least likely to make bail, the ones most likely to commit petty offenses, to have mental health issues, to be considered flight risks, and to be unable to afford restitution. It is not surprising, then, that they remain overrepresented in jail populations. Criminologist John Irwin contends that, more than anything else, jails are "dumping grounds for the poor" and catchalls for uneducated, unemployed, homeless, and impoverished offenders. He refers to these disorderly and disorganized persons as "rabble" and contends that the jail was invented and continues to be operated in order to manage society's rabble.[13] One study found that Irwin's "rabble" theory may be overstated, but the fact still remains that the jail is a social institution in which the poor are overrepresented.[14]

The jail population is made of those who are seen as nuisance in the community, such as the homeless, or those who have mental health issues and no other placement is possible. They tend to be victims in jail and have difficulty protecting themselves. The mentally ill offenders may have committed no crimes but still find themselves in jail. It is not that unusual to hear a mentally ill inmate scream or cry hour after hour.

Adjustment to Jail

The jail climate is critical to the adjustment of inmates and the quality of work experience for staff. If staff and inmates are getting along, inmates are following the regulations and procedures, and rule violations and violence are at a minimum, the jail climate is much different than in a negative environment in which the jail is ripe for a disturbance, riot, or hostage situation.[15] In some jails, especially large urban ones, pretrial confinement is disruptive and traumatic, especially for a person who has not been to jail before. In this culture, the strong prey on the weak, and an adequate adjustment to jail requires that inmates have the ability to protect themselves. Self-protection becomes particularly challenging if an inmate is not connected to a gang.

Most detained prisoners live in an uncertain world. The uncertainties of jail include questions about the length of confinement, chances of obtaining pretrial release, and the results of the court process. Jail inmates also must deal with inactivity and boredom. The collective impact of the jail environment can lead to tension, anxiety, alienation, and guilt. If not handled in constructive ways, the stress of jail confinement can escalate to crisis proportions, resulting in psychological breakdowns.

JAIL ADMINISTRATION AND STRUCTURE

LO3 Discuss jail administration and structure

The most important features defining how jails function consist of the type of jail administration, the variation in size of other characteristics, the supervision of inmates, and the commitment to programs. County sheriffs usually have operational responsibility for the jails. In some jails, the programs that are offered are quite impressive; in other jails, especially small ones, programs may be few or nearly nonexistent.

Local and State Administration and Politics

In more than 3,000 counties in the United States, the sheriff runs the jail. A major problem with this means of jail administration is that sheriffs are politically accountable to county voters, so jails are one of the most political institutions in adult corrections. Sheriffs have received a lot of criticism for their jail administration. Some of the criticism may be deserved, but they also are criticized for things over which they have little control—for example, there may be totally inadequate jail facilities, but the sheriff is unable to get enough money to repair them or build a new facility.

However, there are increasing numbers of sheriffs who are attempting to run their jails in a professional way. They have been willing to implement the minimum standards for local jails and detention facilities developed by the National Sheriffs Association. As illustrated by the career of Arnett Gaston earlier in this chapter, they use good management techniques, develop effective staff training, and do everything in their power to make the jail into a humane institution for short-term detainees. They also attempt to anticipate or prevent problems before they take place.

Jail Administrative Alternatives

There are three alternatives to local control of jails:

- *State-run jails.* Four states (Connecticut, Delaware, Rhode Island, and Vermont) currently have full operational responsibility for jails. Except for five locally operated jails, Alaska, too, has a state-operated jail system. Although state-run jails offer greater operational efficiency than locally operated jails, political opposition by the counties is one important reason why more states are not likely to select this approach.
- *Cooperative (regional) arrangements.* A widely used alternative to local or state control is regional or multicounty arrangements. Kentucky, Virginia, West Virginia, North Dakota, South Dakota, Nebraska, and Kansas were the first states to adopt regional jails. This arrangement typically takes place when a jurisdiction with an adequate jail is willing to contract with neighboring cities and counties to house prisoners on a per diem basis or when a group of local governments decides that no existing facility is adequate and then decides to build a new regional jail or "detention center." Furthermore, local governments may decide to specialize and house different populations, such as juveniles, females, pretrial detainees, or convicted felons awaiting transportation

CORRECTIONAL LIFE

Chris: You're in Jail

I was in the largest jail lockup in the United States, the Los Angeles County Jail. This jail is a cement monolith that houses in excess of 1,000 men on any given day. Over 50 percent of the 150,000-plus inmates in California's 33 prisons originated from Los Angeles County. This jail is affectionately known throughout the state as the "concrete jungle." It houses the most dangerous lockups in the state, if not the country. L.A. County is a training ground for young L.A. gang members. It's where they earn their "bones"—that is, it is where they stab rival gang members and show their "homies" that they are "down" and willing to die for the clique, the gang. For the unaffiliated inmates that are not in gangs, L.A. County is a treacherous maze. Civility is taken as a weakness. Like prison, the use of violence is the only way to gain respect. You either learn to fight and defend your person, or become a victim who is mentally and physically abused. There is no middle ground. The culture is primitive. Rehabilitation or redemption doesn't figure into the equation. Life in the concrete jungle is all about survival.

to state prisons. Transportation problems, multi-jurisdiction funding problems, and turf disputes limit or prohibit the even wider use of cooperative arrangements among local governments.

- *State-subsidized programs.* State subsidies provide a third way to reach beyond locally operated jails, with their politics and financial constraints. Almost 60 percent of the states provide technical assistance to local governments having jail problems, and about 50 percent provide training for jail personnel. In addition, some subsidy programs assist jails in complying with state standards and in making capital improvements ordered by courts.

In addition to state and local control, there has been some effort to turn jails over to private management.

Compare the new-generation jail with more traditional jails

TYPES OF JAIL SUPERVISION AND SURVEILLANCE

The four generations of jail supervision are the linear/intermittent surveillance of inmates, the indirect or podular/remote surveillance of inmates, the direct or podular/direct supervision of inmates, and the new OmniView Total Supervision (OVTS). The supervision of inmates varies in each type of supervision. See Exhibit 5.1, which compares the four generations of jail supervision and examines the differences in supervision.

EXHIBIT 5.1

Types of Supervision in Jail

	Characteristics of Supervision	Evaluation
First-generation jails	From time to time, staff tour the long row of cells in this linear design. Supervision consists of staff peeking into cells. Staff–inmate interaction takes place through bars.	The weakness of this design is found in the inability of staff to see more than one or two cells at a time. This weakness results in high rates of sexual and physical assaults, suicides, and unexpected medical emergencies.
Second-generation jails	These jails are designed to provide indirect or remote surveillance. Supervision is indirect because the officers' station is inside a secure room which is separated from the inmates' living area. Observation takes place through protective windows in front of a console or desk. Microphone and speakers in the living area permit officers to hear and speak with inmates.	The problems with this supervision is that while staff can observe activity in the day room, they are unable to respond quickly to problems. In this form of supervision, consistent with first-generation jails, inmates and staff are separated.
New-generation jails	This is a direct-supervision model which places the correctional officers' station within the inmates' living area or pod, which means that officers can speak with and see inmates. During the day, inmates stay in the day room or open area. Typically, they need permission to go into their cells, and if they do, they must return quickly.	Direct-supervision jails offer many advantages, including effective supervision of inmates; improved communication between staff and inmates; safety of staff and inmates; and improved classification and orientation of inmates.
Fourth-generation jails	The OmniView Total Supervision (OVTS) jail has a centrally placed high-strength mirrored glass control center with a panoramic view that provides 100 percent surveillance of the entire living access facility. The complete interior of the cell units, recreation area, stairwells, entryway, and multipurpose rooms are totally visible.	A major advantage of this supervision is that it establishes zero-tolerance for incidence of inmate rape. It can be utilized in single, double, or multiple occupancy cells without any loss of total supervision, which promises increased security as well as operation cost savings for all classification needs. A disadvantage of this type of supervision is the lack of privacy for inmates (they are constantly being watched).

First-Generation Jails: Linear/Intermittent Surveillance

First-generation jails are designed to provide linear/intermittent surveillance of inmates, which involves staff providing supervision of inmates from time to time as they tour the linear cellblocks (see Figure 5.5). A typical first-generation jail has inmates living in dormitories or multiple-occupancy cells. In this model, staff–inmate interaction usually takes place through bars. The layout is similar to that of a hospital in which long rows of rooms open onto a corridor. Electronic surveillance has been used to compensate for the weakness of the linear design. But officers monitoring banks of video screens find it difficult to maintain effective watchfulness because of preoccupation with other activities, having to view too many cameras, and fatigue. Management in first-generation jails assumes that they hold violent inmates who express their rage by victimizing each other, assaulting staff members, destroying property, and attempting to escape. Nonetheless, because officers can usually see into only one or two cells at a time, these facilities experience high rates of inmate sexual assaults, fights, suicides, accidents, and unexpected medical emergencies.[16]

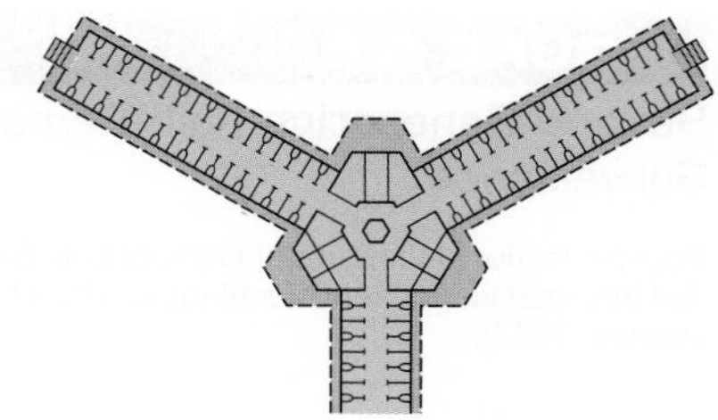

FIGURE 5.5
First-Generation Jail: Intermittent Surveillance

Source: National Institute of Corrections, *Direct Supervision, Jail Informative Packet* (Washington, DC: U.S. Department of Justice, 1993).

first-generation jails Focus on staff providing linear/intermittent surveillance of inmates, which they do by patrolling the corridors and observing inmates in their cells.

second-generation jails Staff use remote supervision as they remain in a secure control booth surrounded by inmate pods or living areas.

new-generation jail A facility with a podular architectural design that emphasizes the interaction of inmates and staff.

Second-Generation Jails: Indirect/Remote Surveillance

Second-generation jails are designed to provide indirect or podular/remote surveillance. Because the officers' station is inside a secure room and separated from the inmates' living area, supervision is indirect. Observation is enabled through protective windows in front of a console/desk. Microphones and speakers inside the living unit permit officers to hear and communicate with inmates (see Figure 5.6). This approach gives rise to several problems:

- Although the staff can observe activity in day rooms, they are unable to respond quickly to problems.
- If a problem occurs in a pod, the officer has to call "out front" for assistance.
- The flow of information between officers and inmates is drastically reduced.
- On-duty staff often overlook minor infractions because they believe it is not worth the trouble to call for assistance.
- Staff lacks knowledge of individual inmates and thus has to make guesses about levels of stress when trouble seems to be brewing in the pod.[17]

This form of jail construction, as with first-generation jails, has the basic problem that inmates and staff are separated.

AP Images/Reed Saxon

Traditional, first-generation jails are known for their violence and brutality. In Los Angeles County, sheriff's deputies inspect a cell block at the Men's Central Jail in downtown Los Angeles. In the wake of allegations that a culture of violence flourished in the jail, reform efforts have been undertaken to reduce conflict.

New-Generation Jail: Direct Supervision

The **new-generation jail**, or direct-supervision model, originated at three metropolitan correctional centers (MCCs) operated by the Federal Bureau of Prisons in the early 1970s, and is based on the direct or podular/direct supervision of inmates, a method that uses the physical

FIGURE 5.6

Second Generation Jail: Remote Surveillance

Source: National Institute of Corrections, *Direct Supervision, Jail Informative Packet* (Washington, DC: U.S. Department of Justice, 1993).

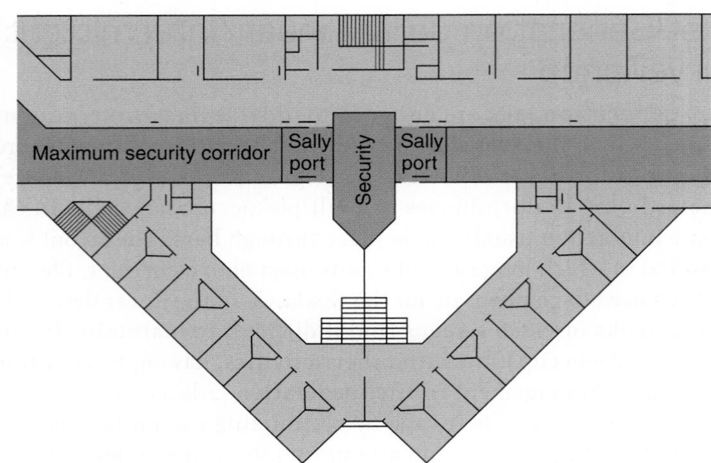

CRITICAL THINKING

Which generation of jail supervisions is the most appropriate for the types of offenders that we incarcerate the most? LO5

plant to manage the jail population. Increasingly popular, there are nearly 500 new-generation jails currently being employed around the United States (see Figure 5.7).[18]

Richard Werner identified five components that structure the new-generation model:

- To create a new understanding of the role of the officer in the institution
- To take officers out of control rooms and place them in living areas where they could interact directly with inmates
- To implement decentralized, small living units (functional unit management)
- To promote the use of noninstitutional environments
- To define this new system and to identify its management principles[19]

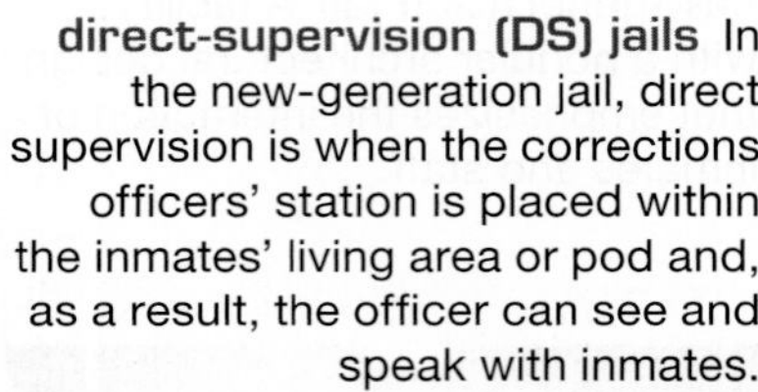

direct-supervision (DS) jails In the new-generation jail, direct supervision is when the corrections officers' station is placed within the inmates' living area or pod and, as a result, the officer can see and speak with inmates.

Direct-supervision (DS) jails place the correctional officers' station within the inmates' living area, or pod, which means the officer can see and speak to inmates. During the day, inmates stay in the open area (day room). Generally, they are not permitted to go into their cells except with permission. If they do so, they must quickly return. The officer controls door locks to cells from the control panel. He or she also carries a small radio worn on the front of the shirt that permits immediate communication with other jail staff if the need arises. In addition, the day room is covered by a video camera monitored in the central control room.

Direct supervision offers many advantages: effective control and supervision of inmates; improved communication between staff and inmates; safety of staff and inmates; manageable and cost-effective operations; improved classification and orientation of inmates, especially programming for specialized offender groups; staff ownership of operations; and the ability to shut a pod down when populations are low.

However, there are also some disadvantages with this model, including the difficulty of selling the jail to a public that tends to see the layout as a means of "coddling" prisoners, the amount of training needed to make the transition to the new style of supervision, and the fact that the overcrowding issue makes this design hard to implement.[20] Christine Tartaro's examination of a national survey of new-generation jails

FIGURE 5.7

Direct-Supervision Jail

Source: National Institute of Corrections, *Direct Supervision, Jail Informative Packet* (Washington, DC: U.S. Department of Justice, 1993).

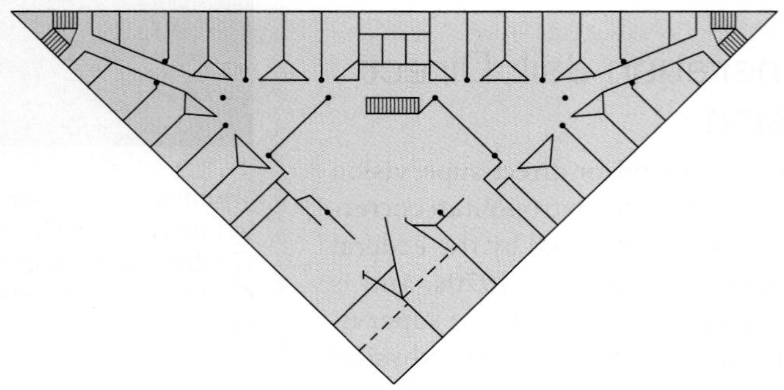

found that many of these jails fail to include important components of the ideal direct-supervision jails, such as normalized living environments, in their facilities.[21]

Yet national surveys further show that direct-supervision jails are an effective means of inmate management and have been accepted as best practice by agencies at the federal, state, and local levels and by accrediting organizations. Direct-supervision facilities are consistently perceived by staff and inmates to have safe environments and experience fewer violent or security-related incidents than traditional jails.[22]

Joel Gordon

New-generation jails feature more direct contact between correctional officers and inmates and a greater degree of supervision and control. Here, a corrections officer watches inmates from the control desk in a podular cellbock in the female facility at the Orange County (Florida) Jail.

Fourth-Generation Jail: Total Supervision

The **OmniView Total Supervision (OVTS)** jail and prison is a concept that is being utilized in several locations. The OVTS incarceration facility encompasses a centrally placed, high-strength mirrored glass control center with a panoramic view that provides 100 percent surveillance of the entire inmate access facility. The complete interior of the cell units, recreation area, stairwells, entryway, and multipurpose rooms are totally visible.[23]

This new correctional facility design complies with the **Prison Rape Elimination Act (PREA)** in that it establishes a zero-tolerance standard for the incidence of prison rape in U.S. prisons. The design of the OVTS cell can be utilized in single, double, or multiple occupancy cells without any loss of total supervision, which promises to provide increased security as well as increased operational cost savings for all classification needs (see Figure 5.8).

OmniView Total Supervision (OVTS) An incarceration facility that has a centrally placed, high-strength mirrored glass control center with a panoramic view that provides 100 percent surveillance of the entire facility.

Prison Rape Elimination Act (PREA) A program dedicated to collecting national prison rape statistics, data, and conducting research; a program dedicated to the dissemination of information and procedures for combating prison rape; a program to assist in funding state programs.

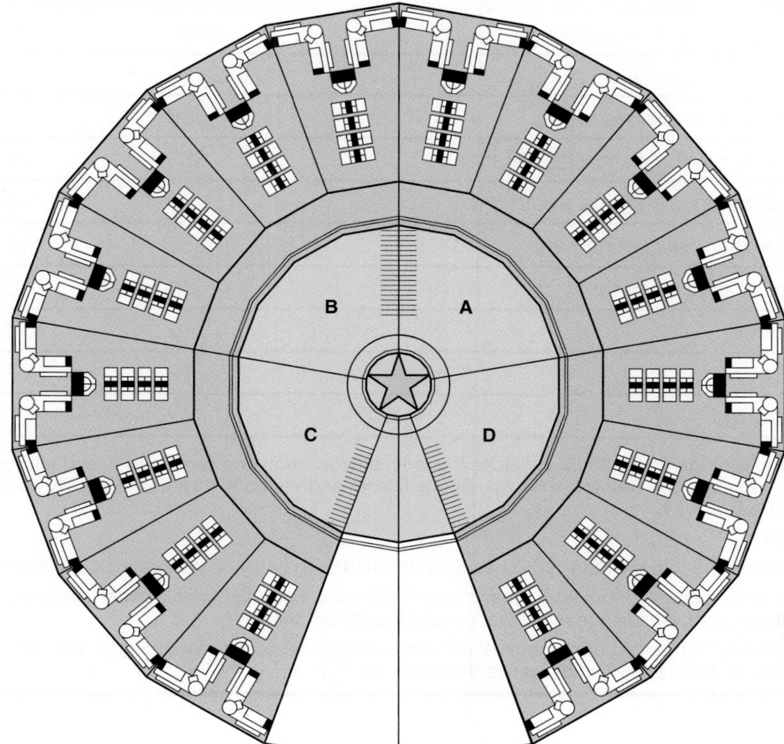

FIGURE 5.8

OmniView Total Supervision

Source: Comparison of Incarceration Supervision Types: Final Analysis, www.radialomniview.com/pdf/scan0002.pdf (accessed March 22, 2012).

MARVIN FONG/The Plain Dealer /Landov

A view of the master **control room** inside the Cuyahoga County **Jail**, Thursday, December 11, 2008, in Cleveland, OH. Read more about the jail here: http://sheriff.cuyahogacounty.us/en-US/Cuyahoga-County-Corrections-Center.aspx.

JAIL PROGRAMS

The lack of programs has long been a criticism of jails. It is difficult for small jails to develop a variety of programs because they lack space, staff, and fiscal resources. They are frequently dependent on volunteers. Large jails have more programs, but overcrowding makes it difficult to offer adequate programming for each inmate. Nevertheless, more programming exists now than was present a generation ago. See Table 5.1 for the programs found in a recent nationwide survey of jails, which are the most current data available.

This survey revealed that nearly half of all jails (46 percent) provided work release or prerelease programs; about 25 percent performed reception, diagnosis, or classification functions; approximately 12 percent had a youthful offender confinement function; 10 percent had drug or alcohol treatment; and about 1 percent had a boot camp.[24]

- North Dakota (91 percent), Minnesota (85 percent), and Pennsylvania (83 percent) were states that had the largest percent of jails that offered work release and prerelease functions.

Describe jail-based treatment programs LO5

FOR GROUP **DISCUSSION**

Create a model of jail supervision that has the potential to reduce violence, keeps correctional staff engaged, and is cost effective. You can use aspects of all of the supervision models or none of them.  LO4  LO5

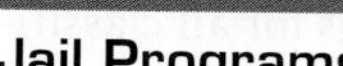

TABLE 5.1

Jail Programs

Function	Number	Percent[a]
General population confinement	3,184	97
Returned to custody	2,142	65
Work release or prerelease	1,496	46
Reception, diagnosis, or classification	805	25
Hospitalization or medical treatment	421	13
Youthful offender confinement	382	12
Alcohol or drug treatment	314	10
Boot camp	19	1
Other[b]	72	2
Not reported	12	^

Note: Data as of March 31, 2006. Excludes the federal jurisdiction and combined prison-jail systems in Alaska, Connecticut, Delaware, Hawaii, Rhode Island, and Vermont. Includes 15 locally operated jails in Alaska.

^Less than 1%.

[a]Percentages sum to more than 100% because jail jurisdictions may have more than one function.

[b]Includes drug, alcohol, or other treatment; psychiatric care; housing inmates under state jurisdiction for a limited period; jurisdiction maintenance; and law library services.

Source: James Stephan and Georgette Walsh, *Census of Jail Statistics* (Washington, DC: U.S. Department of Justice; Bureau of Justice Statistics, 2011), p. 5.

CAREERS IN CORRECTIONS

Carol Higgins O'Brien

Assistant Superintendent/ Warden of Human Services

Carol Higgins O'Brien has been working in corrections for about 30 years. Currently she works at the Middlesex (Massachusetts) Sheriff's Office at the House of Corrections.

In Massachusetts, we have county corrections where pretrial detainees are held in jails. Sentenced inmates can receive up to two and a half years, usually for misdemeanors but sometimes felonies.

We currently house approximately 800 inmates. This number can vary and a few years ago there were 1,200 inmates here. The main building was built in the 1920s and has three old-style tiers; the new facility is four years old and has a podular design with the direct-supervision concept. The podular units are where most of the programs take place. We also have a community work building for minimum security, a work release house, and an electronic monitoring program where inmates live in the community, at home, or in a program and wear an electronic monitoring bracelet and attend a day reporting center.

As assistant superintendent/warden of human services, my responsibilities include treatment, classification, program assessment, educational and vocational programs, religious programming, and substance abuse programs. We have several programs we are proud of. Here are a few examples:

- Digital imaging print shop that teaches inmates the newest version of printing and graphic arts design, providing viable employment opportunities upon release
- Culinary arts program that teaches this industry and provides a certificate from a local technical high school and community college credits
- A custodial training program is about to begin, which will lead to custodial certification

One of the problems we face here is that inmates stay a short amount of time, which means that the time for programming and preparation for reentry is limited. As I tell inmates, they often lack the tools necessary for successful reentry; we try to give them those tools, and fill their toolbox during their stay to help facilitate greater success upon the return to the communities they came from. There is also the major problem with budget constraints. We need to do more with less. The question we face is: how creative can you be and think outside of the box, so we can utilize the resources we have? A further problem is helping staff deal with the stressful environment of a correctional facility. This is not a normal work environment and our staff needs to be able to manage the stress. We are also trying to predict future human behavior and we all know that is not an exact science.

I really love what I do. My movement through my career has always kept my job fresh. It is also very refreshing when your staff like their jobs and like what they do. I see fulfillment and the feelings of success when an inmate is ready to be released and is more equipped than he was when he came here to stay out of trouble; his toolbox is full. For example, I ran into an offender I had worked with in a state prison a few years ago. He wanted to thank me for helping him. He said he was clean and sober, was happily married, and had his own business.

See Chapter 15 for more detailed information on careers in corrections.

- Massachusetts (45 percent), Kentucky (37 percent), and New Jersey (36 percent) were states that had the largest percent of jails that offered alcohol or drug treatment functions.[25]

Larger jails in the United States now generally provide GED and adult basic education programs, drug and alcohol treatment programs, counseling, work release, and jail industries, including inmate work programs and inmate vocational programs. Jails also are required to provide religious services, some exercise equipment, and access to a law library for long-term convicted inmates. Jails are constitutionally mandated to make available adequate health care delivery systems. Some jails have exemplary health care delivery systems; others offer nearly no health care. Some of the crucial health care issues confronting individuals in the jail setting are the following:

- Communicable diseases such as tuberculosis, HIV, sexually transmitted disease, hepatitis, and measles
- Chronic diseases such as hypertension, cardiovascular disease, diabetes, renal/liver disease, and lung diseases
- Chemical/substance abuse
- Prenatal care
- Smoking
- Mental health, including caring for the homeless and the mentally incompetent, and preventing suicide

AP Images/Pat Sullivan

Jail-based rehabilitation programs use a variety of different methods. Here, Kathryn Griffin-Townsend reacts as Harris County jail inmates sing her praises during a group session on June 4, 2013, in Houston. Griffin started and runs the prostitution rehabilitation program We've Been There Done That.

One of the most encouraging aspects of jail programming is the increasing number of programs that are offered to some qualifying jail inmates, including weekend programs, electronic monitoring, day reporting, community service, other pretrial supervision, work programs, and treatment programs. Another important jail program is the interventions conducted in several jails across the nation. These programs attempt to give prisoners greater authority in the operation of their living units while at the same time using staff to teach them to control unwise behavior, instill constructive conduct, and improve communication skills. Evaluations of therapeutic community programs have revealed that they can reduce recidivism and drug use, especially when coupled with community-based aftercare.[26] In addition to the programs at the Middlesex, Massachusetts, House of Corrections, as described by Carol Higgins O'Brien, see Exhibit 5.2, "Examples of Innovative Jail Programming."

EXHIBIT 5.2

Examples of Innovative Jail Programming

A model program operated in the Boulder, Colorado, County Jail has an impressive array of programs offered for inmates:

- A work release dormitory is connected to but separate from the main jail.
- A public health detox facility provides 24-hour inpatient detox services for up to 20 clients, plus a transitional residential program, daily treatment support groups, and sobriety monitoring services for clients who are sober.

(*continued*)

- The jail has all the programs that larger jails usually provide, including adult basic education programs, drug and alcohol treatment programs, and inmate vocational programs.
- A number of other programs are offered, partly because of an extensive volunteer program where volunteers work directly with inmates at the jail. Volunteers provide such services as literacy tutoring; Prison Dharma Network, which focuses on meditation and Buddhist spiritual teachings; the "Production Day" program, which has a goal of eight hours of productive activity every day; teaching crocheting and knitting, so that female offenders can create lap robes to be distributed to nursing facilities, particularly those housing low income residents; and the Boulder County Jail Garden, where master gardeners mentor inmate workers to take care of vegetable and flower gardens.

The L.A. County Jail, the largest jail in the nation, has impressive educational programs:

- About 3,000 of the 19,000 inmates are enrolled in degree and trade programs.
- The jail has contracted three charter schools to teach. The jail also uses deputies and assistants to teach life skills classes.
- Inmates with subject matter specialization can earn special status by teaching courses ranging from real estate investment to kinesiology. Career classes include landscaping, dog grooming, commercial painting, and welding.

Another jail with an impressive number of programs is the Washington County Jail in Hillsboro, Oregon. In this facility, inmates can participate in a wide array of programs:

- Religious programs
- Drug and alcohol prevention services
- Religious-based life skills and substance abuse classes
- Cognitive and behavioral groups targeting violence prevention, problem-solving skills, and social control
- Women's groups on anger management and domestic violence prevention
- Life skills classes on computer skills and finding and keeping employment
- Education
    - General Educational Development (GED) testing preparation
    - Basic adult education classes
    - GED completion
    - Individual tutoring
    - Credit recovery
    - High school completion
    - English-as-a-second-language (ESL) classes
- Intensive cognitive restructuring and skill-building programs
- In-depth drug and alcohol relapse–prevention groups

Shortly after an inmate arrives, and as a long-term plan for the inmate's successful transition back to the community, jail program counselors assess those inmates assigned to them. The latest assessment tools help counselors not only identify the inmates' history but also gain insights into what motivates them and what support factors could make them more productive when they leave jail. The goal is to reserve jail beds and save jail costs by identifying low-risk offenders. Those with a lower likelihood of returning to jail can be quickly returned to the community before they lose their job, house, and family ties. This allows jail counselors to spend more time with inmates who are at a high risk to return to jail.

Sources: Boulder County Sheriff's Office, http://www.bouldercountysheriff.org; California Board of State and Community Corrections, http://www.bscc.ca.gov/; Washington County Jail, Hillsboro, Oregon, http://www.co.washington.or.us/sheriff/jail/; Prison Fellowship, Michigan, http://www.prisonfellowship.org/programs/reentry/out4life/coalitions/Michigan (sites accessed June 2014).

CRITICAL THINKING

If you were a legislator concerned with reducing the jail population, what additional programs and services would you provide to the inmates in order to reduce recidivism? LO5

JAIL OFFICERS

The job of the more than 200,000 correctional officers in jails (sometimes designated as jail officers, corrections deputies, or sheriff's deputies) has changed in recent years.[27] Both the emergence of the new-generation jail as well as the changes resulting from the movement toward professionalism in the jail have been major factors contributing to this change.

Changing Roles

In the past, when a male applicant was interviewed for an entry-level position in the jail, he might be asked whether he could fight or liked to fight. It was widely accepted that the way to establish and maintain control over the jail population was through brute force. As a result, those who worked in the jail were expected to be physically able to handle inmates. There was little or no training given to recruits. It was also widely accepted that police deputies would spend a few years working in the jail and would be transferred to the streets when they had proven their mettle within the jail. In addition, those deputies who had disciplinary problems on patrol would be reassigned to the jail.[28]

Today, officers who work in the jail, especially more progressive ones, are seen as professionals. Women compose one-third of all jail employees, but minority employees are underrepresented in terms of their proportion among inmates. Officers are well trained in correctional academies and know how to negotiate and mediate conflicts with inmates. They are equipped to write reports, because of the realization that the vast preponderance of litigation for the sheriff comes from problems that emerge in the jail. These officers are not the rejects of law enforcement who could not make it on the streets, but individuals who have the capacity for promising careers in jail administration. The greater parity in pay and benefits has also resulted in improved morale and job longevity.[29]

Yet the role of the officer in a jail context does have its challenges. The population of the jail constantly changes, and the officer is interacting with persons from a wide variety of ethnic and social backgrounds. Working with everyone from career criminals to those who were arrested for the first time, the officer needs to be able to respond in a professional manner to as many known situations as can reasonably be expected to occur. The officer must understand that any violation of constitutional rights of an inmate may have the highest potential for personal or agency liability. In addition, occupational stress can be a problem.

The vast majority of research has been conducted on correctional officers in the prison work environment, but there is beginning to be an interest in examining the role of officers in jails. In one study examining stress among jail correctional officers in a northeastern state, the results indicated that perceived danger, role problems, job satisfaction, and organizational strengths were significant predictors of both occupational and general stress. Gender and salary predicted occupational stress, while training and correctional experience predicted general stress.[30] Another study, based on interviews with officers

CORRECTIONAL LIFE

As a correctional officer, when I enter the jail every night, I never know what kind of problems I am going to be faced with. Entering the jail is like entering a different world. It is very difficult to explain to other people what it is like working in a jail environment.

To make it in a modern correctional environment, a correctional officer must have good insight into human behavior. A good officer must also keep his or her sense of humor in such a negative environment as a jail. The average officer and staff member must be able to deal with inmates who have very serious emotional problems.

In a jail environment, inmates have to play by a different set of rules in order to survive. In other words, inmates have to become "jail wise." As a line officer, you have to also become "jail wise" if you want to keep your sanity and live to receive your pension someday.

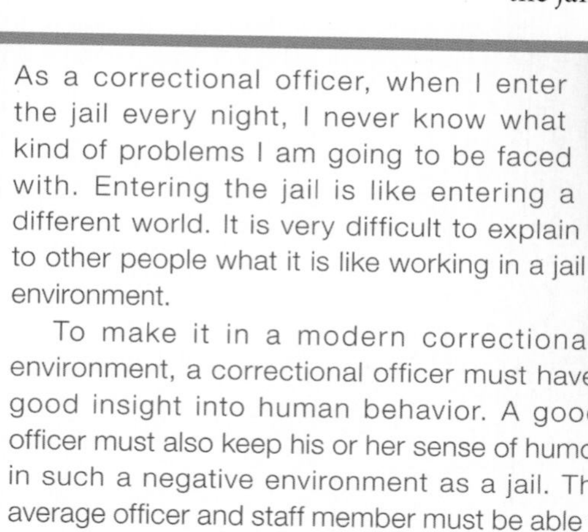

Richard: Jail Wise

at a large southeastern jail, found that male and female officers react to conflict situations in a similar manner, although it seems that the inmate's sex is a salient factor in officers' decisions on how to resolve conflict.[31]

ISSUES OF JAIL CONFINEMENT

The most serious issues facing the jail involve crowding, mental health placements, violence, and suicides. Like other correctional institutions in the United States, jails have not escaped the skyrocketing influx of prisoners. Mental hospitals have traditionally provided for the mentally ill, but as shrinking budgets have caused many state hospitals to close their doors, the mentally ill now circulate between mental health clinics, homelessness, and jail. Violence, especially in large facilities with linear supervision, continues to be a way of life in the jail.[32] Overcrowding and idleness among heterogeneous populations provide an ideal setting for the strong to take advantage of the weak. Suicides have always been a problem within the jail context.

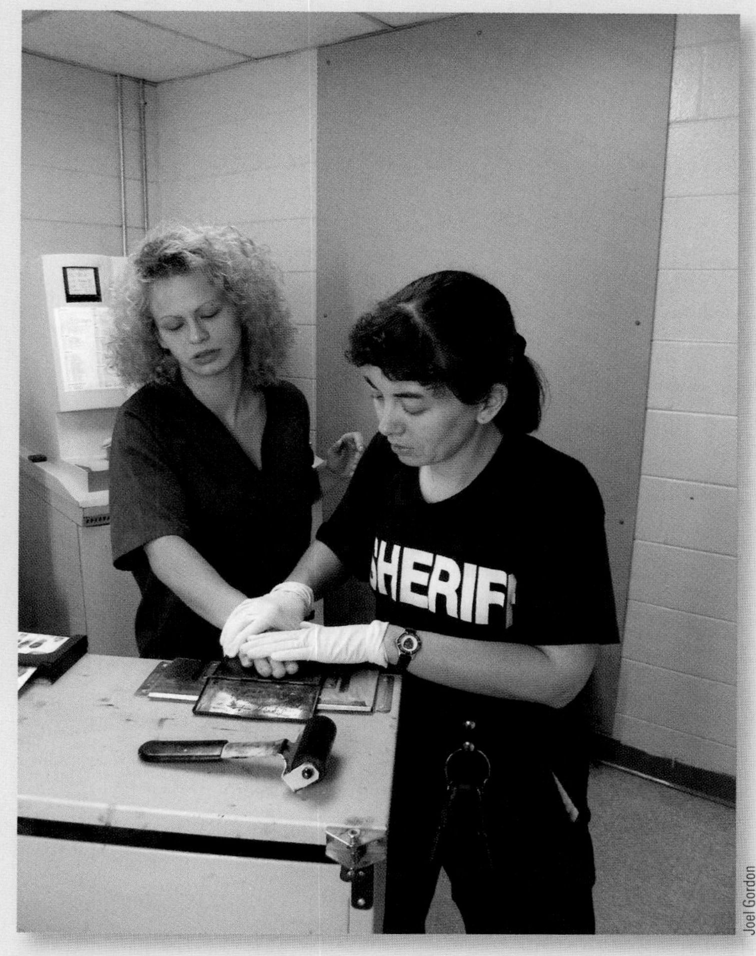

Joel Gordon

Jail officers engage in a variety of tasks, including processing inmates as they arrive at the facility. One of the first steps is fingerprinting, which today is usually done digitally but in some cases, as in this jail, it is done the old way with ink and rollers.

Jail Crowding

While not all jails are overcrowded, some are and still others are under court order to find ways to reduce the number of prisoners. What causes jail crowding and what can be done to alleviate it?

A contributing factor to jail crowding is that in some states many thousands of state and federal prisoners are being held in local jails. What makes jail crowding such a serious problem is that jails have even fewer alternatives for dealing with overcrowded facilities than do federal and state institutions. The Federal Bureau of Prisons and states can transfer inmates from one facility to another. Parole boards in some overcrowded states release prisoners early. Such options are not usually available to jail administrators, who are dependent on bail reform acts, speedy trials, and the benevolence of judges to alleviate overcrowded jail conditions.

LO6 Recognize the legal and administrative issues of jail confinement

Overcrowding is particularly acute in large urban jails, which hold more than 50 percent of the U.S. jail population. The Manhattan Detention Complex in New York City, the Cook County Jail in Chicago, the Los Angeles County Jail, the old District of Columbia jail, and the jails in Atlanta, Dallas, and Houston have continually suffered from overcrowded conditions.

One of the problems resulting from overcrowding is inmate idleness. A long-accepted adage is that busy inmates create fewer problems than idle inmates. A few jails run work farms, and the city workhouses usually have labor gangs. But in existent jail programs, makeshift work and maintenance tasks usually are not adequate. The endless empty hours in day rooms, accompanied by the usual restricted movement within the jail, result in restless prisoners. In first- and second-generation jails, idleness is one of the factors contributing to high rates of physical and sexual assaults among inmates.[33]

MYTH **Jailers are rejects from law enforcement who are untrained and uneducated, running the jail with brutality and treating inmates cruelly.**

FACT **Today, many jail officers are professionals, well trained in correctional academies to negotiate and mediate conflicts with inmates, write reports, and handle administrative duties. They are relatively well paid and have the capacity for promising careers in jail administration.**

Courtesy of Clem Bartollas

CAREERS IN CORRECTIONS

Gina Curcio

Former jail officer at Essex County House of Corrections in Middleton, Massachusetts; currently criminal justice faculty, North Shore Community College, Lynn, Massachusetts

"In corrections, there really is no typical day on the job! Some days will be really quiet with not much going on, and other days there may be numerous fights, medical emergencies, or other disturbances within the same shift.

"Also, while most correctional officers do have an assigned post (a specific housing unit or a specific area of the facility, such as the kitchen, infirmary, central control, transportation, or programs), it is not uncommon for officers to be pulled to work in different areas in order to ensure appropriate staffing throughout the facility. This gives officers some variety in their work assignments and also allows them to learn how to work in other areas of the jail.

"Correctional officers perform a number of duties, including but not limited to: monitoring inmates; documenting all incidents/altercations in official reports; enforcing unit rules and regulations; conducting timed and random rounds to ensure inmate census and safety; developing working relations with inmates to link them to appropriate programs and services; conducting cell searches (known as "shakedowns") for contraband; organizing hourly movement of inmates from the housing unit to programs, visits, the infirmary, recreation, etc.; responding to fights and other types of inmate disturbances; and updating daily unit logs regarding unit activities (chow, recreation, visits, mail, etc.).

"This job is incredibly important because correctional officers are the first line of defense between incarcerated individuals and the public. Moreover, over the past 30 years or so, working in corrections has really been transformed into a profession. Today, correctional officers are trained not only to respond to facility disturbances but also to be proactive and try to prevent disturbances before they happen. For example, training academies and on-the-job training typically include training on how to sense tension on a housing unit and to lock a housing unit in (lock them into their cells) to prevent possible fights.

"As a former jail officer, I can definitely say that I loved working in corrections. It is an exciting, challenging, and rewarding job, and my experience working in corrections has absolutely provided me the opportunity to grow as a person. As a correctional officer, I was able to help inmates resolve issues and connect them to appropriate services and programs that could help them address their criminogenic risks and needs and reduce their chances of recidivism upon release."

See Chapter 15 for more detailed information on careers in corrections.

However, not all jails are overcrowded. And at a time in which prison populations are decreasing in many jurisdictions, it is to be anticipated that more and more jails will be below capacity.

Mental Health Placements

The steadily increasing number of mentally ill inmates is one of the most serious issues facing jail administration. Federal statistics reveal that the number of mentally ill inmates in U.S. jails and prisons has quadrupled in recent years. More than half of all prison and jail inmates report mental health problems, including symptoms of major depression as well as manic and psychotic disorders.[34]

- Jail inmates who had a mental health problem (24 percent) were three times as likely as jail inmates without (8 percent) to report being physically or sexually abused in the past.

- Twenty-one percent of jail inmates reported having a history of a mental health problem.
- Twenty-four percent of jail inmates reported at least one symptom of psychotic disorder.
- Fourteen percent of jail inmates reported that they had used prescribed medication for a mental problem in the year before arrest or since admission.[35]

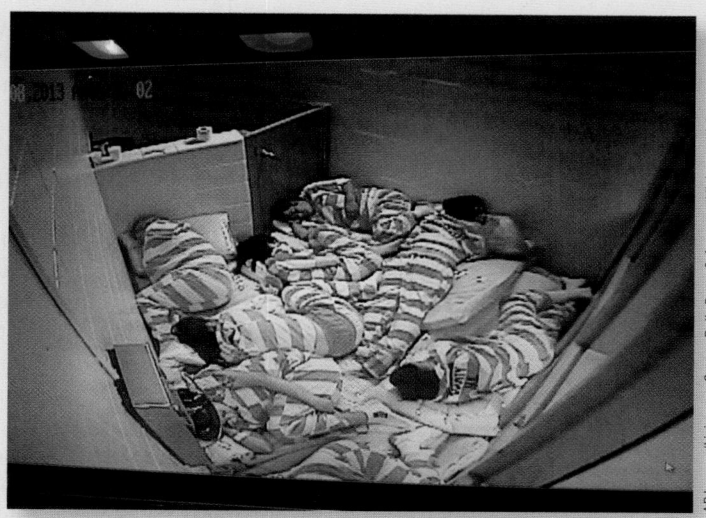

AP Images/Livingston County Daily Press & Argus and livingstondaily.com through the Michigan Freedom of Information Act

Jail overcrowding remains an issue. Eight female prisoners are shown sleeping on the floor of an intake cell in the Livingston County (Michigan) Jail in 2013. Sheriff Bob Bezotte says overcrowding has forced the jail to have some of the female inmates sleep on the floor of a small cell with a single toilet. The sheriff is pushing for a new jail; there are 31 beds for women, but the jail averages more than 60 females on any given day.

The short incarceration lengths tend to limit opportunities for treatment, especially in rural jails, and, consequently, few inmates receive the mental health services they need.[36] Furthermore, jails are often underfunded and unprepared to care for inmates with special needs, especially inmates with mental health issues. Mental health resources, in addition, are largely contingent on jail size.

Traditionally patients with mental health needs or illness were placed in psychiatric hospitals or psychiatric wards of local hospitals. Some of these facilities may specialize in short-term or outpatient therapy for low-risk patients; others specialize in long-term treatment or therapy. Some of these units are voluntary admittance; others, particularly for those who are a significant danger to themselves or to others, may involve involuntary commitment.

Mentally ill offenders are often arrested because community-based treatment programs do not exist, are filled to capacity, or are inconveniently located. The mental health units are especially filled at certain times of the year, and so a patient who needs such a setting must be confined in jail. The downsizing or elimination of community-based mental health treatment has also resulted in increasing numbers of the diagnosed mentally ill being sent to jail. Officials affirm that persons with severe mental illness are commonly jailed for such minor breaches of the law as vagrancy, trespassing, alcohol-related charges, disorderly conduct, or failing to pay for a meal.

Major cuts in state budgets to fund mental health clinics and state hospitals have made jails a necessary placement for the mentally ill offender who is serving pretrial detention or a postconviction sentence (see Exhibit 5.3).

Web App 5.1
Listen to the National Public Radio (NPR) segment (or read the transcript online) "Nation's Jails Struggle with Mentally Ill Prisoners," and discuss what can be done. http://www.npr.org/2011/09/04/140167676/nations-jails-struggle-with-mentally-ill-prisoners LO6

EXHIBIT 5.3

Psychiatric Patients with No Place to Go but Jail

In Illinois, the Cook County Jail has become the state's largest de facto mental health institution. About 11,000 prisoners are housed at the jail at any one time, and the Cook County Sheriff, Tom Dart, estimates that about 2,000 of them suffer from some form of serious mental illness, which is far more than the state-owned Elgin Mental Health Center, which has 582 beds.

Sheriff Dart says the system "is so screwed up that I've become the largest mental health provider in the state of Illinois." However, the situation is about to get worse, according to the sheriff and mental health experts, because Chicago plans to shut down health centers to help balance the budget.

It costs an estimated $143 a day to house a typical detainee in the Cook County Jail. But the cost to house someone with serious mental health issues is two or three times that amount. Sheriff Dart reports that prisoners with mental health problems are in a disproportionate number of fights and make more suicide threats and, as a result, managing them takes more resources.

"And then," he adds, "there's the human side of it. Not treating people with mental illness is bad enough, but treating them like criminals? Please, what have we become?"

Source: Bridget O'Shea, "In Chicago, Mental Health Patients Have No Place to Go," New York Times, February 18, 2012, http://www.nytimes.com/2012/02/19/health/in-chicago-mental-health-patients-have-no-place-to-go.html (accessed June 2014).

Mentally ill prisoners pose a special problem for the jail. Officers' lack of training makes it difficult for them to provide effective intervention for mentally ill prisoners. Treating mentally ill inmates also is more time consuming and difficult than normal inmates. For example, it takes time to monitor whether these inmates are taking their medication or not taking more than they should be taking. Ideally, the mentally ill prisoner would be transferred to a psychiatric facility, but these facilities are often reluctant to accept troublesome prisoners with criminal histories.

One does not have to be around a jail very long to discover the inability of mentally ill individuals to adjust to this environment. They may slump in a corner of their cell in a fetal position; they may be severely withdrawn and appear to be out of touch with what is happening to them. They may spend a good part of the day moaning or groaning in a loud voice. They may have conversations with imaginary partners or protectors. Or they may make ongoing attempts to injure themselves or commit suicide.

The Substance Abuse and Mental Health Services Administration (SAMHSA), particularly its Center for Mental Health Services (CMHS), makes federal funding available for programs designed to divert those with mental illness from jail to support services in mental health treatment programs. During the past decade, SAMHSA funded 20 proposals to implement prebooking and postbooking jail diversion programs.[37]

Violence

Violence in the jail setting consists of collective violence or riots, physical assaults (inmate/inmate, inmate/staff, and staff/inmate), and inmate suicides. Unlike long-term correctional facilities, or prisons, whose history has been checkered with riots and mass disturbances, jails have infrequently had problems with mass disturbances (such as hunger strikes of inmates or destruction of property) and almost never have inmates been organized enough to become involved in a riot and take over a cellblock.

Inmate/inmate physical assaults, including rapes, are the most frequent types of violence. The good news is that physical and sexual assaults take place less frequently in newer jails, with direct supervision of inmates. The bad news is that assaults continue to be a problem in older jails, especially large urban jails. In these jails, women and first-offending males are the most likely victims. Proactive jail administrators have contributed to the reduction of physical assaults (see the Voices Across the Profession feature).

There appears to be less violence in jail facilities as direct supervision and other contemporary programs take effect. Nonetheless, jail violence is still common and some blatant examples surface from time to time. Child molesters are most at risk and subject to extreme violence from other inmates. For example, in 2011, John Chamberlain, a California man awaiting trial on a misdemeanor charge of possessing child pornography, was punched, kicked, and stomped on until he was dead. Five inmates were tried and convicted of murder in the case, and during the trial a former inmate testified that he saw other prisoners beating Chamberlain, who crawled under a bunk for protection. Another witness said he saw attackers beat, pour hot water on, urinate on, and sexually assault Chamberlain while the victim screamed.[38]

Jail Suicides

The problem of jail suicide continues to plague jail administrators and is one of the leading causes of jailhouse death. According to the most recent data (2011), suicide accounts for more than half (61 percent) of all jail deaths. The annual mortality rate in

VOICES ACROSS THE PROFESSION

Arnett Gaston

Former Commanding Officer, Rikers Island

"We thought a lot of our violence was gang activity, because we have a lot of gangs in our jails, but we found that it was more individual action based on smaller groups of inmates. Yet, because part of the problem with violence was associated with gang activity, this led us to set up a gang task force to investigate the activities of the gangs. We were able to diminish much of the gang violence, but equally important, we were able to get a lot of valuable information on gangs—how they operated and what they did. From this, we developed a digitalized imaging system, where we could have a complete picture file on every person in the gang—their markings, their tattoos, and their status in the gang. We were able to share this with the NYPD [New York Police Department], and they were so impressed that they adopted their own digitalized imaging system."

jails (122 deaths per 100,000 inmates) has actually been in decline. Despite that, since 2000, suicide accounted for an annual average of 41 deaths per 100,000 jail inmates (heart disease accounted for 31 deaths per 100,000 during this period). In all, about 300 jail inmates take their own lives each year. And while suicide is the 10th leading cause of death in the U.S., taking more than 38,000 lives per year, the jail suicide rate is double the national average.[39] Figure 5.9 shows the recent trends in jail suicide and heart disease deaths.

Reasons for the relatively high suicide rate may include that those entering jail are cut off from drugs and alcohol which they may have used for self-medication on the outside, they realize they may be facing a long prison sentence, and for the first time they are cut off from the support of family and friends. The attempt to determine the intent behind an often intoxicated or despondent inmate's verbal and physical actions can appear to be an exercise in futility.[40]

Christine Tartaro and Rick Ruddell's national study of suicide found that the prevalence of suicide is two to five times greater in smaller jails than in larger jails. Their study also revealed that special-needs inmates and long-term inmates had higher levels of suicide attempts.[41] A study of suicide victims in jails and prisons in the Netherlands revealed that bullying and suicide risk are related and that a distinction should be made between mild and serious features of bullying and their influence on suicide.[42]

Almost all jails have suicide prevention programs.[43] If inmates are considered a high risk for suicide, they may be monitored with suicide watch programs, in which inmates are placed in specially equipped cells that do not contain anything (belts, sheets, blankets) that can be used for a suicide attempt and in which there is frequent supervision (generally every 30 minutes or so). Cameras are sometimes placed in the cell to maintain ongoing supervision. See Exhibit 5.4 for more on suicide prevention in local jails.

The TechnoCorrections feature shows how jail administrators are attempting to use technology to monitor the whereabouts of inmates, with the goal of reducing violence by increasing control over inmate movements.

FIGURE 5.9

Jail Mortality Rate by Cause of Death

Source: Bureau of Justice Statistics, Death in Custody Reporting Program, 2000–2011.

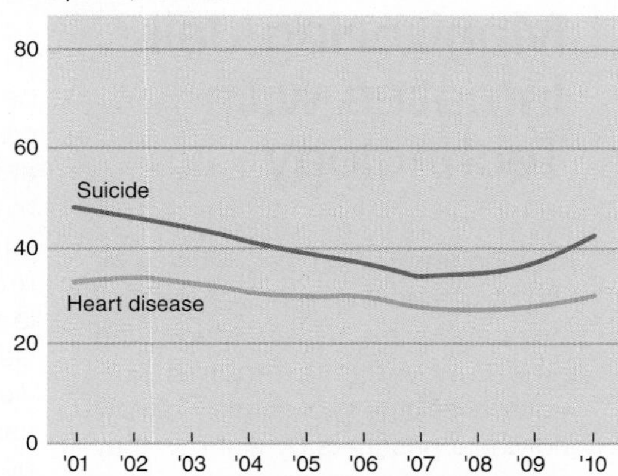

Note: Estimates based on 3-year moving averages centered on the middle year, For example, data for 2010 includes 2009, 2010, and 2011.

EXHIBIT 5.4

Suicide Prevention in Local Jails

Lindsay M. Hayes's recent article on suicide prevention in local jails suggests that more is needed in the prevention of suicides than placing inmates on suicide watch. This usually includes closed-circuit television monitoring, suicide-resistant jail cells, safety smocks, and new technology. According to Hayes, this is simply observing suicidal inmates and waiting for them to attempt suicide.

Hayes proposes that a more adequate and effective suicide prevention plan would include the following:

- *Assessment of suicide an ongoing process.* For example, research formerly revealed that 50 percent of suicides took place within the first 24 hours of confinement, but now research has found that less than 25 percent of suicides take place within the first 24 hours.
- *Suicide risk despite denial.* The direct statements of inmates who deny they are suicidal should not necessarily be relied upon, especially if they have a history of suicidal behavior.
- *Meaningful suicide prevention training.* Useful and annual suicide prevention training to all staff must be provided.
- *One size does not fit all.* Decisions regarding the management of suicidal inmates should be based on that individual's clinical needs and not simply on the resources that are available.
- *Only qualified mental health professional should determine the lack of suicide risk.* The decision that an inmate is no longer suicidal must always be made by a qualified mental health professional, following a comprehensive risk assessment.
- *Suicide precautions should not appear to be punitive.* The jail must avoid creating barriers that discourage an inmate from accepting mental health services should they feel suicidal.
- *Inmates viewed as manipulative can also be suicidal.*
- *Few or no inmates on suicide prevention can be a red flag.* A lack of inmates on suicide prevention does not necessarily mean there are no currently suicidal inmates in the facility. It may be that the facility does not provide adequate supervision for troubled inmates.
- *Avoiding obstacles to prevention.* In order for suicide prevention efforts to be meaningful, all obstacles to prevention must be avoided. For example, one negative attitude is: "If someone really wants to kill themselves, there's generally nothing you can do about it."

Source: Lindsay M. Hayes, "Suicide Prevention in Correctional Facilities: Reflections and Next Steps," National Center on Institutions and Alternatives, 2012, http://www.ncianet.org/suicide-prevention-in-correctional-facilities-reflections-and-next-steps/ (accessed June 2014).

TECHNOCORRECTIONS

Monitoring Jail Inmates with Technology

Keeping track of inmates within a jail can be challenging, especially as they move about the facility. Monitoring inmate movements requires correctional officers to accurately identify individual prisoners by sight as they pass through security posts and to be in frequent telephone and radio communication between officers at two or more security posts. They must check paper passes authorizing inmates' movements and create records to note when prisoners leave one area and enter another. Despite the best precautions and well-thought-out practices, mistakes can be made, officers' attention can be diverted, and tardy inmates not noticed or searched for promptly. This process can be critical since assaults and even murders have been committed by inmates as they moved from one part of a prison or jail to another.

BIOMETRICS

Biometrics—using physiological or behavioral characteristics such as iris, retinal, and facial recognition;

(continued)

hand and finger geometry; fingerprint and voice identification; and dynamic signature—is now being used to keep track of jail inmates. Biometrics systems are usually deployed using a three-step process. First, a camera, scanner, or other sensor takes an image or picture. Second, that image is made into a pattern called a biometric signature. For example, with fingerprints the signature comprises minute points along a finger's ridges, splits, and end lines. Voice recognition involves patterns of cadence, pitch, and tone. Hand and finger geometry measures physical characteristics such as length and thickness. Third, the biometric signature is converted into a template using a mathematical algorithm. Templates contain biometric and other data in the form of numbers that are either embedded on a plastic card or stored in a database. Some systems use a card that can be inserted in or held near a scanner that feeds the information on the card into a computer. The computer compares the biometric signature captured by the scanner with those already in its files to find the correct match.

The Biometric Inmate Tracking System (BITS) has been tested in the U.S. Navy's prison in Charleston, South Carolina. All biometric methods—iris, facial, retinal, finger and hand geometry, voice, and fingerprint—were tested, and the fingerprint recognition method, now used in conjunction with hand geometry, was judged to work best. It provided the most accurate and reliable matches at about one-third the cost of iris, facial, and retinal methods. The fingerprint method also moved prisoners through the gates faster than the others. That's a prime consideration when, for example, correctional specialists are moving 50 or more prisoners at once from housing or work areas to the galley at mealtime. Fingerprint readers are also easier to use and more durable than other readers.

Evaluation of the system indicates that it can be a very effective way of monitoring inmates, freeing jail officers from handling paper passes and allowing them to spend more time actually watching inmates in their area. While final evaluations have not been completed, project staff are optimistic that with further testing and analysis, biometrics technology can be used successfully in U.S. prisons and jails to identify and track inmates.

RADIO FREQUENCY IDENTIFICATION (RFID) TECHNOLOGY

Corrections officials are also beginning to use radio frequency identification (RFID) technology to monitor and track jail inmates. RFID uses small transponders called tags to track movements. RFID tags can be attached to or incorporated into a variety of objects, such as wristbands. Each tag has an integrated circuit and a tiny antenna to handle radio signals and can be used with a network of sensors—called RFID readers—to track movements. For example, a few correctional institutions have used the systems to provide information on prisoners' movements and to alert staff if there is an unusual concentration of people in a certain area. Movement information can be stored in computers and could prove useful in investigations to determine who was present in a certain part of a building at a particular time. Although RFID technology is mature and has been used to track inventory in warehouses, its use in correctional facilities is relatively new and untested but still holds great promise.

FOR CRITICAL THINKING AND WRITING

While we are testing new technology on incarcerated inmates, what else should we be testing? Vaccines? Would it be ethical to offer inmates early release if they undergo experiments testing technological or biological regimens, even if they "volunteer"?

Sources: Philip Bulman, "Using Technology to Make Prisons and Jails Safer," *NIJ Journal* 262 (2009), http://www.nij.gov/journals/262/corrections-technology.htm (accessed June 2014); Christopher Miles and Jeffrey Cohn, "Tracking Prisoners in Jail with Biometrics: An Experiment in a Navy Brig," *NIJ Journal* 253 (2006), http://www.ojp.usdoj.gov/nij/journals/253/tracking.html (accessed June 2014).

TRENDS SHAPING THE JAIL

Discuss the future trends of the jail

In recent years, a number of promising proposals for jail reform have been recommended and implemented. The direct supervision of inmates that is found in the new-generation jail is becoming increasingly common across the nation. Indeed, nearly half or more of the recently constructed jails provide direct supervision.

The Commission on Accreditation of Corrections of the American Correctional Association (ACA), the National Sheriff's Association, and the federal government are proposing minimum standards for the construction and operation of jails. Thirty-two states have established standards for jails, and in 25 states these standards are mandatory. In 2004, the ACA published the *Performance-Based Standards for Adult Local Detention Facilities: Fourth Edition*, which promised to provide a "new generation" of jail standards.

In addition, seven states in recent years have enacted legislation that transfers control of local jails to state government, and many more states have established procedures for state inspection of local jails. Furthermore, regional jails, serving multiple cities or counties, have become a large part of the landscape of American jails. Privatization of the jail, whether in providing particular services or in taking over the operation of the jail, is becoming increasingly widespread on the correctional landscape.

The quality of life in jail, particularly for non-urban jails, has experienced improvement. In some jails, programming has been expanded to include drug treatment, jail industries, boot camps, and self-help programs. Jail inmates have increasingly been released from jail for day reporting and treatment, community service, work release, and weekend release. One of these programs is the subject of the Evidence-Based Corrections feature. Finally, more extensive in-service training, as well as college-educated officers, is being used to improve jail operations.

THINKING LIKE A CORRECTIONS PROFESSIONAL

You are the undersheriff (in charge) at the Y County Jail. The rated capacity is 350, but the population for the last six months has exceeded 500. No relief is in sight. The budget is tight, and the food is meager and unappetizing. An 18-year-old inmate asks for an interview with you. He tells you that the older men in the tank to which he is assigned attempted to sexually assault him after lights-out. He wants protection. He is serving a year and a day for auto theft and has nearly all of it left to serve. How would you handle this situation?

Sexual exploitation is not your only problem. The traffic in cocaine and marijuana in Y County is heavy and poorly controlled by the police. A lot of stuff is coming into the jail. A study by the district attorney's investigative staff finds that officers are bringing much of it for sale to inmate gang leaders. The investigators recommend that all officers be routinely frisked when they arrive at work. You know that many officers will protest that this is unfair to the law-abiding majority of the staff. Will you adopt the district attorney's recommendation anyway? If so, how will you deal with the protest by correctional officers that is sure to follow? What measures would you employ to eliminate traffic in drugs inside the jail?

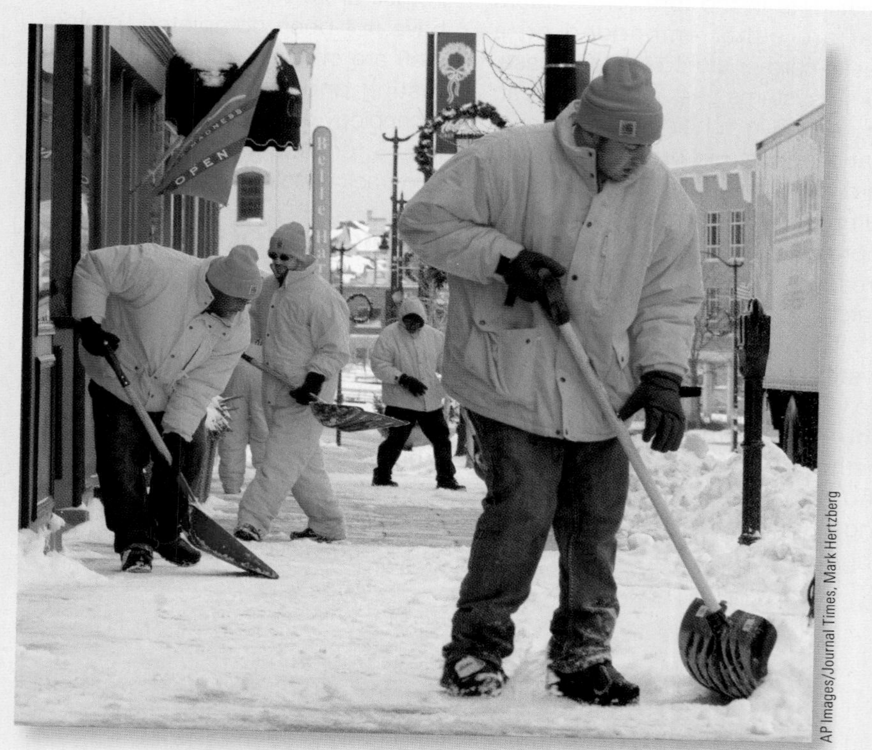

AP Images/Journal Times, Mark Hertzberg

Racine County (Wisconsin) Jail inmates wear jackets and snowsuits identifying them as Sheriff's Community Workers as they shovel downtown sidewalks. The jail inmates, who are on work release, are shoveling sidewalks under a jail program to help take care of city streets. Downtown merchants who were interviewed said they welcome the initiative because not all sidewalks are quickly shoveled by building owners.

EVIDENCE-BASED CORRECTIONS

Iowa's Jail-Based Assessment and Treatment Project

The Jail-Based Assessment and Treatment Project is being tested in three Iowa counties (Polk, Scott, and Woodbury) and focuses on caring for jail inmates suffering from substance abuse and criminal thinking. Clients are admitted to the project and begin their treatment while in jail. Clients take part in substance abuse and criminal thinking treatment, individual and group therapy sessions, support groups, educational classes, and discharge plan development. The program continues in the community with an outpatient component followed by aftercare. The same case manager who works with participants in jail follows them in the community during their outpatient and aftercare phases.

The district attorney, public defender, and probation/parole officer refer potential project participants to the jail assessment team. The in-jail portion of the project lasts from 45 days to 4 months, during which participants concentrate on their criminal thinking and substance abuse treatment simultaneously. Each participant has a case manager and a treatment counselor. Case managers and treatment counselors begin developing a discharge plan in jail once the participant enters the program.

Program participants are released to community outpatient treatment for six to nine months for them to continue their criminal thinking and substance abuse treatment in individual and group therapy sessions. Following outpatient treatment, participants enter the aftercare stage. Aftercare consists of a peer support group once a week. A team that usually includes a case manager, counselor, and probation officer works with program participants in the community for up to one year after release and assists them with educational and employment services and staying engaged in their treatment. Participants have the same case manager in the community that they had in jail.

Each county contracts with a private treatment agency to provide assessments and treatment in jail and in the community. Project stakeholders include public health staff, judges, probation officers, county sheriffs, risk assessment officers, public defenders, district attorneys, treatment staff, and staff from the local mental health centers. These stakeholders keep in close contact with one another to maintain communication, voice concerns, and discuss various problems such as waiting lists and referrals.

DOES IT WORK?

The Iowa Consortium for Substance Abuse Research and Evaluation, located at the University of Iowa, conducts ongoing evaluations of the Jail-Based Assessment and Treatment Project to determine the effectiveness of treatment services. The study measures outcomes along three variables—abstinence, rearrest, and employment—with follow-up interviews six and twelve months after admission to the project. (In Woodbury and Scott Counties, the typical participant will have been out of jail for about four months when the six-month interview is conducted. The typical Polk County participant will have been out of jail for about two months.) Six months after admission to the project, 77 percent of clients had abstained from drug use, 93 percent had not been rearrested, and more than half (52 percent) were employed full time, compared with 31 percent who were employed just before entering the program. Twelve months after admission, 69 percent had abstained from drug use, 84 percent had avoided arrest, and 56 percent were employed full time. These data are evidence of the program's effectiveness.

FOR CRITICAL THINKING AND WRITING

What questions might you want to ask before declaring this program a success? Here is a hint: Who gets referred? Are they the "average" inmate, or are troublemakers and those most likely to recidivate removed from consideration? How about this: Are inmates who give the staff problems removed from the program prior to release and therefore not counted if they recidivate later?

Source: Adapted from Amy L. Solomon, Jenny W. L. Osborne, Stefan F. LoBuglio, Jeff Mellow, and Debbie A. Mukamal, *Life After Lockup, Improving Reentry from Jail to the Community* (Urban Institute: Washington, DC, 2008), http://www.ojp.usdoj.gov/BJA/pdf/LifeAfterLockup.pdf (accessed June 2014).

SUMMARY

LO1 Describe the history and development of the jail

Although initially conceived in England as a place for detaining suspected offenders until they could be tried, jails gradually came to serve the dual purposes of detention and punishment. In America, the early colonial jails consisted of small rooms that housed up to 30 prisoners. The fee system was used in which inmates were required to pay for their own food and services, including wood and coal for heat; those who could not pay were fed scraps until they starved to death Pennsylvania jails established by reformer William Penn in the seventeenth century became the model for other states. In 1773, the Walnut Street Jail was constructed in Philadelphia in which prisoners were be employed in hard labor in the institution and released during the day to repair and clean streets and highways.

LO2 Identify the makeup of the jail population

The makeup of the jail continues to be largely poor, adult, male, and minority inmates, but the numbers of female inmates have increased in recent years.

LO3 Discuss jail administration and structure

Jails are highly political institutions, with the sheriff, an elected official, responsible for jail operations. There are three alternatives to local control of jails: state-run jails, cooperative (regional) arrangements, and state-subsidized programs.

LO4 Compare the new-generation jail with more traditional jails

In recent years, a new-generation jail has increasingly replaced the traditional linear-design jail. New-generation jails still must often deal with problems of overcrowding, but direct supervision of inmates, increased programming, and improved staff morale make this jail a more desirable placement for inmates.

LO5 Describe jail-based treatment programs

Large jails typically provide a variety of programs, including GED and adult basic education programs, drug and alcohol treatment programs, counseling, work release, and jail industries.

LO6 Recognize the legal and administrative issues of jail confinement

Jail crowding, mental health services, and the possibility of violence are three of the most serious issues facing the jail.

LO7 Discuss the future trends of the jail

Voluntary and state-required jail standards, as well as regional or multi-county arrangements of jails, are other hopeful signs that the jails of the twenty-first century will be an improvement over those of the nineteenth and twentieth centuries.

CRITICAL THINKING QUESTIONS

1. Jails have been regarded as totally inadequate institutions. Why was that description frequently accurate in the past? Why is it less likely to be true today?
2. Is there such a thing as a good jail? Imagine yourself inside a good one and describe it.
3. Direct-supervision jails seem so much better than linear-design jails. What problems do you see in direct-supervision jails? How much do you believe the new-generation jail is likely to improve the overall quality of jails in the United States?
4. What programs do you believe a large urban jail needs to offer?

NOTES

1. Petula Dvorak, "Were the Female Guards Indicted in Baltimore Jail Scheme Predators or Prey?" *Washington Post*, April 25, 2013; "14 More Officers Indicted in Baltimore Jail Corruption Case," *Fox News.com*, November 24, 2013, http://www.foxnews.com/us/2013/11/24/14-more-officers-indicted-in-baltimore-jail-corruption-case/ (accessed June 2014).
2. "14 More Officers Indicted in Baltimore Jail Corruption Case."
3. Dvorak, "Were the Female Guards Indicted in Baltimore Jail Scheme Predators or Prey?"
4. Ibid.
5. Margaret Wilson, *The Crime of Punishment, Life and Letters Series*, no. 64 (London: Jonathon Cape, 1934), p. 186.
6. Jack Lynch, "Cruel and Unusual: Prisons and Prison Reform," *Colonial Williamsburg Journal*, http://www.history.org/Foundation/journal/Summer11/prison.cfm (accessed June 2014).
7. *National Jail and Adult Detention Directory 2012* (College Park, MD: American Correctional Association, 2012).

8. Todd D. Minton and Daniela Golinelli, *Jail Inmates at Midyear 2013—Statistical Tables* (Washington, DC: U.S. Department of Justice, 2014), http://www.bjs.gov/content/pub/pdf/jim13st.pdf (accessed June 2014).
9. Ibid. Data in this section come from Minton and Golinelli.
10. Human Rights Watch, *Old Behind Bars: The Aging Prison Population in the United States* (New York: Human Rights Watch, 2012). See also Robynn Kuhlmann and Rick Ruddell, "Elderly Jail Inmates: Problems, Prevalence and Public Health," *California Journal of Health Promotion* 3 (2005): 49–60.
11. See Pauline K. Brennan, "Sentencing Female Misdemeanants: A Examination of the Direct and Indirect Effects of Race/Ethnicity," *Justice Quarterly* 23 (March 2006): 60–95.
12. Bonnie Green, Jeanne Miranda, Anahita Darowalla, and Juned Siddique, "Trauma Exposure, Mental Health Functioning, and Program Needs of Women in Jail," *Crime and Delinquency* 51 (2005): 133–151.
13. John Irwin, *The Jail: Managing the Underclass in American Society* (Berkeley: University of California Press, 1985), pp. 26–38.
14. John A. Backstrand, Don C. Gibbons, and Joseph P. Jones, "What Is in Jail? An Examination of the Rabble Hypothesis," *Crime and Delinquency* 38 (1992): 219–229.
15. Gary F. Cornelius, *The American Jail: Cornerstone of Modern Corrections* (Upper Saddle River, NJ: Prentice Hall, 2008), p. 97.
16. For the three generations of jails, see William "Ray" Nelson, "New Generation Jails," http://prop1.org/legal/prisons/97jails.htm (accessed June 2014); Allen R. Beck, "Deciding on a New Jail Design," http://www.justiceconcepts.com/design.htm (accessed June 2014).
17. Beck, "Deciding on a New Jail Design."
18. Stephen I. Saunders, III, *Direct Supervision Jails: A New Management Model for the 21st Century*, http://www.fdle.state.fl.us/Content/getdoc/08dd615a-20f2-4367-9dd4-c6b23a45278d/Saunders.aspx (accessed June 2014).
19. R. Werner, "The Invention of Direct Supervision," *Corrections Compendium* 30 (2005): 4–7, 32–34.
20. Nelson, "New Generation Jails."
21. Christine Tartaro, "Watered Down: Partial Implementation of the New Generation Jail Philosophy," *Prison Journal* 86 (2006): 284–300.
22. Richard Werner, "Effectiveness of the Direct Supervision System of Correctional Design and Management: A Review of the Literature," *Criminal Justice and Behavior* 33 (June 2006): 403.
23. Ann Coppola, "Out, Out Blind Spot," Corrections.com, February 11, 2008, http://www.corrections.com/articles/17626-out-out-blind-spot (accessed June 2014).
24. James Stephan and Georgette Welsh, *Census of Jail Facilities, 2006* (Washington, DC: Bureau of Justice Statistics, 2011), p. 5.
25. Ibid.
26. Jeffrey Bouffard and Faye Taxman, "Looking Inside the 'Black Box' of Drug Court Treatment Services Using Direct Observations," *Journal of Drug Issues* 34 (2004): 195–218.
27. *Sourcebook of Criminal Justice Statistics* (Washington, DC: Bureau of Justice Statistics, 2014), http://www.albany.edu/sourcebook/tost_1.html#1_h (accessed June 2014).
28. Comments made by F. E. Knowles, February 2007.
29. Ibid.
30. Tammy L. Castle and Jamie S. Martin, "Occupational Hazard: Predictors of Stress Among Jail Correctional Officers," *American Journal of Criminal Justice* 31 (2006): 65–82.
31. Nancy L. Hogan, Eric G. Lambert, John R. Hepburn, Velmer S. Burton, Jr., and Francis T. Cullen, "Is There a Difference? Definitions of and Response to Conflict Situations," *Women and Criminal Justice* 15 (2004): 143–150.
32. Leslie Lunney, "Nowhere Else to Go: Mentally Ill and in Jail," *Jail Suicidal Mental Health Update* (Washington, DC: National Center on Institutions and Alternatives and the National Institute of Corrections, 2000), p. 13.
33. See Christine Tartaro, "The Impact of Density on Jail Violence," *Journal of Criminal Justice* 30 (2002): 499–510.
34. Human Rights Watch, *U.S. Number of Mentally Ill in Prisons Quadrupled*, September 5, 2006. See also Doris J. James and Lauren E. Glaze, *Mental Health Problems of Prison and Jail Inmates* (Washington, DC: U.S. Department of Justice; Bureau of Justice Statistics, 2006).
35. James and Glaze, *Mental Health Problems of Prison and Jail Inmates*, pp. 1–2.
36. Melanie M. Race and colleagues, *Mental Health Services in Rural Jails*, Maine Rural Health Research Center, August 2010.
37. Substance Abuse and Mental Health Services Administration, http://www.samhsa.gov (accessed June 2014).
38. Vik Jolly and Larry Welborn, "Inmates Guilty of Second-Degree Murder in Jail-Beating Death," *Orange County Register*, October 25, 2011, http://www.ocregister.com/articles/murder-323704-beating-chamberlain.html (accessed June 2014).
39. Centers for Disease Control and Prevention, National Suicide Statistics at a Glance, 2013, http://www.cdc.gov/violenceprevention/suicide/statistics/leading_causes.html (accessed June 2014).
40. For the research on the previous studies on jail suicide, see Melinda M. Winter, "County Jail Suicides in a Midwestern State: Moving Beyond the Use of Profiles," *Prison Journal* 83 (June 2003): 132–133.
41. Christine Tartaro and Rick Ruddell, "Trouble in Mayberry: A National Analysis of Suicides and Attempts in Small Jails," *American Journal of Criminal Justice* 31 (2006): 81–104.
42. Eric Blaauw, Frans Willem Winkel, and Ad J. F. M. Kerkhof, "Bullying and Suicidal Behavior in Jails," *Criminal Justice and Behavior* 28 (June 2001): 279–299.
43. James L. Stephan, *Census of Jails, 1999* (Washington, DC: U.S. Department of Justice, August 2001), p. 41.

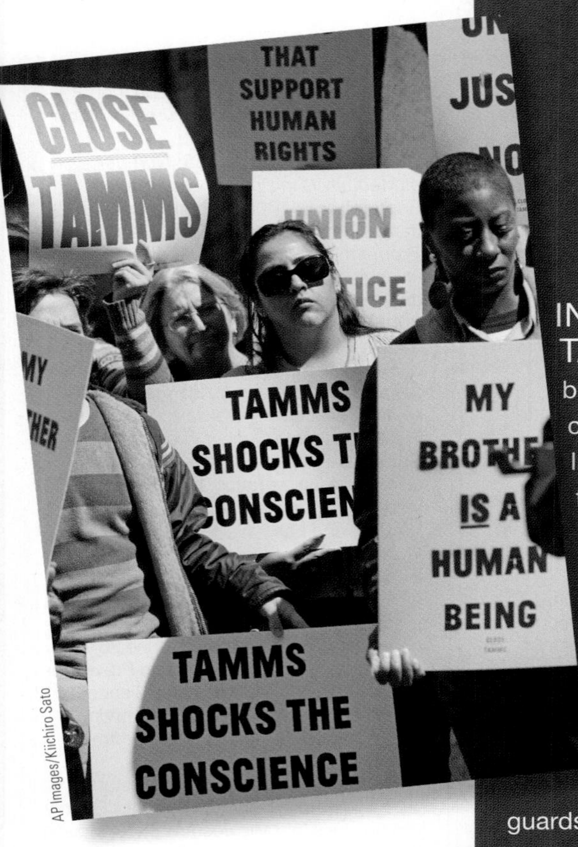

AP Images/Kiichiro Sato

Mothers of prisoners at Tamms Correctional Center march through downtown Chicago to show their support of Governor Pat Quinn's proposal to close the southern Illinois prison, a supermax security lockup for the "worst of the worst" offenders in Illinois. They took aim at the correctional officers union, who were opposed to the prison's closure because it would mean layoffs for guards and other personnel. The mothers said the issue is about "human dignity, not jobs."

IN 1998, THE STATE OF ILLINOIS OPENED THE TAMMS CORRECTIONAL CENTER, a supermax prison built without a cafeteria, yard, chapel, or classrooms. Phone calls and community activities were limited, and contact visits were not allowed. Inmates could only leave their cells for a shower or to exercise alone; food was pushed through a slot in the door. Not surprisingly, the consequences of this isolation were inmates' severe depression, hallucinations, cutting their bodies, or attempted suicide.

The first inmates at Tamms were transferred there from other prisons in Illinois for a one-year shock therapy in order to break down their disruptive behavior and to make them more compliant. Ten years later, more than one-third of the inmates had been there since it opened.

Tamms has had its supporters. The most vocal ones were the guards union, the nearby towns that welcomed the well-paid jobs at Tamms, and state officials who thrived on the tough-on-crime policies.

From 2006 on, there were efforts to reform what took place at Tamms. The prison union and legislatures representing local people fought back. By 2011, the attempted reforms were stalled, in spite of a federal court ruling that inmates at Tamms had been deprived of their due process rights.[1]

An inmate who spent eight years and four months at Tamms supermax prison had this to say about his experience:

I thought I was going up for parole, but instead they shipped me to Tamms. They told me that I was an influential inmate who needed to be separated from the other inmates. I had not received a ticket for a disciplinary offense for 20 years. The place was deplorable. I had a concrete slab for a mattress, a concrete desk, and a concrete toilet. If my wife and family had not supported and visited me, I would have gone mad. The savage ways of this institution was so bad that you would not believe it unless you were there.[2]

This glimpse of a supermax prison in Illinois reminds one of the Dark Ages of corrections when prisoners were brutalized and treated inhumanely. Fortunately, prison reformers in Illinois, members of the legislature, inmates' families, and inmates themselves were able to put pressure and close the facility. Tamms was closed on January 4, 2013.

6

Prisons

Robert Galbraith/Reuters/Landov

LEARNING OBJECTIVES

LO1 Identify the extent to which prisons mirror the larger society

LO2 Describe the age, gender, and racial makeup of those sent to prison

LO3 Discuss the federal jurisdiction over prisons

LO4 Explain whether state jurisdictions are similar from one state to another

LO5 Summarize how many prisoners are housed in private facilities and whether there is common agreement on the effectiveness of these facilities

LO6 Discuss the security types of correctional institutions

LO7 Describe what prisons look like

LO8 Define the basic responsibilities of a correctional administrator

LO9 Explain the proactive management style

PREVIEW OF KEY CONCEPTS

penal harm
UNICOR
Richardson v. McKnight
Correctional Services Corp. v. Malesko
minimum-security prisons
medium-security prisons
maximum-security prisons
segregation
supermax prison
Madrid v. Gomez
radial design
telephone-pole design
courtyard design
campus design
proactive warden

ne of the tragedies of our time is that correctional institutions—whatever form they may take—do not seem to correct, and many former prisoners recidivate soon after reentering society. Although no completely accurate statement of the recidivism rate is available and various studies differ somewhat, it is estimated that more than half of all inmates will be back in prison within six years of their release. That means that each year about 240,000 former prisoners return to prison because they failed on parole.[3]

Prisons maintained by the Federal Bureau of Prisons and every state government are very expensive to our society. The most recent government figures reveal that prisons cost taxpayers about $40 billion each year, up from about $12 billion in 1986. This amounts to an annual cost of about $125 per year for every American citizen.[4]

penal harm A current movement that believes the purpose of corrections is to punish offenders as severely as possible.

Today the just desert/incapacitation philosophy of sentencing is dominant, a policy that seems effective since the crime rate has declined as the number of people in prison has risen. The connection between a declining crime rate and rising prison population is not lost on politicians who energize their political campaigns by supporting policies favoring long-term institutions and putting people behind bars.[5] Advocates of the *no frills*, or **penal harm**, movement argue that if prison is a punishing experience, criminals will be deterred from crime and current prisoners will be encouraged to go straight. Besides, why should individuals who have engaged in antisocial activities receive benefits behind bars that are sometimes unavailable to the honest and law-abiding, such as higher education courses?

The provision of quality care and treatment remains a goal of modern corrections. It is considered a responsibility of a free and democratic society to provide quality care to inmates in institutional settings. Prison reformers, ever since the founding of the Pennsylvania Prison Society in 1787, have believed that an important aspect of quality care is to maintain constant vigilance over those placed in long-term institutions, especially those from disadvantaged backgrounds. There is common agreement among many that quality institutional care of inmates includes providing vocational and educational programs for those who desire them; treating inmates with dignity and respect; avoiding verbal or physical abuse of inmates; and being open to new ways of improving inmate care, perhaps much different from the past. In comparison to Tamms, discussed in the opening vignette, the supermax prison in Oak Park Heights in Minnesota is considered one of the model prisons in the United States. It deployed a model in which inmates were treated with dignity and respect, inmates and staff were both safe, and professional behavior was expected from staff at all times. The Voices Across the Profession feature in this chapter is contributed by its current warden, Kent Grandlienard. Is this how the treatment of prisoners is viewed in the United States today? Does the general public believe that prison inmates are treated with dignity and respect?

The purpose of this chapter, as well as the institutional chapters that follow, is to evaluate, describe, and analyze the state of prisons in contemporary society. What do they do, and how are they doing it? What are they supposed to be? This chapter focuses on describing prisons—what the jurisdictions over them are, what the main types are, what they look like, and how they are governed.

TO WHAT EXTENT DO PRISONS MIRROR THE LARGER SOCIETY?

Identify the extent to which prisons mirror the larger society

An important consideration in corrections is the relationship between the prison and the wider society. James Jacobs's classic analysis of the Stateville Penitentiary in Illinois concludes that the social organization and moral values of the larger society, as well as major society changes, are found in the micro-society within prison walls.[6] Donald Clemmer's classic study of the prison community at Menard Correctional Center in Illinois also notes the existence of numerous parallels between the prison and the free

Kent Grandlienard

VOICES ACROSS THE PROFESSION

Phrases … like "the incarceration is the punishment," "firm, fair, and consistent," "safe, secure, human," and "provide inmates with the opportunity for change" … were the new mantra in corrections.

Kent Grandlienard
Warden, Oak Park Heights Prison

It was 1981, and I was a recent college graduate who had just moved to the town of Stillwater, Minnesota, home of the state's first territorial prison. I had reluctantly left my safe college job at a local lumber company to begin my new job as a corrections counselor at the Stillwater State Prison, the state's largest adult male prison at that time. The economy was tight and employment opportunities somewhat limited, so the word around town was that now was a good time to get into corrections, because in keeping with the town's rich prison history, a new state-of-the-art maximum security facility would soon be opening just up the hill from Stillwater, in neighboring Oak Park Heights. In conjunction with that facility's opening, there would be more career opportunities, as many of the current Stillwater staff were leaving the old prison to transfer to the new one. I began hearing about not only this new facility and all of its unique features, but that it was being planned and run by former Stillwater Warden Frank W. Wood.

Little did I know that my new job at Stillwater would not only provide me with lifelong career opportunities in corrections, or that I would eventually become the warden at MCF/OPH—what I call the "house that Frank built"—but that I was entering an new era in corrections, an era that Warden Wood and then Minnesota Department of Corrections (MN-DOC) Commissioner Orville Pung's philosophy were changing forever. Antiquated and stereotypic terms were being replaced and used in promoting a new degree of professionalism among corrections staff—like prison guards being called "corrections counselors" and prisons being called "facilities." Even the staff uniforms were changing, from the dull, dingy brown shirts at Stillwater to a crisp-white and much more professional look at Oak Park Heights (uniforms that eventually the entire MN-DOC adopted). Accordingly, this philosophy also brought about expectations of how inmates were viewed and treated. Phrases from Warden Wood like "the incarceration is the punishment," "firm, fair, and consistent," "safe, secure, human," and "provide inmates with the opportunity for change," along with Frank's example of what is now called "management by walking around," were the new mantra in corrections. These phrases and philosophy continue to be the foundation of all Minnesota correctional facilities to this day, and I am proud to be a part of continuing that philosophy.

world. Clemmer writes, "In a sense the prison culture reflects the American culture, for it is a culture within it."[7]

There are those who argue that rather than the prison being a microcosm of the larger society, it is a distorted image of that society. In its analysis of the 1971 Attica Prison rebellion, the New York State Special Commission on Attica stated, "While it is a microcosm reflecting the forces and emotions of the larger society, the prison actually magnifies and intensifies these forces, because it is so enclosed."[8]

An examination of the relationship between the prison and society reveals that poverty, racial and gender discrimination, violent crime, and mental illness are found in more exaggerated forms within the prison. The vast majority of prisoners come from pockets of poverty. They have grown up in disorganized communities, have been victims of racial and sexual discrimination, have varying degrees of emotional disturbance, and have victimized others. As these individuals come into the prison, they must deal with the deprivations of confinement in an environment full of racial unrest and division. Predators in the outside world may become victims in this enclosed world. For those who have emotional problems, the world of the prison is even more chaotic.

It is challenging for inmates, regardless of their background, to find they are in an environment that is failing to prepare them for their readjustment to the wider society once they are released. The setting of the prison frequently makes survival the prime concern of prisoners, rather than gaining skills or a positive attitude. So, within the distorted setting of the prison, inmates often leave less able to make it in the wider society than when they were admitted to prison, sometimes many years before.

We will now examine the characteristics of the U.S. prison population, how it breaks down in terms of age, gender, race/ethnicity, and criminal offenses.

INMATE POPULATIONS

Federal and state correctional authorities today have jurisdiction over almost 1,500,000 prisoners. The federal system now holds more than 12 percent of these prisoners, while the remainder are in state institutions. After years of increase despite a steadily decreasing crime rate, the number of correctional inmates has recently begun to stabilize and even decline.[9] What are the characteristics of this inmate group?

Describe the age, gender, and racial makeup of those sent to prison 

Age

White male prisoners tend to be older than African American and Hispanic inmates; 18 percent are aged 45 to 54 and over 11 percent are aged 40 to 44. Women aged 35 to 39 make up the largest percentage of sentenced female prisoners overall (nearly 20 percent). This is true for white, African Americans, and Hispanic female prisoners.[10]

FOR GROUP DISCUSSION

Why do white male prisoners tend to be older than African American and Hispanic inmates? Can this be related to the poverty, racial, and gender discrimination that is seen outside of prison walls? LO2

Gender

As Figure 6.1 shows, males now make up about 93 percent of sentenced prisoners and females make up about 7 percent.

Race

Today, African American males make up about 40 percent of the inmate population, white men 30 percent, and Hispanic men 20 percent. Nearly half of the sentenced females are white; African American women make up 26 percent of all sentenced female inmates and Hispanic women about 17 percent. The rate of incarceration has increased for white women and declined for African American women.

Offense Characteristics

Violent offenders make up more than 53 percent of all sentenced inmates in state prisons. Drug offenses represent the most serious charge for about 17 percent of state prisoners and property offenses for about 18 percent. Offense distributions differ between male and female state prisoners. More than half of males are sentenced for violent offenses, compared to 35 percent of females. Drug, weapons, and immigration offenders make up more than three-quarters of the sentenced federal prison population.

Robin Nelson/PhotoEdit

Federal and state correctional facilities hold more than 1,600,000 prisoners. This population has grown steadily despite a declining crime rate. The vast majority of prisoners come from pockets of poverty, have been victims of racial and sexual discrimination, have varying degrees of emotional disturbance, and have victimized others. These young men are inmates of Baldwin Inmate Boot Camp in Hardwick, Georgia.

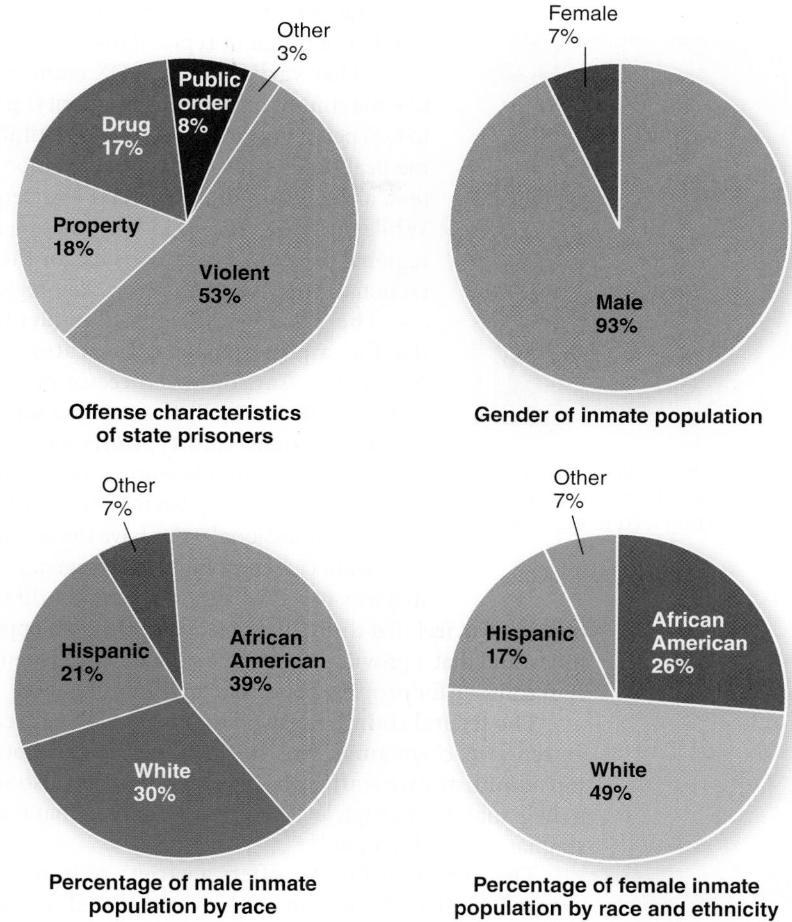

FIGURE 6.1

Inmates Under the Jurisdiction of Federal and State Correctional Systems

Source: Heather C. West and William J. Sabol, *Prisoners in 2011* (Washington, D.C.: Bureau of Justice Statistics, December 2012), pp. 6-9.

There are racial and ethnic differences in the prison population: African American and Hispanic inmates are more likely to be sentenced for violence and drug offenses than whites, who are more likely to be sentenced for property offenses.[11]

JURISDICTION OVER PRISON SYSTEMS IN THE UNITED STATES

The Federal Bureau of Prisons, state departments of corrections, and prisons funded and administered by private corporations have jurisdiction over prisons in the United States.

Federal Bureau of Prisons

LO3 Discuss the federal jurisdiction over prisons

The Federal Bureau of Prisons was established in 1930 to ensure the administration of the 11 federal prisons in operation at that time; today, the Bureau of Prisons oversees more than 100 correctional institutions (including some privately operated facilities), 6 regional offices, a central office in Washington, D.C., 2 staff training centers, and 28 community corrections offices. The BOP is responsible for the custody and care of more than 216,000 federal offenders, of whom 85 percent are confined in bureau-operated correctional institutions or detention centers. The remaining offenders are confined through agreements with state and local governments or through contracts with privately operated community correctional centers, detention centers, and juvenile facilities.[12]

Three inner and outer security fences surround the medium-security federal prison in Marion, Illinois. Once the nation's most secure prison, this federal lockup has housed everyone from spies to a Columbian drug lord to dapper mob boss John Gotti.

The Bureau of Prisons administers a number of different types of institutional settings. They vary from the ADX (administrative maximum or maximum security) prison to U.S. penitentiaries, correctional institutions, medical centers, prison camps, detention centers, and metropolitan correctional centers. While the main office is in Washington, D.C., regional directors are responsible for the correctional settings and offices in their regions.

The Bureau of Prisons has identified itself as a professional organization since Norman C. Carlson was director of corrections (1970–1987). Both management and nonmanagement staff typically view themselves as professionals who work as a team. Correctional officers also tend to view themselves as professionals who have the possibility of upward career mobility in the agency.[13] The majority of staff at all levels, from the director's office down, feel that the BOP offers excellent career opportunities, and that it provides up-to-date skilled management and staff training for people who want to make a difference.

The Cheltenham, Maryland, Federal Law Enforcement Training Center (FLETC) offers training to law enforcement and correctional personnel in the Washington, D.C., area.

The federal training centers do an able job of creating an *esprit de corps* among institutional personnel. Rotating top administrative staff every two or three years also seems to help maintain a high level of professionalism that reduces stagnation and burnout.[14]

The Bureau of Prisons offers a variety of inmate programs.[15] Nearly 50,000 inmates have completed residential drug treatment programs since 1990. In one study, individuals released to the community for at least six months after they completed the federal drug residence program were 73 percent less likely to be arrested for a new offense and 44 percent less likely to test positive for drug use, when compared to inmates who did not complete the program. The BOP has had thousands of inmates complete a general equivalency diploma (GED), and many others have completed vocational training and other educational programs. In addition, the BOP has developed a number of new life skills programs in recent years.[16]

UNICOR The trade name used by Federal Prison Industries.

Federal Prison Industries (FPI), or **UNICOR**, would like to think of itself as the gold standard for inmate vocational programs. FPI employs more than 20,000 inmates, about 25 percent of the sentenced and medically eligible federal inmate population. FPI has up-to-date equipment, develops a strong work ethic, and pays considerably more than state prisoners receive from prison industry.[17] Yet, there is considerable question about the BOP's exploiting inmates in UNICOR by the wages they pay, which are a very small portion of the profits it makes.

The Bureau of Prisons further deserves praise because it has been willing to receive the most hard-to-control inmates from state prisons, thereby making the inmate population more manageable in state facilities. This has sometimes created problems of inmate control in federal facilities, but with the construction of high-security supermax areas in many state facilities across the nation, states may become more willing to place these difficult inmates in their own high-security housing units.

The BOP may be the standard-setter of correctional facilities, but it has had its problems. These include a disastrous fire at FCI Danbury, Connecticut, in which several inmates lost their lives; 21 inmate murders at the Atlanta Federal Penitentiary; an incident at the Marion (Illinois) Federal Penitentiary that claimed the lives of two staff members (two more were stabbed in one day); a riot at the Atlanta Penitentiary, in which inmates nearly burned the entire facility to the ground; and a federal facility in California at which some 40 staff were arrested and charged with corruption. There are other instances of staff brutality as well as staff corruption.[18] Prison crowding is at least as serious a problem in BOP facilities as it is in state institutions.[19] Federal penitentiaries also have serious problems generated by sexual exploitation, inmate defiance, and drug trafficking. In addition, inmates must endure boredom, regimentation, personal indignities, the deprivations of imprisonment, and the difficulty of daily survival.[20] The ideals of professionalism are often not realized on a daily basis, and some staff fall far short of what it means to be a professional.[21]

Web App 6.1
Visit the Bureau of Prisons website at http://www.bop.gov/. Write a brief essay comparing and contrasting the prison types listed under Federal Prison Facilities. LO3 LO6

What type of job and skills within the prison system translate into inmates becoming productive members of society upon release? LO3

State Departments of Corrections

There are 50 separate state departments of corrections as well as one for the District of Columbia. The systems are difficult to compare and evaluate because of differences in ideology, structure, and programs. The quality of previous correctional leaders, the resources available, and the volume of inmates have largely shaped what takes place in corrections within a state.

LO4 Explain whether state jurisdictions are similar from one state to another

Some states have few correctional institutions (New Hampshire, 6; Utah, 5; Wyoming, 4). Other states have many (Texas, 107; North Carolina, 88; Florida, 85). Within each state is considerable variation in the quality of institutions. There may be a maximum-security prison that resembles an old castle and a new minimum-security facility with an innovative and campus design. If one were to visit these facilities, it would be difficult to believe both are managed within the same jurisdiction.

IMPROVING STATE SERVICES Though the problems are immense, state correctional institutions are better than they were in the past. State departments of corrections have become concerned about improving institutional standards. By the late 1970s, state correctional administrators began to apply for institutional accreditation through the Commission on Accreditation of the American Correctional Association. Now nearly all of the 50 states have participated in the accreditation process, and 500 correctional institutions have been accredited or are in the process of accreditation.[22]

Most state departments of corrections have begun to emphasize preservice and in-service training, requiring that newly hired correctional officers must receive some type of training before they begin work in the institution. This training may take place at the state corrections academy, at the institution, or at some other location. Top institutional administrators are increasingly receiving in-service training.

State corrections departments are also now more receptive to institutional research and evaluation. In addition, directors/commissioners of state systems and wardens/superintendents of state prisons are now more open and honest about institutional problems.[23] Despite these advancements, departments of corrections often have underdeveloped programming, insufficient prison industries for inmates, and lack of resources for anything other than prison construction. Exhibit 6.1 discusses how state correctional systems are now dealing with the crises they face on a daily basis.

Private Prisons

Private prisons are much different from federal or state prisons, which are under governmental jurisdiction. The private sector's involvement in corrections is not new. Private industry used prison labor in several ways during the early nineteenth century. The contract labor system used prison labor to manufacture goods for private companies, which furnished tools and materials and supervised the work of inmates. In the piece-price system, contractors furnished raw materials and paid prisoners for the

EXHIBIT 6.1

State Correctional Systems and Dealing with Crisis

The study of state corrections today is actually an examination of corrections responding to crisis. The most promising strategies to help corrections respond to crisis include prison construction, developing clarity of mission, managing corrections effectively, integrating correctional services, training staff, and upgrading standards.

Prison Construction

Nearly every state has undergone major prison construction in the past 30 years. The end result is that many of the facilities built in the nineteenth century or early in the twentieth century are no longer in use.

Developing Clarity of Mission

Connecticut, Minnesota, and Texas have not had the drift, or confusion, that has been a debilitating problem for many correctional agencies, for they are clear about their mission. Connecticut's mission has been to develop a safe and humane system. The Community Corrections Act focuses Minnesota's mission on community-based corrections. Work discipline and education were the bases of the Texas control model, until a federal court decision changed this model in the 1980s. In the past 20 years, a number of other states have focused their mission on the goal of a safe and humane system.

Managing Corrections Effectively

Most correctional systems are set up very much in the bureaucratic tradition—working toward greater efficiency, clear accountability, higher performance standards, more flexible programming, and better allocation of resources. Under the leadership of Frank Wood, both as a prison warden and later commissioner of corrections, Minnesota is one of those states that has distinguished itself in its proactive management of correctional institutions.

Integrating Correctional Services

Only seven states can claim integrated departments that have brought together most of the nine categories of correctional institutions (adult institutions, juvenile institutions, adult probation, juvenile probation, misdemeanor probation, local jails, juvenile detention, parole, and juvenile aftercare). Yet in nearly every department of state corrections, some effort has been expended to develop better integrated services within the system.

Training Staff

Staff training offers one of the brightest hopes for internal change in state corrections, and staff development has become a major emphasis of those states' corrections departments. State correctional academies in New York, California, and Illinois appear to offer the most extensive training programs, both in length of training and the level of staff involvement. Many states offer pre-service and in-service training programs for all levels of correctional staff in state correctional academies.

Upgrading Standards

A system-wide acceptance of correctional standards also offers a major hope for internal change in state corrections. The standards supported by the Commission on Accreditation for Corrections are the most promising so far proposed. The ACA (American Correctional Association) standards, which were developed by corrections practitioners, have already upgraded the correctional programs of nearly every state.

completed goods on a per piece basis. The convict lease system provided prisoners "on loan" to work in farming, construction, mining, and on plantations, under the complete control of the lessee.[24] It should be noted that this is not what private companies do today.

Summarize how many prisoners are housed in private facilities and whether there is common agreement on the effectiveness of these facilities

The private sector now provides prisoners' work programs and medical, education, and psychological services; financing for prison or jail construction; and management and operation of prisons or jails. Two companies operate over half of the contracts of private correctional facilities: the Corrections Corporation of America and the GEO Group Inc. (formerly Wackenhut Corrections). The Corrections Corporation of America (CCA) operates facilities with 75,000 inmates in 61 correctional institutions. The GEO Group operates slightly fewer facilities and houses fewer inmates. Other companies, such as Management and Training Corporation, LCS Correctional Services, and Emerald Corrections, also hold multiple prison contracts throughout the United States.[25] Privately operated facilities are generally located in the southern and western regions of the United States and include both federal and state offenders.[26] (See Figure 6.2 and Exhibit 6.2.)

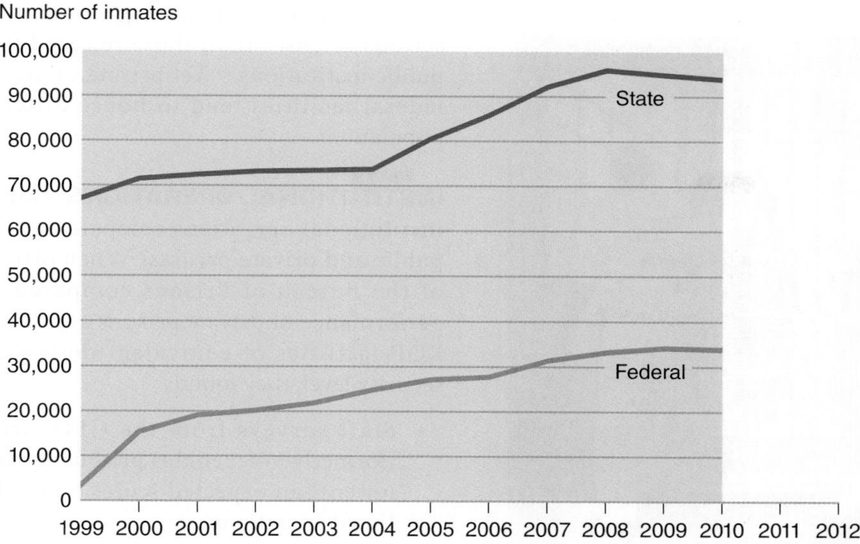

FIGURE 6.2

Private Prison Populations

Source: Based on Cody Mason, *Too Good to Be True: Private Prisons in America*, p. 6. The Sentencing Project.

COST-EFFECTIVENESS Evaluation studies on the cost-effectiveness of private versus public institutions have been inconclusive.[27] Private prisons do seem cheaper to build, but the question pertains to the quality of private services. Mason's 2012 report, *Too Good to Be True*, concludes: "The available evidence does not point to any substantial benefits to privatizing prisons."[28]

LOWER RATES OF RECIDIVISM While some research has found that private providers have lower rates of recidivism, other studies found no difference in the rate of recidivism between public and private facilities.[29] A recent study used data from a large cohort of Oklahoma inmates and found that private prison inmates had a greater risk of recidivism.[30] Some evidence does exist that inmates released from private

EXHIBIT 6.2

Developments in Privatization

- Gary Johnson's platform during his initial 1994 run for governor of New Mexico included a pledge to privatize every prison in the state. By the time he left office in 2003, 44.2 percent of the state's prisoners were in privately run facilities.
- Ohio opened its first private prison in 2000 with the goal of saving $1.6 million per year. This raised the number of inmates held privately in Ohio from zero in 1999 to over 3,000 in 2010.
- North Carolina canceled two contracts with CCA due to concerns about the company's failure to meet contract requirements and banned the practice of bringing in prisoners from out of state. California instituted a similar ban, and Arkansas ended two contracts with Wackenhut (GEO) in 2001.
- In 2004, Nevada Governor Kenny Guinn ended CCA's contract with the state after the company was alleged to have provided substandard services.
- Vermont agreed to start sending prisoners to CCA facilities in Tennessee and Kentucky in 2004. This helped bring the proportion of inmates held privately from zero in 2003 to over 20 percent in 2004. This trend led to Vermont holding over 34 percent of its prison population privately in 2008, before declining to 27 percent by 2010.
- In 2011, California ended contracts for several GEO Group facilities as part of its Criminal Justice Realignment Plan to reduce populations and spending.
- States such as Florida, Ohio, Arizona, New Hampshire, and Utah have been considering beginning or expanding private prison contracting.

Source: From Cody Mason, *Too Good to Be True: Private Prisons in America*, p. 3. Copyright © 2012 by The Sentencing Project. Reproduction of this document in full or in part, and in print or electronic format, only by permission of The Sentencing Project.

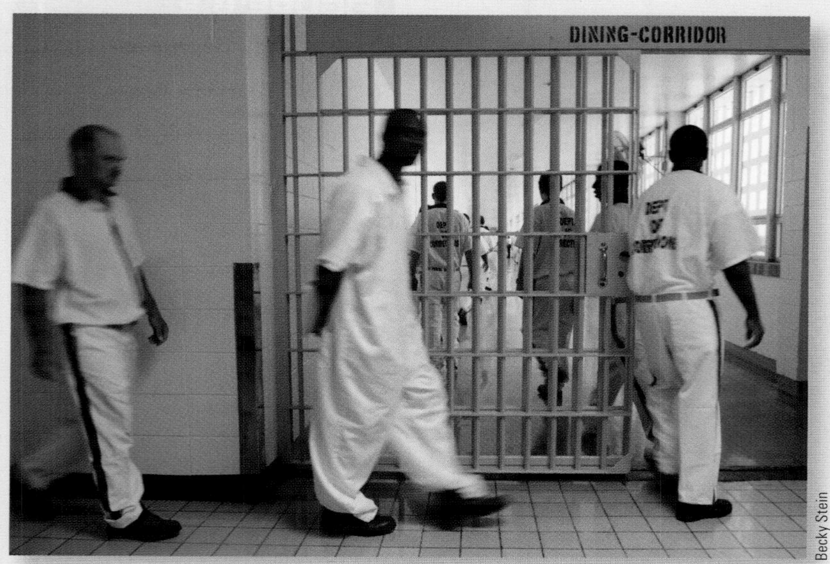

Becky Stein

Inmates in a state facility in Georgia are shown walking to an afternoon activity. Though problems persist, state correctional institutions are much better than they were in the past. Great strides have been made to improve professionalism and the quality of correctional life. Nevertheless, the quality of corrections varies from state to state and among correctional administrators and officers within states.

prisons who do reoffend may commit less serious offenses than those released from public institutions.[31] Yet private, state, and federal facilities tend to house different populations.

INSTITUTIONAL OPERATIONS How do institutional operations compare between public and private prisons? When officials of the Bureau of Prisons compared the performance of private prisons and several BOP facilities of equivalent design and security level, they found:

- Staff surveys from the GEO Group (formerly Wackenhut) prisons revealed lower than expected scores on institutional operations.
- Staff had higher institutional commitment in the private prison.
- The private facility had higher staff turnover than the comparison BOP prisons.
- An inmate survey revealed that inmates perceived worse sanitation and food services at the private facility, while security and gang-activity levels were about the same as the BOP prisons.
- The private prison had higher rates of most kinds of inmate misconduct, including a higher than expected level of drug use at the private facility in comparison to the BOP prisons.[32]

Questions exist on whether private providers skimp on services and programs in order to reduce costs. Some private services providers have been sued because their services were inadequate, causing harm to inmates.[33] It is further reported that private prisons have higher rates of escapes, greater levels of institutional violence, more shoddy construction, and more poorly trained and inexperienced staff than federal and state facilities.[34] Mason's 2012 evaluation questioned the quality of services in private operations.[35] See Exhibit 6.3 for a comparison of institutional operations in private and state-run prisons.[36]

LEGAL ISSUES The increased involvement of private enterprise in corrections raises a number of important financial, legal, and moral questions that have not been

EXHIBIT 6.3

Comparison of Private and Federal/State Facilities

Proponents of private operators contend that they run prisons more effectively and at less cost than public agencies. They claim they can do this because privatization:

- Increases the capacity of prisons because private corporations can build prisons more quickly
- Responds with greater flexibility to correctional needs by cutting red tape
- Attracts employees who are younger and more enthusiastic than public employees
- Brings fresh ideas into the correctional system

In contrast, critics of private prisons argue that private prisons cannot be compared to federal or state prisons because they:

- May build their facilities more quickly but too often the quality of the facilities leaves much to be desired
- Have no lower and probably higher rates of recidivism
- Have higher rates of inmate misconduct
- Provide inferior services to inmates compared to federal and state facilities
- Offer inadequate compensation to staff, who at times barely make more than minimum wage
- Pose ethical and moral issues that are yet to be resolved

adequately addressed. One of the major legal issues is whether private correctional officers have less immunity from lawsuits than state employees. In ***Richardson v. McKnight***, the Supreme Court held that correctional officers employed by a private firm are not entitled to a qualified immunity from suit by prisoners, charging a section 1983 violation.[37] The case of ***Correctional Services Corp. v. Malesko*** defines the protections and rights of prisoners in private corporations' facilities. The U.S. Supreme Court ruled that although Malesko could sue an employee of the private correctional corporation for violating his constitutional rights (he was forced to walk up stairs when he had a heart condition), he could not sue the correctional corporation itself.[38] The *Malesko* decision shields the private prison corporation from suits brought under the federal civil rights statute. Interestingly, the state is still liable, even if the private corporation is not.[39]

THINKING LIKE A CORRECTIONS PROFESSIONAL

You have just been hired as a consultant to the state prison system because of your expertise on private prison management. The governor requests your opinion about a proposal received from the well-known and respected Penal Corporation of America, which is offering to privatize a medium-security prison and guarantees substantial savings to the state. The governor asks for your advice and wants to know the pros and cons of privatization and whether she should go along with the plan. You tell her that this is a complex problem and you will submit a memorandum within a few days. Outline the contents of your memorandum.

TYPES OF CORRECTIONAL FACILITIES

LO6 Discuss the security types of correctional institutions

Correctional institutions can be first divided into male and female institutions. See Exhibit 6.4 for a comparison between prisons for men and those for women. Institutions have further been traditionally designed as minimum-, medium-, and maximum-security facilities. Maximum-security prisons have been further divided into reformatories, state penitentiaries, correctional centers, and state prisons. Beginning in the 1990s, supermax prisons were built around the nation.

Security is the byword of all prisons, especially maximum-security and supermax facilities. Correctional workers are made aware that each inmate is a potential escape risk and, therefore, the utmost security must be maintained. More secure prisons are designed to eliminate hidden corners where people can congregate, and passages are constructed so that they can be easily blocked off to quell disturbances.

EXHIBIT 6.4

Comparison of Men's and Women's Prisons

Men's Prisons	Women's Prisons
Usually much larger, sometimes expanding to several thousand inmates	Usually much smaller
Generally has one security classification	Traditionally, all security classifications are in the same facility
Usually little contact between correctional staff and inmates	Correctional staff and inmates have much more friendly interaction
Violence characterizes prison life, especially in maximum-security prisons	Violence can take place, but it is not characteristic of prison life
Sexual assaults and rape are not uncommon events in prison life	Sexual interaction is much more likely to be by consensus
Male inmates see their prison life as one of survival	In some women's prisons, prisoners become involved in family-like structure
The rackets, including drugs, are usually highly developed	The rackets are much less developed in women's prisons; drugs for example, are found much less in women's prison facilities
Men's prisons typically have many vocational and treatment programs	Women's prisons have fewer treatment and vocational programs

Web App 6.2 The Corrections Corporation of America (CCA) is a private correctional agency that designs, builds, manages, and operates correctional facilities and detention centers on behalf of several federal agencies and state governments. Visit the CCA website at http://www.cca.com/. Write a paper on the benefits of private corrections. LO5

Richardson v. McKnight Supreme Court held that correctional officers employed by a private firm are not entitled to a qualified immunity from suit by prisoners, charging a section 1983 violation.

Correctional Services Corp. v. Malesko Defines the protections and rights of inmates in private corporations' facilities.

minimum-security prisons Prisons with relaxed perimeter security, sometimes without fences or any other means of external security.

Minimum-Security Prisons

Minimum-security prisons, in contrast to other types of prisons, have far more relaxed perimeter security, sometimes without fences or any other form of external security. Inmates usually have less than a year before release when they are moved to minimum security. The inmates live in less-secure dormitories, which are regularly patrolled by correctional officers. As in medium-security facilities, they have communal showers, sinks, and toilets. The inmates work, go to school, and have vocational classes. They get more freedom, so they are permitted to work outside jobs such as road crews and exterior maintenance. These facilities have generous visitation policies with contact visitation, sometimes even short home furloughs, and a safer environment for both staff and inmates.

Web App 6.3
For a state jurisdiction comparison, visit http://www.corrections.com/links/show/30. This page of Corrections.com links to all state correctional agencies. Using your state and a state similar in population size, compare the Department of Corrections facilities and inmate populations. LO2 LO4 LO6

Medium-Security Prisons

Inmates who are placed in **medium-security prisons** may sleep in dormitories on bunk beds, with lockers to store their possessions, or they may be double-bunked (two inmates per cell). They are often out of their cells most of the day. Inmates are usually allowed to work, take courses and get a GED, have visits, and use the yard.

medium-security prisons Prisons with single or double fencing, guarded towers or closed-circuit television monitoring, sally-port entrances, and zonal security systems to control inmate movement within the institution.

Medium-security prisons typically have single or double fencing, guarded towers or closed-circuit television monitoring, sally-port entrances, and zonal security systems to control inmate movement within the institutions. In medium-security prisons, the emphasis is on controlled access to programs. Prisoners assigned to medium custody can be locked down in emergencies, but it is expected that they will participate in industrial and educational activities. The rationale behind medium-security facilities is that a good deal of freedom and movement and the availability of programs are allowed within a technologically secured perimeter.

MYTH Privately run institutions are much more effective than those run by the government. Cutting state bureaucracy is both effective and efficient.

FACT There is little conclusive evidence that private institutions are any better than state-run facilities. Private institutions have their own set of problems.

Maximum-Security Prisons

Most **maximum-security prisons** are large physical plants. Some of the older maximum-security facilities are surrounded by stone walls with guard towers at strategic places. These walls may be 25 or more feet high. But new maximum-security facilities tend to be surrounded by several fences because of the expense of stone walls.

Maximum-security prisons are sometimes divided into close security and maximum security. In close security, inmates usually have one- or two-person cells that are observed from a remote control station. Each cell has its own toilet and sink. Inmates may leave their cells for work assignments or programs and may otherwise be allowed in a common room in the cellblock or an exercise yard. The fences are usually double fences with watchtowers housing armed guards, sometimes with a third, lethal-current electric fence in the middle.[40]

maximum-security prisons Prisons in which complete control of any and all prisoners can be applied at any time.

segregation A punishment unit in which inmates are separated from other inmates and are fed in their cells. Unlike the past, inmates must be adequately fed and permitted some time out of their cells to exercise.

Maximum-security prisons also usually have two types of **segregation**: isolation and administrative segregation. Isolation is punishment; the prisoner is sent for a specific number of days to a solitary cell without contact with other inmates. Administrative segregation is just what the term implies: the prisoner is removed from the main population because his or her behavior is considered dangerous to others. The removal may be for a specific or indefinite period of time, the latter being subject to case review.

In maximum-security prisons, all inmates usually have individual cells with sliding doors controlled from a secure remote control station. Inmates are often allowed out of their cells one out of twenty-four hours. When out of their cells, inmates remain in the cellblock or an exterior cage. Movement out of the cellblock or "pod" is tightly restricted, using restraints and escorted by correctional officers.[41]

The assumption that underlies maximum-security prisons is that the physical characteristics of the prison will be such that complete control of prisoners can be applied at any time.

Supermax Prisons

The **supermax prison**, based on isolation of prisoners, a system that can be traced to the old Pennsylvania model, is known by many names—security housing units, administrative segregation, intensive management unit, and extended control unit.[42] More than 40 states have either built supermax prisons or added high-security units to existing facilities in order to contain problem prisoners.[43] More than 20,000 male and female inmates are now housed in 57 supermax facilities.[44] They house such well-known gang chiefs as Jeff Fort and Larry Hoover, anti-abortion activist and Olympic Park Bomber Eric Rudolph, and terrorists such as Richard Reid, Terry Nichols, and Zacarias Moussaoui.

AP Images/Mary Altaffer

There are many notorious maximum-security prisons, and no less among them is the famed Sing Sing Correctional Facility in Ossining, New York, which stands on a scenic bluff overlooking the Hudson River, about 30 miles north of New York City. The phrase going "up the river" was coined with Sing Sing in mind. It was also the place of some famous executions, including Ruth Snyder, a woman convicted of killing her husband for insurance money. Her execution in Sing Sing's electric chair on January 12, 1928, was photographed and became a national sensation; she was the first woman to be electrocuted since 1899. Altogether, 614 men and women have been executed at Sing Sing.

Take for instance the 484-bed federal facility (ADX) in Florence, Colorado. This prison has the most sophisticated security measures in the United States, including 168 video cameras and 1,400 electronically controlled gates. Inside the cells, all furniture is immovable; the bed, the desk, and TV stand are made of cement. All potential weapons, including toilet seats, toilet handles, and soap dishes, have been removed. The cement walls are 5,000-pound quality, and steel bars are placed so they crisscross every eight inches inside the institution. Cells are angled so that prisoners can see neither each other nor the outside scenery. This cuts down on communications and denies inmates a sense of location, to prevent escapes. The newer prisons have totally automated the traditional jobs of correction officers such as opening cell doors and surveillance.[45]

supermax prison Most secure of all prison systems, in which there is typically a 23-hour lockdown.

In some supermax prisons, there are security housing units (SHUs), pronounced "shoes," for inmates who are deemed to be a special danger to the security of the prison. Within these units, two categories of inmates are housed. The first category is administrative detention (AD), which is used to house inmates who are acknowledged as posing a threat to the general population, though inmates may also be placed in this unit for their own protection. The second category is disciplinary segregation (DS), which is reserved for those inmates who have been found guilty of a serious prison rule violation. Supermax facilities have both supporters and detractors; see Exhibit 6.5.

AP Images/Steve Miller

A day room in the Northern Correctional Institution in Somers, Connecticut, can be seen, with prisoner cells above, as a guard escorts a prisoner out of a shower. This supermax facility is where death row and the most dangerous inmates are housed.

EXHIBIT 6.5

The Pros and Cons of Supermax Prisons

Pros

- Supermax prisons are needed to control inmates whose behavior is so disruptive that they are unmanageable when left in the general inmate population.
- Some inmates are simply too dangerous for the average prison setting. Gang leaders, disruptive inmates from other institutions, and inmates who incite riots are those most likely to be placed in supermax facilities or units.
- Administrators uniformly agree that supermax prisons improve system-wide prison safety, order, and control, as well as contribute to many positive unintended effects.

Cons

- Supermax prisons inflict excessive levels of pain and harm.
- Because they have difficulty controlling their disruptive behavior, mentally ill prisoners are disproportionately represented in these prisons.
- Inmate-on-inmate violence is not reduced through the use of punitive confinement.
- Inmates released directly from supermax prisons are especially dangerous to society because of the harsh conditions of confinement.
- Because a high percentage of the inmates are African Americans, placement in supermax prisons may be racially motivated.

Sources: Daniel P. Mears and Jennifer L. Castro, "Wardens' Views on the Wisdom of Supermax Prisons," *Crime and Delinquency* 52 (July 2006): 421–422; Roy D. King, "The Rise and Rise of Supermax: An American Solution in Search of a Problem?" *Punishment and Society* 2 (1999): 163–186; Lorna A. Rhodes, *Total Confinement: Madness and Reason in the Maximum Security Prison* (Berkeley: University of California Press, 2004); and Hans Toch, "The Contemporary Relevance of Early Experiments with Supermax Reform," *Prison Journal* 83 (2003): 221–228.

CORRECTIONAL LIFE

William: Serving Time in a Maximum-Security Prison

"Serving time in prison is a very weary task. Most outsiders know, or think they know, what the real prison is, but there is no way one can truthfully comprehend prison unless they have experienced prison. Prison is loneliness that sinks its teeth into the souls of men, an emptiness that leaves a sick feeling inside. It is uncertainty that smothers and stifles, it is a memory that comes in the night, its cry like the screams of a trumpet; it is frustration, futility, despair, and indifference. Prison is men who no longer know the love of a woman, their children, and the clean fresh air of a spring night. Prison is where men hope when hope seems futile. Prison is walking in the visiting room to see the worried, careworn face of the mother who anxiously studies the face of her son; still the same loved son, her pride and joy, who now wears a prison number."

SUPERMAX VIOLENCE In the late 1980s and 1990s, the security housing units (SHUs) of the Corcoran State Prison and the Pelican Bay Prison brought the California Department of Corrections considerable adverse publicity because of the levels of violence found in these facilities. At Corcoran's SHU, staff violence reached unbelievable levels. Under an "integrated yard policy," rival groups and known enemies were routinely brought together to fight in the small group exercise yards. For nine years, inmates were used as pawns by staff in these set-up fights. Correctional officers promoted their champions and even wagered on the fights for entertainment. An estimated 8,000 of these "gladiator fights" took place between 1988 and 1997.[46]

Officers in Corcoran used guns to control the yards, and more than 2,000 shooting incidents took place. Hundreds were wounded and five were killed. An independent analysis of the five lethal shootings revealed that none was justified by the department of corrections' own criteria; yet, the "shooting review board" routinely justified every shot ever fired in the SHU yards. In a wrongful-death lawsuit brought on behalf of one inmate gunned down in the yards, former California Corrections Director Dan McCarthy testified that "The rate of violence in the Corcoran SHU in its first year of operation was absolutely the highest rate I have ever seen in any institution anywhere in the country."[47]

Pelican Bay Prison, located in Crescent City, California, was opened in 1989 to move the state's worst offenders out of antiquated facilities such as San Quentin and Folsom. Pelican Bay has two areas: the maximum-security prison and the more notorious supermaximum-security housing unit. The 1,200 inmates in the SHU live 24 hours a day in an X-shaped, windowless bunker. Everything is gray concrete: the walls, the beds, and immovable stools. It is impossible to move more than eight feet in any direction within the cells. There is a skylight two stories up, but on an overcast day, it is dark and so are the cells.[48]

According to testimony given in the legal case ***Madrid v. Gomez*** (1995), excessive and unnecessary force and abuse were common in the special housing unit at Pelican Bay. Examples of the violence at Pelican Bay found in *Madrid v. Gomez* included:

Madrid v. Gomez The judge in this case found that staff at the Pelican Bay Prison in California had used excessive and unnecessary force on inmates.

- Inmates were left naked in outdoor holding cages during inclement weather.
- Beatings occurred even after inmates had been restrained.
- Verbal harassment and racial taunting were commonplace.
- Inmates were shot for fistfights both on the outdoor recreation yards and inside the cellblocks.
- One mentally ill inmate suffered second- and third-degree burns over a third of his body when he was given a bath in scalding water in the prison infirmary a week after he had bitten an officer.

The judge agreed with the prisoners in this class-action suit and ruled in their favor, stating, "Dry words on paper cannot adequately capture the senseless suffering and sometimes wretched misery that defendants' [prison staff and administration] unconstitutional practices leave in their wake."[49]

The effectiveness of the supermax prison is discussed further in the Evidence-Based Corrections feature.

EVIDENCE-BASED CORRECTIONS

Supermax Prisons

While the supermax prison may reassure some correctional experts who applaud a facility designed to house the nation's most dangerous offenders, the question remains: does it work any better than a traditional maximum-security facility?

Some of the most significant evaluations of supermax prisons have been conducted by justice scholar Daniel Mears and his associates. Mears finds that most correctional administrators agree on the definition of the core meaning of a supermax prison: a stand-alone unit or part of another facility designated for violent or disruptive inmates. It typically involves up to 23-hour-per-day, single-cell confinement for an indefinite period of time. Inmates in supermax housing have minimal contact with staff and other inmates. In addition, Mears finds that wardens generally believe that supermax prisons serve to achieve at least four critical goals—increasing safety, order, and control throughout prison systems and incapacitating violent or disruptive inmates. However, Mears finds a great deal of difference over the stated or perceived goals of supermax prisons. There is less agreement about whether they improve inmate behavior throughout prison systems; decrease riots, the influence of gangs, or escapes; successfully punish, reduce the recidivism of, or rehabilitate violent or disruptive inmates; or deter crime in society.

There were also some surprising positive effects. Supermax prisons increase privacy, reduce danger, and even provide creature comforts (such as TV sets) that are unavailable in general-population prisons. Staff report less stress and fear because they have to contend with fewer disruptive inmates. There can also be positive effects in other correctional institutions such as improving living conditions and outcomes for general population inmates by removing the most dangerous offenders from their midst.

On the other hand, Mears and his associates uncovered some negative effects associated with the use of the supermax prison. Staff may have too much control over inmates—a condition that damages staff–inmate

(*continued*)

relationships. Long hours of isolation may be associated with mental illness and psychological disturbances. Supermax inmates seem to have a more difficult time readjusting upon release. A stay in a supermax prison inhibits reintegration into other prisons, communities, and families. Mears and Jennifer Castro surveyed wardens and found that even though they seem to favor supermax prisons, they also expressed concern that the general public considers supermax institutions inhumane, that they drain limited funds from state budgets, and that they produce increases in litigation and court interventions, as well as increased recidivism and reentry failure among released inmates. In sum, it remains unclear whether the benefits of these prison facilities outweigh their costs.

FOR CRITICAL THINKING AND WRITING

Are we giving up on any hope of rehabilitation when we put someone in a supermax prison? Do you think it is possible for someone to turn his or her life around under this strict correctional regiment? What is the point of putting someone in 23-hour-a-day lockdown? Security? Punishment?

Sources: Daniel Mears, "An Assessment of Supermax Prisons Using an Evaluation Research Framework," *Prison Journal* 88 (2008): 43–68; Daniel Mears and Jennifer Castro, "Wardens' Views on the Wisdom of Supermax Prisons," *Crime and Delinquency* 52 (2006): 398–431; Daniel Mears and Jamie Watson, "Towards a Fair and Balanced Assessment of Supermax Prisons," *Justice Quarterly* 23 (2006): 232–267; Daniel P. Mears, *Evaluating the Effectiveness of Supermax Prisons* (Washington, DC: Urban Institute, 2006), http://www.urban.org/uploadedPDF/411326_supermax_prisons.pdf (accessed June 2014).

Describe what prisons look like **LO7**

WHAT PRISONS LOOK LIKE

The four most widely used architectural designs in American prisons are the radial design, the telephone-pole design, the courtyard design, and the campus style (see Figure 6.3). The 1980s and 1990s were years of constant prison construction, and facilities built in those decades—mostly medium- and minimum-security prisons—have influenced the description of a typical American prison. What this means is that the maximum-security prisons depicted in 1930s movies—the prototype of prisons in the past—are no longer the dominant type of institution for adults. During the late twentieth century, technological innovations, usually to promote security, further altered the appearance of prisons.

Architectural Design for Today's Prisons

The structural design of early prisons was created to produce a specific outcome: moral reformation. The isolated cells were intended to facilitate contemplation, work, and penitence. Since Jeremy Bentham's circular Panopticon in the nineteenth century, institutional security or control, rather than reformation, has been the basic function of prison architecture.

radial design In this wheel-shaped configuration, corridors radiate like spokes from a control center at the hub.

In prisons with a **radial design**, the corridors extend like spokes from a control center at the hub. Eastern State Penitentiary in Philadelphia was the first prison to utilize the radial design. The federal penitentiary at Leavenworth (Kansas) and state penitentiaries at Rahway and Trenton (New Jersey) are other prisons with radial designs.[50]

FIGURE 6.3

Prison Designs Used in the United States

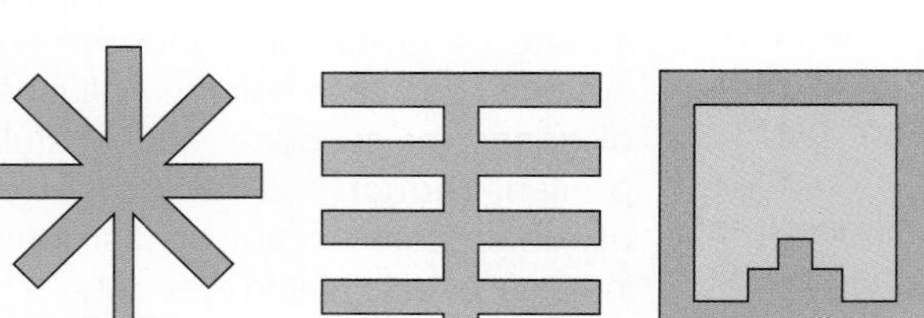
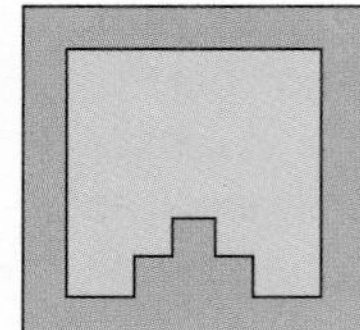
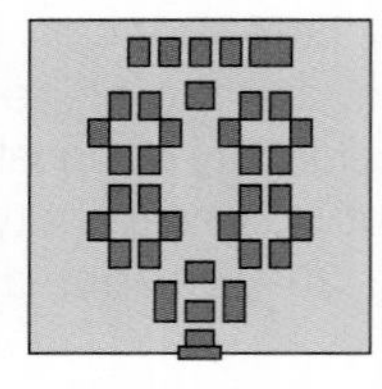

The **telephone-pole design**, which has long central corridors, is more common for prisons built during the twentieth century. This design, the most widely used for maximum-security prisons in the United States, was used for the federal penitentiary in Marion (Illinois), and state correctional institutions at Graterford (Pennsylvania), Somers (Connecticut), and Jackson (Georgia). The telephone-pole design makes it possible to house prisoners by classification levels. A major disadvantage of this layout is that militant convicts can barricade a corridor. In the event of a riot or a hostage-taking situation, inmates can take control of a cell house and make it difficult for guards to recapture control.

telephone-pole design This prison has a long central corridor serving as the means for prisoners to go from one part of the prison to another. Extending out from the corridor are cross-arms containing housing, school, shops, and recreation areas.

courtyard design A prison design in which corridors surround a courtyard. Housing, educational, vocational, recreational, prison industry, and dining areas face the courtyard.

campus design Open prison design that allows some freedom of movement; the units of the prison are housed in a complex of buildings surrounded by a fence.

The **courtyard design**, likely to be found in newer prisons, has housing units. The Washington Corrections Center for Women at Purdy (Gig Harbor) became a showplace among women's prisons and is built around multilevel and beautifully landscaped courtyards. The attractive buildings provided security without fences until a number of escapes in the mid-1970s resulted in the construction of eight-foot fences. Small housing units with pleasant living rooms reflect the expectation that the women will behave like human beings and also imply that they will be treated as such. The education, recreation, and training areas are ample and roomy. Away from the courtyard are attractive apartments, each containing a living room, kitchen, dining space, two bedrooms, and a bath. Women who are close to release or are on work or educational release occupy these apartments.[51]

The **campus design**, used for minimum-security and a few medium-security prisons, utilizes an open design that allows some freedom of movement. Small housing units are scattered among the educational, vocational, recreational, and dining units of the prison. Women's prisons frequently use the campus design. The campus design is likely to be found in showplace institutions that have more generous visiting policies than do typical institutions, allow more furloughs, offer better services and programs, and permit the placement of inmates who provide a safer environment for both staff and inmates.

Changing Form of the Prison

More than half of U.S. prisons today are less than 20 years old. A major advantage of new prison construction across the nation is that these facilities permit the tearing down or closing of many of the old, dungeon-like prisons.

Some of the newly constructed prisons across the nation do not look like prisons. The Minnesota Correctional (Facility) in Oak Park Heights is one of the more technologically advanced and secure prisons in the nation. This three-story facility has some walls below ground level, and living space that faces out to a sunken central courtyard. The subterranean design saves energy, and the prison has a heat-reclaiming unit. Within this innovative facility, the freedom of movement becomes more restricted and closely monitored as inmates approach the institution's security perimeters. This restriction makes it possible to minimize guard-tower surveillance and thereby reduces costs. A sophisticated computer monitors the opening and closing of doors and other routine events. Other security elements at Oak Park Heights include a closed-circuit television monitoring system and an electronic alarm network on the roof of the facility and on the perimeter's double security fence.[52] The use of technology to maintain security in closed prison institutions is the subject of the TechnoCorrections feature.

AP Images/Matt Rourke

The Eastern State Penitentiary in Philadelphia. The penitentiary took in its first inmate in 1829, closed in 1971, and reopened as a museum in 1994.

Using Technology in Prison Security

Only a few years ago, using technology to maintain prison security was unknown. Now prison technology offers innovations that provide substantial savings in staffing costs and operations. A few of the more intriguing technological developments include:

- *Ground-penetrating radar.* Ground-penetrating radar (GPR) is able to locate tunnels inmates use to escape. GPR works almost like an old-fashioned Geiger counter, but rather than detecting metal, the system detects changes in ground composition, including voids such as those created by a tunnel.
- *Heartbeat monitoring.* Now it is possible to prevent escapes by monitoring inmates' heartbeats! The Advanced Vehicle Interrogation and Notification system (AVIAN) works by identifying the shock wave generated by the beating heart, which couples to any surface the body touches. The system takes in all the frequencies of movement, such as the expansion and contraction of an engine or rain hitting the roof, and determines if there is a pattern similar to a human heartbeat.
- *Nonlethal electrified fences.* Nonlethal electrified containment fences stop inmates without causing severe harm or death. If an inmate tries to climb or cut through the perimeter fence, he or she will receive a nonlethal jolt of electricity, which causes temporary immobilization. At the same time, the system initiates an alarm to staff that an attempt has occurred and identifies its location.
- *Backscatter imaging system for concealed weapons.* This system utilizes a backscatter imager to detect weapons and contraband. The primary advantage of this device over current walk-through portals is that it can detect nonmetallic as well as metallic weapons. It uses low-power X-rays equal to about five minutes of exposure to the sun at sea level. Although these X-rays penetrate clothing, they do not penetrate the body.
- *Body-scanning screening system.* This is a stationary screening system to detect nonmetallic weapons and contraband in the lower body cavities. It uses simplified magnetic resonance imaging (MRI) as a noninvasive alternative to X-ray and physical body cavity searches. The stationary screening system makes use of first-generation medical MRI.
- *Transmitter wristbands.* These wristbands broadcast a unique serial number by radio frequency every two seconds so that antennas throughout the prison can pick up the signals and pass the data via a local area network to a central monitoring station PC. The wristbands can sound an alert when an inmate gets close to the perimeter fence or when a prisoner does not return from a furlough on time. They can even tag gang members and notify guards when rivals get into contact with each other.
- *Personal health status monitor.* The personal health status monitor uses acoustics to track the heartbeat and respiration of a person in a cell. More advanced health status monitors are now being developed that can monitor five or more vital signs at once and, based on the combination findings, can produce an assessment of the inmate's state of health. This more advanced version of the personal health status monitor may take another decade to develop, but the current version may already help save lives that would otherwise be lost to suicide.
- *Personal alarm location system.* It is now possible for prison employees to carry a tiny transmitter linking them with a computer in a central control room. In an emergency, they can hit an alarm button and transmit to a computer that automatically records whose distress button has been pushed. A map of the facility appears onscreen, showing the exact location of the staff member in need of assistance.
- *Under-vehicle surveillance system.* An under-vehicle surveillance system utilizes a drive-over camera that records a video image of the license plate and the underside of any vehicle entering or leaving the secure perimeter of the prison. This system allows prison staff to check each vehicle for possible escape attempts and keeps a digital recording of every vehicle that enters or exits the prison.
- *Biometric recognition.* The facial recognition biometric system utilizes facial recognition by matching more than 200 individual points on the human face with a digitally stored image. The system is used to control access in buildings and rooms inside buildings; it will become more and more common in the near future.

(*continued*)

FOR CRITICAL THINKING AND WRITING

These methods are in use today and are merely the forerunners of a technological revolution that is changing the administration of prisons while at the same time improving security. Do you see any downside to technocorrections? Are we relying too much on technology to control our lives not only in prison but on the outside too?

Sources: Jeff Goodale, Dave Menzel, and Glen Hodgson, "High-Tech Prisons: Latest Technologies Drive Cost Savings and Staff Efficiencies," *Corrections Today* 67 (July 2005): 78; John Ward, "Jump-Starting Projects to Automate Correctional Processes," *Corrections Today* 66 (2006): 82–83; John Ward, "Security and Technology: The Human Side," *Corrections Today* 66 (2004): 8; Frank Lu and Laurence Wolfe, "Technology that Works: An Overview of the Supervision and Management Automated Record Tracking (SMART) Application," *Corrections Today* 66 (2004): 78–81; Gary Burdett and Mike Rutford, "Technology Improves Security and Reduces Staff in Two Illinois Prisons," *Corrections Today* 65 (2003): 109–110; Tony Fabelo, "Technocorrections: The Promises, the Uncertain Threat," *Sentencing and Corrections: Issues for the 21st Century* (Washington, DC: National Institute of Corrections).

CORRECTIONAL ADMINISTRATION: HOW ARE PRISONS RUN?

LO8 Define the basic responsibilities of a correctional administrator

The warden or superintendent is ultimately responsible for everything that takes place within the prison. The warden delegates the responsibility for custodial services and for program services to assistant or associate wardens (see Figure 6.4). In large correctional institutions, an associate warden for management services and an associate warden for industrial and agricultural services are charged with the responsibility for those areas. The associate wardens, in turn, rely on middle managers and line staff to operate the various departments within their sphere of responsibility. Institutional administrators encompass establishment of policy, planning, civil suits, institutional monitoring, staff development, and fiscal management.[53]

Establishment of Policy

Wardens determine policy for their particular institutions, although major policy changes must be cleared with the central office. One of the challenges of determining policy stems from the number of groups that must be satisfied: the legislature, the director of corrections, the various levels of institutional staff, the public, and the inmates.

Planning

The warden is expected to develop goals and methods for their achievement. Some top administrators look to modern management principles to be helpful tools in the goal-setting process. If no long-range plan exists, most wardens know they will become involved in crisis-centered management and will have to face the same problems day after day. Staff burnout and inappropriate reactions to organizational problems are the consequences of crisis-centered management.

Dealing with Civil Suits

Civil lawsuits by inmates constitute another area in which planning is needed. Administrators who are sued by prisoners must spend much of their time responding to charges, preparing affidavits, and testifying in court. This time-consuming process is not only frustrating and draining on administrative resources but also intimidating. Administrators may end up paying exorbitant attorneys' fees or sustaining extensive

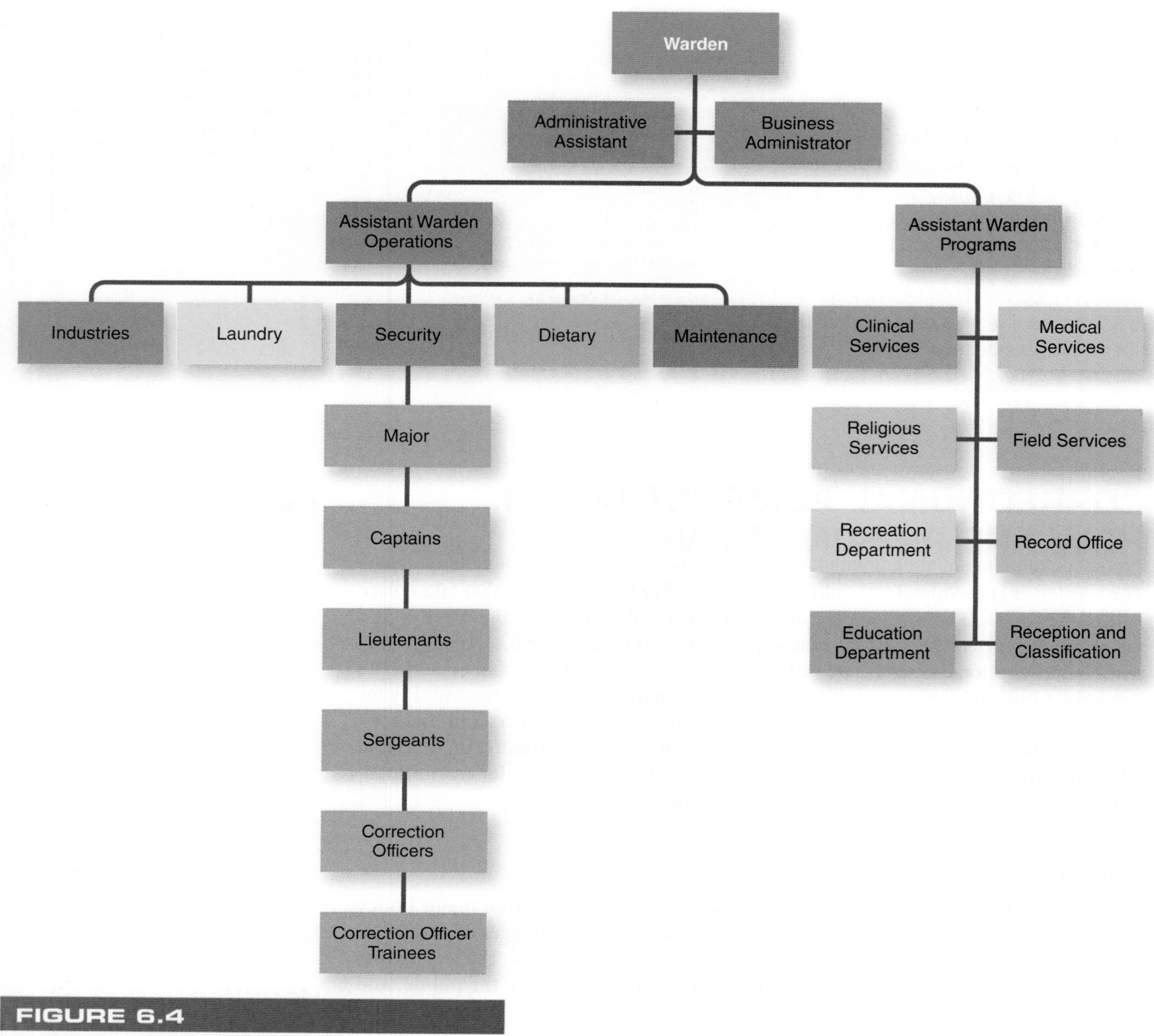

FIGURE 6.4

Institutional Table of Organization

Source: Illinois's Menard Correctional Center.

damages. Court decisions that impose new procedures, standards, and personnel requirements on a correctional system can also be expensive, time-consuming, and full of problems for administrators.

Institutional Monitoring

proactive warden An approach to prison management that is focused on anticipating problems before they occur.

The effective institutional administrator must have adequate information about what is taking place within the facility and must provide for special inmate needs. To keep informed, wardens must find ways to maintain good communication with prisoners. Prisoners with special needs, such as mentally restricted and emotional disturbed prisoners, sex offenders, or AIDS inmates, pose management problems for administrators and will be the subject of Chapter 12.

Staff Development

The warden is expected to develop training programs for new staff and to make changes in job assignments when necessary. The warden's style of leadership affects the way subordinates do their jobs. Most institutional administrators believe that staff morale and job involvement are enhanced when all levels of personnel participate in decision making, but the degree of personnel involvement is a decision that the top manager must make.

Fiscal Management

"A good warden," as correctional administrators are fond of saying, "always has a handle on the budget." Fiscal management should be a year-round process. There should be periodic (perhaps monthly) staff meetings to keep abreast of developments and the status of the budget. The warden should maintain his or her own file on changes that will be needed and others that will be recommended for the next year's budget.

Scott Olson/Getty Images

Warden Shelith Hansbro holds 3-month-old Alexis while visiting with inmates at the Decatur Correctional Center in Illinois. Alexis, who was born while her mother was serving a 54-month sentence for burglary, lives with her mother at the prison, part of the Moms with Babies program at the minimum security facility. The program allows incarcerated women to keep their newborn babies with them for up to two years while serving their sentence. The program boasts a zero percent recidivism rate compared to the statewide rate of 51 percent.

Proactive Wardens

An increasing number of wardens across the nation have become committed to a proactive approach. The **proactive warden** is committed to anticipating and preventing problems before they take place. The proactive warden puts a greater emphasis

LO9 Explain the proactive management style

CAREERS IN CORRECTIONS

Kent Grandlienard
Warden, Minnesota Correctional Facility, Oak Park Heights

"As a corrections administrator is always trying to recruit or promote our business, today's era of 'public employee bashing' by some politicians and the media, who seemingly demonize many public employees for simply having a job and/or the benefits that go with it, is disheartening. Choosing a career like corrections where the work can be both incredibly dangerous and equally lackluster on any given day, and of course with no 'perks' (e.g., holiday bonuses, profit sharing, or stock options), is not necessarily the type of job many young people covet. My entry into corrections as a recent college graduate was somewhat happenstance, but I was clearly drawn into the 'public safety and service' element of the job. Yes, I saw job stability, benefits, and career opportunities as a tradeoff to the lower wages and 'perks' that many of those in the private sector received. But being a dedicated public servant, especially in a correctional facility, and knowing that we are providing a very important public safety service and at the same trying to instill change in individual offenders to help prevent them from reoffending or victimizing others, can be a very rewarding part of this profession."

 See Chapter 15 for more detailed information on careers in corrections.

on programming for inmates and staff development. He or she also emphasizes the importance of direct communication and rapport between the warden and staff, the warden and inmates, and the staff and inmates.[54]

The proactive warden typically sees the context of the prison as a dynamic community with the capacity to change in a positive direction. Proactive wardens generally have the ability to think and conceptualize well, the character development to know the right moral positions to take, the creativity to be a problem solver with sometimes very complex issues, the willingness to look upon the prison as a learning community, and the willingness to take a proprietary interest in the institution.[55] Frank Wood, former warden of two prisons in Minnesota and Commissioner of the Minnesota Department of Corrections, identified several ways in which proactive wardens are different from other wardens (see Exhibit 6.6).

EXHIBIT 6.6

The Proactive Warden

- Proactive wardens believe they can make a difference. They believe that prisons can be run in such a way that inmates and staff have hope and confidence in and respect for each other.
- Proactive wardens believe in treating inmates with dignity and respect. Treating inmates with dignity and respect has to do with how the staff interact with inmates on a daily basis.
- Proactive wardens have a hands-on approach. They spend a good deal of time walking the cellblocks, visiting inmates in their cells, touring the yard, and talking with staff at their assignments. With this management-by-walking-around philosophy, proactive wardens believe they will obtain information necessary to avoid or defuse pending problems.
- Proactive wardens realize the importance of a supportive team. A major concern of these wardens is to build a team of supportive staff.
- Proactive wardens are receptive to technological innovations. They are quick to use the technological advantages that recently have become available to corrections.
- Proactive wardens model the behaviors that they want to elicit from inmates and staff. They believe that a necessary component of a human-relations approach is their willingness to demonstrate to others what involvement in and understanding of others entails.
- Proactive wardens have a plan and the commitment to execute this plan for reform of the existing institution. They have clarity in their goals and principles. Having developed their principles over the years, they are continually working on how these principles could be more effectively attained or realized in a prison context.

Source: Derived from Clemens Bartollas, *Becoming a Model Warden* (Lanham, MD: American Correctional Association, 2004), pp. 69–71, 74–76.

SUMMARY

LO1 Identify the extent to which prisons mirror the larger society

There are numerous parallels between the prison and the free world and in many respects the prison is a microcosm of the wider society. It can be argued that the prison is a distorted image of the larger society, with the problems of the larger society found in an exaggerated form in the prison.

LO2 Describe the age, gender, and racial makeup of those sent to prison

The prison population is made up of males (93 percent) who tend to be young and minority. Violent offenders make up a little more than 50 percent of all sentenced inmates in state prisons.

LO3 Discuss the federal jurisdiction over prisons

The Federal Bureau of Prisons is the largest prison system, as it oversees more than 100 correctional institutions, 6 regional offices, a central office in Washington, D.C., 2 staff training centers, and 28 community corrections offices. The Bureau of Prisons has had its problems, but it has long been advocated as the standard-setter of American corrections. Its advantages over state prison systems include better-trained staff, higher salaries, and more adequately funded programs and operations.

LO4 Explain whether state jurisdictions are similar from one state to another

Correctional systems of the 50 states and the District of Columbia are difficult to compare and evaluate because of differences in ideology, structure, and programs. Yet there has been marked improvement in state correctional systems in recent years.

LO5 Summarize how many prisoners are housed in private facilities and whether there is common agreement on the effectiveness of these facilities

Private prisons are gaining in number and popularity, and now have more than 100,000 inmates. There is disagreement about the quality and effectiveness of private prisons.

LO6 Discuss the security types of correctional institutions

The security levels of prisons vary from minimum-security to supermax correctional facilities. Security is the byword of all prisons, especially maximum-security and supermax facilities. Today, prison cells are still very small, prison keepers are required to keep prisoners docile if they want to keep their jobs, and solitary confinement is a way of life in the most secure prisons across the nation.

LO7 Describe what prisons look like

The four most widely used architectural designs in American prisons are the radial design, the telephone-pole design, the courtyard design, and the campus design.

LO8 Define the basic responsibilities of a correctional administrator

Correctional administrators are responsible for the establishment of policy, planning, dealing with civil suits, institutional monitoring, staff development, and fiscal management.

LO9 Explain the proactive management style

A proactive warden is committed to anticipating and preventing problems before they take place in the prison. This management style believes in treating inmates with dignity and respect, puts an emphasis on programming for inmates and staff development for staff, and holds to the importance of direct communication between the warden and staff and the warden and inmates. An increasing number of wardens see themselves as proactive in their approach.

CRITICAL THINKING QUESTIONS

1. Are all prisons like the "Big House" depicted in movies of the 1930s? Explain your answer using examples from your reading.
2. You wake up one morning and find yourself in prison. Based on your reading of this chapter, describe the sort of prison you hope it will be.
3. Why did the popularity of supermax prisons increase during the 1990s?
4. If you have not visited a prison, make arrangements to do so. Compare what you see with what you have read.
5. What are the advantages of a proactive approach to prison administration?

NOTES

1. Laurie Jo Reynolds and Stephen F. Eisenman, "Tamms Is Torture: The Campaign to Close an Illinois Supermax Prison," *Creative Time Reports*, May 6, 2013, http://creativetimereports.org/2013/05/06/tamms-is-torture-campaign-close-illinois-supermax-prison-solitary-confinement/ (accessed June 2014).
2. Interviewed on February 5, 2014.
3. E. Ann Carson and William J. Sabol, *Prisoners in 2011* (Washington, DC: Bureau of Justice, 2012).
4. Tracey Kychelhahn and Tara Martin, *Justice Expenditure and Employment Extracts, 2010 – Preliminary* (Washington, DC: Bureau of Justice Statistics, 2013).
5. Thomas Stucky, Karen Heimer, and Joseph Lang, "Partisan Politics, Electoral Competition, and Imprisonment: An Analysis of States over Time," *Criminology* 43 (2005): 211–247.
6. James B. Jacobs, *Stateville: The Penitentiary in Modern Society* (Chicago: University of Chicago Press, 1977).
7. Donald Clemmer, *The Prison Community* (New York: Holt, Rinehart & Winston, 1966), p. 298.
8. *Attica: The Official Report of the New York State Special Commission on Attica* (New York: Praeger, 1972), p. 82.
9. Lauren Glaze and Erinn Herberman, *Correctional Populations in the United States, 2012* (Washington, DC: Bureau of Justice Statistics, 2013), http://www.bjs.gov/content/pub/pdf/cpus12.pdf (accessed June 2014).
10. Ibid., pp. 6–7.
11. Ibid., pp. 8–9.
12. Federal Bureau of Prisons, http://www.bop.gov/ (accessed June 2014).
13. See Bartollas's biography of Norman C. Carlson, *A Model of Correctional Leadership: The Career of Norman A. Carlson* (Alexandria, VA: American Correctional Association, 2010).
14. Ibid.
15. For a description of the BOP programs, see Mary Bosworth, *The U.S. Federal*

Prison System (Thousand Oaks, CA: Sage Publishers, 2002).
16. BOP website.
17. Ibid.
18. Bartollas, *A Model of Correctional Leadership: The Career of Norman A. Carlson*.
19. In interviews, three former directors of the Bureau of Prisons—Norm Carlson, Michael Quinlin, and Kathleen Hawk Sawyer—all made this point.
20. For a vivid picture of life within a federal penitentiary, see Pete Earley, *The Hot House: Life Inside Leavenworth Prison* (New York: Bantam Books, 1992).
21. Michael G. Santos has written several books describing his incarceration in federal facilities. For example, see Michael G. Santos, *About Prison* (Belmont, CA: Wadsworth, 2004).
22. Information provided by the American Correctional Association, 2012.
23. Impressions gained from administrators of state departments of corrections and the Federal Bureau of Prisons.
24. Mark Colvin, *Penitentiaries, Reformatories, and Chain Gangs: Social Theory and the History of Punishment in Nineteenth-Century America* (New York: St. Martin's Press, 2000), pp. 243–246.
25. Cody Mason, *Too Good to Be True: Private Prisons in America* (Washington, DC: The Sentencing Project, January 2012), p. 2.
26. Corrections Corporation of America, http://www.cca.com/; The GEO Group, Inc., http://www.geogroup.com/ (sites accessed June 2014).
27. J. Maahs and T. Pratt, "Are Private Prisons More Cost-Effective than Public Prisons? A Meta-Analysis of Evaluation Research Studies," *Crime and Delinquency* 45 (1999): 358–371.
28. Mason, *Too Good to Be True*, p. 17.
29. Gerald G. Gaes, Scott D. Camp, and William G. Saylor, "The Performance of Privately Operated Prisons: A Review of Research," http://www.bop.gov/resources/research_projects/published_reports/pub_vs_priv/oreprpriv_cm2.pdf (accessed June 2014); William Bales et al., "Recidivism: An Analysis of Public and Private State Prison Releases in Florida," 2003, http://www.dc.state.fl.us/pub/recidivismfsu/RecidivismStudy2003.pdf (accessed June 2014); William Bales, Laura Bedard, Susan Quinn, David Ensley, and Glen Holley, "Recidivism of Public and Private State Prison Inmates in Florida," *Criminology and Public Policy* 4 (2005): 57–82; Lonn Lanza-Kaduce, Karen Parker, and Charles Thomas, "A Comparative Recidivism Analysis of Releases from Private and Public Prisons," *Crime and Delinquency* 45 (1999): 28–47.
30. Andrew L. Spivak and Susan F. Sharp, "Inmate Recidivism as a Measure of Private Prison Performance," *Crime and Delinquency* 54 (2008): 282–508.
31. Charles Thomas, "Recidivism of Public and Private State Prison Inmates in Florida: Issues and Unanswered Questions," *Criminology and Public Policy* 4 (2005): 89–100; Travis Pratt and Jeff Maahs, "Are Private Prisons More Cost-Effective than Public Prisons? A Meta-Analysis of Evaluation Research Studies," *Crime and Delinquency* 45 (1999): 358–371.
32. H. G. Lappin, T. R. Kane, W. G. Saylor, and S. D. Camp, *Evaluation of the Taft Demonstration Project: Performance of a Private-Sector Prison and the BOP* (Washington, DC: U.S. Department of Justice, Federal Bureau of Prisons, 2005).
33. Danica Coto, "Medical Care Company Names in Numerous Jail Lawsuits," *Charlotte Observer*, August 30, 2004.
34. Sasha Abramsky, "Incarceration, Inc.," *The Nation*, July 19 and 26, 2004; Gaes, Camp, and Saylor, "The Performance of Privately Operated Prisons"; "Lawmakers Press for Private Prison Closure," *Corrections Digest* 36 (March 2005): 1–2.
35. Mason, *Too Good to Be True*, p. 17.
36. Charles W. Thomas is a strong advocate of private facilities. See Thomas, "Recidivism of Public and Private State Prison Inmates in Florida: Issues and Unanswered Questions."
37. *Richardson v. McKnight*, 521 U.S. 399 (1997).
38. *Correctional Services Corporation v. Malesko*, 534 U.S.61, 122 S.Ct. 515 (2001).
39. Ahmed A. White, "Rule of Law and the Limits of Sovereignty: The Private Prison in Jurisprudential Perspective," *American Criminal Law Review* 38 (2001): 111–147.
40. "Prison Security Levels," *Fire on the Line* prison guard blog, June 7, 2006.
41. Ibid.
42. Maureen L. O'Keefe, "Administrative Segregation from Within: A Corrections Perspective," *Prison Journal* 88 (2008): 123.
43. Daniel P. Mears, "Evaluating the Effectiveness of Supermax Prisons," Urban Institute, May 10, 2006; and Mears, "A Critical Look at Supermax Prisons," *Corrections Compendium* 30 (2005): 6–7.
44. Mears, "Evaluating the Effectiveness of Supermax Prisons."
45. Jeffrey Ian Ross, "Supermax Prisons," *Social Science and Public Policy* 44 (2007): 60–64; Corey Weinstein, "Even Dogs Confined to Cages for Long Periods of Time Go Berserk," in *Building Violence: How America's Rush to Incarcerate Creates More Violence*, ed. John P. May and Khalid R. Pitts (Thousand Oaks, CA: Sage Publications, 2000), p. 121.
46. Kate King, Benjamin Steiner, and Stephanie Ritchie Breach, "Violence in the Supermax: A Self-Fulfilling Prophecy," *Prison Journal* 88 (March 2008): 144–168.
47. Ibid.
48. Laura Sullivan, "Life in Solitary Confinement: At Pelican Bay Prison, a Life in Solitary," NPR, March 7, 2008.
49. *Madrid v. Gomez*, 889 F.Supp. 1146 (N.D.Cal. 1995).
50. William G. Nagel, *An American Archipelago: The United States Bureau of Prisons* (Hackensack, NJ: National Council on Crime and Delinquency, 1974), p. 1.
51. William G. Nagel, *The New Red Barn: A Critical Look at the Modern American Prison* (New York: Walker, 1973), p. 36.
52. Minnesota Department of Corrections, "A New High Security Facility for Minnesota" (St. Paul, MN: Department of Corrections, n.d.), p. 2.
53. Richard Gramley, a former Illinois warden, defined the basic responsibilities of the correctional administrator and helped shape this discussion.
54. Clemens Bartollas, *Becoming a Model Warden* (Lanham, MD: American Correctional Association, 2004), pp. 71–72.
55. Ibid p. 72.

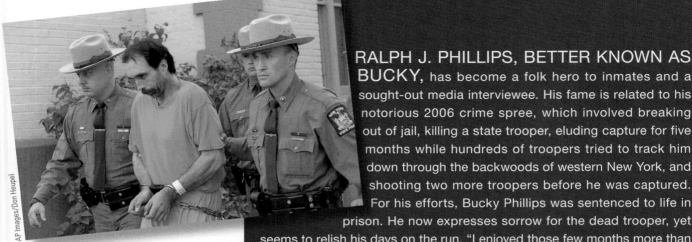

AP Images/Don Heupel

Ralph J. Phillips, better known as Bucky, is shown being escorted by New York State law enforcement officers. Bucky's notoriety is related to his 2006 crime spree, which involved breaking out of jail, killing a state trooper, eluding capture for five months while hundreds of troopers tried to track him down through the backwoods of western New York, and shooting two more troopers before he was captured.

RALPH J. PHILLIPS, BETTER KNOWN AS BUCKY, has become a folk hero to inmates and a sought-out media interviewee. His fame is related to his notorious 2006 crime spree, which involved breaking out of jail, killing a state trooper, eluding capture for five months while hundreds of troopers tried to track him down through the backwoods of western New York, and shooting two more troopers before he was captured. For his efforts, Bucky Phillips was sentenced to life in prison. He now expresses sorrow for the dead trooper, yet seems to relish his days on the run. "I enjoyed those few months more than I've enjoyed any other time in my life," he says. He is especially proud of his maneuvers to remain free: how he led two troopers on a twisted route deep into the woods and watched as a helicopter came to help find them; how he disguised himself several times as a trooper with a uniform he had obtained from an acquaintance, even chatting with another trooper who never recognized him; and how he moved around mostly at night and spent long stretches in the woods, eating rabbits and fish and sleeping on the ground. He assaulted a bounty hunter who kept his picture hanging from his rearview mirror.[1]

Using what he calls "cat and mouse" tactics, Bucky would purposely allow himself to be seen and then would flee as far as Ohio, Kentucky, and West Virginia in stolen cars, only to return back to his home ground. At times, he monitored trooper activity with a police scanner. He became aware that he had become something of a cult figure when he saw strangers walking on a road with shirts bearing the name "Bucky." He also learned that there were signs and shirts reading "Run, Bucky, Run" and "Where's Bucky?" Another sign of his growing fame: a restaurant called Grandma's Kitchen created and began serving customers the "Bucky Burger."[2]

On October 19, 2011, he was charged with violating prison regulations after a search of his cell turned up escape tools.[3]

7

The Prison Experience: Males

Robert Gumpert/Redux

LEARNING OBJECTIVES

 LO1 Describe the relationship between classification and institutional security

 LO2 Discuss the difficulties of confinement for male inmates

 LO3 Review the characteristics, norms, and language of "Big House" prisons of the past

 LO4 Explain the changing social structure of prisons, including gangs, racial tensions, contraband, and sex in prison

 LO5 Classify the forms of violence that take place in prison settings

 LO6 Explain the reasons for prison violence

 LO7 Articulate the changing roles and challenges of correctional officers in men's prisons

PREVIEW OF KEY CONCEPTS

- total institution
- no-frills policy
- prison classification
- external classification systems
- internal classification systems
- Big House
- Gresham Sykes
- inmate code
- Donald Clemmer
- prisonization
- prison culture
- deprivation model
- importation model
- situational model
- administrative-control model
- argot
- prison gang
- security threat groups (STGs)
- contraband
- sexual victimization
- Prison Rape Elimination Act (PREA)
- protective custody
- prison violence
- inmate disturbance
- prison riot

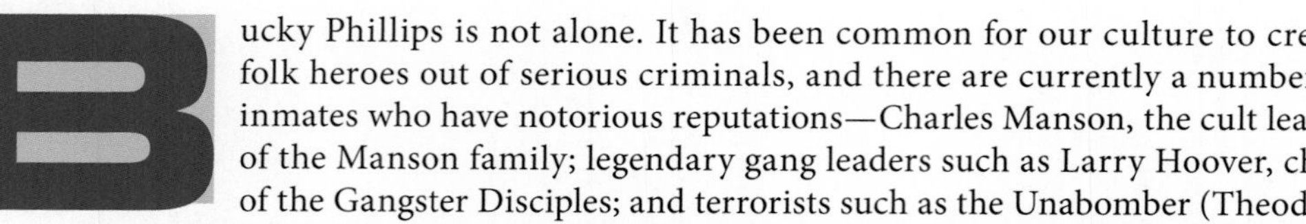

Bucky Phillips is not alone. It has been common for our culture to create folk heroes out of serious criminals, and there are currently a number of inmates who have notorious reputations—Charles Manson, the cult leader of the Manson family; legendary gang leaders such as Larry Hoover, chief of the Gangster Disciples; and terrorists such as the Unabomber (Theodore Kaczynski), shoe bomber Richard Reid, Oklahoma City terror bomb conspirator Terry Nichols, and Zacarias Moussaoui, the French citizen who was convicted of conspiring to kill U.S. citizens as part of the 9/11 attacks and who is now serving a life sentence without parole in the supermax prison in Florence, Colorado.

In contrast to this notoriety, the average inmate lives a life bereft of glamour and fame. Usually far from home with little or no contact with loved ones, inmates feel alienated. They must learn to adapt to a world of deprivation, doing without comforts and pleasures they enjoyed in the free world. Boredom is ever present. The experienced convict eventually learns to do time but has to fight against going "stir crazy." Furthermore, the total impact of incarceration—one negative experience stacked on the next—hardens a person. Male inmates, especially, learn that the best way to avoid being hurt is to repress their emotions. As one ex-offender puts it, "It took me a long time after I got out before I could feel anything. I was so used to making sure that nobody messed with me that I didn't trust nobody. I couldn't let anyone close to me. I didn't know what it felt like to love somebody. Man, I was dead."[4]

Because survival is uncertain in large dangerous institutions, men are likely to arm themselves for self-protection. In most state and federal prisons, the male prisoner also must deal with inmate gangs. As a gang member in a Midwestern prison noted, "In here you can't fly alone; you've got to join an organization if you want to survive."[5] Moreover, racial conflict is acute. Racial tension sometimes erupts in sexual victimization, in stabbings and killings, and in mass disturbances. Considerable evidence exists that incarceration has a negative impact on individuals.[6] For example, criminologist Michael Massoglia has written widely on the relationship between incarceration and negative health in subsequent years following release.[7]

total institution Term coined by Irving Goffman to describe an institution that has total control over all aspects of those confined there.

no-frills policy Inmates will receive the bare minimum of food, services and programs, and medical care required by law.

CRITICAL THINKING

Does a no-frills policy and deprivation make offenders worse or better? Do you think the no-frills policy results in reduced recidivism?

ENTERING PRISON

Prisons in the United States are looked upon as **total institutions**. This means that inmates are segregated from the outside world, are kept under constant scrutiny and surveillance, and are forced to obey strict official rules to avoid facing formal sanctions. With their personal possessions taken from them, they must conform to institutional dress and personal appearance norms. Many human functions are strictly curtailed or limited. Some institutions employ a **no-frills policy** that was passed as an amendment to the 1994 crime bill. What this no-frills policy means is stripping prisons of weight rooms, no cable TV (even if they have a TV that works), no computers, no air conditioning (dormitories are like a blast furnace in the summer), and mediocre food (beans, potatoes, and noodles are repeatedly served in some prisons). Educational and treatment programs have also been cut, making prison life as harsh as possible. The purpose is to convince offenders that prison is no place to be and they had better not return.

There are two important processes for the inmate entering prison: the classification process and the difficulties of adjustment. These processes have much in common for both male and female prisoners.

Describe the relationship between classification and institutional security

Classification

Inmates quickly learn what the term *total institution* really means. Their first experience usually occurs in a classification or reception center, where they are given a battery of psychological and intelligence tests and are evaluated on the basis of their background, offense history, personality, and treatment needs. Specialists attempt to develop a profile that includes criminal and social history, education, job skills and work history, substance abuse, and health. Based on this information, the offender is assigned to the most appropriate custody classification and prison. Violent offenders, high-profile gang members, and hard-core and repeat offenders will usually go to the maximum-security unit. Offenders with learning disabilities may be assigned to an institution that specializes in educational services, mentally disordered offenders will be held in a facility that can provide psychiatric care, and so on. Some states have instituted rigorous classification instruments designed to maximize the effectiveness of placements, thereby cutting down on the cost of incarceration.[8] However, some inmates may find that because of overcrowding they cannot be placed in an institution that meets their needs. Instead, they may find themselves in an overcrowded institution, housing more experienced and/or more dangerous inmates, that lacks the proper treatment they need to aid in their rehabilitation.

prison classification A method of assessing inmate risks and needs that balances the security concerns of the institution with treatment needs of the individual.

CRITICAL THINKING

List five categories or aspects that you would include in the classification system and which offenders or certain populations they would apply to. LO1

Prison classification is a method of assessing inmate risks that balances the security needs of the institution with treatment needs of the individual. Because inmates are a heterogeneous group, possessing a variety of behavioral problems, treatment needs, and psychological conditions, it is important to evaluate them so they can be placed in the proper institution and obtain the appropriate treatment and care. Effective classification can reduce prison infractions and create a safer environment for both inmates and staff. Exhibit 7.1 describes a typical classification report.

EXHIBIT 7.1

Nick's Orientation to Prison

Nick is a 22-year-old white offender who has been sentenced to prison for repeated use of drugs, which resulted in having his probation provoked. As he is transported from the county jail to one of the prison receiving centers, he is extremely fearful. He has heard the horror stories of a new inmate being repeatedly raped. In the next eight weeks, Nick experiences the following classification processes in this western state.

Needs Assessment

- **Health:** At his initial assessment, it was identified that he had asthma.
- **Intellectual Ability:** He scored high on his IQ text and is among the top 5 to 10 percent of inmates.
- **Behavioral/Emotional Problems:** He has a high rate of anxiety and seems to be fearful of his institutional placement.
- **Alcohol Abuse:** None appears to be present.
- **Drug Abuse:** Substance abuse has been his problem throughout adolescence and young adulthood, leading to his current incarceration.
- **Educational Status:** He has one year left to obtain his high school education.
- **Vocational Status:** Currently lacks skills necessary to obtain and hold satisfactory employment.

Institutional Placement

His risk assessment did not suggest a serious institutional risk or the likelihood of prison misconduct. But because of his runaway behavior at two previous juvenile institutional placements, it is recommended that he will be placed in a medium-security facility, surrounded by double fences.

Indicators and Characteristics that Determine How Nick Was Treated

- Nick had no history with violent offenses and so he was determined to be an inmate who would not be likely to create problems.
- He had escaped several times from previous stays at juvenile facilities, and so it was determined that he could be an escape risk.
- His previous history with asthma made it necessary to place him where proper medical services would be available.
- He had scored much higher than average on an IQ test, which made education an important consideration. He should be placed in an education program, first earning his G.E.D. and then taking further educational courses.
- With his drug history, the decision was made that he would need to be placed in a drug treatment group.
- Nick further scored high in anxiety, and he would need to be referred to a psychiatrist to see if medication would be appropriate.

FIGURE 7.1

Prison Classification Process

Source: J. Austin and P. Hardyman, *Objective Prison Classification: A Guide for Correctional Agencies* (Washington, DC: U.S. National Institute of Corrections, 2004).

Admission to prison

Initial external classification
- Custody assessment
- Program needs assessment
- Facility designation

Transfer to facility

Initial internal classification
- Housing assignment
- Program assignment
- Work assignment

Transfer to designated housing area

Reclassification
- External classification
  - Custody
- Internal classification
  - Program
  - Housing
  - Work
  - Facility
  - Community programs

EXTERNAL VS. INTERNAL CLASSIFICATION There are both external and internal classification decisions to be made (see Figure 7.1). James Austin's nationwide review of prison classification systems highlights the difference between external and internal classification. He states that while external classification places an inmate at a custody level that will determine where he or she will be housed, internal classification determines the cell or housing unit, as well as the facility programs (e.g., education, vocational, counseling, and work assignments) to which the prisoner will be assigned.[9]

External classification systems are now being used in all federal and state prison systems in the United States. Each offender is assessed using an objective risk classification system (using data such as the sentence length, the seriousness of the committed offense, and the offender's criminal history) and is assigned to a minimum, medium, maximum, or supermax prison facility.[10]

Internal classification systems focus on those decisions that are made for the incoming prison population. This review may include assessment of:

- Dangerousness as well as other types of assessments (physical health, mental health, gang affiliation, and flight/escape risk)
- Prison rule infractions, grievances, institutional punishments or sanctions, and reclassification decisions[11]

external classification systems Determine the level of security and control needed for the incoming prison population.

internal classification systems Determine the cell or housing unit where inmates will be housed as well as facility programs to which they are assigned.

EVALUATION OF CLASSIFICATION The National Institute of Corrections worked with eight states over a seven-year period to develop, pilot-test, implement, and evaluate internal prison classification systems. Seven models were tested. Colorado, Connecticut, and Florida developed computerized, objective, behavior-based models for housing and program assignments. Oregon developed an objective model that was based on behavioral and compatibility indicators for its female prison population, although preliminary results suggest that the system works equally well for male inmates. New Jersey developed a behavior-based model for identifying the aggression levels of its maximum-custody inmates. Washington State analyzed the utility of the Adult Internal Management System (AIMS) for case management of minimum-custody inmates with long sentences. South Dakota and Missouri further developed a personality-based system, the Adult Internal Classification System (AICS), modeled after AIMS. The diversity of the models developed suggests that there is no "best model," nor should there be one. The instruments and process must be tailored and validated to the specific populations for which they will be used.[12]

Despite its problems, classification has a number of advantages:

- An effective classification system can reduce institutional tension by placing inmates in the prison in which they can function more effectively.
- An effective classification system can better ensure a safe environment for both staff and inmates.
- An effective classification system can avoid placing inmates in more secure and expensive housing than they really need.
- Institutions with inmate gang problems may require that gang members or leaders of rival gangs be separated from each other and a classification system is therefore indispensable.
- Inmates with special needs, including HIV inmates, the elderly, inmates with mental health problems, and sex offenders, require that they be placed in the most appropriate institutional settings.[13]

Difficulties of Adjustment

Discuss the difficulties of confinement for male inmates 

After they arrive at the correctional institution that will perhaps house them for many years, inmates go through a variety of attitude and behavior changes as their sentence unfolds. When they arrive at prison, they are stripped, searched, showered, and assigned living quarters. Their treatment may seem harsh and inhuman, so it is not surprising that many of the men will become depressed when considering the long duration of the sentence and the loneliness and dangers of prison life. They soon realize they must learn the ins and outs of survival: which persons can be befriended, and which are best avoided?[14] To avoid victimization, inmates must learn to adopt a defensive lifestyle.[15] They must discover areas of safety and danger. Studies suggest that with limited resources and extensive personal limitations prior to their confinement, most inmates find that the challenges of incarceration further deplete their meager resources, which increases the difficulties of adjusting to prison life.[16]

FOR GROUP DISCUSSION Break the class into small groups to discuss whether or not an offender being classified into a particular category or group would have an increased potential for victimization and further difficulty adjusting.

Mental Health Services

A Special Report by the Bureau of Justice Statistics found that more than half of all prison and jail inmates had mental health problem, including 705,600 inmates in state prisons, and 78,600 inmates in federal prisons. These estimates constituted an estimated 56 percent of state prisoners and 45 percent of federal prisoners.[17] These were made up of the following categories:

- Female inmates had higher rates of mental health problems than male inmates. In state prisons, 73 percent of females and 55 percent of males, and in federal prisons, 61 percent of females and 44 percent of males were diagnosed with mental health problems.
- Prevalence of mental health problems varied by racial or ethnic group. Among state prisoners, 62 percent of white inmates, 55 percent of African Americans, and 46 percent of Hispanic inmates were found to have mental health problems.
- Rate of mental health problems varied by age. Inmates age 24 or younger had the highest rate of mental health problems, and age 55 or older had the lowest rate.
- Nearly 63 percent of state inmates who had a mental health problem had used drugs the months before their arrest, compared to 49 percent of those without a mental health problem.
- More than one in three state prisoners who had a mental health problem had received treatment since admission.[18]

Big House A type of large fortress-like prison that dominated corrections in the early part of the twentieth century.

TRADITIONAL MALE INMATE CULTURE: THE BIG HOUSE ERA

LO3 Review the characteristics, norms, and language of "Big House" prisons of the past

The so-called **Big House**—large maximum-security prisons that emphasized security and control—dominated American corrections from the 1930s through the 1950s. This type of prison emerged and spread, with considerable help from Hollywood, which portrayed this prison to the general society. States built large fortress-like institutions—Sing Sing, San Quentin, Alcatraz, and Stateville—that became stark representations of the prison experience. The Big House was a walled facility with large cellblocks that often contained three or more tiers of one- or two-man cells. Big House prison populations showed considerable homogeneity. Most of the inmates were white, were property offenders, and had spent several stints in prison during the course of their criminal careers.[19] "Convicts," as they were known then, developed a unified culture and kept their distance from the "hacks" or guards.

Todd Buchanan/Getty Images

Large, menacing prisons dominated during the Big House era. This five-story cellblock in B House at the maximum security Statesville Correctional Center housed over 2,000 felons.

In the Big House, old "cons" informed new prisoners that the guards were in control and the inmates had to make the best

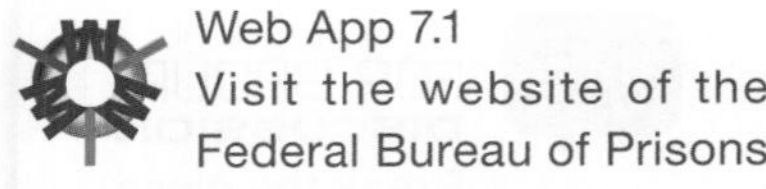

Web App 7.1
Visit the website of the Federal Bureau of Prisons at http://www.bop.gov/about/history/ to learn about the history of Alcatraz prison.

EXHIBIT 7.2

Social Roles in the Big House Prison

- Rats and center men, who hoped to relieve their pains by betrayal of fellow prisoners
- Gorillas and merchants, who relieved deprivations by preying on their fellow prisoners, taking their possessions by force or the threat of force
- Wolves, punks, and fags, who engaged in homosexual acts either voluntarily or under coercion to relieve the deprivation of heterosexuality
- Real men, who endured the rigors of confinement with dignity, as opposed to ball busters, who openly defied authority
- Toughs, who were overtly violent, who would fight with anyone, strong or weak, and who "won't take anything from anybody"
- Hipsters, who talked tough but were really "all wind and gumdrops"

Source: Gresham Sykes, *The Society of Captives: A Study of a Maximum Security Prison* (Princeton, NJ: Princeton University Press, 1958), pp. 64–108.

Gresham Sykes Developed a typology of prison social roles and inmate culture.

of it or face severe consequences. To make their time easier, convicts developed their own social roles, informal codes of behaviors, and language. In an influential study, sociologist **Gresham Sykes** delineated a typology of inmate social roles (see Exhibit 7.2).

Sykes found that inmate social roles, other than "real men," provided ways to reduce the rigors of their own prison life at the expense of fellow prisoners. Convicts fulfilling the social role of the "real men" were loyal and generous and tried to minimize friction among the other inmates. They tried to maintain social cohesion under trying circumstances and set an example that produced inmate solidarity.[20]

Inmate Social Code

inmate code An unwritten but powerful code regulating inmates' behavior; inmates codes are functional to both inmates and prison administrators because they tend to promote order within the walls.

During the Big House era, an informal **inmate code** of behavior developed and dominated the inmate culture. It was based on the following tenets:

- Don't interfere with inmate interests.
- Never rat on a con.
- Do your own time.
- Don't exploit fellow inmates.
- Be tough; be a man; never back down from a fight.
- Don't trust the "hacks" (guards) or the things they stand for.[21]

The inmate code was functional not only to prisoners but to prison administrators.[22] The code promoted order. It encouraged each prisoner to serve his sentence rather than create problems. Prisoners understood that disorder within the walls would mean that informal arrangements between prisoner leaders and staff would be set aside and prisoners would lose privileges it had taken them years to attain. The code also protected the self-respect of inmates because they knew they were maintaining order not for the staff but for themselves. "Hacks" were the enemy, and a convict who was worthy of his role within the prison made his animosity toward the enemy very clear.[23]

Nevertheless, inmates and guards in the Big House knew that they depended on each other. Inmates maintained order and performed many of the tasks of running the institution. In turn, guards permitted inmates to violate certain rules and to gain privileges that were contrary to policy. What took place was an exchange. Staff and inmates accommodated each others' needs while maintaining a hostile stance toward each other.

Prisonization

Among the most influential research on the Big House culture was the research by **Donald Clemmer** in his seminal study of the Southern Illinois Penitentiary (now the Menard Correctional Center). Clemmer claimed that the solidarity of the inmate world prevented prisoners from being rehabilitated. He coined the term **prisonization**, defining it as the "taking on in greater or lesser degree of the folkways, customs, and general culture of the penitentiary."[24] "Prisonization," he added, "is a process of assimilation, in which prisoners adopt a subordinate status, learn prison argot (language), take on the habits of other prisoners, engage in various forms of deviant behavior such as homosexual behavior and gambling, develop antagonistic attitudes toward guards, and become acquainted with inmate dogmas and mores."[25] Clemmer felt that when prisoners adapted to prison life they began surrendering their individuality and became dependent upon the system.

Clemmer's emphasis was on the unique situation of the prison as a community composed of unwilling members under the coercive control of state employees. The prison was viewed as a closed system, despite the fact that staff and the prisoners themselves were bringing in the outside culture and its values. Clemmer thought that all convicts were prisonized to some extent and possibly as many as 20 percent were completely prisonized. And he was convinced that upon release the highly prisonized offenders were likely to return to crime. Just as immigrants coming to the United States would be "Americanized" to a greater or lesser degree, so would a convict entering prison be more or less prisonized.[26]

In maximum-security prisons, inmates are well supervised and security is very tight. Inmates convicted of dangerous crimes such as murder are closely watched. Here, Grade B death row inmates exercise in 8-foot by 10-foot exercise cages and must enter and leave the grounds in handcuffs. Some, like the man in the black hat, are only allowed to exercise by themselves.

Clemmer's research was highly regarded by penal experts, and numerous attempts were made to validate his findings. In one notable study conducted in the Washington State Reformatory, Stanton Wheeler found strong support for Clemmer's concept of prisonization. But Wheeler found that the degree of prisonization varied according to the phase of an inmate's institutional stay: an inmate was most strongly influenced by the norms of the inmate subculture during the middle stage of his or her prison stay (with more than six months remaining).[27]

Donald Clemmer's research highlighted the influence of **prison culture** on the psychological well-being of inmates. What intrigued prison experts was how that culture developed in the first place. Did it arise spontaneously within prison walls or did it reflect the inmate's previous life on the outside? The two explanations for prison

Donald Clemmer Known for his research at Southern Illinois Penitentiary; coined the term *prisonization*, which defines how inmates learn to adapt to prison while taking on the prison culture.

prisonization The process by which inmates learn and internalize the customs and culture of prison.

prison culture The values, norms, and attitudes that inmates form in terms of institutional survival.

CRITICAL THINKING

Between the deprivation and importation models, which do you think is more related to the current prison atmosphere? Do inmates import their outside world and skills into the facility, which in turn creates volatility, or do they react to the deprivations of prison life? LO3

culture that have received the most attention are the deprivation model and the importation model. According to the **deprivation model**, developed by Gresham Sykes, inmate behavior is a product of the prison environment. The model describes the prisoner's attempt to adapt to the deprivations imposed by incarceration.[28] According to the **importation model**, the prison culture is imported from the outside world.[29] Consequently, inmate culture is affected as much by the values of newcomers and events on the outside as it is by traditional inmate values.[30] Two newer models that have received some attention are the **situational model** and the **administrative-control model**. The situational model emphasizes the effect of such factors as prison conditions, rules, and climate on inmate adjustment.[31] In contrast, the administrative-control model looks upon prison administrators as a vital influence on inmate behavior. Prisons characterized by strong leadership and proactive staff interaction with inmates experience less misconduct and violence than facilities that are poorly managed and administered.[32]

deprivation model A model that views the losses experienced by an inmate during incarceration as one of the costs of imprisonment.

importation model A model that suggests that the influences prisoners bring into the prison affect their process of imprisonment.

situational model A model that suggests that prison culture is influenced by situations rather than remaining constant and can vary over time and place.

administrative-control model A model that contends that the management style of the prison has influence over what takes place in inmate culture.

argot A form of slang inmates use in prison settings to express how they feel.

Prison Language or Argot

Referring to thousands of conversations and interviews, as well as to inmate essays and biographies, Clemmer was able to identify a unique language, or **argot**, that prisoners use. The specific demands on language by a subgroup are frequently expressed through slang. Argot, which was originally defined as the jargon or language of thieves but also applied to other groups, is a particular form of slang. It can be argued that a prisoner lives, functions, and thinks within the framework defined by the argot and, therefore, the argot centers on the functions that it serves for the inmate.[33]

With the demise of inmate solidarity and the inmate code in prisons across the United States, the commonly recognized or used argot language has decreased. There still remain a number of terms that appear widely used from one prison to another; see Exhibit 7.3.

EXHIBIT 7.3

Argot Language Used by Inmates

- Back-me-ups—friends you can count on in a fight
- Beef—a charge for the commission of a crime
- Bogus—anything false, counterfeit
- Bracelets—handcuffs or shackles
- Buy the farm—inmate who has committed suicide
- Cellie—cellmate
- Ding—mentally ill inmate
- Do a hitch—serve a prison term
- Easy time—one who is able to serve a sentence relatively trouble-free
- Fish—new inmate
- House—cell
- Jacket—label
- Kite—communication between prisoners and staff
- Pruno—prison-distilled wine made from fruit and other ingredients
- Rat—prisoner who provides information to the administration about other inmates
- Shank—prisoner-made knife or other sharp weapon
- Snitch—same as rat
- Standup guy—strong inmate who will not sell out to staff
- Yard—exercise area for inmates

Sources: Some of these are found in Lorna A. Rhodes, *Total Confinement: Madness and Reason in the Maximum Security Prison* (Berkeley: University of California Press, 2004), and others are common knowledge of the authors.

CONTEMPORARY MALE PRISON CULTURE

As the Big House era came to an end in the final decades of the twentieth century, prison culture underwent a dramatic change, taking on new forms in its structure, language, and mores. The influence of the inmate social code waned and with it the control over the inmate population by the right guys and real men. In its place has been an invasion of prison gangs and resulting racial conflicts, as well as changes in sexual expression.

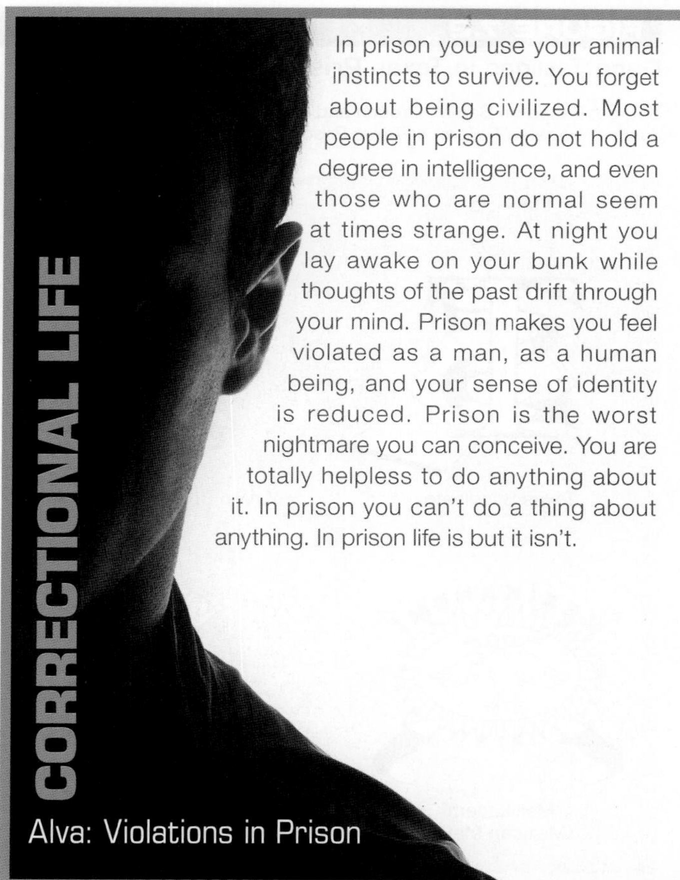

CORRECTIONAL LIFE
In prison you use your animal instincts to survive. You forget about being civilized. Most people in prison do not hold a degree in intelligence, and even those who are normal seem at times strange. At night you lay awake on your bunk while thoughts of the past drift through your mind. Prison makes you feel violated as a man, as a human being, and your sense of identity is reduced. Prison is the worst nightmare you can conceive. You are totally helpless to do anything about it. In prison you can't do a thing about anything. In prison life is but it isn't.
Alva: Violations in Prison

Prison Gang Structures

Prison gangs exist in 40 states and in the Federal Bureau of Prisons. In some states, especially California, Illinois, and Texas, prison gangs are the dominant force in inmate life. In nearly all of the other states that have prison gangs, they pose security problems and cause increased levels of violence. Prison gangs have recently been called **security threat groups (STGs)**.

ORIGINS AND DEVELOPMENT OF PRISON GANGS In the late 1960s and 1970s, street gang members were being sent to prison in increasing numbers. It was not long before prison gangs appeared in New York, Pennsylvania, Ohio, Arizona, Michigan, and Iowa. By the 1990s, prison gangs were found in all of the larger prison systems and many of the small ones.

In California, the Mexican Mafia (chiefly from East Los Angeles) vies for power with Nuestra Familia (consisting of rural Chicanos). African Americans in California are organized into the Black Guerrilla Family, the Black Muslims, the Black Panthers, and other groups; the Neo-Nazis and the Aryan Brotherhood are white gangs that have organized to provide protection against abuse and intimidation.

In the Illinois prison system, the Gangster Disciples, the Black Gangster Disciple Nation, the Conservative Vice Lords, and the Latin Kings vie for control. James Jacobs claims that the most important factor contributing to violence at Stateville was the presence of these four Chicago street gangs.[34] All of these "super gangs" originated in the slums of Chicago, and many of the leading figures were gang leaders when in free society. Jacobs found that formal agreements among the gang leaders assured incarcerated members that members of other gangs would not molest them. Inmates unaffiliated with a gang—around 50 percent of those at Stateville—were fair game for thievery, intimidation, blackmail, assault, and sexual pressure.[35]

Prison gangs in Texas are also increasing their control over prison life. Formed in 1975 by a group of prisoners who had served time in the California prison system, the Texas Syndicate is the oldest and the second largest inmate gang in the Texas prison system. A Texas offshoot of the Mexican Mafia, Mexikanemi (or Soldiers of Aztlan), was formed in 1984 and is the largest inmate gang in Texas. The Aryan Brotherhood of Texas and the Texas Mafia are two other powerful inmate gangs. Figure 7.2 shows the tattoo insignia of these four gangs. Both the Texas Syndicate and Mexikanemi are organized along paramilitary lines. Regardless of rank, both inmate gangs require their members to abide by a strict code of conduct known as the "constitution."[36]

LO4 Explain the changing social structure of prisons, including gangs, racial tensions, contraband, and sex in prison

prison gang A group of inmates who are bound together by mutual interests, have identifiable leadership, and act in concert to achieve a specific purpose that generally includes the conduct of illegal activity.

security threat groups (STGs) The name that law enforcement and corrections officials give to groups that exhibit ganglike activity.

Web App 7.2
Visit the Gangs OR Us site at http://www.gangsorus.com/ about STGs and the flow from street to prison and back again to prison. LO4

FIGURE 7.2

Gang Tattoos in Texas Prisons

Source: Based on Ben M. Crouch and James W. Marquart, *An Appeal to Justice: Litigated Reform of Texas Prisons* (p. 210).

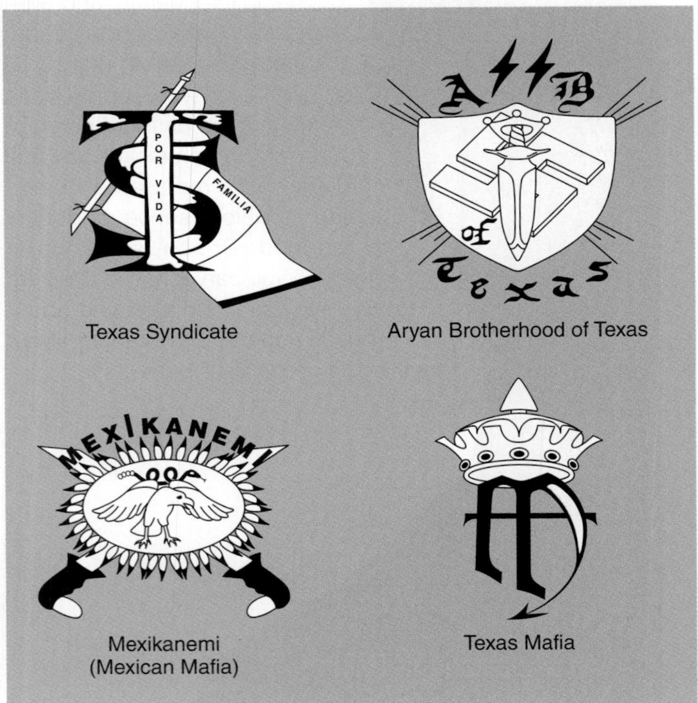

The Federal Bureau of Prisons (BOP) identifies the Aryan Brotherhood, Mexican Mafia, Texas Syndicate, and Black Guerrilla Family as particularly troublesome for prison officials. In addition, the BOP has identified as security threat groups (STGs) other gangs such as the Arizona Aryan Brotherhood, Black Gangster Disciples, Hells Angels, and Jamaican Posse.[37]

ECONOMIC VICTIMIZATION Prison gangs usually specialize in economic victimization. They typically force all independent operators out of business and either divide among themselves the spoils of drugs and other inmate contraband or fight to the death to determine who will establish a monopoly within the prison.[38] A survey of security threat groups in prisons found that they dominated the inmate rackets, including the illegal sex trade, illicit food business, loan sharking scams, gambling scams, "extortion" rackets, and drug trafficking.[39]

GANGS AND VIOLENCE High levels of violence may occur when gangs are in conflict with each other. Interracial conflict disrupts institutional life when large gangs organized along racial and ethnic lines make it a deliberate policy to attack other racial and ethnic gangs. Another problem is that imprisoned gang leaders usually have tight control over what takes place within the prison where they are confined. Imprisoned gang leaders have incited prison disturbances, the taking of hostages, and inmates' refusal to work or come out of their cells.[40]

Gangs have gained control in some prisons because officials are afraid that violence will be commonplace unless gang demands are met and leaders appeased. As one prison official in Illinois put it, "We felt that we had to stay on their good side or they would take the lid off the prison."[41] According to Larry Hoover, the legendary leader of the Gangster Disciples, gangs can incite a riot any time they want. In fact, according to Hoover, the gangs had agreed, especially the Vice Lords and the Gangster Disciples, that they would maintain peace within the prison, including cutting down on prison rapes, if the administration would meet their demands.[42]

The prison gang problem is serious and getting bigger. Prison gangs spread from one state to another in several ways. Inmate gang members may be transferred to a federal or another state correctional institution, where they spread their gang's ideas. Gang members who move from one state to another and are then imprisoned for criminal activities may organize a gang in prison. Also, the leaders of some street gangs send gang members to other states specifically to establish a gang organization, and those organizers end up sentenced to prisons in that state.

COMBATING GANGS It was clear by the early 1990s that prison officials had to take away the gangs' authority over prison life. Every attempt was made to suppress the expression of gang activity within the prison. Any demonstration of gang membership or activity was a disciplinary offense and could even lead to an institutional transfer to a more secure facility, including federal facilities. Suspected gang members were closely followed by staff and even segregated from other members.[43] Prison officials developed intelligence networks to discover what was taking place with gangs and who was involved.

TECHNOCORRECTIONS

Nonlethal Weapons in Prison

The use of nonlethal weapons to control inmate populations has become commonplace. Many of these weapons are manufactured by TASER International, Inc., the leading manufacturer of electronic control devices (ECDs). Generally speaking, a taser is an electroshock weapon that uses electrical current to disrupt voluntary control of muscles, producing what is called *neuromuscular incapacitation.*

The Shockwave area denial system by Taser can be used in correctional settings. The Shockwave system is a mobile, remote force-multiplier that uses neuromuscular incapacitation technology to deny access to strategically important areas in a prison. The device consists of a six-shot ECD that covers a 20-degree arc with 25-foot cartridges in units that can be stacked side by side or vertically, or can be daisy-chained together. The Shockwave device is used to defuse violent crowd situations by deploying multiple taser cartridges across a wide area arc. It can be triggered from a remote location, thereby reducing danger to prison security forces.

What Are the Risks?

Critics complain that taser devices cause extreme pain and even death. The American Civil Liberties Union alleges that tasers subject their victims to a 50,000-volt shock followed by 100-microsecond pulses of 1,200 volts. Since 2001, more than 500 people in the United States have died after officers tased with this weapon. However, a study by the National Institute of Justice finds that ECDs may be safer than believed. The researchers found that although exposure to ECDs is not risk free, there is no conclusive medical evidence within the state of current research that indicates a high risk of serious injury or death from the direct effects of ECD exposure; using ECD devices is safe in the vast majority of cases.

While the potential for moderate or severe injury related to ECD exposure is low, darts may cause puncture wounds or burns. Puncture wounds to an eye by a barbed dart could lead to a loss of vision in the affected eye. There is currently no medical evidence that ECDs pose a significant risk for induced cardiac dysrhythmia when deployed reasonably. Nor is there medical evidence to suggest that exposure to an ECD produces sufficient metabolic or physiologic effects to produce abnormal cardiac rhythms in normal, healthy adults.

FOR CRITICAL THINKING AND WRITING

These findings suggest that the use of taser weapon technology will remain a standard security measure behind prison walls. Do you have problems with their use and if so why? As an alternative, would you consider the use of heavy medication, "chemical straitjackets," as a means of controlling the inmate population?

Sources: Rebecca McCray and Emma Andersson, "Tasers No Longer a Non-Lethal Alternative for Law Enforcement," American Civil Liberties Union, May 3, 2012, https://www.aclu.org/blog/criminal-law-reform/tasers-no-longer-non-lethal-alternative-law-enforcement (accessed July 2014); National Institute of Justice, "Study of Deaths Following Electro Muscular Disruption," 2011, https://www.ncjrs.gov/pdffiles1/nij/233432.pdf (accessed June 2014); David Griffith, "TASER Showcases Shockwave Area Denial System at Urban Shield" *Police: The Law Enforcement Magazine*, http://www.policemag.com/blog/editors-notes/story/2008/12/taser-showcases-shockwave-area-denial-system-at-urban-shield.aspx (accessed July 2014). For more recent information on taser usage, see also http://aclu-or.org/content/aclu-use-tasers (accessed June 2014).

Prison officials have also stepped up security measures and control mechanisms to control gangs and violence. The TechnoCorrections feature discusses one commonly used method of inmate control.

Some corrections departments are making a diligent effort to prosecute gang members for crimes they have committed in the prison. Others have enforced the rule against "unauthorized activity or assembly," in which known gang members are unable to associate with each other. And a few simply lock up identified gang members and leave them in segregation while they are incarcerated. Pelican Bay State Prison in

VOICES ACROSS THE PROFESSION

Steven Ayers
Prison Captain, Oak Park Heights Maximum Security Prison, Minnesota

As captains, being responsible for overall security of the prison, we do have our difficulties and challenges. An emerging challenge right now is the offenders' abuse of over-the-counter and prescription medications. Offenders go to great lengths to try to get high on drugs, and without access to illegal drugs, they have resorted to abusing these types of drugs. Another issue is that security threat groups used to be clearly defined along racial lines. Now the groups are made up of a mix of races and there is in-fighting with the younger and older members within the groups. This has made it much more challenging to track and monitor groups in our facility. Management of offenders suffering from mental illness in prison taxes staffing resources. Our goal is to help them so they can serve their sentences in the general population, but it can be very difficult for them to make it successfully in that environment.

AP Images/Reed Saxon

Intergang conflict can take a toll on correctional facilities. Here, dozens of burned-out bunks are seen in a dormitory damaged by a fire set during a riot at the California Institution for Men in Chino, California. The riot, which left more than 200 injured and two buildings destroyed, was triggered by an ongoing racial conflict between black and Hispanic gangs that dominate the prison.

California actually mandates that identified gang members go through declassification programs and renounce their gang ties.[44]

Changing Racial Patterns

By the 1990s, prisons were more racially polarized than ever before. Racial tension and hostility became so intense that different racial and ethnic groups avoided each other as much as possible. They sat on different sides of the dining room and when assembling to watch movies or television. Even a slight disagreement among races—for example, over changing a television channel—could quickly spark violence. If an inmate was stabbed and the stabbing did not appear to have racial overtones, there might not be any further problems. But if a person from one racial or ethnic group stabbed an inmate from a different group, retaliation usually followed.

Today, much attention is paid to the racial integration of inmates. The most significant issue is whether it is practical to adopt a policy of enforced integration.[45] Chad Trulson and James Marquart used 10 years of inmate-on-inmate assault data in Texas and compared the rates of violence between prisoners who were racially integrated and those who were racially segregated. Trulson and Marquart found that violence among integrated inmates was lower than the level of violence found among segregated inmates.[46] They argue that successful racial integration was achieved in Texas because prison officials removed disruptive inmates from the general prison population and matched compatible inmates. They conclude that housing inmates randomly is the only realistic and legally defensible strategy of prison desegregation.[47]

Conflict among gangs is the norm, regardless of ethnic or racial makeup. It is not unusual for a Hispanic gang to battle an African American gang for dominance among the prison population. Or Hispanic gangs may war among themselves for prison dominance. Intraracial gang conflict is as common as interracial.[48]

MYTH Prisons are high-security institutions where control is tight and inmates are closely monitored.

FACT Many prisons are controlled by inmate gangs rather than the correctional staff. Within prison walls, gangs run such activities as the illegal sex trade, the illicit food business, loan sharking scams, gambling, extortion, and drug trafficking.

contraband Unauthorized materials possessed by prisoners.

Prison Contraband

Contraband can be defined as any unauthorized substance or material possessed by inmates, such as weapons, drugs, alcoholic beverages, prohibited appliances, and clothing. Gambling, institutional privileges, special food and canteen services, and prostitution can also be acquired through the contraband market. Contraband can also be items that would assist in an escape, such as ropes or ladders, or wire cutters that could cut a security fence. The definition of contraband has varied over time. Though cigarette smoking was commonplace in years past, tobacco products are considered contraband in some prisons today.

Inmates, of course, desire contraband. Drugs and alcohol substitutes can ease the pains of confinement. Weapons may be used as a means to protect oneself against other inmates or even to attack staff. Contraband can help start a riot or aid in escapes. In order to control contraband, staff must spend a considerable amount of time searching inmates' cells and lockers. Staff are aware that the more contraband that can be retrieved from a prison, the safer the prison will be for both inmates and staff and the less chance that serious problems will erupt.

AP Images/Pat Sullivan

High-tech tools are now being used to control or limit prison contraband. A screen in the warden's office at the Stiles Unit of the Texas Department of Criminal Justice displays the view from security cameras at the prison in Beaumont, Texas. New technology at the prison unit will divert calls, texts, emails, and Internet log-in attempts from contraband phones.

HOW CAN CONTRABAND GET INTO A PRISON? There are a number of ways that contraband comes into the prison:

- Contraband can be brought in by visitors. The extensiveness of this problem has resulted in more careful screening of visitors.
- Contraband may be introduced into the prison by corrupt prison staff, who can turn a lucrative profit by selling it to inmates. Some prisons have found it necessary to occasionally search staff when they come to work, over the strong objection of correctional employee unions.

FOR GROUP **DISCUSSION**

Discuss some ways to punish inmates for contraband. Should incentives or good conduct credits be provided for inmates who are not involved in the trade and sale of contraband? **LO4**

- Contraband can be made by prisoners. They may make a knife, for example, out of a bedspring. Inmates have always demonstrated amazing ingenuity in what they use to make contraband.
- Inmates may be able to steal contraband from other areas of the prison, such as food or knives from the kitchen or tools from vocational shops. Inmates can also steal metal from the metal shop and use this to fashion deadly weapons.

Sex in Prison

Sex among inmates in men's prisons usually occurs in three different contexts:

- Consensual sex involving affection and/or sexual release
- Coercive sexual behavior that combines force and domination
- Sex for hire, the purchase of sexual release at various levels of domination

sexual victimization Forcing an inmate to submit sexually to one or more inmates.

Prison Rape Elimination Act (PREA) This act established "zero tolerance" for rape in custodial settings, required data collection on the incidence of rape in each state, and established a National Prison Rape Elimination Commission.

While sex among inmates was not unknown in the Big House era, it has undergone significant change in the contemporary correctional setting. Today, the violence and brutality of inmates toward other inmates is expressed in **sexual victimization** as well as in stabbings or slayings. Many new arrivals in prison, especially white males who have committed minor crimes, are "on trial" and may become victimized if they fail to show their toughness and resiliency. The juvenile inmate especially has a difficult time, as these inmates tend to be very vulnerable. If first-time inmates, including juveniles, have the willingness and capacity to fight, they will usually pass the trial. If not, then prison time will indeed be "hard time."[49]

CORRECTIONAL LIFE

A Victim Speaks

My name is _______ and I am 23 years old and although my past criminal record isn't at its best, at heart I'm still a great kid!

After being locked up for about six months, I suffered from something many young males would hate to speak on and that's rape. I was raped at Eastern Mississippi Correctional Facility. I was beat brutally and had several facial and rectum injuries from this attack. I was raped, robbed, and assaulted by several prisoners. I was held hostage during the attack in a cell. I was threatened with knives and tormented by these inmates for several hours. After being a victim of rape by another male I am suffering still from anxiety, depression and stress issues because of my attacks.

HOW COMMON IS SEXUAL ASSAULT? In 2003, President George W. Bush signed the **Prison Rape Elimination Act (PREA)** to "provide for the analysis of the incidence and effects of prison rape in federal, state, and local institutions and to provide information, resources, recommendations, and funding to protect individuals from prison rape."[50] A data collection instrument was developed in order to sample 10 percent of all facilities in the United States to measure the extent of jail and prison sexual victimization.[51] The act established three programs in the Department of Justice:

- A program dedicated to collecting national prison rape statistics and data, and to conducting research
- A program dedicated to the dissemination of information and procedures for combating prison rape
- A program to assist in funding state programs[52]

The most recent federal data show:

- Administrators of adult correctional facilities reported 8,763 allegations of sexual victimization in 2011, a statistically significant increase over the 8,404 allegations reported in 2010 and 7,855 in 2009.
- The number of allegations has risen since 2005, largely due to increases in prisons, where allegations increased from 4,791 allegations to 6,660 in 2011 (up 39 percent).
- About 52 percent of substantiated incidents of sexual victimization in 2011 involved only inmates, while 48 percent of substantiated incidents involved staff with inmates.
- Among the estimated 1,390 youths who reported victimization by staff, 89 percent were males reporting

sexual activity with female staff, and 3 percent were males reporting sexual activity with both male and female staff.

- In 2011–12, an estimated 4 percent of state and federal prison inmates and 3 percent of jail inmates reported experiencing one or more incidents of sexual victimization by another inmate or facility staff in the past 12 months or since admission to the facility, if less than 12 months.
- About half of all allegations (51 percent) involved nonconsensual sexual acts (the most serious, including penetration) or abusive sexual contacts (less serious, including unwanted touching, grabbing, and groping) of inmates with other inmates. Nearly half (49 percent) involved staff sexual misconduct (any sexual act directed toward an inmate by staff) or sexual harassment (demeaning verbal statements of a sexual nature) directed toward inmates.
- An estimated 44 percent of substantiated inmate-on-inmate sexual victimizations involved physical force or threat of force, while 11 percent of staff-on-inmate sexual victimizations involved physical force, abuse of power, or pressure. Victims were physically injured in 18 percent of substantiated incidents of inmate-on-inmate sexual victimization, compared to less than 1 percent of incidents of staff-on-inmate victimization.[53]

It is most likely that the government survey undercounts the true incidence of sex assaults in prison. Why the difficulty in getting an accurate count? Inmates are reluctant to report rape to both researchers and prison administrators.[54] The inmate social code demands that inmates be strong and show no sign of weakness. Although the assailant in a sexual assault gains respect and status, the victim may fear that his fellow inmates may perceive him as weak and vulnerable. Inmates fear that if they report sexual assault they will be harassed or face retaliation by other inmates. Some independent research efforts indicate that at least 20 percent of all inmates are raped during their prison stay.[55] Christopher Hensley and colleagues found that 18 percent of inmates reported inmate-on-inmate sexual threats and that 8.5 percent reported that they had been sexually assaulted.[56] In another study, Hensley found that 14 percent of the inmates had been sexually targeted by other inmates.[57]

MYTH Prisons are highly dangerous places, and most inmates are sexually assaulted.

FACT Prison rape is actually less pervasive than previously believed, and most male inmates are spared sexual assaults.

Not all research finds such high levels of violent sex. When Mark Fleisher examined sexual violence in men's high-security and women's medium- and high-security prisons, he found that sexual violence was uncommon. Most sex was consensual, rather than forced, and was used to win favors or privileges.[58]

Regardless of whether sexual assaults are seen as epidemic or as relatively infrequent, few would deny that sexual victimization has many unfortunate effects. It curbs victims' freedom to act; indeed, many victims feel that their only viable alternative is to check into **protective custody**. Sexual victimization also leads to feelings of helplessness and depression, the threat of AIDS, damaged self-esteem, possible self-destructive acts such as self-mutilation or suicide, lowered social status, psychosomatic illnesses, increased difficulty in adjusting to life after release, and possibly even increased risk of recidivism.

protective custody A form of segregation, not for punishment but intended to isolate potential victims from predators.

ELIMINATING SEXUAL ASSAULT Anyone who has worked in an adult prison knows how difficult it is to eliminate or even dramatically reduce sexual assaults. Double-celling and dormitories make it impossible to protect vulnerable inmates. The inmate culture, with its discouragement of those who give testimony against predators, is another obstacle to a safe facility. In addition, the physical size of correctional facilities, the overcrowded conditions, and the number of areas of indefensible space are greater restrictions to keeping vulnerable inmates safe.

Using video cameras in those areas in which inmates are more vulnerable may reduce sexual assaults. It is also important for inmates to understand that they will

EVIDENCE-BASED CORRECTIONS

Eliminating Prison Rape

The Prison Rape Elimination Act of 2003 (PREA) established a "zero-tolerance standard" for prison rape and mandated that the U.S. Department of Justice (DOJ) "make the prevention of prison rape a top priority in each prison system." One of the goals of PREA was to increase the data and information on the incidence of prison rape to help improve management and administration in regard to sexual violence in correctional facilities. The law also created an independent National Prison Rape Elimination Commission, which was charged with studying the impact of sexual assault in correction and detention facilities and developing national standards to address the problem. Now there is more information available and correctional administrators have a more complete picture of sexual violence in prisons, providing them with the information and assistance they need to address this complex problem.

One research effort to assess prison violence was conducted by James Austin and his associates, which looked at sexual violence in the Texas prison system, the third largest prison system in the nation. The researchers chose this system because it had the highest rate of alleged incidents (550 alleged incidents, for a rate of 3.95 per 1,000 prisoners); on the other hand, it also has one of the lowest substantiation rates (less than 3 percent). In studying the number and nature of sexual assault allegations in this system from 2002 to 2005, they assembled "lessons learned" to help reduce sexual assaults across all correctional systems.

Among their findings in *Sexual Violence in the Texas Prison System*:

- White inmates are attacked more than any other race. Nearly 60 percent of the 43 "sustained" incidents—those proven to be true by an investigation—involved a white victim.
- Victims are generally younger than their assailants. The average age of victims in "sustained" cases was three years younger than the assailants.
- Mentally ill or intellectually impaired inmates are more likely to be victimized. Although only 12 percent of the allegations involved a mentally ill or intellectually impaired prisoner, this percentage is 8 times the proportion of mentally ill inmates in the general prisoner population (1.6 percent).
- Cellblocks with solid cell fronts may contribute to sexual assault. Solid cell fronts, while permitting privacy for the inmates and reducing noise within the unit, also provide the degree of privacy that permits sexual assaults to occur. Unlike older prison designs, in which the cell fronts consist of bars, solid doors limit visual observation by staff and, to some degree, soundproof the cells to the point that staff have difficulty hearing what is going on in individual cells.

The researchers made several recommendations, including that officials provide more structured opportunities to report sexual assault and that prisoners who have been implicated in such incidents be closely monitored. The researchers also recommended that a better system of categorizing victims and assailants be considered, and provided a characteristics checklist for correctional officials to use to help identify potential victims and assailants.

Another study, by Mark Fleisher and Jessie Krienert, looked at the sociocultural causes of prison sexual violence in men's and women's high-security prisons across the United States. Using a large cross-section of inmates (408 males and 156 females in 30 prisons across 10 states), they identified major attitudes and beliefs that inmates have about prison sexual assault, including:

- Inmate culture has a complex system of norms on sexual conduct. An act of sexual violence that occurs in one context may be interpreted differently in another context. Interpretation depends on the pre-assault behavior of the victim and the assailant, as well as other inmates' perceptions of the causes of the sexual violence.
- Inmates "self-police" against unwanted sexual predators and maintain protective relationships to facilitate safety from physical and sexual abuse.
- Inmate sexual culture allows inmates to disagree on the meaning of sexual violence in similar contexts. Some inmates may interpret sexual violence as rape, whereas other inmates may interpret a similar act as other than rape. The response of a victim toward an aggressor after the act of sexual violence plays a key role in an inmate's interpretation of sexual violence.
- Inmates judge prison rape as detrimental to the social order within the prison community—prison rapists are unwelcome.

(*continued*)

As a result of this evidence, many states have created new policies and procedures to change the correctional culture, thereby affecting the attitudes of staff and inmates. Some now mandate training for all staff on inappropriate sexual conduct and sexual violence and offer inmate education on reporting mechanisms and services for victims. However, problems still remain such as inmate unwillingness to report victimization, staff fear of false allegations, lack of staff training, and delayed reporting of incidents. Despite these issues, with the implementation of PREA and the active engagement of correctional officials, a multifaceted effort to understand the extent of prison sexual violence and to identify solutions for reducing it is well under way.

FOR CRITICAL THINKING AND WRITING

Is it possible to get valid information about prison rape since so many victims are reluctant to report attacks? Might it be possible to set up inmate-run anti-rape units that would be responsible for preventing rape, identifying rapists, and reducing sexual assaults? Or is this self-help approach doomed to fail?

Sources: Pat Kaufman, "Prison Rape: Research Explores Prevalence, Prevention," *NIJ Journal* 259 (2008), http://www.nij.gov/nij/journals/259/prison-rape.htm (accessed June 2014); James Austin, Tony Fabelo, Angela Gunter, and Ken McGinnis, *Sexual Violence in the Texas Prison System*, National Institute of Justice, September 2006, http://www.ncjrs.gov/pdffiles1/nij/grants/215774.pdf (accessed June 2014); Mark Fleisher and Jessie Krienert, *The Culture of Prison Sexual Violence*, National Institute of Justice, 2006, http://www.ncjrs.gov/pdffiles1/nij/grants/216515.pdf (accessed June 2014).

be prosecuted if convicted of sexual assault and that all charges of sexual assaults against them will be fully investigated. But probably the most important way to protect inmates is a vigorous and valid classification process in which more vulnerable inmates are isolated from those who may take advantage of them. The Evidence-Based Corrections feature discusses research on sexual violence in prison and how correctional administrators are using the knowledge to improve conditions.

EXPRESSIONS OF PRISON VIOLENCE

LO5 Classify the forms of violence that take place in prison settings

Prison violence is usually interpreted to mean a prison riot or mass disturbances, but it also means violence of inmates toward each other, toward staff, and staff's violence toward inmates. Prison violence also includes self-inflicted violence, when inmates attempt to hurt themselves or may even have successful suicide incidents.

prison violence Can vary from riots to staff assaults, inmate assaults, staff assaults of inmates, or self-inflicted violence.

Riots and Other Major Disturbances

Inmate disturbances can be nonviolent or violent. Nonviolent disturbances include hunger strikes, sit-down strikes, work stoppages, voluntary lock-downs (staying in one's cell even when the cellblock is open), excessive numbers of inmates reporting on sick call, and the filing of grievances by nearly everyone in a cellblock or even in the entire institution. Violent inmate disturbances include crowding around a correctional officer and intimidating him or her so that a disciplinary ticket is not written, assaulting officers, sabotaging the electrical, plumbing, or heating systems, burning or destroying institutional property, and **prison riots**—attempts to take control, with or without hostages, of a cellblock, a yard, or an entire prison.

inmate disturbance A disturbance, either violent or nonviolent, that brings disruption or even closes down the prison.

prison riot Collective response of inmates that is violent, in which they strike out against what they consider unfair prison conditions.

The most well-known prison riots took place at the Attica Correctional Center in Attica, New York, in 1971 and at the New Mexico State Prison in Santa Fe in 1980. During recent decades, riots have taken place in numerous correctional facilities across the United States. A few examples include:

- *William G. McConnell Unit in Beeville, Texas (1999).* The disturbance started when an inmate pried his way out of his cell and made it through three security doors. He stabbed a correctional officer and released 83 inmates from their cells. They were subdued by a tactical team an hour later.[59]

- *New Castle, Pennsylvania (2007).* About 500 inmates were involved in this riot in which two staff members and seven inmates suffered minor injuries at a facility that is operated by a private company.[60]
- *Three Rivers, Texas, Federal Prison (2008).* This disturbance left one prisoner dead and 22 others injured. Criminal intelligence sources said they believe the riot might have been between Mexican American inmates who consider themselves Chicanos and inmates who have closer ties to Mexico.[61]
- *Oklahoma State Reformatory at Granite, Oklahoma (2008).* Two inmates died and 15 more were injured during rioting in an exercise yard. This disturbance between black and Native American inmates was sparked by one inmate spitting on another.[62]

PATRICK TEHAN/MCT/Landov

A dormitory suffered heavy fire damage after a recent riot at the California Institution for Men in Chino, California.

HOW RIOTS OCCUR Riots may be spontaneous or planned to achieve some goal. Planning a riot usually requires a degree of inmate solidarity. When prison riots break out today, they tend to be more like the New Mexico riot rather than the inmate revolt at Attica. At Attica, inmates had a high degree of organization, solidarity, and political consciousness. The New Mexico riot was notable for inmates' fragmentation, lack of effective leadership, and disorganization. Indeed, the 1980 New Mexico riot showed the extent to which relations between prisoners had fragmented during the 1970s. Political apathy and fighting among inmates had replaced the politicization and solidarity of earlier years.[63]

Inmate Assaults on Staff

Inmates commit more than 16,000 annual assaults against staff. This is a little more than one-third of the number of assaults against other inmates. About one-sixth of the inmate-on-staff assaults require medical attention. About 70 percent of inmate assaults on staff are referred for prosecution.[64]

In one study, S. C. Light carried out a content analysis of official records dealing with nearly 700 prisoner-staff assaults in New York State.[65] He focused on the themes, or the immediate context, of the assaults and discovered that six themes accounted for over four-fifths of the cases. In decreasing order of frequency, these themes were:

- *Officer's command.* Assault followed an explicit command to an inmate.
- *Protest.* Assault occurred because the victim considered himself/herself victimized by unjust or inconsistent treatment by a staff member.
- *Search.* Assault occurred during search of an inmate's body or cell.
- *Inmates fighting.* Assault resulted from an officer intervening in a fight between inmates.
- *Movement.* Assault took place during the movement of inmates from one part of the prison to another.
- *Contraband.* Assault followed a staff member suspecting an inmate of possessing contraband items.[66]

Correctional officers are particularly concerned about being physically and sexually violated by inmates during hostage takings during a riot. One study examined 33 hostage takings and forced confinements spanning 11 years in Canadian institutions and found that of the 20 hostage takings, 7 had involved sexual assaults of staff. In this study, sexual assaults were always against women and 36.6 percent of the women were sexually assaulted.[67] Hostage taking can also result in violence toward male correctional officers, as took place during the violent conclusion of the Attica siege in September 1971, in which 11 officers and staff died,[68] and the standoff in Lucasville, Ohio, in April 1993, in which three officers died.[69]

Inmates versus Inmates

Inmate-on-inmate violence comes as no surprise. The prison environment combines a number of factors that contribute to inmates' assaults on each other. These factors include inadequate supervision by staff members, architectural designs that promote rather than inhibit victimization, the easy availability of deadly weapons, the housing of violence-prone inmates in close proximity to relatively defenseless victims, a high level of tension produced by close quarters and crosscutting conflicts among both individuals and groups of inmates, and feedback systems through which inmates feel the need to take revenge for real or imagined slights for past victimizations.[70]

Understandably, inmates make every effort to protect themselves. Weaponry has replaced fists as the primary means of self-protection in men's institutions. A variety of objects can be weapons: chisels, screwdrivers, sharpened shanks of spoons, broomsticks, baseball bats, clubs, chunks of concrete, stiff wire, heavy-gauge metal, metal from beds, boiler plate metal, and zip guns. Smuggled weapons also appear. Correction officers collect barrelfuls of knives and other weapons during shakedowns in some institutions.

Staff Assaults on Inmates

While riots and prisoner-on-prisoner assaults tend to make headlines, severe beating of inmates by prison staff have occurred throughout much of U.S. corrections history.[71] All kinds of punitive and sadistic practices have taken place. As you may recall, federal surveys have found that a majority of sexual assaults reported by inmates involve correctional staff members. James Marquart's examination of the maximum-security Eastham Unit in Texas in the 1980s found widespread staff brutality toward inmates. In explaining this abuse, Marquart concluded that physical coercion was deeply embedded in the guard subculture.[72]

Today, there is less evidence of staff's inappropriate use of force on inmates. Prisoners' rights organizations continue to accuse staff of retaliating against rioting inmates after regaining control of cellblocks. Most of the criticism of staff brutality against prisoners has come from those who have examined high-security units or supermax prisons. Fay Dowker and Glenn Good documented a number of instances of staff brutality in high-security units or prisons. For example, in Missouri's Potosi Correctional Center, prison officials apply the "double-litter restraint" to difficult prisoners. The prisoner's hands are cuffed behind him, his ankles are cuffed, and he is forced to lie face down on a cot. A second cot is then tightly strapped upside down over the inmate and the ends are strapped shut, which totally encloses and immobilizes him.[73] In addition, as previously discussed, correctional officers in California's Corcoran and Pelican Bay Prisons have received attention for their use of force against inmates.

Exhibit 7.4 summarizes the explanations for violence in prisons on an individual and a collective basis:

Self-Inflicted Violence: Prison Suicide

Between 2001 and 2010, suicide was among the five leading causes of deaths in prison in all but two years. The number of prison suicides slowly increased during this period, from about 170 to 215 per year.[74] White prison inmates were, on average, three times

EXHIBIT 7.4

Explanations for Prison Violence

There is no single explanation for either collective or individual violence, but many theories are proposed for why it takes place.

Individual Violence

- *History of prior violence*. Before inmates were incarcerated, many were violence-prone individuals who used force to get their own way.
- *Psychological factors*. Many inmates suffer from personality disorders. It is not surprising that people with extreme psychological distress may resort to violence to dominate others or that inmates with personality disorders are violently abused by others.
- *Prison conditions*. The prison experience itself causes people to become violent.
- *Lack of dispute-resolution mechanisms*. Many prisons lack effective mechanisms that enable inmate grievances against either prison officials or other inmates to be handled fairly and equitably.
- *Basic survival.* Inmates resort to violence in order to survive. The lack of physical security, inadequate mechanisms for resolving complaints, and the code of silence promote individual violence by inmates who might otherwise be controlled.

Collective Violence

- *Inmate-balance theory.* Inmate-balance theory is based on the belief that collective disorders occur when prison officials go too far in asserting their authority.
- *Administrative-control theory.* According to this theory, collective violence is caused by prison mismanagement, lack of strong security, and inadequate control by prison officials. Poor management may inhibit conflict management and set the stage for violence.
- *Overcrowding.* As the prison population continues to climb, unmatched by expanded capacity, prison violence may increase.

Sources: Kristine Levan, *Prison Violence: Causes, Consequences and Solutions* (Farnham, UK: Ashgate Publishing, 2012); James Byrne, Faye Taxman, and Donald Hummer, *The Culture of Prison Violence* (New Jersey: Prentice Hall, 2007).

more likely than black inmates to commit suicide; prison suicide is most common among young married white males. Age had little influence over suicide rates, with prisoners committing suicide at nearly equal rates across age groups, though juveniles have high rates of suicide. Suicide generally occurs early in confinement, and hanging is the usual method. Some prison homicides are in fact suicides, because inmates let themselves be murdered by violent inmates. Inmates have been known to charge the fence, knowing that guards will shoot them down. Furthermore, prisoners on death row who have lost their will to live may call off their appeals, letting the state carry out the suicidal act.

Explain the reasons for prison violence LO6

- The prison experience itself, marked by deprivation, overcrowding, and violence, increases the likelihood of prison suicide.[75]
- Prisoners typically experience less social control than the general population and lower levels of integration with other people and groups. These loners are more likely to feel alienated and depressed, hence they have higher rates of suicide.[76]
- Most inmates bring psychological and emotional problems to prison when they arrive and these preconditions are related to suicide. One study of the mental health records of all 76 suicides that occurred between 1993 and 2001 in the New York Department of Correctional Services found that 95 percent had a substance abuse history, 70 percent displayed agitation or anxiety prior to the suicide, and 49 percent had a behavioral change.[77]

Steven Ayers

CAREERS IN CORRECTIONS

"This is what drives and motivates me—that we can make a difference in offenders' lives."

Steve Ayers

Prison Captain, Oak Park Heights Maximum Security Prison, Minnesota

"The following list describes a typical day in the life of a prison captain. This is where the real prison work occurs:

- We read the incident reports/captain's report from the previous 24 hours.
- We prepare for the warden's executive morning meeting, held Monday through Friday.
- In the warden's executive meeting, we review all reports and develop a plan of action for the day. We update the warden on any projects/initiatives we are working on.
- We represent the interests of the correctional officers to the executive level staff.
- We are always trying to prevent major incidents such as offender physical altercations, assaults on staff, contraband in the facility, and suicides. If they occur, we work to ensure they are handled appropriately and minimize the negative impacts.
- We are responsible for developing emergency plans, officer post orders, and security policies and routinely conduct drill on our plans. We conduct weekly inspections of the entire facility.
- We respond to real and imagined concerns of offenders, and assist staff with work issues they are experiencing.
- We search, search, and search to try to keep the 'neighborhood' safe.

The security division job consists of 99 percent routine/normal operations with 1 percent responding to emergency incidents that take place. We work with staff to avoid complacency in carrying out their duties. Every three years we have a security audit, and I ensure that we are in compliance with the security standards and policies."

See Chapter 15 for more detailed information on careers in corrections.

GUARDING THE PRISON

Historically, the paramilitary model has been used for security in most institutions. Custodial staffs wear uniforms and badges; are assigned titles such as sergeant, lieutenant, captain, and major; use designations such as company, mess hall, drill, inspection, and gig list; and maintain a sharp division between lower- and higher-ranking officers. The procedures and organizational structures that control inmates are also militaristic in form. For many years, prisoners marched to the dining hall and to their various assignments. They removed their hats in the presence of a captain and stood at attention when the warden approached.

Although the prison has been stripped of some of its regimentation, the paramilitary model is alive and flourishing. Associate wardens of custody or operations are ultimately responsible for knowing the whereabouts of all inmates at all times. Correctional officers' captains, few in number, are usually assigned to full-time administrative responsibilities or to shift command. Lieutenants are known as troubleshooters. They roam the institution dealing with volatile incidents. The lieutenant's job is to be right there with fellow officers. The lieutenants take troublesome inmates out of their cells and walk them to segregation. Sergeants, like army sergeants, manage particular units, such as cell houses or the hospital, and supervise several other officers.

Lou Dematteis/Reuters/Corbis

California State Correctional Officer A. Lopez closes the door to the type of cell that awaits the most serious criminal offenders in maximum-security prisons. Scott Peterson, who gained national notoriety for killing his wife Laci, is actually housed in this cell in San Quentin State Prison.

The Changing Role of Correctional Officer

Higher salaries, improved standards, greater training, and unionization are signs that the role of correctional officer is undergoing change. Correctional officers are beginning to make a living wage in most states (see Chapter 15 for career details). Over half of the states now require a high school diploma or a GED certificate as their minimum employment requirement. Many states have academy training programs for pre-service and in-service officers, which appear to be effective in ensuring that officers bring basic skills to their jobs. The Federal Bureau of Prisons requires three years of college for correctional officers.

Correctional officers in the majority of states are now unionized. The growth of unions among correctional officers has encouraged them to seek greater rights, more recognition, and higher pay. The unions that represent correctional officers include AFSCME (American Federation of State, County, and Municipal Employees), the Service Employees International Union (SEIU), the International Brotherhood of Teamsters, and state employee associations. Officers in Connecticut, New Jersey, New York, and Ohio have gone on strike to protest low wages or poor working conditions. When correctional officers walk out, other personnel, the state police, and sometimes even the National Guard are forced to run the institution until the strike is settled.

Articulate the changing roles and challenges of correctional officers in men's prisons

Conflicting Goals and Expectations

The greatest problem faced by correctional officers is the duality of their role: maintainers of order and security and advocates of treatment and rehabilitation. Added to this basic dilemma is the changing inmate role. In earlier times, correctional officers could count on inmate leaders to help them maintain order, but now they are faced with a racially charged atmosphere in which violence is a way of life. Correctional work in some institutions can be filled with danger, tension, boredom, and little evidence that efforts to help inmates lead to success. Correctional officers experience alienation and isolation from inmates, the administration, and each other. It is not surprising that correctional officers perceive significant levels of stress related to such job factors as lack of safety, inadequate career opportunities, and work overload.[78] However, those who have high levels of job satisfaction, good relations with their coworkers, and high levels of social support seem to be better able to deal with the stress of the correctional setting.[79]

MYTH **Prison guards are ruthless people who enjoy their position of power over inmates, fight rehabilitation efforts, and have a "lock psychosis" developed from years of counting, numbering, and checking on inmates.**

FACT **Correctional officers are public servants who are seeking the security and financial rewards of a civil service position. Most are in favor of rehabilitation efforts and do not hold any particular animosity toward inmates.**

Women Officers in Men's Prisons

It is not unusual to find women working as correctional officers in men's prisons. The enactment of equal employment legislation, especially Title VII, which prohibited sex discrimination in hiring by state and local government, opened the doors for women in men's prisons. *Dothard v. Rawlinson* (1977) and *Gunther v. Iowa State Men's*

Reformatory (1979) are the two most important U.S. Supreme Court cases examining whether women are qualified to work in men's prisons. The former was an Alabama lawsuit filed by Diane Rawlinson, a recent college graduate in correctional psychology, who was denied a job as a correctional officer because she was five pounds below the minimum weight requirement. Her class-action suit challenged the state height and weight requirements. The suit also charged that a department of corrections regulation preventing female officers from "continual close proximity" to prisoners in maximum-security prisons for men (known as the no-contact rule) was discriminatory. The U.S. Supreme Court, in a 5–4 decision, overturned a lower court decision that had invalidated the no-contact rule. The Supreme Court was unwilling to let women work in a maximum-security prisons for men in Alabama because of the danger of sexual attack and because the vulnerability of women to attack would weaken security and endanger other prison employees.[80]

In the *Gunther* decision, the Court dismissed security issues as a reason for limiting women's employment in Iowa. The *Gunther* decision said that job requirements to strip-search male inmates or witness male inmates in showers constituted an attempt to protect women from working as a correctional officer.[81]

Some critics have questioned the wisdom of such assignments; they believe that women are not fit for the job because they are not strong enough, are too easily corrupted by inmates, or are poor backups for officers in trouble. Women have been criticized as being a disruptive influence because inmates compete for their attention or refuse to follow their orders. Critics also say that the presence of women violates inmates' privacy, especially when women are working shower areas or conducting strip searches. However, in a number of cases, the courts have generally tried to protect both women's right to employment and inmates' privacy as much as possible.[82]

Those supporting the employment of female officers in men's prisons argue that departments of corrections can achieve privacy by means of administrative policies preventing women from doing strip searches. The installation of modest half-screens, fogged windows that permit figures to be seen, or privacy doors on toilet stalls offers solutions to privacy issues. Security does not have to be sacrificed, and these modifications can be made to the physical environment at little cost.

VOICES ACROSS THE PROFESSION

Respect gets respect.

Barbara Casey
Correctional Officer, Fort Dodge Correctional Center, Iowa

As a female working in a male facility, you definitely have to be thick-skinned. Addressing inappropriate comments is a must, but how they're addressed is a key to the law of corrections—respect gets respect. In my 15 years of working at the Fort Dodge Correctional Facility, I have only had a few incidents. I tend to have a mothering behavior with younger offenders and at all times keep in mind my behavior is always being watched by offenders. I always try to display prosocial behavior. Even in working the segregation units, I have observed older offenders addressing younger offenders on their manners to female staff. At Fort Dodge Correctional Facility, we have offender mentors and officers work with the mentors in how to help younger and special-needs offenders adapt to incarceration. With that being said, the female officer has to be aware and identify if you are being manipulated by an offender. He may be setting you up for future favors. He may point out he did you a favor or told you something that was said about you and he handled it for you. It is very important to immediately address that behavior and stop it. Otherwise offenders will pick that out as a weakness and expound on it.

THINKING LIKE A CORRECTIONS PROFESSIONAL

As the warden of an adult prison, you hear from inmates who work in the kitchen that correctional officers are taking food home that was intended for inmates. What would you do to investigate these charges? Would you dismiss these accusations because you believe that your officers would not become involved in such inappropriate behavior? Would you hand this investigation over to your associate warden for operations and trust that he or she will handle the investigation in an appropriate way? Would you hand this investigation over to a security staff member, such as a captain, but stay involved yourself?

If it was discovered from the investigation that two correctional officers were regularly taking meat and other food intended for inmates, how would you handle this situation? Would it be sufficient grounds for termination?

Officers' Response to Problems on the Job

Like the prison culture, problem-solving skills are passed down from one generation of correctional worker to another. Old-timers tell new correctional officers about acceptable behavior on the job. Experienced officers know that all officers will be punished severely for violations of security. A mistake that leads to an escape may cost them several weeks "in the streets" (suspension) or may even result in termination. Any erosion of security makes it more likely that inmates will initiate a disturbance and that the disturbance will mushroom into a full-scale riot. Moreover, experienced officers know that inmates cannot be given too much leeway or they will end up controlling the institution and abusing their keepers. These officers try to teach newly certified correctional staff how to strike a balance between rigidly enforcing all the rules and allowing the inmates to gain control. Finally, experienced officers know that the best hope for security is fair treatment of inmates. Simply put, an inmate who is treated fairly and with respect is much less likely to become a security problem than a prisoner who feels humiliated and abused by staff.

Nevertheless, there are always a few officers who become involved in corrupt and illegal behavior that jeopardizes security and violates the law. They may agree to bring contraband into the institution because they have been set up by inmates. Some officers carry contraband for profit. Inmates who are trafficking drugs into the institution or have a drug appetite themselves seem to be able to raise large amounts of cash. According to offenders who have spent time in federal and state institutions, inmates walk and talk with each new officer and soon figure out who can be corrupted. An example is an officer in a Midwestern state who was caught in a strip search with two large bags of marijuana taped across his chest. Investigators found that he had been bringing drugs into the prison for some time and had been able to buy a Cadillac and expensive clothes with his additional tax-free income.[83]

Job Enrichment: A Challenge for Administrators

There is no question that most correctional officers want to help inmates, provide them with human services, and help them to rise as much as possible above the limitations of their institutional setting. These officers relate to inmates as human beings and see themselves as being consistent, fair, and flexible.[84] The challenge is to motivate all line staff to rise to this level of professionalism.

VOICES ACROSS THE PROFESSION

This is what drives and motivates me—that we can make a difference in offenders' lives.

Steven Ayers
Prison Captain, Oak Park Heights Maximum Security Prison, Minnesota

I really look forward to coming to work every day. I work hard on trying to do the "right thing" even though at times it may not be viewed favorably by staff and/or offenders. One needs to work on staying positive in a potentially negative work and living environment. I relieve any stress the job creates by staying physically fit. The job is filled with so much variety and there is always something refreshing and new. This is what drives and motivates me—that we can make a difference in offenders' lives. It is very fulfilling when an offender informs me that I have made a positive difference in his life, big or small. This business is not for everyone, as you need to be able to separate what the offender had done to get to prison and treat them humanely at all times. Ninety-five percent of the offenders will someday be released back into society, so we need to work on creating an environment that is positive to hopefully allow them to be better people, not worse.

Barbara Casey

CAREERS IN CORRECTIONS

Barbara Casey
Correctional Officer, Fort Dodge (Iowa) Correctional Center

"**Job Description:** Our basic task is to supervise incarcerated offenders. We must maintain security for the offenders, staff, and facility.

A Day on the Job: Each shift is given a pass-down from the previous shift. Our captain reports on any changes that have occurred within the last 24 hours, activities, behaviors that may have caused lock-ups or level reductions, trips off grounds and returns, new arrivals. Each officer receives assignments. Upon reporting to your assigned post, the officer receives another pass-down from the officer who is currently working that post. At that time the officer shares any information that will assist in the supervising of that area.

Activities Performed: While supervising the offenders, the officer performs security searches (pat and property). We work with offenders on their behavior and supervise their activities. Officers are trained in reentry skills and are taught to role model prosocial behavior and contribute to the positive reentry of the offender to society without victimization. Several officers contribute in the treatment classes that are taught at the facility. Officers also participate in classification so they can help offenders stay with their goals and case plan for release. We are expected to communicate indicators to counselors and the psychologist."

See Chapter 15 for more detailed information on careers in corrections.

SUMMARY

LO1 Describe the relationship between classification and institutional security

Classification of inmates is an important consideration for institutional security. Classification involves both external classification, in which an inmate is sent to a particular custody level institution, and internal classification, in which the prisoner is assigned to a housing area and programs.

LO2 Discuss the difficulties of confinement for male inmates

The difficulties of confinement for male inmates, especially in maximum-security placements, include protecting oneself against the dangers of prison society and dealing with the loneliness and boredom of daily life.

LO3 Review the characteristics, norms, and language of "Big House" prisons of the past

The traditional male inmate culture, or the Big House era, had social roles, an inmate code, and prison language or argot. All this led to a solidarity of inmate culture.

LO4 Explain the changing social structure of prisons, including gangs, racial tensions, contraband, and sex in prison

The contemporary prison is a violent and unpredictable environment in which to do time. Prison gangs are found in most state correctional systems and the Federal Bureau of Prisons. Racial conflict within the walls is a relatively new feature of prison structure. Sexual assaults may be less prevalent than in the past, but many new inmates, especially those who have not done time before, will be tested.

LO5 Classify the forms of violence that take place in prison settings

The forms of violence that take place in prison settings include collective violence or riots, inmate assaults on inmates, inmate assaults on staff, staff assaults on inmates, and prison suicides. Inmate assaults on staff occur frequently in today's prisons, but the number of assaults on staff is about a third of the number of assaults against other inmates. Staff assaults on inmates still take place, though much less frequently than in the past. Prison suicide rates have dipped sharply in recent years; today suicides constitute about 7 percent of all state prisoners' deaths. Most large prisons, especially maximum-security ones, experience a riot at one time or another.

LO6 Explain the reasons for prison violence

There are many theories as to why prison violence takes place, ranging from individual violence to collective violence. Individual explanations of prison violence include history of prior violence, psychological factors, prison conditions, lack of dispute-resolution mechanisms, and basic survival. Collective violence explanations include inmate-balance theory, administrative-control theory, and overcrowding.

LO7 Articulate the changing roles and challenges of correctional officers in men's prisons

Higher salaries, improved standards, greater training, and unionization are signs that the role of correctional officer is undergoing change. The greatest problem faced by correctional officers is the duality of their role in maintaining order and security and advocating treatment. In addition, correctional officers today are experiencing greater alienation and isolation from inmates. Furthermore, the correctional officer's role has shifted in recent years, as part of the growing professionalization of the prison. There are increasing numbers of officers who wish to treat inmates fairly, with consistency, and humanely.

CRITICAL THINKING QUESTIONS

1. You are the warden of a correctional facility that has extremely high rates of violence among racial and ethnic groups. What will your strategy be for diffusing the racial and ethnic tension?
2. Is it more difficult for an inmate to do time today than during the Big House era?
3. What causes prison riots and inmate violence? What can a prison administrator do to reduce violence?
4. Is it possible to communicate and to develop a relationship with prison gang members? What would be the purpose of such a relationship?
5. Why do you think there is so much contraband in prison? What can be done to restrict its availability?

NOTES

1. "Phillips Case: Ex-Fugitive 'Bucky' Phillips Pleads Guilty to Shooting Trooper," *Niagara Gazette*, November 29, 2006.
2. Ibid.
3. Associated Press, "Inmate Who Killed Trooper Is Said to Have Escape Tools," October 19, 2011, http://www.nytimes.com/2011/10/20/nyregion/ralph-phillips-who-killed-trooper-is-accused-of-harboring-escape-tools-in-dannemora-prison.html (accessed June 2014).
4. Interviewed in 1995.
5. Interviewed in 1999.
6. For an article relating imprisonment and the life course, see Charles E. Loeffler, "Does Imprisonment Alter the Life Course? Evidence on Crime and Employment from a Natural Experiment," *Criminology* 51 (2013): 137–166.
7. See Michael Massoglia, Martin Y. Iguchi, James Bell, Rajeev N. Ramchard, and Terry Fain, "How Criminal System Racial Disparities May Translate into Health Disparities," *Journal of Health Care for the Poor and Underserved* 16 (2005): 48–56.
8. Richard Berk, Heather Ladd, Heidi Graziano, and Jong-Ho Baek, "A Randomized Experiment Testing Inmate Classification Systems," *Criminology and Public Policy* 2 (2003): 215–242.
9. J. Austin, *Findings in Prison Classification and Risk Assessments* (Washington, DC: U.S. National Institute of Corrections, 2003), p. 2.
10. James M. Byrne and April Pattavina, "Institutional Corrections and Soft Technology," in *The New Technology of Crime, Law and Social Control*, ed. James M. Byrne and Donald J. Rebovich (Monsey, NY: Criminal Justice Press, 2007), p. 247.
11. Ibid., pp. 264–265.
12. Patricia L. Hardyman, James Austin, Jack Alexander, Kelly Dedel Johnson, and Owan C. Tulloch, *Internal Prison Classification Systems: Case Studied in Their Development and Implementation* (Washington, DC: National Institute of Corrections, 2002), p. 22.
13. Ibid., p. 1.
14. Christopher Hensley, Mary Koscheski, and Richard Tewksbury, "Examining the Characteristics of Male Sexual Assault Targets in a Southern Maximum-Security Prison," *Journal of Interpersonal Violence* 20 (2005): 667–679.
15. John Wooldredge, "Inmate Lifestyles and Opportunities for Victimization," *Journal of Research in Crime and Delinquency* 35 (1998): 480–502.
16. Andy Hochstetler, Daniel S. Murphy, and Ronald L. Simons, "Damaged Goods: Exploring Predictors of Distress in Prison Inmates," *Crime and Delinquency* 50 (2004): 436.
17. Doris J. James and Lauren E. Glaze, *Mental Health Problems of Prison and Jail Inmates*, Bureau of Justice Statistics Special Report (Washington, DC: U.S. Department of Justice, 2006), p. 1.
18. Ibid.
19. The early twentieth-century prison writings describe this prison environment.
20. Ibid.
21. Adapted from Gresham M. Sykes and Sheldon L. Messinger, "The Inmate Social System," in *Theoretical Studies in the Social Organization of the Prison*, ed. Richard A. Cloward (New York: Social Science Research Council, 1960), pp. 6–8.
22. Gresham Sykes, *The Society of Captives: A Study of a Maximum Security Prison* (Princeton, NJ: Princeton University Press, 1958), pp. 64–108.
23. For a new book on the convict code, please refer to Rebecca Trammell, *Enforcing the Convict Code* (Boulder, CO: Lynne Rienner, 2012).
24. Donald Clemmer, *The Prison Community* (New York: Holt Rinehart & Winston, 1958), p. 209.
25. Ibid., pp. 299–300.
26. Ibid.
27. Stanton Wheeler, "Socialization in Correctional Institutions," *American Sociological Review* 26 (1961): 697–712.
28. Sykes, *The Society of Captives*.
29. Ibid., pp. 142–155.
30. See Daniel P. Mears, Eric A. Stewart, and Ronald L. Simons, "The Code of the Streets and Inmate Violence: Investigating the Salience of Imported Belief Systems," *Criminology* 51 (2013): 695–728.
31. Shanhe Jiang and Marianne Fisher-Giorlando, "Inmate Misconduct: A Test of the Deprivation, Importation, and Situational Models," *Prison Journal* 82 (2002): 335–358.

32. Andy Hochstetler and Matt DeLisi, "Importation, Deprivation, and Varieties of Serving Time: An Integrated-Lifestyle-Exposure of Prison Offending," *Journal of Criminal Justice* 33 (2005): 257–266; Clemens Bartollas, *Becoming a Model Warden: Striving for Excellence* (Lanham, MD: American Correctional Association, 2004).
33. B. Useem and M. Reisig, "Collective Action in Prisons: Protests, Disturbances, and Riots," *Criminology* 37 (1999): 735–760, at 735.
34. James B. Jacobs, *Stateville: The Penitentiary in Mass Society* (Chicago: University of Chicago Press, 1977), p. 146.
35. Ibid.
36. Ben M. Crouch and James W. Marquart, *An Appeal to Justice: Litigated Reform of Texas Prisons* (Austin: University of Texas Press, 1989).
37. D. Orlando-Morningstar, *Prison Gangs* (Washington, DC: Federal Judicial Center, 1997).
38. Ibid., and Lee Bowker, *Prison Victimization* (New York: Elsevier, 1980).
39. George W. Knox, "The Problem of Gangs and Security Threat Groups (STGs) in American Prisons Today: A Special NGCRC Report," *Journal of Gang Research* 12 (2004): 1–76.
40. Personal interview, 2009.
41. Personal interview, 2009.
42. Personal interview, 2009.
43. Mark S. Davis and Daniel J. Flannery, "The Institutional Treatment of Gang Members," *Corrections Management Quarterly* 5 (2001): 37–46.
44. John Hancock, "Combating Gang Activity in Prison," Corrections.com, 2008, http://www.corrections.com/news/article/18097 (accessed June 2014).
45. Chad R. Trulson, James W. Marquart, Craig Hemmens, and Leo Carroll, "Racial Desegregation in Prison," *Prison Journal* 88 (2008): 270–299; Chad Trulson and James W. Marquart, *Judicial Intervention, Desegregation, and Inter-Racial Violence: A Case Study of Inmate Desegregation in a Southern Prison System*, unpublished manuscript (Huntsville, TX: Sam Houston State University, 2002).
46. Chad R. Trulson and James W. Marquart, "Inmate Racial Integration: Achieving Racial Integration in the Texas Prison System," *Prison Journal* 82 (2002): 498–525.
47. James W. Marquart and Chad R. Trulson, "First Available House: Desegregation in American Prisons and the Road to *Johnson v. California*," *Corrections Compendium* 31 (2006): 1–5.
48. Hancock, "Combating Gang Activity in Prison."
49. For the influence that correctional officers can have on contributing to or defusing a rape-prone culture, see Helen M. Eigenberg, "Correctional Officers and Their Perceptions of Homosexuality, Rape, and Prostitution in Male Prisons," *Prison Journal* 80 (December 2000): 415–433. For a recent book on sex in male prisons, see Catherine D. Marcum and Timothy L. Castle, *Sex in Prison: Myths and Realities* (Boulder, CO: Lynne Rienner Publishers, 2013). See also Richard B. Felson, Patrick Cundiff, and Noah Painter-Davis, "Age and Sexual Assault in Correctional Facilities: A Blocked Opportunity Approach," *Criminology* 50 (2012): 887–912; Merry Morash, Seok Jin Jeong, and Nancy Zang, "An Exploratory Study of the Characteristics of Men Known to Commit Prisoner-on-Prisoner Sexual Violence," *Prison Journal* 90 (2010): 161–178.
50. 108th Congress, 2003, 117 Stat 972. See also Brenda V. Smith, "Analyzing Prison Sex: Reconciling Self-Expression with Safety," *Columbia Journal Gender and Law* 185 (2006).
51. Bureau of Justice Statistics, *Data Collection for the Prison Rape Elimination Act of 2003* (Washington, DC: U.S. Printing Office, 2004).
52. S. 1435[108]: Prison Rape Elimination Act of 2003; Public Law No: 108–79.
53. Bureau of Justice Statistics, PREA Data Collection Activities, 2014, May 8, 2014, http://www.bjs.gov/index.cfm?ty=pbdetail&iid=4989 (accessed July 2014).
54. Kristine Levan Miller, "The Darkest Figure of Crime: Perceptions of Reasons for Male Inmates to Not Report Sexual Assault," *Justice Quarterly* online (2009): 1–21.
55. Jesse Walker, "Rape Behind Bars," *Reason* 35 (2003): 10–12.
56. Hensley, Koscheski, and Tewksbury, "Examining the Characteristics of Male Sexual Assault Targets in a Southern Maximum-Security Prison," pp. 667–679.
57. Christopher Hensley, Richard Tewksbury, and Tammy Castle, "Characteristics of Prison Sexual Assault Targets in Male Oklahoma Correctional Facilities," *Journal of Interpersonal Violence* 18 (2003): 595–606.
58. Mark S. Fleisher and Jessie L. Krienert, *The Myth of Prison Rape: Sexual Culture in American Prisons* (New York: Rowman & Littlefield, 2008).
59. Jennifer Stump, "Unit Riots at Beeville Prison," *Caller*, December 21, 1999.
60. *The Sun*, Yuma, Arizona, April 25, 2007.
61. *San Antonio Express News*, March 28, 2008.
62. "At Least Two Dead in Oklahoma Prison Riot," *USA Today*, May 19, 2008.
63. Mark Colvin, *From Accommodation to Riot: The Penitentiary of New Mexico in Crisis* (Albany: State University of New York Press, 1990).
64. Camille Graham Camp, *The Corrections Yearbook: Adult Correction 2002* (Middletown, CT: Criminal Justice Institute, 2003), p. 50.
65. S. C. Light, "Assaults on Prison Officers: Interactional Themes," *Justice Quarterly* 78 (1991): 243–251.
66. Ibid.
67. Donna L. Mailloux and Ralph C. Serin, "Sexual Assaults During Hostage Takings and Forcible Confinements: Implications for Practice," *Sexual Abuse: A Journal of Research and Treatment* 13 (2003): 161–170.
68. See "New York: Attica Survivors File $30M Suit for Damages," *Corrections Digest* 33 (2002): 7.
69. For the difficulties of negotiating with inmates during hostage taking, see Steven J. Romano, "Achieving Successful Negotiations in a Correctional Setting," *Corrections Today* 65 (April 2005): 114–118.
70. Colvin, *From Accommodation to Riot*. For an account of an attempt by inmates to defuse violence among inmates, see Christine Walrath, "Evaluation of an Inmate-Run Alternative to Violence Project: The Impact of Inmate-Inmate Intervention," *Journal of Interpersonal Violence* 16 (2001): 697–711.
71. For a history of violent behavior by staff members, see Mark Fleisher, *Warehousing Violence* (Newbury Park, CA: Sage Publications, 1989).
72. Crouch and Marquart, *An Appeal to Justice: Litigated Reform of Texas Prisons*.
73. Fay Dowker and Glenn Good, "The Proliferation of Control Unit Prisons in the United States," *Journal of Prisoners on Prisons* 4 (1993): 95–110; Holly J. Buckhalter, "Torture in U.S. Prisons," *Nation*, July 3, 1995, pp. 17–18.
74. Margaret E. Noonan, "Mortality in Local Jails and State Prisons, 2000–2010, Statistical Tables," Bureau of Justice Statistics, 2012, http://www.bjs.gov/content/pub/pdf/mljsp0010st.pdf (accessed June 2014).
75. M. P. Huey and T. L. McNulty, "Institutional Conditions and Prison Suicide: Conditional Effects of Deprivation and Overcrowding," *Prison Journal* 85 (2005): 490–514.
76. Christine Tartaro, "An Application of Durkheim's Theory of Suicide to Prison Suicide Rates in the United States," *Death Studies* 29 (2005): 413–422.
77. Bruce B. Way, Richard Miraglia, Donald A. Sawyer, Richard Beer, and John Eddy, "Factors Related to Suicide in New York State Prisons," *International Journal of Law and Psychiatry* 28 (2005): 207.
78. Joseph Micielli, *The Stress and the Effects of Working in a High Security Prison* (Rockville, MD: National Institute of Justice, 2008).
79. Stephen Owen, "Occupational Stress Among Correctional Supervisors," *Prison Journal* 86 (2006): 164–181; Eugene Paoline, Eric Lambert, and Nancy Hogan, "A Calm and Happy Keeper of the Keys: The Impact of ACA Views, Relations with Coworkers, and Public Views on the Job Stress and Job Satisfaction of Correctional Staff," *Prison Journal* 86 (2006): 182–205; Mike Vuolo and Candace Kruttschnitt, "Prisoners' Adjustment, Correctional Officers, and Context: The Foreground and Background of Punishment in Late Modernity," *Law and Society Review* 42 (2008): 307–314.
80. *Dothard v. Rawlinson*, 433 U.S. 321 (1977); *Gunther v. Iowa State Men's Reformatory*, 612 F.2d 1079 (6th Cir. 1979); *Ford v. Ward*, 471 F. Supp. 1095 (S.D.N.Y. 1978).
81. *Gunther v. Iowa State Men's Reformatory; Ford v. Ward.*
82. *Dothard v. Rawlinson; Gunther v. Iowa State Men's Reformatory; Ford v. Ward.*
83. Incident reported to Bartollas.
84. From a survey of corrections officers done in Kentucky, this study found that rehabilitation received the strongest support of the various correctional ideologies, with female officers being more supportive of rehabilitation than males. See Richard Tewksbury and Elizabeth Ehrhardt Mustaine, "Correctional Orientations of Prison Staff," *Prison Journal* 88 (June 2008): 207–233.

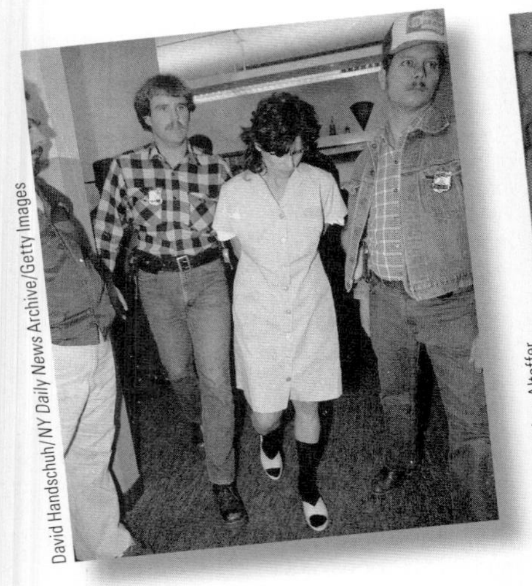

David Handschuh/NY Daily News Archive/Getty Images

AP Images/Mary Altaffer

While some women's prisons are supportive and provide rehabilitation services, others are troubled and destructive. Here, inmates walk the halls in formation at Tutwiler Prison for Women in Wetumpka, Alabama. Tutwiler inmates have seen more than their share of problems. According to the U.S. Justice Department, corrections officers have raped, beaten, and harassed women inside the prison for at least 18 years. More than a third of the employees have had sex with prisoners, which is sometimes the only currency for basics like toilet paper and tampons. The conditions in Tutwiler are so bad that the federal government says they are most likely unconstitutional.

ON THE MORNING OF WEDNESDAY, SEPTEMBER 17, 2003, Kathy Boudin was released on parole from the Bedford Hills Correctional Facility. Boudin's departure ended a 22-year stay at the prison that left its mark on fellow prisoners and the programs that are available for their rehabilitation and health.[1]

On October 20, 1981, Kathy Boudin served as a decoy in the passenger seat of a U-Haul van in Nanuet, New York, from which armed men emerged and shot Nyack police officer Waverly Brown and police sergeant Edward O'Grady following the robbery of a Brinks armored truck. Boudin was one of 19 people convicted of participation in this Brinks robbery crime. She was incarcerated after her arrest and pleaded guilty in 1984 to first-degree robbery and second-degree murder. Her sentence was 20 years to life.

In the years that followed her incarceration, she reshaped her life as an inmate. Boudin started to work at the prison's Children's Center in 1984. She was the inmate coordinator of the parenting classes and the teen program. In 1994, the college-in-prison programs were discontinued throughout the nation. Kathy approached Michelle Fine, professor of psychology at the Graduate Center of City University of New York, and they worked together to reestablish college at the prison in Bedford. Eventually, they were able to get 12 colleges and universities to give faculty pro bono. Two staff people coordinated the program within the prison, and it worked very well. In her 22 years in the Bedford Hills Correctional Facility, Boudin either initiated or was involved in more than a dozen programs for inmates.[2]

Kathy Boudin was paroled in 2003, the third time she went up for parole. She accepted a job as an AIDS counselor at St. Luke's-Roosevelt Hospital Center in New York City. Since her release, she has received her Ed.D. from Columbia University, Teachers College and is presently an adjunct assistant professor at Columbia Teachers College and Sheinberg Scholar-in-Residence at NYU Law School. She is also a consultant to the Osborne Association in the development of a Longtermers Responsibility Project taking place in the New York State Correctional Facilities utilizing a restorative practice approach. Boudin also has been a consultant for Vermont Corrections, the Women's Prison Association, and Family Justice. Boudin has focused her work on the HIV/AIDS epidemic and criminal justice issues, including: women in prison; the mother–child relationship and parenting from a distance; adolescent relationships with incarcerated parents; restorative justice; and basic literacy inside correctional institutions.[3]

Women like Kathy Boudin who commit violent crimes are not typical of female offenders confined in long-term correctional institutions. Nor do many women prisoners have the impact on prison life (or in the community subsequent to their release) that Kathy has had. The average woman in prison, as this chapter will convey, is more likely to be a troubled, undereducated drug or property offender.

8

The Prison Experience: Females

AP Images/Dave Martin

LEARNING OBJECTIVES

 LO1 Identify the main reason for the fact that more than 100,000 women are in prison

 LO2 Identify the findings of the classic studies of social structure in women's prisons

 LO3 Discuss the contemporary studies of women doing time in prison

 LO4 Ascertain that providing sufficient programs for incarcerated women with children is critical

 LO5 Identify the serious issues of health care in women's prisons

 LO6 Discuss professionalism in women's prisons

PREVIEW OF KEY CONCEPTS

Elizabeth Fry
Ward and Kassebaum
butch
femme
Giallombardo
fictive families
Hefferman
kinship networks
the mix
Human Rights Watch
correctional counselor

The treatment of women behind bars has come to the forefront of corrections. One reason is that there are now more females involved in the justice system, and their unique problems and issues have been identified. Before 1960, few women were in prison and independent women's prisons were relatively rare; most were attached to male institutions. Only four institutions for women were built between 1930 and 1950. In comparison, 34 women's prisons were constructed during the 1980s as crime rates soared.[4]

Men are almost 14 times more likely than women to be incarcerated in a federal or state prison; while the female inmate population is still relatively small, there are now more than 100,000 women in prison. However, like male inmates, there has been a recent decline in the number and rate of women being held behind bars, from 65 female prisoners per 100,000 U.S. female residents in 2011 to 63 in 2012. In 2012, the number of female prisoners (108,866 inmates) fell to the lowest level since 2005—a 2.3 percent decrease from 2011.[5]

In Voices Across the Profession, Judy Anderson, former warden of the Camille Griffin Graham Correctional Institution in South Carolina, suggests that women prisoners have gender-specific needs, and this is an important factor in providing them adequate programming.

PRISONS FOR WOMEN: HISTORY AND CHARACTERISTICS

In the early days of prison history, women were confined in separate quarters in men's prisons and, like men, suffered from filth, overcrowding, and hard conditions. Women lodged in the Auburn penitentiary in New York were subject to beatings and sexual abuse by the male guards. African American and poor women were disproportionately incarcerated in all parts of the United States.

Elizabeth Fry Quaker who brought reform to women confined in prison.

Even before the end of slavery, Quaker abolitionists and suffragists were at the forefront of the prison reform movement. In the early 1800's **Elizabeth Fry** of England helped organize the women confined at London's Newgate Gaol. Her brave and innovative work at Newgate with incarcerated women and their children was testimony to the fact that, with decent treatment, women convicts were redeemable. Fry challenged the rampant sexual abuse of institutionalized women and advocated that they be under the authority of other women and confined to their own institution. She also sought to substitute for the Quaker system of absolute silence a system that permitted inmates to communicate with each other and help each other reform. Fry was able to instill hope and dignity where there had been only despair. Today Elizabeth Fry Societies in Canada play an active role in exposing abuses in women's prisons.[6]

The Indiana Women's Prison, the first separate prison for women, was founded by a Quaker couple in 1873. Four years later, Massachusetts built an all-females state reformatory. Another American Quaker helped found the progressive women's reformatory at Bedford Hills. Other states gradually followed, and separate institutions for men and women became the norm, although there were exceptions. Fry's program, which emphasized women helping women, rehabilitation, religious education, and obedience, was instituted throughout North America.[7]

Many significant aspects of contemporary corrections were pioneered by female administrators in charge of institutions for female offenders—for example, educational instruction, work release, and vocational activities. Prison reformers regarded women as good candidates for rehabilitation, partly because they were considered less dangerous than their male counterparts.

During the progressive era, cottage-style reformatories were developed as an alternative to harsh custodial institutions. Inmates of the custodial prisons, mostly African American women, suffered from the filthy conditions and violence inflicted by male guards. The new reformatories were usually staffed by women and aimed

VOICES ACROSS THE PROFESSION

It is meaningful when you see an inmate grow and believe that she can be successful when she returns to the community.

Judy Anderson
Former Warden, Camille Griffin Graham Women's Prison, South Carolina

Women do their time more as process, while men are more interested in the bottom line. For example, women are able to forgive more easily than do men. They are usually not as violent. Men fight and move on. Women involved in a fight are upset; they need to do a lot of talking with verbal responses. For women, the bottom line is that everything is rational.

When I think about job satisfaction, it means a lot to me when I see staff members grow, accept new responsibilities, and move on with their careers. It is meaningful when you see an inmate grow and believe that she can be successful when she returns to the community. It means a great deal when you can make some system changes and have an impact on the field of corrections. I also like the fact that no two days are exactly alike and that I am also growing on the job.

to correct women's moral behavior. Women were sentenced to the reformatories for various sexual offenses, including pregnancy outside marriage and unlawful sexual intercourse. By 1935, the progressive era was over, and reformatories and custodial prisons were merged. The legacy of the "cottage system" is evident at the woman's federal prison in Alderson, West Virginia, and in many state prisons, such as Bedford Hills in New York.[8]

The 1960s and 1970s, a period of civil rights awareness and protest by various oppressed groups, was also a time of reformist zeal concerning women in prison. Compassion was expressed for women who killed their husbands in self-defense and were charged with murder. There was also a huge outcry over politically active prisoners such as Angela Davis and Joan Little. Davis was charged with abetting the escape of a violent prisoner, and Little was tried for killing her jailer during the act of rape.

The period of retrenchment of social services and the War on Drugs, which got under way in the 1980s and is continuing well into the twenty-first century, parallel a mass media campaign dramatizing crimes of violence. Women of color have been the most adversely affected by mandatory drug sentencing laws, mainly the harsh sentencing for crack cocaine. Another factor affecting both male and female prisoners is the vested interests of major corporations—the prison-industrial complex—and many local communities in the building and maintaining of prisons for their economic well-being.

RISE OF WOMEN'S IMPRISONMENT

Identify the main reason for the fact that more than 100,000 women are in prison

Why is the female inmate population still so high? In addition to women now committing more serious crimes, sentencing changes have helped put more women behind bars. Mandatory minimum sentences provide the same punishment for conspiracy to commit crimes, such as driving the getaway car, as for the instigator of the crime itself. According to the American Civil Liberties Union, women are increasingly caught up in the ever-widening net cast by current drug laws such as conspiracy laws

MYTH Sentencing reform movements help keep people in the community and reduce incarceration.

FACT While males may benefit from sentencing reforms, females suffer. Judicial discretion traditionally benefited women. Now gender-neutral sentences have placed more women behind bars.

and accomplice liability laws that extend criminal liability to the arrested offender's partners and relatives.[9] Accordingly, almost half of the women in prison today under these mandatory sentencing laws have been convicted of conspiracy. Sentencing laws fail to consider the reasons—including domestic violence, economic dependence, or dependent immigration status—that compel many women to remain silent. Mandatory minimum laws often subject women to the same—or in some cases harsher—sentences than the principals in the drug trade who are ostensibly the target of those policies.[10] This is an example of what we might call "equality with a vengeance," an equality of punishment meted out to women who violate the law.

Female offenders are more likely than males to be convicted of a nonviolent crime and be incarcerated for a low-level involvement in drug offenses, such as driving a boyfriend to make a drug deal. The female offender may end up serving a longer sentence than the boyfriend simply because she is less likely to work out a plea arrangement.[11]

CRITICAL THINKING

How much of female crime consists of victimless crime? Should victimless crimes be punished the same as criminal offenses that have a victim? LO3

While the equality movement is under way, the prison is still a gendered organization, and some correctional administrators recognize that women often bring with them a set of needs that are different from the burdens faced by male inmates.

Characteristics of Women in Prison

Incarcerated women have typically had a troubled family life. Significant numbers were at-risk children, products of broken homes and the welfare system. Over half have received welfare at some time during their adult lives. As juveniles, they experienced a pattern of harsh discipline and abuse. Many claim to have been physically or sexually abused. This pattern continued in adult life; many female inmates were victims of domestic violence.[12]

AP Images/Rich Pedroncelli

Inmate Serina Diaz spends time with her granddaughter, Elena Montes, 7 months, during a visit at the Folsom Women's Facility in California. Diaz had the opportunity to spend time with her family through a nonprofit program called Get on the Bus, which arranges for children of inmates to visit their parents in California prisons around Mother's Day and Father's Day. This type of program is critical since so many female inmates are mothers.

Not surprisingly, many female offenders display psychological problems, including serious psychopathology.[13] One survey of incarcerated women in 12 nations, including the United States, found that 4 percent had psychotic illnesses; 12 percent, depression; and 42 percent, a personality disorder, including 21 percent with antisocial personality disorder.[14]

A significant number of female inmates report having substance abuse problems; more than two-thirds are serving time for nonviolent drug offenses.[15] Surveys show that about three-fourths have used drugs at some time in their lives, and almost half were involved with addictive drugs, such as cocaine, heroin, or PCP. Little difference exists in major drug use between male and female offenders when measured over their life span or at the time of their current arrest.

The cultural baggage that inmates bring into the prison setting is the end product of the drug wars on the streets and the War on Drugs in society. Caught up in the drug wars are minority women (Hispanic and African American) involved with gang members, foreigners arrested at airports as couriers for international drug syndicates, and violent and nonviolent offenders arrested for crime indirectly related to drug use. Race and class intersect in predictable ways to ensure that the persons most feared and resented by society are those who are shut away. Today, as Meda Chesney-Lind suggests, "street crime" has become a code word for "race." And racial tensions in the free community lay the groundwork for ethnic differences and resentments behind prison bars.[16]

The incarceration of so many women who are low-criminal risks yet face a high risk of exposure to HIV and other health issues because of their prior history of drug abuse presents a significant problem. One study of incarcerated women found that one-third of the sample reported that before their arrest they had traded sex for money or drugs; about one-quarter of these women reported trading sex for money or drugs "weekly or more often."[17] Such risky behavior significantly increases the likelihood of their carrying the AIDS virus or other sexually transmitted diseases.

The picture that emerges of the female inmate is troubling (see Exhibit 8.1). After a lifetime of emotional turmoil, physical and sexual abuse, and drug use, it seems improbable that overcrowded, underfunded correctional institutions can forge a dramatic turnaround in the behavior of at-risk female inmates. Many have lost custody of their children, a trauma that is more likely to afflict those who are already substance abusers and suffer from depression.[18] It should come as no surprise then that many female inmates feel strain and conflict, psychological conditions related to violent episodes.[19]

EXHIBIT 8.1

Characteristics of Women in Prison

- Women in prison lack a solid employment history.
- They often have a history of poor physical health.
- They have a history of financial problems.
- They exhibit a distinct lack of education.
- They have received experiences of physical and sexual abuse.
- They have a history of substance misuse.
- They often have mental health and other problems.
- They are likely to be primary caregivers for their children.

Source: Amanda Noblet, "Women in Prison: A Review of the Current Female Prison System: Future Directions and Alternatives," *Internet Journal of Criminology 2008*, http://www.internetjournalofcriminology.com (accessed June 2014).

FOR GROUP **DISCUSSION**

Using Exhibit 8.1 as the basis for your group discussion, answer these questions: Would addressing these characteristics in the community reduce female criminal activity? Which of these characteristics can be and should be addressed first, and how? Select a group spokesperson and present your ideas to the class. **LO1**

GENDER DIFFERENCES IN CLASSIFICATION

There are different gender-based approaches to the classification of offenders entering the correctional system. Some institutions continue to use "gender-neutral" assessments in their classification models. Included in these evaluations are measures related to education, employment, finances, living arrangements, and quality of family life, leisure time activities, antisocial friends, substance abuse, mental health, and criminal thinking. These dynamic risk/needs assessments have been shown to predict institutional misconduct.[20]

While traditional classification models can be effective, contemporary correctional systems are now recognizing the special needs of women and creating gender-specific classification schemes. Female inmates have a high incidence of often overlapping challenges, which include drug and alcohol histories, mental illness, childhood physical and sexual victimization, current intimate partner violence, and limited or lack of work experience. Gender-specific classification helps correctional administrators develop the proper *wrap-around services*, which address the multiple needs of female inmates and help in the coordination of services among multiple providers, helping them create a continuum of care that can develop over time.[21] Gender-specific classification has become increasingly popular among correctional administrators wishing to become responsive to the special needs of female prisoners.[22]

Identify the findings of the classic studies of social structure in women's prisons LO2

DOING TIME

The classic studies of women in prison found that prison culture for women was much different from that of men and revolved around sexual alliances with other female inmates. However, more recent studies have found that severe overcrowding, scarcity of resources, and emphasis on security now creates a much more austere and severe environment. Women tend to be placed in a higher security level than they need and are forced to suffer indignities such as intrusive searches.[23] As a result, women prisoners have a different response to imprisonment than was typically found in the past.

Classic Studies

There are three classic studies of women in prison: Ward and Kassebaum, Giallombardo, and Hefferman (see Exhibit 8.2).[24]

Ward and Kassebaum Classic study that claimed women adapted to imprisonment by forming homosexual alliances.

butch The dominant, or male, role in a homosexual relationship in the prison society.

femme The docile, or female, role in a homosexual relationship in the prison society.

Giallombardo Classic study that identified that women were involved in fictive families in adapting to imprisonment.

fictive families A grouping of unrelated individuals who have assumed the traditional family roles of mother, father, grandparents, and so on.

- **Ward and Kassebaum**: In their 1965 study of the Frontera Correctional institution in California, David A. Ward and Gene Kassebaum found that women attempted to deal with the painful conditions of confinement by establishing homosexual alliances. The researchers describe these prison love affairs as appearing to be unstable, short lived, explosive, and involving strict differentiation between the roles of "butch" and "femme." **Butch** is a dominant, or male, role. **Femme** is a docile, or female, role. The person in the butch role is expected to be strong, in control, and independent, and to pursue the femme.
- **Giallombardo**: Rose Giallombardo's 1966 study of the federal reformatory for women in Alderson, West Virginia, indicated a major difference between male and female prisoners. Among female inmates, membership in **fictive families** was more common than participation in homosexual activities and occurred earlier than sexual involvement. Giallombardo reported that the women at Alderson established familiar relationships similar to the relationships of the free world. A sort of family life—with "mothers" and "fathers," "grandparents," and "aunts" and "uncles"—was at the very center of inmate life at Alderson and provided a sense of belonging and identification that enabled inmates involved

EXHIBIT 8.2

Comparison of Classic Studies

Study	Prison Studied	Basic Finding
Ward and Kassebaum	Frontera Correctional Institution in California	Women cope with prison by establishing homosexual alliances.
Giallombardo	Federal reformatory for women in Alderson, West Virginia	Some women form fictive families in prison.
Hefferman	District of Columbia's women's reformatory in Occoquan, Virginia	Fictive kinship structure was present.

Sources: David A. Ward and Gene Kassebaum, *Women's Prisons and Social Structure* (Chicago: Anderson, 1965; Rose Giallombardo, *Society of Women: A Study of a Women's Prison* (New York: Wiley, 1966); Esther Hefferman, *Making It in Prison: The Square, the Cool, and the Life* (New York: Wiley, 1972).

Could fictive families in women's prisons be considered a security threat group (STG)? LO3

in "family affairs" to do easy time. Unlike male prisoners, the women at Alderson did not design the social system to combat the social and psychological deprivations of prison.

- **Hefferman**: The 1972 research of Esther Hefferman at the District of Columbia's women's reformatory in Occoquan, Virginia, also supported the hypothesis that fictive kinship structure is present in women's prisons. Hefferman, along with Giallombardo, emphasized the concept of latent cultural identity as a factor leading to the formation of the fictive family. By this she meant the pre-institutional identity the female offender brings with her into the prison setting. Hefferman argued that women construct the kinship structure because they are socialized to conceive of themselves, their needs, and their peer relations primarily in terms of family roles and situations.

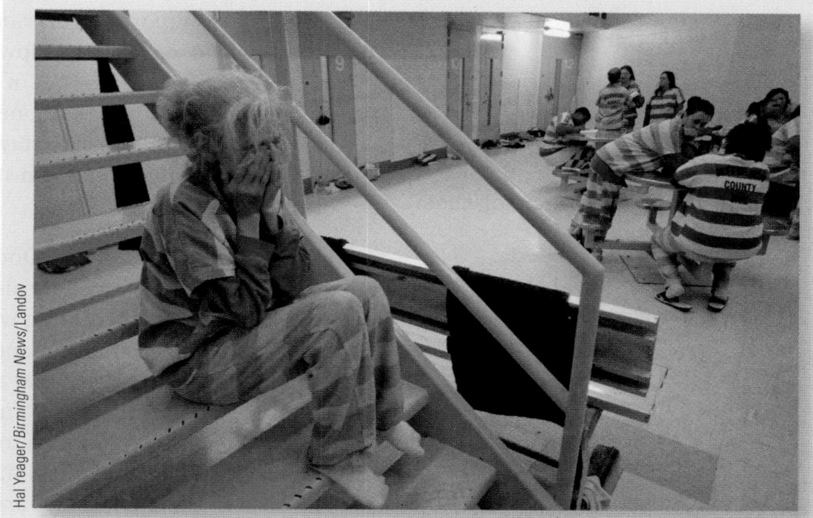
Hal Yeager/Birmingham News/Landov

Prisons can be overcrowded, but many inmates are alone and isolated. Though women tend to form substitute family-like groupings, not all do—and for those who don't, the prison experience can be devastating.

Contemporary Prison Experience for Women

Several contemporary studies continue to document the existence of same-sex relations in women's prisons, but the widespread opinion today is that **kinship networks** are nowhere near as defined as one might believe reading the early studies.[25] In contrast, contemporary studies emphasize that social structure and relationships are only a small part of how women do prison time. Similarities do exist in how women do time today compared to the past, but the increased size of women's prisons, the emphasis on security, and the de-emphasis on programming have affected how women cope with prison life.

Barbara Owen's classic account, *In the Mix: Struggle and Survival in a Women's Prison* is a study that took place at the Central California Women's Facility, the world's largest female correctional facility. The basic question that framed her study was: how do women prisoners do time?[26] The following are her findings:

- The culture that develops in a women's prison is "markedly different from the degradation, violence, and predatory structure of male prison life" because "the culture of the female prison seeks to accommodate these struggles rather than to exploit them."
- The phase of a woman's criminal record and the number of previous prison terms contribute greatly to the prison experience.
- Women prisoners, in comparing their imprisonment experiences to those of men prisoners, generally agreed that men show more solidarity than women.
- Women are confined to administrative segregation for three major reasons: fighting, drug-related offenses, and assaults on staff.
- Three general categories of exploitative relationships took place: (1) begins with a nonpayment of a friendly loan of food or cigarettes; (2) pursues a relationship with a naïve woman prisoner for exploitative purposes; and (3) involves outright extortion where an inmate who is thought to be weak is pressured to surrender her goods to another prisoner, either one time or as ongoing extortion.
- Race tends to be de-emphasized much more than would be found in male prison culture and is not critical to prison culture.
- No formal gang culture exists.

Hefferman Classic study that found the presence of fictive families in women's adaptation to prison life.

kinship networks A type of prison socialization in which women deal with incarceration by becoming part of make-believe families.

LO3 Discuss the contemporary studies of women doing time in prison

- Commitment to a criminal identity and stage in one's criminal and prison career are the most important contributions to one's style of doing time.
- The convict code has the following tenets: "Mind your own business," "The police are not your friend: stay out of their face," "If asked by staff, you do not tell," "Do not allow rat-packing; fight one on one only," "Take care of each other."
- In doing time, it is wise to stay out of "**the mix**," which is any behavior that can bring trouble or conflict with staff and other prisoners (e.g., involvement in drugs or fights).

the mix Owen's term for women's involvement in problematic prison behaviors and activities.

Mark Pogrebin and Mary Dodge's interviewing of former female inmates who had done time in a western state also discovered that an important element of prison life for many women was dealing with fear and violence. Some reported that violence in women's prisons is common and that many female inmates undergo a process of socialization fraught with danger and volatile situations.[27] Confinement for women may produce severe anxiety and anger because of separation from families and loved ones and the inability to function in normal female roles. Unlike men, who direct their anger outward, female prisoners may turn to more self-destructive acts to cope with their problems. Female inmates are more likely than males to maim themselves and attempt suicide. One common practice among female inmates is self-mutilation, or carving. This ranges from simple scratches to carving the name of their boyfriend on their body or even complex statements or sentences ("To mother, with hate").[28]

CRITICAL THINKING

Describe what prison for females might be like if they did not have fictive families and they stayed out of "the mix." Do you think they would have a better or worse experience in prison? Why?

Candace Kruttschnitt and Rosemary Gartner observed women's interactions in two California women's prisons, the Central Institution for Women (CIW) and the Valley State Prison for Women (VSPW), a high-security facility.[29] They found that imprisonment for women has changed over the past 40 years because today administrators place greater emphasis on custody and security, practice greater austerity, and give less attention to individuals. As a result, less is expected of prisoners, and in turn, inmates expect less from the prison administration and more from each other. Because administrators are preoccupied with the security and management of prisoners rather than rehabilitation, female inmates have become disaffected, suspicious, and isolated.[30]

While the structure of female social relations may be changing, Kruttschnitt and Gartner's study found that sexual relationships were still "very much a part of life" in prison. The researchers reason that because of the public's greater acceptance of same-sex relationships, there is now less regulation of prisoners' lives.[31]

Kruttschnitt and Gartner found that the prisoners in the two prisons they studied had three major ways of negotiating, or coping with, prison life:

- *Adopted style.* In this model, women associate with other prisoners and enjoy their associations. Few of these women report having problems with correctional officers.
- *Convict style.* This model involves spending time with only one or two others, or alone, and, as with the adopted style, these women enjoy their associations with other inmates. However, unlike the adopted class, they are highly likely to have difficulty dealing with correctional officers.[32]
- *Isolate style.* This model is characterized by preferring to be alone when not locked up in cells. Alienated from other prisoners, this negative and singular style gives female inmates the feeling that they have no control over their prison environment.

MYTH Women form quasifamily structures in prison, with "mothers and fathers," "grandparents," and "aunts and uncles."

FACT In contemporary prisons, female inmates may be more prone to mistrust their friendships with other women prisoners and refrain from forming close relationships.

The influence of the prison environment is seen in that in more punitive environments, women prisoners are least likely to approach their confinement in an adopted, as opposed to an isolate, manner. Women prisoners are also far more outspoken about what they see as inhumane treatment, abuse from staff, and arbitrary restrictions.

So, though women prisons are usually less violent, involve less gang activity, and do not reflect the racial tensions found in men's prisons, interpersonal relationships might be less stable and less familial than in the past. Inmates may be more prone to mistrust their friendships with other women prisoners and believe the primary motivation for interpersonal relationships involves economic manipulation.[33] In an era of high security in prison, female inmates may be forming a society that is more like males'.

Candace Kruttschnitt and Rosemary Gartner also interviewed 38 prisoners at the Valley State Prison for Women. Every one reported that the overriding concern was with control and security and that there was limited interest in helping inmates. Inmates felt that there was nothing for them to do except follow the rules. Prisoners felt that the institutional orientation was fundamentally aimed at maintenance and security. Some women even interpreted treatment by staff as intentional punitiveness. The women further felt that the administration had de-emphasized the potential for rehabilitation. The end result of this austere environment was poor relations among inmates.[34]

It may be this emphasis on control and security will increasingly take place in women's prisons, and this, in turn, will affect how women do time in the future. As it has in the Valley State Prison for Women, it will affect women prisoners' relationships with staff and other inmates, the quality of the prison environment, and the programming that is offered inmates. See Exhibit 8.3 for a comparison of contemporary studies of women in prison.

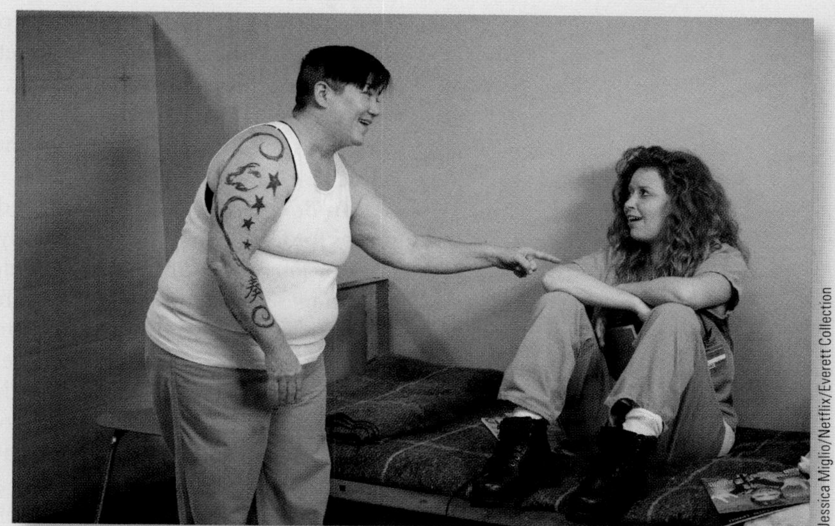
Jessica Miglio/Netflix/Everett Collection

Women in prison are much more likely to form close, family-like bonds than males. This photo captures a scene from the critically acclaimed TV series *Orange Is the New Black*, whose focus is the bonds that develop during incarceration.

EXHIBIT 8.3

A Comparison of Contemporary Studies of Women in Prison

Researchers	Location	Main Findings
K. Faith; Forsyth et al.; Tewksbury and Koscheski; Severance	Studies located primarily in southern prisons	Documented the same-sex relations in women's prisons that were found in the classic studies
Barbara Owen	Central California Women's Facility	Found that women's imprisonment is similar to that of men in terms of inmate solidarity, exploitative relationships, gang culture, and inmate code
Pogrebin and Dodge	Western prisons	Revealed that fear and violence, including self-destructive coping mechanisms, are characteristic of inmates' lives
Kruttschnitt and Gartner	Central Institution for Women (California)	Found that female inmates have become more dissatisfied, suspicious, and isolated
Kruttschnitt and Gartner	Valley State Prison for Women (California)	Found that the overriding concern is with control and security, with limited interest in helping inmates

SPECIAL ISSUES IN THE INCARCERATION OF WOMEN

The problems posed by the lack of treatment opportunities, gender-specific programs, motherhood in prison, the quality and adequacy of prison health care, and the sexual victimization of women prisoners are five pressing issues in women prisons.

Programs and Treatment Opportunities for Women Prisoners

Vocational programming for men in prison is extensive, including barbering, auto repair, painting, welding, machine shop, baking, sheet metal work, furniture repair, air conditioning repair, blueprint reading, and medical emergency training. Vocational programs for women are usually much more limited: beauty culture, secretarial training, computers and data processing, business machine operation, baking, and food operation. Women prisoners claim that they are being unfairly trained, with the lack of adequate treatment and vocational programs, making it difficult for them to complete in the job market when they are released.

In *Barefield v. Leach* (1974) a federal court ruled that the opportunities and programs for female inmates were clearly inferior to those for male inmates.[35] Two decades later in *Pargo v. Elliott* (1995), a federal court again examined the issue of unequal treatment. The justices compared the various programs available to female inmates, controlling for custody classification, and compared them to those available to male inmates. After scrutinizing all of the claims, the court found no evidence of invidious discrimination. It also determined that the programs and services available to women and men inmates as a whole, or according to custody level, were substantially similar to those received by any male inmate given the various institutional needs and circumstances.[36] The court added that any differences were related to legitimate enological interests such as security and rehabilitation.[37] So it is possible that the treatment gap between programs for male and female offenders may be closing.

Gender-Specific Programs for Women Prisoners

The failure to gain relief from the courts in terms of equality of programs and treatment services withstanding, the recent emphasis has been increased implementation of gender-specific programs. Because women have different pathways to crime than men, they experience imprisonment as a whole differently than men. It stands to reason that they would benefit from gender-specific programming.

Gender-specific programming includes the following:

- Nurturing and reinforcing "femaleness" as a positive identity with inherent strengths
- Providing women with decision-making and life skills that assist their development and growth
- Teaching empowerment such as using their voice, speaking for themselves, and recognizing that they have choices
- Recognizing the dangers and risks that women face because of gender; this acknowledges that their lives have been likely affected by sexism, victimization, poverty, and racism
- Providing programs that tap women's cultural strengths rather than focusing primarily on the individual
- Furnishing education about women's health, including pregnancy, contraception, and disease prevention
- Giving women a voice in program design, implementation, and evaluation
- Providing adequate financing to ensure that comprehensive programming will be sustained long enough for women prisoners to integrate the benefits[38]

Motherhood in Prison

An estimated 80,000 incarcerated women, or about two-thirds of the women incarcerated in U.S. state prisons and nearly 60 percent of women confined in federal prisons, are parents and are mothers to nearly 320,000 children under age 18.[39] Furthermore, most of these women were the heads of single-parent households prior to their confinement.[40]

The separation of women prisoners from their children can be traumatic for both mothers, children and other family members[41] Prisons, and especially women's prisons, generally are located in remote, rural areas. Over time, family ties are broken.

Yet prisoners' family relationships are very important not only for mental health reasons but for postrelease success. See Figure 8.1 for predictors of children's adjustment following parental incarceration and reunion.

While their mothers are incarcerated, children most frequently stay with maternal grandmothers, but other caretakers include the child's father or other relatives. Female inmates find solace in the fact that their children are placed with their own mothers, and feel relatively confident that they will encounter minimal difficulties when taking the children back upon release. If no suitable family alternatives are available, children may be placed in foster homes or put up for adoption; this solution makes it very difficult for mothers to regain custody after release.[42]

Imprisoned women are burdened with the knowledge that their own behavior has caused the separation from their children, a condition that generates feelings of emptiness, helplessness, guilt, anger, and bitterness. They also fear loss or rejection by the children. With prolonged separation, mothers fear their children might establish stronger bonds of affection with caretakers than with them. Furthermore, mothers fear that teenage children staying with maternal grandparents may be arrested because of inadequate supervision.[43]

Even more problems await inmates who are pregnant. The likelihood of pregnancy is high during imprisonment, with some prisoners sentenced to prison when they are already pregnant, and others becoming pregnant during home furloughs, work release, conjugal visits, or even through sexual relations or rape by prison staff. Studies of pregnancy outcome among women prisoners have revealed high rates of perinatal mortality and morbidity. The termination of prison pregnancy may not be possible even if the inmate desires it; under other circumstances the inmate may be forced by prison officials to have an abortion.[44]

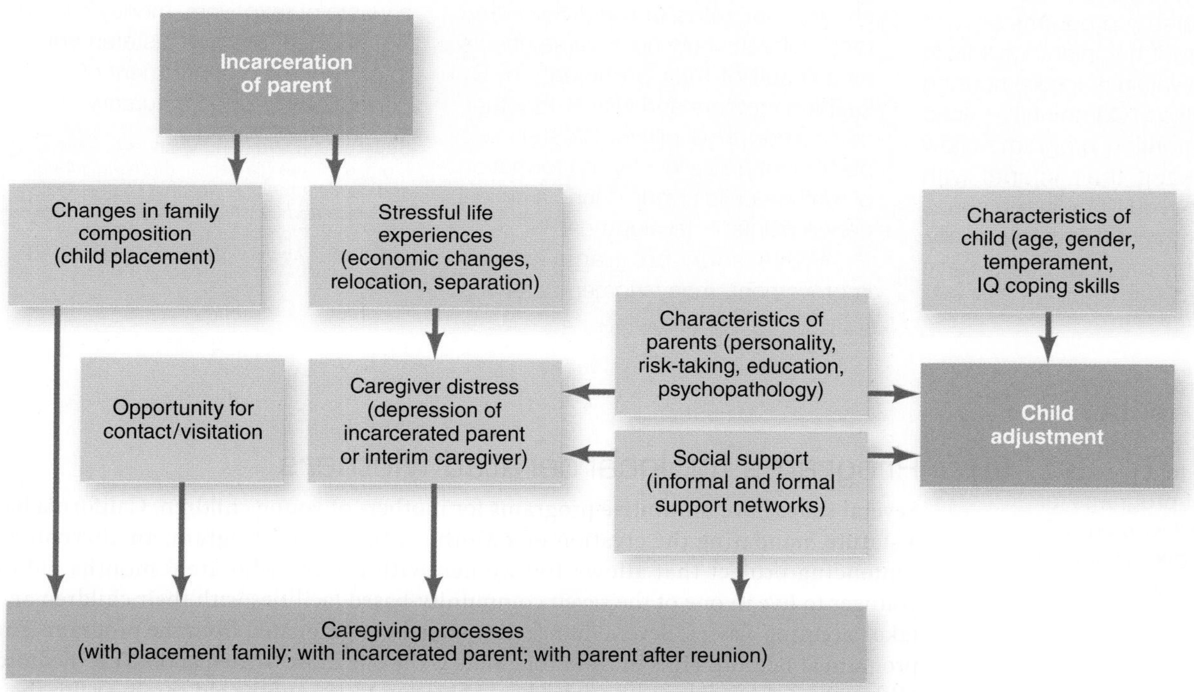

FIGURE 8.1

Predictors of Children's Adjustment Following Parental Incarceration and Reunion

Sources: Family Strengthening Policy Center, "Supporting Families with Incarcerated Parents" (Washington, DC: National Human Services Assembly, 2005), p. 9. Adapted from R. Parke and K. A. Clarke-Stewart, *Effects of Parental Incarceration on Young Children* (Washington, DC: U.S. Department of Health and Human Services, 2002).

EVIDENCE-BASED CORRECTIONS

Prison Nursery Programs

It is now estimated that 4 percent of women in state prisons and 3 percent of women in federal prisons were pregnant at the time of admittance; about 6 percent of women in local jails were pregnant at the time of admittance. Despite this trend, there is no national policy that dictates what happens to children born to mothers who are under correctional supervision. The overwhelming majority of children born to incarcerated mothers are separated from their mothers immediately after birth and placed with relatives or into foster care. In a handful of states, women have other options: prison nurseries and community-based residential parenting programs.

Prison nursery programs allow a mother to parent her infant for a finite period of time within a special housing unit at the prison. Community-based residential parenting programs allow mothers to keep their infants with them while they fulfill their sentences in residential programs in the community. In either case, most mothers have committed low-level nonviolent offenses, face relatively short sentences, and will continue as their children's primary caregiver upon release.

A national study sponsored by the Women's Prison Association found that the number of prison-based nursery programs is growing, but such programs are still rare. Though every state has seen a dramatic rise in its women's prison population over the past three decades, only nine states (New York, Nebraska, Washington, Ohio, Indiana, South Dakota, Illinois, West Virginia, and Wyoming) have prison nursery programs in operation or under development.

Despite the fact that they are still few in number, research shows that these programs benefit mothers and children. When adequate resources are available for prison nursery programs, women who participate show lower rates of recidivism, and their children show no adverse effects as a result of their participation. By keeping mothers and infants together, these programs prevent foster care placement and allow for the formation of mother–child bonds during a critical period of infant development.

While such programs are an improvement, many women parenting their infants in prison nurseries could be doing so in the community instead. Most women in prison nursery programs present little risk to public safety. Community corrections programs have been shown to protect public safety and reduce recidivism at a fraction of the human and economic costs of prison. In the community, programs could operate according to prevailing community child health and development standards. Mothers would be able to access educational and vocational services while participating in a mother–child program, as they will be expected to serve as both mothers and employees after their release.

FOR CRITICAL THINKING AND WRITING

Are prison nurseries valuable or just a waste of taxpayers' money? If you like the idea, prepare a statement to convince the department of corrections to open a nursery.

Source: Chandra Kring Villanueva, Sara From, and Georgia Lerner, *Mothers, Infants and Imprisonment, A National Look at Prison Nurseries and Community-Based Alternatives* (New York: Women's Prison Association, 2009), http://www.wpaonline.org (accessed June 2014).

Ascertain that providing sufficient programs for incarcerated women with children is critical

Programs for Incarcerated Mothers

Several states have innovative programs for mothers of young children. California has a statute mandating the creation of a Mother-Infant Care Program, an alternative-sentencing project that allows 100 women with infants who are 6 months old or younger to live in one of the seven community-based facilities with their children and take parenting classes. Several hundred women have graduated from the program. The program at Bedford Hills in New York State is the one most written about. The Bedford Hills program provides a nursery where babies up to 18 months old can live with their mothers. A playroom is available for older children, who are encouraged to come and visit with their moms. The mother–child bonding has been excellent in this program, and the women learn child care skills. The Nebraska Correctional Center for Women, similarly, has a prison nursery and overnight visits for older children to maintain the bonds between mother and child. Children can stay up to five days a month. According to the male warden, the presence of children has a harmonizing effect on the whole population.[45] The Evidence-Based Corrections feature discusses an evaluation of these programs.

Inmate mothers are also treated well in some other countries. For example, the European Committee for Children of Imprisoned Parents (EUROCHIPS) advocates that attention be paid to the needs of children in maintaining ties with their incarcerated parents. The Swedish Prison and Probation Service ordered the following for all prisons in Sweden:

- Special leave will be granted for important events concerning children.
- Children should be allowed to telephone and speak directly to the parent. (In the past, children could only leave a message and ask the parent to call back, which frequently occurred several hours later.)
- Each new prisoner should be asked about his/her children.
- Flexible visiting hours for children need to be provided.[46]

Lucy Nicholson/Reuters/Landov

Family visits can mean a lot to female inmates, giving them a chance to maintain close family ties.

FOR GROUP DISCUSSION

Discuss how your group would propose to create a program for inmate mothers that would provide punishment, deterrence, and rehabilitation. How often can they see their children? What goals do they have to achieve? LO4

Prison Health Care

The quality of health care in women's prisons varies from very good to grossly inadequate. Women in prison have unique health care needs that sometimes are not being met. As the prison population ages, these needs become critical.[47] Compared to men, women in prison have higher rates of illness. On the bright side, prison administrators now provide ready access to female-specific health care services, and initial physical and pelvic examinations, mammograms, and routine pregnancy screenings are performed. However, despite progress, problems still exist:

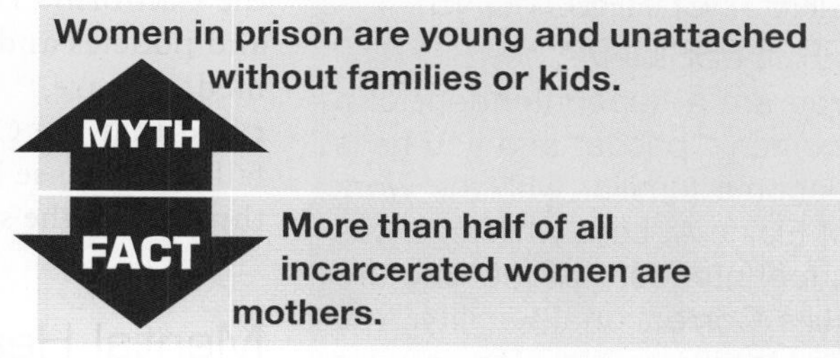

MYTH Women in prison are young and unattached without families or kids.

FACT More than half of all incarcerated women are mothers.

LO5 Identify the serious issues of health care in women's prisons

- *Failure to refer seriously ill inmates for treatment and delays in treatment.* Women inmates suffering from treatable diseases such as asthma, diabetes, sickle cell anemia, cancer, late-term miscarriages, and seizures have little or no access to medical attention, sometimes resulting in death or permanent injury. Instances of failure to deliver life-saving drugs for inmates with HIV/AIDS have also been noted.
- *Lack of qualified personnel and resources and use of nonmedical staff.* There are too few staff to meet physical and mental health needs. This often results in long delays in obtaining medical attention; disrupted and poor quality treatment causing physical deterioration of prisoners with chronic and degenerative diseases, such as cancer; overmedication of prisoners with psychotropic drugs; and lack of mental health treatment. The use of nonmedical staff to screen requests for treatment is also common.
- *Charges for medical attention.* In violation of international standards, many prisons/jails charge inmates for medical attention, on the grounds that charging for health care services deters prisoners from seeking medical attention for minor

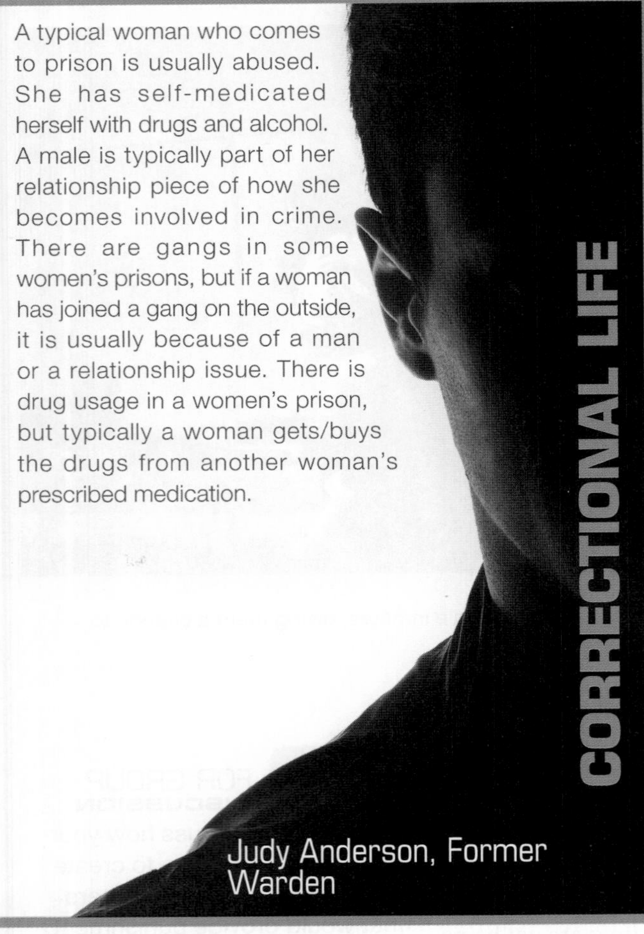

matters or because they want to avoid work. In some supermax prisons, where prisoners cannot work at all, the U.S. Justice Department has expressed concern that charging prisoners impedes their access to health care.

A typical woman who comes to prison is usually abused. She has self-medicated herself with drugs and alcohol. A male is typically part of her relationship piece of how she becomes involved in crime. There are gangs in some women's prisons, but if a woman has joined a gang on the outside, it is usually because of a man or a relationship issue. There is drug usage in a women's prison, but typically a woman gets/buys the drugs from another woman's prescribed medication.
CORRECTIONAL LIFE
Judy Anderson, Former Warden

- *Inadequate reproductive health care.* The National Institute of Corrections has stated that provision of gynecological services for women in prison is inadequate. Only half of the state prison systems surveyed offer female-specific services such as mammograms and Pap smears, and often entail a long wait to be seen.
- *Shackling during pregnancy.* Shackling of all prisoners, including pregnant prisoners, is policy in federal prisons and the U.S. Marshals Service and exists in almost all state prisons. Only two states have legislation regulating the use of restraints (belly chains, leg irons, and handcuffs). Shackling during labor may cause complications during delivery such as hemorrhage or decreased fetal heart rate. If a caesarian section is needed, a delay of even five minutes may result in permanent brain damage to the baby.
- *Lack of treatment for substance abuse.* The gap between services available and treatment needs continues to grow. The number of prisoners with histories of drug abuse is growing, but the proportion of prisoners receiving treatment has declined during the past decade.
- *Lack of adequate or appropriate mental health services.* A large percentage of women inmates experience sexual or physical abuse before coming to prison and suffer from posttraumatic stress disorder. Very few prison systems provide counseling. Women attempting to access mental health services are routinely given medication without opportunity to undergo psychotherapeutic treatment.[48]

THINKING
LIKE A CORRECTIONS PROFESSIONAL

You are a superintendent of a women's prison, and you have become familiar with the work of Elaine A. Lord while she was superintendent of the Bedford Hills Correctional Facility. You would like to develop in your facility the type of programming that is present at Bedford Hills. What steps would you take to accomplish this? What would you do first, second, and so forth? In thinking this out, be certain to include involvement of staff, inmates, and funding.

In some cases, impetus for change has come through civil litigation. In *Plata v. Davis* (2002), the largest-ever prison class-action lawsuit, inmates alleged that California officials inflicted cruel and unusual punishment by their deliberate indifference to serious medical needs. The settlement agreement required that the California Department of Corrections improve its medical care procedures and policies and devote significant resources to ensure timely access to proper medical care.[49] In another California case, *Budd v. Cambra* (2002), the court ruled that the California Department of Corrections violated the law when it failed to license health care facilities that provide in-patient treatment to inmates throughout the state.

Mental Health Care

It is estimated that more than half of all inmates have mental health problems and that female inmates have higher rates of mental health problems than males.[50] This is a particularly important issue considering the toll mental conditions have on cognitive, emotional, and volitional functions of the personality. Mental disorders make it difficult for a female inmate to function in the prison environment and those who suffer emotional distress are more likely to be victimized, cut themselves, and attempt suicide than their peers. Effective treatment of the mentally ill inmate faces many obstacles, including lack of proper resources and funding.[51]

Elaine A. Lord, former superintendent of Bedford Hills Correctional Institution, describes the difficulty of running an institution in which a large percentage of the residents are seriously mentally ill.[52] The wild behavior of some of the most disturbed inmates occupied the time of prison staff and resulted in many problems, including self-harm cutting and attacks on staff and other inmates. As the population exploded at Bedford Hills, giving attention to the needs of these seriously ill women was not possible. In the segregation units, women were constantly yelling and banging on the walls. A lawsuit was brought against the institution for the havoc that existed in the disciplinary unit. "Legal action is not always bad news for superintendents," as Lord states. "In some cases it actually forces necessary changes for procedures that open new ways of reacting to residents or groups or provides funding for staff and space for new programs." Thanks to the court case, additional mental health staff members were added and special therapy groups were run in the segregation unit.

Web App 8.1
The Bedford Hills College Program was founded by a task force chaired by then-superintendent Elaine Lord and comprised of education specialists and incarcerated students at the Bedford Hills Correctional Facility. Visit the Prison Studies Project website at http://prisonstudiesproject.org/2011/08/bedford-hills-college-program/ to learn more about Bedford Hills and other prison education programs. How do educational programs in prisons reduce recidivism rates, especially for women?

Sexual Abuse

It is common for female inmates to engage in same-sex relationships. Those involved in some form of pseudo-families try to create the type of family they wished they had on the outside. While most of these relationships are consensual, it is not unknown for women to be pressured into a sexual alliance by being threatened with social isolation unless she becomes involved in a sexual alliance with another inmate.

Human Rights Watch An international nongovernmental organization that is concerned with the rights of individuals, such as prisoners.

The Bureau Justice Statistics surveys of confined prison inmates have consistently found higher rates of inmate-on-inmate sexual victimization among females than males. In the latest survey, 4.7 percent of female inmates compared to only 1.9 percent of the male inmates reported being sexually victimized by another inmate.[53] When the rate of sexual victimization was limited to nonconsensual sexual acts, the difference between females and males was almost 5 times greater.[54]

Sexual abuse is also found when inmates are harassed, assaulted, or even raped by male correctional staff. Women prisoners are aware that they can lose their jobs or be thrown into "the hole" (isolation cell) if they do not do what male staff want.

Until recently, relatively little attention has been paid to the sexual assaults on female prisoners by their male guards. The International Women's Day organization documented more than 1,000 cases of sexual abuse of U.S. prisoners by correctional staff.[55] Extensive documentation was also provided by the Women's Rights Project of **Human Rights Watch**, an international nongovernmental organization. *All Too Familiar: Sexual Abuse of Women in U.S. State Prisons*, a 347-page report drawn from firsthand interviews, court records, and records of guards' disciplinary hearings, is astonishing in the graphic detail provided of everyday experiences of women in state prisons. It revealed that the extent of correctional officer-on-inmate abuse behind the closed doors of prisons is staggering.[56]

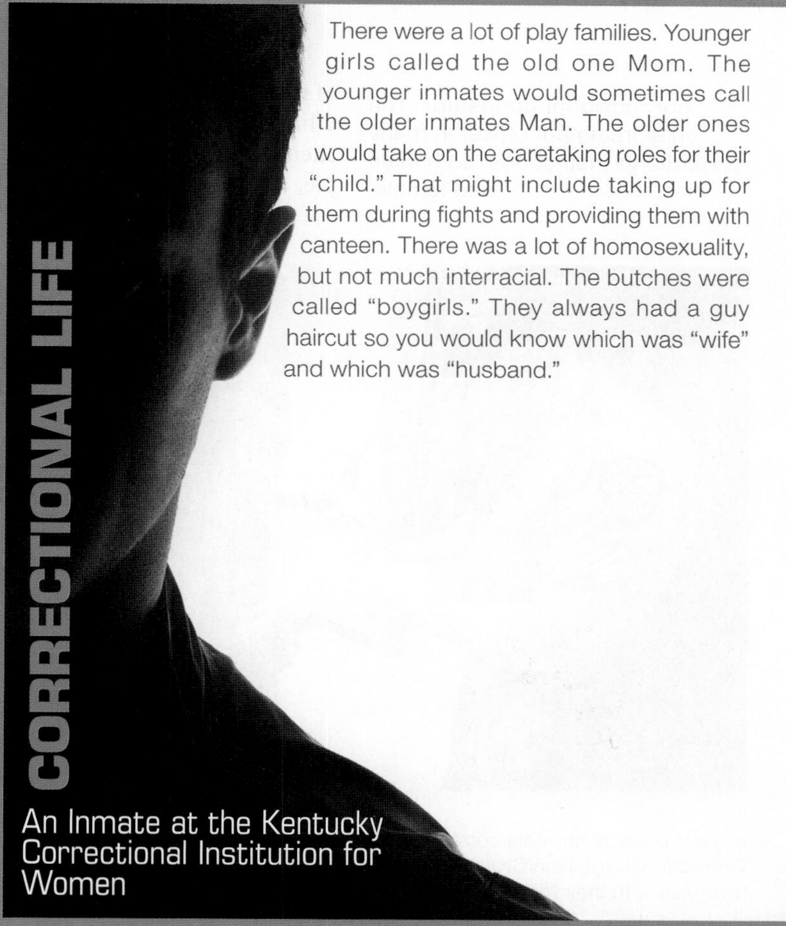

There were a lot of play families. Younger girls called the old one Mom. The younger inmates would sometimes call the older inmates Man. The older ones would take on the caretaking roles for their "child." That might include taking up for them during fights and providing them with canteen. There was a lot of homosexuality, but not much interracial. The butches were called "boygirls." They always had a guy haircut so you would know which was "wife" and which was "husband."

An Inmate at the Kentucky Correctional Institution for Women

CAREERS IN CORRECTIONS

Judy Anderson
Former Warden

"As warden, I basically saw myself as the mayor of a large urban city, which has a high crime rate and a large population of indigent people. The warden is responsible for providing all the services for inmates, which involves food, housing, education, medical, work, clothing, and anything in between.

"Women come to prison through different pathways than men. They do time differently; they reenter and transition to the community differently. Consequently, we tailor our service delivery to meet their needs, not duplicate what is done with men. What we try to do is to be gender responsive, which recognizes the behavioral and social differences between female and male offenders, but we still have a long way to go. In the corrections system, most of our policies and procedures are designed for the majority, the men."

See Chapter 15 for more detailed information on careers in corrections.

correctional counselor The chief treatment officer in many correctional institutions, both male and female.

There continues to be extensive litigation concerning the sexual mistreatment of female inmates. Scandals have erupted in Alabama, California, Georgia, Hawaii, Ohio, Louisiana, Michigan, Tennessee, New York, and New Mexico.[57] Most of them came to light only because of publicity surrounding legal suits. For example, a jury awarded $15.4 million to 10 current and former prisoners at Michigan's Robert Scott Correctional Facility for sexual abuse by male guards.[58] This sad story of sexual abuse was repeated a number of times in court filings, including a class action suit against New York Department of Corrections correctional officers, officials, and supervisors.[59]

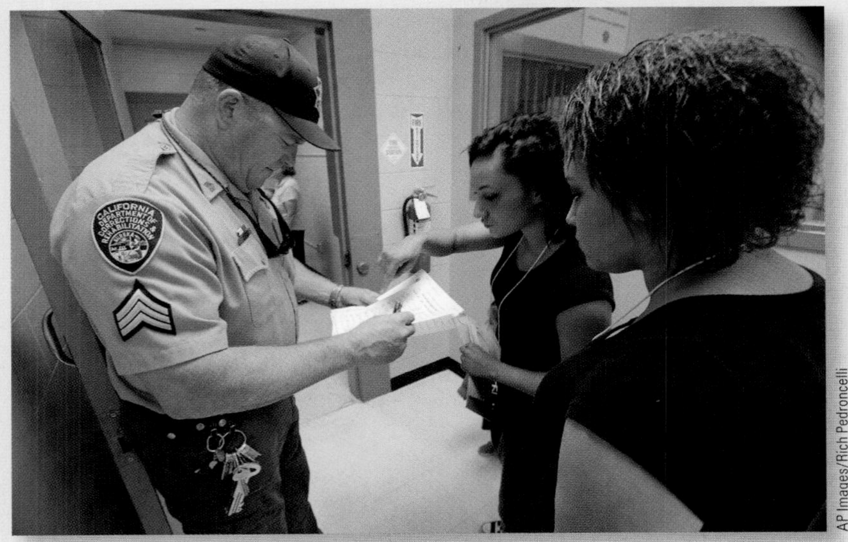
AP Images/Rich Pedroncelli

It is not unusual for male correctional officers to work in women's prisons. Here, Correctional Sgt. Ron Crother checks in Samantha and Summer La France before their visit with their mother at the Folsom Women's Facility in California.

Corrections Staff in Women's Prisons

Correctional administrators, correctional counselors and case workers, and women and men correctional officers are three categories of staff who have contact with inmates. Women have been superintendents of women's prisons since late in the nineteenth century, but today increasing numbers of women are being appointed wardens of men's prisons.

The **correctional counselor** is the basic treatment officer in many adult correctional institutions. Female correctional counselors serve several functions in women's and men's prisons (see Chapter 15).

Volunteer choir director Tina Hutchenson hugs an inmate who earned an associate's degree by attending classes at the Tennessee Prison for Women prison in Nashville. Nine inmates earned their diploma in a program offered by Lipscomb University. The graduates can continue on to earn bachelor's degrees.

PROFESSIONALISM IN WOMEN'S PRISONS

LO6 Discuss Professionalism In Women's Prisons

There is a growing movement to make the staff in women's prisons more competent and professional. What defines professionalism in a women's prison?

- A commitment to develop programming for inmates that deals with their present and helps them plan for the future
- A desire to treat inmates with dignity and respect
- A wide commitment to engage staff in prison management and operations
- A refusal to accept abusive treatment from staff toward inmates
- A determination to provide a safe environment for both inmates and staff
- A realization that staff training is a necessary aspect of a humane prison
- A desire to model positive behavior, both within and outside of the prison
- A willingness to pursue accreditation of their facility

SUMMARY

LO1 Identify the main reason for the fact that more than 100,000 women are in prison

The female prison population is now more than 100,000. The rise in female imprisonment is traced largely to the mandatory harsh minimum sentences for drug possession and dealing.

LO2 Identify the findings of the classic studies of social structure in women's prisons

Classic studies indicated that the social structure in women's prisons included both make-believe families and same-sex relationship models. In recent decades, it appears that there is less evidence of make-believe families in women's prisons.

LO3 Discuss the contemporary studies of women doing time in prison

These studies examine daily experiences of women in prison:

- Some studies continue to find the existence of same-sex relations in women's prisons.
- Barbara Owen focuses on how women deal with the culture of prison life, especially those who are committed to a criminal identity.
- Pogrebin and Dodge discovered that an important aspect of prison life was dealing with fear and violence.
- Kruttschnitt and Gartner looked at how women negotiate or cope with prison life in one prison, and in another more secure women's prison, they examined how women deal with a facility which has as its dominant concern maintaining order and security, rather than helping inmates. They also considered how the increased control and security have affected how women cope with prison life.

LO4 Ascertain that providing sufficient programs for incarcerated women with children is critical

Motherhood in prison represents a serious issue for inmate mothers and a daunting challenge for correctional administrators. Only nine states maintain nurseries for the children of female inmates.

LO5 Identify the serious issues of health care in women's prisons

These issues include inadequate reproductive care, shackling during pregnancy, lack of substance abuse treatment, lack of mental health services, failure to refer seriously ill inmates for treatment, delays in treatment, lack of qualified personnel and resources, and use of nonmedical staff. Adequate prison health care poses a difficult challenge because of rising costs, but nonetheless, it is a constitutionally mandated right for women prisoners.

LO6 Discuss professionalism in women's prisons

Professionalism in a women's prison includes a desire to treat inmates with dignity and respect, a goal of maintaining a safe and humane environment for inmates, a refusal to be involved with abusive treatment toward inmates or corruption in any form, and a commitment to develop programming for inmates that will help them deal with the present and plan for the future.

CRITICAL THINKING QUESTIONS

1. Women are committing more crimes, but the real increase shows up in drug-related crimes. Why do you think that women are involved in more drug-related crimes now than in the past?
2. The typical female offender has children. How does motherhood affect her doing time?
3. "Women's inmate society establishes a substitute group in which women can identify or construct family patterns similar to those in the free world." Describe the family structure in a women's prison.
4. Sexual abuse of inmates is a problem in some women's prisons. What can be done to reduce exploitation?
5. How do the subcultures of men's and women's prisons differ?
6. Do you support a separate but equal women's criminal justice system? Why or why not?

NOTES

1. Abby Luby, Record Review, 2003, http://abbylu.com/pdfs/PROFILES/Kathy%20Boudin%27s%20Impact.pdf (accessed June 2014). See also articles on Kathy Boudin in the *New York Times*, May 18, 2003.
2. Ibid.
3. Faculty web page for the Columbia University School of Social Work, where Boudin is an adjunct assistant professor, http://socialwork.columbia.edu/faculty/adjunct-faculty/kathy-boudin (accessed June 2014).
4. Nicole Hahn Rafter, *Partial Justice* (New Brunswick, NJ: Transaction Books, 1990), pp. 181–182.
5. E. Ann Carson and Daniela Golinelli, *Prisoners in 2012 – Advance Counts*, (Washington, DC: Bureau of Justice Statistics, 2013), http://www.bjs.gov/content/pub/pdf/p12ac.pdf (accessed July 2014).
6. American Friends Service Committee, *Struggle for Justice: Report on Crime and Justice in America* (New York: Hill & Wang, 1971), p. 16.
7. Ibid.
8. For a history of women's prisons, see Samuel Walker, *Popular Justice: A History of American Criminal Justice* (New York: Oxford University Press, 1980).
9. American Civil Liberties Union, *Caught in the Net: The Impact of Drug Policies on Women and Families*, March 15, 2005, http://www.aclu.org/drug-law-reform/caught-net-impact-drug-policies-women-and-families (accessed June 2014).
10. Ibid.
11. Polly Radosh, "Reflections on Women's Crime and Mothers in Prison: A Peacemaking Approach," *Crime and Delinquency* 48 (2002): 300–316.
12. Seena Fazel and John Danesh, "Serious Mental Disorder in 23,000 Prisoners: A Systematic Review of 62 Surveys," *Lancet* 359 (2002): 545–561.
13. Rebecca Jackson, Richard Rogers, Craig Neuman, and Paul Lambert, "Psychopathy in Female Offenders: An Investigation of Its Underlying Dimensions," *Criminal Justice and Behavior* 29 (2002): 692–705.
14. Fazel and Danesh, "Serious Mental Disorder in 23,000 Prisoners."
15. Ann Carson and Daniela Golinelli, *Prisoners in 2012 – Advance Counts*.
16. Meda Chesney-Lind and Lisa Pasko, *The Female Offender: Girls, Women, and Crime*, 2nd ed. (Newbury Park, CA: Sage Publications, 2004).
17. Gary Michael McClelland, Linda Teplin, Karen Abram, and Naomi Jacobs, "HIV and AIDS Risk Behaviors Among Female Jail Detainees: Implications for Public Health Policy," *American Journal of Public Health* 92 (2002): 818–826.
18. Christine Grella and Lisa Greenwell, "Correlates of Parental Status and Attitudes Toward Parenting Among Substance-Abusing Women Offenders," *Prison Journal* 86 (2006): 89–113.
19. Lee Ann Slocum, Sally Simpson, and Douglas Smith, "Strained Lives and Crime: Examining Intra-Individual Variation in Strain and Offending in a Sample of Incarcerated Women," *Criminology* 43 (2005): 1067–1110.
20. Ibid.
21. Merry Morash, "A Great Debate Over Using the Level of Service Inventory-Revised (LSI-R) with Women Offenders," *Criminology and Public Policy*, 8 (2009): 177.
22. See Ibid.
23. Sally Abrahamson, "Prisons Must Cease Re-Traumazing Women: A Call for Gender-Responsive Programs that End the Cycle of Violence," American University School of Law, 2009.
24. David A. Ward and Gene Kassebaum, *Women's Prisons and Social Structure*

(Chicago: Anderson, 1965); Rose Giallombardo, *Society of Women: A Study of a Women's Prison* (New York: Wiley, 1966); Esther Hefferman, *Making It in Prison: The Square, the Cool, and the Life* (New York: Wiley, 1972).

25. K. Faith, *Unruly Women: The Politics of Confinement and Resistance* (Vancouver, BC, Canada: Press Gang Publishing, 2003); Craig J. Forsyth, Rhonda D. Evans, and D. Buck Foster, "An Analysis of Inmate Explanations for Lesbian Relationships in Prison," *International Journal of Sociology of the Family* 30 (2002): 66–77; C. Hensley, R. Tewksbury, and M. Koscheski, "Inmate-to-Inmate Sexual Coercion in a Prison for Women," *Journal of Offender Rehabilitation* 37 (2002): 77–87; Theresa A. Severance, "The Prison Lesbian Revisited," *Journal of Gay and Lesbian Social Services* 17 (2004): 39–57.
26. Barbara Owen, "In the Mix: Struggle and Survival in a Women's Prison (Albany: State University of New York Press, 1998), pp. 1–2.
27. Mark Pogrebin and Mary Dodge, "Women's Accounts of Their Prison Experiences: A Retrospective View of Their Subjective Realities," *Journal of Criminal Justice* 29 (2001): 531–541.
28. Robert Ross and Hugh McKay, *Self-Mutilation* (Lexington, MA: Lexington Books, 1979).
29. Candace Kruttschnitt and Rosemary Gartner, *Marking Time in the Golden State: Women's Imprisonment in California* (Cambridge, UK: Cambridge University Press, 2005).
30. Ibid., p. 118.
31. Ibid., p. 92.
32. Ibid., p. 92., pp. 133–134.
33. Kimberly R. Greer, "The Changing Nature of Interpersonal Relationships in a Women's Prison," *Prison Journal* 80 (December 2000): 442–468.
34. Kruttschnitt and Gartner, *Marking Time in the Golden State*, pp. 101, 105, 107.
35. *Barefield v. Leach*, No. 1-0282 slip. Op. (D.N.M._), December 18, 1974.
36. *Pargo v. Elliott*, 49 F3d 1355 (1995).
37. Ibid.
38. Office of Juvenile Justice and Delinquency Prevention, "What Does Gender-Specific Programming Look Like?" in *Guiding Principles for Promising Female Programming*, 1998, http://www.ojjdp.gov/pubs/principles/ch2_6.html (accessed June 2014).
39. Family Strengthening Policy Center, "Supporting Families with Incarcerated Parents," (Washington, DC: National Human Services Assembly, 2005), p. 2. See also Jacquelyn L. Sandifer, "Evaluating the Efficacy of a Parenting Program for Incarcerated Mothers," *Prison Journal* 88 (2008): 423–445.
40. Craig J. Forsyth, "Pondering the Discourse of Prison Mamas: A Research Note," *Deviant Behavior: An Interdisciplinary Journal* 24 (2003): 269–280.
41. Phyllis E. Berry and Helen M. Eigenberg, "Role Strain and Incarcerated Mothers: Understanding the Process of Mothering," *Women and Criminal Justice* 15 (2003): 101.
42. Joycelyn M. Baunach, "Parenting Programs in Women's Prisons," *Women and Criminal Justice* 14 (2002): 131–140.
43. Ibid.
44. Kristine Siefert and Sheryl Pimlott, "Improving Pregnancy Outcome During Imprisonment: A Model Residential Care Program," *Social Work* 46 (April 2001): 125–134.
45. For a description of these programs, see Katherine Stuart van Wormer and Clemens Bartollas, *Women and the Criminal Justice System* (Boston: Allyn & Bacon, 2007), pp. 164–165.
46. British Broadcasting Company (BBC), "Mothers in Prison," *Woman's Hour*, November 20, 2001.
47. General Accounting Office, *Women in Prison: Issues and Challenges Confronting U.S. Correctional Systems* (Washington, DC: U.S. Department of Justice, 1999).
48. Amnesty International, http://www.amnestyusa.org/our-work/issues/women-s-rights/violence-against-women (accessed June 2014).
49. Frank D. Russo, "California Senate Vote Today on $7 Billion Prison Health Care Construction Bill," *California Progress Report*, http://www.californiaprogressreport.com/site/california-senate-vote-today-7-billion-prison-health-care-construction-bill (accessed June 2014).
50. Doris J. James and Lauren E. Glaze, *Mental Health Problems of Prison and Jail Inmates* (Washington,DC: U.S. Department of Justice; Bureau of Justice Statistics Special Report, 2006), p. 1.
51. See Julio Arboleda-Flórez, "Mental Patients in Prison," *World Psychiatry* 8 (2009): 187–189.
52. E. A. Lord, "The Challenges of Mentally Ill Female Offenders in Prison," *Criminal Justice and Behavior* 35 (2008): 928–942.
53. Bureau of Justice Statistics, "Former National Prisoner Survey" (Washington, DC: U.S. Department of Justice, 2008).
54. Ibid.
55. International Women's Day, 2001. For examinations of the seriousness of this issue, see Cathy McDaniels-Wilson and Joanne Belknap, "The Extensive Sexual Violation and Sexual Abuse Histories of Incarcerated Women," *Violence Against Women* 14 (2008): 1090–1127; Ashley G. Blackburn, Janet L. Mullings, and James W. Marquart, "Sexual Assault in Prison and Beyond: Toward an Understanding of Lifetime Sexual Assault Among Incarcerated Women," *Prison Journal* 88 (2008): 351–377.
56. Human Rights Watch, Women's Rights Project, *All Too Familiar: Sexual Abuse of Women in U.S. State Prisons* (New York: Human Rights Watch, 1996).
57. Chesney-Lind and Pasko, *The Female Offender*.
58. Tina Lam, "Jury Awards Women $15.4 Million for Sexual Abuse in Prison," *Detroit Free Press*, http://www.usatoday.com/news/nation/2008-02-02-prison-abuse_N.htm (accessed June 2014).
59. Kari Lyderson, "Red Tape Lets Guards Rape Women Prisoners, Suit Argues," *New Standard*, http://www.november.org/stayinfo/breaking06/RapeSuit.html (accessed June 2014).

AP Images/The Daily Texan/Rebeca Rodriguez

Adequate medical care is among the legal rights granted to inmates. Ernest Sanders (60) and Clifton Haygood (53) are both receiving medical care at Kilby Correctional Facility in Mt. Meigs, Alabama. The Kilby facility, built in 1969, provides hospital services to include comprehensive medical, dental, and mental health care. Sanders has kidney problems and Haygood was just told by the doctor that his colon cancer is in remission.

IN 1987, MICHAEL MORTON WAS CONVICTED OF MURDER, accused of killing his wife, Christine. On October 4, 2011, Michael Morton walked out of a Williamson County (Texas) courtroom a free man after his murder conviction was overturned because of DNA evidence that another man had actually killed his wife. It turns out that a bandana found at the scene of another murder contained the blood of Christine Morton and another man, Mark Alan Norwood, a known felon who lived in the area. Michael Morton served nearly 25 years in prison before being released. In 2013, Norwood was convicted of the murder of Christine Morton and sentenced to life in prison; he is also currently accused of killing another woman, Debra Baker, in 1988.

After Morton was set free, Barry Scheck, co-director of the Innocence Project, a nonprofit organization that takes on cases such as Morton's, told the press, "Mr. Morton was the victim of serious prosecutorial misconduct that caused him to lose 25 years of his life and completely ripped apart his family. Perhaps even more tragically, we now know that another murder might have been prevented if law enforcement had continued its investigation rather than building a false case against Mr. Morton."[1] Morton would have never been convicted if the prosecution had turned over as required evidence pointing to his innocence. Among the evidence that was kept from the defense:

- A statement by the victim's mother, who told police that the couple's 3-year-old child witnessed the murder and provided a chilling account of watching a man who was not his father beat Christine to death.
- A report that a neighbor had on several occasions observed a man park a green van on the street behind the Mortons' house, then get out and walk into the wooded area off the road.
- A report that a check made out to Christine Morton by a man named John B. Cross was cashed with Christine's forged signature nine days after her murder.[2]

These omissions were not lost on lawmakers: on May 16, 2013, Texas Senate Bill 1611 was signed into law. Called the Michael Morton Act, it is designed to ensure a more open trial discovery process by removing obstacles for accessing prosecutorial evidence before trial. The bill became law on January 1, 2014.[3]

The Morton case is one of many that show that courts can make a mistake and innocent individuals are routinely sentenced to long terms in prison or even given the death penalty. It follows then that many prison inmates are not actually guilty of the crimes that put them behind bars. They would be at a significant legal disadvantage if their civil rights were denied. If prison inmates were unable to obtain legal representation or denied the right to bring their case to court, people like Michael Morton would never be able to earn their freedom.

9

Prisoners' Rights

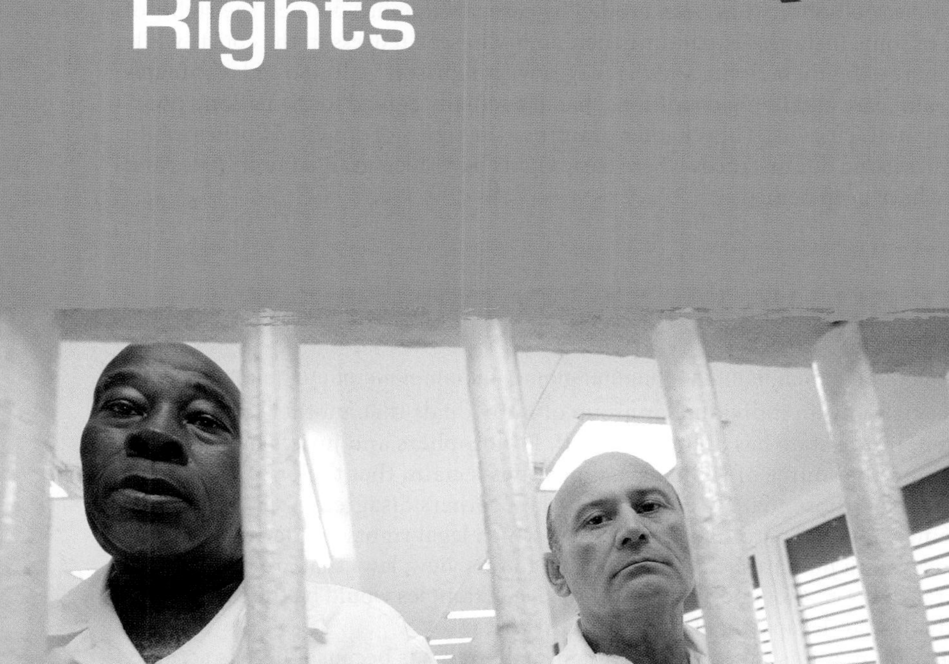

Michel Mercier/The Huntsville Times /Landov

LEARNING OBJECTIVES

 Discuss what is meant by the term *prisoners' rights*

 Discuss the foundation of prisoners' rights

 Identify the First, Fourth, Eighth, and Fourteenth Amendment substantive rights that the courts have awarded inmates

 Summarize the legal services that are available to inmates

 Discuss the rights that have not been given to inmates

PREVIEW OF KEY CONCEPTS

- principle of least eligibility
- Bill of Rights
- statutes
- case law
- landmark decision
- *habeas corpus*
- hands-off doctrine
- restraining hands doctrine
- Section 1983
- Prison Litigation Reform Act (PLRA)
- substantive rights
- First Amendment
- jailhouse lawyers
- Fourth Amendment
- Eighth Amendment
- cruel and unusual punishment
- Fourteenth Amendment
- Innocence Projects
- grievance process
- corrections ombudsman

Proving innocence is only one aspect of the need for maintaining civil rights behind prison walls. Inmates also want to hold on to their constitutionally guaranteed rights, such as the right to practice religion and be free from cruel and unusual punishment while confined in a correctional facility. Over the past 50 years, the nation's court system has dealt with these issues and others. For many years the **principle of least eligibility** defined the rights that prisoners receive in prison. This principle states that prisoners should receive no better services and privileges than the least advantaged honest citizen in society. Every honest citizen should have a better life than prisoners. However, the confining nature of the principle of least eligibility has been eroded by case law that has defined the rights of prisoners, in some instances expanding their ability to seek redress in the courts while in others increasing their rights and privileges within prison walls. So today inmates may get health care and living conditions that are actually denied to the nation's poorest, albeit honest, citizens. This chapter examines the rights of convicted prisoners in some detail, setting out instances where basic rights have been granted to inmates and where they have been denied.

principle of least eligibility States that prisoners should receive no better services than the general public receives. It means that the least advantaged in society should have a better life than do prisoners.

Discuss what is meant by the term *prisoners' rights*  LO1

WHAT DO WE MEAN BY PRISONERS' RIGHTS?

A *right* is a claim by an individual or group of individuals that another individual, a corporation, or the state has a duty to fulfill. Philosophers and jurists have written volumes about the source of rights. Legal positivists claim that the only rights anyone possesses are those that are conferred by law[4]; others disagree, asserting that all human beings possess "natural" rights—from which legal rights are derived—necessary for survival in human society.[5] According to this view, laws that are inconsistent with natural rights cannot and should not survive. Examples would be the race laws of Nazi Germany and the apartheid laws of South Africa.

One reason that it is difficult to define inmate rights is because there is actually more than one view on the topic.

- *Legalistic/due process view.* Convicted felons do not have rights other than those conferred on them by law. In the United States, those rights are derived by the courts from the Constitution of the United States, from the state constitutions, and from the laws that Congress and the state legislatures enact. Inmates are entitled to due process of the law even in confinement.
- *Crime control view.* Inmates are criminals who have harmed others and must be made to pay for their misdeeds. Convicted criminals have, by definition, forfeited their right to freedom and liberty. The suffering they endure in confinement serves to deter future criminal behaviors. The fewer rights inmates have, the greater the deterrent effect of punishment.
- *Humanistic view.* Inmates are humans who have made mistakes and are being punished. Prisons are places of punishment, but they should not be punishing. If inmates are given the same rights and privileges as any citizen, their anger and resentment toward society will diminish, thereby aiding the rehabilitation process.

FOR GROUP **DISCUSSION**

In your group, discuss which view—legalistic/due process, crime control, or humanistic—makes the United States prison system obsolete and which makes it most efficient and why. LO1

Considering these opposing viewpoints, in this chapter we use the following definition, which is a combination of humanistic and legalistic/due process, when we refer to inmate rights: Inmates must be given all the rights conferred on them by law, including due process rights, but their status as convicted felons has caused them to lose certain rights that free citizens have, including freedom and the ability to come and go as they wish.

FOUNDATIONS OF PRISONERS' RIGHTS LAW

LO2 Discuss the foundation of prisoners' rights

The U.S. Constitution is the principal source of prisoners' rights, but federal and state statutes, legal precedents, federal civil rights lawsuits, and writs of *habeas corpus* are also important sources of prisoners' rights.

U.S. Constitution

Substantive criminal law primarily defines crimes, but the law of criminal procedure consists of the rules and procedures that govern the pretrial processing of criminal suspects and the conduct of criminal trials. The body of the Constitution and the first 10 amendments (added to the Constitution on December 15, 1791, and known as the **Bill of Rights**) are the main sources of the procedural law. The purpose of these amendments was to prevent the government from usurping citizens' personal freedoms. The U.S. Supreme Court's interpretation of these amendments has served as the basis for the creation of legal rights of the accused. Exhibit 9.1 sets out the most important amendments affecting inmates' rights.

Bill of Rights The name given to the first 10 amendments to the U.S. Constitution, which are looked upon as fundamentally important in the processing of criminal defendants.

Statutes

States may award rights to prisoners beyond those granted by the U.S. Constitution or state constitution. **Statutes** tend to be written in more specific terms than are the U.S. Constitution or state constitutions. For example, the U.S. Supreme Court was

Statutes States may award rights to prisoners beyond those granted by the U.S. Constitution or state constitution.

EXHIBIT 9.1

Amendments to the Constitution that Affect Inmates' Rights

- The *First Amendment* grants freedom of religion, speech, the press, and assembly.
- The *Fourth Amendment* bars illegal "searches and seizures," a right especially important for the criminal justice system because it means that police officers cannot indiscriminately use their authority to investigate possible crime or arrest a suspect.
- The *Fifth Amendment* limits the admissibility of confessions that have been obtained unfairly. In the landmark case of *Miranda v. Arizona*, the Supreme Court held that a person accused of a crime has the right to refuse to answer questions when placed in police custody.[6]
- The *Sixth Amendment* guarantees a defendant the right to a speedy and public trial by an impartial jury, the right to be informed of the nature of the charges, and the right to confront any prosecution witnesses. It also contains the right of a defendant to be represented by an attorney, a privilege that has been extended to numerous stages of the criminal justice process, including pretrial custody, identification and lineup procedures, preliminary hearings, submission of a guilty plea, trial, sentencing, and postconviction appeal.
- The *Eighth Amendment* bars excessive bail or excessive fines imposed, as well as cruel and unusual punishment inflicted. This prohibition protects both the accused and convicted offenders from actions regarded as unacceptable by a civilized society, including corporal punishment and torture.
- The *Fourteenth Amendment* is the vehicle used by the courts to apply the protection of the Bill of Rights to the states. It affirms that no state may "deprive any person of life, liberty, or property, without due process of law."

Web App 9.1
Use a web search engine to find information about statutes and rights awarded to inmates in your state. Which do you feel are appropriate and which are excessive or misplaced? LO2

asked in 1998 whether the Americans with Disability Act applied to state prisoners. In a unanimous decision the Court ruled that the statute's language included state prisoners.[7] The U.S. Congress is responsible for statutes dealing with problems concerning the entire nation. Congress passes laws defining federal crimes and punishments, authorizes programs in terms of criminal justice policies, and allocates funds for federal criminal justice agencies. Each state legislature enacts laws that govern the acts of that state and the individuals within that jurisdiction. In addition, state legislatures appropriate funds for state agencies, including corrections.

Legal Precedents

case law The body of judicial precedent that is built on legal reasoning and previous interpretations of statutory laws.

landmark decision When a precedent establishes an important principle, or represents a change or new law.

Previous court decisions, called **case law**, also affect court decisions. Judges create law or modify existing law when they make a decision in a particular case. They are guided by the Constitution and its Bill of Rights, state and federal statutes, and decisions in other cases. The precedent on an issue represents the collective body of judicial principles that a court considers when interpreting the law. Judges consider the principles involved in former decisions and apply them to the cases being decided. When a precedent establishes an important principle, or represents a change or new law, that precedent is known as a **landmark decision**. For example, in the important case *Holt v. Sarver*, federal courts intervened in the state prison system of Arkansas and addressed complaints of physical abuse by guards and inmate trustees on members of the general inmate population.[8] Trustees had been put in charge of fellow inmates and ruled with an iron hand. The Court found their abuse a violation of the Eighth Amendment's prohibition against cruel and unusual punishment. Following this decision, similar litigation was introduced in many other states, all but ending the trustee system in U.S. prisons.

Federal Civil Rights Lawsuits

Civil rights are rights that have been guaranteed and protected by the government. These laws are a protection against the denial of an individual's civil rights based on race, sex, age, religion, national origin, physical limitation, or previous condition of servitude. Civil rights lawsuits have covered issues such as public education, public housing, employment, voting, access to public facilities, and corrections. The U.S. Supreme Court has played a significant role in increasing government protections of civil rights to prisoners, including the right to sue people whom they feel violated their rights during trial. For example, in one recent case, two Mississippi men wrongfully sent to prison filed federal lawsuits against the medical experts who testified the men left bite marks on two slain children.[9]

Writ of *Habeas Corpus*

habeas corpus A Latin expression meaning "you have the body." A writ of *habeas corpus* brings a person before a court or judge to determine the legality of his or her restraint in custody.

Habeas corpus represents the principal means by which state inmates attack the constitutionality of their convictions in federal courts. *Habeas corpus* has been called "the great writ of liberty." It is the means to show that individuals have the right to be free from arbitrary arrests. *Habeas corpus* permits a federal judge to find a due process violation sufficient enough to overturn the judgment of numerous state judges and 12 jurors. Today, critics charge that *habeas corpus* often releases the convicted on technical principles of law, rather than on grounds of innocence or even for reasons of clemency. The Antiterrorism and Effective Death Penalty Act of 1996 greatly restricts the power of federal judges to award relief to state prisoners who file two or more *habeas corpus* applications. If an inmate asserts a claim that has been previously presented in a federal *habeas corpus* petition, the claim must be dismissed in all cases. See Figure 9.1 for the trends in *habeas corpus* petitions filed in U.S. District Court.

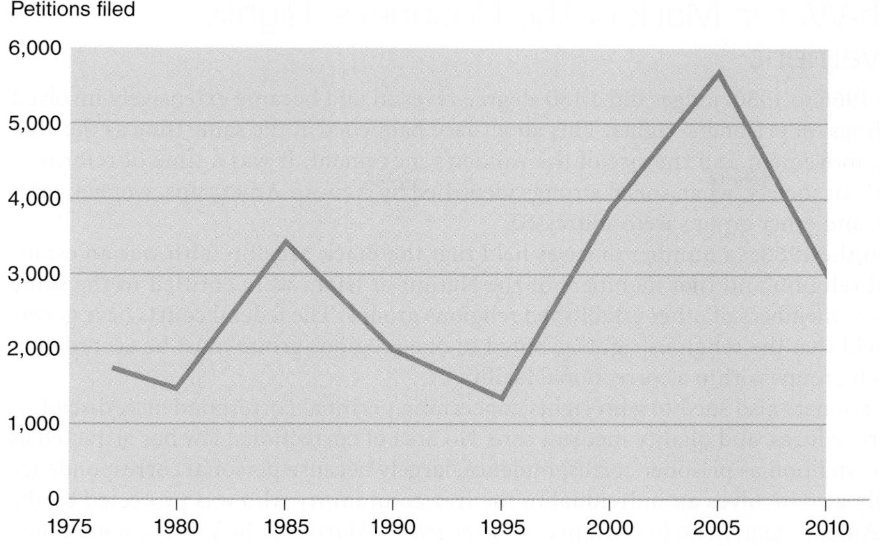

FIGURE 9.1

Trends in *Habeas Corpus* Petitions Filed in U.S. District Court

Sources: John Scalla, *Prisoners Petitions Filed in U.S. District Courts, 2000, with Trends, 1980–2000* (Government Printing Office: Bureau of Justice Statistics, 2002); *Sourcebook of Criminal Justice Statistics* online, www.albany.edu/sourcebook/ (accessed March 28, 2012).

hands-off doctrine The idea that persons sentenced to prison are not entitled to the same constitutional protections they enjoyed before conviction.

DEVELOPING PRISONERS' RIGHTS

While the above sources of law are the basis of prisoners' rights, they were not automatically applied or adopted. Quite the opposite. Prior to 1960, it was generally accepted that a convicted individual forfeited all rights not expressly granted by statutory law or correctional policy. Inmates were considered to be *civilly dead*. Convicted offenders, reasoned the U.S. Supreme Court, should expect to be penalized for their misdeeds and part of their punishment was the loss of freedoms ordinary citizens take for granted.

An examination of judges' actions over the years makes it possible to distinguish three phases of the prisoners' rights movement: (1) the convicted felon as-slave-of-the-state phase, (2) the high-water mark of the prisoners' rights movement, and (3) the crime control response of the federal and state courts.

Convicted Felons as Slaves of the State

For most of the history of the United States, the prisoner has been a slave of state corrections—that is, prisoners lost all their rights when sentenced to prison. An 1871 case, *Ruffin v. the Commonwealth of Virginia*, expressed it this way: "[The prisoner] has, as a consequence of his crime, not only forfeited his liberty, but all his personal rights except those which the law in its humanity accords to him. He is for the time being the slave of the state."[10] One reason why prisoners lacked rights was that federal and state courts were reluctant to intervene in the administration of prisons unless the circumstances of a case clearly indicated a serious breach of the Eighth Amendment protection against cruel and unusual punishment. This judicial policy is referred to as the **hands-off doctrine**. The courts used three basic justifications for their neglect of prison conditions:

- Correctional administration was a technical matter best left to experts rather than to courts ill-equipped to make appropriate evaluations.
- Society as a whole was apathetic to what went on in prisons, and most individuals preferred not to associate with or know about offenders.
- Prisoners' complaints involved privileges rather than rights. Prisoners were considered to have fewer constitutional rights than other members of society.[11]

AP Images/JIM COLE

Robert Tulloch was sentenced to life in prison in New Hampshire for killing two Dartmouth professors when he was 17 years old. Recently, Tulloch and three other New Hampshire teens serving life sentences argued to be resentenced under a U.S. Supreme Court ruling that says mandatory life sentences for juveniles amount to cruel and unusual punishment. Tulloch was granted a new sentencing hearing, but it is unlikely his prison term will be reduced.

High-Water Mark of the Prisoners' Rights Movement

From 1966 to 1980, judges did a 180-degree reversal and became extensively involved in rulings on prisoners' rights. This about-face happened at the same time as the civil rights movement and the rise of the women's movement. It was a time of reform in American society, when social wrongs identified by African Americans, women, prisoners, and other groups were addressed.

In the 1960s, a number of cases held that the Black Muslim faith was an established religion and that members of the Nation of Islam were entitled to the same rights as members of other established religious groups. The federal courts have generally held that the religious rights granted to one religious group must be accorded to all such groups within a correctional facility.

Prisoners also sued to gain rights concerning personal correspondence, disciplinary procedures, and quality medical care. No area of correctional law has attracted as much attention as prisoner correspondence, largely because personal correspondence usually also involves an individual in the free community who was protected by the First Amendment. In an important case, *Procurier v. Martinez*, the U.S. Supreme Court ruled that "Censorship of prison mail works as a consequential restriction on the First and Fourteenth Amendment rights of those who are not prisoners."[12] What this meant is that citizens in the outside community have the right to correspond with prisoners without censorship of their mail. More recent court rulings have extended the rights of prison officials to censor inmate mail; see this section of First Amendment rights later in this chapter.

The high-water mark of the prisoners' rights movement was the *Wolff v. McDonnell* decision.[13] McDonnell, a prisoner, had filed a class-action suit against the state of Nebraska, claiming that its disciplinary procedures, especially those pertaining to the loss of "good time" (time subtracted from a sentence for good behavior), were unconstitutional.

The state court ruled that the defendant had not received the minimum requirements for disciplinary procedures. He petitioned the U.S. Supreme Court to restore the good time he had lost and to assess damages against corrections officials. The Supreme Court ruled that the state of Nebraska had properly enacted laws pertaining to the granting and revoking of good time. Nevertheless, the procedure used to revoke good time was found to be in violation of the due process rights granted in the Fourteenth Amendment.

A final major victory for inmates was in the area of medical rights. In *Estelle v. Gamble*, the court ruled that deliberate interference with serious medical needs constitutes cruel and unusual punishment.[14] Significantly, the suit also demonstrated that a complaint of system-wide deprivation of medical care receives a more sympathetic hearing than do complaints alleging inadequate medical care for an individual.

Crime Control Response by the Court

restraining hands doctrine Supreme Court doctrine that gave correctional administrators freedom from excessive lower court interference.

In the 1970s, court opinions shifted toward a more balanced position between prisoners' rights and legitimate institutional interest. This so-called **restraining hands doctrine** of the U.S. Supreme Court was obvious in four cases: *Baxter v. Palmigiano, Enomato v. Clutchette, Mecham v. Fano,* and *Montanye v. Haymes.*[15]

Of these, the *Mecham v. Fano* decision most clearly expressed the restraining-hands doctrine because of its ruling that the prisoner is subject to the rules of the prison system: "Given a valid conviction, the criminal defendant has been constitutionally deprived of his liberty to the extent that the state may confine him and subject him to the rules of its prison system so long as conditions of confinement do not otherwise violate the Constitution."[16]

The 1981 *Rhodes v. Chapman* case, which held that the Southern Ohio Correctional Facility was not in violation of the Eighth Amendment for double-celling inmates, was an even greater victory for prison officials.[17] In *Rhodes*, the Court ruled that double-bunking of prisoners was not cruel and unusual punishment. The Court ruled that conditions of confinement must not involve the wanton and unnecessary infliction of pain, nor may they be grossly disproportionate to the severity of the crime warranting imprisonment. But conditions that are not cruel and unusual under contemporary standards are not unconstitutional. To the extent such conditions are restrictive and even harsh, such as double-bunking, they are part of the penalty that criminals pay for their offenses against society.

Turner v. Safley remains the leading standard for evaluating prisoner free-expression claims.[18] Leonard Safley, a Missouri inmate, became involved with a female inmate at the Renz Correctional Institution in Cedar City, Missouri, which housed both male and female inmates at the time. After he was transferred to another prison, he planned to marry and wanted to correspond with his fiancée. Prison officials did not approve of the correspondence or the intended marriage, which in fact took place under court order. The case eventually landed in the U.S. Supreme Court, and while the Court struck down the restriction on inmate marriages, it ruled that inmate-to-inmate correspondence could be restricted. This case is significant because it changed the standard of review and made it possible for prison officials to make decisions on how to preserve the safety of the prison and inmates.[19]

In 1991, the Supreme Court ruled in the *Wilson v. Seiter* decision that uncomfortable conditions are not unconstitutional but are part of the penalty that inmates pay for committing crimes. The inmates claimed that the prison was too cold in the winter and too hot in the summer. The Court emphasized that to be in violation of constitutional rights, prison officials have to show deliberate indifference to inmates' basic needs. This became the standard for suits brought under **Section 1983**.[20] See Exhibit 9.2.

Section 1983 Provides for civil action for the deprivation of their rights by an agent of government in which the plaintiff can receive punitive damages as well as the costs of the litigation.

CRITICAL THINKING

Should inmates be barred from filing suit after they have exhausted all administrative remedies? LO2

EXHIBIT 9.2

Section 1983

Section 1983 of Title 42 of the United States Code provides, in part:

> § 1983. Civil action for deprivation of rights "Every person who, under color of any statute, ordinance, regulation, custom, or usage, of any State or Territory or the District of Columbia, subjects, or causes to be subjected, any citizen of the United States or other person within the jurisdiction thereof to the deprivation of any rights, privileges, or immunities secured by the constitution and laws, shall be liable to the party injured in an action at law, suit in equity, or other proper proceeding for redress . . ."

Under this federal statute, persons who are deprived of their rights under the Constitution by someone acting under "color of law" (federal, state, or local) can bring a federal cause of action for damages and other relief.

Elements of a Cause of Action

Three elements are required to bring an action under 42 U.S.C. 1983. The plaintiff must prove the following:

1. He or she was deprived of a specific right, privilege, or immunity secured by the Constitution or U.S. laws.
2. The alleged deprivation was committed under color of state law.
3. The deprivation resulted in injuries suffered by the plaintiff.

Damages

A victim may recover compensatory damages, injunctive relief, and (except in the case of municipal defendants) punitive damages. The prevailing plaintiff can also recover the costs of the litigation and reasonable attorney's fees.

VOICES ACROSS THE PROFESSION

Conditions of confinement in most correctional entities have been denigrated dramatically. We are back to the 1950s, with little hope of relief in sight.

Dr. Allen Ault
Former Commissioner of Corrections in Colorado, Georgia, and Mississippi

In 1996, Congress passed the Prison Litigation Reform Act (PLRA), which was developed for a coalition of state attorneys general whose purpose was to curb the discretion of the federal courts in these types of actions. Their motivation was to reduce the workloads and expense of dealing with the numerous cases filed under the auspices of Section 1982 of the Civil Rights Act. The major effect of the provisions of the PLRA is that inmates now have the burden, individually and not as a class, to prove that a corrections practice or condition has a direct detrimental effect on their physical or mental well-being.

The PLRA has had the desired impact intended by the authors of the bill. Court intervention into corrections practice and conditions of confinement is almost nonexistent. Currently, legislative and executive branches of government have no fear of court action to ameliorate their detrimental actions. Many county, state, and federal correctional agencies have had their budgets cut drastically, some by over 50 percent, even though prisoner population has not been reduced. As a result, conditions of confinement in most correctional entities have been denigrated dramatically. We are back to the 1950s, with little hope of relief in sight.

Prison Litigation Reform Act (PLRA) Passed by Congress in 1996, this act limits the ability of inmates to complain about conditions of confinement and to allege violations of their constitutional rights.

LIMITING RIGHTS The inmate rights revolution soon clogged the appellate courts, prompting calls for limitations on inmate-sponsored litigation. The **Prison Litigation Reform Act (PLRA)**, which was passed by Congress and signed by President Clinton in 1996, limits the ability of prisoners to complain about conditions of confinement and to allege violation of their constitutional rights. The PLRA requires prisoners to either pay the full fee when filing a complaint ($150 in 1998) or to make an initial down payment followed by periodic installment payments. A three-strikes provision of this act prohibits an indigent prisoner from filing new lawsuits when the prisoner has previously filed frivolous or meritless claims. The PLRA appears to have had the greatest impact on civil rights prisoners, from whom the number of petitions filed dropped 20 percent from 1996 to 1997 and another 11 percent from 1997 to 1998.[21]

In Voices Across the Profession, Dr. Allen Ault, former commissioner of corrections in Colorado, Georgia, and Mississippi, defines the impact that the Prison Litigation Reform Act has had on prisoners' rights. And in another Voices feature, Alvin J. Bronstein, former director of the National Prison Project of the American Civil Liberties Union, puts the gains and losses of the prisoners' rights movement into perspective.

Inmates are also required to exhaust administrative remedies before they can take their complaints to the court system. The U.S. Supreme Court has decided two cases that define the scope of the exhaustion requirement—one dealing with a request for monetary relief and the other with allegations of excessive use of force. In *Booth v. Churner* (2001), a unanimous Court ruled that an inmate must go through the administrative processes before monetary relief could be granted.[22] In *Porter v. Nussle* (2002), a unanimous Court also made it clear that prisoners must use their grievance systems before going to court; there are no exceptions to this rule, even in situations where a grievance system cannot respond to an inmate's request for relief.[23]

Alvin J. Bronstein

VOICES ACROSS THE PROFESSION

There is hope with a new generation of correctional administrators who are a cut above a lot of correctional administrators from the past in terms of inmates' concerns.

Alvin J. Bronstein
Director Emeritus of the National Prison Project of the ACLU

Unfortunately, the gains of the 1960s, 1970s, and 1980s in terms of prisoners' rights were largely replaced by the Prison Litigation Reform Act of 1996. I stepped down from the Prison Project in January of 1996, and the Congress celebrated my departure by passing the Prison Litigation Reform Act in May of 1996. It was the result of a whole bunch of distortions by the National Association of Attorneys General, who published a top 10 list of all those cases that they claimed were causing problems. For example, in one of these cases they claimed that the prisoner was suing because he ordered creamy peanut butter from the commissary and got regular peanut butter. In fact, the peanut butter was not the real issue, but was mentioned as a minor example of the prison's inefficiency in a complaint that also described massive overcrowding and terrible medical care, which they ignored. Without any hearings, Congress passed it as a last-minute amendment to the commerce department's budget.

It has made it very difficult for prisoners' litigation projects because of the onerous terms and exhaustion requirements of the act, including difficulties in filing and getting attorneys. Attorneys would no longer be getting fees at market rate, and it has been harder to get them involved. In contrast, I can remember in 1987 we had pending lawsuits in 27 states—major cases involving entire state systems, such as Tennessee, Alabama, Colorado, New Mexico, Maine, and Rhode Island. We had seven lawyers in our office, and we could not run around the country and take care of these cases without competent local lawyers being willing to help us.

SUBSTANTIVE RIGHTS OF INMATES

LO3 Identify the First, Fourth, Eighth, and Fourteenth Amendment substantive rights that the courts have awarded inmates

Through a slow process of legal review, the courts have granted inmates a number of **substantive rights** that have significantly influenced the entire correctional system. The most important of these rights are discussed in the following sections. Prisoners have sued to establish rights in four areas: (1) the right to physical security and the minimum conditions necessary to sustain life, (2) the right to receive their constitutionally guaranteed safeguards, (3) the right to challenge the legality of their convictions through the courts, and (4) the right to receive the benefit of reasonable standards and procedural protections. See the Timeline for the most significant U.S. Supreme Court decisions on prisoners' rights.

substantive rights A right, such as life, liberty, or property, that is held to exist for its own sake and to constitute part of the legal order of society.

First Amendment Rights

The rights of prisoners under the **First Amendment**—freedom of religion, speech, the press, and assembly—have been subject to significant legal challenges.

First Amendment Congress shall make no law respecting an establishment of religion, or prohibiting the free exercise thereof; or abridging the freedom of speech, or of the press; or the right of the people peaceably to assemble, and to petition the government for a redress of grievances.

RELIGION Freedom of religion is a fundamental right guaranteed by the First Amendment. In general, the courts have ruled that inmates have the right to assemble and pray in the religion of their choice, but that religious symbols and practices that interfere with institutional security can be restricted. Administrators can draw the line if religious needs become cumbersome or impossible to carry out for reason of cost

TIMELINE

SIGNIFICANT U.S. **SUPREME** COURT DECISIONS ON PRISONERS' RIGHTS

Wolff v. McDonnell (1974)
Disciplinary measures are necessary to lose "good time."

Procunier v. Martinez (1974)
Censorship of inmate mail is subject to some restrictions.

Ruiz v. Estelle (1975)
Texas's correctional system is unconstitutional.

Estelle v. Gamble (1976)
Lack of proper medical care by the state is cruel and unusual punishment.

Meachum v. Fano (1976)
Inmate is subject to the rules of the prison system.

Theriault v. Carlson (1977)
The First Amendment does not protect religions that are shams and are devoid of religious sincerity.

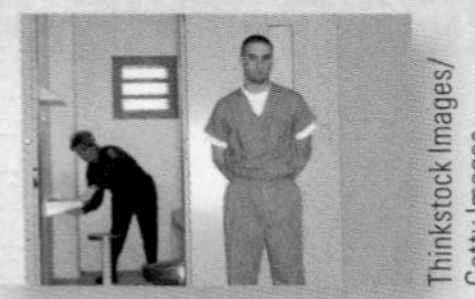

Thinkstock Images/Getty Images

Bell v. Wolfish (1979)
Unannounced cell searches are necessary for security and order.

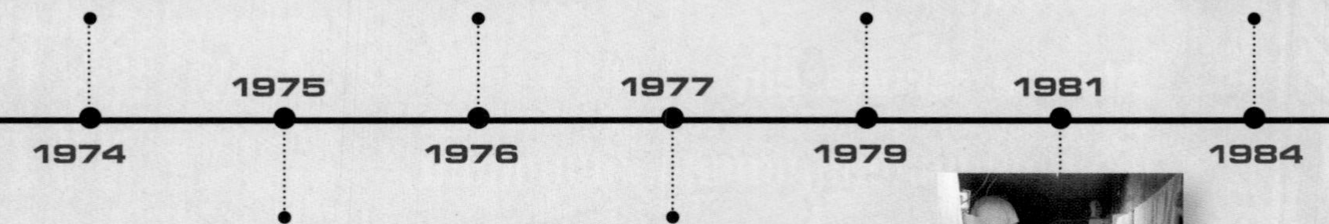

Rhodes v. Chapman (1981)
Double-celling is not unconstitutional.

AP Image/Rich Pedroncelli/File

Hudson v. Palmer (1984)
The Fourth Amendment does not apply to cell searches.

Whitley v. Albers (1986)
A prisoner shot during a riot does not suffer cruel and unusual punishment if the action was taken to maintain discipline rather than to cause harm.

Joel Gordon Photography

The courts have generally upheld freedom of religion behind bars, as long as religious practices do not interfere with institutional security. Here, a Jummah Congregational Prayer and Sermon session for Bilalian and African American Muslim inmates is led by the imam, Chaplain F. Rashid, in the Orange County (Florida) Jail.

or security. Granting special privileges can also be denied on the grounds that they will cause other groups to make similar demands. The federal courts have consistently held that the religious rights granted to one religious group must be accorded to all such groups within a correctional institution. Religious freedom has been looked upon as a preferred freedom; thus, the burden of proof is on institutional administrators when they wish to limit religious practices.[24] However, the courts usually have not required prison administrators to provide special diets, nor are they willing to allow the free exercise of religion to jeopardize the security and safety of the institution.

Religious rights resulted from lawsuits filed by smaller religious groups demanding that prison administrators give their parishioners the same religious rights granted members of established churches. Many of these legal actions were filed by the Nation of Islam, also known as the Black Muslims, an organization founded in Detroit by Wallace Fard Muhammad in 1930 with the goal of resurrecting the spiritual, mental, social, and economic

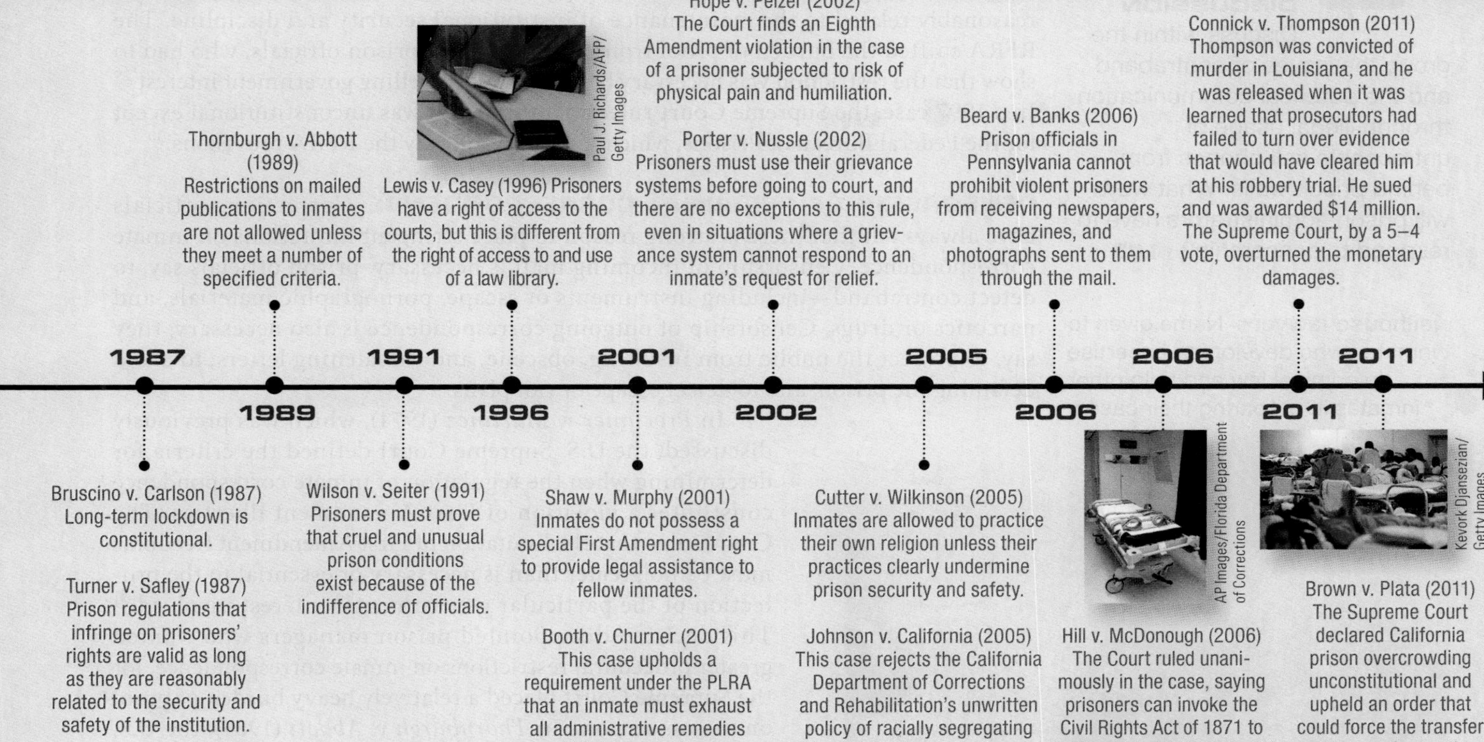

1987
Bruscino v. Carlson (1987) Long-term lockdown is constitutional.
Turner v. Safley (1987) Prison regulations that infringe on prisoners' rights are valid as long as they are reasonably related to the security and safety of the institution.
1989
Thornburgh v. Abbott (1989) Restrictions on mailed publications to inmates are not allowed unless they meet a number of specified criteria.
1991
Wilson v. Seiter (1991) Prisoners must prove that cruel and unusual prison conditions exist because of the indifference of officials.
1996
Lewis v. Casey (1996) Prisoners have a right of access to the courts, but this is different from the right of access to and use of a law library.
Paul J. Richards/AFP/Getty Images
2001
Shaw v. Murphy (2001) Inmates do not possess a special First Amendment right to provide legal assistance to fellow inmates.
Booth v. Churner (2001) This case upholds a requirement under the PLRA that an inmate must exhaust all administrative remedies available before filing a suit over prison conditions.
2002
Hope v. Pelzer (2002) The Court finds an Eighth Amendment violation in the case of a prisoner subjected to risk of physical pain and humiliation.
Porter v. Nussle (2002) Prisoners must use their grievance systems before going to court, and there are no exceptions to this rule, even in situations where a grievance system cannot respond to an inmate's request for relief.
2005
Cutter v. Wilkinson (2005) Inmates are allowed to practice their own religion unless their practices clearly undermine prison security and safety.
Johnson v. California (2005) This case rejects the California Department of Corrections and Rehabilitation's unwritten policy of racially segregating inmates in double cells each time they are transferred to a new facility.
2006
Beard v. Banks (2006) Prison officials in Pennsylvania cannot prohibit violent prisoners from receiving newspapers, magazines, and photographs sent to them through the mail.
2006
Hill v. McDonough (2006) The Court ruled unanimously in the case, saying prisoners can invoke the Civil Rights Act of 1871 to challenge a state's choice of drugs used in administering a lethal injection.
AP Images/Florida Department of Corrections
2011
Connick v. Thompson (2011) Thompson was convicted of murder in Louisiana, and he was released when it was learned that prosecutors had failed to turn over evidence that would have cleared him at his robbery trial. He sued and was awarded $14 million. The Supreme Court, by a 5–4 vote, overturned the monetary damages.
2011
Brown v. Plata (2011) The Supreme Court declared California prison overcrowding unconstitutional and upheld an order that could force the transfer or release of more than 30,000 convicted felons over the next two years.
Kevork Djansezian/Getty Images

conditions of the black men and women of America. The Nation of Islam also promoted the belief that worship of Allah will bring about universal peace. The courts eventually allowed Black Muslim ministers to conduct services and to permit Muslim prisoners access to the Quran and other religious materials. Subsequent rights were granted to other religious groups, such as Buddhists.[25]

While the Supreme Court recognized the right of inmates to practice their religion, the most important case on this issue limited absolute religious freedom and placed the security of an institution above the right to attend religious services. In *O'Lone v. Estate of Shabazz*, Muslim inmates in a minimum-security classification requested permission to attend services held in another section of the prison.[26] They argued that these services were essential to the practice of their religion. The request was denied on the basis of security. The Court upheld the denial, holding that "[w]hen a prison regulation impinges on inmates' constitutional rights, the regulation is valid if it is reasonably related to legitimate penological interests."[27]

In an important 2005 case, *Cutter v. Wilkinson*, the Court ruled that the Religious Land Use and Institutionalized Persons Act of 2000, which was intended to protect the rights of prisoners, is not an unconstitutional government promotion of religion.[28] Writing for the majority, Justice Ruth Bader Ginsburg stated, "It confers no privileged status on any particular religious sect, and singles out no bona fide faith for disadvantageous treatment." *Cutter* allows inmates to practice their own religion unless their practices clearly undermine prison security and safety.

RELIGIOUS FREEDOM RESTORATION ACT (RFRA) In 1993, Congress passed the Religious Freedom Restoration Act (RFRA) as a reaction to concerns about restraining free exercise of religion. Congress rejected corrections officials' request to

FOR GROUP **DISCUSSION** Discuss within the group the issues of contraband and the potential communication through illegal usage of untraceable cell phones from behind prison walls. What ways will prison administrators have to respond to censorship? LO3

jailhouse lawyers Name given to inmates who develop an expertise in criminal law and help other inmates in preparing their cases.

exclude jail and prison inmates from aspects of the act. Prior to this act, the inmate's exercise of religion could be restricted by prison officials if the restrictions were reasonably related to the maintenance of institutional security and discipline. The RFRA shifted the burden of proof from the prisoner to prison officials, who had to show that the restriction was necessary because of a compelling government interest.[29] In a 1997 case, the Supreme Court ruled that the RFRA was unconstitutional except for the Federal Bureau of Prisons, which must still abide by the RFRA provisions.[30]

CENSORSHIP OF PERSONAL CORRESPONDENCE Corrections officials have always felt that there is strong reason to place stringent limitations on inmate correspondence. Censorship of incoming mail is necessary, prison officials say, to detect contraband—including instruments of escape, pornographic materials, and narcotics or drugs. Censorship of outgoing correspondence is also necessary, they say, to protect the public from insulting, obscene, and threatening letters; to avoid defaming the prison; and to detect escape or riot plans.

In *Procunier v. Martinez* (1974), which was previously discussed, the U.S. Supreme Court defined the criteria for determining when the regulation of inmate correspondence constitutes a violation of First Amendment liberties. The Court ruled that the limitation of First Amendment freedoms must be no greater than is necessary or essential to the protection of the particular governmental interest involved.[31] This decision disappointed prison managers who wanted greater procedural restrictions on inmate correspondence, for the Supreme Court placed a relatively heavy burden of proof on prison censors. In *Thornburgh v. Abbott* (1989), the U.S. Supreme Court attempted to clear up lower court rulings concerning mailed publications with this ruling that publications must meet one of a number of criteria.[32] The Court went on to rule that unless one of these standards is met, the restrictions on the receipt of published material are not allowed.[33] In a 2001 case, *Shaw v. Murphy*, the Supreme Court ruled that inmates do not have a right to correspond with other inmates even if it concerns legal advice if prison administrators believe such correspondence undermines prison security.[34] In *Beard v. Banks* (2006), the Third Circuit Court of Appeals held that prison officials in Pennsylvania could not prohibit even the most violent prisoners from receiving photographs, newspapers, and magazines sent to them through the mail.[35]

Inmate Calvin Crawford is shown during a videotaped interview conducted by the *Naples Daily News* at a Florida state prison. Crawford, 35, has been in prison since 1992 when he was convicted in the shooting death of Judah Hamad, 22, a Fort Pierce grocery store owner. Inmates are permitted to speak to the press, but it is not a federal requirement that there be no administrative restrictions on the interview process. See the actual video interview at www.naplesnews. com/videos/detail/letter-inmate/.

ACCESS TO COURTS, LEGAL SERVICES, AND MATERIALS Without the ability to seek judicial review of conditions causing discomfort or violating constitutional rights, the inmate must depend solely on the slow and often insensitive administrative mechanism of relief within the prison system. Therefore, the right of easy access to the courts gives inmates hope that their rights will be protected during incarceration. Courts have held that inmates are entitled to have legal materials available and be provided with assistance in drawing up and filing complaints. Inmates who help others, so-called **jailhouse lawyers**, cannot be interfered with or harassed by prison administrators.

FREEDOM OF THE PRESS AND OF EXPRESSION With the lifting of the hands-off doctrine, courts have consistently ruled that only when a compelling state interest exists can prisoners' First Amendment rights be modified; correctional authorities must justify the limiting of free speech by showing that granting it would threaten institutional security. In one case, the court upheld the punishment of a prisoner who circulated materials calling for a collective protest against the administration.[36]

What about talking to the media? In *Pell v. Procunier* (1974), California inmates challenged prison rules that prohibited them from conducting interviews with the press. The Supreme Court ruled that prisoners do not have an automatic right to meet the press, because the legitimate state interest in security, order, and rehabilitation has to be considered.[37] The *Pell* decision solidified the balance test established in *Martinez*, but it also gave corrections officials the major role in determining when the interests of security, order, and rehabilitation were involved.

AP Images/Walla Walla Union-Bulletin/Jeff Horner

While prisons are places of punishment, the courts have ruled that they cannot be punishing places. Certain privileges must be allowed. Here, in Washington State Penitentiary, inmate Torrey Baker whips up a tamale in a sandwich bag within the confines of his cell. Inmates at the Walla Walla prison have produced "The Convict Cookbook," which includes recipes that can be made inside a cell without a stove.

CENSORSHIP OF PUBLICATIONS AND MANUSCRIPTS The extent to which prison officials can censor the publications prisoners receive and can restrict the freedom of prisoners to publish articles and books while in prison has been the subject of much litigation. Although the courts have cautiously advised a broadening of these rights, they have reserved discretionary responsibility to prison administrators.

Web App 9.2
Use a Web search engine to search for "prison art" or "inmate artwork". If you or a loved one were a victim of the inmate artist, what type of reaction would you have if that inmate was selling his or her artwork for profit? Is this an appropriate expression of freedom to have as an incarcerated inmate? LO3

RIGHT TO ASSEMBLE Prisoners' right to assemble is also restricted. The emergence of prisoner unions in 10 states in the early 1970s brought about litigation on this subject.[38] *Goodwin v. Oswald* (1972) brought a decision upholding the right of prisoners to form unions. The Supreme Court stated that nowhere in state or federal law is the formation of prisoner unions outlawed or prohibited.[39] However, in *Jones v. North Carolina Prisoners' Union* (1977), the Supreme Court held that a state regulation prohibiting prisoners from soliciting others to join a union and barring union meetings did not violate the First Amendment.[40]

The *Jones* decision represented another setback for prisoners' rights. On the one hand, the Supreme Court extended the position in *Pell*, in which prison officials were looked to as the party that would decide when institutional security and order were threatened. On the other hand, the *Jones* decision extended the power of prison officials to limit First Amendment rights if they believed the potential existed for disruption of order.[41] See Exhibit 9.3 for these First Amendment cases.

FOR GROUP **DISCUSSION**
Based on the issues that prisons have with contraband, create a list of appropriate protections that inmates should have under the Fourth Amendment. LO3

Fourth Amendment Rights

The basic issue in the **Fourth Amendment** is proper search and seizure. The courts have consistently held that the protection the Fourth Amendment provides against unreasonable searches and seizures does not extend to prison. For example, *Moore v. People* (1970) concluded that searches conducted by prison officials "are not unreasonable as long as they are not for the purpose of harassing or humiliating the inmate in a cruel or unusual manner."[42]

Cell searches have raised the privacy issue. In *Bell v. Wolfish* (1979), the Supreme Court made it clear that unannounced cell searches, or "shakedowns," were necessary for security and order.[43] *Hudson v. Palmer* (1984) further shattered any hope that

Fourth Amendment The right of the people to be secure in their persons, houses, papers, and effects, against unreasonable searches and seizures, shall not be violated, and no warrants shall issue but upon probable cause, supported by oath and affirmation, and particularly describing the place to be searched, and the persons or things to be seized.

EXHIBIT 9.3

First Amendment Cases

- *O'Lone v. Estate of Shabazz.* The Supreme Court limited absolute religious freedom and placed the security of the prison above the right to attend religious services.
- *Cutter v. Wilkinson.* The Supreme Court ruled that inmates are allowed to practice their own religion unless their practices clearly undermine prison security and safety.
- *Procurier v. Martinez.* The Supreme Court defined the criteria for determining whether regulation of inmate correspondence constitutes a violation of First Amendment liberties.
- *Thornburgh v. Abbott.* The Supreme Court ruled that publications must meet one of a number of current criteria to determine whether receipt would not be allowed.
- *Shaw v. Murphy.* The Supreme Court ruled that inmates do not have a right to correspond with other inmates even if it concerns legal action if prison administrators believe such correspondence undermines prison security.
- *Beard v. Banks.* The Third Court of Appeals held that prison officials in Pennsylvania could not prohibit even the most violent prisoners from receiving photographs, newspapers, and magazines sent to them through the mail.
- *Pell v. Procunier.* The Supreme Court ruled that prisoners do not have an automatic right to meet the press because legitimate state interest in security, order, and rehabilitation has to be considered.
- *Goodwin v. Oswald.* The Supreme Court stated that nowhere in state or federal law is the formation of prisoner unions outlawed or prohibited.
- *Jones v. North Carolina Prisoners' Union.* The Supreme Court held that a state regulation prohibiting prisoners from soliciting others to join a union and barring union meetings did not violate the First Amendment.

the Fourth Amendment would limit cell searches. The Court ruled that "the Fourth Amendment has no applicability to a prison cell."[44] Strip searches also have been allowed by the courts, which generally have permitted prison officials to conduct pat searches and body-cavity examinations in the name of institutional order and security.[45] See Exhibit 9.4 for cases concerned with Fourth Amendment rights.

Eighth Amendment Rights

Eighth Amendment Excessive bail shall not be required, nor excessive fines imposed, nor cruel and unusual punishments inflicted.

In the prison setting, the **Eighth Amendment** has been applied to living conditions, especially with painful executions, excessive corporal punishment, medical experimentation, and abuse of labor. The three principal tests of conformance with

EXHIBIT 9.4

Fourth Amendment Cases

- *Moore v. People.* The Supreme Court ruled that searches conducted by prison officials are not unreasonable unless they are designed to harass or humiliate the inmate in a cruel or unusual manner.
- *Bell v. Wolfish.* The Supreme Court made it clear that unannounced cell searches and shakedowns were necessary for security and order.
- *Hudson v. Palmer.* The Supreme Court ruled that the Fourth Amendment has no applicability to a prison cell, and cell searches, including strip searches, are necessary in the name of institutional order and security.

the Eighth Amendment deal with these questions: Does the punishment shock the conscience of a civilized society? Is the punishment unnecessarily cruel? Does the punishment go beyond legitimate penal aims? Considerable case law concerns violation of the Eighth Amendment by means of solitary confinement, physical abuse, deadly force, the death penalty, denial of access to medical treatment and services, and segregation.

SOLITARY CONFINEMENT The courts have generally supported the separation of troublesome prisoners from the general prison population. They have ruled that separation is necessary to protect the inmate, other prisoners, and the staff, and to prevent escapes. Although several courts have ordered the release of inmates from harsh solitary confinement, most courts have been unwilling to interfere unless the conditions were clearly "shocking," "barbarous," "disgusting," or "debasing." Court decisions often disagree whether cruel and unusual punishment existed when prisoners were denuded, exposed to the winter cold, and deprived of such basic necessities of hygiene as soap and toilet paper. For example, a federal district court in *Knop v. Johnson* (1987) ruled that cruel and unusual punishment existed when the state of Michigan failed to provide inmates with winter coats, hats, and gloves.[46] In *Harris v. Fleming* (1988), the federal court found that cruel and unusual punishment did not exist when an Illinois inmate was deprived of toilet paper for five days and soap, toothpaste, or a toothbrush for ten days.[47]

PHYSICAL ABUSE Not until the mid-1960s did a court decide that the disciplinary measure of whipping a prisoner with a leather strap constituted cruel and unusual punishment.[48] More recently, as discussed in Chapter 6, the court ruled in the *Madrid v. Gomez* decision (1995) that excessive and unnecessary force was used at the Pelican Bay State Prison in California in a variety of ways and circumstances.[49] There are two critical issues involving physical abuse:

- *Inmate on inmate.* The courts have generally been unwilling to impose liability on prison officials for failing to protect prisoners from physical abuse and sexual assault from other inmates. However, the courts have ruled that prison officials are liable for damages if they display indifference to attacks on inmates occurring inside the prison. The test of liability is "deliberate indifference" that requires something more than mere negligence and less than maliciousness.[50]
- *Correctional officer on inmate.* In one of the most influential cases in terms of force, *Hudson v. McMillian* (1992), Hudson, a Louisiana prison inmate, testified he had suffered minor bruises, facial swelling, loosened teeth, and a cracked dental plate after receiving a beating by two prison guards. The magistrate hearing the case ruled that respondents (staff) had violated the Eighth Amendment's prohibition on cruel and unusual punishments, and awarded Hudson damages. The court of appeals reversed the decision, holding that prisoners' charges of excessive force must prove "significant injury" and that Hudson could not prevail because his injuries were minor and required no medical attention. The case was appealed to the Supreme Court, which ruled that as long as force is used in a good faith effort to maintain control, there is no liability. It is only in instances when prisoners can prove that correctional officers acted maliciously that liability is held.[51]

MYTH Inmates can be abused by correctional officers and there is nothing they can do to get help.

FACT Inmates can sue for damages if they are injured by correctional staff members. However, they must show that the correctional officers acted maliciously and were not using force merely to maintain control of an unruly inmate.

DEADLY FORCE The use of deadly force in prison is not uncommon. However, the wanton use of force by guards is off limits and deadly force is permissible only to prevent the commission of a felony or the infliction of severe bodily harm.[52]

The courts have ruled that the use of deadly force can be used to prevent an inmate from escaping if a state has classified escape as a felony. Nevertheless, the courts have ruled that to avoid civil and criminal liability, deadly force must be used only as a last resort—after all other reasonable means have failed.

In *Whitley v. Albers* (1986), the Court set the standard for the use of deadly force. During the course of a riot at the Oregon State Penitentiary, a prison officer was taken hostage and placed on the upper tier of a two-tier cellblock. In an attempt to free the hostage, one of the officers shot an inmate in the knee. The Supreme Court ruled that prison officials are not liable for the use of deadly force unless it can be shown that they acted in a "wanton" manner, which is a difficult standard for attorneys to meet.[53]

MEDICAL TREATMENT AND SERVICES In early prisons, inmates' right to medical treatment was restricted through the "exceptional circumstances doctrine." Using this policy, the courts would hear only those cases in which the circumstances totally disregarded human dignity, while denying hearings to less serious cases. The cases that were allowed access to the courts usually represented a situation of total denial of medical care.

To gain their medical rights, prisoners have resorted to class-action suits (suits brought on behalf of all individuals affected by similar circumstances—in this case, poor medical attention). In the most significant case, *Newman v. Alabama* (1972), the entire Alabama prison system's medical facilities were declared inadequate.[54] The Supreme Court cited the following factors as contributing to inadequate care: insufficient physician and nurse resources, reliance on untrained inmates for paramedical work, intentional failure in treating the sick and injured, and failure to conform to proper medical standards. The *Newman* case forced corrections departments to upgrade prison medical facilities.

It was not until 1976, in *Estelle v. Gamble*, that the Supreme Court clearly mandated an inmate's right to have medical care.[55] Gamble had hurt his back in a Texas prison and filed suit because he contested the type of treatment he had received and questioned the lack of interest that prison guards had shown in his case. The Supreme Court said, "Deliberate indifference to serious medical needs of prisoners constitutes the 'unnecessary and wanton infliction of pain,' proscribed by the Eighth Amendment."[56] Gamble was allowed to collect monetary damages for his injuries.

In the *Pennsylvania Department of Corrections v. Yeskey* (1998) decision, Yeskey was sentenced to 18 to 30 months in a Pennsylvania prison. It was recommended by the sentencing court that he be placed in a motivational boot camp for first-time offenders. Successful completion of the boot camp would have made him eligible for parole in six months. However, prison officials refused his admission to the program because of his medical history of hypertension. Yeskey then filed suit alleging that his exclusion violated the Americans with Disabilities Act of 1990 (ADA). In a unanimous opinion written by Justice Antonin Scalia, the Supreme Court affirmed the lower court ruling, as it held that no "public entity" may discriminate against qualified disabled individuals due to their disability. The significance of this case is that the ADA also applies to state prisons.[57]

MYTH Prisons are hellholes lacking in basic human services such as proper medical care.

FACT The Supreme Court has mandated that inmates get proper medical care, and failure to provide adequate health services leaves them vulnerable for litigation. The provisions of the Americans with Disabilities Act of 1990 (ADA) must also be respected within prison walls.

Today, inmates are guaranteed medical treatment when there is a serious medical need in order to avoid the "unnecessary and wanton infliction of pain."[58] This has been defined as (1) "whether a reasonable doctor or patient would perceive the medical need in question as important and worthy of comment or treatment; (2) whether the medical condition significantly affects daily activities; and (3) the existence of chronic and substantial pain."[59] Additionally, courts may find a "serious medical need" if a condition "has been diagnosed by a physician as mandating treatment or ... is so obvious that even a lay person would easily recognize the necessity of a doctor's attention."[60]

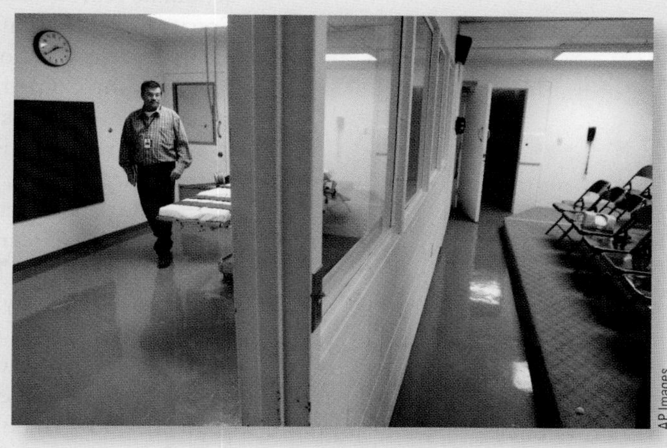

A warden's assistant at the Oklahoma State Penitentiary walks past the gurney in the execution chamber. On April 29, 2014, inmate Clayton Lockett died of a heart attack approximately 40 minutes after the state began administering midazolam, the first drug in a three-drug protocol. Witnesses said he began to nod, mumble, and writhe on the gurney. The Department of Corrections promised a full review of Oklahoma's execution procedures while abolitionists called for a moratorium on executions.

CRUEL AND UNUSUAL PUNISHMENT The concept of **cruel and unusual punishment** is founded in the Eighth Amendment of the U.S. Constitution. The term itself has not been specifically defined by the Supreme Court, but the Court has held that treatment constitutes cruel and unusual punishment when it does the following:

- Degrades the dignity of human beings[61]
- Is more severe (disproportional) than the offense for which it has been given[62]
- Shocks the general conscience and is fundamentally unfair[63]
- Is deliberately indifferent to a person's safety and well-being[64]
- Punishes people because of their status, such as race, religion, and mental state[65]
- Is in flagrant disregard of due process of law, such as punishment that is capriciously applied[66]

State and federal courts have placed strict limits on disciplinary methods that may be considered inhumane. Corporal punishment all but ended after the practice was condemned in *Jackson v. Bishop* (1968).[67] Although the solitary confinement of disruptive inmates continues, its prolonged use under barbaric conditions has been held to be in violation of the Eighth Amendment. Courts have found that inmates placed in solitary have the right to adequate personal hygiene, exercise, mattresses, ventilation, and rules specifying how they can earn their release.

cruel and unusual punishment
Punishment that involves torture or the infliction of unnecessary and wanton pain.

In *Hope v. Pelzer* (2002), the Supreme Court ruled that correctional officials who knowingly violate the Eighth Amendment rights of inmates can be held liable for damages.[68] Larry Hope, an Alabama prison inmate, was twice handcuffed to a hitching post for disruptive conduct. He was handcuffed above shoulder height, and when he tried moving his arms to improve circulation, the handcuffs cut into his wrists, causing pain and discomfort. He spent seven hours on the hitching post, during which he was given one or two water breaks but no bathroom breaks, and a guard taunted him about his thirst. Hope filed a suit against three guards charging them with violating his civil rights. The U.S. Supreme Court ruled that Hope's allegations established an Eighth Amendment violation. It ruled that among the "'unnecessary and wanton' inflictions of pain [constituting cruel and unusual punishment forbidden by the amendment] are those that are 'totally without penological justification.'" This determination is made in the context of prison conditions by ascertaining whether an official acted with "deliberate indifference" to the inmate's health or safety, a state of mind that can be inferred from the fact that the risk of harm is obvious. The Court reasoned that any safety concerns had long since ended by the time Hope was handcuffed to the hitching post, because he had already been subdued, handcuffed, placed in leg irons, and transported back to prison. The *Hope* case shows that correctional officials can be sued if their behavior violates an inmate's constitutional rights and that they or any reasonable person should have surmised that the behavior was in violation of accepted practices.

OVERALL PRISON CONDITIONS Prisoners have long had the right to the minimal conditions necessary for human survival, such as the necessary food, clothing, shelter, and medical care to sustain human life. A number of attempts have been made to articulate reasonable standards of prison care and to make sure they are carried out. Courts have held that, although people are sent to prison for punishment, it does not mean that prison should be a punishing experience.[69] In the 1994 case of *Farmer v. Brennan*, the Court ruled that prison officials are legally liable if, knowing that an inmate faces a serious risk of harm, they disregard that risk by failing to take measures to avoid or reduce it. Furthermore, prison officials should be able to infer the risk from the evidence at hand; they need not be warned or told.[70]

In the pending case *Dockery v. Epps*, the focus is on the basic rights of prisoners during their incarceration. This federal lawsuit was filed on May 2013 on behalf of prisoners at the East Mississippi Correctional Facility (EMCF). This for-profit prison is characterized as hyperviolent, grotesquely filthy, and dangerous. EMCF is operated "in a perpetual state of crisis" where prisoners are at "grave risk of death and loss of limbs." The facility, located in Meridian, Mississippi, is supposed to provide intensive treatment to the state's prisoners with serious psychiatric disabilities, many of whom are locked down in long-term solitary confinement.[71]

Although inmates retain the right to reasonable care, if there is a legitimate purpose for the use of governmental restrictions, they may be considered constitutional. For example, it might be possible to restrict reading material, allow strip searches, and prohibit inmates from receiving packages from the outside if the restrictions are legitimate security measures. If overcrowded conditions require it, inmates may be double-bunked in cells designed for a single inmate.[72]

RACIAL SEGREGATION On August 8, 2009, a riot in the California prison at Chino left hundreds injured, buildings burned, and property destroyed.[73] The disturbance was sparked by racial tensions between Latino and black inmates, and later sparked a great deal of controversy over the issue of racial segregation in prison: Should prisons be segregated to prevent violence among gangs like the Aryan Brotherhood, the Mexican Mafia, and the Black Guerrilla Family? Or should prisons be integrated like other institutions because any form of segregation is inherently unconstitutional?

The Alabama case of *Washington v. Lee* (1966) was the first judicial intervention on the desegregation of prisons.[74] Federal Judge Frank Johnson held that "this court can conceive of no consideration of prison security or discipline which will sustain the constitutionality of state statutes that on their face require complete and permanent segregation of the races in all Alabama penal facilities." The state was therefore ordered to provide for the total desegregation of all prisons within one year. This was done.[75] In the 2005 case *Johnson v. California*, Supreme Court reaffirmed the *Lee* decision when it ruled that racial segregation of prison inmates, in their cells or anywhere on prison grounds, is an inappropriate form of racial classification.[76] It left it open for lower courts to decide, using a standard of strict scrutiny, when segregation is inappropriate and unconstitutional. *Johnson* focused on the policy of segregating inmates upon their arrival at a prison. The Court ruled that if racial segregation was allowed for incoming inmates it would also be justified "in the dining halls, yards, and general housing areas." Segregation would only be allowed if a prison administrator could prove that there was a compelling interest in prison safety. The Court recognized that "prisons are dangerous places, and the special circumstances they present may justify racial classifications in some contexts." But these are only in the most extreme circumstances. It remains to be seen in light of the Chino riots whether the resolve to racially integrate prisons will be dampened and that courts—even when using a "strict scrutiny" standard—will find that integration, in many instances, is just too dangerous. Exhibit 9.5 sets out some critical Eighth Amendment cases that help define cruel and unusual punishment.

Fourteenth Amendment All persons born or naturalized in the United States, and subject to the jurisdiction thereof, are citizens of the United States and of the State wherein they reside. No State shall make or enforce any law which shall abridge the privileges or immunities of citizens of the United States; nor shall any State deprive any person of life, liberty, or property, without due process of law; nor deny to any person within its jurisdiction the equal protection of the laws.

Fourteenth Amendment Rights

Due process is the major issue in the **Fourteenth Amendment**, especially related to disciplinary hearings and inmates helping each other to prepare their cases for appeal.

EXHIBIT 9.5

Critical Eighth Amendment Cases

- *Knop v. Johnson.* A federal district court ruled that cruel and unusual punishment existed when the state of Michigan failed to provide inmates with winter coats, hats, and gloves.
- *Harris v. Fleming.* The federal court found that cruel and unusual punishment did not exist when an Illinois inmate was deprived of toilet paper for five days and soap, toothpaste, or a toothbrush for ten days.
- *Hudson v. McMillan.* The Supreme Court ruled that as long as force is used in a good faith effort to maintain control, there is no liability. It is only in instances when prisoners could prove the correctional officers acted maliciously that liability is held.
- *Whitley v. Albers.* The Supreme Court ruled that prison officials are not liable for the use of deadly force unless it can be shown that they acted in a "wanton" manner, which is a difficult standard for attorneys to meet.
- *Newman v. Alabama.* The Supreme Court ruled that the entire Alabama prison system medical facilities were inadequate and ordered that they be improved.
- *Estelle v. Gamble.* The Supreme Court ruled that "deliberate indifference" to "serious medical needs" of prisoners constitutes the "unnecessary and wanton infliction of pain," a violation against the prohibition of cruel and unusual punishment.
- *Pennsylvania Department of Corrections v. Yeskey.* The Supreme Court held that no public entity may discriminate against qualified disabled individuals due to their disability. The significance of this case is that the American Disability Act also applies to state prisons.
- *Jackson v. Bishop.* Corporal punishment all but ended after the practice was condemned in this case decided by the U.S. 8th Circuit Court.
- *Hope v. Pelzer.* The Supreme Court ruled that correctional officials who knowingly violate the Eighth Amendment rights of inmates can be held liable for damages.
- *Farmer v. Brennan.* The Supreme Court ruled that prison officials are legally liable if, knowing that an inmate faces a serious risk of harm, they disregard that risk by failing to take measures to avoid or reduce it.
- *Washington v. Lee.* The federal court in this Alabama case ordered the total desegregation of all prisons within one year.
- *Johnson v. California*. The Supreme Court ruled that racial segregation of prison inmates, in their cells or anywhere on prison grounds, is inappropriate use of racial classification.

DUE PROCESS RIGHTS IN DISCIPLINARY HEARINGS The 1974 *Wolff v. McDonnell* decision has been heralded as a landmark because of its impact on correctional administration and prisoners' rights.[77] In reviewing disciplinary procedures, the Supreme Court held that they were not equivalent to criminal prosecution and that during disciplinary hearings prisoners do not have the full due process rights of a defendant on trial. Nevertheless, the Court specified certain minimum requirements for disciplinary proceedings:

- The inmate must receive advanced written notice of the alleged rules infraction.
- The prisoner must be allowed sufficient time to prepare a defense against the charges.
- The prisoner must be allowed to present documentary evidence on his or her own behalf and therefore may call witnesses, as long as the security of the institution is not jeopardized.

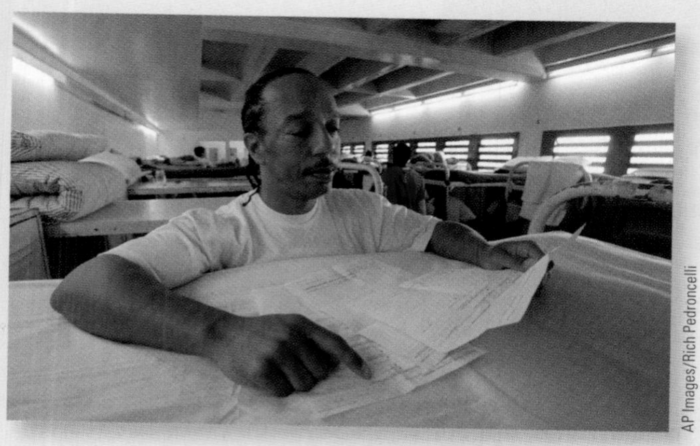

Inmate John Rankins looks over a disciplinary report filed against him for refusing to take a bunk assignment with an inmate of a different race at the Sierra Conservation Center in Jamestown, California. Rankins refused the bunk assignment for fear of being assaulted by other inmates. Despite efforts by California prison officials to end one of the nation's last vestiges of institutionalized, government-mandated racial segregation, powerful race-based gangs violently oppose attempts at desegregation in prison housing units. Blacks, whites, and Hispanics are willing to sleep side by side in bunk beds spaced an arm's length apart, but would brawl or risk longer sentences rather than accept an inmate of another race in a bed above or below them in the same bunk bed stack.

- The prisoner is permitted to seek counsel from another inmate or a staff member when the circumstances of the disciplinary infraction are complex or the prisoner is illiterate.
- The prisoner is to be provided with a written statement of the findings of the committee, the evidence relied upon, and the rationale for the action. A written record of the proceedings must also be maintained.[78]

Wolff v. McDonnell was significant because it standardized certain rights and freedoms within correctional facilities. Although inmates received some procedural safeguards to protect them against the notorious abuses of disciplinary meetings, they did not receive all the due process rights of a criminal trial. Nor did the Court question the right of corrections officials to revoke the "good time" of inmates.

LEGAL ASSISTANCE TO INMATES Until well past the time when the hands-off doctrine passed into obsolescence, correctional authorities were obsessed by their belief that prisoners should not trouble the courts with their complaints. Particularly discouraged were "writ writers," who prepared complaints for themselves and other prisoners. In many states, the preparation of writs was a disciplinary offense, calling for a session of punitive isolation.[79] Access to the courts was vigorously prevented. In 1941, the Supreme Court took notice of the obstacles to writs of *habeas corpus* in *Ex parte Hull.*[80]

Hull had filed for a writ of *habeas corpus*, only to have the papers he filed returned to him by prison officials without submission to the court. When ordered by the Supreme Court to show cause why Hull's petition for a writ should not be granted, the warden replied that he had issued a regulation that all such petitions had to be referred to the legal investigator for the parole board. The regulation went on to say that "documents submitted to [the investigator], if in his opinion are properly drawn, will be directed to the court designated or will be referred back to the inmate." Justice Frank Murphy's opinion pronounced this regulation invalid: "The state and its officers may not abridge or impair petitioner's right to ... apply for a writ of *habeas corpus*."

In *Bounds v. Smith* (1977), in a 5–4 decision, the Court ruled that the state of North Carolina had a duty to provide adequate law libraries in each of its correctional facilities.[81] Although the state's proposal for a standard library is rather generous in its content, including the standard legal referral and state statutes, other states have gone far beyond North Carolina in the provision of law libraries, some of them so extensive as to be the envy of practicing attorneys.

In *Johnson v. Avery* (1969), the Supreme Court ruled that institutional officials may not prohibit inmates from assisting one another with legal work unless the institution provides reasonable legal assistance to inmates.[82] This decision denied the constitutionality of a Tennessee prison regulation that provided: "No inmate will advise, assist or otherwise contract to aid another, either with or without a fee, to prepare writs or other legal matters ... Inmates are forbidden to set themselves up as practitioners for the purpose of promoting a business of writing writs." The Court ruled that inmates have the right to receive assistance from jailhouse lawyers. The Court also stated that the activities of the jailhouse lawyer could

EXHIBIT 9.6

Fourteenth Amendment Cases

- *Wolff v. McDonnell.* The Supreme Court held that disciplinary procedures were not equivalent to criminal prosecution and that during disciplinary hearings prisoners do not have formal due process rights of the defendant on trial.
- *Ex parte Hull.* The Supreme Court held that the state or prison officials may not impair a petitioner's rights to apply for a writ of habeas corpus.
- *Bounds v. Smith.* The Supreme Court ruled that the state of North Carolina had a duty to provide adequate law libraries in each of its correctional facilities.
- *Johnson v. Avery.* The Supreme Court ruled that institutional officials may not prohibit inmates from assisting one another with legal work unless the institution provides reasonable legal assistance to inmates.

be restricted as to time and place, and that jailhouse lawyers could be prohibited from receiving fees for their services.[83] See Exhibit 9.6 for a selection of Fourteenth Amendment cases.

PROVIDING LEGAL SERVICES TO INMATES

LO4 Summarize the legal services that are available to inmates

While inmates have gained rights, it is critical to provide them with legal counsel so that they can avail themselves of their legal benefits and privileges. The **Innocence Projects** provide representation and investigative assistance to prison inmates who claim to be innocent of the crimes for which they were convicted. (See the Evidence-Based Corrections feature.)

Innocence Projects These projects, found in a number of states, provide free legal assistance for those cases in which question remains regarding the legality of their convictions.

EVIDENCE-BASED CORRECTIONS

Wrongful Convictions

A wrongful conviction occurs when a person is convicted who is actually innocent of the crime and was no way involved in the incident that brought them to trial. While this turn of events can be devastating to those involved, such as Michael Morton, the subject of our opening vignette, no one actually knows how many prison inmates were innocent and wrongfully convicted. There are a number of reasons why the number of wrongful convictions remains unknown:

- No official or even unofficial statistics are kept.
- An acquittal is not a good measure of actual innocence.
- It is very difficult to unravel a case of actual innocence.
- Many prisoners falsely claim innocence.
- Criminal justice system personnel (police and prosecutors) deny that wrongful convictions occur and do not cooperate in uncovering miscarriages of justice.

There are now about 1 million felony convictions per year in state and federal courts. So even at a rate of .005 innocent people being falsely convicted each year, it is possible to estimate that 5,000 factually innocent persons are convicted of felonies in any given year.

To shed light on this important issue, legal scholar Samuel Gross examined hundreds of criminal cases

(continued)

over a 15-year period in which the convicted person was exonerated. Gross puts the number of exonerations at 340 between 1989 and 2003, the period he studied. Most known exonerations were for murder and rape cases. Yet a far larger number of serious felonies, including robbery, have not generated known cases of actual innocence. There is typically no biological evidence in robberies (and therefore no chance for DNA analysis) and the opportunities for mistaken eyewitness identification are greater. It stands to reason that many people imprisoned for robbery in the United States are actually innocent.

Gross also found that in 88 percent of the rape cases in the study, DNA evidence helped free the inmate. But biological evidence is far less likely to be available or provide definitive proof in other kinds of cases. Only 20 percent of the murder exonerations involved DNA evidence, and almost all of those were rape-murders. About 90 percent of false convictions in the rape cases involve misidentification by witnesses, and these errors very often occur across races: black men accused of raping white women made up a disproportionate number of exonerated rape defendants. Interracial rapes are uncommon, accounting for less than 10 percent of all rapes. But in half of the rape exonerations, black men were falsely convicted of raping white women. And while 29 percent of those in prison for rape are black, 65 percent of those exonerated of the crime are African American. Gross concludes that white Americans are much more likely to mistake one black person for another than to do the same for members of their own race.

FOR CRITICAL THINKING AND WRITING

Gross found that the leading causes of wrongful convictions for murder were quite different. These include false confessions and perjury by co-defendants, informants, police officers, or forensic scientists. In sum, the evidence found by Gross suggests that wrongful convictions in murder cases are quite common and that giving inmates access to the courts to address these wrongs is essential. Assuming Gross is correct and the chances for wrongful convictions in murder cases are significant, does this mean that capital punishment is too risky to be used as a punishment?

Source: Samuel Gross, Kristen Jacoby, Daniel J. Matheson, Nicholas Montgomery, and Sujata Patil, "Exonerations in the United States, 1989 Through 2003," *Journal of Criminal Law and Criminology* 95 (2005): 523–560.

grievance process A formalized arrangement in which inmates can register their complaints about the conditions of their confinement.

The **grievance process** is another means available for inmates who feel that they have been unjustly treated or have been denied their rights. Nearly all of the grievance processes are set up by either the institution or the department of corrections. Grievances usually are submitted to someone in the institution and then go through a number of steps until they may end up in the director's office. If they cannot be resolved to the inmate's satisfaction on one level, they proceed to the next. Institutions vary on whether there is a time limit on processing the various steps.

AP Images/Jason DeCrow

On April 9, 2014, Martin Tankleff, bottom right, who was wrongfully convicted of murdering his parents in 1988, speaks at a rally on the steps of City Hall in New York. The rally was held by a group of New York City men who claim they were framed by police detective Louis Scarcella decades ago to voice their demand for prosecutors to speed up an ongoing review of the detective's cases. They claim they were convicted on evidence fabricated by the now-retired detective.

A **corrections ombudsman** is a further means sometimes available for inmates who feel that they have been unjustly treated. In those states that have a corrections ombudsman, he or she is empowered to investigate complaints that are:

- Alleged to be contrary or inconsistent with the law or department of corrections practice
- Based on mistaken facts or irrelevant considerations
- Inadequately explained when reasons should have been revealed
- Inefficiently performed
- Unreasonable unfair or otherwise objectionable, even though in accordance with law

The corrections ombudsman does not investigate when:

- The complainant could reasonably be expected to use a different remedy or action.

- The complaint is trivial, frivolous, vexatious, or not in good faith.
- The complaint has been too long delayed to justify present examination.

If an investigation discovers that a complainant has been treated improperly by a state agency, the office works with the agency involved to resolve the complaint through appropriate corrective action. Ombudsman programs can serve such functions as investigating allegations, monitoring facilities, conducting research, educating the community, providing recommendations for improvement, and, if needed, bringing litigation.

A number of states have statewide corrections ombudsmen, including California, Iowa, Michigan, Minnesota, Montana, New Jersey, Texas, and Wisconsin. These programs have been successful at improving conditions in adult prisons by monitoring the relationship between prisoners and prison officials. The success of these programs depends upon the ombudsman's authority to pursue remedies and his or her ability to manage the competing interests of inmates and officials. If prisoners feel that the ombudsman lacks the ability to address their complaints adequately, they will be reluctant to be cooperative. However, if prison officials feel that the ombudsman is unreasonable, they will be reluctant to implement recommendations and may create additional obstacles to safeguarding prisoners' rights.[84]

Alyssa Schukar/The New York Times/Redux

Shon Hopwood became a jailhouse lawyer while serving a 13-year sentence for armed robbery. After leaving prison he earned a law degree with financial support from the Bill and Melinda Gates Foundation. What's more, Hopwood won a clerkship for a judge on the U.S. Court of Appeals for the District of Columbia Circuit, which is generally considered the second most important court in the nation, after the Supreme Court.

corrections ombudsman An ombudsman (a Swedish word that means "representative") is a person or body that protects citizens against governmental abuses.

CAREERS IN CORRECTIONS

Corrections Ombudsman—New Jersey

"The ombudsman's role has a long and honorable tradition as a means of protecting against abuse, bias, and other improper treatment or unfairness. The office of the corrections ombudsman provides a mechanism for the continuing resolution of issues, problems, or complaints of inmates sentenced within New Jersey's correctional system regarding their living conditions and other matters.

"The office investigates complaints when an inmate has failed to get satisfactory results through available institutional channels.

"Serving as a designated neutral, the corrections ombudsman is an advocate for fairness who also acts as a source of information and referral, aids in answering questions, and assists in the resolution of concerns during critical situations.

"Since the office is independent from and external to the correctional facilities, it ensures objectivity and credibility among inmates and staff. In considering any given instance or concern, the interests and rights of all parties who may be involved are taken into account."

Source: State of New Jersey Office of the Corrections Ombudsman, http://www.state.nj.us/correctionsombudsman/ (accessed July 2014).

See Chapter 15 for more detailed information on careers in corrections.

THINKING LIKE A CORRECTIONS PROFESSIONAL

You are a corrections ombudsman and discover that a warden of a maximum-security prison has been resistant to inmates' concerns. He has problems with a particular attorney who has become quite an advocate with inmates, whom he sees as continually challenging his authority in putting forward what she defines as rights of prisoners. He does not even want to permit this attorney to enter the prison.

How will you intercede in this situation? If the warden persists in disallowing the attorney's admittance to the prison, what will you do?

THE IMPACT OF THE PRISONERS' RIGHTS MOVEMENT

Today, there is both good news and bad news about prisoners' rights. The good news is that over the past 40 years some of the bad conditions of the worst prisons have been corrected and prisoners have made gains in several areas. The improvements are undeniable and would not have been achieved without judicial intervention. Prisoners have made the greatest gains in the right to send and receive letters, but they also have made strides in their right to communicate with lawyers and the courts. Furthermore, the courts have permitted the right of religious freedom as long as it does not jeopardize institutional security. Courts also have been willing to rule on the totality of conditions in a prison setting when prisoners appeared to be undergoing severe dehumanization and deterioration in their mental and physical well-being. It can be argued that many of these improvements are probably irreversible and that the states can be trusted to maintain constitutionally acceptable prisons. Alvin J. Bronstein says, "We also feel that there is hope with a new generation of correctional administrators who are a cut above a lot of correctional administrators from the past in terms of inmates' concerns. It is also helpful that the American Correctional Association is more sensitive than it has been to inmates' concerns and rights."

The bad news is that overcrowding and its associated evils are reappearing and will be difficult to correct. Further bad news is that in too many states prisoners are expected to do "hard time" and not to enjoy the amenities that they were given in the past. With this social and political context, it has been more difficult for prisoners to win "cruel and unusual punishment" lawsuits. Another source of bad news is that federal courts, which were actively involved in prisoners' rights from the 1960s on, withdrew their receptivity to inmate suits in the 1990s. A final source of bad news is that the Prison Litigation Reform Act (PLRA), passed by Congress and signed by President Clinton in 1996, has limited the ability of prisoners to allege violations of their constitutional rights.

Discuss the rights that have not been given to inmates **LO5**

Prisoners may retain basic human rights, but they are not entitled to the same degree of constitutional protections that they enjoyed before conviction. The conditions of confinement can never satisfy prisoners. Convicts and their plight attract little public sympathy, so action to correct intolerable conditions is usually delayed until a crisis occurs. At that point, remedies must be drastic and thus costly, far more so than would be the case if farsighted planning, development, and fiscal support were available to implement changes as soon as they are needed.

SUMMARY

LO1 Discuss what is meant by the term *prisoners' rights*

Inmates must be given all the rights conferred on them by law, including due process rights, but their status as convicted felons has caused them to lose certain rights that free citizens have, including freedom and the ability to come and go as they wish.

LO2 Discuss the foundation of prisoners' rights

The U.S. Constitution is the principal source of prisoners' rights, but federal and state statutes, legal precedents, federal civil rights lawsuits, and writs of *habeas corpus* are also important sources of prisoners' rights.

LO3 Identify the First, Fourth, Eighth, and Fourteenth Amendment substantive rights that the courts have awarded inmates

Prisoners have made the greatest gains in the First, Fourth, Eighth, and Fourteenth Amendments, which include the right to send and receive letters, the right to communicate with lawyers and the courts, and the right of religious freedom as long as it does not jeopardize institutional security. Courts have also given relief on the totality of conditions in a prison setting when prisoners appeared to be undergoing severe dehumanization and deterioration in their mental and physical well-being.

LO4 Summarize the legal services that are available to inmates

Inmates are free to find attorneys who will provide legal services for them (usually *pro bono*). In addition, there are a number of Innocence Projects throughout the nation; inmates might be successful in persuading one of these projects to take their case on. A few states have corrections ombudsmen, a non-system representative who is charged to protect citizens against legal abuse, and if inmates are doing time in a state that has a corrections ombudsman, this may be an available legal service. The grievance process is another available service, where inmates can complain through this formalized arrangement if they feel they have been unjustly treated.

LO5 Discuss the rights that have not been given to inmates

The good news about prisoners' rights is that some of the worst conditions of prisons have been corrected and inmates have made gains in several areas. The bad news is that overcrowding continues to be a problem in many prisons, inmates have lost some of the amenities they were given in the past, federal courts are not as actively involved in prisoners' rights as they were in the past, and the Prison Litigation Reform Act has limited the ability to allege violations of their constitutional rights.

CRITICAL THINKING QUESTIONS

1. What did it mean to say that a convicted felon was "civilly dead"?
2. Summarize the most important cases establishing the hands-off doctrine.
3. Why is the right to due process so difficult to disentangle from institutional priorities?
4. Considering the concept of least eligibility, should inmates get greater medical care from the state than the average citizen? Should they be entitled to costly procedures such as a heart transplant?
5. Why has the implementation of prisoners' rights been so difficult for the courts?

NOTES

1. Christina Caron, "Michael Morton Set Free After Spending Nearly 25 Years in Prison, Exonerated by DNA Evidence for His Wife's Murder," ABC News, October 4, 2011, http://abcnews.go.com/US/michael-morton-free-25-years-prison-exonerated-wifes/story?id=14663445 (accessed July 2014).
2. Ibid.
3. Brandi Grissom "Perry Signs Michael Morton Act," *Texas Tribune*, May 16, 2013, http://www.texastribune.org/2013/05/16/gov-rick-perry-signs-michael-morton-act/ (accessed July 2014).
4. Andrei Marmor, "The Nature of Law," *Stanford Encyclopedia of Philosophy* (Stanford, CA: Center for the Study of Language and Information, revised 2007).
5. John Locke was a great proponent of natural rights. See John C. Attig, *The Words of John Locke from the Seventeenth Century to the Present* (Westport, CT: Greenwood Press, 1985).
6. *Pennsylvania Department of Corrections v. Yeskey*, 524 U.S. 206 (1998).
7. *Miranda v. Arizona*, 384 U.S. 436, 86 S.Ct. 1602, 16 L.Ed.2d 694 (1966).
8. *Holt v. Sarver*, 309 F.Supp. 362 (E.D. Ark. 1970), affirmed, 442 F.2d 304 (8th Circuit, 1971).
9. "Exonerated Mississippi Men Sue over Bite Mark Testimony," *Picayune Item*, April 4, 2009, http://picayuneitem.com/statenews/x2079286911/Exonerated-Miss-men-sue-over-bite-mark-testimony (accessed July 2014).
10. *Ruffin v. Commonwealth*, 62.790, at 796 (1871).
11. National Advisory Commission on Criminal Justice Standards and Goals, *Corrections* (Washington, DC: Government Printing Office, 1973), p. 18.
12. *Procunier v. Martinez*, 416 U.S. 396 (1974).
13. *Wolff v. McDonnell*, 418 U.S. 539 (1974).
14. *Estelle v. Gamble*, 429 U.S. 97 (1976).
15. *Baxter v. Palmigiano*, 425 U.S. 308 (1976); *Enomato v. Clutchette*, 428 U.S. 308 (1976); *Meacham v. Fano*, 427 U.S. (1976); *Montanye v. Haymes*, 96 S.Ct. 2543 (1976).
16. *Meacham v. Fano*.
17. *Rhodes v. Chapman*, 29 Cr. L. rptr. 3061 (1961).
18. *Turner v. Safley*, 428 78, 1987.
19. For a review of this case, see David L. Hudson, Jr., "*Turner v. Safley*: High Drama, Enduring Precedent," First Amendment Center, http://www.firstamendmentcenter.org/turner-v-safley-high-drama-enduring-precedent (accessed July 2014).
20. *Wilson v. Seiter*, 501 U.S. 294 (1991).
21. "Legislation Has Mixed Effect on Petitions," *Third Branch* 31 (1999). For a review of the courts and the PLRA, see Barbara Belbot, "Report on the Prison Litigation Act: What Have the Courts Decided So Far?" *Prison Journal* 84 (2004): 290–316.
22. *Booth v. Churner*, U.S. 731 (2001).
23. *Porter v. Nussle*, 534 U.S. 516 (2002).
24. See Christopher E. Smith, *Law and Contemporary Corrections* (Belmont, CA: Wadsworth, 1999).
25. *Cruz v. Beto*, 405, U.S. 319 (1972).
26. *O'Lone v. Estate of Shabazz*, 482 U.S. 342, 107 S.Ct. 1400, 96 L.Ed.2d 282 (1987).
27. Ibid., at 349.
28. *Cutter v. Wilkinson*, 544 U.S. 709 (2005).
29. Philip L. Reichel, *Corrections: Philosophies, Practices, and Procedures* (Boston: Allyn & Bacon, 2001), p. 528.
30. *Boerne v. Flores*, 521 U.S. 507 (1997).
31. *Procunier v. Martinez*, 416 U.S. 396 (1974).
32. *Thornburgh v. Abbott*, 490 U.S. 401 (1989).
33. Ibid.
34. *Shaw v. Murphy*, 532 U.S. 223 (2001).
35. *Beard v. Banks*, 548 U.S. 521 (2006).
36. *Roberts v. Papersack*, 256 F.Supp. 415 (M.D. 1966).
37. *Pell v. Procunier*, 417 U.S. 817 (1974).
38. C. Ronald Huff, "Unionization Behind the Walls," *Criminology* 12 (1974): 184–185.

39. *Goodwin v. Oswald*, 462 F.2d 1245-46 (3d Cir. 1972).
40. *Jones v. North Carolina Prisoners' Union*, 433 U.S. (1977).
41. C. Ronald Huff, "The Discovery of Prisoners' Rights: A Sociological Analysis," in *Legal Rights of Prisoners*, ed. G. P. Alpert (Beverly Hills, CA: Sage Publications, 1980), pp. 60–61.
42. *Moore v. People*, 171 Colorado 338, 467 P.2d (1970).
43. *Bell v. Wolfish*, 441 U.S. 520 (1979).
44. *Hudson v. Palmer*, 82 L.Ed.2d 393 (1984).
45. See *Bell v. Wolfish.*
46. *Knop v. Johnson*, 667 F.Supp. 467 (1987).
47. *Harris v. Fleming*, 839 F.2d 1223 (1988).
48. *Jackson v. Bishop*, 404 F.2d 571 (8th Cir. 1968).
49. *Madrid v. Gomez*, 889 F.Supp. 1146 (N.D. Cal. 1995).
50. Ibid., at 843 n.8.
51. *Hudson v. McMillian*, U.S. 1 (1992).
52. *Beard v. Stephens*, 372 F.2d 685 (5th Cir. 1967).
53. *Whitley v. Albers*, 475 U.S. 312 (1986).
54. *Newman v. Alabama*, 92 S.Ct. 1079, 405 U.S. 319 (1972).
55. *Estelle v. Gamble*, 429 U.S. 97 (1976).
56. Ibid.
57. *Pennsylvania Department of Corrections v. Yeskey*, 524 U.S. 206 (1998).
58. *Estelle v. Gamble*, 429 U.S. 97, at 104.
59. *Brock v. Wright*, 315 F.3d 158, 162 (2nd Cir. 2003)
60. *Hill v. DeKalb Reg'l Youth Detention Ctr.*, 40 F.3d 1176, 1187 (11th Cir. 1994).
61. *Trop v. Dulles*, 356 U.S. 86, 78 S.Ct. 590 (1958); see also *Furman v. Georgia*, 408 U.S. 238, 92 S.Ct. 2726, 33 L.Ed.2d 346 (1972).
62. *Weems v. United States*, 217 U.S. 349, 30 S.Ct. 544, 54 L.Ed. 793 (1910).
63. *Lee v. Tahash*, 352 F.2d 970 (8th Cir., 1965).
64. *Estelle v. Gamble*, 429 U.S. 97 (1976).
65. *Robinson v. California*, 370 U.S. 660 (1962).
66. *Gregg v. Georgia*, 428 U.S. 153 (1976).
67. *Jackson v. Bishop*, 404 F.2d 571 (8th Cir. 1968).
68. *Hope v. Pelzer et al.*, 536 U.S. 730 (2002).
69. *Bell v. Wolfish*, 99 S.Ct. 1873–1974 (1979); also see "*Bell v. Wolfish*: The Rights of Pretrial Detainees," *New England Journal of Prison Law* 6 (1979): 134.
70. *Farmer v. Brennan*, 144 S.Ct. 1970 (1994).
71. *Dockery v. Epps*, PC-MS-0007: Docket/ Court 3:13–cv–00326 (S.D. Miss.) State/ Territory Mississippi: Case Type(s).
72. *Rhodes v. Chapman*, 452 U.S. 337 (1981); for further analysis of *Rhodes*, see Randall Pooler, "Prison Overcrowding and the Eighth Amendment: The Rhodes Not Taken," *New England Journal on Criminal and Civil Confinement* 8 (1983): 1–28.
73. "Report Predicted Violence at Chino Prison Dorm Hit by Race Riots," *Los Angeles Times*, August 10, 2009, http://latimesblogs.latimes.com/lanow/2009/08/report-warned-of-violence-at-chino-prison-baracks-hit-by-race-riots.html (accessed Kuly 2014).
74. *Washington v. Lee*, 263 F.Supp. 27 (M.D. Alabama 1966). Affirmed, *Lee v. Washington*, 390 U.S. 333 (1968).
75. Ibid.
76. *Johnson v. California*, 543 U.S. 499 (2005).
77. *Wolff v. McDonnell.* 418 U.S. 539 (1974).
78. *Prisoner Law Reporter*, "Prison Discipline Must Include Notice," hearing of the Commission on Correctional Facilities and Services of the American Bar Association, Vol. 3 (July 1975): 51–53.
79. For examples of the measures taken to stamp out such activities, see Steve J. Martin and Sheldon Ekland-Olson, *Texas Prisons: The Walls Came Tumbling Down* (Austin: Texas Monthly Press, 1987), pp. 32–45, 50–58.
80. *Ex parte Hull*, 312 U.S. 546. Rehearing denied, 312 U.S. 716 (1941).
81. *Bounds v. Smith*, 430 U.S. 817 (1977).
82. *Johnson v. Avery*, 393 U.S. 483 (1969).
83. Smith, *Law and Contemporary Corrections*.
84. "Use of Ombudsman Programs in Juvenile Corrections," U.S. Department of Justice, Office of Juvenile Justice and Delinquency Prevention, http://www.ojjdp.gov/pubs/walls/sect-02.html (accessed July 2014).

© Courtesy of Alan Barrett, California Prison Industry Authority

The diving program at Chino Prison in California has trained hundreds of men in commercial diving, most of whom have made a successful adjustment in the community. The program was first established in 1970 and lasted for 33 years before it was eliminated during budget cuts in 2003. On December 1, 2006, the commercial diving center in Chino was reestablished as part of the renewed rehabilitation efforts of the California Department of Corrections and Rehabilitarion.

A COMMERCIAL DIVING PROGRAM CONDUCTED AT the California Institution for Men at Chino has had quite an effect on inmates. Initiated and created in 1970 by the Marine Technology Training Center, this 11-month training includes a mix of academic and physical work totaling 2,000 hours of instruction, which is more than twice as much as required at some civilian diving schools. The diverse curriculum includes diving physics, navigation, report writing, air systems, welding, seamanship, blueprint reading, diesel engines, and marine construction. The intent of the program is to not only focus on technological skills but also instill a professional attitude of determination, courage, and perseverance.[1]

This diving program was established at Chino under the guidance of Leonard Greenstone, a former U.S. Navy salvage diver and successful commercial diving contractor. Eighty percent of the inmates do not make it through the program, but those who do are skilled deep sea divers capable of patching pipeline underwater. The successful program has trained hundreds of men in commercial diving. Evaluations tracking former graduates find the program has had a remarkable success rate; less than 10 percent of participants have returned to prison.[2]

The Chino divers are given jobs because of the school's strong reputation and a steady need for highly skilled labor in shipping, heavy construction, and the oil industry. Phil Newsum, executive director of the Association of Diving Contractors International, says that Chino graduates are among the best in the industry. "It all comes down to one question, 'Can you do the job?' They have shown over and over that they can."[3]

This is an exciting program and helps fulfill the responsibility of the Federal Bureau of Prisons and the states' departments of corrections, constitutionally mandated by federal and state courts, to provide programs and services to prisoners placed in their care. The federal government's Second Chance Act of 2007 authorized various grants to government agencies and nonprofit groups to provide a variety of services, including employment assistance, housing, substance abuse treatment, and family programming, that can help to reduce reoffending and parole violations.

10 Correctional Programs and Services

LEZLIE STERLING/MCT/Landov

LEARNING OBJECTIVES

 LO1 Identify the role of treatment and services in prisons today

 LO2 Discuss classification for treatment

 LO3 Discuss the individual-level treatment programs

 LO4 Identify the group programs held in prisons

 LO5 Discuss inmate self-help programs

 LO6 Evaluate the quality of prison programs for inmates

 LO7 Evaluate the quality of prison services for inmates

 LO8 Explain how treatment in prison can become more effective

PREVIEW OF KEY CONCEPTS

- risk assessment
- needs assessment
- responsivity principle
- SENTRY
- insight-based therapy
- behavior modification
- cognitive-behavior therapy (CBT)
- Cognitive Thinking Skills Program (CTSP)
- therapeutic community (TC)
- anger management programs
- self-help programs
- service project
- conjugal visits
- Hawes-Cooper Act
- Ashurst-Sumners Act

any states have made efforts to inform soon-to-be-released inmates of specific programs to help them better prepare for reentry. For example, in Maryland, the corrections department Education Libraries service is equipped with computers and other educational tools, which serve all the prerelease institutions in Maryland and help inmates prepare for life on the outside.[4]

It is true that prison programming has declined over time, and it is also true that inmates are more in need of substance abuse and alcohol abuse programs than mental health treatment programs. Inmates now have a greater interest in dealing with their substance abuse addictions, and correctional authorities have the responsibility for providing meaningful treatment programs for those inmates receptive to them.[5]

Jim Weber/The Commercial Appeal / Landov

Some prison programs do work. Here, Jeff Smith works at his job as a carpenter for the Salvation Army. Smith attributes his success to a treatment program he took while serving time for forgery in the Shelby County (Tennessee) Corrections Center. The program, called "Moral Reconation Therapy," was designed by two Memphis psychologists and is now a standard in prisons all across the country.

In addition to treatment programs, state correctional authorities are responsible for providing adequate basic care of inmates, including academic education, vocational training, and religious services. The state or federal government is also required to provide medical and dental services to inmates, which are sometimes extremely expensive with the number of elderly inmates increasing. Recreation has long been important, even though recreational services have been cut with the current "eliminating the frills" emphasis of many correctional systems. The courts have further required that prisons have libraries, particularly libraries that provide the necessary law books for inmates.

What does it mean for the state to provide quality care to inmates? Should inmates have the same quality of medical care as individuals in the free community? How good does the food that the state serves inmates need to be? Does the state have any responsibilities for inmates' education beyond a GED? Does the state need to pay inmates for the work they do? These are the questions and issues that are addressed in this chapter.

Identify the role of treatment and services in prisons today **LO1**

ROLE OF TREATMENT AND SERVICES IN PRISON TODAY

Correctional treatment can be defined as any means to correct an offender's character, habits, attitudes, or behaviors so as to overcome his or her propensity toward crime. At its core, the contemporary correctional system rests on the belief in an individual's ability to change. While this view expresses optimism about the human spirit, most correctional administrators also are well aware that the prison is an extremely unfavorable setting for correctional treatment.[6]

As you may recall, treatment has been part of the correctional experience since the nineteenth century. However, correctional treatment came under pressure more than 30 years ago when sociologist Robert Martinson startled both correctional personnel and the public with the pronouncement that "with few and isolated exceptions, the rehabilitative efforts that have been reported so far have no appreciable effect on recidivism."[7] Douglas Lipton, Judith Wilks, and Martinson had surveyed 231 studies on offender rehabilitation, which are found in their book *The Effectiveness of Correctional Treatment: A Survey of Treatment Evaluation Studies*.[8] Their research review found that there was little benefit from treating inmates in prison.

Despite Martinson's dreary conclusion, a spirited debate over the "nothing works" thesis has continued to rage. Treatment proponents have dismissed Martinson's claim as overreaching. When Paul Gendreau and Robert R. Ross reviewed the published works on correctional rehabilitation programs, they found that many intervention programs reported success.[9] According to Gendreau and Ross, this success rate was "convincing evidence that some treatment programs, when they are applied with integrity by competent practitioners in appropriate target populations, can be effective in preventing crime or reducing recidivism.[10] Even Martinson eventually conceded that "contrary to [his] previous position, some treatment programs *do* have an appreciable effect on recidivism. Some programs are indeed beneficial."[11] Mark W. Lipsey and Francis T. Cullen's comprehensive review of the studies of correctional rehabilitation has found consistently positive effects on reducing recidivism, but they add that considerable variability exists in those effects depending on the type of treatment, its implementation, and the nature of the offenders to which it is applied.[12]

In sum, while Martinson's widely read review cast doubt on the effectiveness of correctional treatment, more recent reviews have found that programs can be highly

CAREERS IN CORRECTIONS

Diana Bailey

Diana Bailey

Workforce Development/ Transition Coordinator, Maryland State Department of Corrections

Diana Bailey works in mobile units to provide transitional information and library services for inmates in the prerelease system.

"We have a variety of formal and informal career assessments of inmates inside the fence. Many offenders, especially when they are locked up for a while, see life as all about them. They have not necessarily thought of themselves in an employment career pathway context, and when you are doing a career assessment about them, they are totally enthralled. We are looking at their learning styles, interests and preferences, and work values. We are trying to work with their interests and skills, which many of them never knew they had. Teachers get to be creative in ferreting out their core competencies, trying to package their potential and to utilize their potential as much as possible.

"Students also develop career portfolios, and they take those to either the one-stop career center or whatever service provider they may be linked up with. So, hopefully, they can hit the ground running when they get back to the community. When they leave the institution, for the most part, we have no further contact with them. We are hopeful that the providers can do their magic that we started inside the fence.

"We also have at our maintaining institutions career centers that are very much like you would see in a public library. They have all the offender-specific and customized career development resources that would be useful for inmates doing career exploration or getting their résumé development taken care of. They usually will have sample applications and cover letters to help inmates, because most of them will be on their own when they leave us. Our goal is that they will have the skills to know what the career process is and to take it to the next step."

See Chapter 15 for more detailed information on careers in corrections.

MYTH Prison programs don't work. Only nondangerous offenders who volunteer have any hope of benefiting from treatment within prison walls.

FACT High-risk offenders, even those who are forced into treatment, do very well, maybe even better than less dangerous volunteers. For both groups, those who complete the treatment regimen fare best.

effective under particular circumstances and with specific inmate populations, especially for those inmates who complete the programs. In the midst of these hopeful possibilities for treatment, there are at least two deterrents today that discourage the wider use of institutional programs:

- Overcrowded institutions, filled with inmate gangs, violence, and racial conflicts, require that the focus be on security and institutional survival.
- The "no frills" institutional emphasis found in many states cuts back on programming and treatment, as much as constitutionally is permitted.

Discuss classification for treatment LO2

CLASSIFICATION FOR TREATMENT

In order to provide the most effective treatment, inmate needs are assessed at a classification center. Treatment effectiveness is thought to be maximized by matching inmate needs with the proper treatment modality. Proper classification is crucial to the efficient application of treatment because offenders are a diverse group, possessing a variety of behavioral issues and styles, as well as varying states of psychological health.

FOR GROUP **DISCUSSION** Create an "offender" by completing the needs assessment in Exhibit 10.1 and then discuss with your group some programs that could be developed that may rehabilitate or change the offender's shortcomings. LO2

There are a number of classification systems used in American corrections. The earliest and the one that is most commonly used is **risk assessment**, used to assign inmates to high-, medium-, and low-risk caseloads. Another classification system is the **needs assessment**, used to record staff assessment of prisoners' problems, as well as the magnitude of these problems. Needs assessments are particularly essential for inmate reentry programs. See Exhibit 10.1, which includes needs related to prison adjustment. A third possible classification is the risk/needs assessment. The most widely used system of risk/needs assessment is the Level of Service Inventory-Revised (LSI-R). It includes such factors as criminal history, education/employment, leisure/recreation activities, companions, alcohol/drug use, and emotional/personal state. Even when inmates have been classified according to risk and needs assessment, there is an important consideration of their treatment amenability or likelihood of achieving success in the program, which is defined as the **responsivity principle**.[13]

SENTRY, another classification method that has contributed to both treatment and the safety of inmates as well as staff, remains the primary automated inmate management system for the Federal Bureau of Prisons. It provides immediate access to the current institutional population or community facility population. SENTRY further calculates all aspects of inmates' sentences and is the means by which inmates are assigned to specific facilities. SENTRY identifies inmates the court has determined need special evaluation, such as the need to separate inmates who have threatened each other, and records inmates' participation in disruptive groups and street gangs.[14]

Similar to the classification discussion in Chapter 5, which was focused more on institutional security rather than treatment, prison crowding makes it difficult to be able to provide an adequate assessment program concerning the treatment needs of inmates.

risk assessment Designed to predict new offenses or prison misconduct.

needs assessment Attempts to offer treatment-relevant information, such as social adjustment, hygiene, and level of family support.

responsivity principle Maintains that programs should consider offenders' situations as well as characteristics that may become barriers to success in a correctional program.

SENTRY This system tracks and provides appropriate staff with access to critical inmate information, such as assignments, program completions, and inmate movement in every Federal Bureau of Prisons facility or while an inmate is in transit.

CORRECTIONAL TREATMENT METHODS

More than half of all prison inmates have experienced symptoms of a mental health problem or have had a recent history of mental disturbance. Consequently, all federal prisons and most state prisons and jail jurisdictions provide mental health services to inmates, including screening inmates at intake for mental health, problems,

EXHIBIT 10.1

Assessment of Client Needs

INITIAL INMATE CLASSIFICATION
ASSESSMENT OF NEEDS

NAME ______________________ Last First MI **NUMBER** ______________________

CLASSIFICATION CHAIRMAN ______________________ DATE ____/____/____

TEST SCORES:

______ I.Q.

______ Reading

______ Math

NEEDS ASSESSMENT: Select the answer that best describes the inmate.

	1	2	3	
HEALTH:	**1** Sound physical health, seldom ill	**2** Handicap or illness that interferes with functioning on a recurring basis	**3** Serious handicap or chronic illness, needs frequent medical care	______ **code**
INTELLECTUAL ABILITY:	**1** Normal intellectual ability; able to function independently	**2** Mild retardation, some need for assistance	**3** Moderate retardation, independent functioning severely limited	______ **code**
BEHAVIORAL/EMOTIONAL PROBLEMS:	**1** Exhibits appropriate emotional responses	**2** Symptoms limit adequate functioning, requires counseling, may require medication	**3** Symptoms prohibit adequate functioning, requires significant intervention, may require medication or separate housing	______ **code**
ALCOHOL ABUSE:	**1** No alcohol problem	**2** Occasional abuse, some disruption of functioning	**3** Frequent abuse, serious disruption, needs treatment	______ **code**
DRUG ABUSE:	**1** No drug problem	**2** Occasional abuse, some disruption of functioning	**3** Frequent abuse, serious disruption, needs treatment	______ **code**
EDUCATIONAL STATUS:	**1** Has high school diploma or GED	**2** Some deficits, but potential for high school diploma or GED	**3** Major deficits in math and/or reading, needs remedial programs	______ **code**
VOCATIONAL STATUS:	**1** Has sufficient skills to obtain and hold satisfactory employment	**2** Minimal skill level, needs enhancement	**3** Virtually unemployable, needs training	______ **code**

Source: Patricia Van Voorhis, Michael Braswell, and David Lester, *Correctional Counseling and Rehabilitation*, 6th ed. (Cincinnati: Anderson, 2007), p. 143.

Mentally ill inmates present a unique problem for correctional administrators. Here, public defender Jennifer Johnson (right) applauds client Carmen Morales for making improvements during a hearing at the Behavioral Health Court in San Francisco. Behavioral Health Court (BHC), a collaborative court with the San Francisco Superior Court, addresses the complex needs of mentally ill defendants with co-occurring substance use disorders by diverting them from jail and into appropriate community treatment. In this program, judges can offer a chance for users to go to rehab, get jobs, move into houses, find primary care physicians, and even remove their tattoos. There is enough data now to show that these alternative courts reduce recidivism and save money.

providing therapy or counseling by trained mental health professionals, and distributing psychotropic medications.[15]

Rehabilitation efforts begin early in the inmates' correctional experience and continue on until its end. While in the classification center, inmates are typed and presented with a series of conditions designed essentially to change and/or control their lifestyle, including getting help for a variety of problems (such as alcoholism, drug abuse, mental illness, etc.), mandatory meetings with treatment personnel, and a series of restrictions if they fail to partake in a treatment regime. Failure to abide by these conditions may result in loss of privileges, reduced good time, ineligibility for early release programs, and other penalties.

This section presents a selection of therapeutic methods—individual, group, and self-directed programs that have been used nationally in correctional settings—and identifies some of their more salient features.

Individual-Level Treatment Programs

A number of different individual techniques are used within the prison, including insight-based therapy, behavior therapy, and cognitive-behavior therapy. These are reviewed below.

Discuss the individual-level treatment programs **LO3**

INSIGHT-BASED THERAPY It is common for prisons to employ **insight-based therapy** techniques for the treatment of mental and emotional disorders. There are many different types of insight-based therapy techniques, but in general they utilize insight, persuasion, suggestion, reassurance, and instruction so that inmates may see themselves and their problems more realistically and develop the desire to cope effectively with their fears and problems. (See Exhibit 10.2.)

EXHIBIT 10.2

Insight-Based Therapies

Type	Treatment Goal	Qualifications of Therapist	Length of Treatment Period	Response from Offenders
Psychotherapy	Lead inmates to insight	Psychiatrist, psychologist, social worker	Long-term	Will examine individual problems with therapist
Transactional analysis	Lead inmates to insight	Psychiatrist, psychologist, trained nonprofessional, staff	Usually several months	Will examine individual problems in a group context and will learn a new approach to interpersonal relationships
Reality therapy	Help inmates to obtain basic needs	Psychiatrist, psychologist, trained nonprofessional, staff	Short period of time	Will learn to cope with reality, model responsible behavior, and determine right from wrong

Psychiatrists, clinical psychologists, and psychiatric social workers have used various versions of insight-based therapies in American prisons since the early twentieth century. Prisoners are encouraged to talk about past conflicts that cause them to express emotional problems through aggressive or antisocial behavior. The insight that inmates gain from this individual therapy supposedly helps them resolve the conflicts and unconscious needs that drove them to crime. As a final step, the inmate becomes responsible for his or her own behavior.

insight-based therapy Typically involves treatment designed to encourage communication of conflicts and insight into problems, with the goal being relief of symptoms, changes in behavior, and personality growth.

Insight-based therapies have some fundamental limitations in a prison context. Inmates usually do not see themselves as having emotional problems and are reluctant to share their inner thoughts with therapists. There are also staffing problems. Professional mental health staff make up only about 3 percent of agency staff, and they must provide a range of mental health services in U.S. prisons.[16] These staff are overworked because more than half of all prison and jail inmates have some form of mental health problem.[17] As a result, correctional treatment staff often have little time to conduct ongoing therapy. Instead, the few trained therapists in U.S. prisons are swamped with classification work and emergency cases.

Web App 10.1
Go to the Prison Policy Initiative website to read an article about incarceration and mental illness: http://www.prisonpolicy.org/blog/2000/04/01/massdissent/. What reasons are given for incarceration not being a solution for mental illness? LO3

BEHAVIOR THERAPY A second form of individual treatment, behavior therapy, rests on the assumption that desirable behaviors that are rewarded immediately and systematically will increase, and undesirable behaviors that are not rewarded or are punished will diminish or be extinguished. Behavior therapy uses positive and negative reinforcement to encourage desirable and extinguish undesirable behaviors. **Behavior modification** is the principal behavior therapy technique and is still practiced informally in a great many correctional institutions. It works like this: inmates receive additional privileges as they become more accepting of the institutional rules and procedures and as they give evidence of more positive attitudes. The Evidence-Based Corrections feature looks at one successful attempt at modifying inmate behavior.

Behavior modification A technique in which rewards or punishments are used to alter or change a person's behavior.

EVIDENCE-BASED CORRECTIONS

Getting Ready Program

The Getting Ready program is Arizona's common-sense approach to prerelease preparation designed to reduce postrelease recidivism. It is aimed at giving inmates better coping skills that can help them ease the shock of reentry.

The program begins on day one of incarceration and continues to the conclusion of every inmate's sentence. Getting Ready redefines the officer–offender relationship, shifting many responsibilities from the staff to the inmates and empowering both groups to function at substantively high levels. For example, officers do not tell inmates when to get up and when to go to sleep. Getting Ready does not just preach about what you ought to be doing when you get back to the real world. It brings the real world—what they call a "parallel universe"—into prison so that inmates in every custody level acquire and practice basic life skills from the first to the last day of their incarceration. In a sense, it involves adapting the prison life to resemble life in the community. One example is health care. Because health care costs are rising, Getting Ready helps prepare inmates to lower their medical costs upon release. It teaches them healthy habits—not smoking, eating healthy foods, exercising, and complying with medical directions—activities that will result in a lower co-pay on the outside. The parallel universe model has also been applied to inmates' work assignments. The program uses the U.S. Department of Labor's *Dictionary of Occupational Titles* to determine job categories and salaries and revises inmate pay to reflect what someone could expect to receive proportionately for performing this work in the community.

The same principle is applied to education. An inmate is not required to complete or further his education, but until he earns a GED—assuming

(*continued*)

he is academically able, which encompasses the vast majority of the population—he can be employed only in entry-level jobs, earning entry-level wages. Like in the real world, once they earn a GED, many other employment opportunities open up. In Getting Ready, a GED becomes a prerequisite to job training, better work assignments, and higher wages.

Getting Ready uses a three-tiered earned incentive system that changes the traditional paradigm. This system recognizes good behavior—greater acceptance of responsibility and better decision making—with rewards or incentives that can be earned over time, are appropriate to each custody level, and are prized by the population. Inmates who do well have the possibility of eating their meals in a less regimented setting, followed by a show or televised sports event, and the opportunity to buy snacks not ordinarily sold in the commissary.

Evaluations of the program indicate that since it was implemented, violence has been reduced, with inmate-on-inmate assaults decreasing 46 percent, inmate-on-staff assaults down 33 percent, suicides down 67 percent, and sexual assaults down 61 percent. The average one-year return rate for all releases in the two years before and after Getting Ready started improved 2.75 percent. Within this group of releases were 1,500 inmates who completed Getting Ready in its entirety. This group has done considerably better, as much as two years after release, than inmates of comparable risk who were not in the program.

FOR CRITICAL THINKING AND WRITING

In the Getting Ready program, an inmate has to work very hard to earn a visit in which family members are allowed to bring food, and not all inmates in every custody level are eligible. Do you think such special treatment will create resentment and unrest among those who are not in the program?

Source: Dora Schriro, "Getting Ready: How Arizona Has Created a 'Parallel Universe' for Inmates," *National Institute of Justice Journal* 263 (2009) http://www.nij.gov/journals/263/getting-ready.htm (accessed July 2014).

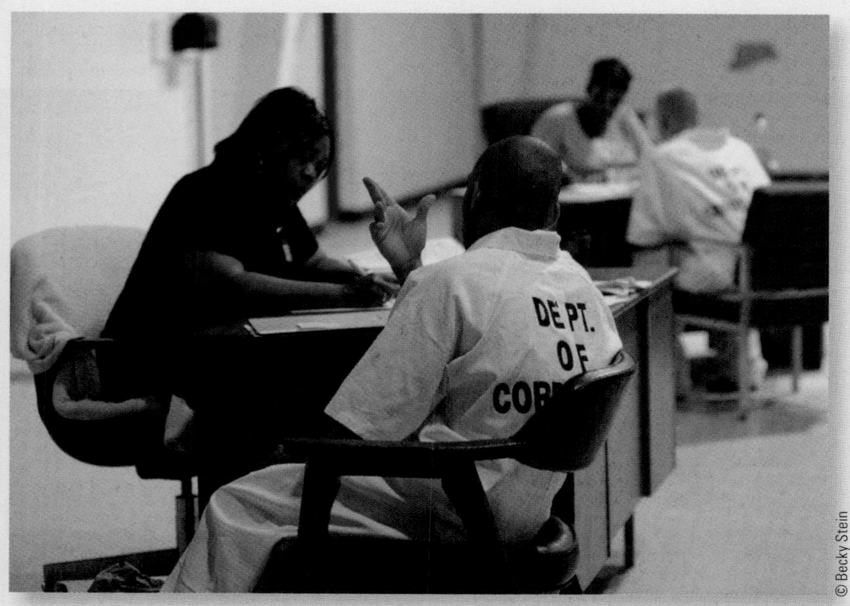

A counselor doing a mental health evaluation in the intake area at Georgia Diagnostic and Classification Prison in Jackson, Georgia. It is both a reception center (where inmates are evaluated and classified according to security level, mental health status, etc.) and a maximum-security prison where death row inmates are housed.

COGNITIVE-BEHAVIOR THERAPY

Cognitive-behavior therapy (CBT) for offenders is based on the assumption that the foundations for criminal behavior are dysfunctional patterns of thinking. The intent is that by altering routine misinterpretations of life events, offenders can modify antisocial aspects of their personality and consequence behaviors. The goal of these interventions is to identify cognitive deficits linked to criminality, such as impulsivity, a concrete thinking style that impinges on the ability to appreciate the feelings and thoughts of others, impairments in self-defeating behavior, egocentricity, inability to reason critically, peer interpersonal problem-solving skills, and a preoccupation with self.[18]

CBT in offender treatment targets the choices, thoughts, attitudes, and meaning systems that are associated with antisocial behavior as well as deviant lifestyle. It usually uses a training approach to teach new skills in areas where offenders showed deficits, such as generating alternative solutions, rather than reacting on first impulse; interpersonal problem awareness, evaluating consequences, opening up and listening to other perspectives; resisting peer pressure, soliciting feedback, taking on the person's well-being into account, and deciding on what is the most beneficial course of action.[19]

Cognitive-behavior therapy (CBT) Therapy based on the assumption that the foundations for criminal behavior are dysfunctional patterns of thinking.

The CBT therapists act as teachers, and lessons are generally taught to groups in classroom settings. The lessons may include group exercises involving role-play, homework assignments, rehearsal, and intensive feedback and generally follow detailed lesson plans and structured curriculum.[20] People taking part in CBT learn specific skills that can be used to solve the problems they confront all the time as well as skills they can use to achieve legitimate goals and objectives. CBT first concentrates on developing skills to recognize distorted or unrealistic thinking when it happens, and then works toward changing that thinking or belief to mollify or eliminate problematic behavior.[21]

The most widely adopted of the cognitive-behavioral interventions is the **Cognitive Thinking Skills Program (CTSP)** developed by Robert Ross and Elizabeth Fabiano, which is now a core program in the Canadian Correctional System and has been implemented in the United States, Australia, New Zealand, and some European countries.[22]

CTSP was developed through a systematic review of all published correctional programs that were associated with reduced criminal recidivism. The researchers identified 100 evaluations of effective programs and discovered that all were designed to target offenders' thinking. Rigid thinking could be minimized by teaching participants creative thinking skills and providing them with prosocial alternatives to use when responding to interpersonal problems. Teaching offenders techniques of self-control could improve social adjustment. These interventions are core components of CTSP.[23]

A review of the literature leads to the conclusion that the combining element of cognition and behavioral approaches is found in the principle of self-reinforcement. This concept says that behavioral and cognitive changes reinforce each other. When cognitive change leads to changes in behavior, what takes place is a sense of well-being that strengthens the change in thought and, as a result, further strengthens the behavioral changes. This self-reinforcing feedback process is a key element of that cognitive-behavioral approach and is the basis for helping offenders understand the cognitive-behavioral process (see the "Cognitive-Behavioral Roadmap" in Figure 10.1).[24]

COGNITIVE-BEHAVIOR THERAPY EFFECTIVENESS There is considerable research support that shows positive effects of cognitive-behavioral approaches with offenders:[25]

- A meta-analysis of 69 studies covering both behavior and cognitive-behavioral programs determined that the cognitive-behavioral programs are more effective in reducing rates of recidivism than the behavior programs. The mean reduction was about 30 percent for treated offenders.[26]
- Other meta-analysis of correctional treatment concluded that cognitive-behavioral methods constituted critical aspects of effective correctional treatment.[27]
- Another study determined that the most effective interventions are those that employ cognitive-behavioral techniques to improve cognitive function.[28]
- There is strong evidence that positive results are more likely to take place among certain subgroups. For example, CTSP seems to be more effective with offenders over age 25 and with property offenders.[29] See Figure 10.2 for the recidivism effects for skill-building programs.

CRITICAL THINKING

Do the mentally ill belong in a prison setting? Which type of therapy is most appropriate in a prison setting, if any? If none are appropriate, how should we handle the treatment of the mentally ill? LO3

Cognitive Thinking Skills Program (CTSP) A cognitive-behavioral intervention, developed by Ross and Fabiano, designed to improve offenders' thinking processes.

FOR GROUP DISCUSSION

Cognitive-behavior therapy is one of the more effective programs for sex offenders. Your group should discuss what other therapeutic prison programs might benefit sex offenders, or should we focus more on punishment than rehabilitation? Visit the Bureau of Justice Assistance website at https://www.bja.gov/evaluation/program-corrections/sops1.htm for more information to support your evaluation of sex offender treatment programs in prison. Chapter 12 on special populations also discusses sex offender treatment in prison. LO3

Group Programs

LO4 Identify the group programs held in prisons

In addition to individual-level therapies, most correctional institutions maintain group counseling programs. These programs help inmates to:

- Better control their emotions (understanding why they feel the way they do, learning how not to get too nervous or anxious, solving their problems creatively)
- Communicate effectively with others (understanding what people tell them and communicating clearly when they write)

FIGURE 10.1

The Cognitive-Behavioral Roadmap:

The Process of Learning and Change

Source: Based on Wanberg and Milkman, *Criminal Conduct and Substance Abuse Treatment: Strategies for Self-Improvement and Change: Pathways to Responsible Living : The Participant's Workbook.*

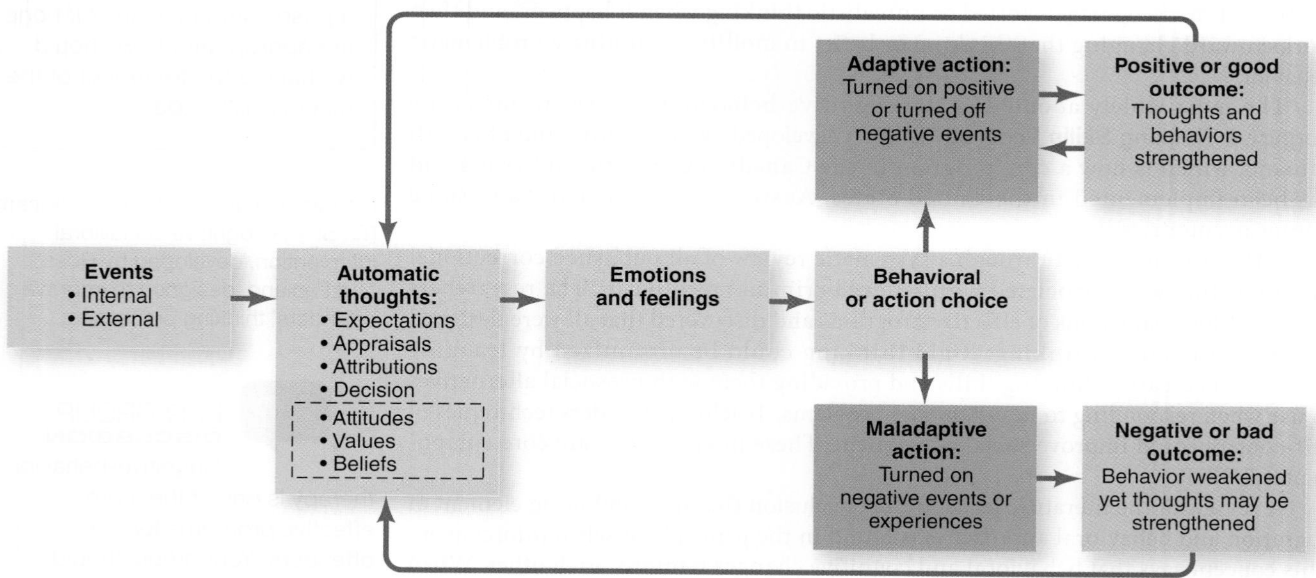

FIGURE 10.2

Mean Recidivism Effects for Skill-Building Programs

Source: Based on Mark Lipsey et al., *Improving the Effectiveness of Juvenile Justice Programs : A New Perspective on Evidence-Based Practice* (p. 26) as found at the following URL: http://cjjr.georgetown.edu/pdfs/ebp/ebppaper.pdf. Center for Juvenile Justice Reform, Georgetown Public Policy Institute.

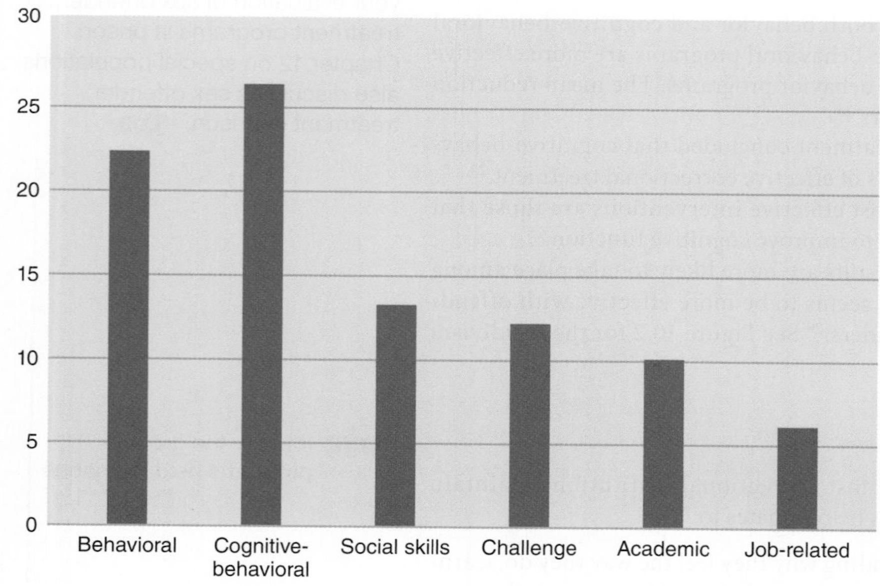

- Deal with pressing legal concerns (keeping out of legal trouble and avoiding breaking laws)
- Efficiently manage general life issues (finding a job, dealing with difficult coworkers, being a good parent)
- Develop and maintain supportive social relationships (getting along with others, making others happy, making others proud)[30]

Some of the more common programs are discussed below.

DRUG AND ALCOHOL TREATMENT PROGRAMS The Federal Bureau of Prisons instituted its current drug treatment program 20 years ago and has adapted it in the years that followed to incorporate advances in correctional understanding of the problem. It uses cognitive-behavioral treatment and is implemented in a well-designed, evidence-based, modified therapeutic community. This extensive program includes drug abuse education, nonresidential drug abuse treatment for short-term offenders, and the Residential Drug Abuse Program (RDAP). This is the most intensive treatment program following the CBT model of treatment and is wrapped in a modified therapeutic model in which inmates learn what it is like in a prosocial community. Inmates live in a unit separate from the general population.

Translation Drug Abuse Treatment (TDAT) requires a continuation of drug abuse treatment in the community upon transfer to a residential reentry center (RRC). The primary responsibility of the regional TDAT staff is the monitoring of inmates' treatment progress during their stay in the RRC. Regional TDAT staff have developed a complex network of community-based contact to deliver treatment to inmates residing in an RRC or on home confinement. The regional TDAT key personnel work closely with probation to establish continual treatment as inmates leave Bureau custody and move to supervised release.[31]

Few states have developed this history or such a well-developed model for dealing with drug or alcohol offenders in prison, but there is an attempt in nearly every correctional system to provide some programming for these offenders. Treatment studies that have been done in prison populations have found that when drug programs are well integrated, using effective program elements and implemented carefully, these programs:

- Reduce relapse
- Reduce criminality
- Reduce recidivism
- Reduce inmate misconduct
- Reduce mental illness
- Reduce behavioral disorders
- Increase the level of the inmates' stake in societal norms
- Increase levels of education and employment upon returning to the community
- Improve health and mental health symptoms and conditions
- Improve relationships[32]

Stephen Bahr and colleagues found that effective drug treatment programs (1) focused on high-risk offenders, (2) provided strong inducements to receive treatment, (3) included several types of interventions simultaneously, (4) provided intensive treatment, and (5) included an aftercare component.[33]

THERAPEUTIC COMMUNITIES The **therapeutic community (TC)** treatment approach focuses on the total environment and uses all the experiences of that environment as the basic tools for therapeutic intervention. Evolving from the work of famed psychiatrist Maxwell Jones, this approach attempts to give persons within the therapeutic unit greater authority in the operation of their living units.[34]

therapeutic community (TC) A community treatment group designed to divert drug users from the criminal justice system; therapeutic communities vary in how much control they are given in prison settings.

An evaluation of the California Substance Abuse Treatment Facility (CSATF) found that it was associated with significant advantages for management of the prison—including lower rates of infractions, reduced absenteeism among correctional staff, and virtually no illicit drug use among prisoners.[35] While at one time more than 1,400 inmates received treatment, budget cuts have reduced that number to around 300 today.[36]

The Amity Prison TC in the J. Donovan Correctional Facility, a medium-security prison near San Diego, is one of the best-known therapeutic community programs. It provides intensive treatment to 200 male inmates who reside in a housing unit the last 9 to 12 months of their prison term. All participants are volunteers, and formal programming occurs four hours a day on weekdays; there is also a postrelease program. Evaluations find that the Amity treatment group has significantly lower rates of reincarceration, longer time to reoffending, and higher levels of employment when compared to a control group who did not receive similar treatment measures.[37]

Self-contained therapeutic communities are difficult to establish in an institutional setting. Prison authorities are reluctant to delegate responsibility and authority to therapeutic communities and change rules to accommodate an atypical prison social system. However, therapeutic communities' recent success with treating drug abuse in prison has resulted in the increased development and use of these programs.[38] TCs have reduced recidivism when there is postprison support and follow-up treatment.[39] To ease acceptance of these programs, Therapeutic Communities of America has developed minimum standards and translated these standards into a formal accreditation process. The intent is to standardize the screening and selection process and to translate the broad standards into finding the ideal curriculum for various offenders. For example, how would a curriculum for mothers be different than for single men?[40]

CRITICAL THINKING

Should drug offenders who have not committed additional crimes be sent to prison for treatment? How would you create a better plan of action for drug offenders? Or do you believe the prison is instrumental in reducing drug abuse? Why? LO4

ANGER MANAGEMENT There is common agreement that anger is linked to violent criminal behavior in the community; to violent behavior, self-harm, and institutional conflict in the prison environment; and to failure to adjust on parole and post-institutional release. As a result, **anger management programs** are desired because of inmates' need for violence reduction techniques.[41] One survey of group psychotherapy services in correctional facilities indicated that anger therapy may be the most frequent form of group therapy offered within prison settings.[42] Anger management is frequently a part of drug treatment and sex offender treatment programs. Cognitive-behavioral approaches are often used as a means of helping inmates find ways to control their anger.

anger management programs Programs designed to help inmates manage their anger, especially in interpersonal relations.

self-help programs Programs from which inmates seek self-improvement, such as anger management, or express ethnic or cultural goals.

Yet, unlike other forms of prison treatment, such as drug abuse, little or no data are kept on anger management groups. One study that took place in a Midwestern low-security prison did find that those participants assigned to a treatment group had significant reduction in anger compared to those placed in the control group.[43]

Inmate Self-Help Programs

Discuss inmate self-help programs LO5

Departments of corrections frequently encourage inmates to establish **self-help programs**. These are run primarily by the inmates themselves and often express ethnic and cultural goals. Self-help groups meet in the evening or on the weekends. They usually are required to have staff sponsorship and establish governing bylaws and procedures.

VOICES ACROSS THE PROFESSION

Corrections work demands professionalism, courage, and commitment. Challenges in the field represent opportunities for our staff to shine in accomplishing seemingly impossible goals through dedicated teamwork.

Cathy Fontenot
Assistant Warden of Programming, Louisiana State Penitentiary, Angola

As an assistant warden, I have safely emergency-housed thousands of inmates evacuated from historic hurricanes and floods, have eaten last meals with death row inmates, have traveled abroad and across the United States to audit and observe prisons, have attended the Academy Awards, and have facilitated victims in both forgiving their offenders and in gaining knowledge that has moved them along their journey toward healing. Corrections work demands professionalism, courage, and commitment. Challenges in the field represent opportunities for our staff to shine in accomplishing seemingly impossible goals through dedicated teamwork. Modern corrections work has the ability to impact every part of the criminal justice system and due to all that we've learned in "what works" is leading to safer and better public safety in our world. What could be more rewarding than that?

Self-help programs offered in prison include Alcoholics Anonymous, Gamblers Anonymous, Toastmasters, Jaycees, Lifers, Dale Carnegie, Check Anonymous, Native American Spiritual and Cultural Awareness Group, yoga, transcendental meditation, tai chi, Insight Incorporated, Positive Mental Attitude (PMA), assertiveness training, anger management, stress management, life skills, moral development, and emotional maturity instruction.

HELPING OTHERS As part of the self-help initiative, some inmates are eager to become involved in **service projects**. These projects may have both self-help and service aspects or may focus on a needed institutional or community service. Some service projects are ongoing; others arise because of a disaster or emergency in the community. Service projects have included providing child care for prison visits, fighting forest fires and floods, adopting war orphans, doing peer counseling, recording books for the blind, training service dogs, donating blood, caring for rescued horses, participating as paramedics or in other lifesaving roles, and umpiring Little League games in the community.[44]

service projects A worthy cause, such as disaster relief or peer counseling, in which inmates willingly participate.

In 2013, FCI (Federal Correctional Institution) Morgantown began a Veterans-to-Veterans Service Dog Training Program. The service dog program provides training and certification to 21 inmates who will become service dog trainers. The inmates have been carefully screened and selected for this particular training. All of them are military veterans and train dogs for veterans in the community who have mobility impairments and/or posttraumatic stress disorder (PTSD). The inmate trainers and the dogs assigned to them all reside in a housing unit designated specifically for inmate-veterans at FCI Morgantown.[45]

SELF-DEVELOPMENT The current recidivism rate may be high, but some inmates leaving prison are able to live law-abiding and productive lives. Some success stories incorporate self-development while in prison, ranging from religious experience (such as conversion to Islam) to involvement in a self-help program, or even getting help and guidance from another inmate. Success on the outside may also be aided by improving self-discipline or the development of internal resources, sometimes aided by reading. As one inmate put it:

> We have to have a "strong mind" to make it in here. This is how I made it through three years of segregation. When we have a "strong mind," we have a feeling of self, a continuity to life, and an enhanced faculty of reasoning. It has to do with one not having any feelings of inferiority and worthlessness. A strong mind will help us to know who we are, what we are; it will help us accept and respect who and what we are, and know that virtually everything and every situation we encounter in life offer us a valuable lesson, which if fully understood, makes us wiser.

This inmate and his strong mind had no more disciplinary problems during the remainder of his 15-year incarceration, and upon his release he remained law abiding and a positive force in his community.[46]

© Joyce Dopkeen/*New York Times*/Redux

Sharon Richardson, an inmate at Bedford Hills Correctional Facility, in Bedford Hills, New York, and her yellow Labrador, Mitzie, show what Mitzie has learned. The dog has been trained to stare at Richardson every time she says, "Watch me." Richardson is one of about 30 women at the prison who take part in a program run by an organization called Puppies Behind Bars, which has inmates at several prisons in New York, New Jersey, and Connecticut help train service dogs to assist disabled people, including veterans returning from Iraq and Afghanistan.

Well, for people who are guilty who are incarcerated, my message to them would be: The system is not going to rehabilitate you. You have to want it for yourself, so you need to be proactive. Take advantage of the educational opportunities that are there. Read nonfiction books, don't waste your time or get caught up in prison politics. Try to orient everything you do towards your future life when you're eventually free. There have been a lot of worthwhile accomplishments by people who have committed crimes that have resulted in their conviction, but they have done a lot of meaningful things both individually and that have benefitted society.

For more about Jeffrey Deskovic, see Chapter 11.

CORRECTIONAL LIFE

Jeffrey: A Former Inmate

PRISON EDUCATION, VOCATIONAL, AND RELIGIOUS PROGRAMS

In addition to counseling and treatment, a correctional institution is responsible for providing all the necessary services to care for the physical, educational, recreational, and spiritual needs of inmates.

Evaluate the quality of LO6 prison programs for inmates

Academic Education

In adult institutions, academic education is usually available through adult basic education (ABE) programs, secondary and general education studies, postsecondary education programs, and social education programs. In a great many correctional systems, mandatory education is required of those inmates who manifest clearly defined educational deficiencies. College courses have been provided through live instruction, correspondence courses, television hookups, and release time, which allows inmates to attend educational institutions in the community. Community colleges have offered inmates courses leading to a two-year degree.

Improving inmates' educational skills may reduce recidivism through several mechanisms:

- Inmates who attain sufficient reading and writing skills for functional literacy may increase the possibility of lawful employment after release from prison. Postrelease employment is an important consideration in staying crime-free. Therefore, educational programming in prison may reduce recidivism by improving job opportunities.

VOICES ACROSS THE PROFESSION

When they see a copy of their résumé, which looks cool and has legitimate skills on it, they feel really good about it.

Diana Bailey
Workforce Development/Transition Coordinator, Maryland State Department of Corrections

The persons we are working with inside in the prisons frequently do not see themselves in terms of self-esteem or self-concept or as being part of any normal mainstream group. When they see a copy of their résumé, which looks cool and has legitimate skills on it, they feel really good about it. That is part of the skill development to get them ready for the horribly competitive workforce process they are going to be involved with when they get out.

- The educational process may be helpful in reducing recidivism by facilitating the conscientiousness, maturation, and dedication that educational achievement requires. This view proposes that education may equip inmates to evaluate their environments and their decisions more thoughtfully and, as a result, make decisions that will assist them in remaining out of prison when released.
- The educational setting within the prison gives inmates an opportunity to interact with civilian employees in the context of a goal-oriented and nonauthoritarian relationship.[47]

Research studies have found that educational program participation was related to reduced rates of recidivism.[48] One effort compared the impact of correctional education on rearrest, reconviction, and incarceration in Maryland, Minnesota, and Ohio, and found that participation in education resulted in lower rates of recidivism.[49] The key findings in this study:

- For rearrest, correctional education participants had statistically significant lower rates of rearrest (48 percent) when compared to the control group of nonparticipants (57 percent).
- For conviction, correctional education participants had statistically significant lower rates of reconviction (27 percent) when compared to the control group of nonparticipants (35 percent).
- For reincarceration, correctional education participants had statistically significant lower rates of reincarceration (21 percent) when compared to the control group of nonparticipants (31 percent).[50]

However, in spite of evidence that postsecondary correctional education (PSCE) reduces recidivism and improves institutional adjustment, prisoners have been denied access to higher education and Pell Grants, which provide college loans with beneficial repayment rules.[51] College prison programs have also been reduced, primarily because increasingly prison systems believe that prisoners do not need the frills of postsecondary schooling.[52]

Vocational Training

The need for vocational training has always been evident, because most inmates are educable and trainable but lack any regular work experience or any demonstrable skills in a trade. The basic purpose of vocational training, then, is to prepare inmates for jobs in the community.

The variety of vocational programs offered in men's prisons is impressive. Indeed, the Federal Bureau of Prisons UNICOR program employs approximately 16 percent of work-eligible inmates. They gain marketable job skills in prison-based facilities while working in factory operations, such as metals, furniture, electronics, textiles, and graphic arts. Work assignments pay from 23 cents to $1.15 per hour.[53] In prisons across the nation, there are similar programs offering skill training in printing, barbering, welding, meat cutting, machine shop work, electronics, baking, plumbing, computer programming, television and radio repair, bus repair, air conditioning maintenance, automotive body and fender repair, sheet metal work and repair, painting, blueprint reading, and furniture repair and upholstering.

Fewer vocational programs exist for women in correctional institutions. Vocational programs for women typically include cosmetology, secretarial training, business machine operation, data processing, baking and food preparation, and child care. But recently this pattern has been changing in some women's prisons. For example, Bedford Hills in New York offers women training in auto mechanics, electronics, and video technology, and the women's prison in Nebraska provides a course in truck driving.

FOR GROUP DISCUSSION

If your group represented a group of business owners, what skills, education, and training would an ex-offender have to have in order for you to hire him or her? Discuss your beliefs about hiring ex-offenders. Do they deserve a second chance? **LO6**

VOICES ACROSS THE PROFESSION

The success stories may be few and far between, but when we have one, it's great.

Diana Bailey
Workforce Development/Transition Coordinator, Maryland State Department of Corrections

As a professional educator and a career development professional, the creativity of making a program and service delivery system for this population has been a real challenge. When it works, it is fabulous. When it does not work, it provides a high level of frustration. We think, what else could we have done? In many cases, [the problem is the] lack of support systems when they leave us. Increased skills give them improved self-esteem and more legal income necessary for economic self-sufficiency. Money means a lot to people; it gives them choices they might not have otherwise. The success stories may be few and far between, but when we have one, it's great.

Another approach increasing in popularity involves inmates in animal training. The state of Florida maintains several such programs. For example, CARE (Canine Assisted Re-Entry) dogs spend nine weeks at Baker Correctional Institution's Work Camp being trained by inmates who serve as trainers, handlers, and caretakers. The inmates teach the dogs to sit, stay, come, and walk by their owner's side without pulling on the leash. At the end of the nine weeks, the dogs are tested to make sure they have learned all their skills before graduation from the program. The inmates have been trained by professional dog trainers in the hope that they will be able to find employment in animal services upon release.

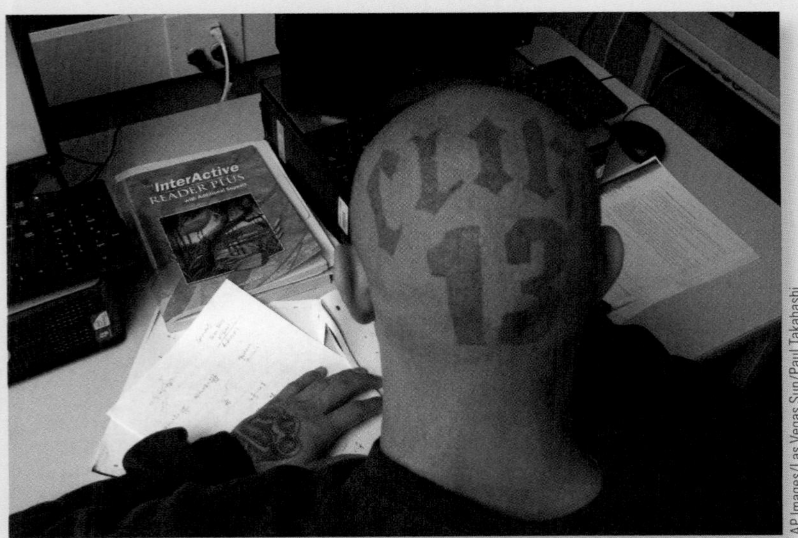

AP Images/Las Vegas Sun/Paul Takahashi

Inmates routinely take courses in an effort to earn a GED, receive specialized training, and even acquire college credit. Here, an inmate works on a reading assignment during a class at the High Desert State Prison, about 40 miles northwest of Las Vegas. More than 300 inmates at the prison receive adult education and vocational training from the Clark County School District through a partnership with the Nevada Department of Corrections.

Another Florida program, FEATS (Force-free Education and Training Solutions) is located at the Northwest Florida Reception Center (NFRC). The program teaches inmates to train and care for dogs and provides them with valuable technical and interpersonal skills while increasing the adoptability of shelter dogs that may otherwise have been euthanized. Each dog is assigned to a team of three inmates: a trainer, an assistant trainer, and a caregiver. The inmates, with their assigned dogs, attend weekly training sessions with a professional instructor and are responsible for continuing the dog's training throughout the week. For eight weeks the dogs live full time with the inmates and become crate trained, housetrained, receive necessary socialization with people and other dogs and learn basic obedience.[54]

Prison job fairs are offered in some prisons. The Federal Bureau of Prisons, Texas prisons, and Wisconsin prisons are among those correctional systems holding job fairs. [55]

Participation in vocational programs is seen as a means of reducing recidivism, based on the premise that the acquisition of vocational skills such as goal-setting, motivation, commitment, and technical and nontechnical knowledge increases ex-offenders' legitimate employment opportunities following release.[56] David B. Wilson and colleagues found from an examination of 33 evaluations of vocational and work programs that "participants are employed at a higher rate and recidivate at a lower rate than nonparticipants."[57] Nonetheless, a sobering reality is that the crowded conditions in today's prisons only permit a small percentage of inmates to participate in vocational programs.

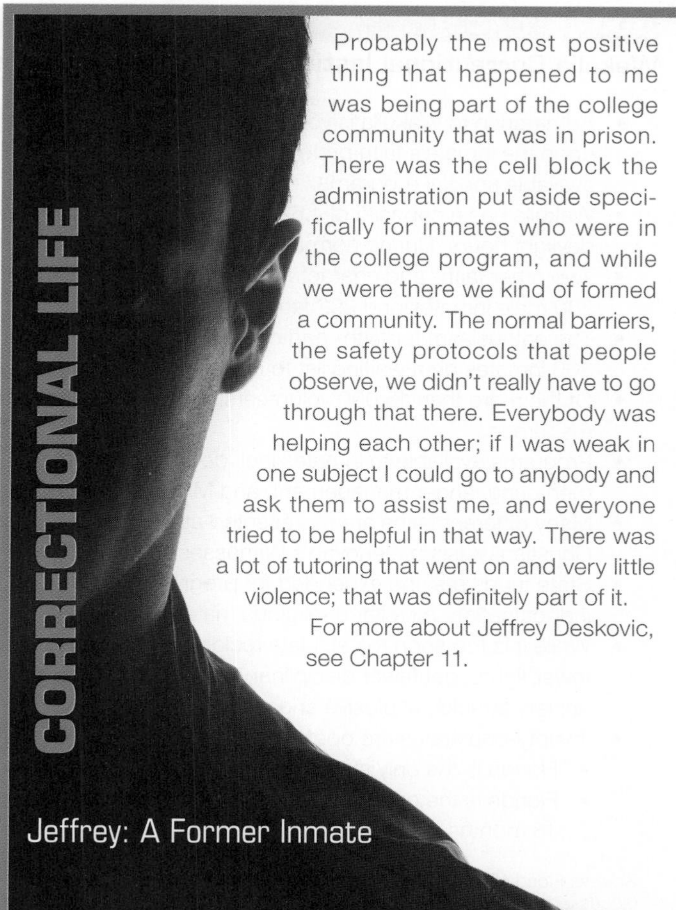

Probably the most positive thing that happened to me was being part of the college community that was in prison. There was the cell block the administration put aside specifically for inmates who were in the college program, and while we were there we kind of formed a community. The normal barriers, the safety protocols that people observe, we didn't really have to go through that there. Everybody was helping each other; if I was weak in one subject I could go to anybody and ask them to assist me, and everyone tried to be helpful in that way. There was a lot of tutoring that went on and very little violence; that was definitely part of it.

For more about Jeffrey Deskovic, see Chapter 11.

Religion

Religious instruction and services are always provided in federal, state, and private prisons. Full-time Protestant and Roman Catholic chaplains are available in most prisons. In some prisons, rabbis and imams come in from the outside community to conduct services for Jewish and Muslim inmates. Religious services include Sunday Mass and morning worship, confession, baptism, instruction for church membership, choir, and religious counseling.

The emphasis on religion in prison has recently grown, due in part to President George W. Bush's creation of a White House Office of Faith-Based and Community Initiatives. In 2003, Florida Governor Jeb Bush dedicated the first faith-based prison in the United States, a 750-bed medium-security facility for men in Lawtey, Florida. In 2004, Florida converted what was then the all-male Hillsborough Correctional Institution to the nation's first faith-based correctional facility for women. At least five states—Texas, Kansas, Minnesota, Florida, and Iowa—have opened new prison facilities in which the central philosophy involves religious teaching. In March 2004, the Corrections Corporation of America (CCA) announced its interest in developing faith-based correctional facilities. In 2014, CCA announced that it now employs chaplains and program facilitators who offer inmate residents a variety of worship services, faith-based counseling, and religious resources to address practical and spiritual needs. These professionals design and deliver a continuum of care that approaches and treats the inmate as "the total person." By addressing such social problems as addiction, education, and faith in integrative programs and therapeutic living communities, CCA clients are provided with a variety of rehabilitative opportunities.[58] See Exhibit 10.3 for what takes place in a Florida faith- and character-based prison. The Urban Institute conducted an evaluation of both

AP Images/Damian Dovarganes

Inmate Robert Ross, 32, a full-time clerk and a leader in the seminary training program, plays guitar during services at the California Rehabilitative Center chapel in Norco. The program, called The Urban Ministry Institute (TUMI), started as an experiment in Norco's prison and expanded to at least 18 California prisons and nearly 900 inmates, including women, thanks to a gift from a Malibu real estate entrepreneur. The program aims to transform inmates into church leaders, pastors, teachers, and evangelists. The TUMI curriculum is divided into 16 eight-week courses covering biblical studies, theology and ethics, Christian ministry, and urban mission.

EXHIBIT 10.3

Wakulla Correctional Institution, Crawfordville, Florida: A Faith- and Character-Based Prison

- Admittance to Wakulla is voluntary, as is program participation by the inmates. Entry into the program does not depend upon the inmate's faith preference or lack thereof, but rather on his or her behavior and desire to participate in the available special programs.
- Wakulla has a capacity of 1,622 inmates. Faith- and character-based activities take place each day of the week during daylight hours. During normal work hours, inmates are assigned to regular work assignments or education classes.
- Two other faith- and character-based institutions in Florida—Lawtey and Hillsborough Correctional Institutions—house 780 male inmates and 292 female inmates, respectively.
- The enthusiasm for faith- and character-based programs has been overwhelming, evidenced by the more than 300 inmates on a waiting list to enter such a program.
- Of the more than 15,000 volunteers statewide, more than 600 support the Wakulla program with services and other resources.
- Programs available to inmates include Victim Impact Panels, life skills, personal growth, family life, parenting, AA, NA, mentoring, anger management, and MAD DADS (Men Against Destruction/Defending Against Drugs and Social-Disorder).
- Many different faiths are represented at Wakulla, including inmates with no faith preference. Some of the faiths include Christianity, Islam, Jehovah's Witnesses, Seventh-Day Adventist, Judaism, Mormonism, Nation of Islam, and Buddhism.
- State funds may be expended for programs that further secular goals, but not for programs that further religious indoctrination. All related religious materials are donated.
- While it is too soon to calculate recidivism rates, inmates in faith- and character-based programs have proven to have fewer fights, get fewer disciplinary reports, and may even have fewer crisis mental health events (seasonal depression, anxiety attacks, explosive anger, etc.).
- Twenty-one states are operating or developing faith-based residential programs, but among these:
  - Florida is the only state with an entirely faith- and character-based institution.
  - Florida is the only state where the duration of the program can last until release. The duration for other states is 12 to 18 months.

Source: Florida Department of Corrections, Wakulla Correctional Institution, http://www.dc.state.fl.us/secretary/press/2005/FaithBasedWakulla.html (accessed July 2014).

You are the chairperson of a congressional committee that has been asked to evaluate faith- and character-based prisons. How will you do this? Do you think that your committee and you will visit existing faith- and character-based prisons? Will your committee and you consider the following questions?

- How is it possible for a faith- and character-based prison to exist and still honor the separation of church and state?
- Could this type of program be placed in another prison (a unit or cellblock) if it were not state financed?

What other questions do you think you will consider? What will your final recommendations be?

Lawtey and Hillsborough, the two Florida faith- and character-based correctional institutions and found that overall, "staff, inmates, and volunteers overwhelmingly find value in the FCBI [faith- and character-based institution] model and believe that it is achieving its goals of changing inmate behaviors, preparing inmates for successful reentry, and ultimately reducing recidivism."[59]

PROVIDING SERVICES TO INMATES

In addition to treatment, prison authorities provide basic human services to inmates. In some cases, these services are the result of legal cases brought by inmates demanding better treatment. The courts have mandated that medical services, visitation with family, and the use of a sufficient law library are constitutional rights of prisoners.

Medical Services

Medical services have become one of the most important issues of corrections, particularly because of infectious disease (HIV, AIDS, hepatitis B, hepatitis C, tuberculosis), female health issues, and elderly prisoners'

Courtesy of Clem Bartollas

CAREERS IN CORRECTIONS

Cathy Fontenot
Assistant Warden of Programming, Louisiana State Penitentiary, Angola

"In August of 2002, I was promoted to assistant warden of programming at the Louisiana State Penitentiary, the state's largest and only maximum-security prison for adult males. The assistant warden of programming is responsible for all the services and programs afforded to inmates, such as recreation, chaplaincy, education, vocation, prerelease, visitation, classification, records, visitation, and mailroom, as well as the training academy. I have served as head public information and relations officer for the famous prison, which includes supervision over inmate media outlets like *The Angolite*, Angola's award-winning news magazine; KLSP, the nation's only FCC licensed radio station on prison grounds; and KLSP-TV, the prison's own television station. I've had the great fortune to work under the tenure of Warden Burl Cain, the longest-serving warden in America, and under his leadership have been involved with establishing progressive programming such as hospice, the on-site accredited branch of the New Orleans Baptist Theological Seminary college degree program, the 2013 ACA's Innovative Corrections Award recipient program, the New Orleans/LSP Court Ordered Reentry Workforce Development Program, the Louisiana State Penitentiary Museum, and the world-famous Angola Prison Rodeo and Arts and Crafts Festival. Many states and also international corrections systems, media, and tourists have visited us to see firsthand what we call moral rehabilitation at work."

See Chapter 15 for more detailed information on careers in corrections.

medical concerns. Key questions are: What kind of services should the state and the federal government provide for inmates? And what can the state and federal government afford? The quality of medical care varies from state to state and even from one prison to another within that state. Inmates suffer from a wide variety of health problems: An estimated 44 percent of state inmates and 39 percent of federal inmates reported a current medical problem other than a cold or virus. These include arthritis, hypertension, and other serious conditions.[60]

LO7 Evaluate the quality of prison services for inmates

While medical attention can be spotty, most inmates do get to see a medical professional for their health needs. Among inmates who reported a medical problem, more than 70 percent of state and federal inmates saw a medical professional; more than 8 in 10 inmates prisons report receiving a medical exam or a blood test since admission.[61]

MYTH Prisoners are kept away from their families, resulting in divorce and family breakup.

FACT Many states, including California, New York, and Connecticut, allow conjugal visits that give inmates private time with their families that can last up to two days.

Mental Health Services

Because a large portion of inmates suffer mental health problems, it is imperative that there are sufficient care workers and correctional counselors available to handle the mental health needs of the prison population. Recruiting treatment providers, such as psychiatrists who can prescribe medication and clinical psychologists who can do in-depth therapy at least for a brief period of time, is among the most pressing needs of the correctional system.

Visitation

Many inmates are married or have close families and friends, and a stay in prison strains relationships. To help inmates deal with the disruption caused by a prison sentence, most correctional institutes allow visitation privileges.

The quality of the visitation process has improved in recent years. Visiting arrangements tend to fall into the following categories: (a) closed visits, (b) limited-contact visits, (c) informal-contact visits, (d) freedom of grounds, and (e) conjugal or family visits. For a while, the general trend was to permit prisoners much more physical contact than they had been allowed in the past, but this trend began to change in the final years of the twentieth century.

conjugal visits A visit lasting one or two days during which prisoners can enjoy private visitation with their families.

Conjugal visits, or family visits, are permitted in a few states for inmates who have earned privileges. Conjugal visits usually mean that prisoners enjoy 24 or 48 hours of privacy with their families. A trailer is frequently provided for the visit. The spouse or other family member brings food to prepare, and a correctional officer checks on the inmate once a day or so. These programs have been expanded in most participating states to include female prisoners. Mississippi instituted a program of conjugal visitation in the 1950s, but recently the conjugal program in that state was ended; in 1968, the California Correctional Institution at Tehachapi instituted family visitation. More recently, Connecticut, New York, and Washington began programs of family visitation.

The Library

In recent years, prison libraries have been expanded and made available to all inmates. Inmates in most prisons are now permitted to obtain books from the state library if they are not available at the prison. In contrast to the days when the books were kept in the warden's office or in other inaccessible places, well-equipped law libraries generally are available for inmate use.

Handout/Mct/Landov

There are many prison industry programs operating around the nation. Here, federal inmates in Leavenworth disassemble old electronics at a prison industries recycling facility. Can this training help them get jobs on the outside in a world with high unemployment? Would someone hire an ex-inmate rather than a nonoffender even if the former had experience working in a prison industry?

Prison Industries

Several prison industries programs developed in the late nineteenth century: contract system, piece-price system, lease system, and public account system. The first three of these systems involved partnerships between the state and private business that resulted in marketing the goods produced by inmate labor to the public. The major difference in these systems was found in who supervised the inmate labor: the state supervised prisoners under the piece-price system; private business supervised inmates under the contract and lease systems. The public account system involved direct sales by state-run industries to the public.

Resistance from labor unions and local businesses resulted in the passage of state and federal law in the twentieth century that prohibited inmate-made goods from competition in the free market. The **Hawes-Cooper Act** of 1929 permitted states to bar out-of-state prison-made goods from sale in the receiving state. In 1935, the **Ashurst-Sumners Act** was enacted, making transportation of prison-made goods in interstate commerce a federal crime. The passage of this final piece of federal legislation resulted in most of those few states that had not yet adopted the state-use system soon doing so. These acts essentially put an end to the interstate transport of prison products, which means that the employment of prison labor has resulted in the production of materials exclusively for use in institutions of the state or its subdivisions and not for sale.

Hawes-Cooper Act The Hawes-Cooper Act was passed on January 19, 1929, and mandated that prison-made goods and merchandise transported from one state to another were to be subject to the existing laws of the importing state.

Ashurst-Sumners Act The 1935 Ashurst-Sumners Act was the product of cooperation between organized labor and business, and stemmed from the competition between the prisons and the free market.

There are several approaches to prison industry:

- *The prison provides space and a labor pool of inmates to hire.* With this model, a company supervises the inmates and makes all decisions related to personnel, wages, and products. An example of this is the Free Venture Model, a federal program that began in Connecticut and now extends to 16 states, which attempts to achieve productive labor with private-sector efficiency, wages, and relevance. The goal of the Free Venture Model is a realistic work environment with a full workday. Inmate wages are based on output, and training for job skills can be transferred to work in the community.[62] Another well-known example takes place at the Eastern Oregon Correctional Institution in Pendleton, Oregon. Oregon Corrections Enterprises is the employer, and inmates make a line of T-shirts, jeans, and jackets, known as Prison Blues.
- *The prison becomes a temporary personnel service.* One example of this is telemarketing from prison. About a dozen states, including Arizona, California, Iowa, and Oregon, have call centers in state and federal institutions in which inmates are employed in telemarketing jobs.[63]
- *The institution employs inmates for prison industry and pays them a wage.* Federal Prison Industries is the most noteworthy example of a correctional system developing a highly successful industrial program for inmates. FPI has continually made a profit through the sale of goods to federal agencies; it is entirely self-sustaining and operates without appropriating any funds. FPI pays prisoners reasonably well, at least in comparison with the pay they would receive in most state systems.

Typically, inmates choose to become involved in prison industry because it enables them to earn much-needed money, even though the hourly wages for most states are pitifully low. Inmates can make 20 to 30 cents an hour in state prisons, over $1.00 an hour in Federal Prisons Industries (UNICOR), or, if working for private industry in some prisons, $10 to $15 dollars an hour.

Making Correctional Treatment More Effective

LO8 Explain how treatment in prison can become more effective

Evaluation of education, vocation, and work programs indicates that they may be able to lower recidivism rates and increase postrelease employment.[64] Research shows that inmates who have completed higher levels of education find it easier to gain employment upon release and consequently are less likely to recidivate over long periods.[65]

It is also possible that a combination of efforts rather than a single approach can have beneficial results—such as combining institutional treatment with postrelease aftercare.[66] So although not all programs are successful for all inmates, many treatment programs are effective, and some participants, especially younger clients, have a better chance of success on the outside than those who forgo treatment.[67]

Effective programs are set up by an inspired individual or group of individuals, have unified teamwork on the part of the staff, have a transmittable philosophy of life, trust offenders with decision-making responsibilities, help offenders develop

EXHIBIT 10.4

Principles and Components of Effective Programs

- Teach interpersonal skills.
- Teach academic skills training, which includes adult basic education and general equivalency diplomas. This teaches the offender how to participate in education activities and how to read, write, and utilize basic arithmetic.
- Provide vocational skills training, which teaches how to acquire and maintain employment in order to fulfill financial obligations and how to engage in purposeful activity and postrelease employment.
- Make use of behavioral modification techniques.
- Use cognitive-behavioral therapy. This focuses on engaging in accurate self-appraisal and goal setting, solving problems effectively, maintaining self-control, and displaying prosocial values.
- Stress improving moral reasoning.
- Offer sex-offender interventions, particularly cognitive restructuring, which teaches the inmate to control self-destructive or other destructive behavior.
- Provide drug abuse treatment. Combine in-prison therapeutic communities with follow-up community treatment.

Sources: David Wilson, Leana Bouffard, and Doris Mackenzie, "A Quantitative Review of Structured, Group-Oriented, Cognitive-Behavioral Programs for Offenders," *Criminal Justice and Behavior* 32 (2005): 172–204; Mark Lipsey and David Wilson, "Effective Intervention for Serious Juvenile Offenders: A Synthesis of Research," in *Serious and Violent Juvenile Offenders: Risk Factors and Successful Interventions*, ed. Rolf Loeber and David Farrington (Thousand Oaks, CA: Sage Publications, 1998); Joan Petersilia, *When Prisoners Come Home* (New York: Oxford University Press, 2003), pp. 176–177.

needed skills, are regarded as unique and different by offenders, avoid conflict with formal decision makers, avoid isolation from social institutions (such as the family and the school), and provide a support network following release or graduation (see Exhibit 10.4).[68]

The strategy for improving the effectiveness of correctional treatment has argued for some time that it is necessary to discover what works for which offenders in what contexts. In other words, correctional treatment could work if *amenable* offenders were offered *appropriate* treatment by *matched* workers in environments *conducive* to producing maximal effects.

Accordingly, if offenders are placed in the right programs at the optimal time for them to benefit from treatment, then program integrity becomes a matter of major importance.[69] Program integrity requires that effective intervention delivers the services to the offenders that they claim to deliver, that treatment has sufficient strength to accomplish goals, that program personnel are equipped to deliver the specified services, and that treatment is not only matched to the interest and needs of offenders but has the flexibility to be modified according to the changing interests and needs of offenders.[70] Effective implementation of treatment ultimately depends on research to provide the information on who should get what treatment, when treatment is best given, and what frequency and intensity of treatment are necessary. It would certainly appear that the increasingly wide use of evidence-based practices will improve the effectiveness of correctional treatment.

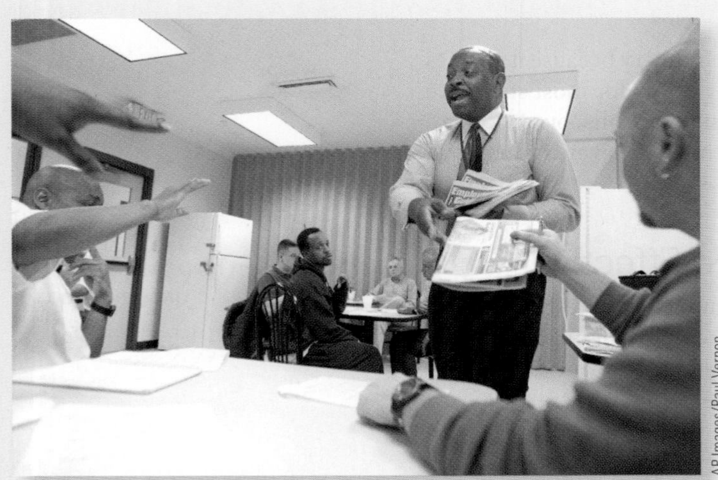
AP Images/Paul Vernon

Community correctional centers enable residents to keep jobs in the community, helping to maintain their bond to family and friends. Here, William Palmer, employment services representative with Alvis House Community Corrections Center, passes out copies of the employment guide to Alvis House residents during an education consulting session at a facility in Columbus, Ohio.

VOICES ACROSS THE PROFESSION

Corrections is an ever-changing, rewarding, and challenging profession that demands physical and mental toughness balanced with true compassion for those in need.

Cathy Fontenot
Assistant Warden of Programming, Louisiana State Penitentiary, Angola

I am passionate about the work we are doing to allow victims to live without or with less fear, to break the cycle of violence in individuals, families, and communities, and to dedicate my life to the service of my coworkers, family, friends, and the public. Corrections is an ever-changing, rewarding, and challenging profession that demands physical and mental toughness balanced with true compassion for those in need. We are working to improve recidivism results through creative programming aimed at using inmate lifers as mentors to short-term offenders destined for release. We strive to enhance professional development opportunities and training techniques among our correctional officers, staff, and volunteers. I remain excited by the many ways we can reassure and educate the public of the many successes modern correctional environments are able to achieve in reentry preparation and in creating less violent prisons.

SUMMARY

LO1 Identify the role of treatment and services in prisons today
The role of treatment and services in prisons today is to provide opportunities for inmates to profit from confinement and to provide adequate, basic care of inmates.

LO2 Discuss classification for treatment
The role of classification is to define the needs of inmates as well as the available programs that can meet those needs.

LO3 Discuss the individual-level treatment programs
The three main individual techniques used within the prison include insight-based therapy, behavior therapy, and cognitive-behavior therapy. The treatment programs that are offered within prisons today tend to be more drug- and behavior-oriented than in the past and much less based on psychological models and insight.

LO4 Identify the group programs held in prisons
The therapeutic community (TC) and anger management programs are two of the most widely used group treatments in prison. The therapeutic community approach focuses on the total environment and uses all the experiences of that environment as the basic tools for therapeutic intervention. Anger management programs are designed to help inmates manage their inappropriate anger outbursts.

LO5 Discuss inmate self-help programs
Inmate self-help programs are run primarily by the inmates and are designed to help inmates improve themselves, such as anger management, or express ethnic or cultural goals.

LO6 Evaluate the quality of prison programs for inmates
Prison programs include academic education, vocational training, and religious instruction and services. The quality of these programs varies from one prison to another, but they do face the problem that prison overcrowding makes it difficult for inmates to have available popular vocational training programs.

LO7 Evaluate the quality of prison services for inmates
The constitutionally mandated services provided to inmates include medical services, visitation, the library, and recreation. Inmates have long complained about some of these services, especially medical care, but overall they have recently been provided quality medical care.

LO8 Explain how treatment in prison can become more effective
If offenders are placed in the right programs at the optimal time for them to benefit from treatment, the likelihood increases that they will benefit from treatment. It is also possible that a combination of efforts rather than a single approach can have beneficial results.

CRITICAL THINKING QUESTIONS

1. Would you support giving inmates with psychological issues mood altering drugs to maintain or control their behavior?
2. In some prisons, inmates receive excellent care. Is it fair for them to receive better medical care than many citizens in the community?
3. Do you think that prisoners should have to pay for their food, board, medical care, and other services? Why or why not?
4. You are inside. The parole board tells you to get some therapy. Every choice mentioned in this chapter is available to you. Which will you choose? Why?
5. Is it exploitation of inmates for prison industries to make large profits but pay inmates so little?

NOTES

1. California Department of Corrections and Rehabilitation, *Staff News: Communicating with Professionals in Corrections and Parole*, December 15, 2006, pp. 1, 7.
2. Ibid.
3. Kevin Johnson, "Prison Diving Program Anchors Former Inmates," *USA Today*, July 14, 2008. For a more recent article, see "Program Offers California Inmates A Second Chance Through Diving," CBS SF Bay Area, February 8, 2012, http://sanfrancisco.cbslocal.com/2012/02/06/program-offers-california-inmates-a-second-chance-through-diving/ (accessed July 2014).
4. Maryland State Department of Education, http://marylandpublicschools.org/msde/ (accessed July 2014).
5. Statements recently expressed to one of the authors by inmates he interviewed in various prisons across the nation.
6. Rudiger Ortmann, "The Effectiveness of Social Therapy in Prison: A Randomized Experiment," *Crime and Delinquency* 46 (April 2000): 214–232.
7. Robert Martinson, "What Works? Questions and Answers About Prison Reform," *Public Interest* (Spring 1974): 21–54.
8. Douglas Lipton, Robert Martinson, and Judith Wilks, *The Effectiveness of Correctional Treatment: A Survey of Treatment Valuation Studies* (New York: Praeger Press, 1974).
9. Paul Gendreau and Robert Ross, " Effective Correctional Treatment: Bibliotherapy for Cynics," *Crime and Delinquency* 27 (1979): 463–489.
10. Robert R. Ross and Paul Gendreau, eds., *Effective Correctional Treatment* (Toronto: Butterworth, 1980), p. viii; Paul Gendreau and Robert R. Ross, "Revivification or Rehabilitative Evidence," *Justice Quarterly* 4 (September 1987): 349–407.
11. Robert Martinson, "New Findings, New Views: A Note of Caution Regarding Sentencing Reform," *Hofstra Law Review* 7 (1979): 244.
12. Mark W. Lipsey and Francis T. Cullen, "The Effectiveness of Correctional Rehabilitation: A Review of Systematic Reviews," *Annual Review of Law and Social Science* 3 (2007): 297–320. See also Francis T. Cullen, "The Twelve People Who Saved Rehabilitation: How the Science of Criminology Made a Difference," *Criminology* 43 (2005): 1–42; Doris Layton MacKenzie, *What Works in Corrections: Reducing the Criminal Activities of Offenders and Delinquents* (New York: Cambridge University Press, 2006); Edward E. Rhine, Tina L. Mawhorr, and Evalyn C. Parks, "Implementation: The Bane of Effective Correctional Programs," *Criminology and Public Policy* 5 (2006): 347–358.
13. Patricia Van Voorhis, Michael Braswell, and David Lester, *Correctional Counseling and Rehabilitation*, 6th ed. (Cincinnati: Anderson, 2007), pp. 137, 146.
14. Office of the Inspector General, "Select Application Controls Review of the Federal Bureau of Prisons Sentry Database System," July 2003, http://www.usdoj.gov/oig/reports/BOP/a0325/app8.htm (accessed July 2014).
15. Doris James and Lauren Glaze, *Mental Health Problems of Prison and Jail Inmates* (Washington, DC: Bureau of Justice Statistics, 2006), http://bjs.ojp.usdoj.gov/content/pub/pdf/mhppji.pdf (accessed July 2014).
16. Eve Kupersauin, "Inmates Getting MH Care, but Quality Unknown," *Psychiatric News* 36 (2001): 6.
17. James and Glaze, *Mental Health Problems of Prison and Jail Inmates*.
18. Gerald G. Gaes, Timothy J. Flanagan, Lawrence L. Motiuk, and Lynn Stewart, "Adult Correctional Treatment," in *Crime and Justice, 26th Edition: Prisons*, ed. Michael Tonry and Joan Petersilia (Chicago: University of Chicago Press, 1999), pp. 374–375.
19. Harvey Milkman and Kenneth Wanberg, *Cognitive-Behavioral Treatment: A Review and Discussion for Correctional Professionals* (Washington, DC: National Institute of Corrections, 2007), p. 5.
20. Ibid.
21. Sesha Kethineni, and Jeremy Braithwaite, "The Effects of a Cognitive-Behavioral Program for At-Risk Youth: Changes in Attitudes, Social Skills, Family, and Community and Peer Relationships," *Victims and Offenders* 6 (2011): 93–116.
22. Patricia Van Voorhis, Lisa M. Spruance, P. Neal Ritchey, Shelley Johnson Listwan, and Renita Seabrook, "The Georgia Cognitive Skills Experiment: A Replication of Reasoning and Rehabilitation," *Criminal Justice and Behavior* 31 (2004): 282–305.
23. Ibid.
24. Ibid.
25. Ibid.
26. Frank S. Pearson, Douglas S. Lipton, Charles M. Cleland, and Dorline S. Yee, "The Effects of Behavioral/Cognitive-Behavioral Programs on Recidivism," *Crime and Delinquency* 48 (2002): 476–496.
27. Milkman and Wanberg, *Cognitive-Behavioral Treatment*, p. xix.
28. Ibid.
29. Pearson, Lipton, Cleland, and Yee, "The Effects of Behavioral/Cognitive-Behavioral Programs on Recidivism."
30. Dianna Newbern, Donald Dansereau, and Urvashi Pitre, "Positive Effects on Life Skills Motivation and Self-Efficacy: Node-Link Maps in a Modified Therapeutic Community," *American Journal of Drug and Alcohol Abuse* 25 (1999): 407–410.
31. Federal Bureau of Prisons, *Substance Abuse Treatment*, http://www.bop.gov/inmates/custody_and_care/substance_abuse_treatment.jsp (accessed July 2014).
32. Ibid.
33. Stephen J. Bahr, Amber L. Master, and Brian M. Taylor, "What Works in Substance Abuse Treatment Programs for Offenders?" *Prison Journal* (December 2012): 12–14.
34. Maxwell Jones, *Social Psychiatry in Prison* (Baltimore: Penguin Books, 1968).
35. Michael Prendergast, David Farabee, and Jerome Cartier, "The Impact of In-Prison Therapeutic Community Programs on Prison Management," *Journal of Offender Rehabilitation* 32 (2001): 3–78.

36. Personal conversation with facility staff, March 28, 2012.
37. Ibid.
38. Gerald Melnick, Josephine Hawke, and Harry K. Wexler, "Client Perceptions of Prison-Based Therapeutic Community Drug-Treatment Programs," *Prison Journal* 84 (2004): 121–127.
39. George De Leon, Gerald Melnick, George Thomas, David Kressel, and Harry K. Wexler, "Motivation for Treatment in a Prison-Based Therapeutic Community," *American Journal of Drug and Alcohol Abuse* 26 (2000): 33–46.
40. W. N. Welsh and G. Zajac, "A Census of Prison-Based Drug Treatment Programs: Implications for Programming, Policy, and Evaluation," *Crime and Delinquency* 50 (2004): 108–133.
41. Ibid.
42. Steven D. Vannoy and William T. Hoyt, "Evaluation of an Anger Therapy Intervention for Incarcerated Adult Males," *Journal of Offender Rehabilitation* 39 (2004): 40.
43. Vannoy and Hoyt, "Evaluation of an Anger Therapy Intervention for Incarcerated Adult Males," p. 40.
44. For animal programs in prison, see Gennifer Furst, *Animal Programs in Prison: A Comprehensive Assessment* (Boulder, CO: Lynne Rienner Publishers, 2011).
45. Ibid.
46. One of the authors talked with this inmate when he came off segregation and has followed his career, February 17, 2014.
47. Gaes, Flanagan, Motiuk, and Stewart, "Adult Correctional Treatment," pp. 374–375.
48. Lauren O'Neill, Doris Layton MacKenzie, and David M. Bierie, "Educational Opportunities Within Correctional Institutions: Does Facility Type Matter?" *Prison Journal* (2007): 311–327; J. Bouffard, D. L. MacKenzie, and L. Hickman, "Effectiveness of Vocational Education and Employment Programs for Adult Offenders: A Methodology-Based Analysis of the Literature," *Journal of Offender Rehabilitation* 31 (2000): 1–41; David B. Wilson, Catherine A. Gallagher, and Doris L. MacKenzie, "A Meta-Analysis of Corrections-Based Education, Vocation, and Work Programs for Adult Offenders," *Journal of Research in Crime and Delinquency* 47 (2000): 347–368.
49. Stephen J. Steurer, Linda Smith, and Alice Tracy, *OCE/CEA: Three-State Recidivism Study*, report submitted to the Office of Correctional Education (Washington, DC: Correctional Education Association; Department of Education, 2001).
50. Ibid.
51. Joshua Page, "Eliminating the Enemy: The Import of Denying Prisoners Access to Higher Education in Clinton's America," *Punishment and Society* 6 (2004): 357–378.
52. United States General Accounting Office, *Prisoner Releases: Reintegration of Offenders into Communities* (Washington, DC: U.S. General Accounting Office: 2001).
53. Federal Bureau of Prisons, UNICOR, http://www.bop.gov/inmates/custody_and_care/unicor.jsp (accessed July 2014).
54. Florida Department of Corrections, "Want to Know More About Our Inmate Dog Training Programs?" http://www.dc.state.fl.us/apps/utopia/learn.html (accessed July 2014).
55. Dan Benson, "Prison Job Fair Gives Inmates a Rehearsal for Life Outside," *Journal Sentinel*, September 29, 2008.
56. Wilson, Gallagher, and MacKenzie, "A Meta-Analysis of Corrections-Based Education, Vocation, and Work Programs for Adult Offenders," p. 361.
57. Ibid.
58. Corrections Corporation of America, "Inmate Programming with Corrections Corporation of America," http://cca.com/Media/Default/documents/CCA-Resource-Center/Inmate_Program_Overview.pdf (accessed July 2014).
59. LaVigne, Brazzell, and Small, *Evaluation of Florida s'Faith- and Character-Based Institutions: Final Report*.
60. Bureau of Justice Statistics, *Medical Problems of Prisoners* (Washington, DC: U.S. Department of Justice, 2008).
61. Ibid.
62. Connecticut Department of Corrections, *Free Venture Model in Correction* (Hartford, CT: Department of Corrections, n.d.).
63. Jon Swartz, "Inmates vs. Outsourcing," *USA Today*, July 6, 2004.
64. Wilson, Gallagher, and MacKenzie, "A Meta-Analysis of Corrections-Based Education, Vocation, and Work Programs for Adult Offenders," pp. 347–368.
65. Mary Ellen Batiuk, Paul Moke, and Pamela Wilcox Rountree, "Crime and Rehabilitation: Correctional Education as an Agent of Change—A Research Note," *Justice Quarterly* 14 (1997): 167–180.
66. Megan Kurlychek and Cynthia Kempinen, "Beyond Boot Camp: The Impact of Aftercare on Offender Reentry," *Criminology and Public Policy* 5 (2006): 363–388.
67. David Farrington and Brandon Welsh, "Randomized Experiments in Criminology: What Have We Learned in the Last Two Decades?" *Journal of Experimental Criminology* 1 (2005): 9–38.
68. Dr. Martin Groder, the late psychiatrist and pioneer of therapeutic communities, advocated these common elements of effective programs throughout his career. We discussed these principles during interviews one of the authors had with Dr. Groder; the last was in 2002.
69. Evidence-based practices are one of the common requirements of correctional programs today; this has to do with referring and using other programs that have been found to be effective. See Edward J. Latessa, "The Challenge of Change: Correctional Programs and Evidence-Based Practices," *Criminology and Public Policy* 4 (2004): 547–560.
70. See Lipsey and Cullen, "The Effect of Correctional Rehabilitation: A Review of Systematic Reviews," pp. 297–320.

Jeffrey Mark Deskovic with one of his lawyers, Barry Scheck, at a news conference, September 20, 2006, upon his release from prison. Deskovic was wrongly imprisoned for 16 years for killing a young girl; another man, Steven Cunningham, was the actual killer.

IN 1997, STEVEN CUNNINGHAM, while serving a 20-to-life sentence for murder, told authorities that he had also killed a 15-year-old girl named Angela Correa 10 years earlier. His confession (along with DNA evidence) eventually helped clear Jeffrey Mark Deskovic, one of Correa's high school classmates, who was wrongfully imprisoned for 16 years for the crime. Retesting of DNA recovered from Correa's body had matched it to Cunningham. Cunningham at first denied his role in the killing, but eventually confessed to raping and strangling Correa, a sophomore at Peekskill High School in New York.[1]

Deskovic, like many freed inmates, struggled to rebuild his life. For six months, he got by on $137 a month in disability checks and $150 in food stamps from the federal government. Earning money through speech and newspaper articles about wrongful convictions, he paid rent for the first time in his life, for an apartment the county subsidized because of his depression and posttraumatic stress disorder. He enrolled at Mercy College in Dodds Ferry, New York, on a $22,000 scholarship, but found relationships with females as well as his male peers difficult.[2]

While some correctional experts believe that anyone can be successfully treated and rehabilitated in prison, others point to repeat killers such as Steven Cunningham and say that they are untreatable, unrepentant, and should never be released or paroled. There is little if any evidence that incarceration reduces an offender's risk of reoffending upon return to the community.[3] Cunningham knew another innocent man had been convicted for a crime he himself had committed, but chose to say and do nothing for 16 years, even though he was already in prison! Perhaps he thought that he might one day be paroled and a second murder conviction would ruin his chances for early release. Should violent criminals ever be given the chance of early release? Is it fair to the victim of the crime and/or future victims?

11 Parole and Release to the Community

MICHAEL LLOYD/The Oregonian/Landov

LEARNING OBJECTIVES

 LO1 Describe parole practices today

 LO2 Discuss how the parole board functions

 LO3 Identify the rules for parolees released to the community

 LO4 Summarize the procedures involved in the revocation of parole

 LO5 Describe why people fail on parole

 LO6 Identify some of the rights that ex-offenders have lost

PREVIEW OF **KEY CONCEPTS**

ticket of leave
parole
discretionary parole
mandatory parole release
parole board
parole guidelines
intensive supervision parole (ISP)
technical violations
Morrissey v. Brewer
revocation of parole
disenfranchisement laws

Parole is one of the most controversial aspects of the criminal justice process. What makes parole so controversial is that there are offenders such as Steven Cunningham who, in the public's mind, should never be let out of prison, while others such as Jeffrey Mark Deskovic should not be in prison at all. Some people find it offensive when a notorious child killer is even considered for early release even though there is evidence that they have been model prisoners. Take the case of Eric M. Smith, who was denied parole in 2014 for the seventh straight time. In 1993, when he was 13 years old, Smith was convicted of killing 4-year-old Derrick Robie in Steuben County, New York. He was 13 when he lured Derrick into a wooded area near the boy's home, strangled him, smashed his head with a rock, and sodomized him with a stick. After looking over the facts, the parole board said the "serious and brutal" crime is more compelling than Smith's clean disciplinary record, positive prison programming, and release plans. Smith is next scheduled to appear before the parole board in April 2016.[4] Was the parole board correct in denying Smith parole? If someone is kept in prison for more than 20 years for an act they committed when they were 13 years old, why even bother considering parole? If they haven't changed sufficiently in 20 years, what makes anyone think they can change in 22? And is the nature of the crime more important when considering parole than the nature of the parolee? These are all important questions to be answered.

This chapter considers the problems and possibilities of parole, including other means of returning inmates to the community. We will first discuss parole practices and then examine the importance of reentry for ex-offenders leaving prison.

PAROLE PRACTICES

As you may recall (Chapter 1), the origins of parole can be traced to the work of Alexander Maconochie, superintendent of a penal colony on Norfolk Island, Australia. Maconochie issued "marks" encouraging positive behavior and let inmates serve their sentences in stages, each increasing in responsibility. The final stage was a **ticket of leave.**

ticket of leave In Maconochie's system of graduated release, this was the final stage.

Later, influenced by Maconochie, Sir Walter Crofton established the "Irish mark system" in which inmates could earn early release by positive behavior (see Exhibit 11.1). The Irish mark system was well received, appeared to have low rates of recidivism, and penologists from the United States began to urge bringing these ideas of graduated release to the United States.[5]

EXHIBIT 11.1

Irish Mark System

In 1854, Walter Crofton, a retired navy officer, was sent to introduce the progressive state system at the prison at Mountjoy, near Dublin. The complete program became known as the Irish mark system. The system applied to convicts serving terms of three years or more.

- The first stage was eight or nine months, depending on the convict's conduct. The first three months was spent in solitary confinement (no work) and on reduced rations (no meat). After that, he would be put on full rations and given sedentary but unskilled labor. Service and instruction would expose him to religion and literacy classes to make sure he would not leave prison without knowing how to read and write.

(*continued*)

- When fully eligible for the second stage, the prisoner would be moved to Spike Island, off the southern coast of Ireland, or if he happened to be skilled at a craft, to a construction site at Philipstown, where convicts were building a new prison. The second stage included four classes: third, second, first, and the "advanced" class. In each class, a prisoner had to earn good marks for a maximum of nine a month—three for good conduct, three for good work on an assigned job, and three for intelligence. Prisoners were punished for rule violations by the loss of marks. Time in the advanced class was determined by the length of the sentence to be served and the number of marks awarded. With a maximum number of marks, a sentence of 15 years could be served in 10 years.
- The third or intermediate stage was spent at Luck Common, 15 miles from Dublin, where convicts were housed in dormitories, worked at land reclamation, and were given vocational training to fit them for employment when finally released. This was minimum custody confinement.
- In the final stage, prisoners were released on license or "ticket of leave" when it was felt they were so changed in attitude and behavior that they would be unlikely to return to crime. Just to be certain, they were required to report periodically to the police. The license expired at the conclusion of the sentence. They were made to understand that if there were signs of a relapse into criminal ways, they would be returned to prison.

Source: Mary Carpenter, *Reformatory Prison Discipline, as Developed by the Rt. Hon. Sir Walter Crofton* (London: Longman, Greer, Green, and Dyer, 1872), pp. 5–22.

parole The conditional release from confinement of an offender serving an indeterminate sentence.

Zebulon R. Brockway presented a paper on the Irish mark system at the First Correctional Congress in 1870, and when he was appointed superintendent of Elmira Reformatory (opened in 1876), he adopted the mark system. Brockway would release inmates conditionally to the community once they demonstrated reformation, and there they would be supervised by state agents. Parole, as it was called, rapidly spread across the United States. But it was not until 1944 that all states had adopted the indeterminate sentence and the use of parole.

© Chester Higgins Jr./*New York Times*/Redux

After many years behind bars, nothing seems familiar to parolees. The pace of life sometimes startles them, causing them to feel like outsiders in their own communities. The Fortune Society is dedicated to helping inmates make a successful adjustment back into society and believes in a world where all who are at-risk, incarcerated, or formerly incarcerated can become positive, contributing members of society. Their work supports successful reentry of formerly incarcerated men and women and promotes alternatives to incarceration. In this photo, Betty Wilson teaches Nolen Ruiz how to make vegetarian lasagna at the Fortune Society, where former prisoners can learn to cook for their families.

Extent of Parole Today

Today, most inmates return to society and try to resume their lives. For the majority of these inmates, their reintegration into society comes by way of **parole**—the planned community release and supervision of incarcerated offenders before the expiration of their full prison sentences. Parole is a vast enterprise (see Figure 11.1). Consider the most recent data available (2012):

- The total adult parole population was more than 850,000, with nearly 1 million adults moving onto or off parole during the year.
- Both parole entries (down 9 percent) and exits (down 7 percent) declined between 2011 and 2012.
- The state parole population fell about 0.6 percent, from an estimated 745,000 to 740,400, while the federal parole population grew 3.5 percent, from 107,000 to about 110,000.
- Fifty-eight percent of parolees completed their term of supervision or were discharged.
- The reincarceration rate among parolees at risk for violating their conditions of supervision continued to decline, dropping to 9 percent from about 12 percent in 2011.[6]

FIGURE 11.1

Estimated Parole Entries and Exits

Source: Bureau of Justice Statistics, Annual Parole Survey, 2000–2012.

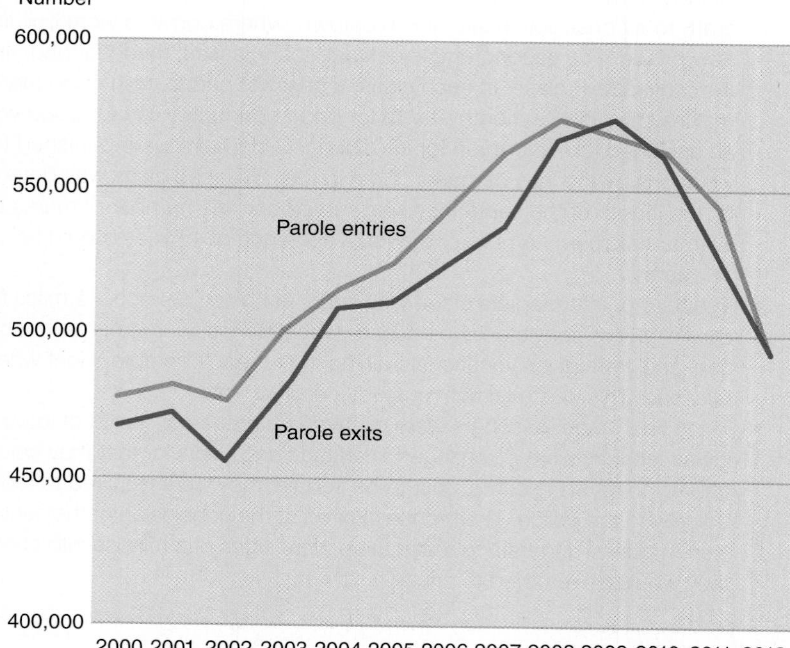

Describe parole practices today **LO1**

Principles of Parole

Regardless of its format, parole is based on the following principles:

- The state extends to offenders a privilege by releasing them from prison before their full sentence is served.
- The state also enters a release contract with offenders in exchange for their promise to abide by certain conditions.
- Offenders who violate the law or the conditions of parole can be returned to prison to complete their sentences.
- The state retains control of parolees until they are dismissed from parole.

Types of Parole

The format of parole is determined by statutory requirement. In indeterminate sentencing states, after an inmate has served the minimum sentence his or her case is reviewed by a parole board, a duly constituted body of men and women who review inmate cases and determine whether offenders have reached a rehabilitative level sufficient to deal with the outside world. The board also dictates what specific parole rules parolees must obey. After reviewing the case, they have the discretion to release the inmate to serve the remainder of his or her sentence in the community.

discretionary parole The decision to release inmates is made by a parole board.

mandatory parole release Inmate is released on parole when the unserved portion of the maximum prison term equals good time.

This use of **discretionary parole** has been abolished in 13 states and the federal government, and four states have abolished discretionary parole for certain offenses (see Exhibit 11.2 for the states that have abolished it). In the remaining jurisdictions that use determinate sentencing models, the amount of time a person must remain in prison is a predetermined percentage of the sentence, assuming there are no infractions or escape attempts. Referred to as **mandatory parole release**, under this model the inmate is released when the unserved portion of the maximum prison term equals his or her earned good time (less time served in jail awaiting trial).[7] See Figure 11.2 for the percentage of parolees by type of release.

Most inmates leave prison before the completion of their sentence and are placed on parole. Here, Michael Franzese (left), a former captain in the Colombo crime family, leaves the ball park after coaching an all-star Little League team. Franzese spent three years in federal prison in the late 1980s for racketeering and tax conspiracy. Then, he says, he decided to leave the Mafia. Much to his surprise and that of many law enforcement officials, the decision has not proven fatal. After another stint in prison for parole violation from 1991 to 1994, Franzese says he left his life of crime and has planted new roots in Los Angeles—promoting hip-hop concerts, developing real estate, and pursuing his true passion, coaching Little League baseball.

FIGURE 11.2

Entries to Parole by Type of Entry

Source: Bureau of Justice Statistics, Annual Parole Survey, 2000–2012. In some states, sentences can be reduced by more than half with a combination of statutory and earned good time. If the conditions of their release are violated, mandatory releasees can have their good time revoked and be returned to the institution to serve the remainder of their unexpired term.

Entries to parole, by type of entry, 2000–2012

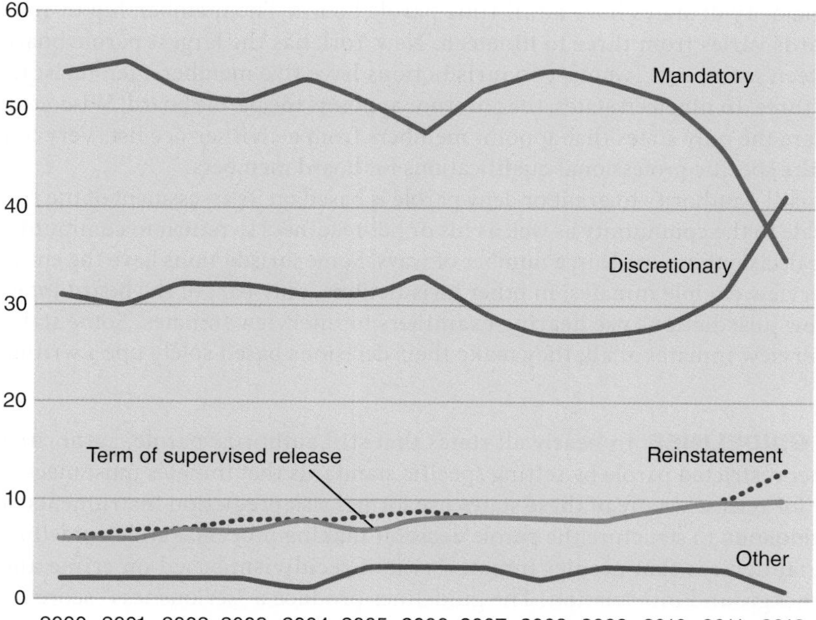

EXHIBIT 11.2

The Abolition of Discretionary Parole

All Offenders	Certain Violent Offenders
Arizona	Alaska
Delaware	Louisiana
Federal government	New York
Florida	Tennessee
Indiana	
Kansas	
Maine	
Minnesota	
Mississippi	
North Carolina	
Oregon	
Virginia	
Washington	
Wisconsin	

MYTH Every inmate, save those serving life for murder, has a right to get parole if they behave well in prison.

FACT The Supreme Court has ruled that there is no legal right to parole. All inmates are entitled to is an opportunity to be heard by a parole-granting authority and a statement of reasons if their parole is denied.

The remaining inmates are released for a variety of reasons, including expiration of their term, commutation of their sentence, and court orders to relieve overcrowded prisons.[8] In a few instances, inmates are released after their sentence has been commuted by a board of pardons or directly by a governor or even the president of the United States. About 15 percent of prison inmates are released after serving their entire maximum sentence without any time excused or forgiven. And despite the efforts of correctional authorities, about 7,000 inmates escape every year from state and federal prisons (the number of escapes is actually declining, due in part to better officer training and more sophisticated security measures).[9]

Describe how the parole board functions **LO2**

The Parole Board

The capricious and arbitrary manner in which parole boards, especially in the past, decided when an inmate was ready for release had drawn strong criticism from inmates, prison reformers, and practitioners in the criminal justice system. The riot of Attica in 1971 and the subsequent report that identified parole as a source of inmate discontent have also contributed to the unfavorable scrutiny of parole boards. The unfairness of parole boards is legendary among inmates. Stories defying logic are told of how nondrinking inmates have been turned down for parole until they agree to join an Alcoholics Anonymous group in the prison. In addition, there has been a tendency to blame the parole board when a parolee commits a serious crime in the community, especially a sex offense.

parole board An official panel that determines whether an inmate serving an indeterminate sentence is ready for parole.

The **parole board** is administered by an independent agency (autonomous model) or is part of a single large department that runs all state correctional programs (consolidated model). The parole board is an independent agency in all but five states (Maryland, Michigan, Minnesota, Ohio, and Texas), but parole field services are administered by the department of corrections in two-thirds of the states.

The duties of the parole board are as follows:

- To select and place prisoners on parole
- To aid, supervise, and provide continuing control of parolees in the community
- To determine when the parole function is completed and to discharge from parole
- To determine whether parole should be revoked, if violations of conditions occur

The majority of states have a full-time parole board. The membership of state parole boards varies from three to nineteen. New York has the largest parole board with nineteen members. Twenty-two jurisdictions have five members; ten jurisdictions have three. In nineteen states, the governor appoints the parole board; Wisconsin and Ohio are the only states that appoint members from a civil service list. Very few states require specific professional qualifications for board members.

Web App 11.1
Go to your state's Division of Parole website to learn about the parole board. Suggest the characteristics of offenders that should be paroled. Are there offenders who should *not* be paroled? **LO2**

The board's authority to grant or deny parole is based on its assessment of the risk of the inmate to the community as well as his or her readiness to return to community life. Parole decisions are made in a number of ways. Some jurisdictions have the entire board interview eligible inmates; in other jurisdictions, only part of the board interviews. A few jurisdictions use hearing examiners to interview inmates. Some states do not interview inmates at all; they make their decisions based solely upon written reports.

parole guidelines Actuarial devices predicting the risk of recidivism based on information about the offender and the crime.

PAROLE GUIDELINES In nearly all states that still authorize parole, authorities have further restricted parole by setting specific standards that inmates must meet to be eligible for release. Many of these states use formal risk prediction instruments or **parole guidelines** to structure the parole decision-making process. Parole guidelines are actuarial devices that predict inmates' risk of recidivism based on crime and offender background information. The guidelines produce a "seriousness" score for each offender by summing the points assigned for various background characteristics (higher scores mean greater risk). Prisoners with the least serious crimes and the lowest statistical probability of reoffending are the first to be released.[10]

Many guidelines are based on the U.S. Parole Commission's salient factor score (SFS). In use since 1981, the salient factor score is based on:

- Number of previous convictions/adjudications
- Number of previous commitments that were more than 30 days
- Age at current offense
- Recent three-year prison commitment-free period
- Heroin/opiate or other drug dependency
- Whether inmate is older

The SFS places the inmate in one of four risk categories: very good, good, fair, or poor. Accordingly, parole officials consider this score in deciding whether parole is to be granted and, if so, what level of supervision will be needed.[11]

Despite these advantages, few states currently rely primarily on parole guidelines or risk prediction instruments for making release decisions. Maryland, Ohio, Pennsylvania, Virginia, and Washington do still use risk assessment instruments, but in each of these instances, risk assessment scores are strictly advisory.[12]

CRITICAL THINKING

If you had to create five new parole guidelines for today's offenders, what would they be? Would you allow sex offenders to be paroled? Drug offenders? Murderers? What factors would be the basis for your release decision? LO2

PAROLE GRANT HEARINGS Discretionary parole decisions are made at a parole grant hearing. At this hearing, the full board or a selected subcommittee reviews information, may meet with the offender, and then decides whether the parole applicant has a reasonable probability of succeeding outside of prison. Each parole board has its own way of reviewing cases.

In a few states, such as Ohio, parole board members meet face to face with the applicant before a decision is made. A face-to-face meeting can be beneficial because the hearing panel can get feedback from inmates to more thoroughly evaluate parole readiness. Parole board officials, many of whom have varied professional training and experience, can use these meetings to assess an inmate's sincerity and readiness for release.[13] In addition, parole boards will look at the inmate's crime, institutional record, and willingness to accept responsibility before making the release decision. Some jurisdictions rely on standardized tests that predict whether a potential parolee may recidivate upon release.[14] Inmates who maintain their innocence may find that denying responsibility for their crimes places their release date in jeopardy. The requirement that they admit guilt or culpability is especially vexing for those inmates who are actually innocent and who actively refuse to accept their institutional label of "convicted criminal."[15]

One of the major issues concerning parole board decision making is whether it has racial disparity effects. Kathryn D. Morgan and Brent Smith's study of parole in Alabama found that race did not have a significant impact on decisions at the preliminary screening stage or the parole release stage. They found that 42 percent of the African American inmates up for parole were released, compared to 43 percent of the white inmates, a finding that supports equal treatment in the parole grant decision.[16]

Most states have recently taken measures to ensure due process at parole grant hearings. For example, about half of the states now permit counsel to be present and witnesses to be called. Verbatim transcripts are frequently kept of the hearings. Furthermore, inmates are typically provided with both a written and an oral explanation of the parole decision. However, inmates continue to be denied access to their files, which means they are unable to determine why their case was decided the way it was.

AP Images/Elise Amendola

Inmate Frederick Christian speaks on his own behalf during a hearing before the state parole board in Natick, Massachusetts. Christian had been in prison for 20 years for a premeditated robbery that resulted in two dead and one injured. His parole request was granted in a 6–0 vote.

Identify the rules for parolees released to the community **LO3**

Characteristics of Those on Parole

Regardless of the method of their release, former inmates face the formidable task of having to readjust to society. This means regaining legal rights they may have lost on their conviction, reestablishing community and family ties, and finding employment. After being in prison, these goals are often difficult to achieve. The typical characteristics of adults on parole are that they are predominantly male; are divided between white and African American as well as a strong Hispanic or Latino representation; are being supervised by a parole officer and have a sentence length of one year or more; and were sentenced for drug, violent, or property offenses, in that order (see Figure 11.3).

FIGURE 11.3

Characteristics of Adults on Parole

Source: Laura M. Maruschak and Thomas P. Bonczar, *Probation and Parole in the United States, 2012* (Washington, DC: U.S. Department of Justice, Bureau of Justice Statistics, 2013), p. 21.

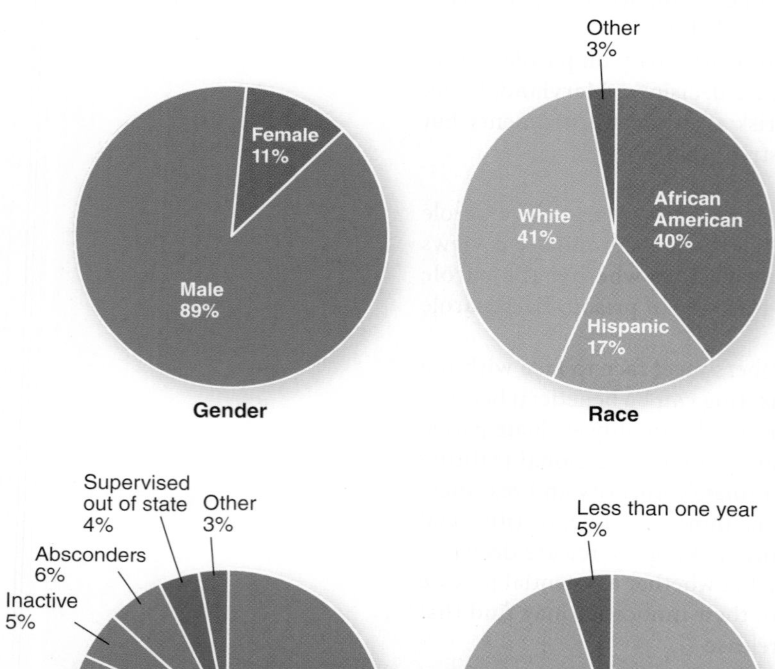

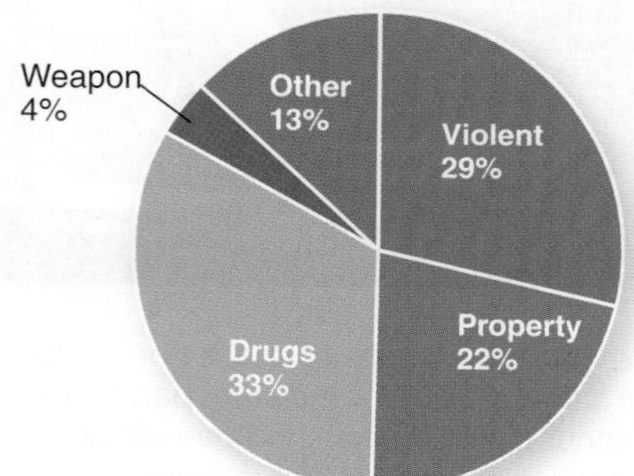

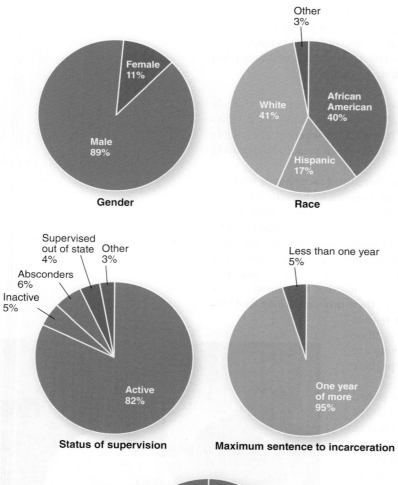

The Parolee in the Community

Once released into the community, the typical parolee is given a set of rules and conditions that must be obeyed—standard conditions applicable to all parolees and special conditions tailored to particular parolees. Standard conditions may include:

- Reporting to the parole agent within 24 hours of prison release
- Not carrying weapons
- Reporting changes of address and employment
- Not traveling more than 50 miles from home or not leaving the county for more than 48 hours without prior approval from the parole officer
- Obeying all parole agent instructions
- Seeking and maintaining employment or participating in education/work training
- Not committing crimes
- Submitting to search by police and parole officers[17]

Special conditions of parole may include:

- Participating in an appropriate educational or vocational program, as indicated by the parole's parole officer
- Participating in educational achievement testing in order to ascertain intellectual capacity, educational skill level, or learning ability
- Participating in psychological or psychiatric evaluation, as instructed by the offender's supervising officer
- Participating in mental health treatment/case management/rehabilitation training program

© Jennifer Reynoldson

VOICES ACROSS THE PROFESSION

Mentoring and changing lives is meaningful work that has a significant impact on the offender as well as the community.

Jennifer Reynoldson
Probation/Parole Officer Supervisor

As a probation/parole officer supervisor in the largest judicial district in Iowa, there are multiple facets to effectively supervising community-based offenders on probation and parole. Research clearly shows that the implementation and utilization of evidence-based practices into daily case work with offenders has an impact on reducing recidivism and promoting positive change with offenders. It is the mission of the district as well as each officer to protect the public, employee, and offender during the course of their daily case management work with offenders. As a supervisor, it is my responsibility to work with probation and parole officers to ensure that they are utilizing the most successful techniques to assist in this process.

The fundamentals of evidence-based practices include assessing offender risk, identifying criminogenic need areas, and targeting those areas with cognitive-based interventions to reduce risk. It is the philosophy of the department that offenders will be supervised according to their risk and need level rather than by charge type. This means that a high-risk offender who is only on supervision for simple misdemeanor will receive the same intensive supervision as a felony offender with the same amount of risk. Why would we do that? If you are the victim of domestic violence and your partner has tried to stab you with a knife, beaten you in front of your children, or held you hostage, and then is charged with a simple assault charge, it becomes clear why our department has chosen to focus on risk rather than charge type. As a side note, domestic violence calls are the most dangerous made by law enforcement and corrections.

We focus our limited resources on medium- to high-risk offenders and are able to reduce their risk significantly if evidence-based practices are incorporated into all aspects of their case management. Evidence-based practices also clearly demonstrate that the most effective parole officers are those who can effectively build a working alliance and develop good rapport with the offenders they supervise. Effective officers will utilize a strength-based approach during office appointments that incorporates motivational interviewing techniques to help promote change. Think about your own experience in college, high school, or even grade school. Who was your favorite teacher and why? Most answer that their favorite teacher was funny, cared about them, and taught them things they didn't know before. The same can be said for our most successful parole officers. Those who have those traits get the best results.

- Informing any prospective employer of an offender criminal history if the offender will be employed in a position of financial responsibility
- Not entering a specified county or counties without prior written approval by the parole officer
- Prohibiting certain financial activities by offenders who have been convicted of theft or fraud or who have a propensity for engaging in theft or fraudulent criminal behavior

Parolees who violate these rules may have parole revoked and be sent back to the institution to serve the remainder of their sentence. Once in the community, the parolee is supervised by a trained staff of parole officers who help him or her search for employment and monitor the parolee's behavior and activities to ensure that the conditions of parole are met. In Voices across the Profession, probation/parole officer supervisor Jennifer Reynoldson offers her perspective on some of the challenges faced by these officers.

Parole is generally viewed as a privilege granted to deserving inmates on the basis of their good behavior while in prison. Parole has two conflicting sides, however. On the

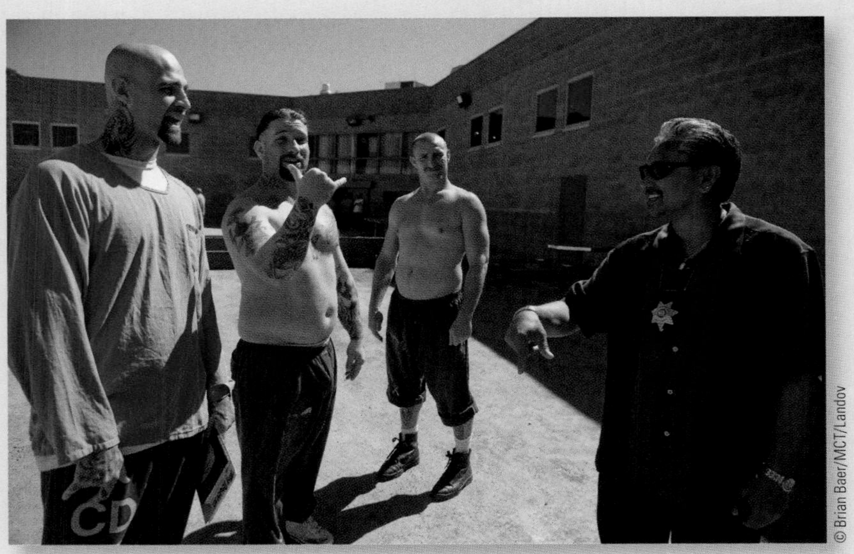
© Brian Baer/MCT/Landov

Parole officers' work takes them to many different locales where they must help people with a variety of serious social and personal problems. Here, parolees Tony DeWeese, Blaine Clayton, and Jason Marshal talk with parole officer Roland Asuncion in the yard during a break in classes at the drug treatment program for parolees in Folsom, California.

one hand, the paroled offender is allowed to serve part of the sentence in the community, an obvious benefit for the deserving offender. On the other hand, since parole is a privilege and not a right, the parolee is viewed as a dangerous criminal who must be carefully watched and supervised. The conflict between the treatment and enforcement aspects of parole has not been reconciled by the criminal justice system, and the parole process still contains elements of both.

To overcome these roadblocks to success, the parole officer may have to play a much greater role in directing and supervising clients' lives than the probation officer. In some instances, parole programs have become active in creating new postrelease treatment-oriented programs designed to increase the chances of parole success. In other instances, parole agencies have implemented law enforcement–oriented services that work with local police agencies to identify and apprehend parolees who may have been involved in criminal activity.[18]

THE PAROLE OFFICER

State parole agencies now employ nearly 65,000 full-time and 2,900 part-time workers, almost equally split between male and female full-time parole officers. Their average caseload is 38 active parolees for each full-time position devoted to parole supervision.[19] There are some communities in which parole officers continue to see service as an important part of the job. But for the most part, parole officers are seen and view themselves as control agents.[20]

Parole officers have much in common with probation officers. Both perform duties that are investigatory and regulatory. They face similar role conflicts and frustrations. Both cope with excessive caseloads, both lack community resources, and both may be inadequately trained. In fact, in many states the same officer provides both probation and parole services. In separated departments, state-administered parole services usually pay officers somewhat better than do county-funded probation services. Parole officers also tend to be older and more experienced in the criminal justice system than probation officers.

Surveillance and Constraint

Parole agents are powerful legal actors. Some states equip them with legal authority to carry and use firearms. Parole agents have legal authority to search persons, places, and property without fulfilling the requirement imposed by the Fourth Amendment. They are able to order arrests without probable cause and to confine without bail. Parole agents also are able to recommend revocation of parole for new crimes or for technical violations of the conditions of parole.

Agents' authority extends into the wider community. Their power to search applies to households where a parolee is living and to businesses where a parolee is working.[21] The search does need to be done within a constitutional framework. Because of the power and privilege, the relationship that develops between parole officer and parolee is much more adversarial than supportive. Parolees see officers'

© James Young

VOICES ACROSS THE PROFESSION

I see offenders coming out of prison all the time depressed, saying, "I am a felon, no one will hire me." You have to say to them, "Some won't—let's find the ones who will."

James Young
Probation/Parole Officer

I currently supervise high-risk parolees. I carry a lower caseload than most agents to be able to supervise the offenders I have more effectively. The offenders I supervise all have curfews, they are required to report in the office more frequently, and they are placed on a color code to submit to drug and alcohol tests. Once I sign them up to parole they are given a color. They are then required to call a phone number twice a week. If their color comes up, they must come into the office the next morning and provide a urine sample. Since this is not one of the best parts of the job, the duties are shared by all probation and parole officers on a rotating basis. The positive results are then reported to the supervising officer for referring the offender to treatment or report to the court.

My street partner and I also conduct home checks and pre-parole checks; we will enter the offender's house and visit with the offender and their family members. We take note of the offender or family member's demeanor, cleanliness of the home, who is in the home, whether anyone is drinking or looking suspicious. We may check rooms, refrigerators, or areas outside the house for contraband. We do not carry weapons. We have pepper spray and a handheld radio to keep in contact with Polk County Sheriff's dispatch. They record all calls and check on us if we have been in a home for an extended period of time.

The area of parole that I am most excited about is what we call the reentry program. Years ago our only concern was for the public, and we would watch the offender until they made a mistake or broke a parole condition and send them right back to the institution. Now we work with the offender, place them in programming that will help them get a job, take care of their mental health needs, connect them with the programs that will help them with basic daily needs, and most of all involve the family and their prosocial friends to help them get though this difficult period of transition in their life. I see offenders coming out of prison all the time depressed, saying, "I am a felon, no one will hire me." You have to say to them, "Some won't—let's find the ones who will." If you can move an offender from the institution to the home, provide them with solid information, point them in the right direction for meaningful work, and have regular contacts with spouses, parents, and adult children to help, you can have an offender who feels good about himself. He is productive, he is being a father again and supportive of his spouse, with a very good chance of staying out of the institution.

weapons (in those states that approve carrying of weapons) and handcuffs and know the officers can have them returned to prison. In turn, parole officers know that some parolees are dangerous and capable of assaulting them.

Supervision of Parolees

Five states' agencies account for nearly half of the adults under parole supervision: California, Texas, Illinois, New York, and Pennsylvania.[22] A number of technologies are being used to aid supervision by parole agencies nationwide. These include concealed weapons detection instruments to increase officer safety, and face and voice recognition technologies. Parole officers also use drug and alcohol testing, remote alcohol and drug monitoring, new technologies for monitoring sex offenders, such as penile plethysmographs, and computer surveillance software.[23] These technologies are changing the nature of parole supervision, the manner in which drug and alcohol tests are conducted, and locating and tracking parolees within geographical boundaries.[24] The TechnoCorrections feature discusses the use of GPS to monitor sex offenders.

Monitoring Sex Offenders in the Community

Electronic monitoring has been used to keep probationers under surveillance and is now being adopted for use with parolees. One prominent example is New Jersey's Sex Offender Monitoring Pilot Project Act, which became law in August 2005. The State Parole Board is empowered to subject the State's highest-risk sex offenders to round-the-clock Global Positioning System (GPS) monitoring. Data suggest GPS monitoring has contributed to a lower recidivism rate than nationwide data indicates for high-risk sex offenders. Under GPS monitoring, offenders' movements are recorded, time-stamped and stored, and used as evidence in the investigation of any new sex crimes. The State Parole Board regularly provides this data to other law enforcement agencies, to assist in their investigations.

The program was required because the state parole board's caseload of sex offenders is one of the largest in America, mainly due to the passage of Supervision for Life sentencing guidelines for sex offenders. Today, sex offenders make up nearly a third of the parole caseload, with a net increase of about 45 new sex offenders each month.

An analysis of 225 sex offenders who were subject to GPS monitoring in New Jersey found that only one of these high-risk sex offenders had been charged with a new sex crime while under GPS supervision. The lone offender was arrested at the crime scene, but even if he had left the scene, the GPS data was available to pinpoint his presence at the time and place of the crime, and was ready to serve as a vital aid to the investigation.

The following case examples demonstrate ways in which the state parole board's GPS monitoring has intercepted violations by sex offenders and has helped law enforcement agencies work together to protect the public.

- In Sussex County, GPS tracking data revealed that a sex offender was repeatedly staying at an address other than his registered address. The unauthorized address turned out to be the residence of his girlfriend, who had an infant in the home. This data was turned over to the prosecutor's office. The sex offender was investigated and charged with violations of Megan's Law for failing to stay at his approved address.
- In Burlington County, a sex offender's past victim reported the sex offender was stalking her. A review of GPS tracking data revealed that the sex offender had been at the former victim's place of employment and near her home. This information was turned over to the prosecutor's office.
- In Union County, the GPS monitoring program tracked a Tier III sex offender to a residential mental health treatment facility where it turned out he was employed. Parole officers investigated and determined the sex offender did not register his employment with the prosecutor's office as required under Megan's Law. The prosecutor was notified, and the subject was suspended from his employment as it was determined that his commitment offense involved elderly victims.

The New Jersey project's success may herald increased use of GPS monitoring for parolees in the community.

FOR CRITICAL THINKING AND WRITING

In 2014, paroled sex offenders Franc Cano, 27, and Steven Dean Gordon, 45, were arrested on charges of raping and killing four women in Southern California. They allegedly wore GPS trackers while committing their crimes, and police said that data from the devices was one of the investigative tools used to put the case together. Authorities could not (or would not) explain how Cano and Gordon allegedly managed to carry out the killings while under supervision. Does a case such as this make you question the value of GPS devices to monitor parolees?

Sources: New Jersey Parole Board, "Report on New Jersey's GPS Monitoring of Sex Offenders," http://www.state.nj.us/parole/docs/reports/gps.pdf (accessed July 2014); Fox News, "Police Say Accused California Serial Killers Wore GPS trackers While Committing Crimes," April 15, 2014, http://www.foxnews.com/us/2014/04/15/2-sex-offenders-charged-with-rapes-murders-4-california-women/ (accessed July 2014).

INTENSIVE SUPERVISION PAROLE (ISP) The most at-risk parolees are placed on **intensive supervision parole (ISP)**. These programs use limited caseload sizes, treatment facilities, the matching of parolee and supervisor by personality, and shock parole (which involves immediate short-term incarceration for parole violators to impress them with the seriousness of a violation). ISP clients are required to attend more office and home visits than routine parolees. ISP may also require frequent drug testing, a term in a community correctional center, and electronic monitoring in the home. More than 17,000 parolees are under intensive supervision; 1,400 of these are monitored electronically by computer.

intensive supervision parole (ISP) More extensive supervision than is given for most parolees.

Evaluations of ISP programs have produced mixed results. Some show that they may actually produce a higher violation rate than traditional parole supervision because limiting caseload size allows parole officers to supervise their clients more closely and spot infractions more easily.[25] However, some evaluations do show that under some conditions a properly run ISP program can significantly reduce recidivism upon release. The key factors may be parole officer orientation (a balance between social service and law enforcement seems to work best) and a supportive organizational environment in which the program is being run.[26]

Web App 11.2
Go to the Family Watchdog website (http://www.familywatchdog.us/) to understand what type of information is tracked on sex offenders in the community and who is a registered sex offender in your area. LO3

The fact that so many parolees have had their parole revoked, resulting in their return to prison, has attracted the interest of policy makers. While some commit new crimes, a large percentage of parolees return to prison for **technical violations**: they have violated the conditions of their parole, for example, leaving the jurisdiction without permission.[27] In California, two-thirds of parolees returned to prison are parole violators.[28]

technical violations Parole violations that pertain to behavior that is not crime, such as the failure to refrain from alcohol use.

Is There a Legal Right to Parole?

What happens if the parole authority denies early release, but the inmate believes he is deserving of parole? Perhaps he has witnessed other inmates receiving parole who have similar institutional records. Can he question the parole board's decision via the courts? The Supreme Court answered this question in 2011 when it ruled in the consolidated cases of *Swarthout v. Cooke* and *Cate v. Clay* that due process requirements are satisfied when a prisoner has an opportunity to be heard and is provided a statement of the reasons why parole is denied; there is in essence no absolute or legal right to receiving parole. The first case, *Swarthout v. Cooke*, involved Damon Cooke, who was incarcerated in California for attempted first-degree murder. In 2002, the California Board of Prison Terms rejected his parole request. California law provides that if the board denies parole, the prisoner can seek judicial review. Subsequently the California superior court, the California court of appeal, and the California supreme court all denied Cooke's petitions, prompting him to seek federal assistance. Similarly, *Cate v. Clay* began with the 1978 conviction of Elijah Clay for first-degree murder. In 2003, the board found Clay suitable for parole, but the governor reviewed the case and found Clay unsuitable for parole. After going through the state process, Clay filed a claim in federal court. The district court concluded that the governor's reliance on the nature of Clay's original offense rather

In some jurisdictions, a unified department of probation and parole carries out field investigations. Here, Chelsea Klostreich (left) and Lucinda Carroll (center), parole and probation officers with Washington County, Oregon, check on the household of a man on parole for a domestic violence charge. The officers travel in pairs for safety.

than his prison behavior violated his right to due process. The Ninth Circuit affirmed, concluding that the governor's decision was unreasonable.

The Supreme Court reversed both decisions, holding that the due process clause requires fair procedures in parole hearing. However, it held that both Cooke and Clay received adequate process because they were allowed an opportunity to be heard and were provided a statement of the reasons why parole was denied. The courts do not have the right to step in and conclude the parole board (and governor's) decisions were faulty. If the process is fair, then the inmate must live with the outcome.[29]

Summarize the procedures involved in the revocation of parole LO4

Parole Revocation

There are also legal issues involved when a parolee violates the rules of his release. This process begins when the parole officer decides if and when to file a complaint against a parolee. In some states, regulations guide or even mandate specific responses to violations, which restricts parole officers' discretion. However, in the majority of jurisdictions parole officers have significant discretionary power.[30] Tara Opsal and colleagues found that, in Colorado, parole officers used race, ethnicity, gender, pivotal categories, and therapeutic needs to construct and made the decision when and whether to file a complaint.[31]

Morrissey v. Brewer Supreme Court ruled on procedures for revocation of parole.

revocation of parole A formal procedure that takes place when a parole board, after listening to the parolee and his or her parole officer and their witnesses, decides that parole must end because the offender committed a new crime or violated the conditions of parole.

In ***Morrissey v. Brewer*** (1972), the U.S. Supreme Court first ruled on procedures for **revocation of parole**. Morrissey was a bad-check writer who had been paroled from the Iowa State Penitentiary. Seven months after his release, his parole was revoked for a technical violation, and he was returned to prison. At about the same time, a second petitioner, Booher, was returned to prison without opportunities on a technical parole violation. Both men petitioned for *habeas corpus* on the grounds that they had been denied due process of the law and returned to prison without opportunities to defend themselves at an open hearing. The two cases were consolidated for appeal and eventually reached the U.S. Supreme Court.

In his opinion, Chief Justice Warren Burger laid down the essential elements of due process for parole revocation. The first requirement was a hearing before an "uninvolved" hearing officer, who might be another parole officer or perhaps an "independent decision maker," who would determine whether there was reasonable cause to believe that a parole violation had taken place. If so, the parolee might be returned to prison, subject to a full revocation hearing before the parole board.

The actual revocation procedures begin when the parole officer requests a warrant based on an alleged violation of parole. A parole officer, a warrant officer, or a police officer can issue a warrant. Once parolees are in custody, they are given a list of the charges against them. The next step in this process, which tends to vary from state to state, gives prisoners an opportunity to challenge at a preliminary hearing the allegation of violation and to confront adverse witnesses, including parole officers. The hearing officer is usually a senior officer, whose chief task is to determine whether there are reasonable grounds for believing that parolees have violated one or more of the conditions of parole—that is, whether there is "probable cause." If probable cause exists, parolees are held in custody for a revocation hearing. If probable cause is not found, parolees are returned to supervision.

A more comprehensive revocation hearing is held to determine whether the violation of parole is serious enough to justify returning parolees to prison. If parole is not revoked, parolees are returned to supervision. Jurisdictions vary greatly in determining how much time revoked parolees should spend in prison. They also vary in their decisions on whether parolees should receive credit for the time they spend under parole supervision. In complying with the requirements of due process imposed in *Morrissey v. Brewer*, parole officers and parole boards have focused their attention on the processing of violating cases. However, instead of receiving praise from the political system for its get-tough approach, the parole system has received criticism for its high return rates, because of the ongoing problem of prison overcrowding and its fiscal implications.

FOR GROUP **DISCUSSION**

Discuss what types of assistance, program, and services should be offered by parole agencies and agents to reduce technical violations. LO4

HOW SUCCESSFUL IS PAROLE?

Despite all efforts to treat, correct, and rehabilitate incarcerated offenders, a majority still return to prison shortly after their release.[32] An important federally sponsored study of more than 270,000 prisoners released in 15 states found that within three years of release, two-thirds of parolees were rearrested, half were reconvicted, and about 25 percent resentenced to prison. In all, more than half of those released are back in prison, serving time for a new prison sentence or for a technical violation of their release, such as failing a drug test, missing an appointment with their parole officer, or being arrested for a new crime (see Figure 11.4).[33] A similar study of about 300,000 parole discharges found that more than half either absconded or were returned to jail or prison.[34]

These data show that most offenders fail upon reentry into the community, and failure is most likely to take place soon after release (see Table 11.1).

Recently, the Bureau of Justice Statistics released the findings of a study of the five-year post-release offending patterns of persons released from prisons in 30 states beginning in 2005. The study used different measures of recidivism, including a new arrest, court adjudication, conviction, and incarceration for either a new sentence or a technical violation. It also documents the extent to which the released prisoners committed crimes in states other than the one in which they were released.

Not unlike other studies, this most recent one found that about two-thirds (67.8 percent) of released prisoners were arrested for a new crime within three years, and three-quarters (76.6 percent) were arrested within five years. Within five years

FIGURE 11.4

Estimated Percent of the At-Risk Parole Population Returned to Incarceration

Source: Bureau of Justice Statistics, Annual Parole Survey, 2000–2012.

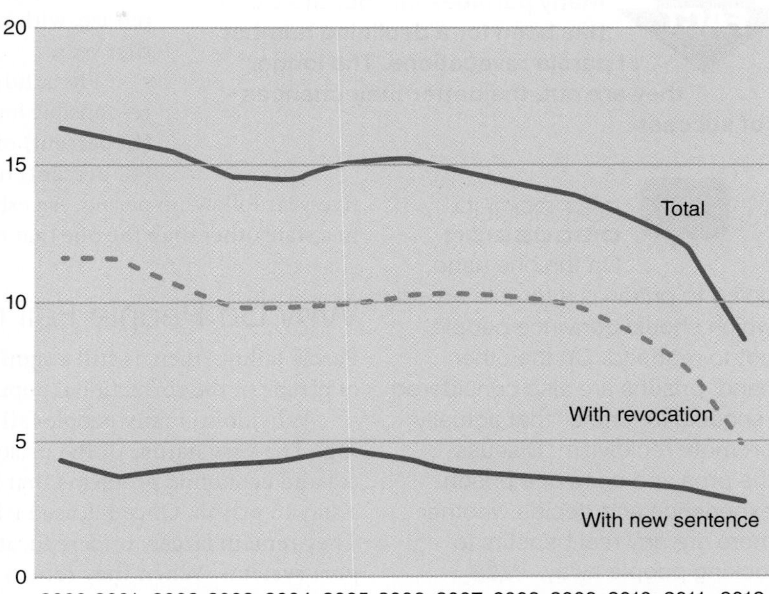

TABLE 11.1

Success on Parole

Study	Populations	Outcome
Hughes and James	270,000 released prisoners in 15 states	Two-thirds arrested within three years for felony or serious misdemeanor; about 25 percent were back in prison.
Lowenkamp and Latessa	7,306 offenders placed in community-based programs	Programs were more effective with higher-risk offenders than with lower-risk ones. Moderate and high-risk offenders had a 70 percent success rate.
U.S. Department of Justice 2002 Trends Study	297,851 parole discharges	45.3 percent were successful completions and 51.7 percent were returned to jail or prison.
U.S. Department of Justice 2005	503,800 parole discharges	45 percent were successful completions and 38 percent were returned to jail or prison.

Sources: Timothy Hughes and Doris James, "Inmates Returning to the Community After Serving Time in Prison," http://www.bjs.gov/content/pub/pdf/reentry.pdf (accessed July 2014); Christopher T. Lowenkamp and Edward J. Latessa, "Increasing the Effectiveness of Correctional Programming Through the Risk Principle: Identifying Offenders for Residential Placement," *Criminology and Public Policy* 4 (2005): 263–290; Bureau of Justice Statistics, *New Release*, April 2004; Bureau of Justice Statistics, *Bulletin*, November 2006.

Describe why people fail on parole **LO5**

of release, 82 percent of property offenders, 77 percent of drug offenders, 74 percent of public order offenders, and 71 percent of violent offenders were arrested for a new crime. Younger inmates were more likely to fail than older ones. Within five years of release, 84 percent of inmates who were age 24 or younger at release were arrested, compared to 79 percent of inmates ages 25 to 39, and 69 percent of those age 40 or older.

MYTH Most former inmates succeed on parole.

FACT Many parolees fail, but the trend has been for a declining number of parole revocations. The longer they are out, the better their chances of success.

Parole violations occurred fairly soon after release. More than a third (37 percent) of all prisoners who were arrested within five years of release were arrested within the first six months after release, with more than half (57 percent) arrested by the end of the first year.

The study found that relatively few chronic offenders were responsible for a significant portion of all postrelease crime: A sixth (16 percent) of released prisoners were responsible for almost half (48 percent) of the nearly 1.2 million arrests that occurred in the five-year follow-up period. An estimated 11 percent of released prisoners were arrested in a state other than the one that released them during the five-year follow-up period.[35]

FOR GROUP **DISCUSSION**

On the one hand, going to prison is a terrible ordeal which should convince people not to reoffend. On the other hand, prisons are also considered "schools for crime" that actually promote recidivism. Discuss the pros and cons of a prison experience and decide whether there are any real benefits to locking people away. **LO5**

Why Do People Fail on Parole?

Parole failure, then, is still a significant problem, and there are hundreds of thousands of people in the correctional population who fail on the outside each year.

Why do so many people fail on parole? And why are more people now succeeding? The very nature of the prison experience itself may be a factor: the psychological and economic problems that lead offenders to recidivism are rarely addressed by a stay in prison. Once released from prison, offenders face a multitude of difficulties. They remain largely undereducated, unskilled, and usually without solid family support systems. When they return to society, it may be to the same destructive neighborhood and social groups that prompted the original law-violating behavior.[36] It is also possible that parole failure is tied to the releasee's own lifelong deficits. Most research efforts indicate that a long history of criminal behavior, an antisocial personality, and childhood experiences with family dysfunction are all correlated with postrelease recidivism.[37]

AP Images/Kyle Green

Sarah Pearce gets a hug from Rick Visser, an attorney who worked on her case for four years, as she is released on March 14, 2014, in Caldwell, Idaho. Pearce was released after serving 11 years, 215 days for six felony guilty verdicts relating to a vicious attack on passing motorist Linda LeBrane in June 2000. Third District Judge Juneal Kerrick, who in January 2004 sentenced Pearce to 15 years to life, amended her sentence to time served, plus five more years of supervised release. An additional three years of prison time could be imposed if she violates her probation. Without the amended sentence, the earliest Pearce could have gained parole would have been August 2017. What factors will help her be successful? What obstacles does she have to overcome?

PERSONAL MARRIAGE AND FAMILY ISSUES

Recidivism may be a by-product of the disruptive effect a prison experience has on personal relationships. Ex-inmates may find their home life torn and disrupted when they are finally released.[38] Wives of inmates report that they have to face the shame and stigmatization of having an incarcerated spouse while withstanding a barrage of calls from their jealous husbands on the "inside," who try to monitor their behavior and control their lives. Family visits to the inmate become traumatic and strain relationships because they often involve strip searches and other invasions of privacy.[39] Sensitive to these problems, some states have instituted support groups designed to help inmates' families adjust to their loneliness and despair.[40]

State correctional authorities have developed programs that help inmates adjust to reentry, by providing prerelease treatment or postrelease care. Christopher Lowenkamp and Edward Latessa studied more than 7,000 offenders placed in 53 community-based residential programs as part of their parole. Offenders who successfully completed residential programming were compared with offenders under parole/postrelease control who were not placed in residential programs. Lowenkamp and Latessa found that residential programs were particularly effective with higher-risk offenders and that residential treatment helped the most troubled inmates make a successful reentry into society.[41]

The Evidence-Based Corrections feature discusses another initiative designed to help inmates successfully return to society.

EVIDENCE-BASED CORRECTIONS

Serious and Violent Offender Reentry Initiative (SVORI)

The Serious and Violent Offender Reentry Initiative (SVORI) program is designed to improve reentry outcomes along five dimensions: criminal justice, employment, education, health, and housing. SVORI programs are encouraged to implement a multiphased approach. Although the structure varies, programs usually plan at least one prerelease phase and at least one postrelease phase. The prerelease, institutionally based phase generally entails the selection of eligible participants and the initiation of SVORI programming and services. During the prerelease phase, most programs begin the development of a reentry plan for each participant. This plan usually assesses basic needs (e.g., medical services, food, shelter, and clothing). Most programs plan to provide a wide array of services to SVORI participants, including case management, treatment plan development, and release plan development. A transition team develops a schedule involving case management, employment services, supervision and monitoring, transitional housing, treatment, and aftercare. As in the prerelease phase, the program offers a wide range of services to SVORI participants in the post-release phase including:

- Substance abuse treatment
- Mental health counseling
- Medical and/or dental services
- Employment and/or education training
- Housing assistance
- Faith-based services
- Other services such as parenting skills, domestic violence awareness, life skills, and/or anger management

Many SVORI programs offer participants support from the community following the completion of their parole term. During this sustaining phase, program administrators encourage participants to maintain contact with personal social support networks and to be involved in community reintegration activities.

A number of detailed evaluations of the programs have been undertaken, and the findings have been mixed. The evaluators have determined that participants in SVORI programs are more likely to receive services than comparable nonparticipants. From release through 15 months postrelease, SVORI participants appear to be doing well—moderately better than non-SVORI participants—across a wide range of outcomes. About one-third report living in their own residences. In contrast to pre-incarceration findings, few reported that they currently lived with people who abused alcohol or drugs. Nearly three-fourths had worked since release. However, results indicate that, compared to non-SVORI participants, SVORI participants show no discernible differences on outcomes with respect to recidivism, housing, substance abuse, and physical and mental health. What seemed to be the problem? Simply put, offenders face important challenges upon returning to their communities. These challenges include finding suitable housing and employment and obtaining affordable health care (including substance abuse treatment and mental health counseling). Results from the SVORI evaluation support the notion that successful reentry of returning offenders cannot be tied to one process (such as, in this example, the provision of services).

FOR CRITICAL THINKING AND WRITING

Working seems to be a significant factor in parole success. What can be done to encourage employers to hire parolees, especially when there are high unemployment rates?

Sources: Christy Visher and Pamela Lattimore, "Study Examines Prisoners' Reentry Needs," NIJ Update, April 2008, http://www.ncjrs.gov/pdffiles1/nij/222475.pdf (accessed July 2014); National Institute of Justice, "Evaluation of the Serious and Violent Offender Reentry Initiative," July 26, 2011, http://nij.gov/topics/corrections/reentry/evaluation-svori.htm (accessed July 2014).

CRITICAL THINKING

After reading about SVORI, do you think it's the criminal justice system's right to mandate relocation of offenders upon release? Do they have a better chance of not reoffending by returning to different circumstances? What type of aftercare should be provided if this were to happen? LO5

Losing Rights

Identify some of the rights that ex-offenders have lost LO6

Ex-inmates may find that going straight is an economic impossibility. It is particularly difficult in the present job market, with so many out of work. Many employers are reluctant to hire people who have served time. Even if a criminal record does not automatically prohibit all chance of employment, why would an employer hire an ex-con when other applicants are available? If they lie about their prison experience and are later found out, ex-offenders will be dismissed for misrepresentation. Research shows that former inmates who gain and keep meaningful employment are more likely to succeed on parole than those who are unemployed or underemplo yed.[42] One reason that ex-inmates find it so difficult to make it on the outside is the legal restrictions they are forced to endure. These may include bans on certain kinds of employment, limits on obtaining licenses, and restrictions on their freedom of movement. One survey found that a significant number of states still restrict the activities of former felons.[43] In general, states have placed greater restrictions on former felons as part of the get-tough movement. These have been described as "invisible punishments" that reduce the rights and privileges of those convicted of crimes.[44]

However, courts have considered individual requests by convicted felons to have their rights restored. It is common for courts to look at such issues as how recently the criminal offense took place and its relationship to the particular right before deciding whether to restore it. An additional frustration results from the civil disabilities imposed on convicted felons. The get-tough movement of the 1980s increased the statutory restrictions placed on parolees. Ex-offenders confront legal and social barriers that stand between them and job opportunities. Examinations of statutory barriers indicate that as many as 300 occupations require licenses that are unobtainable by persons with felony convictions. Felons are not likely to find work as nurses, barbers or beauticians, real estate salespersons, or cashiers, or to work in places where alcoholic beverages are sold. Limited work experience, lack of training, difficulty in accepting supervision, and unrealistic expectations about income and promotion also put ex-offenders seeking jobs at a disadvantage. Dealing with the public and with coworkers is not a skill learned in prison, so ex-offenders are unlikely candidates for any job calling for interaction with strangers.

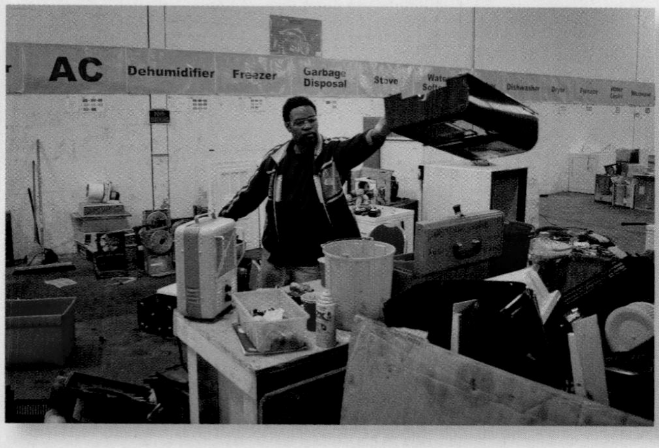

disenfranchisement laws Civil disabilities facing parolees when they return to the community.

The **disenfranchisement laws** or civil disabilities extend into many other areas of the convicted felon's life. Fourteen states permanently deny convicted felons the right to vote (most other states restrict this right until felons fulfill their sentences). Their criminal records may preclude them from retaining parental rights, may be grounds for divorce, and may bar them from serving on a jury, holding public office, and owning firearms. Eight jurisdictions require ex-offenders to register with a police department on release from prison.

A number of experts and national commissions have condemned the loss of rights of convicted offenders as a significant cause of recidivism. Consequently, courts have generally moved to eliminate the most restrictive elements of postconviction restrictions.[45]

Bloomberg/Getty Images

Ex-cons often have a hard time getting a job, but change may be coming. Here, ex-convict Archmiguel "Arch" Murphy deconstructs a dehumidifier for scrap metal at the Better Futures Minnesota warehouse in Minneapolis. As companies such as Target and Walmart remove questions about criminal history from applications, state and local governments are passing laws that could help ex-offenders get job interviews.

What Can Be Done to Improve Parole Effectiveness?

One way of improving parole effectiveness is to analyze the factors that predict parole success or failure and then build programs around the results. A number of attempts have been made to isolate these factors. In one such attempt, Joe Graffam and colleagues conducted a large-scale study to examine the employability of ex-offenders and prisoners. They found that aside from those with an intellectual or psychiatric disability, those with a criminal background were deemed as less likely than other disadvantaged groups to obtain and maintain employment. They found that six broad domains influence the reintegration of ex-offenders:

- Personal conditions
- Rehabilitation and counseling support
- Employment and training support
- Social network/environment
- Accommodation
- The criminal justice system[46]

Similarly, Christy Visher and Jeremy Travis found that recidivism is affected by several factors: (a) personal and situational characteristics, including peers, family, community, and state-level policies, (b) incarceration experiences, and (c) the period after release.[47]

CORRECTIONAL LIFE

Jeffrey: An Ex-Offender Outside

I think the hardest thing about coming out of prison to the free world is finding a job. I was born with two strikes, being black and male. Then, once a man gets a criminal record, that is the third strike. They say they want you to make it, but everywhere you go—state agency, job interview with private employer—you are met with the same look. It is the look that says you're unwanted, and no matter how many help-wanted signs are in the windows, it always seems they want everyone's help but mine. What makes it even more difficult is that while we were in prison we gained very few viable skills, nothing that can really help you out in society. So that when you get out, most of us are unequipped to make it.

It may be possible to create effective parole programs built around these criteria. For example, California created a statewide, community-based correctional program that was intended to reduce parole recidivism. The Preventing Parolee Crime Program (PPCP) provided employment services, housing assistance, substance abuse treatment, and literacy training to thousands of parolees. The study found that the PPCP produced modest reductions in recidivism and parole absconding, and created the potential for substantial long-term cost savings. The fact that its positive effects were strongest for parolees who completed their services taught the lesson that future program designers and administrators should consider including mechanisms to improve service utilization and parolee retention.[48]

Criminologist Joan Petersilia has a number of recommendations to improve parole effectiveness. They include the following:

- *Parole offices should incorporate neighborhood parole supervision.* The key components of what some consider the new parole model are to strengthen parolees' linkages with law enforcement and the community, to offer a full-service model of parole, and to attempt to change the ex-offenders' lives through personal, family, and neighborhood interventions.
- *Parole administrators should establish and test reentry courts and community partnerships.* The motive is to engage the broader community and the justice system in monitoring and assisting ex-offender reintegration. This has been called the Reentry Partnership Initiative (RPI).
- *Policy makers should establish procedures for ex-prisoners to regain full citizenship.* This issue is one of establishing some procedure by which some parolees can move beyond their criminal records.[49]

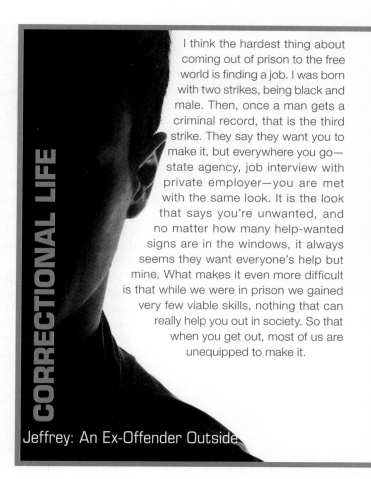

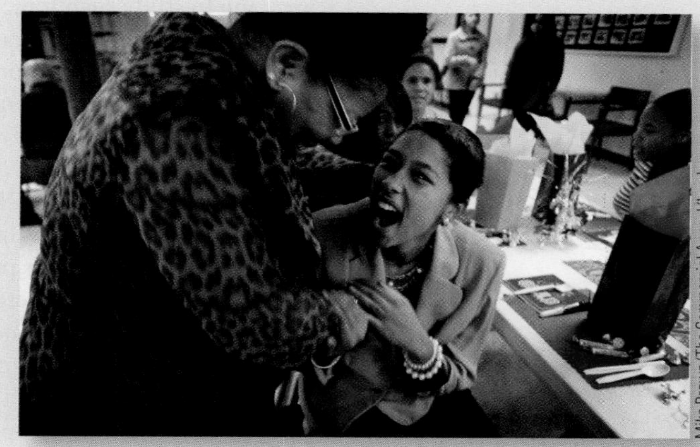

Mike Brown/The Commercial Appeal/Landov

Kellie Johnson, 20, (right) reacts when she hears that Janice Jones (left) has some big news for her. Upon her graduation from the HopeWorks parole preparation program, Johnson will be hired for her very first job. She took part in HopeWorks to try to turn her life around and put it back on track after serving 22 months in prison for robbery.

THINKING
LIKE A CORRECTIONS PROFESSIONAL

The new governor of your state believes that ex-offenders should be given more rights. She has appointed you as chair of a special task force to prepare a report for her. What rights will you recommend that a released inmate ought to have? Which privileges should inmates be allowed to become full citizens?

TARGETING TIME, PLACE, AND OFFENDERS Corrections expert James Byrne suggests that another effective approach may be front-loading the intensity of parole supervision—that is, closely supervising parolees as soon as they are released from prison and cutting back on supervision as they adjust to the community. We know that most people fail on parole soon after they are released from prison; about 10 percent of all offenders are arrested during their first month back in the community. Therefore, concentrating community supervision resources at the start of an offender's parole term might be effective, since that is when they are more likely to reoffend.[50]

Byrne also suggests that resources may be directed at parolees who pose the greatest threat to the community. To date, 31 states have passed legislation allowing the use of lifetime community supervision for targeted groups of offenders, most notably sex offenders and offenders convicted of homicide. While these offenders actually have a low reoffending rate, their close supervision may be reassuring to the community, their victims, and the community corrections agencies responsible for supervising the offender.

Finally, Byrne suggests that effective parole supervision must be community oriented. Community supervision strategies should consider community-level risks posed by parolees and then assign community corrections officers to specific geographic areas rather than to specific caseloads. Those areas that need the most help are already at risk to crime and lack resources to prevent its occurrence. Parole officers assigned to these areas can make the most difference.[51]

Second Chance Act

On April 9, 2008, President George W. Bush signed the Second Chance Act into law. Receiving bipartisan support in both chambers of Congress, the bill was supported by a broad spectrum of leaders representing law enforcement, corrections, the courts, and local government. This first-of-its-kind legislation authorizes various grants to government agencies and nonprofit groups to provide employment assistance, substance abuse treatment, housing, family programming, mentoring, victim support, and other services that can help reduce reoffending and violations of probation and parole. If properly financed and carried out, the act could cut recidivism and ruinous prison costs for states by helping them develop programs that former inmates need to build viable, crime-free lives. The Second Chance Act provides millions of dollars in funding to study such topics as smart probation projects; treatment of returning adults and juveniles with co-occurring substance abuse and mental health disorders; adult and juvenile reentry demonstration projects; adult mentoring programs; technology career training projects for incarcerated adults and juveniles; and demonstration field experiments to test a parole reentry model.[52]

HAVING FEWER PRISONERS Developing postrelease programs might even be more effective if the size of the correctional system was reduced and fewer inmates held behind bars. Greater parole and aftercare resources could then be targeted to a smaller number of inmates returning to society. But would a reduced emphasis on incarceration produce a higher crime rate, something no one really wants? Not according to a recent (2014) study conducted by the Sentencing Project that examined prison population reduction efforts in three states, New York, New Jersey, and California. Each has reduced their prison populations by about 25 percent during the past decade at a time when the nationwide state prison population rose by 10 percent. While downsizing their prisons, the violent crime rate fell at a higher rate in these three states than it did nationwide; property crime rates also decreased in all three. If prison populations can be reduced by 25 percent with little or no adverse effect on the crime rate, then the savings could be directed at helping those being released from prison achieve better results in the community.[53]

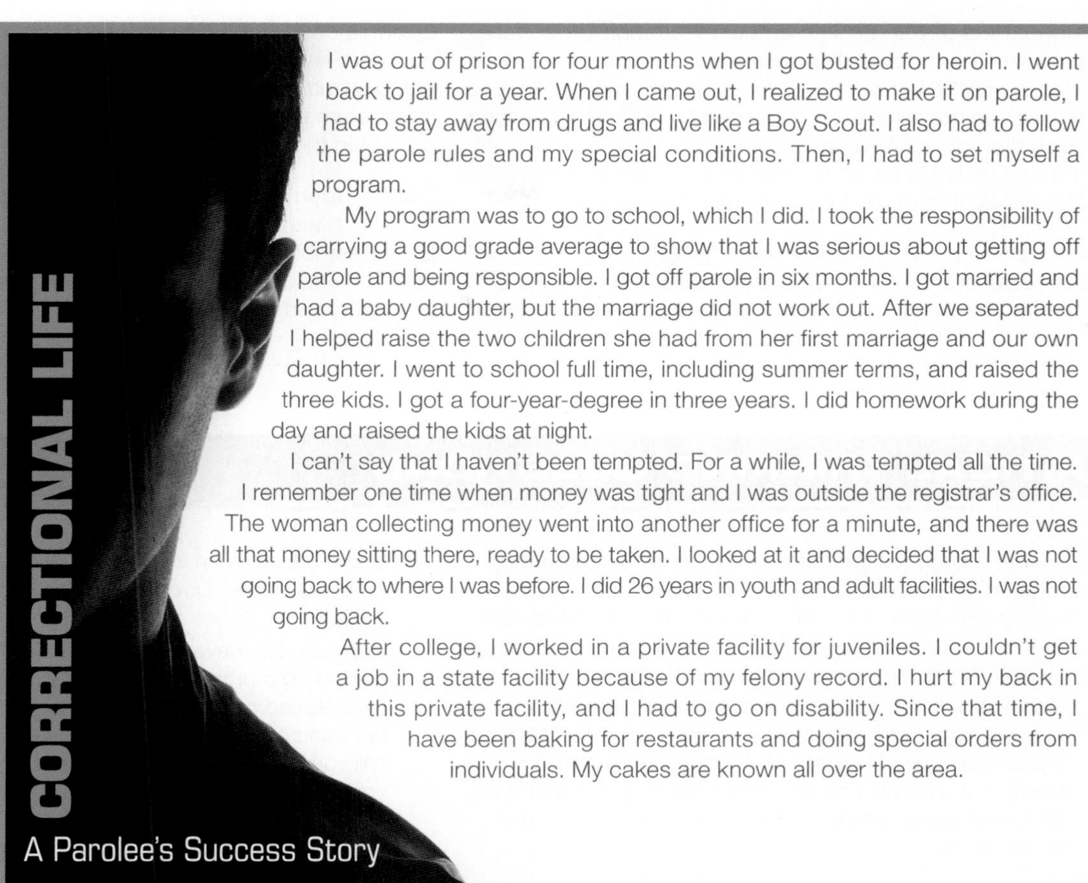

I was out of prison for four months when I got busted for heroin. I went back to jail for a year. When I came out, I realized to make it on parole, I had to stay away from drugs and live like a Boy Scout. I also had to follow the parole rules and my special conditions. Then, I had to set myself a program.

My program was to go to school, which I did. I took the responsibility of carrying a good grade average to show that I was serious about getting off parole and being responsible. I got off parole in six months. I got married and had a baby daughter, but the marriage did not work out. After we separated I helped raise the two children she had from her first marriage and our own daughter. I went to school full time, including summer terms, and raised the three kids. I got a four-year-degree in three years. I did homework during the day and raised the kids at night.

I can't say that I haven't been tempted. For a while, I was tempted all the time. I remember one time when money was tight and I was outside the registrar's office. The woman collecting money went into another office for a minute, and there was all that money sitting there, ready to be taken. I looked at it and decided that I was not going back to where I was before. I did 26 years in youth and adult facilities. I was not going back.

After college, I worked in a private facility for juveniles. I couldn't get a job in a state facility because of my felony record. I hurt my back in this private facility, and I had to go on disability. Since that time, I have been baking for restaurants and doing special orders from individuals. My cakes are known all over the area.

SUMMARY

LO1 Describe parole practices today

Discretionary parole has now been abolished in 13 states, but for those states that have parole it is based on the following principles:

- The state extends to offenders a privilege by releasing them from prison before their full sentence is served.
- The state also enters a release contract with offenders in exchange for their promise to abide by certain conditions.
- Offenders who violate the law or conditions of parole can be returned to prison to complete their sentences.
- The state retains control of parolees until they are dismissed from parole.

LO2 Discuss how the parole board functions

Parole decisions can be made with an entire board interviewing eligible inmates; in other jurisdictions, only part of the board interviews eligible inmates. Hearing examiners are used in some jurisdictions to interview inmates. Some states, rather than interviewing inmates, make their decisions based solely upon written reports. Nearly all states still authorizing parole have further restricted parole by setting specific standards that inmates must meet to be eligible for release. Some states use formal risk prediction instruments or parole guidelines to structure the parole decision-making process.

LO3 Identify the rules for parolees released to the community

The parolee released to the community is typically given a set of rules and conditions that must be obeyed. These include reporting to the parole officer within 24 hours; not carrying weapons; obeying all parole agent instructions; not traveling more than 50 miles from home or leaving the county without permission; not committing crimes; seeking and maintaining employment.

LO4 Summarize the procedures involved in the revocation of parole

Revocation of parole takes place when a parole board decides, while granting the parolee due process rights, that parole must end because the offender committed a new crime or violated the conditions of parole. The actual revocation procedures begin when the parole officer requests a warrant based on an alleged violation of parole. The next step involves parolees being given an opportunity to challenge at a preliminary hearing the allegation of violation and to confront adverse witnesses. If probable cause is found to exist by the hearing officer, the parolee is held in custody for a revocation hearing.

LO5 Describe why people fail on parole

People fail on parole for a number of reasons: the very nature of the prison experience itself; a multitude of difficulties faced upon release, include remaining largely undereducated, unskilled, and usually without solid family support systems; and personal marriage and family issues. In addition, they frequently must return to the same neighborhoods and social groups that prompted their law-violating behavior in the first place.

LO6 Identify some of the rights that ex-offenders have lost

Legal restrictions that parolees face include bans on certain kinds of employment, limits on obtaining licenses, loss of voting privileges, and restrictions on the freedom of movement.

CRITICAL THINKING QUESTIONS

1. "Parole boards are arbitrary and discriminatory and they ought to be abolished," says John Q. Liberal. "Yes, but so is the whole criminal justice system," says Sally Moderate. "At least the boards are trying to remedy inequities." What are likely to be the reasons behind each opinion?
2. Technical violators of parole are filling our prisons and aggravating problems related to prison crowding. What is your evaluation of technical violations of parole? For example, if a parolee moves in with his girlfriend and does not tell his parole officer, is this justification for returning him to prison?
3. Some states claim that an ex-offender's record should be made public. Does an ex-offender have any rights of privacy?
4. Suppose you have been convicted of a felony and have served 30 months in your state's penitentiary. You will be released on parole next week. How will your parents, husband or wife, children, and friends receive you? What will you do about getting a job? Will the university readmit you without any special processing? How are you going to discuss the last 30 months with your friends, some of whom do not know that you were in prison?

NOTES

1. Fernanda Santos, "Inmate Enters Guilty Plea in '89 Killing," *New York Times*, March 15, 2007.
2. Fernanda Santos, "Vindicated by DNA, but a Lost Man on the Outside," *New York Times*, November 25, 2007, http://www.nytimes.com/2007/11/25/us/25jeffrey.html (accessed July 2014).
3. David Farabee, *Rethinking Rehabilitation: Why Can't We Reform Our Criminals?* (Washington, DC: AEI Press, American Enterprise Institute, 2005).
4. Nalina Shapiro, "Convicted Child Killer Is Denied Parole," WVIB News, April 14, 2014, http://wivb.com/2014/04/14/convicted-child-killer-is-denied-parole/ (accessed July 2014).
5. A. A. Bruce, *Parole and Indeterminate Sentences* (Springfield, Illinois, Parole Board, 1928).
6. Laura M. Maruschak and and Thomas P. Bonczar, "Probation and Parole in the United States, 2012," *Bureau of Justice Statistics Bulletin* (Washington, DC: U.S. Department of Justice, 2013), http://www.bjs.gov/content/pub/ascii/ppus12.txt (accessed July 2014).
7. Ibid.
8. Kathryn D. Morgan and Brent Smith, "The Impact of Race on Parole Decision-Making," *Justice Quarterly* 25 (June 2008): 413.
9. Ibid.
10. Joan Petersilia, *When Prisoners Come Home: Parole and Prisoner Reentry* (New York: Oxford University Press, 2003), p. 71. See also "What Works in Community Corrections: An Interview with Dr. Joan Petersilia," the Pew Center on the States, Public Safety Performance Project, November 2007, http://www.pewtrusts.org/en/research-and-analysis/reports/0001/01/01/what-works-in-community-corrections (accessed July 2014).
11. Petersilia, *When Prisoners Come Home*.
12. Ibid., p. 72.
13. Sandra Crockett Mack and Khalil Osiris, "Successful Reentry, One Case at a Time," *Corrections Today* 69 (2007): 50–55.
14. Caroline Kröner, Cornelis Stadtland, Matthias Eidt, and Norbert Nedopil, "The Validity of the Violence Risk Appraisal Guide (VRAG) in Predicting Criminal Recidivism," *Criminal Behavior and Mental Health* 17 (2007): 89–100.
15. Kathryn Campbell and Myriam Denov, "The Burden of Innocence: Coping with a Wrongful Imprisonment," *Canadian Journal of Criminology and Criminal Justice* 46 (2004): 139–164.
16. Morgan and Smith, "The Impact of Race on Parole Decision-Making."
17. Petersilia, *When Prisoners Come Home*, p. 82.
18. Brian Parry, "Special Service Unit: Dedicated to Investigating and Apprehending Violent Offenders," *Corrections Today* 63 (2001): 120.
19. Thomas P. Bonczar, *Characteristics of State Parole Supervising Agencies, 2006* (Washington, DC: Bureau of Justice Statistics Special Report, 2008), p. 1.
20. James M. Byrne, "The Social Ecology of Community Corrections: Understanding the Link Between Individual and Community Change," *Criminology and Public Policy* (May 2008).
21. Patrick A. Langan and David J. Levin, *Recidivism of Prisoners Released in 1994* (Washington, DC: Bureau of Justice Statistics, 2002).

22. Bonczar, *Characteristics of State Parole Supervising Agencies, 2006*.
23. Byrne, "The Social Ecology of Community Corrections."
24. Petersilia, *When Prisoners Come Home*, p. 90.
25. David Z. Zanis, Frank Mulvaney, Donna Covello, Arthur I. Alterman, Barry Savity, and William Thompson, "The Effectiveness of Early Parole to Substance Abuse Treatment Facilities on 24-Month Criminal Recidivism," *Journal of Drug Issues* (2003): 223–236.
26. Mario Paparozzi and Paul Gendreau, "An Intensive Supervision Program that Worked: Service Delivery, Professional Orientation, and Organizational Supportiveness," *Prison Journal* 85 (2005): 445–466.
27. James A. Wilson, "Bad Behavior or Bad Policy? An Examination of Tennessee Release Cohorts, 1993–2001," *Criminology and Public Policy* 3 (2005): 485–526.
28. Joan Petersilia and Robert Weisberg, "Parole in California: It's a Crime," *Los Angeles Times*, April 23, 2006, http://articles.latimes.com/2006/apr/23/opinion/op-petersilia23 (accessed July 2014).
29. *Swarthout v. Cooke* and *Cate v. Clay*, 562 U.S. __ (2011).
30. Tara Opsal, Sara Steen, and Peter Lovegrove, "Understanding Parole Officers' Assessment of Risk and Need: The Role of Race, Ethnicity, and Gender in Filing Revocation Complaints," unpublished paper, 2011. See also Jeff Lin, Ryan Grattet, and Joan Petersilia, "'Back-End Sentencing' and Reimprisonment: Individual, Organizational and Community Predictors of Parole Sentencing Decisions," *Criminology* 4 (2010): 759–795.
31. Opsal, Steen, and Lovegrove, "Understanding Parole Officers' Assessment of Risk and Need."
32. Wilson, "Bad Behavior or Bad Policy?"
33. Timothy Hughes and Doris James, "Inmates Returning to the Community After Serving Time in Prison," http://www.bjs.gov/content/pub/pdf/reentry.pdf (accessed July 2014).
34. Bureau of Justice Statistics, *New Release*, April 2004; and Bureau of Justice Statistics, *Bulletin*, November 2006.
35. Matthew Durose, Alexia Cooper, and Howard N. Snyder, *Recidivism of Prisoners Released in 30 States in 2005: Patterns from 2005 to 2010* (Washington, DC: Bureau of Justice Statistics, 2014), http://www.bjs.gov/content/pub/ascii/rprts05p0510.txt (accessed July 2014).
36. Jeremy Travis and Joan Petersilia, "Reentry Reconsidered: A New Look at an Old Question," *Crime and Delinquency* 47 (2001): 291–313.
37. James Bonta, Moira Law, and Karl Hanson, "The Prediction of Criminal and Violent Recidivism Among Mentally Disordered Offenders: A Meta-Analysis," *Psychological Bulletin* 123 (1998): 123–142; Arthur J. Lurigio, "Effective Services for Parolees with Mental Illnesses," *Crime and Delinquency* 47 (2001): 446–461; Larry Brimeyer, "Iowa Implements Mental Health Re-entry Program," *Corrections Today* 65 (2003): 38–41; Jeffrey Draine, Nancy Wolff, Joseph E. Jacoby, Stephanie Hartwell, and Christine Deucios, "Understanding Community Re-entry of Former Prisoners with Mental Illness: A Conceptual Model to Guide New Research," *Behavioral Sciences and the Law* 23 (2005): 689–707.
38. Beth Huebner, "Racial and Ethnic Differences in the Likelihood of Marriage," *Justice Quarterly* 24 (2007): 156–183.
39. Laura Fishman, *Women at the Wall: A Study of Prisoners' Wives Doing Time on the Outside* (New York: State University of New York Press, 1990).
40. Leslee Goodman Hornick, "Volunteer Program Helps Make Inmates' Families Feel Welcome," *Corrections Today* 53 (1991): 184–186.
41. Christopher T. Lowenkamp and Edward J. Latessa, "Increasing the Effectiveness of Correctional Programming Through the Risk Principle: Identifying Offenders for Residential Placement," *Criminology and Public Policy* 4 (2005): 263–290. For an article that challenges the findings of Lowenkamp and Latessa, see James M. Byrne and Faye S. Taxman, "Crime (Control) Is a Choice: Divergent Perspectives on the Role of Treatment in the Adult Corrections System," *Criminology and Public Policy* 4 (2005): 291–310.
42. T. E. Hanlon, D. N. Nurco, R. W. Bateman, and K. E. O'Grady, "The Response of Drug Abuser Parolees to a Combination of Treatment and Intensive Supervision," *Prison Journal* 78 (1999).
43. Kathleen Olivares, Velmer Burton, and Francis Cullen, "The Collateral Consequences of a Felony Conviction: A National Study of State Legal Codes Ten Years Later," *Federal Probation* 60 (1996): 10–17.
44. Jeremy Travis, "Invisible Punishment: An Instrument of Social Exclusion," in *Invisible Punishment: The Collateral Consequences of Mass Imprisonment*, ed. Marc Mauer and Meda Chesney-Lind (Washington, DC: New Press, 2002), p. 16.
45. See, for example, *Bush v. Reid*, 516 P.2d 1215 (Alaska, 1973); *Thompson v. Bond*, 421 F.Supp. 878 (W.D. Mo., 1976); *Delorne v. Pierce Freightlines Co.*, 353 F.Supp. 258 (D. Or., 1973); *Beyer v. Werner*, 299 F.Supp. 967 (E.D. N.Y., 1969).
46. Joe Graffam, Alison Shinkfield, Barbara Lavelle, and Wenda McPherson, "Variables Affecting Successful Reintegration as Perceived by Offenders and Professionals," *Journal of Offender Rehabilitation* 40 (2004): 147–171.
47. Christy A. Visher and Jeremy Travis, "Transitions from Prison to Community," *Annual Review of Sociology* 29 (2003): 89–113.
48. Sheldon X. Zhang, Robert E. L. Roberts, and Valerie J. Callanan, "Preventing Parolees from Returning to Prison Through Community-Based Reintegration," *Crime and Delinquency* 52 (October 2006): 551–571. In a 2012 issue of *Criminology and Public Policy* devoted to employment-based reentry for parolees, there is strong emphasis placed on how to improve the effectiveness of reentry programs for parolees that target employment: *Criminology and Public Policy* 11 (February 2012).
49. Petersilia, *When Prisoners Come Home*, pp. 172–211.
50. James Byrne, *The New Generation of Concentrated Community Supervision Strategies: Focusing Resources on High Risk Offenders, Times, and Places*, report prepared for the Public Safety Performance Project, the Pew Charitable Trusts, Washington, DC, 2009.
51. Ibid.
52. U.S. Department of Justice, "Justice Department Announces More than $62 Million to Strengthen Reentry, Probation and Parole Programs," November 14, 2103, http://www.justice.gov/opa/pr/2013/November/13-ag-1217.html (accessed July 2014).
53. Mark Mauer and Nazgol Ghandnoosh, "Fewer Prisoners, Less Crime: A Tale of Three States," The Sentencing Project, 2014, http://sentencingproject.org/doc/publications/inc_Fewer_Prisoners_Less_Crime.pdf (accessed July 2014).

© Gloria Killian

As a former law student, Gloria Killian was assigned to the prison law library, where she worked for 14 years providing legal assistance to other inmates. She worked extensively with battered women and developed specialized legal services for many different areas of the prison. After being incarcerated for 16 years, Killian's conviction was overturned on appeal. Once released, she started her own nonprofit organization, Action Committee for Women in Prison, whose mission is to advocate for the humane and compassionate treatment of incarcerated women and to work for the release of all women who are unjustly imprisoned.

THERE ARE A NUMBER OF TRAGIC STORIES of aging prisoners in the California correctional system who are ineligible for parole. One of the most touching is that of Helen Leheac, who at 88 years old was nearly blind and deaf, her mind enfeebled by Alzheimer's, and in the terminal stages of kidney failure. Helen had hoped to be released from prison and spend her last days in a transitional home for formerly incarcerated women.[1] But after she had served 19 years behind bars on a conspiracy-to-murder conviction, the parole board told her that she remained a risk to public safety if she were freed and denied her request for release.

On January 5, 2009, Helen died of pneumonia in a hospital near the Central California Women's Facility (CCWF) in Chowchilla, where she was confined. She was shackled at her waist and ankles, with two guards at her bedside.

Gloria Killian, a former inmate of the California Institution for Women (CIW) in Corona and now a strong prisoners' rights advocate, comments, "It's a terrible injustice, what's going on in those prisons. There's nothing worse than being sick and being in prison. These people are not a threat to society. They couldn't hurt a fly if they wanted to. And besides, it's too expensive to keep them incarcerated."

"The board gives us a release date, and the governor takes it away," said Jane Benson, 60, a prisoner of 22 years at CIW. She succeeded in persuading the parole board to free her the fourth time she came up for parole. But she said her luck ran out when her papers reached the governor's desk.

12 Special Prison Populations

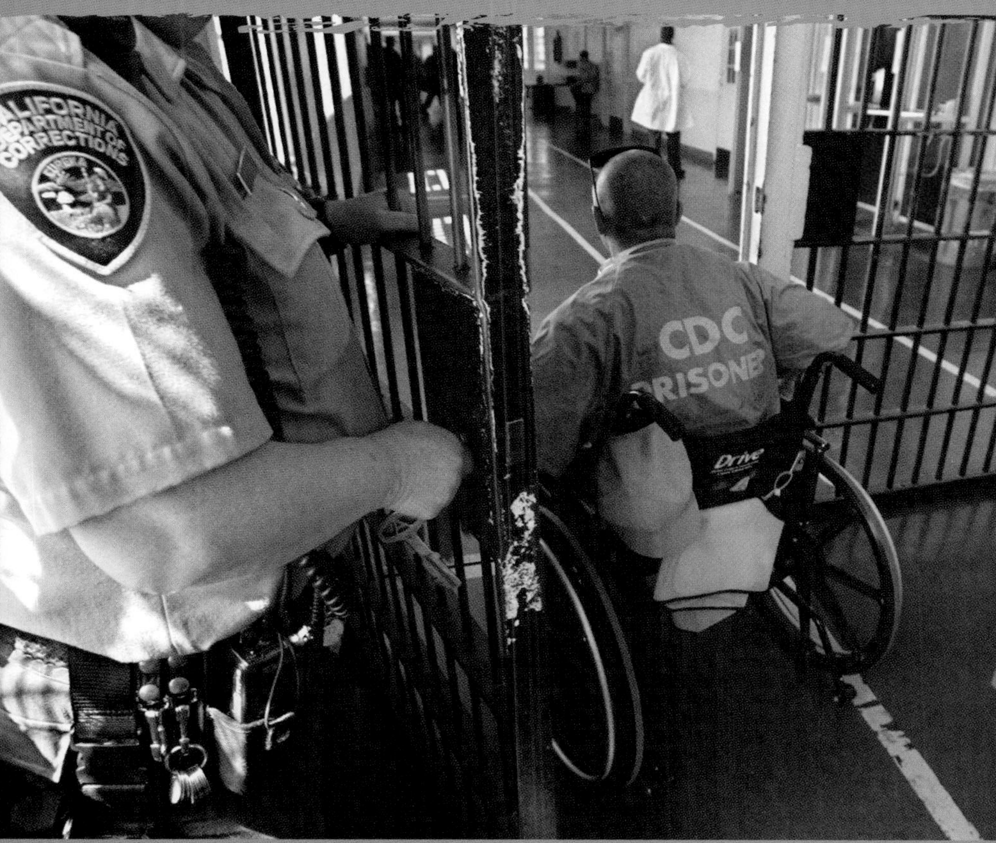

AP Images/Rich Pedroncelli, file

LEARNING OBJECTIVES

Describe the problems of inmates with a substance-involved history

Recognize what challenges and problems sex offenders bring to the prison

Name some of the issues terrorists present to the correctional system

Explain the prison experience of HIV inmates

Describe the world faced by chronic mentally ill inmates while they are in prison

Explain the plight of elderly inmates while incarcerated and what is involved in their care

Discuss the problems faced by illegal immigrants in U.S. prisons

PREVIEW OF KEY CONCEPTS

special offense inmates
special needs inmates
special population inmates
sex offenders
Megan's Law
terrorist
ticking bomb scenario
family detention centers

With tougher sentencing laws, it is projected that by 2030 there will be 33,000 geriatric inmates in California prisons alone, costing the state at least a $1 billion a year.[2] Elderly inmates provide unique management problems for staff. How is it possible to treat this special needs group in a manner that is compassionate and humane? It also illustrates how the prison population today is not a homogenous community but as diverse and varied as the nation itself. Inmates bring with them a myriad of social problems, and this chapter will consider a variety of inmate types, grouped in the following three categories: **special offense inmates**—inmates with substance abuse histories, sex offenders, and terrorists; **special needs inmates**—HIV inmates and inmates with chronic mental health issues; and **special population inmates**—elderly inmates and inmates who are illegal immigrants. Problems posed by each type to the correctional environment and to community settings when they are released are discussed in some detail, followed by a discussion of the programs that are being employed to help members of these subgroups adjust to the institution and to the community upon their release.

special offense inmates Inmates who are involved in substance abuse, are sex offenders, or are terrorists.

special needs inmates These include HIV inmates and inmates with chronic mental health issues.

special population inmates These include the elderly prisoner and the illegal immigrant inmate.

Mary Leftridge Byrd, a corrections professional for more than 30 years, served as superintendent of three correctional institutions housing women and men, and is currently the federal security director for the Transportation Security Administration (TSA) at Hartsfield-Jackson Atlanta International Airport. In Voices Across the Profession, she discusses what she liked about being a warden, including working with difficult or special populations, and what she feels she accomplished in her work in corrections.

SPECIAL OFFENSE INMATES

Special offense inmates are linked together because of their prior criminal/deviant behavior issues. Some are violent offenders, others are substance abusers, and some present problems to correctional administrators because they engage in multiple-offense patterns, such as violent drug-gang members, and others are domestic or international terrorists. Three special offense inmates are considered in this section: inmates with substance abuse histories, which includes such offenders as street-level drug dealers, drug traffickers, "mules" who carry drugs for others, and alcoholics whose crimes are directly related to drinking problems; the **sex offenders** group, which includes rapists and pedophiles; and terrorists.

sex offenders A variety of offenders including pedophiles and rapists.

Corrections and Substance-Involved Inmates

LO1 Describe the problems of inmates with a substance-involved history

The problems of substance-involved inmates are certainly not a small matter: many offenders report that they were under the influence of drugs and alcohol when they committed crime.[3] Nearly 50 percent of inmates in federal prisons are drug offenders.[4] Nearly 30 percent of inmates in state prisons are serving time for drug offenses.[5] (See Exhibit 12.1 for drug abuse history of inmates in prison.)

PROBLEMS OF WORKING WITH SUBSTANCE-INVOLVED INMATES

Narcotics or alcohol can become a special challenge when an inmate comes into the prison addicted and may crash from a sudden withdrawal. A sudden withdrawal from alcohol, for example, can throw the inmate's system into shock and may cause cardiac arrest, kidney failure, or hallucinations. Another challenge of working with substance-abuse inmates is the cost of medical treatment for inmates dealing with substance abuse.

Some inmates, desperate to continue their substance-abusing lifestyle, will actually produce homemade alcohol within the institution. An alcohol-based contraband that is found in nearly every prison is called "prison hooch" or sometimes "rook," which is a concentrated form of alcohol and can be made in a variety of ways. Much of

Mary Leftridge Byrd

VOICES ACROSS THE PROFESSION

When asked about my management philosophy—no matter what office I am leading—I need only six words: "Do justly, walk humbly, love mercy."

Mary Leftridge Byrd
Federal Security Director for the TSA at Hartsfield-Jackson International Airport and former prison warden

I have served as superintendent or warden of institutions that house mentally ill women and men who live in the same housing areas as those who have had long histories of drug abuse and addiction. I have also been involved with those who had histories of domestic violence, both as survivors and as perpetrators. Inmates could be elderly or very young and extraordinarily violent or extremely vulnerable. We had inmates who were living with HIV/AIDS. We always needed to remember that beyond the problems inmates bring to us, they were still daughters and sons, fathers and mothers, and relatives to people in the community, and we needed to treat them in a respectful way.

What did I like about being a warden? Where else could I have the opportunity to be involved in ensuring the provision of medical care along with the emotional and spiritual support often needed when someone is seriously or terminally ill? Where else could I have the opportunity to learn a lot about facilities, management, and physical plant maintenance? Where else could I have the opportunity to become active in a dynamic education system without certification? Where else would I have the ability to insist on hanging artwork in a public facility? Where else could I have the opportunity to be directly involved and accountable for the financial administration of a large organization? Where else could I have the opportunity to be involved with the culinary arts on such a large scale? Where else could I get involved in law enforcement as we were there? Think about our K-9 units, contraband interdiction efforts, investigations, sweeps and searches. Where else could I be involved in ministry? There is no question that my work is based on my own spirituality. For years I have believed I am called to do this. The longer I remain in the field, the more readily I acknowledge this calling, but my ministry is based more on behavior than through spoken words.

When asked about my management philosophy—no matter what office I am leading—I need only six words: "Do justly, walk humbly, love mercy." I am ever grateful to be on a journey that gives so much, especially the ever-present privilege to teach and the opportunity to learn.

EXHIBIT 12.1

Substance-Abusing Inmates and Criminal Activity in Prisons

A report by the National Center on Addiction and Substance Abuse (CASA) at Columbia University revealed that substance abuse inmates were involved in these inmate offenses:

- 78 percent of violent crimes
- 83 percent of property crimes
- 77 percent of public order, immigration or weapon offenses, and probation/parole violations

The CASA report also found that substance abuse inmates were:

- Four times likelier to receive income through illegal activity
- Twice as likely to have had at least one parent who abused alcohol or other drugs when they were children
- 41 percent likelier to have some family criminal history
- 20 percent less likely to have completed at least high school
- 20 percent likelier to be unemployed a month before incarceration

Source: Lauren Duran and Sulaiman Berg, *Behind Bars II: Substance Abuse and America's Prison Population*, the National Center on Addiction and Substance Abuse at Columbia University, press release, 2010, http://www.casacolumbia.org/newsroom/press-releases/2010-behind-bars-II (accessed July 2014).

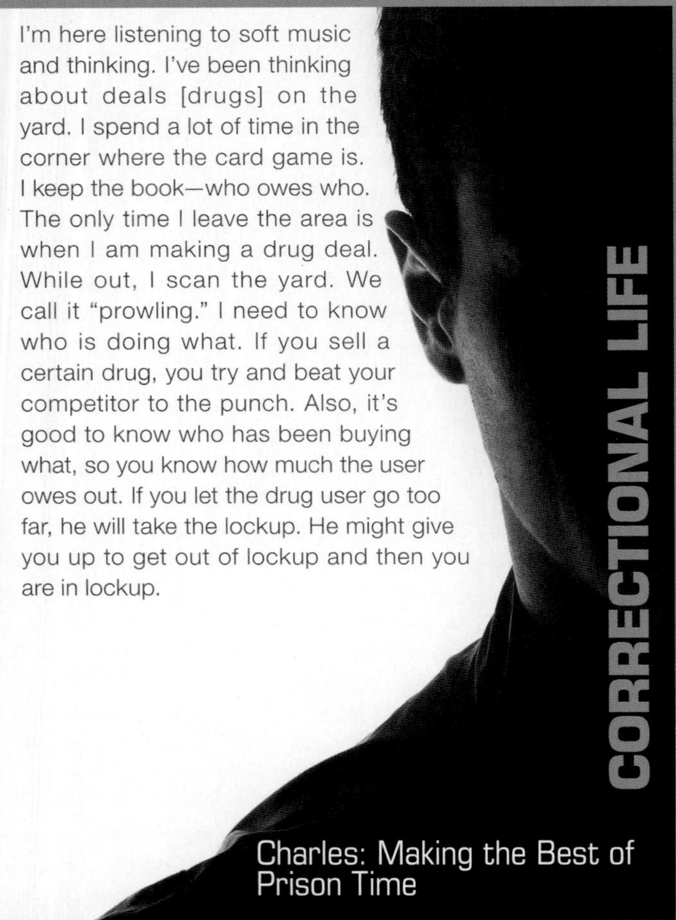

the inmate world in some prisons focuses around the drug/alcohol economy—buying, using, selling, and bartering. Not surprisingly, violence invariably erupts from this economy. In the Correctional Life feature, a long-term Pennsylvania inmate tells how he has learned to do time. He also gives some information on how he sells drugs in prison.

PROGRAMS FOR SUBSTANCE-INVOLVED INMATES About 90 percent of all state and federal prisons in the United States offer some form of substance abuse counseling, and about one in eight inmates have participated in a substance abuse treatment program while incarcerated.[6] Alcoholics Anonymous (AA), Narcotics Anonymous (NA), and other drug programs are also conducted in prisons. Some programs are brought into the prisons by AA or NA members from the community. Others are conducted by staff members.[7]

Evaluations of drug treatment programs have determined that treatment services should be based on the following:

- A clear and consistent treatment philosophy
- An atmosphere of empathy and safety
- The recruitment and maintenance of committed, qualified treatment staff
- Clear and unambiguous rules of conduct
- The use of ex-offenders and ex-addicts as role models, staff, and volunteers
- The use of peer role models and peer pressure
- The provision of relapse prevention programs
- The establishment of continuity of care throughout custody and community aftercare
- The integration of treatment evaluations into the design of the program
- The maintenance of treatment program integrity, autonomy, flexibility, and openness[8]

There is evidence that prisoners assigned to prison-based drug treatment programs have better prison adjustment than those in the general population.[9] There is also evidence that drug-involved offenders are less likely to recidivate if they receive treatment behind prison walls.[10] Offenders who enter and complete in-prison residential treatment are less likely to experience new arrests and substance use during the first six months following release.[11] Nonetheless, despite this success, relatively few at-risk inmates receive treatment while incarcerated.[12] In the Evidence-Based Corrections feature, one of the more widely used and successful programs to treat substance-abusing inmates is discussed.

Recognize what challenges and problems sex offenders bring to the prison

Sex Offenders

About 10 percent of prisoners in state prisons and 1 percent in federal facilities have been convicted of a sex offense. This number varies from one state to another.[13] In 2008, a Texas man named James Kevin Pope was sentenced to 40 life prison terms for sexually assaulting young girls over a two-year period. He received a life sentence for each sex assault conviction. At the request of prosecutors, Pope was sentenced to serve the sentences consecutively, adding up to 4,060 years behind bars; parole eligibility would begin in the year 3209.[14]

While Pope's sentence was extreme, increased prosecution and conviction, as well as longer and harsher sentences, have contributed significantly to increased numbers

EVIDENCE-BASED CORRECTIONS

Therapeutic Communities

Because substance abuse is superprevailing among correctional clients, some correctional facilities have been reformulated into therapeutic communities that apply a psychological, experimental learning process and rely on positive peer pressure within a highly structural environment. The therapeutic community (TC) for the treatment of drug abuse and addiction has existed for about 40 years. In general, TCs are drug-free residential settings that use treatment stages that reflect increased levels of personal and social responsibility. Peer influence, applied through a variety of group processes, is used to help individuals learn and assimilate social norms and develop more effective social skills.

TCs differ from other treatment approaches principally in their use of the community, comprising treatment staff with those in recovery, as key agents of change. This approach is often referred to as "community as method." TC members interact in structural and nonstructural ways to influence attitudes, perceptions, and behavior associated with drug use.

The community itself, including staff and program participants, becomes the primary method of change. They work together as members of a "family" in order to create a culture where community members confront each other's negative behavior and attitudes and establish an open, trusting, and safe environment. The TC approach then relies on mutual self-help. It also encourages personal disclosure rather than the isolation of the general prison culture.

In addition to the importance of the community as a primary agent of change, a second fundamental TC principle is "self-help," a process that ensures that the individual and treatment are the main contributors to the change process. Mutual self-help means that individuals also assume partial responsibility for the recovery of their peers, an important aspect of an individual's own treatment.

IS IT EFFECTIVE?

Treating substance-abuse inmates has proved difficult even with such highly touted programs as the therapeutic community. For three decades, the National Institute on Drug Abuse has conducted several large studies to advance scientific knowledge of the outcome of drug abuse treatment. These studies collected data from over 65,000 individuals submitted to publicly funded treatment agencies, including TCs and other types of program (i.e., methadone maintenance, outpatient drug abuse, short-term inpatient, and drug detoxification programs). Data were collected during the treatment stage and in a series of follow-ups that focused on outcomes that occurred 12 months and longer after treatment.

These studies found that participation in a TC was associated with several positive outcomes. For example, the Drug Abuse Treatment Outcome Study I (DATOS), the most recent long-term study of drug treatment outcomes, shows that those who successfully completed treatment in a TC had lower levels of cocaine, heroin, and alcohol use, criminal behavior, unemployment, and indicators of depression than they had before treatment.

Success rates for TC programs may be shaped by the way individual programs are administered and the effectiveness of treatment delivery. For example, there is evidence that those inmates who recently completed TC programs have significantly lower recidivism rates than non-attendees and are more likely to seek treatment once they return to the community. In addition when run successfully, TC programs seem effective in reducing rearrest and reincarceration rates.

FOR CRITICAL THINKING AND WRITING

1. Do you think that there could be a potential abuse of power in therapeutic communities? Do you trust that those in a position of respect will use their power in a positive way? After all, in TC programs peers take a significant role in the treatment process. TC programs depend upon people who may have addiction problems and personality deficits to help one another. Is there a problem with that approach?
2. TC program evaluations show that those who successfully completed treatment in a TC had lower levels of cocaine, heroin, and alcohol use, criminal behavior, unemployment, and indicators of depression than they had before treatment. Is that conclusive evidence of success? What important questions remain unanswered? Hint: Who determines what a successful completion means and how many people successfully complete the program?

Sources: National Institute of Drug Abuse Research Series, *Therapeutic Community*, http://www.drugabuse.gov/publications/research-reports/therapeutic-community (accessed July 2014); Sheldon X. Zhang, Robert E. L. Roberts, and Kathryn E. McCollier, "Therapeutic Community in a California Prison, Treatment Outcomes After 5 Years," *Crime and Delinquency* 37 (2011): 82; Mitchell Miller and Helen Miller, "Considering the Effectiveness of Drug Treatment Behind Bars, Findings from the South Carolina RSAT," *Justice Quarterly* 28 (2011): 70–86.

Megan's Law Named for Megan Kanka, a seven-year-old girl from New Jersey who was sexually assaulted and murdered in 1994 by a neighbor who, unknown to the victim's family, had been previously convicted for sex offenses against children. Megan's Laws are state and federal statutes that require convicted sex offenders to register with local police and to notify law enforcement authorities whenever they move to a new location. The statutes establish a notification process to provide information about sex offenders to law enforcement agencies and, when appropriate, to the public. The type of notification is based on an evaluation of the risk to the community from a particular offender.

of sex offenders in prisons. Other signs of the get-tough attitude toward sex offenders are laws permitting the indefinite confinement of rapists and child molesters who are viewed as too dangerous for release at the end of their court-imposed sentences. The state of Washington had the first such law, and Kansas, New Jersey, and Wisconsin have adopted similar laws.[15] With their release, these offenders, especially those convicted of offenses against children, are faced with **Megan's Law** and the National Sex Offender Registry. Megan's Law is mentioned in an Evidence-Based Corrections feature in Chapter 3, and in a TechnoCorrections feature Chapter 11, and is the legislation passed by New Jersey that is commonly called by this name. In 1996, Congress passed a tougher version of Megan's Law, which requires states to inform the public when a convicted sex offender considered a danger to the public is released from prison and settles in the neighborhood. States were required to establish a warning system by September 1997 or lose some federal anticrime funds. A National Sex Offender Registry became fully functional in 1999.

PROBLEMS OF WORKING WITH SEX OFFENDERS The child molester, or pedophile, has long had difficulty with prison adjustment. Other inmates, many of whom have families and children on the outside, want to set an example and convince child molesters that they will pay dearly for their crimes. In many prisons, unless pedophiles are placed in protective custody, they are likely to be sexually assaulted or even killed. Yet, in other prisons, prison classification has been successful in placing sex offenders in relatively safe environments; in these institutions, pedophiles are not harmed as they do their time.

Marvin Fong/Plain Dealer/Landov

Ariel Castro pauses while speaking before his sentencing with his attorneys Craig Weintraub, left, and Jaye Schlachet, right, in Cuyahoga County Common Pleas Court in Cleveland, Ohio, on July 26, 2013. Castro was sentenced to prison for life on hundreds of charges, including kidnapping, rape, and holding captive Amanda Berry, Gina DeJesus, and Michelle Knight for nearly a decade. One month into his sentence, he committed suicide.

Many studies have shown the recidivism rate of sex offenders to be relatively low, especially when compared to the recidivism rates of other types of offenders. While their recidivism rate is relatively low, released sex offenders are four times more likely to be rearrested for a sex crime than released non–sex offenders, most occurring in the first 12 months following their release from a state prison. Those with the most frequent pre-prison sex offending record, as measured by number of arrests, were the ones most likely to continue their sex offending career.[16] In Exhibit 12.2, Washington state's program for sex offenders is discussed in some detail.

CIVIL COMMITMENT FACILITIES Legislatures in some states have recently taken another step in controlling sexual offenders by passing laws that permit a diagnosis of sex offenders as sexually violent predators. When a person is convicted of a sex offense, he receives a penal sanction, usually a prison sentence. Once the inmate is nearing release, the state can file a petition to have the offender involuntarily and indefinitely committed to a mental institution or correctional facility that blends both a correctional facility and a mental institution. An evaluation by a mental health professional is required as well as a probable cause hearing to determine whether to label the offender a sexually violent predator. If he is so labeled, and following the completion of his prison sentence, the offender is confined to a mental health facility until judged by mental health professionals to no longer constitute a danger to the community. Sixteen states have now passed laws to involuntarily commit sexually violent predators.[17]

CRITICAL THINKING

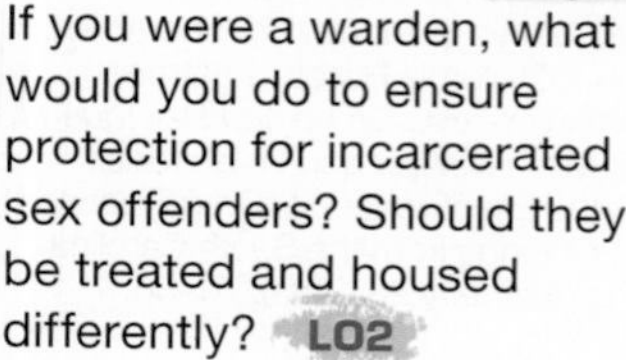

If you were a warden, what would you do to ensure protection for incarcerated sex offenders? Should they be treated and housed differently? LO2

Under these civil commitment programs, almost 3,000 pedophiles, rapists, and other sex offenders are being held indefinitely in civil commitment facilities, secure institutions that provide mental health treatment. They cost taxpayers from four to eight times more than keeping offenders in prison. The U.S. Supreme Court has

EXHIBIT 12.2

Sex Offender Treatment in Prison

An estimated 95 percent of sex offenders sentenced to prison eventually return to the community. That makes the Twin Rivers Sex Offender Treatment Program for men at the Monroe Correctional Complex and a similar program at the Washington Correction Center for Women in Gig Harbor valuable tools in the struggle to help them become law-abiding citizens.

The Department of Corrections knows treatment is not a cure for sexual deviancy. Therefore, the Monroe program's three main goals are:

- Helping offenders learn to reduce and manage risk
- Providing information to help the department and its community partners monitor and manage offenders more effectively
- Evaluating and improving treatment

Treatment begins with comprehensive assessments that include psychological tests, clinical interviews, and other techniques designed to define treatment goals and strategies for each offender. Counselors study what has sparked past offenses and then help to define the attitudes, thinking, and behavior skills that are needed to reduce the likelihood of reoffending. Program participants receive individual and group therapy. Group sessions generally have 12 to 14 members and meet from 6 to 10 hours per day. Additional classes and sessions address sexual deviancy, life skills, and other topics.

Offenders vary widely in their motivation and commitment to change. Treatment is likely to be successful to the extent that offenders are able to:

- Recognize and understand the factors that contributed to their offense(s)
- Monitor themselves and their environment to detect changes indicating that their risk to reoffend is increasing
- Develop the skills necessary to intervene, manage, and reduce risky behavior
- Remain willing and able to apply monitoring and intervention skills in a timely and effective manner, including seeking outside assistance when necessary

Treatment priority is given to the highest-risk offenders. But lower-risk offenders may be admitted for such factors as the offender:

- Used a high level of violence when committing his or her crime
- Likely committed more offenses than his or her official record shows
- Expresses an intention to commit future sex offenses
- Engages in sexually aggressive behavior in prison
- Experiences thoughts and fantasies related to sexually abusive behavior and is bothered by them

Offenders can be terminated from treatment for assaults and fighting, sexual behavior, violating the confidentiality of others in the program, failing to make progress in treatment, or being placed in a high security category (such as maximum). Offenders are expected to continue receiving treatment for up to three years after leaving prison through aftercare programs available throughout the state. The Washington Corrections Center for Women in Gig Harbor offers similar treatment for approximately 10 of the 25 female sex offenders incarcerated there.

Source: Washington State Department of Corrections, "Sex Offender Treatment in Prison," http://www.doc.wa.gov/community/sexoffenders/prisontreatment.asp (accessed July 2014).

upheld the constitutionality of the laws, primarily because their aim is to furnish treatment if possible, not punish offenders twice for the same crime. The Supreme Court weighed in on this issue in 1997, in the case of *Kansas v. Hendricks*.[18] Leroy Hendricks was a repeat child molester. As the end of his prison sentence neared, state prosecutors became concerned that upon his release he would continue victimizing children. In accordance with Kansas's Sexually Violent Predator Act, they filed to have Hendricks civilly committed as soon as he was released from prison. Hendricks appealed, claiming that it violated the law against double jeopardy. The case eventually made it to the Supreme Court, which ruled that the Kansas act did not violate double jeopardy because it was a civil action and was designed to protect the safety of innocent people rather than punish an offender. The Court ruled that indefinite commitment was not equal to a life sentence because the prisoner-cum-patient is "permitted immediate release upon a showing that the individual is no longer dangerous or

Is there a cure for sex offenders? Should sex offenders be treated as if they are ill? Discuss your views with the group, using Exhibit 12.2, "Sex Offender Treatment in Prison," as a basis for your discussion.

mentally impaired." After the decision Leroy Hendricks remained locked up at a cost of $185,000 a year—more than eight times the cost of a prison sentence in that state. When it was announced that he was moving to a group home in 2006, his transfer was protested by community residents. On April 28, 2006, the Kansas Supreme Court prevented the state from moving Hendricks out of a special treatment program for violent sexual predators to a group home in rural Leavenworth County.[19]

Terrorists in Prison

Name some of the issues terrorists present to the correctional system LO3

The Guantánamo Bay Naval Base detention camp is still in operation, though the number of inmates has been steadily declining. According to Human Rights Watch, as of August 2014, a total of 779 detainees have been held at the Guantánamo Bay facility since the September 11, 2001, attacks, 15 of them under age 18. Of the 779, roughly 600 have been released without charges; there are now about 149 detainees remaining. Of these, 78 are awaiting transfer home or to another country; 7 have been convicted in the military commissions after trial or plea bargain. Of the 149 detainees that remain at Guantánamo only six, Abd al-Rahim al-Nashiri, and the September 11, 2001 co-defendants, face any formal charges.[20]

Web App 12.1 View the *60 Minutes* segment "Supermax: A Clean Version of Hell" (http://www.cbsnews.com/news/supermax-a-clean-version-of-hell/) about terrorists in supermax. Do you think terrorists belong in our prison system? Do they understand the deterrent effect? Is this simply a way to safely keep them away from the outside world? LO3

In addition to Guantánamo, many convicted **terrorists** are now being housed in federal maximum-security prisons and are part of the general prison population. The United States Penitentiary Administrative Maximum Facility (ADX) in Florence, Colorado, the most secure supermax federal prison, holds many of the convicted terrorists, including Zacarias Moussaoui, who planned to be one of the 9/11 hijackers; Wadih El Hage, Osama bin Laden's former private secretary; and Ramzi Yousef, the leader of the first World Trade Center attack in 1993.[21]

terrorists One who acts with premeditated and politically directed violence directed against noncombatants.

When (and if) Guantánamo is closed down, its terrorist inmates will be transferred to traditional prisons in the United States or elsewhere. Correctional administrators will then have to decide how to control this special population: should they be given the same rights and privileges of other inmates or kept under much tighter control?

One major issue has been accusations that convicted terrorists held in maximum security prisons are able to freely communicate with the outside world, encouraging future terrorist attacks from their jail cells. Media news reports indicate that individuals convicted of committing terrorist acts against the United States have been allowed to recruit terrorists because the Federal Bureau of Prisons allows them very generous pen pal privileges. In one notorious incident, convicted terrorists were able to contact, from their prison in the United States, individuals in a Spanish terror cell, including Mohamed Achraf, who later allegedly led a plot to bomb Spain's National Court building in Madrid.[22]

MYTH A progressive, democratic society like the United States would never condone the physical torture of people being held in custody.

FACT While official U.S. government policy and doctrine are vehemently opposed to torture, the United States has condoned harsh interrogation techniques that combine physical and psychological tactics, including head slapping, waterboarding, and exposure to extreme cold.

Using Torture

One of the most controversial issues surrounding the treatment of suspected terrorists is the use of torture to gain information. While most people loathe the thought of torturing anyone, some experts argue that torture can sometimes be justified in what they call the **ticking bomb scenario**. Suppose the government found out that a captured terrorist knew the whereabouts of a dangerous explosive device that was set to go off and kill thousands of innocent people. Would it be permissible to engage in the use of torture on this single suspect if it would save the population of a city? Legal scholar Alan Dershowitz argues that torturing terrorists in custody can be justified under some circumstances, especially to prevent damaging terror attacks. To ensure that torture is not used capriciously, Dershowitz proposes the creation of a "torture warrant" that can only be issued by a judge in cases where (a) there is an absolute need to obtain immediate information in order to save lives and (b) there is probable cause that the suspect has such information and is unwilling to reveal it to law enforcement agents. The suspect would be given

ticking bomb scenario This scenario proposes that a dangerous explosive device is set to go off and kill thousands of people and, therefore, it might be necessary to take extreme measures, such as torture, on a subject to extract information from him or her.

EXHIBIT 12.3

Comparison of Special Offense Inmates

Inmate	Number in Prison	Treatment Access	Recidivism Rates
Substance-involved inmates	High percentage	About 1 in every 8 substance-abusing inmates receive adequate treatment	High rates of recidivism upon release
Sex offenders	About 10 percent in state prisons and 1 percent in federal prisons	Relatively few receive adequate treatment	Very low, 5 to 10 percent repeat their criminal offenses
Terrorists	1,100 or so spread over several prisons	N/A	Low for those who have been released from federal prisons

immunity from prosecution based on information elicited by the torture; it would only be to save lives. The warrant would limit the torture to nonlethal means, such as sterile needles being inserted beneath the nails to cause excruciating pain without endangering life.[23]

RARE RECIDIVISM In contrast with the record at Guantánamo, where the Defense Department says that about 25 percent of those released are suspected or known of subsequently joining militant groups, it appears extremely rare for federal inmates with past terrorist ties to plot violence following release. About 300 have been quietly released, and the government keeps a close eye on them. Before prisoners are released, FBI agents generally interview them, and probation officers track them for a number of years.[24] Exhibit 12.3 sets out a comparison of these special offense categories.

SPECIAL NEEDS INMATES

Special needs inmates include a variety of people with particular mental or physical conditions that require that they either be separated from the general prison population and/or receive unique treatment tailored to their particular circumstance. Inmates bring many physical health issues to the prison, including high rates of tuberculosis, hepatitis, and HIV, and these health issues have an effect on budgets, staff, and other inmates. In addition, as a group, inmates have high rates of chronic mental health issues, including depression, anxiety, and some psychosis.

Corrections and the HIV-Infected Inmate

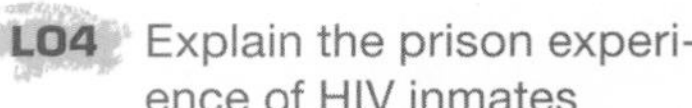

Explain the prison experience of HIV inmates

Inmate populations include a high percentage of individuals in AIDS risk groups, particularly intravenous drug users.[25] However, the number of HIV-infected inmates has been on the decline.

- The rate of HIV/AIDS among state and federal prison inmates declined from 194 cases per 10,000 inmates in 2001 to 146 per 10,000 at year end 2010.
- Between 2001 and 2010, the average annual decline of 16 percent in the national AIDS mortality rate was similar to the decline in small (down 12 percent), medium (down 17 percent), and large (down 19 percent) state prison populations.
- AIDS-related deaths in state prisons declined from 89 in 2009 to 69 in 2010 among males, from 70 to 43 among black non-Hispanics, and from 87 to 60 among all state inmates age 35 or older.[26]

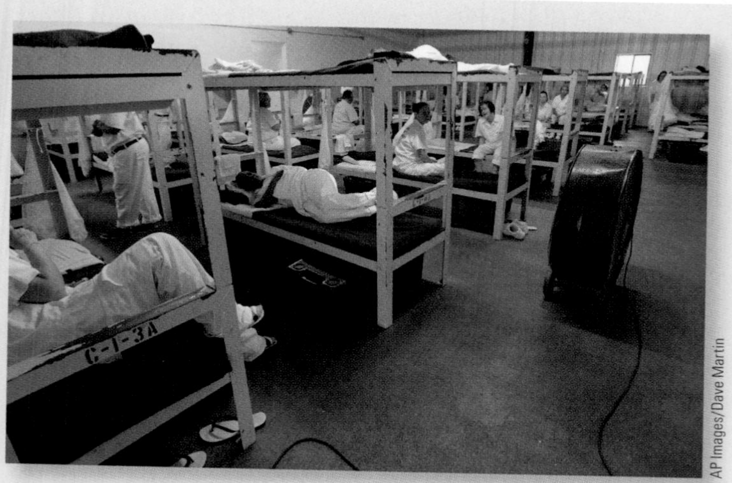

AP Images/Dave Martin

Inmates sit on their bunks in a dorm at Tutwiler Prison for Women in Wetumpka, Alabama. Alabama prison system's policy of keeping HIV-positive inmates segregated from other inmates was struck down as a violation of federal disabilities law. The state was given time to comply with the ruling.

PROBLEMS OF WORKING WITH HIV INMATES HIV inmates are now integrated with the general population in all state prison systems. Working with this population raises a number of questions: Should patients with AIDS be hospitalized, segregated, or paroled? Should officers be notified when an inmate tests positive? How about notifying past or prospective sexual partners? Does educating inmates about safe sex and needle hygiene imply that the state condones sexual behavior and drug use in prison? Does this education obligate prison officials to provide the means for prisoners to practice safe sex and good needle hygiene while imprisoned? Another issue is that in view of the HIPPA health privacy act, there is a prohibition of sharing HIV status of offenders with line officers and the implications of this problem for corrections staff.

PROGRAMS FOR HIV/AIDS INMATES Prison programs increasingly are informing inmates about the risk of unsafe sex and drug abuse. Prison personnel tend to be extremely cautious about contact with and treating inmates with HIV/AIDS. Nonetheless, a number of programs and initiatives have been created. Several states (including Vermont and Mississippi) and local jurisdictions (such as New York City, San Francisco, Philadelphia, and Washington, D.C.) are providing condoms to inmates, while others make bleach available to inmates to disinfect needles. The Centers for Disease Control and Prevention (CDC) is attempting to promote programs for HIV- and AIDS-infected inmates.[27]

- The CDC funds state and local health departments and community-based organizations to provide enhanced HIV testing and other HIV prevention services in a wide range of settings, including prisons and jails.
- It published HIV testing guidance for correctional facilities.
- It funded the evaluation of a program for which voluntary opt-out HIV rapid screening was integrated into the medical intake process at a large county jail in Atlanta with high HIV prevalence. The CDC is helping develop a best practices/model protocol for U.S. jails to implement HIV screening and other medical services during the medical assessment at intake. Persons with HIV will be linked to care and treatment.
- CDC supports Project START, an HIV, STI, and hepatitis prevention program for young men leaving prison. The intervention has been successful in reducing HIV risk behaviors of young men after release from custody, at a cost comparable to other HIV prevention programs. The CDC provides resources and training to providers through the Diffusion of Effective Behavioral Interventions project.
- Through a CDC-funded demonstration project, researchers are trying to decrease risky sexual behaviors among incarcerated adolescent black youth and adult black men at the Atlanta City Detention Center before the inmates return to their communities. Peer educators interview inmates about sexual practices and barriers to adopting HIV risk-reduction behaviors.[28]

Under the Corrections Demonstration Project, four state grantees (California, Florida, New Jersey, and New York) have created HIV prevention/peer education programs within correctional institutions. These services include weekly new inmate orientation to describe the available HIV prevention services (New Jersey) and prerelease health education sessions for inmates who are returning to the community (California).

Three of the state jurisdictions, California, New Jersey, and New York, are offering peer educator training to both HIV-positive and HIV-negative inmates. These programs hope to build associations with correctional officials and medical staff and to implement the needed services in prisons without placing a burden on correctional budgets.

Some prison systems have worked with outside agencies to help HIV/AIDS inmates adjust to prison life and prepare for reentry. In San Quentin prison in California, Centerforce, a private nonprofit institution, has been training inmates as peer HIV educators. Twice a year, volunteers are solicited to receive the comprehensive peer education training and then to work as peer educators within the prison. About 40 peer educators are trained each year. Centerforce personnel conduct focus groups to assess the service needs of inmates living with HIV, and to get feedback from them about primary prevention programs at the prison. Peer educators provide individual support for inmates newly diagnosed in prison and for HIV-positive inmates who have not been previously incarcerated. Centerforce has developed a two-week, eight-session health promotion intervention for HIV-positive inmates preparing to be released from prison. The sessions include such topics as self-esteem, health maintenance, community resources, stress management, substance use, legal issues, and barriers to care after release as well as a resource fair to introduce community service providers. In addition, peer educators conduct one-to-one sessions to help inmates learn techniques to prevent them from acquiring or transmitting HIV after release from prison. During these sessions, an individual's HIV risk is assessed, an individualized risk-reduction plan is created, and referrals are given. Sessions are conducted within two weeks of release from prison.[29]

CRITICAL THINKING 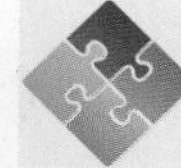

How much of the health care costs should taxpayers have to pay for those that are terminally ill? Is it appropriate to release those ill inmates in order for the state to save money? LO4

Corrections and Chronic Mentally Ill Inmates

LO5 Describe the world faced by chronic mentally ill inmates while they are in prison

According to national surveys, more than half of all prison and jail inmates (56 percent of state prisoners, 45 percent of federal prisoners, and 64 percent of local jail inmates) have a mental health problem. See Exhibit 12.4 for data on inmates who reported symptoms of a mental disorder.

PROBLEMS OF WORKING WITH CHRONIC MENTAL HEALTH INMATES

Prisoners with chronic mental health problems typically have had behavioral problems before incarceration and many get involved in substance abuse. An estimated 61 percent of state prisoners and 44 percent of jail inmates who have a mental health problem had a current or past violent offense. About a quarter of both state prisoners (25 percent) and jail inmates (26 percent) had served three or more prior sentences

EXHIBIT 12.4

Inmates Who Reported Symptoms of a Mental Disorder

- 54 percent of local jail inmates had symptoms of mania, 30 percent major depression, and 24 percent psychotic disorder, such as delusions or hallucinations.
- 43 percent of state prisoners had symptoms of mania, 23 percent major depression, and 15 percent psychotic disorder.
- 35 percent of federal prisoners had symptoms of mania, 16 percent major depression, and 10 percent psychotic disorder.

Female inmates have higher rates of mental health problems than male inmates—in state prisons, 73 percent of females and 55 percent of males; in federal prisons, 61 percent of females and 44 percent of males; and in local jails, 75 percent of females and 63 percent of males.

Source: Doris J. James and Lauren E. Glaze, *Mental Health Problems of Prison and Jail Inmates* (Washington, DC: Bureau of Justice Statistics Special Report, 2006), p. 1.

before incarceration. Inmates with a mental health problem also had high rates of substance dependence or abuse in the year before their admission:

- 74 percent of state prisoners and 76 percent of local jail inmates were dependent on or abusing drugs or alcohol.
- 37 percent of state prisoners and 34 percent of jail inmates said they had used drugs at the time of their offense.
- 13 percent of state prisoners and 12 percent of jail inmates had used methamphetamines in the month before their offense.

AP Images/Troy Maben

A mentally ill inmate (right) talks to members of the mental health treatment team, (from left) psych technician Anthony Ramos, social worker Lee Penchansky, and psychologist Dr. Charlene Green inside the Idaho Maximum Security Institution near Boise, Idaho. The inmate is one of many of Idaho's mentally ill sent to the prison for treatment because there are no other adequate facilities. He is too sick to be treated as an outpatient and too dangerous for lower-level security hospitals.

In addition, these inmates bring other problems to the prison setting. About a quarter of both state prisoners and jail inmates with mental problems also report past physical or sexual abuse. About one in three state prisoners with mental health problems, one in four federal prisoners, and one in six jail inmates had received mental health treatment since admission. Taking a prescribed medication was the most common type of treatment—27 percent in state prisons, 19 percent in federal prisons, and 15 percent in local jails.[30]

Because inmates with chronic mental health problems present such a challenge for correctional administrators, efforts have been made to develop screening instruments to identify and classify them in an efficient manner. These instruments are discussed in Exhibit 12.5.

EXHIBIT 12.5

Mental Health Screening Tools

Considering the significant problems posed by mentally ill inmates, it is important for correctional administrators to develop tools to quickly identify inmates who are in need of special services. Most clinical evaluations are time consuming and expensive, so a brief but effective screening is available. Researchers funded by the National Institute of Justice have created and tested two mental health screening tools and found that they are likely to work well in correctional settings: the Correctional Mental Health Screen (CMHS) and the Brief Jail Mental Health Screen (BMHS).[31]

CMHS

- The CMHS uses separate questionnaires for men and women. The version for women (CMHS-W) consists of eight yes/no questions and the version for men (CMHS-M) contains twelve yes/no questions about content and lifetime indications of serious mental disorders. Six questions regarding symptoms in the inmate's history of mental illness are the same on both questionnaires: the remaining questions are unique to each gender. Some of the questions are:
- Have you ever had worries you just can't get rid of?
- Some people feel that their mood changes frequently—as if they spend every day on an emotional roller coaster. Does this sound like you?
- Do you get annoyed when friends or family complain about their problems? Or do people complain that you are not sympathetic to their problems?
- Have you ever felt like you didn't have any feelings, or felt distant or cut off from other people or from your surroundings?
- Has there ever been a time when you felt so irritable that you found yourself shouting at people or starting fights or arguments? Do you often get in trouble at work or with friends because you act excited at first but then lose interest in projects and don't follow through?
- Do you tend to hold grudges or give people the silent treatment for days at a time?

Each screen takes about three to five minutes to administer. It is recommended that male inmates who answer yes to six or more questions and female inmates who answer yes to five or more questions be referred for further evaluation.

(continued)

BHMS

The BHMS has eight yes/no questions, takes about two to three minutes and requires minimum training to administer. It asks six questions about current mental disorders plus two questions about history of hospitalization and medication for mental or emotional problems. Inmates who answer yes to two or more questions about current symptoms or answer yes to either of the other two questions are referred for further evaluation. Corrections classification officers, intake staff, or nursing staff can administer the screen.

Validation test results show that these tests are effective instruments that can be used to identify depression, anxiety, PTSD, some personality disorders, and the presence of any undetected mental health problems.

Sources: Michael Martin, Ian Colman, Alexander Simpson, and Kwame McKenzie, "Mental Health Screening Tools in Correctional Institutions: A Systematic Review," *BMC Psychiatry* 13 (2013), http://www.ncbi.nlm.nih.gov/pubmed/24168162 (accessed July 2014); Andrew L. Goldberg and Brian R. Higgins, *Brief Mental Health Screening for Corrections Intake*, http://www.ncjrs.gov/pdffiles1/nij/215592.pdf (accessed July 2014); National Institute of Justice, *Mental Health Screens for Corrections*, May 7, 2007, http://www.ncjrs.gov/pdffiles1/nij/216152.pdf (accessed July 2014).

PROGRAMS FOR PRISONERS WITH CHRONIC MENTAL HEALTH ISSUES How did the population of mentally ill inmates get so large? In the 1960s, the government began closing state-run hospitals due to budget cuts and court orders forbidding the institutionalization of mentally ill people unless they received proper treatment. As a result, the number of people hospitalized for mental illness has significantly declined. Fifty years ago, the United States had nearly 600,000 state hospital beds for people suffering from mental illness; today, that number has dwindled to 40,000. Many wound up on the street and in the courts. Many Americans receive mental health treatment in prisons and jails rather than hospitals or treatment centers. New York City's Rikers Island jail alone holds thousands of mentally ill inmates at any given time.

MYTH One reason why male inmates are more violent and dangerous than female inmates is because males have a higher rate of mental illness.

FACT The rate of mental illness among females in prison is actually higher than males. Almost three-quarters of women in prison suffer from mental illness.

While the number of inmates with mental health problems is significant, treatment has been less than adequate and services for mentally ill inmates have been highly criticized. This has prompted advocacy groups to file lawsuits and lobby legislatures to promote relief for the mentally ill inmate. One reason is the charge that mentally ill inmates have been the subject of brutality by correctional officers. One case involving guards at the Rikers Island facility in New York was captured on a video where correctional officers can be seen scrapping with an inmate at his cell's threshold, then pushing their way inside. They spent about three minutes there—they threw the inmate to the floor and repeatedly kicked and punched him in the head and torso. A minute later, a captain entered the cell and was heard by a nearby inmate discussing how to handle the situation; Corrections Department rules permit officers to enter an inmate's cell only when there is an immediate threat, such as a suicide attempt. The video then shows the captain heading to a jail clinic, where she fashions a noose out of the inmate's pants, twisting the legs and tying them together in a loop. Shortly before this incident occurred, another inmate, a mentally ill Marine Corps veteran, died in an overheated cell, while another died after being locked in a cell for seven days, naked and covered in feces.[32]

Exhibit 12.6 sets out the treatment access and postrelease success of special needs inmates.

CRITICAL THINKING

Do the mentally ill belong in our prisons? Is there another place for them to go? If they commit a crime, should the focus be on punishment or treatment? LO5

EXHIBIT 12.6

Comparison of Special Needs Inmates

Inmate	Number in Prison	Treatment Access	Recidivism Rates
HIV-infected	No national data	Providing medical care and some psychological counseling	Postrelease success is typical of the average inmate
Chronic mental health issues	About half of inmates have mental health problems	Usually medication and some direct intervention when crisis situations take place	High recidivism rates when returned to the community

AP Images/Jennifer Simonson

Minnesota Department of Corrections Sgt. Carl Bennett, center, takes part in a role-playing exercise to convince a schizophrenic offender to come out of his cell during crisis intervention training at the Minnesota Correctional Facility in Stillwater. The training is intended to help employees defuse potentially violent situations and avoid use of force with inmates who have mental health issues.

SPECIAL POPULATION INMATES

The third type of unique inmate is those in special populations, whose status creates problems for prison administrators. The elderly prisoner and the illegal immigrant inmate are two forms of special population inmates.

Corrections and the Elderly Inmate

Today there are more than 120,000 inmates aged 50 and over in state or federal prisons, more than twice as many as a decade earlier.[33] The aging of the prison population has come about from longer sentences resulting from the get-tough-on-crime measures that impose truth-in-sentencing, mandatory sentences, and three-strikes laws, and an increasing number of older people convicted of sex crimes and murder.[34] This number is sure to rise: the U.S. population aged 65 and older is estimated to grow from 35 million in 2000 to 78 million in 2050, and the number of those aged 85 and older will increase from 4 million to 31 million.[35] By some estimates, by the year 2030 one-third of the U.S. prison population will be geriatric.[36]

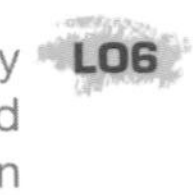

Explain the plight of elderly inmates while incarcerated and what is involved in their care

There are different adjustment rates for elderly prisoners. The longer the amount of time remaining to be served, the harder it usually is for the elderly person to deal with confinement. Background factors, such as level of education and marital status, can also affect the adjustment of the elderly. Some inmates, especially those imprisoned early in life, are more institutionally dependent than others. Some have higher morale and are more involved in programs and prison life than others. There is the problem that in many prisons there is little programming or specialized treatment geared for elderly inmates.[37]

PROBLEMS OF WORKING WITH THE ELDERLY INMATE The elderly prisoner is vulnerable to victimization and requires special attention when it comes to medical treatment, housing, nutrition, and institutional activities. The care of the elderly is extremely expensive. For example, the average cost of housing an inmate over 60 is $70,000 a year, which is about three times the average cost for other prisoners. To cope with this problem, some states have developed a number of strategies to mitigate the rising cost of caring for prisoners, including increased use of telemedicine and the outsourcing of medical services to state universities and other providers. A small number of states have made limited use of Medicaid to help finance rising prison health care costs. The potential benefits of Medicaid financing will increase substantially as the Affordable Care Act takes effect, but only in states that expand their programs. One problem: currently, most state Medicaid programs cover very few childless adults, a population that makes up the bulk of the prison population. In most cases, only pregnant women and disabled inmates are eligible for Medicaid. By expanding Medicaid to all adults with incomes up to 138 percent of the federal poverty line ($11,490 for an individual), virtually everyone who is incarcerated will qualify for the federal-state program. The federal government will pay 100 percent of costs for newly eligible adults from 2014 through 2016 and gradually decrease its share to 90 percent by 2020.[38]

Inmates over 50 are also more likely to have health and mental health problems than noninstitutionalized Americans because they often come from poor backgrounds, have a greater likelihood of drug and alcohol abuse, and have more restricted access to health care.[39]

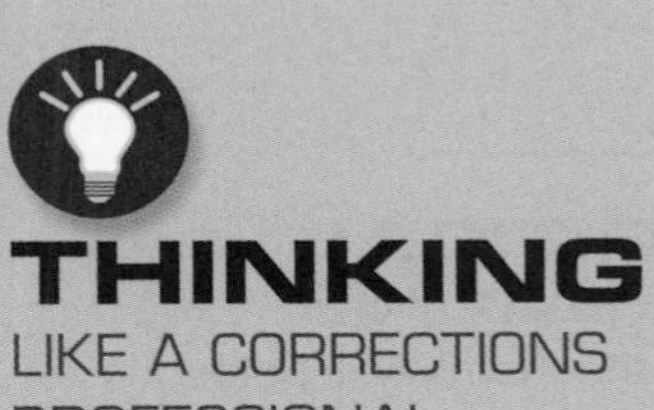

THINKING LIKE A CORRECTIONS PROFESSIONAL

The warden calls you and other lieutenants together and tells you that prison suicides have become a major problem. There have been three so far this month, and the current year has the highest number of suicides in the history of the prison.

As the senior correctional supervisor, he wants you to chair a team to study this problem and make recommendations that will reduce the incidents of suicides. What will you do—first, second, and third? Are prison suicides something that can be reduced through management procedures?

Some elderly prisoners find prison physically difficult to manage. One study of 120 female prisoners aged 55 or older in a California prison found that 69 percent of the women reported that at least one prison activity of daily living was very difficult to perform. These women also had higher rates of hypertension, asthma or other lung disease, and arthritis.[40] Another study found that nearly 40 percent of state inmates 55 and older have a recent history of mental health problems or disorders.[41]

Ronald H. Aday and others have reported that older prisoners need more orderly conditions, safety precautions, emotional feedback, and familial support than younger prisoners. They are particularly uncomfortable in crowded conditions, tend to prefer small groups, and want time alone.[42]

One of the problems of working with elderly prisoners is that increasing numbers of these prisoners have violent records or are sex offenders. One study conducted in the Deerfield Correctional Center in Virginia, which includes a large population of geriatric inmates, found that 75 percent had violent records and nearly 30 percent were sex offenders.[43] This record means that while the elderly demand special care, high security measures still must be maintained.[44]

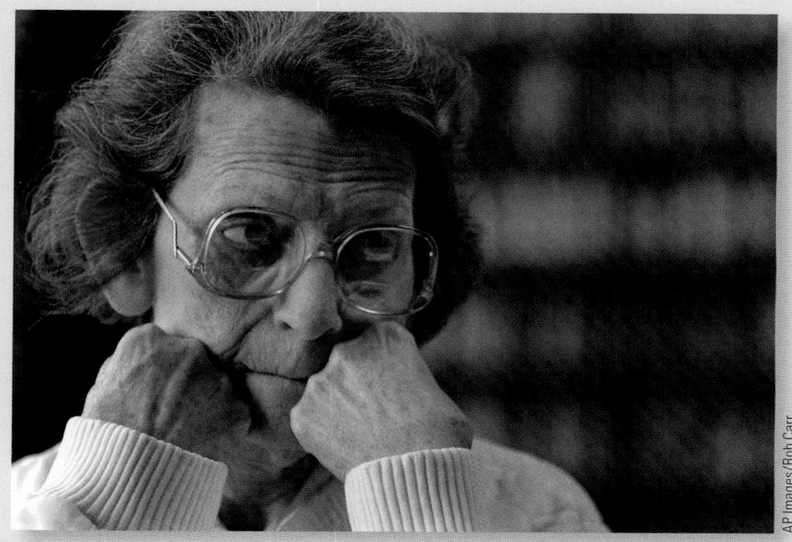

AP Images/Rob Carr

Martha Staggs, 68, listens to a question during an interview at the Julia Tutwiler Prison for Women in Wetumpka, Alabama. Staggs, who was convicted of murdering her husband in 2003, was diagnosed with colon cancer and after surgery the cancer spread to her liver. Her chemotherapy and medical bills total more than $67,000 a year. The cost of elderly or infirm inmates to Alabama's underfunded, overcrowded prison system has prompted several lawmakers to support a bill that would expedite parole dates for those prisoners. Is there any point in keeping someone like Staggs behind bars or would an elderly inmate such as her be better off being treated in the community?

Corrections and the Illegal Immigrant

Few issues create as much controversy as immigration and crime. Concerns over the effects of immigration have existed for a long time, and bans against criminal aliens represented some of the earliest restrictions on immigration in the United States.[45] More recently, policies adopted in the mid-1990s have greatly expanded the scope of acts for which noncitizens may be expelled from the United States. Even so, calls to curtail immigration, especially illegal immigration, appeal to public fears about immigrants' involvement in criminal activities.[46]

CRITICAL THINKING

Is there a deterrent effect to keeping the elderly behind bars? Should they be subject to compassionate release? LO6

Ironically, concern about the criminal activity of immigrants is rampant despite growing evidence that they actually have very low crime rates. According to "Crime, Corrections, and California: What Does Immigration Have to Do with It?"—a report released by the Public Policy Institute of California—immigrants are far less likely than the average U.S. native to commit crime in California.[47] Significantly lower rates of incarceration and institutionalization among foreign-born adults suggest that long-standing fears of immigration as a threat to public safety are unjustified. See Exhibit 12.7 for the key findings.

LO7 Discuss the problems faced by illegal immigrants in U.S. prisons

The findings are striking because immigrants in California are more likely to be young and male and to have low levels of education—all characteristics associated with higher rates of crime and incarceration. Yet the report shows that institutionalization rates of young male immigrants with less than a high school diploma are extremely low, particularly when compared with U.S.-born men with low levels of education. The low rates of criminal involvement by immigrants may be due in part to current U.S. immigration policy, which screens immigrants for criminal history and assigns extra penalties to noncitizens who commit crime.[48]

MYTH Most people are released from prison and there are relatively few elderly inmates.

FACT Today, there are more than 120,000 inmates aged 50 and over in state or federal prisons, more than twice as many as a decade earlier.

EXHIBIT 12.7

Key Findings About Immigrants

- People born outside the United States make up about 35 percent of California's adult population but represent only about 17 percent of the state prison population.
- U.S.-born adult men are incarcerated in state prisons at rates up to 3.3 times higher than foreign-born men.
- Among men aged 18 to 40—the age group most likely to commit crime—those born in the United States are 10 times more likely than immigrants to be in county jail or state prison.
- Noncitizen men from Mexico aged 18 to 40—a group disproportionately likely to have entered the United States illegally—are more than 8 times less likely than U.S.-born men in the same age group to be in a correctional setting (0.48 percent versus 4.2 percent).

Source: Kristin F. Butcher and Anne Morrison Piehl, "Immigration Has Little To Do with California Crime" press release, Public Policy Institute of California, February 25, 2008. Reprinted by permission of Public Policy Institute of California, http://www.ppic.org/main/publication.asp?i=776 (accessed July 2014).

© Jose Cabezas/AFP/Getty Images

Illegal immigrants are an emerging correctional population. The Willacy Detention Center in Raymondville, Texas, is used by the U.S. Immigration and Customs Enforcement (ICE) agency to keep illegal immigrants in detention before they are deported. On December 18, 2008, 116 Salvadoran nationals—83 men and 33 women—were woken up at 4 A.M. and transported in buses under strict surveillance to be flown back to El Salvador. Here, prison guards at the Willacy facility frisk female detainees before embarking for the airport.

Despite the evidence indicating that both legal and illegal immigrants are less crime prone than native-born Americans, John Hagan and Alberto Palloni have found that the public's fear of illegal immigrants leads to higher levels of detention among Hispanic immigrants who actually break the law. Their findings suggest that Hispanics may suffer an increased burden at the pretrial release stage, because of both racism and anti-immigrant attitudes.[49] Stephen Demuth and Darrell Steffensmeier's analysis of this issue found conclusive evidence that anti-immigrant attitudes may contribute to the over-detention of immigrants who do break the law.[50]

PROBLEMS ILLEGAL IMMIGRANTS BRING TO THE PRISON Illegal immigrants have a number of unique problems that must be addressed by correctional administrators. They may be recruited into ethnically compatible gangs. They frequently have difficulty in communicating with staff because their ability to use English is limited. Consequently, the growing number of non–English-speaking inmates requires that correctional staff become bilingual. If needs are not met, prison unrest may result.

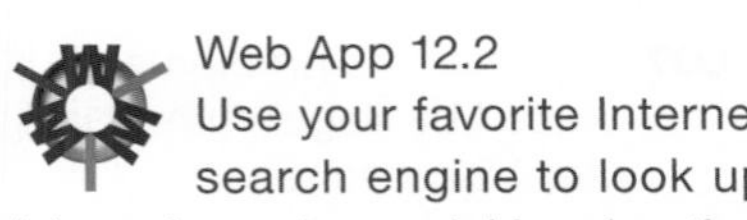

Web App 12.2
Use your favorite Internet search engine to look up Arizona's controversial immigration law SB 1070. Do you think this legislation would have an impact on the number of illegal immigrants we find in our prisons? LO7

family detention centers Minimum-security residential facilities that provide schooling for children, recreational activities, and access to religious services.

PROGRAMS FOR ILLEGAL IMMIGRANTS The Bureau of Immigration and Customs Enforcement (ICE)—the federal agency that has jurisdiction over immigrant detention—is now in the process of creating **family detention centers**, minimum-security residential facilities that would house entire families and provide schooling for children, recreational activities, and access to religious services.

This concept has been condemned by human rights groups and immigrant rights organizations as punitive and unnecessary, but immigration authorities embrace it as a deterrent against families crossing the border as a group and to ensure that immigrants show up for their court hearings and leave the country when ordered deported. Illegal immigrants who commit criminal offenses typically are required to be punished for these offenses, such as being sent to prison and doing their time, before they are subjected to being deported.

When family detention centers began operations, correctional administrators immediately faced protests and lawsuits charging that the children were living in substandard conditions. Children were given hospital scrubs to wear, forbidden to have toys, and allowed only one hour of recreation per day. After a legal settlement, children are now allowed to wear pajamas, move freely around the center, and bring toys into their rooms. There also have been changes made to the facility, including adding individual bathrooms, adding murals, and replacing metal doors.[51]

While the family detention center has been controversial, so too have the working conditions in the detention center. In 2014, at least 60,000 immigrants worked in the federal government's nationwide detention centers—a number that is greater than the work force of any other single employer in the country. What is at issue is the wages: 13 cents an hour, a number that saves the government and the private companies $40 million or more a year by allowing them to avoid paying outside contractors the $7.25 federal minimum wage. Some immigrants held at county jails do not receive a wage and are paid with sodas or candy bars for providing services like meal preparation for other government institutions. The compensation at detention centers is set under guidelines created in 1950 and which have not been changed since; courts have upheld the dollar-a-day compensation. So on any given day, about 5,500 detainees work for $1, in programs run by the federal government and private companies.[52]

washingtonindependent.com

The increased collaboration between the Department of Homeland Security (DHS) and local law enforcement has resulted in large numbers of detained illegal immigrants being held in local jails. Here, illegal immigrants are held at a detention facility in Phoenix, Arizona. Confusion often reigns when local jails go beyond handling regular local criminal matters to holding civil detainees for federal agencies. Questions of custody and responsibility involve both federal and state agencies, and inmates may be charged with both criminal and civil proceedings involving different legal rights.

Michael H. Fogel

CAREERS IN CORRECTIONS

Michael H. Fogel

Forensic Psychologist

"Forensic psychologists are employed in a variety of settings, including correctional facilities, psychiatric hospitals, and court clinics. I am a professor in the Department of Forensic Psychology at The Chicago School of Professional Psychology (TCSPP), and I maintain an independent practice in forensic psychology. At TCSPP, I teach courses for students seeking a master's degree in forensic psychology or a doctoral degree in clinical forensic psychology. In my private practice, I conduct psychological evaluations concerning psycholegal issues. I might be asked by a prosecuting or criminal defense attorney to assess a defendant's competence to stand trial, mental state at the time of the offense, or risk to commit a future act of violence. With each referral question, there are generally accepted standards of practice that guide how I complete the evaluation. One governing guideline is to perform an unbiased and impartial evaluation regardless of the side that retains me and the adversarial nature of the legal system. Indeed, a forensic psychologist is akin to a teacher. Instead of instructing a classroom of students, he or she is educating judges and juries via a written report and/or expert witness testimony about the findings of their evaluation."

"A typical evaluation will include a review of relevant records (e.g., police reports, school records, mental health records), interviews with the defendant, interviews with collateral informants (e.g., family members, witnesses, treatment providers), and the administration of psychological tests and/or forensic assessment instruments. After the evaluation is complete and an opinion has been reached, I will discuss my findings with the prosecuting or criminal defense attorney who retained my services, and will usually be asked to write a report, which will detail my findings and the data upon which they are based. Most often, my reports will stand on their own and expert witness testimony is not required; however, the extent to which an expert is called to testify varies greatly by jurisdiction and the nature of the evaluation."

See Chapter 15 for more detailed information on careers in corrections.

SUMMARY

LO1 Describe the problems of inmates with a substance-involved history

Inmates with a substance-involved history, especially drug-addicted inmates, need treatment while incarcerated and, at the same time, they pose particular challenges to maintaining a lawful environment if they are involved in drug use and trafficking to other inmates.

LO2 Recognize what challenges and problems sex offenders bring to the prison

Sex offenders are more numerous in prison than in the past. The major categories of sex offenders are the rapist and the child molester. It is the child molester who traditionally has had a difficult time in the prison environment, but improved classification in some states has resulted in sex offenders being safer than they have been in the past. Some sex offenders face civil commitment when they are released from prison.

LO3 Name some of the issues terrorists present to the correctional system

Terrorists are presently housed in the Guantánamo Bay facility and in federal facilities on the mainland. Relatively few are housed in Guantánamo and many of these are scheduled to be transferred or released. Only a handful have actually been convicted of crimes. When (and if) Guantánamo is closed down, its terrorist inmates will be transferred to traditional prisons. One major issue has been accusations that convicted terrorists held in maximum security prisons are able to freely communicate with the outside world, encouraging future terrorist attacks from their jail cells.

LO4 Explain the prison experience of HIV inmates

HIV inmates are now integrated in the general population. However, many problems and issues remain to be settled. Should patients with AIDS be hospitalized? Should officers be notified when an inmate tests positive? Does educating inmates about safe sex and needle hygiene imply that the state condones sexual behavior and drug use in prison?

LO5 Describe the world faced by chronic mentally ill inmates while they are in prison

Chronic mentally ill inmates are also highly represented in prison populations. It has been found that half or more of inmates in today's prisons have some form of mental health problem, and with some inmates their behavior is so extreme that they need psychiatric intervention and medication. They face ridicule, harassment, and the possibility of various forms of victimization from other inmates and very little in terms of programs and other means, other than medication, to help them cope with prison life.

LO6 Explain the plight of elderly inmates while incarcerated and what is involved in their care

Elderly inmates are extremely costly to care for, both in maintaining their physical well-being and in providing for them during the final days of their lives. One of the tasks of prison staff is to protect them from exploitative inmates. The management and care of these inmates require proper programming, a safe environment, and a sensitive and concerned staff.

LO7 Discuss the problems faced by illegal immigrants in U.S. prisons

Illegal immigrants are another special population in prison settings. Even though illegal immigrants do pose problems, such as when they become involved in a violent prison gang, they ordinarily present little difficulty during the time they are detained. Their biggest problem is being exploited as cheap prison labor: a dollar a day!

CRITICAL THINKING QUESTIONS

1. Is there a better way to handle vulnerable inmates than to put them in the prison population or to isolate them in protective custody?
2. What should the role of correctional staff be with inmates who are dying?
3. Which group of inmates discussed in this chapter do you think poses the greatest problem for staff?
4. Which group of inmates discussed in this chapter do you think has the greatest problem with prison life?
5. Does the fact that privately run detention facilities pay the illegal immigrants they house a dollar a day make you reconsider the concept of running a correctional facility for profit?

NOTES

1. Viji Sundaram, "Golden Girls Behind Bars: Aging Population Yearn for Freedom," *New America Media*, February 9, 2009, http://news.newamericamedia.org/news/view_article.html?article_id=90940ea33392050bde1225dd95067e36 (accessed July 2014).
2. Ibid.
3. James P. Wojtowicz, Tongyin Liu, and G. Wayne Hedgpeth, "Factors of Addiction: New Jersey Correctional Population," *Crime and Delinquency* 53 (2007): 471–500.
4. William J. Sabol, Heather Couture, and Paige M. Harrison, *Prisoners in 2006* (Washington, DC: Bureau of Justice Statistics, 2007), p. 10.
5. Ibid., p. 24.
6. Sarah Goodrum, Michelle Station, Carl Leukefeld, J. Matthew Webster, and Richard T. Purvis, "Perceptions of a Prison-Based Substance Abuse Treatment Program Among Some Staff and Participants," *Journal of Offender Rehabilitation* 37 (2006): 27–46.
7. See Stephen K. Valle and Dennis Humphrey, "American Prisons as Alcohol and Drug Treatment Centers: A Twenty-Year Reflection, 1988–2000," *Alcoholism Treatment Quarterly* 20 (2002): 83–106.
8. Michael L. Prendergast and Henry K. Wexler, "Correctional Substance Abuse Treatment Programs in California: A History Perspective," *Prison Journal* 84 (2004): 12–13.
9. Michael L. Prendergast, Elizabeth A. Hall, and Harry K. Wexler, "Multiple Measures of Outcome in Assessing a Prison-Based Drug Treatment Program," *Journal of Offender Rehabilitation* 37 (2003): 65–94.
10. Sheryl Pimlott Pubiak, Carol J. Boyd, Janie Slayden, and Amy Young, "The Substance Abuse Treatment Needs of Prisoners: Implementation of an Integrated Statewide Approach," *Journal of Offender Rehabilitation* 41 (2005): 1–19. See also Bernadette Pelissier, "Gender Differences in Substance Use Treatment Entry and Retention Among Prisoners with Substance Use Histories," *American Journal of Public Health* 94 (2004): 1418–1424. See also Steven Belenko, "Assessing Released Inmates for Substance-Abuse-Related Service Needs," *Crime and Delinquency* 52 (2006): 94–113.
11. Bernadette Pelissier, Susan Wallace, Joyce Ann O'Neil, Gerald G. Gaes, Scott Camp, William Rhodes, and William Saylor, "Federal Prison Residential Drug Treatment Reduces Substance Use and Arrests After Release," *American Journal of Drug and Alcohol Abuse* 27 (2001): 315–337. See also Neal P. Langan and Bernadette M. Pelissier, "The Effect of Drug Treatment on Inmate Misconduct in Federal Prisons," *Journal of Offender Rehabilitation* 34 (2002): 21–30.
12. Steven Belenko and Jordan Peugh, "Estimating Drug Treatment Needs Among State Prison Inmates," *Drug and Alcohol Dependence* 77 (2005): 269–281.
13. *Sex Offending and Sex Offenders: Theories, Factors, and Treatment*, InsidePrison.com, April 2006, http://www.insideprison.com/Sex-Offending-and-Offenders.asp (accessed July 2014).
14. Associated Press, "Texas Man Gets 4,060 Years in Prison," *New York Daily News*, July 2, 2008.
15. William M. DiMascio, *Seeking Justice: Crime and Punishment in America* (New York: Edna McConnell Clark Foundation, 1995), p. 22.
16. Matthew Durose, Patrick Langan, Erica Schmitt, *Recidivism of Sex Offenders Released from Prison in 1994* (Washington, DC: Bureau of Justice Statistics, 2003), http://www.bjs.gov/content/pub/pdf/rsorp94.pdf (accessed July 2014).
17. These 16 states are Arizona, California, Florida, Illinois, Iowa, Kansas, Massachusetts, Minnesota, Missouri, New Jersey, North Dakota, South Carolina, Texas, Virginia, Washington, and Wisconsin.
18. *Kansas v. Hendricks*, 521 U.S. 346 (1997).
19. Monica Davey and Abby Goodnough, "Doubts Rise as States Hold Sex Offenders After Prison," *New York Times*, March 4, 2007.
20. Human Rights Watch, "Facts and Figures: Military Commissions v. Federal Courts," August 2014, http://www.hrw.org/features/guantanamo-facts-figures (accessed August 2014).
21. Scott Pelley, "Supermax: A Clean Version of Hell," *60 Minutes*, October 14, 2007.
22. United States Senate, "Schumer: Bureau of Prisons Process Must Be Examined and Fixed Immediately, Pen Pal Privileges for Terrorists Must Stop," March 1, 2005.
23. Alan M. Dershowitz, *Shouting Fire: Civil Liberties in a Turbulent Age* (New York: Little, Brown, 2002); Dershowitz, "Want to Torture? Get a Warrant," *San Francisco Chronicle*, January 22, 2002.
24. Shane, "Beyond Guantánamo," p. 26.
25. Camille Graham Camp and George M. Camp, *The Corrections Yearbook 2002: Adult Corrections* (Middletown, CT: Criminal Justice Institute, 2002), p. 52.
26. Laura Maruschak, *HIV in Prisons, 2001–2010* (Washington, DC: US Department of Justice, 2012), http://www.bjs.gov/content/pub/pdf/hivp10.pdf (accessed August 2014).
27. Centers for Disease Control and Prevention, "HIV in Correctional Settings, 2014," http://www.cdc.gov/hiv/risk/other/correctional.html (accessed August 2014).
28. Ibid.
29. Centerforce, "Collaborative Programs in HIV, STD and Hepatitis Prevention," http://caps.ucsf.edu/centerforce (accessed July 2014).
30. Ibid.
31. Michael Martin, Ian Colman, Alexander Simpson, and Kwame McKenzie, "Mental Health Screening Tools in Correctional Institutions: A Systematic Review," *BMC Psychiatry* 13 (2013), http://www.ncbi.nlm.nih.gov/pubmed/24168162 (accessed August 2014).
32. Michael Schwirtz and Michael Winerip, "New York City Reviewing Rikers Assaults on 129 Inmates," *New York Times*, July 21, 2014, http://www.nytimes.com/2014/07/22/nyregion/new-york-city-reviewing-injuries-dealt-by-rikers-correction-officers.html (accessed July 2014).
33. Christine Vestal, "Study Finds Aging Inmates Pushing Up Prison Health Care Costs," Pew Charitable Trusts, October 29, 2013, http://www.pewtrusts.org/en/research-and-analysis/blogs/stateline/2013/10/29/study-finds-aging-inmates-pushing-up-prison-health-care-costs (accessed August 2014).
34. Ibid.
35. Data from the American Geriatrics Society, http://www.americangeriatrics.org/ (accessed August 2014).
36. Quoted in Steve Tokar, "Prisons Not Adapting to Needs of Aging Inmate Population," University of California Newsroom, 2006.
37. Christine Vestal, "Study Finds Aging Inmates Pushing Up Prison Health Care Costs."
38. Ibid.
39. Anthony A. Sterns and Greta Lax, "The Growing Wave of Older Prisoners: A National Survey of Older Prisoner Health, Mental Health and Programming," *Corrections Today* 70 (August 2008): 70–76.
40. Tokar, "Prisons Not Adapting to Needs of Aging Inmate Population."
41. D. J. James and L. E. Glaze, *Mental Health Problems of Prison and Jail Inmates* (Washington, DC: Bureau of Justice Statistics, 2006). See also Rebecca S. Allen, Laura Lee Phillips, Lucinda Lee Roff, Ronald Cavanaugh, and Laura Day, "Religiousness/Spirituality and Mental Health Among Older Male Inmates," *Gerontologist* 46 (2008): 692–697; Steven J. Caverley, "Older Mentally Ill Inmates: A Descriptive Study," *Journal of Correctional Health Care* 12 (2006): 1–7.
42. Sterns and Lax, "The Growing Wave of Older Prisoners."
43. Eva Russo, "Growing Old Behind Bars," *Richmond Times-Dispatch*, March 4, 2009.
44. Viji Sundaram, "Golden Girls Behind Bars."
45. Daniel Kanstroom, *Deportation Nation: Outsiders in American History* (Cambridge, MA: Harvard University Press, 2007).
46. Kristin F. Butcher and Anne Morrison Piehl, "Crime, Corrections, and California: What Does Immigration Have to Do with It?" Public Policy Institute of California, *California Counts: Population Trends and Profiles* 9 (February 2008): 1, http://www.ppic.org/main/publication.asp?i=776 (accessed July 2014).
47. Ibid.
48. Ibid., pp. 1–2.
49. John Hagan and Alberto Palloni, "Sociological Criminology and the Mythology of Hispanic Immigration and Crime," *Social Problems* 46 (1999): 615–632.
50. Stephen Demuth and Darrell Steffensmeier, "The Impact of Gender and Race-Ethnicity in the Pretrial Release Process," *Social Problems* 51 (May 2004): 222–242.
51. Anna Gorman, "Immigration Agency Plans New Family Detention Centers," *Los Angeles Times*, May 18, 2008.
52. Ian Urbina, "Using Jailed Migrants as a Pool of Cheap Labor," *New York Times*, May 24, 2014, http://www.nytimes.com/2014/05/25/us/using-jailed-migrants-as-a-pool-of-cheap-labor.html (accessed August 2014).

Marvin Fong/The Plain Dealer/Landov

Serial murderer Anthony Sowell received a recommendation of the death penalty from the jury for the murders of 11 women in Cleveland, Ohio. Sowell originally filed an insanity defense but later changed it to not guilty. Is it possible that serial killers like Sowell are truly "mentally sound"? And if they are psychologically impaired, should they be executed?

IN 1985, ANTHONY SOWELL WAS SENTENCED TO PRISON FOR 15 YEARS for abducting and attempting to sexually assault a pregnant woman. He got out in 2005, but the prison experience had done nothing to dampen his disturbed sexual appetites. In September 2009, a woman filed a complaint with police that Anthony Sowell had hit, choked, and raped her in his home. When police arrived with a warrant, they did not find Sowell but did discover two bodies lying in plain sight. Further searches uncovered more bodies scattered around the house, in crawl spaces, in the basement, and carelessly buried in the backyard.

Sowell was arrested and charged with eleven counts of murder, rape, and kidnapping. On July 22, 2011, he was convicted of the murders of the eleven women, and on August 10, 2011, jurors recommended the death penalty. On April 2, 2012, the Supreme Court of Ohio put his execution on hold, pending appeal; the appeals process continues to take place. In addition, there have been numerous civil suits filed charging that Cleveland police had received complaints about Sowell but failed to investigate them in an effective manner. The suits charge that at least five women died at Sowell's hands after police had sufficient evidence to arrest him and search his home.[1]

13

Capital Punishment and the Death Row Inmate

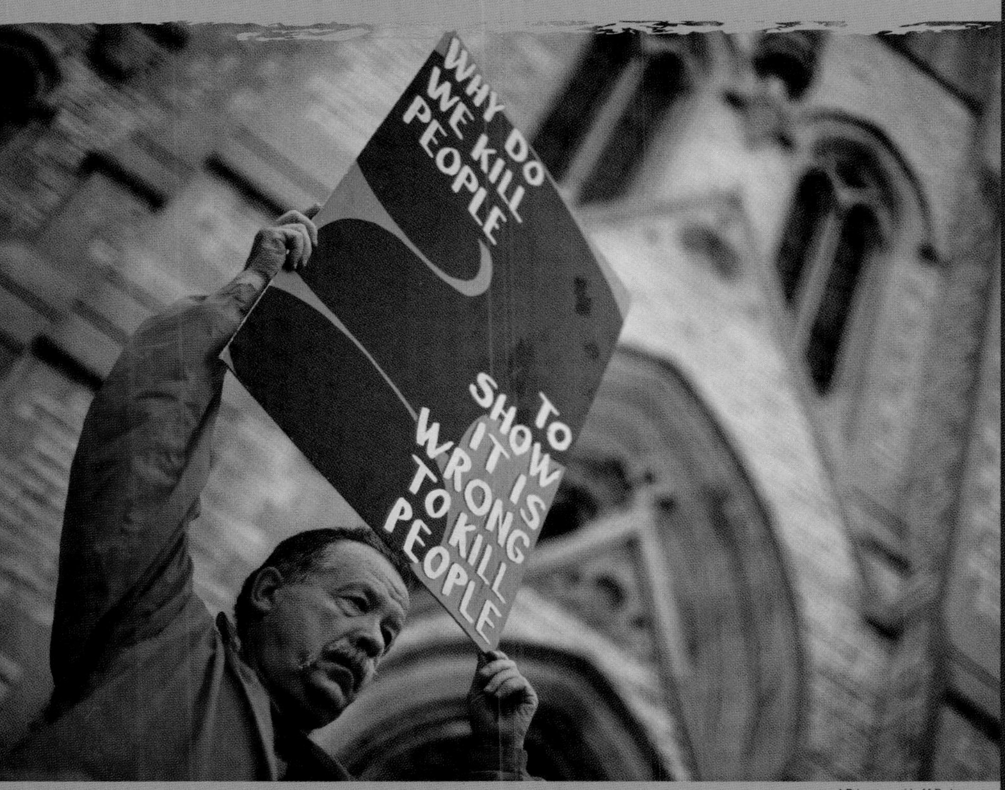

AP Images/Jeff Roberson

LEARNING OBJECTIVES

 Describe what public opinion is concerning the death penalty

 Compare the importance of aggravation versus mitigation concerning the death penalty

 Discuss the position of the U.S. Supreme Court concerning the death penalty

 Identify the position of the Supreme Court concerning the importance of race and the death penalty

 Discuss the Supreme Court's rulings on the execution of mentally impaired inmates and juveniles

 Describe how correctional officers working on death row regard their jobs

 Identify how inmates on death row adjust to their situation

 Evaluate whether the death penalty deters murder

PREVIEW OF KEY CONCEPTS

lethal injection
guilt/innocence phase
punishment phase
Furman v. Georgia
Gregg v. Georgia
aggravation
mitigation
McCleskey v. Kemp
Thompson v. Oklahoma
Stanford v. Kentucky
Roper v. Simmons
death-qualified jury
deathwatch
execution team
retentionist arguments
abolitionist arguments

Capital punishment, as the Anthony Sowell case reveals, is a topic that stirs deep emotional reactions in both supporters and opponents. With this trial, as with every murder trial, the outcome is viewed from different perspectives. The victims' surviving family and children, as well as the police community, strongly supported giving Anthony Sowell the death penalty. The state representative, the prosecutor, played his role in persuading the jury to bring back a recommendation for the death penalty. In contrast, the defendant and his attorneys viewed the proceedings through a much different lens. In this case, as in nearly all death penalty cases, there are flaws in the process. The defendant's prior background and personal problems could be ignored by the judge. We know errors can and have been made in capital trials. Should the chance that an innocent person may be executed outweigh the need for retribution? Should Sowell get off with a life sentence in view of the murders he committed?

In Voices Across the Profession, Kelly Culshaw, a former group supervisor in the Ohio Public Defender's Death Penalty Division and in recent years a federal public defender in Phoenix, Arizona, tells what troubles her about the death penalty.

© Kelly Culshaw

VOICES ACROSS THE PROFESSION

From the trial through to the end, there isn't a lot of rhyme or reason to who gets death and who gets life.

Kelly Culshaw
Attorney

"After being here [Ohio] 10 years, my general impression of the death penalty is that it has some real fairness issues. From the trial through to the end, there isn't a lot of rhyme or reason to who gets death and who gets life. Secondly, it doesn't seem like the death penalty is applied equally. My clients are predominantly from a poor socioeconomic class. They are generally black and most of them have killed a white person. That is how the statistics play out in Ohio. Third, when you look at how relief is granted, you can see the unfairness issues. You can put two cases next to each other that are virtually identical and one gets relief and the other doesn't.

"I like coming to work because I went to law school to become a public defender. That's what I've always wanted to do. I believe in the criminal justice system and the right to a defense. This is a job, especially with death penalty cases, where you can really make a difference.

"What I do and what my office does are extremely important. Regardless of what your personal opinion is concerning the death penalty, most of us would agree that if your state is going to be in the business of killing people, you want to make sure that the Constitution is followed and that the rules are applied as carefully as possible to make sure that the people who get the ultimate penalty are the most deserving."

Kelly Culshaw is cognizant that many of her defendants had poor representation at the trial level and are in desperate need of somebody who will put some time and energy on their case. "It is especially important to be a public defender in the death penalty arena," she adds, "because of the finality of the penalty." That is why she feels that her office and other offices like the Ohio Public Defender's office "must be vigilant about the defendant's constitutional rights."

CAPITAL PUNISHMENT AS A SENTENCE

The ultimate disposition in sentencing is the decision by the court to take the life of a convicted defendant. The survival of capital punishment in the United States has been debated since the earliest days of the republic. In 1787, Dr. Benjamin Rush (1746–1813) of Philadelphia, the most famous physician of his time and a signer of the Declaration of Independence, delivered an oration on the subject that set forth a position taken by religious liberals, especially Quakers, throughout American history. His rationale rests on suppositions that would not be taken seriously in our society, such as "The punishment of murder by death is contrary to reason and to the order and happiness of society."[2] Another strong supporter for eliminating capital punishment was Edward Livingston (1764–1836). At one time United States Attorney for New York as well as mayor of New York City, due to ill health he left those offices to settle in Louisiana and became an influential advocacy of criminal justice law reform. He presented a draft to the Louisiana legislature entitled, "The Crime of Employing the Punishment of Death." Livingston's argument was reasoned and eloquent, but it failed to move the legislators.[3] The most powerful rhetoric in favor of the death penalty came from England, where Sir James Fitzjames Stephen (1829–1894) propounded uncompromising views on the need for severe punishment of all criminals. Summarizing his position, he said, "No other punishment deters men so effectively from committing crimes as the punishment of death."[4]

There have been more than 16,000 executions carried out in the United States, beginning with the execution of Captain George Kendall in 1608. Until the year 2000, the general trend in the second half of the twentieth century was an increase in the number of persons under sentence of death; the number of persons under sentence of death has declined since 2000 (see Figure 13.1). Of the 8,032 people under sentence of death between 1977 and 2012, 16 percent had been executed by 2014, 6 percent died from causes other than execution, and 40 percent received other dispositions. Between 1930 and 2012, a total of 5,179 inmates were executed under civil authority; military authorities carried out an additional 160 executions. Since the Supreme Court reinstated the death penalty statutes in 1976, 1,320 inmates have been executed.

Today there are more than 3,000 inmates under sentence of death in state and federal prisons. Fewer than 50 people are executed yearly (see Figure 13.2).[5] In 2013, nine states executed 39 inmates, which was four fewer than the number executed in 2012. Four states—Texas, Mississippi, Oklahoma, and

FIGURE 13.1

Number of Persons Under Sentence of Death

Source: Tracy L. Snell, *Capital Punishment, 2012 Statistical Tables* (Washington, DC: Bureau of Justice Statistics, U.S. Department of Justice, May 2014).

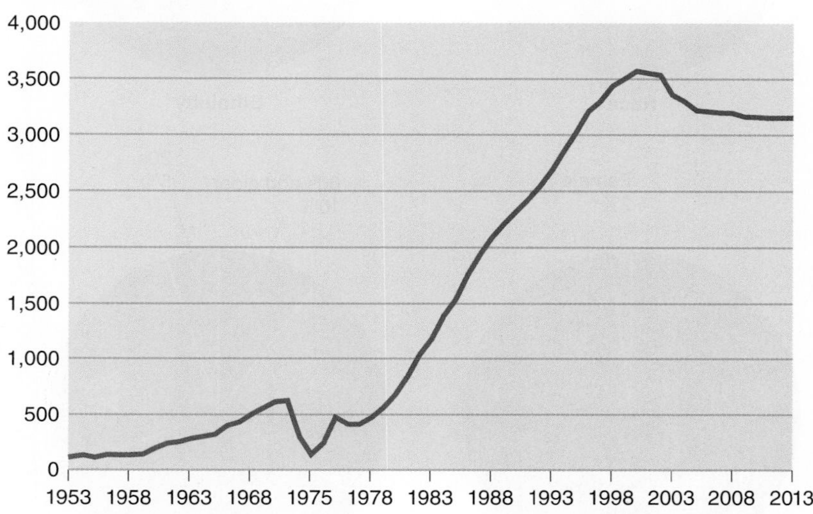

FIGURE 13.2

Number of Persons Executed in the United States

Source: Tracy L. Snell, *Capital Punishment, 2012 Statistical Tables* (Washington, DC: Bureau of Justice Statistics, U.S. Department of Justice, May 2014).

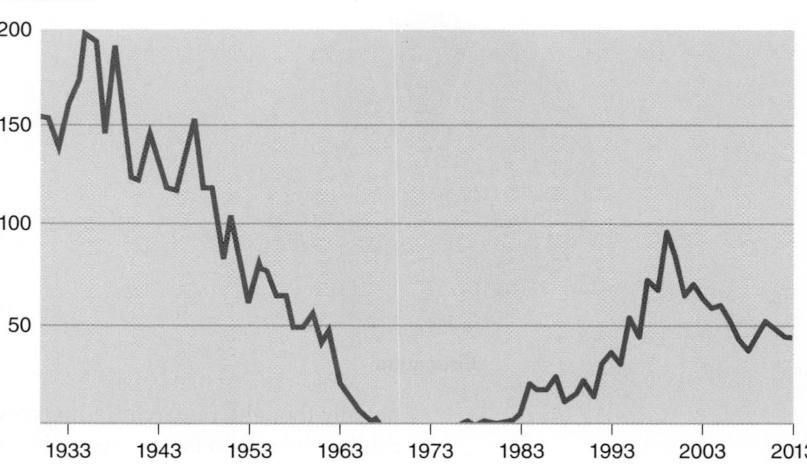

FIGURE 13.3

Demographic Characteristics of Prisoners Under Sentence of Death

Source: Tracy L. Snell, *Capital Punishment, 2012 Statistical Tables* (Washington, DC: Bureau of Justice Statistics, U.S. Department of Justice, May 2014).

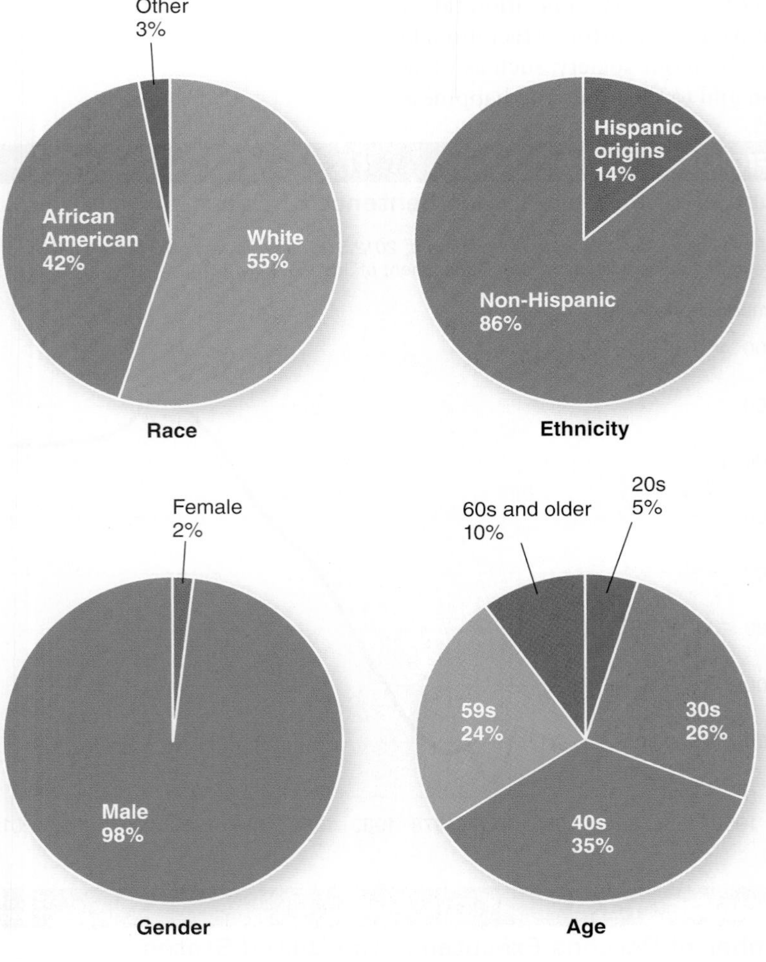

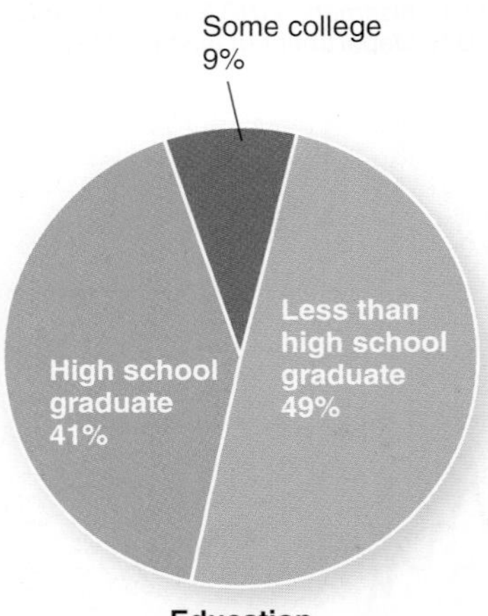

Arizona—have conducted the most executions since the reinstatement. Almost all executions were of men, by lethal injection.[6] Although most of the executions through U.S. history have been for murder and rape, at one time federal, military, and state laws sanctioned the death penalty for other crimes, such as robbery, kidnapping, treason, espionage, and desertion from military service.[7] A series of Supreme Court decisions have restricted the death penalty to mentally sound adults over age 18 who commit murder in the first degree with extenuating or aggravating circumstances.

THE DEATH PENALTY IN CONTEMPORARY SOCIETY

On December 2, 2005, with his final words, "God bless everybody in here," Kenneth Boys became the 1,000th prisoner to be put to death in the United States since capital punishment was reinstated in 1976.[8] The death penalty has become an institution. Two driving forces in this institution are public opinion about capital punishment and political support for the death penalty. Although the death penalty still receives high approval in the United States, it is not as well received internationally.

Death Penalty Profile

In the most recent study of those under sentence of death, 56 percent were white and 42 percent were black. The 388 Hispanic inmates under sentence of death accounted for 14 percent of inmates with a known ethnicity. Ninety-eight percent of inmates under sentence of death were male, and 2 percent were female. The race and gender of those under sentence of death has remained relatively unchanged since 2000 (see Figure 13.3).[9]

Researchers Mark Cunningham and Mark Vigen found that an overwhelmingly large number of death row inmates are Southern males, frequently intellectually limited and academically deficient, with developmental histories of trauma, family disruption, and substance abuse. The rates of psychological disorders among death row inmates are high, with the conditions of confinement seeming to aggravate or precipitate these disorders. In contrast to what is traditionally thought, research findings reveal that the majority of death row inmates do not exhibit violence in prison, even when they are in more open institutional settings.[10]

Lethal injection is now the predominant method of execution and is used in 32 states and the federal government. In addition to lethal injection, 16 states authorized an alternative method of execution (see Figure 13.4). Eight states authorized electrocution; three states, lethal gas; three states, hanging; and two states, firing squad. For states that authorize multiple methods of execution, the method is generally selected by the condemned prisoner. Exhibit 13.1 sets out each state's current death penalty policy.[11]

Public Opinion

American public opinion on the death penalty shifted dramatically during the twentieth century. Ever since 1939, the Gallup Poll has asked the public, "Do you favor or oppose the death penalty for persons convicted of murder?" For several decades in the twentieth century, support for the death penalty gradually declined. As recently as 1978, a Roper poll found that 66 percent of the population opposed the death penalty. As the violent crime rate skyrocketed in the 1980s public opinion changed and a great majority of Americans, more than 80 percent, favored executions.[12] Some evidence indicates, however, that when the public is presented with the alternative of life imprisonment without the possibility of parole (LWOP), there is less support (about 50 percent) for the death penalty.[13]

Web App 13.1
Watch the CBS News report "The Slow Death of the Death Penalty?" at http://www.cbsnews.com/news/the-slow-death-of-the-death-penalty/.

lethal injection The predominant method of execution, used in 35 states and by the federal government.

Web App 13.2
Use a search engine to find articles about how some states are dealing with the shortage of sodium thiopental, one of the main drugs used in lethal injections.

LO1 Describe what public opinion is concerning the death penalty

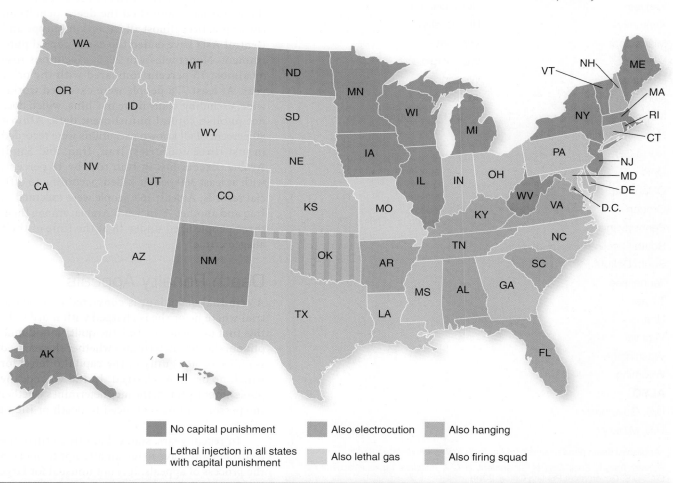

No capital punishment | Also electrocution | Also hanging
Lethal injection in all states with capital punishment | Also lethal gas | Also firing squad

FIGURE 13.4
Modes of Execution

Source: Tracy L. Snell, *Capital Punishment, 2012 Statistical Tables* (Washington, DC: Bureau of Justice Statistics, U.S. Department of Justice, May 2014).

EXHIBIT 13.1

Death Penalty Policy by State

States with the Death Penalty	States without the Death Penalty
Alabama	Alaska
Arizona	Connecticut*
	Hawaii
Arkansas	Illinois
California	Iowa
Colorado	Maine
	Maryland*
Delaware	Massachusetts
Florida	Michigan
Georgia	Minnesota
Idaho	New Jersey
Indiana	New Mexico*
	New York
Kansas	North Dakota
Kentucky	Rhode Island
Mississippi	Vermont
Missouri	West Virginia
Montana	Wisconsin
Nebraska	**ALSO**
Nevada	District of Columbia
New Hampshire	
North Carolina	
Ohio	
Oklahoma	
Oregon	
Pennsylvania	
South Carolina	
South Dakota	
Tennessee	
Texas	
Utah	
Virginia	
Washington	
Wyoming	
ALSO	
U.S. Government	
U.S. Military	

*Abolished death penalty; prisoners on death row on earlier convictions.

Source: Tracy L. Snell, *Capital Punishment, 2012 – Statistical Tables* (Washington, D.C.: U.S. Government Printing Office, 2014).

What factors influence public opinion about the death penalty? Media reports of erroneous executions as well as popular books about people released from death row because they were found to be innocent can influence public perceptions. Former death row inmates who have become public figures and win the sympathy of the general public by their work behind bars can also have an effect.[14]

International Opposition to the Death Penalty

The trend worldwide is to abolish the death penalty. According to human rights watchdog agency Amnesty International, over the last 20 years, the total number of countries carrying out executions dropped from 37 in 1994 to 22 in 2013. The ongoing trend has been to abolish the death penalty. According to their latest research, at the start of 2014, more than two-thirds of the countries in the world have abolished the death penalty in law or practice; almost all nations in Europe and Central Asia have ended the use of capital punishment. Nonetheless, in 2013, executions rose by almost 15 percent compared with the prior year. At least 778 people were executed worldwide, excluding many more in China, which does not publish capital punishment data. Almost 80 percent of all known executions were recorded in just three countries: Iran, Iraq, and Saudi Arabia. Executions in Iran rose by 18 percent, with at least 369 people killed, according to official records. At least 169 people were executed in Iraq and another 79 in Saudi Arabia, among them three people aged under 18 at the time of their alleged crime.[15]

Death Penalty Appeals

A criminal defendant is convicted in a capital trial where he or she is charged with murder. In this first phase of the trial, the **guilt/innocence phase**, the jury determines whether the accused is guilty or not guilty of the capital offense for which he or she is charged. In the second, the **punishment phase**, the jury determines whether the person will be sentenced to death or life in prison.

In recent years, states that often utilize the death penalty have made an attempt to shorten the process of appeals. It is not unusual for large law firms to become involved in a case and provide counsel far superior to what the defendant received at his or her trial. A convicted defendant can decide not to pursue appeals, and his or her execution will take place in a few years.

Most cases are first heard in the state court of appeals. This is usually an automatic direct appeal, and the case will be examined for trial error and to determine if the case is consistent with similar death penalty cases. State review courts seldom overturn a conviction. The U.S. Supreme Court is then petitioned for a writ of *certiorari*, which is a written order to the lower court to send the records forward for a review. If the Supreme Court denies review, as it usually does, the stage of postconviction review begins. At this second stage, with the challenge from death row inmates that they have received ineffective or incompetent trial counsel, new counsel is appointed by the court. The new counsel typically raises questions about the fairness of the trial, such as tainted evidence, incompetent legal representation, or prosecutorial or police misconduct. If the trial court denies the appeal, it may be filed again with the state court of appeals. Typically, the state court of appeals denies the petition, and the defense counsel petitions the U.S. Supreme Court.

MYTH The general public wholeheartedly supports the death penalty.

FACT While it is true that surveys show that a majority of the public supports capital punishment, support erodes when they are given a choice such as life without parole for convicted killers. Wrongful convictions may convince many people that the use of the death penalty is just too risky.

This ends the second stage, and the third stage, the federal *habeas corpus* stage, is filed in the U.S. district court in the state that convicted the defendant. If this petition is denied by the U.S. district court, it is submitted to the U.S. court of appeals. A denial of the petition by the U.S. appeals court will send it forth again to the U.S. Supreme Court to intercede. When all appeals have been exhausted, including efforts to get the U.S. Supreme Court to intercede, the attorneys for the convicted prisoner usually approach the governor of the state and ask for a stay of the execution or clemency (see Figure 13.5).[16]

guilt/innocence phase In a capital trial, the phase in which the jury determines whether the accused is guilty or not guilty of the capital offense for which he or she is charged.

punishment phase In a capital trial, the phase in which the jury determines whether the person will be sentenced to death or life in prison.

A number of reasons exist why the review process takes 10 or more years from conviction to execution:

- *Possibility of error.* Because of the terrible consequences of a false conviction in a death penalty case, it is critical to determine if any error influenced the outcome of the trial process. James S. Liebman and colleagues, in studying 4,578 appeals between 1973 and 1995, found that the overall rate of error in capital punishment cases in the United States was a staggering 68 percent. Two out of every three cases reviewed by the courts during this time period were deeply flawed.[17]
- *Complex process.* Death penalty appeals are very complex and take time to weave from one stage to the other.
- *Appellate delay.* Due to case pressure and overload, appeals courts, especially on the federal level, take a lengthy period of time to respond to a case before them. Federal judges tend to submit findings that are more extensive and better researched than is ordinarily true in those filed by state appeals courts.

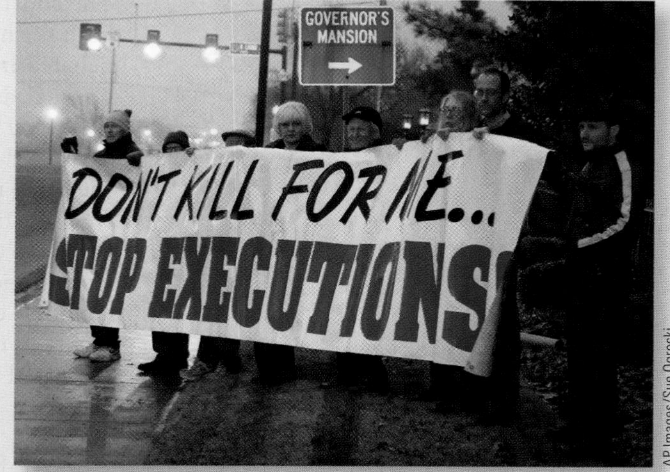

AP Images/Sue Ogrocki

Abolitionists make their opposition to the death penalty an open public issue. Here, death penalty opponents hold a sign outside the governor's mansion in Oklahoma City on January 9, 2014, protesting the execution of Michael Lee Wilson. Twenty years earlier, Wilson robbed a convenience store and beat the manager, Richard Yost, with an aluminum baseball bat 54 times in 131 seconds while he begged for mercy. So that any customers would not be suspicious, Wilson put on Yost's uniform and worked the cash register as Yost lay dying in a pool of blood, beer, and milk behind the cooler doors. Would you have joined the protest if you could?

To reduce the number of appeals, federal court rulings have placed limits on their use in death penalty cases. The Supreme Court dealt with this issue when Warren McCleskey returned to the Supreme Court for another attempt to overturn his sentence.[18] In a decision announced on April 15, 1991, Justice Anthony Kennedy wrote for a 6–3 majority rejecting McCleskey's claim of racial bias and went on to pronounce a new rule on such appeals. Henceforth, "a failure to press at the outset a claim of constitutional defect will be excused only *if* the inmate can show that something

FIGURE 13.5

The Capital Criminal Process: Trial Through State and Federal Postconviction

Source: James S. Liebman, Jeffrey Fagan, and Valerie West, *A Broken System: Error Rates in Capital Cases 1973–1995* (New York: Columbia University School of Law, 2000), p. 22.

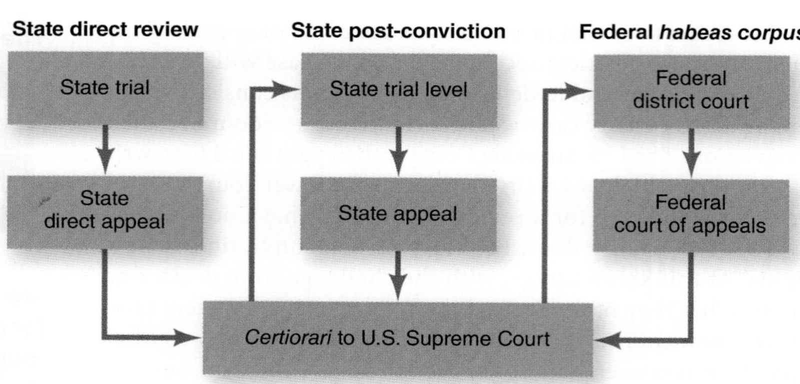

Furman v. Georgia U.S. Supreme Court decision that declared the death penalty unconstitutional.

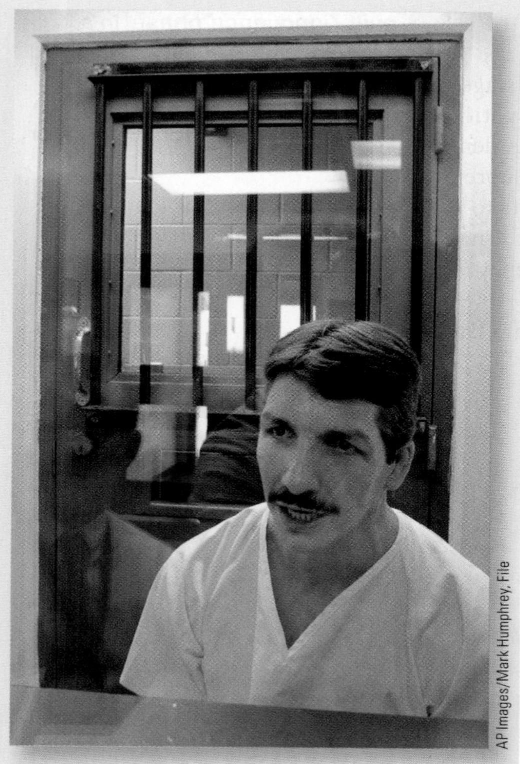

Courts have limited the number and type of appeals in death penalty cases. Here, Paul Dennis Reid, known as "the Fast Food Killer," is shown during an interview. The Tennessee Supreme Court ruled that family and legal advocates for Reid, who was convicted of killing seven people in a series of robberies in Nashville and Clarksville, could continue to appeal his convictions against his wishes. Reid was sentenced to death but died in prison from natural causes before his sentence could be carried out.

AP Images/Mark Humphrey, File

actually prevented raising that issue and can prove that the claimed defect made a difference in the outcome of the verdict or sentence."[19] McCleskey was executed on September 25, 1991.

Another method to limit appeals is to restrict the use of *habeas corpus* (see Chapter 9). Prisoners on death row argue in such a writ that their detention as condemned persons is based on some error in the administration of the law.

Despite the fact that it is difficult to appeal a capital sentence, many cases have been brought before the court system. In the following sections, some of the more important legal rulings are discussed in some detail.

LEGALITY OF THE DEATH PENALTY

The constitutionality of the death penalty has been a major concern to both the nation's courts and its concerned social scientists. Lawyers have debated in the federal courts whether capital punishment is cruel and unusual, as stated in the Eighth Amendment to the Constitution. Whether it is *cruel* depends on one's perspective, but because it is favored by so many and has been in use for so long, the death penalty is not *unusual* and therefore not constitutionally banned per se. It is difficult to argue that the Constitution bans the death penalty, because the creators made reference to capital crimes, and executions were carried out at the time the Constitution was written. But times have changed, and the Constitution is a flexible document. Consequently, there have been numerous legal challenges to the use of the death penalty. Some of the most critical ones are discussed in the following section.

Use of Discretion: Aggravation versus Mitigation

Compare the importance of aggravation versus mitigation concerning the death penalty  LO2

In 1972, in one grand gesture, the U.S. Supreme Court in ***Furman v. Georgia*** swept away the death penalty in every state and spared the lives of men and women on death row.[20] The *Furman* case was the climax of a long battle against the death penalty. One of the campaigners was the NAACP, acutely sensitive to the fact that African Americans have been disproportionately given the death penalty. *Furman* involved an African American man accused and convicted of murder and rape. Georgia law allowed the judge to impose capital punishment at his or her personal discretion. In a 5–4 decision, the Supreme Court relied on the "equal protection" provision of the Fourteenth

Amendment to overturn the sentence, as well as the "cruel and unusual punishment" provision of the Eighth Amendment. In his option, Justice William O. Douglas wrote:

> The high service rendered by the "cruel and unusual" clause is to require legislatures to write penal laws that are even-handed, non-selective, and non-arbitrary, and to require judges to see to it that general laws are not applied sparsely, selectively, and spottily to unpopular groups.[21]

Douglas went on to hold that the Georgia law violated the Fourteenth Amendment because, like the laws of the other states authorizing the death penalty, it provided the courts with so much discretionary freedom that judges could impose capital punishment on only a select group of people—the poor, the unpopular, and racial minorities. The Supreme Court did not completely rule out the use of capital punishment as a penalty. Rather, it objected to the arbitrary and capricious manner in which it was imposed. After *Furman*, many states changed statutes that had allowed jury discretion in imposing the death penalty. In some states, this was accomplished by enacting statutory guidelines for jury decisions; in others, the death penalty was made mandatory for certain crimes only. Despite these changes in statutory law, no further executions were carried out while the Court pondered additional cases concerning the death penalty.

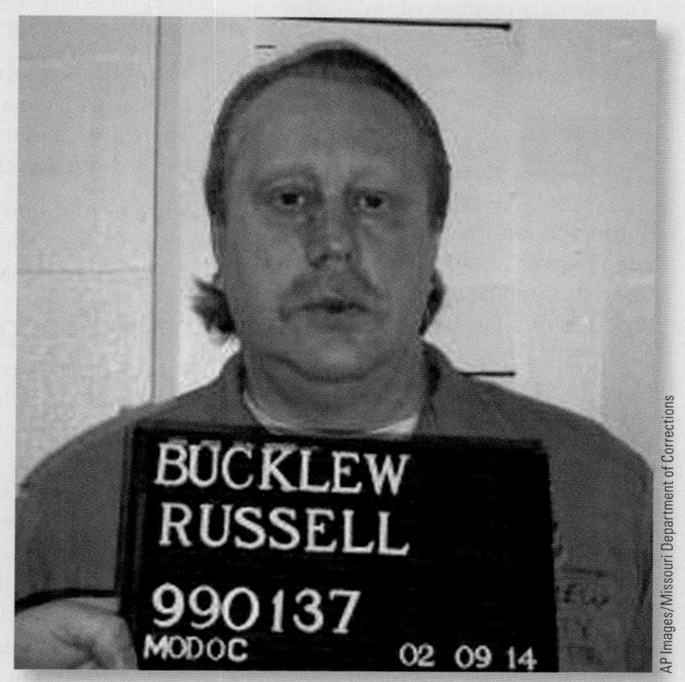

Russell Bucklew was scheduled to die for killing a romantic rival as part of a crime spree in southeast Missouri in 1996. The convicted murderer suffers from a rare illness creates vascular tumors in his head and neck and causes hemorrhages. His lawyers contended that the masses would likely prevent a lethal dose of pentobarbital from circulating properly and would prolong a painful death, violating the constitutional protection against cruel and unusual punishment. The Supreme Court agreed and halted his execution on May 20, 2014, pending further review.

In July 1976, the Supreme Court ruled on the constitutionality of five state death penalty statutes. In the first case, ***Gregg v. Georgia***, the Court found valid the Georgia statute holding that a finding by the jury of at least one "aggravating circumstance" out of ten is required in pronouncing the death penalty in murder cases.[22] In the *Gregg* case, for example, the jury imposed the death penalty after finding beyond a reasonable doubt two aggravating circumstances: (1) the offender was engaged in the commission of two other capital felonies, and (2) the offender committed the offense of murder for the purpose of receiving money and other financial gains (for example, an automobile).[23]

The issue of **aggravation** versus **mitigation** was further defined in the California case *Pulley v. Harris* (1984). Here the question was whether California law was unconstitutional because it did not require that the sentencing court compare the facts of the case with the disposition of other similar cases in order to ensure that the sentence was proportional to the seriousness of the crime.[24] The Supreme Court decided that California's death penalty law could be imposed if the California court could find that one or more of seven "special circumstances" were present: (1) murder for profit, (2) murder perpetrated by an explosion, (3) murder of a police officer on active duty, (4) murder of a victim who was a witness to a crime, (5) murder committed in a robbery, (6) murder with torture, or (7) murder by a person with one or more previous convictions of murder. In *Pulley v. Harris*, the murder was committed in the course of a robbery, a fact that satisfied the constitutional requirement of proportionality, and the Court ruled that Harris was eligible for execution.[25] In a more recent case, *Kansas v. March* (2006), the Supreme Court ruled that the Kansas death penalty scheme, which directs imposition of the death penalty when mitigating factors stand equal with aggravating factors, is constitutional.[26]

Gregg v. Georgia U.S. Supreme Court decision that superseded *Furman v. Georgia* and declared the death penalty constitutional if certain conditions are met.

aggravation When a jury finds a first-degree murder conviction on a defendant at the end of the trial phase, the defendant is then tried in a second phase, referred to as the penalty phase. The task of the prosecution is to establish that the sentence should be death because the aggravating causes in the case exceed mitigating causes.

mitigation During the penalty phase of the jury proceedings, the defense attempts to establish that there are greater mitigating causes than aggravating causes and the jury should bring in a recommendation for less than death (usually for life imprisonment without the possibility of parole).

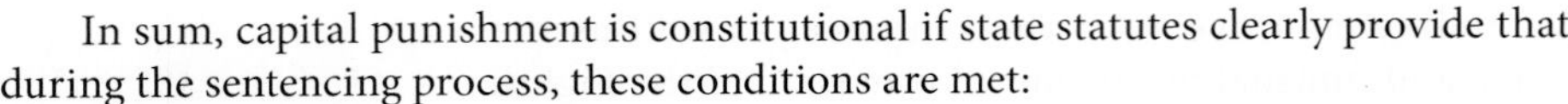

Discuss the position of the U.S. Supreme Court concerning the death penalty LO3

In sum, capital punishment is constitutional if state statutes clearly provide that, during the sentencing process, these conditions are met:

1. The court is informed about the defendant's background and criminal history.
2. Mitigating factors affecting culpability are brought to the attention of the court.
3. There are standards to guide trial courts in making the sentencing decision.
4. Every death sentence is reviewed by a state appellate court.[27]

FOR GROUP DISCUSSION Review the rights of the accused and identify which rights could be infringed upon through death penalty proceedings. LO2

Since resumption of the death penalty, the Court has dealt with a number of critical issues defining when, how, and with whom the penalty can be employed.

Administering Death

Identify the position of the Supreme Court concerning the importance of race and the death penalty LO4

McCleskey v. Kemp The Supreme Court ruled that race did not enter into the decision of the Georgia court and that there was no evidence of racial bias.

Most states have discontinued use of traditional methods of execution such as hanging and the electric chair and now rely on lethal injection. In 2008, the U.S. Supreme Court ruled in *Baze v. Rees* that Kentucky's lethal injection protocol satisfies the Eighth Amendment. Lethal injection is used for capital punishment by the federal government and 35 states, at least 30 of which (including Kentucky) use the same combination of three drugs. Kentucky's lethal injection protocol reserves to qualified personnel, with at least one year's professional experience, the responsibility for inserting the intravenous (IV) catheters into the prisoner.[28] The Court ruled that such procedures are constitutionally acceptable and do not amount to cruel and unusual punishment. Nonetheless, there have been some well-publicized incidents where executions have been botched by administration of ineffective drugs. For example, in 2014, it took Arizona inmate Joseph Rudolph Wood nearly two hours to die after he received a lethal injection with a combination of the sedative midazolam and the painkiller hydromorphone; he spent more than 90 minutes gasping for air every five to 12 seconds before he finally stopped breathing. In other 2014 cases, an Ohio inmate gasped for nearly 30 minutes before expiring, and Clayton Lockett, an Oklahoma inmate, died of a heart attack after prison officials halted his execution because the drugs weren't being administered properly.[29]

New York Daily News Archive/Contributor/Getty Images

In this infamous 1928 photo, Ruth Snyder, sentenced to death for the murder of her husband, is shown being executed in the electric chair in Sing Sing Prison. The final moments of her execution were caught on film by a miniature plate camera strapped to the ankle of Tom Howard, a photographer working for the *New York Daily News*.

Race and the Death Penalty

A significant argument of abolitionists is that the death penalty is used in a racist fashion and therefore violates constitutional guarantees of due process and equal protection. The critical case on this issue concerns the murder trial of ***McCleskey v. Kemp*** (1987).[30] McCleskey was an African American man who was convicted in 1978 of the murder of a white police officer during an armed robbery. He contended that the imposition of the death penalty was cruel and unusual because African American men killing white victims are sentenced to death with greater frequency than white men killing white victims.

In support of this contention, McCleskey presented to the Supreme Court a study by Professor David Baldus showing the following: In Georgia, 22 percent of African American defendants with white victims received the death penalty, but only 8 percent of white defendants with white victims received the death penalty. Only 3 percent of white defendants charged with killing African American victims were sentenced to death. Prosecutors sought the death penalty in the cases of 70 percent of African American defendants killing white victims, but capital punishment was sought for only 32 percent of white defendants killing African American victims. It was argued that the figures showed that Georgia courts and prosecutors were discriminatory in their application of the laws.[31]

Justice Lewis Powell, writing for a 5–4 Supreme Court majority, rejected this argument. He held in this particular case that race did not enter into the decision of the Georgia court, and regardless of national data trends, there was no evidence of bias in the present case.[32] Although the Supreme Court was not swayed by charges of racial bias in the *McCleskey* decision, it has ruled that jury selection cannot be tainted by racial bias. In the 2003 case of *Miller-El v. Cockrell*, an African American defendant was convicted of capital murder in 1986 and sentenced to death. Miller-El's attorneys argued that prosecutors excluded African Americans from jury duty in Dallas County, Texas. The lower courts refused to consider his claim, but the Supreme Court disagreed, saying that the prosecutors had used their peremptory challenges to eliminate 91 percent of the eligible African Americans. The stated reasons for eliminating African Americans from the jury pool also applied to some white jurors who were not challenged and did serve on the jury. The Court further noted that the prosecution used underhanded techniques in order to eliminate African Americans. Moreover, a memo existed that instructed prosecutors to eliminate jurors based on race, ethnic background, and religion.[33]

John Donohue examined capital punishment in Connecticut from 1973 to 2007, a 34-year period, and did a comprehensive evaluation of 4,686 murders. He found that arbitrariness and discrimination were defining features of capital punishment sentences in this state. He especially found the racial effect evident (minority defendants with white victims were far more likely to be sentenced to death than others).[34]

CRITICAL THINKING

Can death be considered cruel and unusual when the execution is not carried out in an appropriate manner? For example, look up the case of Angel Diaz, who was put to death by the state of Florida in a "botched" execution process that lasted 34 minutes. LO3

CRITICAL THINKING

Select a landmark death penalty case and dissect it to discuss the appropriateness of the sanction, issues that may not have been considered, and the deterrent effect of using death as the punishment. LO4

Women on Death Row

After 1976, when the death penalty was reinstated in the United States, there was a lull in the execution of women. See Exhibit 13.2 for the chronological order of women whom the states punished in this way.

EXHIBIT 13.2

Executions of Women

On February 5, 2014, Suzanne Basso, 59, was put to death in Texas for the torture slaying of Louis "Buddy" Musso, a mentally ill man. Basso has lured the New Jersey man to Texas with the promise to marry him. Basso, with five others, beat him and killed him for his money and cashed in on an insurance policy of which she was made the beneficiary. Since the U.S. Supreme Court reinstated the death penalty in 1976, 14 women have been executed in the United States. (In the same time, about 1,400 men have been executed in this nation.) The list of these women consists of:

- Velma Barfield, 52, November 2, 1984, lethal injection in North Carolina for poisoning her fiancé.
- Karla Faye Tucker, 38, February 3, 1998, lethal injection in Texas for killing two people.
- Judy Buenoano, 54, March 30, 1998, electrocution in Florida for killing her husband and son.
- Betty Lou Beets, 62, February 24, 2000, lethal injection in Texas for killing her fifth husband.
- Christina Marie Riggs, 28, May 2, 2000, lethal injection in Arkansas for smothering her two small children.
- Wanda Jean Allen, 41, January 11, 2001, lethal injection in Oklahoma for killing two women.
- Marilyn Plantz, 40, May 1, 2001, lethal injection in Oklahoma for having her husband killed.
- Lois Nadean Smith, 61, December 4, 2001, lethal injection in Oklahoma for killing her son's ex-girlfriend.
- Lynda Lyon Block, 54, May 10, 2002, electrocution in Alabama for murdering a police officer.
- Aileen Wournos, 46, October 9, 2002, lethal injection in Florida for murdering six men.
- Frances Newton, 40, September 14, 2005, lethal injection in Texas for killing her two children and husband.
- Teresa Lewis, 41, September 23, 2010, lethal injection in Virginia for conspiring to kill her husband and stepson.
- Kimberly McCarthy, 52, June 26, 2013, lethal injection in Texas, for the robbery, beating, and fatal shooting of a retired college professor.
- Suzanne Basso, 59, February 5, 2014, in Texas, for the torture, robbery, and slaying of a mentally ill man.

(continued)

Of the women who have been executed, the public outcry was the strongest against the execution of the born-again Christian Karla Fay Tucker, whose interviews on national television captivated the nation and swayed public opinion in her support. In Europe, in early February 1988, editorial writers called the execution of Tucker a "barbaric act." Entreaties from all over the world and from the pope failed to gain clemency. Tucker, despite being an admitted axe murderer who had killed two strangers in a drug-induced rage, galvanized the sympathy of the world.

Source: Crime Library, "Women Executed in America," http://www.crimelibrary.com/photogallery/women-executed-in-america.html (accessed July 2014).

Discuss the Supreme Court's rulings on the execution of mentally impaired inmates and juveniles **LO5**

Execution of Mentally Impaired Prisoners

Amnesty International contends that humanitarian standards require that people with mental impairment not be subjected to the death penalty. Amnesty International cites a 1988 recommendation by the United States Committee on Crime Prevention and Control that "persons suffering from mental retardation or extremely limited mental competence should not be executed for their acts." In 1989, the United States Economic and Social Council adapted a similar resolution. Despite such pronouncements, the mentally impaired continued to be executed in the United States. On August 16, 2000, John Satterwhite, a 53-year-old man who had been diagnosed as having both mental impairment and paranoid schizophrenia, died by lethal injection by the state of Texas. Satterwhite had been sentenced to death for the 1979 murder of Mary Francis Davis during the robbery of a shop in San Antonio.[35]

CRITICAL THINKING 

There are many medications and psychotropic drugs that assist in the well-being of the mentally ill. Is it appropriate to use these drugs to create competency in order to execute an individual? Is this constitutional? **LO5**

In 2002, the Supreme Court ruled in *Atkins v. Virginia* that execution of the mentally retarded was unconstitutional.[36] Daryl Atkins, who had an IQ of 49, was sentenced to death for killing Eric Nesbitt in the parking lot of a 7-Eleven store. Justice John Paul Stevens, writing for the majority, noted that since the *Penry v. Lynaugh* case, in which the Supreme Court had upheld the execution of the retarded, a national consensus had emerged rejecting such execution. He added that the number of states prohibiting such executions had increased from two to eighteen.[37] The Court found his arguments persuasive and ended the practice of executing the mentally challenged.

According to Amnesty International, since 1983 more than 60 inmates diagnosed with mental illness have been executed in U.S. prisons. Amnesty International argues that executing these inmates who cannot understand the nature of or reason for their punishment serves no deterrent or retributive purpose. In addition, common law has traditionally maintained that persons with mental illness may be incapable of pursuing available appeals or preparing themselves for death, in keeping with humanitarian or religious principles.[38]

In 1986, in *Ford v. Wainwright*, the Supreme Court heard the case of a person who became mentally deficient after receiving a death sentence.[39] In prison, Ford began to exhibit extremely delusional behavior. He claimed that the Ku Klux Klan was part of a conspiracy forcing him to commit suicide and that his female relatives were being tortured and sexually abused elsewhere in the prison. Writing for the majority, Justice Thurgood Marshall ruled that the Eighth Amendment prohibits the state from executing persons with mental illness because the accused person must understand that he or she has been sentenced to death and the reasoning behind this decision. Marshall found the alternative offensive to humanity.[40]

A 1991 Arkansas case thrust the execution of the mentally ill into the national limelight. Ricky Ray Rector had killed a police officer and another citizen and then shot himself in the temple, lifting three inches off his brain and leaving him with the competence of a small child. Rector was convicted at trial and given the death penalty. In prison, he howled day and night, jumping around and giving no indication that he realized he was on death row and would be executed. The Supreme Court rejected his appeal. The issue of how competence should be determined is an important consideration complicating whether a mentally ill person should be executed or not. Typically, the state's expert witnesses will find that the defendant is competent, while the defense's expert witnesses will find that the defendant is unable to understand the legal procedures that are taking place. Another issue concerns the morality of treating a person's mental illness so that they can be executed. Although the Court has not directly addressed this issue, the 1990 *Washington v. Harper* ruling found that a state could require an inmate to take a drug to control his schizophrenia.[41]

MYTH The United States is one of the few countries that still executes juvenile offenders who commit murder.

FACT The Supreme Court has ruled that no one who commits a crime under the age of 18 can be given the death penalty.

Execution of Juveniles

International human right treaties prohibit executing anyone under 18 years of age. The International Covenant on Civil and Political Rights, the U.N. Convention on the Rights of the Child, and the American Convention on Human Rights all have provisions to this effect. Indeed, more than 100 countries have laws specifically excluding the execution of juveniles or may be presumed to exclude such executions as they are parties of one of the above treaties. Seven countries since 1990 are known to have executed inmates who were under 18 years of age at the time of the crime—Congo, Iran, Nigeria, Pakistan, Saudi Arabia, the United States, and Yemen. Since 1994, 20 executions of those who were juveniles when they committed the crime have taken place, including 13 in the United States.[42]

FOR GROUP **DISCUSSION** Create a list of aggravating and mitigating circumstances for juveniles that should be considered, in addition to age, at the time of the offense. LO5

The United States is one of the few nations that has executed juvenile offenders. In a 1988 case, ***Thompson v. Oklahoma***, Wayne Thompson was 15 when he was arrested along with his half brother—then age 27—for the shooting and stabbing to death of Charles Keene. The Court ruled by a 5–3 vote that "the Eighth and Fourteenth Amendments prohibit the execution of a person who was under 16 years of age at the time of his or her offense."[43] In the 1989 case ***Stanford v. Kentucky***, the question had to do with the eligibility of a murderer for execution when the crime was committed while he was a minor.[44] Stanford was 17 years and 4 months old when he was sentenced to death. Writing for a divided court, Justice Antonin Scalia ruled that inasmuch as common law prescribed 14 as the minimum age for execution, the sentence of a 17-year-old did not violate the Eighth Amendment proscription against cruel and unusual punishment.[45] All debate over the possible use of capital punishment as a sanction for juveniles ended with the 2005 case of ***Roper v. Simmons*** when the Court held that executing those who commit their crimes as juveniles is neither consistent with the Constitution nor in keeping with the standards of a civilized society.[46]

Thompson v. Oklahoma U.S. Supreme Court decision that prohibits execution of juveniles under age 16 at the time of the offense.

Stanford v. Kentucky U.S. Supreme Court decision allowing the execution of juveniles who were age 17 at the time of the crime.

Roper v. Simmons U.S. Supreme Court decision that disallows the execution of juveniles who committed a capital crime under the age of 18.

Administrative Issues and the Death Penalty

A **death-qualified jury** means that any person opposed in concept to capital punishment is removed during *voir dire*. Defense attorneys are opposed to death-qualified juries because they bar those citizens who oppose the death penalty from serving as jurors. Defense attorneys believe that these citizens may be more liberal and less likely to convict defendants. Consequently, death qualification creates juries that are not representative of the public opposing the death penalty.

death-qualified jury During *voir dire*, any person opposed to capital punishment may be dropped from the jury pool.

In *Witherspoon v. Illinois*, the Supreme Court upheld the practice of removing jurors who are opposed to the death penalty.[47] The Court further made it easier to convict people in death penalty cases when it was ruled that jurors could be excused if their views on capital punishment were deemed by a trial judge to "prevent or substantially impair the performance of their duties."[48] The Court further ruled that jurors can be excused because of their opposition to the death penalty at the guilt phase of a trial, in spite of the fact that the issue of capital punishment would not need to be considered until a separate sentencing hearing.[49] In addition, the Court ruled in *Lockhart v. McCree* (1986) that removing those who oppose capital punishment does not violate the Sixth Amendment provision that juries represent a fair cross-section of the community and, as a result, unfairly tips the scale toward juries that are prone to convict defendants in capital cases.[50] Thus, it would appear that, at least for the present, prosecutors are able to excuse jurors who believe that the death penalty is immoral or wrong.

CRITICAL THINKING

Should juveniles be sentenced to life in prison for crimes that would have been given the death penalty if it was available? LO5

See the Timeline for the significant U.S. Supreme Court decisions on the death penalty.

TIMELINE

LEGAL CHALLENGES **TO** THE DEATH PENALTY

1972 — ***Furman v. Georgia*** Overturns death penalty in Georgia.

1976 — ***Gregg v. Georgia*** Declares death penalty in Georgia is constitutional.

Popperfoto/Getty Images

1984 — ***Pulley v. Harris*** No constitutional requirement for a proportionality review of sentences in comparable cases in a state.

1986 — ***Ford v. Wainwright*** Prohibits the state from executing the insane.

1987 — ***McCleskey v. Kemp*** Rejects racial injustice of the death penalty.

1988 — ***Thompson v. Oklahoma*** Prohibits execution of juveniles under age 16.

Joel Gordon

1989 — ***Penry v. Lynaugh*** Mental retardation is no bar to capital punishment.

Stanford v. Kentucky Eighth Amendment does not prohibit the death penalty for crimes committed at age 16 or 17.

WORKING ON DEATH ROW

The conditions on death row vary among the states that house condemned prisoners. All states except Missouri and Tennessee segregate death row prisoners from the general prison population. Meals are usually served in condemned prisoners' cells. If inmates are permitted to purchase a television, they may do so but generally can receive only local channels. They can read until they fall asleep, no matter how late it might be, because each cell typically has individually controlled light switches. Inmates generally live in windowless cells. They cannot see or hear what is going on outside the prison. Attorneys can almost always visit five or more times each week, and condemned prisoners can have one or two family visits a week. A few days before their scheduled execution, prisoners are frequently taken from their cells to another prison in which the execution will take place.[51]

A number of staff members are involved with death row inmates: classification officers who process newly arriving inmates, the correctional officers and supervisors who are directly responsible for the inmates, mental health personnel, the chaplain, and the emergency medical technicians who insert the IVs that will send three fatal drugs through the condemned inmate's veins.

Describe how correctional officers working on death row regard their jobs **LO6**

Working with Death Row Inmates

A group of correctional officers and supervisors are responsible for inmates on death row. They seem to be positive about their jobs, and inmates, in turn, generally feel that they are being treated with respect.[52] When asked how he liked his job, one death row

1991

AP Images/Press of Atlantic City/Danny Drake

Payne v. Tennessee Eighth Amendment does not prohibit admission of "victim impact" evidence.

2002

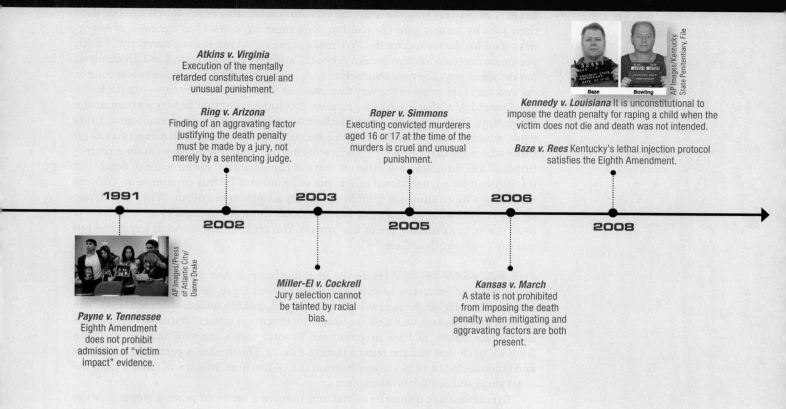

Atkins v. Virginia Execution of the mentally retarded constitutes cruel and unusual punishment.

Ring v. Arizona Finding of an aggravating factor justifying the death penalty must be made by a jury, not merely by a sentencing judge.

2003

Miller-El v. Cockrell Jury selection cannot be tainted by racial bias.

2005

Roper v. Simmons Executing convicted murderers aged 16 or 17 at the time of the murders is cruel and unusual punishment.

2006

Kansas v. March A state is not prohibited from imposing the death penalty when mitigating and aggravating factors are both present.

2008

Baze Bowling

AP Images/Kentucky State Penitentiary, File

Kennedy v. Louisiana It is unconstitutional to impose the death penalty for raping a child when the victim does not die and death was not intended.

Baze v. Rees Kentucky's lethal injection protocol satisfies the Eighth Amendment.

correctional officer replied, "It is a job. These guys are going to die, and we try to treat them decently. We do everything we can for them."[53]

Because of the length of time between conviction and execution, officers working on death row may develop relationships with the inmates and even develop a form of rapport. Officers do experience a sense of loss when inmates are moved to where they will be executed, but they do not usually feel that they are putting them to death. They are merely doing their job. It is easier for officers when inmates are transferred to another facility to be executed than when the executions take place in the same institution.

CRITICAL THINKING

If you were a corrections officer working with death row inmates, would you be able to treat them with humanity and respect? Should the prison system hire only officers who have not been victims of crime? LO6

Execution Teams

Death work culminates in the **deathwatch**, which is generally 24 to 48 hours. It is usually supervised by a team of correctional officers who report to the prison warden; the warden or his or her representative is legally mandated to preside over the execution.

deathwatch The period, generally 24 to 48 hours, before the execution; usually supervised by a team of correctional officers.

Teams are likely to view the execution as a shared responsibility. The deathwatch team officers feed inmates on the "row," observe them, escort them to the shower and exercise areas, prepare them for execution, escort them to the death chamber, and secure them for execution. Members of this team have the responsibility of explaining to condemned inmates what is going to happen to their personal property, when and how long they can talk with family in the final hours before execution, and how the warden has a phone line available to hear any stay of execution that might be forthcoming from the courts or the governor's office.[54]

execution team Those who carry out the execution.

Those who carry out the execution are part of what is known as an **execution team**. The officers who make up the execution team usually say that they cope with their jobs by focusing on the routine. One supervisor, who has the rank of major, described his duties succinctly: "We make sure everything is done correctly."[55] Each person on the team has a particular job to do, and they attempt to do it in a professional but detached way. They see themselves as doing a job that society requires someone to do, and they take pride in the way they conduct themselves as they carry out the law.

Donald A. Cabana wrote a gripping account of the time he was warden of the Mississippi State Penitentiary at Parchman, and supervised two executions. In this book, which is recommended reading, he says, "Capital punishment exacts a toll on those who must carry it out."[56] Nor is working on death row an easy job for a correctional officer. Inmates have different ways of coping with their sentence of death, but it is difficult for a correctional officer not to be affected by this environment. Officers must deal with emotions of guilt because they administered death. When asked, one officer echoed what a number of fellow officers think about these events: "After it is over, you get to thinking about the inmate. You try to block out what happened but you can't—his death is there."[57]

THE PROCESS OF DEATH In the final few hours before death, while procedures vary somewhat from state to state, a prisoner receives his or her final visits from family and attorney. He or she is provided a final meal, usually whatever is requested. The warden and chaplain visit and stay until the execution is over. Witnesses arrive, and the inmate makes the final preparations. In some states, the male inmate receives a fresh set of clothes and the female inmate a dress. The inmate is permitted to shower and is connected to an electrocardiogram (EKG) machine, which will remain until the heart stops and death has taken place.

Executions are quite ritualized and involve a series of precise steps. It is the responsibility of the strap-down team, usually a six-person group, to escort the condemned from their cells to the execution room and secure them to the execution table. Each is assigned responsibility for one body part, such as the left arm or the left leg. This process keeps them from focusing on what they are preparing the condemned for and diffuses responsibility. One officer who performed this duty for 15 years notes, "We each have a duty to do it as efficiently as we can. The day is important enough that we want it to go without a hitch."[58]

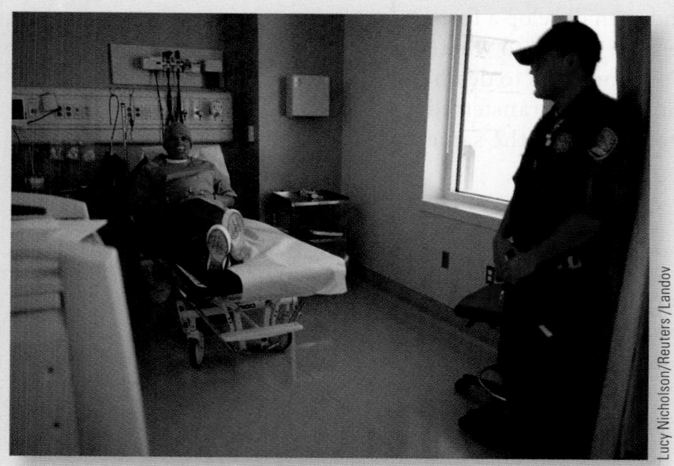

Lucy Nicholson/Reuters/Landov

On June 8, 2012, Albert Ruiz, who was on death row for murder, waits for a medical checkup at San Quentin state prison in California. Ruiz had been on death row since 2003 when he died of natural causes in 2013, at age 51. All of California's death row prisoners are at San Quentin. The state last executed an inmate in 2006.

When the straps are securely fastened, then it is up to the warden to give the signal to begin the execution. The warden usually stands at the head of the person strapped on the gurney, and the prison chaplain stands at his or her feet. When the medical technician or the trained officer injects the two lethal chemicals, death usually comes in a few minutes.

The first drug, sodium thiopental, ensures that the prisoner does not experience any pain associated with the paralysis and cardiac arrest caused by the second and third drugs, pancuronium bromide and potassium chloride. According to the U.S. Supreme Court, the actual insertion of the intravenous (IV) catheter must be made by a person who has at least one year's professional experience. The execution team has the responsibility to mix the drugs and load them into syringes, and the warden and deputy warden must remain in the execution chamber to observe the prisoner and watch for any IV problems while the execution team administers the drugs from another room. If the prisoner is not unconscious within 60 seconds after the sodium thiopental's delivery, a new dose must be given at a secondary injection site before the second and third drugs are administered.[59] A physician examines the body and pronounces death.

The execution process is concluded when the strap-down team reenters the death chamber, unfastens the straps around the body, and transfers it to another gurney. The body is loaded into a waiting hearse and taken to a local funeral home, where it is either claimed by the family or interred by the state. The death certificate usually says "state-ordered homicide."[60]

LIVING ON DEATH ROW

LO7 Identify how inmates on death row adjust to their situation

Inmates living on death row share experiences like no others. There appear to be at least four types of inmate responses to death row:

- Some continue to reiterate their innocence, and they may even go to their execution claiming innocence.
- Some focus on legal appeals and court work.
- Some have a religious experience and adopt a new religious identity.
- Some become quite depressed, ruminating over struggles and difficulties of adjusting to death row.

In the midst of these responses, inmates deal with a variety of anxieties on death row—arranging meetings with their attorneys, waiting for rulings from appeal courts, desiring correspondence from their families, and looking forward to upcoming family visits. Another source of anxiety is when the date of execution is approaching for their incarcerated friends or themselves.

One inmate on death row in Ohio talks about the trauma when a condemned prisoner is taken from death row to the prison where he will be executed:

> Last week they came and got a guy down the cellblock. We had been friends for a number of years, and we had served time together in a number of "joints" in this state. He knew his time was up, but we didn't believe it was going to happen until they came and got him. This place hasn't been the same since that. I don't think I've slept since that. I know my time is coming and, as I told you before, I'm innocent. The state is going to kill an innocent man. I just feel nervous; I can't relax. I can't get it off my mind that my time is coming too.[61]

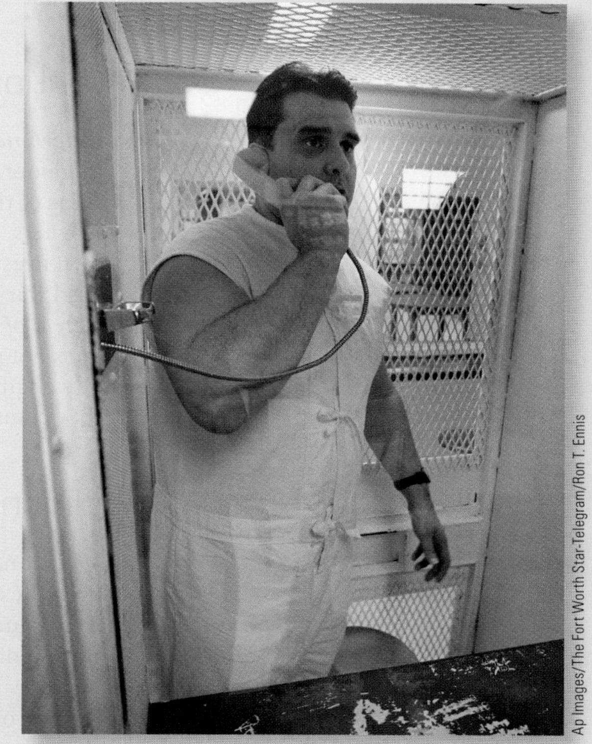

Ap Images/The Fort Worth Star-Telegram/Ron T. Ennis

For some, living on death row means preparing for the end. Here, on February 15, 2012, George Rivas speaks from death row in the Allan Polunsky Unit prison in Livingston, Texas, about his part in the crime rampage of the Texas Seven. On December 13, 2000, Rivas's gang overpowered workers at the Texas Department of Criminal Justice Connally Unit prison in Kenedy and stole the workers' clothes, broke into the prison's armory to get guns, and drove away in a prison truck. They committed several robberies, including two in Houston, and then 11 days later, gunned down Irving, Texas, police officer Aubrey Hawkins. In the end, Rivas was executed by lethal injection on February 29, 2012, at 6:22 p.m.

THE EFFECT OF EXECUTIONS ON NON–DEATH ROW INMATES

Traditionally, an execution in a prison would generate a ruckus from non–death row inmates, which could include inmates banging on their cells, dumping debris out of their cells, or even destruction of property. Today, non–death row inmates have much less response to an execution in their institution, for a number of reasons. First, the states in which executions are taking place generally will transfer inmates from where they had spent a number of years to another institution in which they will be executed in a short period of time, perhaps as little as a month or so. Thus, the executed inmate has not built relationships or familiarity with the inmates where the execution takes place. Second, the place where the condemned inmate is

THINKING
LIKE A CORRECTIONS PROFESSIONAL

In your state, the governor has suspended all executions, citing troubled executions and wrongful convictions in other states, and plans to appoint a commission. You have been appointed to head this commission to consider the humanity and constitutionality of the death penalty. Your commission will include doctors, lawyers, scientists, and law enforcement officials.

As the chair of this commission, what would you do, in the order in which you would do it? (First action, second, third, fourth, etc.) What information would your commission need to make its report? What do you think would be the outcome of your commission's report? For example, if the report should conclude that the problems related to the death penalty make it unconstitutional, what do you think the governor or his successor would do? In answering this question, remember that your state has executed a number of people in the modern era of the death penalty.

held, as well as where the execution itself happens, is set apart from the remainder of the prison. One of the authors has been involved in a number of death penalty cases, and he has always been amazed how you go deeper and deeper into the prison before you reach death row. Third, for those states that execute inmates, this event is frequent enough that it is not considered that unusual. For example, in Texas, inmates see execution as more or less a regular event. Finally, few executions attract much attention anymore outside or inside the prison. Having said all this, non–death row inmates may not have the response to an execution that they have had in the past, but it is still a vivid reminder to these inmates how the state has control of their lives.

ARGUMENTS FOR AND AGAINST THE DEATH PENALTY

Defenders of the death penalty make several arguments supporting their position and, at the same time, those who oppose the death penalty base their arguments on several positions. The following sections outline both the **retentionist arguments** and the **abolitionist arguments**.

Retentionist Arguments

- *Deterrence.* Punishment has a deterrent value. Crime is a rational process, and therefore it only stands to reason that the possibility of a death sentence will deter some of those who are contemplating murder.[62]
- *Fairness.* It is only fair that "cold-blooded" killers pay for their crimes with their own lives. In Walter Berns's eloquent essay, he draws on humanity's anger against Nazi war criminals to justify capital punishment for retribution.[63]
- *Threat of recidivism.* Defenders of the death penalty charge that life imprisonment does not protect society, because prisoners who have committed murder are usually eligible for parole after a period of time, or if they are given a life sentence, they commit another murder while they are incarcerated.[64]

Abolitionist Arguments

- *The moral issue.* Moralists who reject the death penalty as a response to crime, even the crime of murder, hold that it is state-administered homicide. The moralist's argument goes on to a consideration of the inevitable caprice in the administration of the death penalty. In addition, this argument makes the point that the majority of men and women executed have been African American or Hispanic, in spite of all the precautions against prejudice that have been built into the judicial process. Does race influence the death penalty? Consider the Evidence-Based Corrections feature.
- *The constitutional issue.* Challenges to the legitimacy of capital punishment have built their case against the death penalty by the ambiguous language of the Eighth and Fourteenth Amendments. What this challenge is all about is that the death penalty is unconstitutional.
- *The pragmatic issues.* The possibilities of errors, incompetent and inexperienced defense counsels, police officers who are not truthful, and prosecutors who repress evidence are some of the reasons why the wrong individuals are convicted and given the sentence of death. Recent releases from death row because of wrongful convictions are a reminder of the accuracy of this concern. Another pragmatic issue is the costliness of the death penalty; it is several times more expensive than confining an inmate for the duration of his or her life. For example, a recent (2014) study conducted by the Kansas Judicial Council found that the cost of an

retentionist arguments Defenders of the death penalty make several arguments supporting their positions, including its deterrent value, fairness, and the idea that life imprisonment does not sufficiently protect society.

abolitionist arguments Those who oppose the death penalty base their arguments on several positions, including the moral issue, the constitutional issue, and the pragmatic issues.

execution was four times the cost of a life sentence. Examining 34 potentially capital cases from 2004 to 2011, the study showed that criminal defense costs for death penalty trials averaged $395,762 per case, compared to $98,963 per similar case when the death penalty was not on the table. Trial court costs were equally skewed: $72,530 for cases with the death penalty; $21,554 for those without. In the event that the case ended in a guilty plea and did not go to trial, death penalty cases cost about twice as much for defense attorneys ($130,595 versus $64,711) and court costs ($16,263 versus $7,384), compared to cases where death was not sought. One reason was that jury trials averaged 40 days in cases where the death penalty was being sought, but only 17 days when it was not an option. Justices of the Kansas Supreme Court assigned to write opinions estimated they spent 20 times more hours on death penalty appeals than on non-death appeals. Cost differentials did not end at the courthouse door. The Department of Corrections said housing prisoners on death row cost more than twice as much per year ($49,380) as for prisoners in the general population ($24,690).[65]

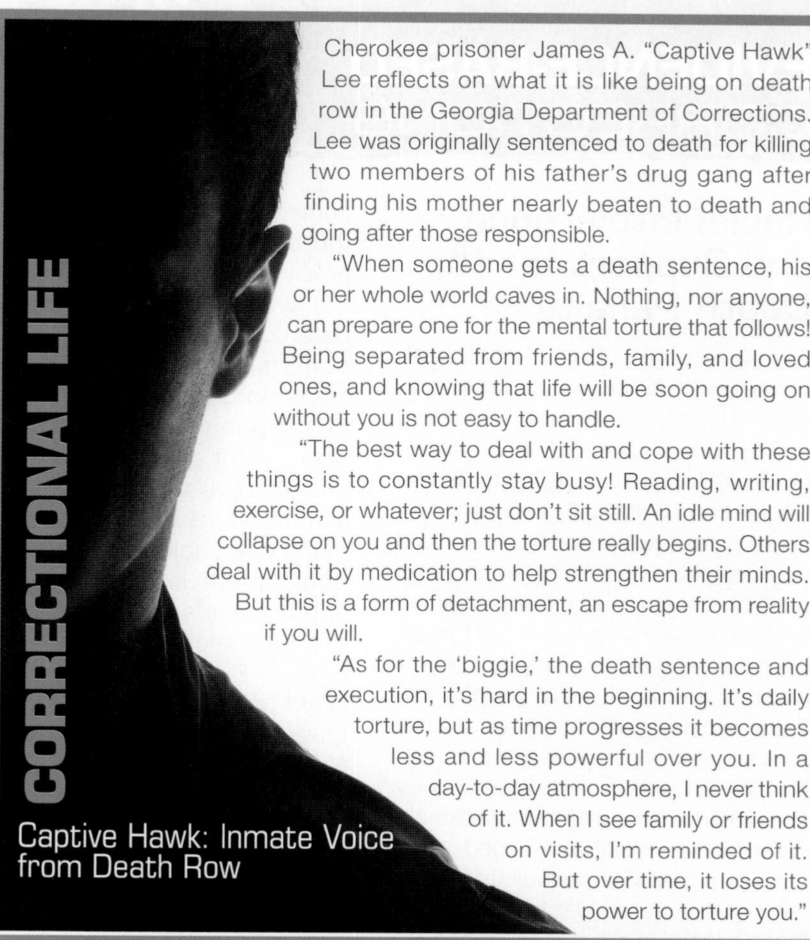

CORRECTIONAL LIFE

Captive Hawk: Inmate Voice from Death Row

Cherokee prisoner James A. "Captive Hawk" Lee reflects on what it is like being on death row in the Georgia Department of Corrections. Lee was originally sentenced to death for killing two members of his father's drug gang after finding his mother nearly beaten to death and going after those responsible.

"When someone gets a death sentence, his or her whole world caves in. Nothing, nor anyone, can prepare one for the mental torture that follows! Being separated from friends, family, and loved ones, and knowing that life will be soon going on without you is not easy to handle.

"The best way to deal with and cope with these things is to constantly stay busy! Reading, writing, exercise, or whatever; just don't sit still. An idle mind will collapse on you and then the torture really begins. Others deal with it by medication to help strengthen their minds. But this is a form of detachment, an escape from reality if you will.

"As for the 'biggie,' the death sentence and execution, it's hard in the beginning. It's daily torture, but as time progresses it becomes less and less powerful over you. In a day-to-day atmosphere, I never think of it. When I see family or friends on visits, I'm reminded of it. But over time, it loses its power to torture you."

AP Images/Rich Pedroncelli

Those opposed to the death penalty include people whom you might think would be supporters. Ronnie Sandoval (left) and Lorrain Taylor comfort each other as they hold photos of their slain children at a news conference where they joined others in supporting a November 2012 ballot initiative to end the death penalty, held in Sacramento, California, August 29, 2011. Sandoval's son, Arthur Carmona, was murdered in Santa Ana in 2008 and Taylor's twin sons were gunned down together in Oakland in 2000. Both mothers spoke against the death penalty and support the initiative that would replace capital punishment with life prison terms.

EVIDENCE-BASED CORRECTIONS

Racial Intolerance and Support for the Death Penalty

Why do people support the death penalty? Is it based on an actual belief that capital punishment deters murder or do other forces influence public attitudes? According to James Unnever and Francis Cullen's research, support for capital punishment, here and abroad, may reflect cross-group conflict and animosity. Public opinion is fueled by perceived or actual threats by outside groups—the dominant group's fear that its privileges are being eroded by the demands of a minority and the minority group's belief that it can enhance its position by challenging the existing racial/ethnic order. Members of the privileged group can claim that their prejudices toward the outsiders are justified because these minorities are disrupting society by being overly criminal. Unnever and Cullen argue that associating criminality with "others" helps justify the belief in harsh criminal justice policies such as the death penalty.

Unnever and Cullen found that data collected in the United States confirmed their views that racial intolerance predicts not only pro–death penalty attitudes but also support for punitive crime control measures. Using survey data from a number of other nations, they found that public support for capital punishment is related to beliefs about racial and ethnic minorities. The data showed that individuals in France, Belgium, the Netherlands, West and East Germany, Italy, Luxembourg, Denmark, Great Britain, Greece, Spain, Finland, Sweden, and Austria who expressed racial and ethnic prejudice were more likely to support harshly punishing criminals. Racial intolerance was one of the most substantive predictors of punitiveness. People with more years of education were less likely and those who were conservatives were more likely to embrace punitive sentiments. However, punitiveness was not related to racial/ethnic intolerance in Portugal and Ireland, possibly because these two countries have more benign race relations than most others.

In conclusion, Unnever and Cullen found that support for capital punishment may rely less on the need for safety and is more likely a response to racial and ethnic conflict and anger.

FOR CRITICAL THINKING AND WRITING

If racial animus and discrimination form the basis for people's opinion of capital punishment, can African Americans convicted of murder ever hope to be given fair treatment? Is that fact alone sufficient to influence your views on the death penalty and whether it meets legal standards of fairness?

Source: James Unnever and Francis Cullen, "Racial-Ethnic Intolerance and Support for Capital Punishment: A Cross-National Comparison," *Criminology* 48 (2010): 831–879.

Evaluate whether the death penalty deters murder LO8

DOES THE DEATH PENALTY DETER MURDER?

Defenders of the death penalty, as stated above, make several arguments supporting their positions. They claim that this punishment is justified because it provides incapacitation and is a deterrent to murder. They assert further that the death penalty provides justice for victims' families, that individuals who commit heinous crimes deserve the death penalty, and that it is proportional.

Contemporary opposition to capital punishment is generally based on beliefs about the possibility of error; the unfair use of discretion; no deterrence effect; racial, gender, and other biases; brutality unacceptable to a free society; and the expense of executions (up to $3 million per execution, which is considerably more than life imprisonment).

Yet the absolute key issue in the death penalty debate is whether this punishment can lower the murder rate. Even with its brutality and cruelty, the claim could be made that the death penalty could be justified if it proved to be an effective deterrent that would save innocent lives. As suggested by this chapter, those who favor the death penalty claim that it has real deterrent value and those who oppose it deny it has real deterrent value. Which position is correct?

The particular focus on the empirical research on the death penalty is whether the death penalty serves as a more effective deterrent than life imprisonment for capital crimes such as homicide. The methods that have been employed include the following:

- *Immediate impact studies.* This approach attempts to calculate the effects a well-publicized execution has on the short-term murder rate.
- *Time-series analysis.* This approach compares long-term trends in capital punishment rates and murder.
- *Contiguous-state analysis.* This approach compares murder rates in states with the death penalty to the murder rates of a similar state that has abolished the death penalty.

AP Images/Lou Krasky

Years on death row take a toll on inmates. Here, a death row inmate stands in his cell at Lieber Correctional Institution near Ridgeville, South Carolina. Inmates at the facility spend about 23 hours a day in a cell so narrow they can touch both walls at the same time and just long enough to accommodate a set of bunk beds, a toilet, and a sink.

The majority of researchers have failed to find any deterrent effect of the death penalty. There is little evidence that murder rates rise when a state abolishes capital punishment any more so than murder rates decrease when the death penalty is adopted. The murder rate is further similar both in states that use capital punishment and neighboring states that have abolished the death penalty.

Despite this lack of empirical verification, some recent studies have concluded that executing criminals may, in fact, bring the murder rate down. Newer studies, using sophisticated data analysis, have been able to uncover a more significant association. James Yunker, using a national data set, has found evidence that there is a deterrent effect of capital punishment now that the pace of executions has accelerated.[66] Economists Hashem Dezhbakhsh, Paul H. Rubin, and Joanna M. Shepherd performed an advanced statistical analysis on county-level homicide data and found that each execution leads to an average of 18 fewer murders.[67]

These efforts contradict findings that capital punishment fails as a deterrent. So on the one hand, the most recent research indicates that if the death penalty was used more frequently, it is possible that the tipping point would be reached, and execution can become an effective deterrent measure. On the other hand, capital punishment still carries significant baggage. According to research sponsored by the Pew Foundation, a majority of death penalty convictions have been overturned, many due to "serious, reversible error," including egregiously incompetent defense counsel, suppression of exculpatory evidence, false confessions, racial manipulation of the jury, "snitch" and accomplice testimony, and faulty jury instructions.[68] However, not all innocent people on death row are eventually exonerated. A recent study by Samuel Gross and his colleagues examined data on both 7,482 defendants who were given death sentences between 1973 and 2004 and death row exonerations during that time. Their complex statistical analysis suggested that about 4 percent of death row prisoners would have eventually been exonerated and that at least 340 people may have been put to death unjustly in the past 40 years.[69] So after years of study, the value of the death penalty remains a topic of considerable debate.

SUMMARY

LO1 Describe what public opinion is concerning the death penalty

American public opinion shifted dramatically in the twentieth century. As recently as 1978, one public opinion poll found that 66 percent of the population opposed the death penalty. However, in the last two decades of the twentieth and into the twenty-first century, with the rising violent crime rates, public opinion changed and a great majority of Americans, more than 80 percent, favored the death penalty. Some evidence exists that when the public is presented with the alternative of life imprisonment without the possibility of parole, the support declines (about 50 percent) for the death penalty.

LO2 Compare the importance of aggravation versus mitigation concerning the death penalty

The first phase of the death penalty trial determines guilt or innocence. If the jury finds that a person is guilty of first-degree murder, then the court process enters the penalty phase. For a person to be condemned to death in the penalty phase, the jury must find that the aggravation factors (why the defendant should be put to death) are greater than the mitigation factors (why the defendant should not be put to death).

LO3 Discuss the position of the U.S. Supreme Court concerning the death penalty

The death penalty has received mixed support from the U.S. Supreme Court, but, with certain exceptions, the Court has consistently found the death penalty does not constitute cruel and unusual punishment.

LO4 Identify the position of the Supreme Court concerning the importance of race and the death penalty

Jury selection cannot be tainted by racial bias, but unless the defense can prove that racial bias is involved, race is not a factor in the execution process.

LO5 Discuss the Supreme Court's rulings on the execution of mentally impaired inmates and juveniles

The Supreme Court has opposed execution of juveniles under 18 and the execution of the mentally impaired.

LO6 Describe how correctional officers working on death row regard their jobs

Correctional workers on death row believe that they have a duty to do and try to perform it as efficiently as they can. They want to treat the condemned with dignity and respect.

LO7 Identify how inmates on death row adjust to their situation

Death row inmates attempt to adjust to their situation in a variety of ways. Some focus on their cases, others have a religious experience and see themselves through their new identity, while many ruminate about the struggles and difficulties they have in adjusting to death row.

LO8 Evaluate whether the death penalty deters murder

There has been continuous debate and much research conducted to determine whether the death penalty deters murder, and at the end of the day, the evidence seems to conclude that the death penalty does not deter murder in our society.

CRITICAL THINKING QUESTIONS

1. Do we need the death penalty to satisfy our need for revenge? Is it possible for society to give up the death penalty?
2. What is the purpose of taking the life of a murderer who is mentally ill?
3. What do you think is the most persuasive argument for the death penalty?
4. What do you think is the most persuasive argument against the death penalty?
5. What do the recent stances of the U.S. Supreme Court suggest will be the future of the death penalty in this nation?

NOTES

1. Rachel Dissell, "Did Cleveland Police Mishandle a 2008 Case Against Serial Killer Anthony Sowell? Detective's Deposition Raises New Questions," *Cleveland Plain Dealer*, October 3, 2013, http://www.cleveland.com/court-justice/index.ssf/2013/10/cleveland_detective_explains.html (accessed July 2014).
2. Dagobert D. Runes, ed., *The Selected Writings of Benjamin Rush* (New York: The Philosophical Library, 1947).
3. Philip E. Mackey, *Voices Against Death: American Opposition to Capital Punishment, 1787–1975* (New York: Burt Franklin, 1976), pp. 14–33.
4. Sir James Fitzjames Stephen, "Capital Punishments," *Fraser's Magazine* 69 (1864): 753–772.
5. Tracy L. Snell, *Capital Punishment, 2012 – Statistical Tables* (Washington, DC: Bureau of Justice Statistics, U.S. Department of Justice, 2014), http://www.bjs.gov/content/pub/pdf/cp12st.pdf (accessed July 2014).

6. Ibid.
7. Tracy Snell, Capital Punishment 2012 (Washington, D.C.: Bureau of Justice Statistics, May 2014).
8. Andrew Buncombe, "U.S. Turns Against Death Penalty as 1,000th Prisoner Is Executed," *Common Dreams News Center*, November 29, 2006.
9. Snell, *Capital Punishment, 2012 – Statistical Tables.*
10. Mark D. Cunningham and Mark P. Vigen, "Death Row Inmate Characteristics, Adjustment, and Confinement: A Critical Review of the Literature," *Behavioral Sciences and the Law* 20 (2002): 191–210.
11. Snell, *Capital Punishment, 2012 – Statistical Tables.*
12. Joseph Carroll, Death Penalty Information Center, "Gallup Poll: Who Supports the Death Penalty?" November 16, 2004, http://www.deathpenaltyinfo.org/gallup-poll-who-supports-death-penalty (accessed July 2014).
13. Ibid.
14. Karen S. Miller, *Wrongful Capital Convictions and the Legitimacy of the Death Penalty* (New York: LFB Scholarly Publishing LLC, 2006); Michael Mello, *The Wrong Man: A True Story of Innocence on Death Row* (Minneapolis: University of Minnesota Press, 2001).
15. Amnesty International, "The Death Penalty in 2013," http://www.amnesty.org/en/death-penalty/death-sentences-and-executions-in-2013 (accessed July 2014).
16. James S. Liebman, Jeffrey Fagan, and Valerie West, *A Broken System: Error Rates in Capital Cases, 1973–1995* (New York: Columbia University School of Law, 2000).
17. Ibid. See also, concerning the possibility of wrongful convictions, D. Michael Risinger, "Innocents Convicted: An Empirically Justified Factual Wrongful Conviction Rate," *Journal of Criminal Law and Criminology* 97 (2007): 761–806; James D. Unnever and Francis T. Cullen, "Executing the Innocent and Support for Capital Punishment: Implications for Public Policy," *Criminology and Public Policy* 4 (2005): 3–38.
18. *McCleskey v. Kemp*, 438 U.S. 586 (1991).
19. Ibid.
20. *Furman v. Georgia*, 408 U.S. 238 (1972).
21. Ibid.
22. *Gregg* v. *Georgia*, 428 U.S. 153, 96 S.Ct. 2909, 49 L.Ed.2d 859 (1976).
23. Ibid., at 205–207, 96 S.Ct. at 2940–41.
24. *Pulley v. Harris*, 104 S.Ct. 881 (1984).
25. Ibid.
26. *Kansas v. March*, 548 U.S. 263 (2006).
27. *Pulley v. Harris.*
28. *Baze et al. v. Rees, Commissioner, Kentucky Department of Corrections, et al.*, 0–7-5439, 217 S.W. 3d 207 (2008).
29. The Telegraph, "Botched Arizona Execution Was 'Torture,' Says John McCain," July 26, 2014, http://www.telegraph.co.uk/news/worldnews/northamerica/usa/10993166/Botched-Arizona-execution-was-torture-says-John-McCain.html (accessed July 2014).
30. *McCleskey v. Kemp.*
31. Ibid.
32. Ibid.
33. *Miller-El v. Cockrell*, 537 U.S. 322 (2003).
34. John Donohue, "Capital Punishment in Connecticut, 1973–2007: A Comprehensive Evaluation from 4,686 Murders to One Execution," http://works.bepress.com/john_donohue/87/ (accessed July 2014). For a discussion of this study, see Lincoln Caplan, "The Random Horror of the Death Penalty," *New York Times*, January 7, 2012, http://www.nytimes.com/2012/01/08/opinion/sunday/the-random-horror-of-the-death-penalty.html (accessed July 2014).
35. Amnesty International website, http://www.amnesty.org (accessed July 2014).
36. *Atkins v. Virginia*, 122 S.Ct. 2242 (2002).
37. Ibid.
38. Amnesty International website.
39. *Ford v. Wainwright*, 477 U.S. 399 (1986).
40. Ibid.
41. *Washington v. Harper*, 494 U.S. 210 (1990).
42. Amnesty International website.
43. *Thompson v. Oklahoma*, 487 U.S. 815 (1988).
44. *Stanford v. Kentucky*, 109 S.Ct. 2969 (1989).
45. Ibid.
46. *Roper v. Simmons*, 543 U.S. 551 (2005).
47. *Witherspoon v. Illinois*, 391 U.S. 550 (1968).
48. *Wainwright v. Witt*, 499 U.S. 412, 105 S.Ct. 844, 83 L.Ed.2d 841 (1985).
49. Ibid.
50. *Lockhart v. McCree*, 476 U.S. 162, 106 S.Ct. 1758, 90 L.Ed.2d 137 (1986).
51. Michael Taylor, "Peterson to Begin Life on Death Row," *San Francisco Chronicle*, March 17, 2005.
52. As an expert witness in nearly 20 death row cases, Bartollas has interviewed inmates on death row and talked with officers responsible for these inmates. It is unusual for conflict to be present among officers and inmates.
53. Ibid.
54. Robert Johnson, *Death Work: A Study of the Modern Execution Process* (Pacific Grove, CA: Brooks/Cole, 1990), pp. 70–71.
55. Sara Rimer, "Working on Death Row: A Special Report: In the Busiest Death Chamber, Duty Carries Its Own Burdens," *New York Times*, December 17, 2000.
56. Donald A. Cabana, *Death at Midnight: The Confession of an Executioner* (Boston: Northeastern University Press, 1996), p. xi.
57. Ken Hausman, "Researcher Enters Minds of Death-Row Officers," *Psychiatry News* 36 (2001): 6.
58. Ibid.
59. *Baze et al. v. Rees.*
60. Rimer, "Working on Death Row: A Special Report."
61. Inmate told Bartollas this in October 2004.
62. This was the argument expressed by James Q. Wilson, Ernest van den Haag, and more recent economists and others.
63. Water Berns, *For Capital Punishment* (New York: Basic Books, 1979).
64. Bartollas has been an expert witness in a number of cases in which inmates who had committed a previous murder committed another murder while incarcerated.
65. Judicial Council, Kansas Legislature, "Report of the Judicial Council Death Penalty Advisory Committee," February 13, 2014, http://www.deathpenaltyinfo.org/documents/KSCost2014.pdf (accessed July 2014).
66. James Yunker, "A New Statistical Analysis of Capital Punishment Incorporating U.S. Postmoratorium Data," *Social Science Quarterly* 82 (2001): 297–312.
67. Hashem Dezhbakhsh, Paul H. Rubin, and Joanna M. Shepherd, "Does Capital Punishment Have a Deterrent Effect? New Evidence from Postmoratorium Panel Data," *American Law and Economics Review* 5 (2003): 344–376.
68. Pew Foundation, "Death Penalty," http://www.pewtrusts.org/en/topics/state-policy (accessed July 2014).
69. Samuel R. Gross, Barbara O'Brien, Chen Huc, and Edward Kennedy, "Rate of False Conviction of Criminal Defendants Who Are Sentenced to Death," Proceedings of the National Academy of Sciences of the United States of America, March 25, 2014.

© Michael Ainsworth/*Dallas Morning News*/Corbis

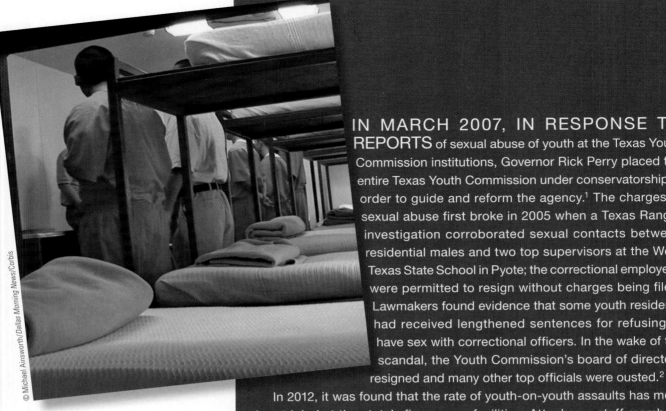

IN MARCH 2007, IN RESPONSE TO REPORTS of sexual abuse of youth at the Texas Youth Commission institutions, Governor Rick Perry placed the entire Texas Youth Commission under conservatorship in order to guide and reform the agency.[1] The charges of sexual abuse first broke in 2005 when a Texas Ranger investigation corroborated sexual contacts between residential males and two top supervisors at the West Texas State School in Pyote; the correctional employees were permitted to resign without charges being filed. Lawmakers found evidence that some youth residents had received lengthened sentences for refusing to have sex with correctional officers. In the wake of the scandal, the Youth Commission's board of directors resigned and many other top officials were ousted.[2]

In 2012, it was found that the rate of youth-on-youth assaults has more than tripled at the state's five secure facilities. Attacks on staff members have also increased. For example, the physical assaults in these facilities among youth increased from 17 assaults per 100 youths in 2007 to 54 per 100 in 2012. Deputy Director Deborah Fowler of [Texas] Appleseed said that the agency is struggling to change the state from punishment to rehabilitation: "I think they've had a really hard time turning the ship. I'm very pessimistic about the ability to really shift the culture."[3]

14

The Juvenile Offender

Ann Johansson/Corbis

LEARNING OBJECTIVES

 LO1 Identify the early development of juvenile justice

 LO2 Identify how sentencing structures in juvenile justice have changed in recent years

 LO3 Explain the disposition of probation, including how it is administered and by whom and recent trends in its use

 LO4 Distinguish between community treatment and institutional treatment for juvenile offenders

 LO5 Discuss the nature of aftercare for juvenile offenders, including recent innovations in juvenile aftercare and reentry programs

 LO6 Explain how the juvenile is transferred and tried in adult court

 LO7 Identify the plight faced by juveniles sent to adult prisons

PREVIEW OF KEY CONCEPTS

juvenile justice system
juvenile delinquent
status offender
parens patriae
community treatment
institutional treatment facility
Juvenile Justice Standards Project
blended sentencing
residential programs
wilderness programs
group homes
family group homes
nonresidential programs
aftercare
judicial waiver
statutorial exclusion

The victimization of youths in the Texas juvenile training schools is a sad commentary on institutionalization in the **juvenile justice system**. However, Texas is not alone. A national Bureau of Justice Statistics survey of 26,550 adjudicated youth held in state-operated and large local or privately operated juvenile facilities found that an estimated 12 percent (representing 3,220 youth nationwide) reported experiencing one or more incidents of sexual victimization by another youth or faculty staff member in the previous months or since admission.

juvenile justice system A system established over 100 years ago to provide for the care of law-violating youth.

- About 2.6 percent of youth (700 nationwide) reported an incident involving a peer and, alarmingly, 10.3 percent (2,730) reported an incident involving facility staff.
- About 4.3 percent of youth (1,150) reported having sex or other sexual activity with facility staff as a result of some type of force; 6.4 percent of youth (1,710) reported contact with facility staff without force or threat.
- Approximately 95 percent of all youth reporting staff sexual misconduct said they had been victimized by female staff; 42 percent of staff in state juvenile facilities were female.[4]

In the midst of this bad news about juvenile institutionalization, there is good news from California. In the last decade, California has closed eight of its eleven juvenile facilities and successfully turned the responsibility for its nonviolent offenders over to the counties. Governor Jerry Brown also wants to complete the transformation and phasing out of the three remaining state facilities that hold 1,000 more serious offenders. The state realizes that it will need to develop different facilities for managing violent young offenders. Spending on the system has dropped by almost half, from nearly $500 million to about $245 million and the state has cut its juvenile offender population from about 10,000 in the mid-1990s to about 1,000 today. Some critics are concerned that without a state juvenile system to hold violent offenders, prosecutors may try more young people as adults, but the state can prevent this by monitoring and penalizing counties that over-prosecute juveniles and by allowing for extended custody in local facilities for those juveniles who have committed more serious crimes.[5]

California's closing of training schools is a hopeful sign that juvenile institutionalization is experiencing widespread reform. Independent of but interrelated with the adult criminal justice system, the juvenile justice system is primarily responsible for dealing with minors who violate the criminal law (**juvenile delinquents**) and also those youth who have not committed crimes but are incorrigible, truants, runaways, or unmanageable—behaviors forbidden for underage children (**status offenders**).

juvenile delinquents An underage minor who engages in antisocial activities that are defined as criminal behavior by the state's legal code.

status offenders A juvenile who engages in an act that is considered illegal because of his or her age, such as running away, disobedience, or truancy.

This chapter examines how youthful offenders are handled by the juvenile justice system. It also considers boot camps and adult prisons as placements for juvenile offenders, juveniles' transfer to adult courts, and the changing sentencing structures for juvenile offenders. These are critical issues because so many juveniles who have been processed through the justice system later end up in the adult correctional system.

The Voices Across the Profession feature gives us a glimpse into the world of Jean Tomlinson, who started working in the juvenile justice field as a juvenile correctional officer. She worked her way up the career ladder and became the first female director of security for the Texas Youth Commission. She was responsible for all the intakes into the system, making certain they were classified correctly and had their adjudication documents, and assigning them to the proper facility after they had been assessed. She eventually became superintendent of a for-profit 155-bed facility for males aged 10 to 15. Then she became the assistant superintendent of a 240-bed facility in south Texas, which was a regional facility.

FOR GROUP **DISCUSSION**

Come up with a list of five status offenses that could lead to delinquent or criminal activity and discuss how each could start as one and end up another.

© Jean Tomlinson

VOICES ACROSS THE PROFESSION

When I talk in my classes about juveniles whose crimes are very similar to adult crimes—such as drug dealers, sex offenders, murderers, attempted murderers, and car thieves—students are amazed.

Jean Tomlinson
Administrator in Juvenile Correctional Institution

I have a real passion for the juvenile justice system and look upon it as my calling. I think [corrections] students today are much more aware of the adult system than they are of juvenile justice issues. When I talk in my classes about juveniles whose crimes are very similar to adult crimes—such as drug dealers, sex offenders, murderers, attempted murderers, and car thieves—students are amazed. I may talk about an 11-year-old sex offender who might have had six or seven victims. [Students] are somewhat naïve about the crimes that kids can commit at an early age. In Texas, once you are involved in the juvenile justice system, you are with them until you are 21.

I feel that we need to focus on a couple of different areas. Interventions with the family are an important area. These children come from broken homes, dysfunctional in so many ways—for example, a child being used as a pornographic object, and the mother making money off of her children. I believe that if a kid is locked up, the family should have counseling and therapy as long as the kid is locked up. The next focus is to separate minor and more serious offenders. In Texas, we put our 11-year-olds in with our 19- and 20-year-olds. The younger kids are still pliable and amenable to rehabilitation, and they want the approval of adults and people around them. After they are 16, they are either really entrenched in gangs or expect to go to the pen and want to go to the pen. And that is when they begin to hurt the guards.

HISTORY OF THE JUVENILE JUSTICE SYSTEM

 Identify the early development of juvenile justice

Juvenile justice in the United States began in the colonial period and continued to use English practices. The family, the cornerstone of the community in colonial times, was the source and primary means of social control of children. The law was uncomplicated: the only law enforcement officials were town fathers, magistrates, sheriffs, and watchmen, and the only penal institutions were jails for prisoners awaiting trial or punishment. Juvenile lawbreakers did not face a battery of police or other authorities, nor did they have to worry that practitioners of the juvenile justice system would try to rehabilitate or correct them. They only had to concern themselves with being sent back to their families for punishment.

As children got older, however, the likelihood increased that they would be dealt with more harshly by colonial law. The state, even in those early days, clearly was committed to raising its children correctly and making them follow society's rules. Indeed, this early practice appears to have been incorporated into the early Massachusetts Puritan code, which was a model for the U.S. Constitution of 1787.

The state became even more concerned about the welfare of its children in the 1800s. Increased urbanization, industrialization, and bureaucratization were changing the face of America. In the cities particularly, increasing numbers of youths were seemingly out of control. Reformers searched for ways to teach them traditional values, and the asylum and the training school were developed to help the state maintain its control.

The Concept of *Parens Patriae*

parens patriae A medieval English doctrine that sanctioned the right of the Crown to intervene in natural family relations whenever a child's welfare was threatened.

The early courts took control of juveniles under the concept of ***parens patriae***, a Latin term used to signify the role of the king as the father of his country. The concept was first used by English kings to establish their right to intervene in the lives of the children of their vassals—children whose position and property were of direct concern to the monarch.[6] As time passed, the monarchy used *parens patriae* more and more to justify its intervention in the lives of families and children in order to protect their general welfare.[7] *Parens patriae* was brought over and used in American courts, being formalized in the case of *Ex parte Crouse* in 1838, which gave the courts a legal basis for intervening in the lives of children. The Bill of Rights, the Pennsylvania Supreme Court ruled, did not apply to minors and the state could legitimately confine minors who needed "protection." This meant that juveniles did not have the right to counsel or trial by jury, and could be confined even in the absence of criminal behavior.

Child Savers and the Origin of the Juvenile Court

By the end of the 1800s, much of the U.S. population lived in urban areas and worked in factories. Cities were large and growing, and waves of immigrants were inundating the nation's shores with millions of people destined to remain poor. Conditions in the cities were shocking; there was much poverty, crime, disease, mental illness, and dilapidation. The cities' children were viewed as unfortunate victims of the urban scene. The concept of *parens patriae* was used by so-called "child savers" to control the lives of poor and immigrant children. The child-saving philosophy can be seen in a statement by Judge Gustav L. Schramm, who was the first juvenile court judge of Allegheny County (Pittsburgh), Pennsylvania: "Neither umpire nor arbiter, [the juvenile court judge] is the one person who represents his community as *parens patriae*, who may act with the parents, or when necessary even in place of them, to bring about behavior more desirable."[8] The child-saving movement culminated in passage of the Illinois Juvenile Court Act of 1899, which established the nation's first independent juvenile court. For the first time the distinction was made between children who were neglected and those who were delinquent. Delinquent children were those under the age of 16 who violated the law. Most important, the act established a court and a probation program specifically for children. In addition, the legislation allowed children to be committed to institutions and reform programs under the control of the state. The key provisions of the act were these:

- A separate court was established for delinquent and neglected children.
- Special procedures were developed to govern the adjudication of juvenile matters.
- Children were to be separated from adults in courts and in institutional programs.
- Probation programs were to be developed to assist the court in making decisions in the best interests of the state and the child.[9]

The attractiveness of the juvenile court philosophy resulted in almost all states setting up juvenile courts. In fact, by 1928, only 2 of 31 states had not passed a juvenile court statute.

Buyenlarg/Archive Photos/Getty Images

On May 5, 1910, an 8-year-old boy charged with stealing a bicycle is brought before a juvenile court judge.

After 60 years of operation, the juvenile court was heavily criticized because it operated informally and defendants were given few constitutional rights. Children would be tried without lawyers and did not have the right to confront witnesses or have juries. Then, in the critical case of *In re Gault* (1967), the Supreme Court granted juveniles due process rights, including an attorney. See the Timeline for Supreme Court decisions of special relevance to juvenile justice.

CONTEMPORARY JUVENILE JUSTICE

Today, every state maintains an independent juvenile system that traditionally is based on a policy of treatment, rehabilitation, and care for needy children. This system is charged with the care and treatment of minor children who have been found to have violated the state's penal code but because they fall under a statutory age limit, which is most commonly 17 or 18 years of age, society has chosen to treat them differently and separately from more experienced and adult offenders.

Keeping within this framework of treatment and rehabilitation, there is a wide choice of correctional treatments available for juveniles. These can be divided into two major categories: community treatment and institutional treatment. **Community treatment** refers to efforts to provide care, protection, and treatment for juveniles in need. These efforts include probation, treatment services (such as individual and group counseling), restitution, and other programs. **Institutional treatment facilities** are correctional centers operated by state and county governments. These facilities restrict the movement of residents through staff monitoring, locked exits, and interior fence controls.

community treatment Treatment provided to juveniles in the community versus an institutional context.

institutional treatment facilities A correctional institution that provides long-term treatment for juveniles.

Similarities Between Juvenile and Adult Justice Systems

The fact is that considerable similarity exists between the juvenile and adult justice systems. Both consist of three basic subsystems and interrelated agencies. The flow of justice in both is supposed to be from law violation to police apprehension, judicial process, judicial disposition, and rehabilitation in correctional agencies. The basic vocabulary is the same in the juvenile and adult systems, and even when the vocabulary differs, the intent remains the same.

Note the following terms that refer to the juvenile and adult systems:

Adjudicatory hearing is a trial.

Aftercare is parole.

Commitment is a sentence to confinement.

Detention is holding in jail.

Dispositional hearing is a sentencing hearing.

Juvenile court officer is a probation officer.

Minor is a defendant.

Petition is an indictment.

Petitioner is a prosecutor.

Respondent is a defense attorney.

Taking into custody is arresting a suspect.

Both the juvenile and adult systems are under fire to get tough on crime, especially on offenders who commit violent crimes. Both must deal with excessive caseloads and institutional overcrowding, must operate on fiscal shoestrings, and face the ongoing problems of staff recruitment, training, and burnout. Exhibit 14.1 further describes the common ground and differences between the juvenile and adult justice systems.

TIMELINE

DEVELOPMENT OF **CORRECTIONS**

SUPREME COURT DECISIONS REGARDING JUVENILES

1966 — Kent v. United States (1966) Courts must provide the "essentials of due process" in transferring juveniles to the adult system.

1967 — In re Gault (1967) In hearings that could result in commitment to an institution, juveniles have four basic constitutional rights.

AP Images/Ernest K. Bennett

1970 — In re Winship (1970) In delinquency matters, the state must prove its case beyond a reasonable doubt.

1971 — McKeiver v. Pennsylvania (1971) Jury trials are not constitutionally required in juvenile court hearings.

© iStock.com/Jason Doiy

1975 — Breed v. Jones (1975) Waiver of a juvenile to criminal court following adjudication in juvenile court constitutes double jeopardy.

1977 — Oklahoma Publishing Company v. District Court (1977)

1979 — Smith v. Daily Mail Publishing Company (1979) The press may report juvenile court proceedings under certain circumstances.

EXHIBIT 14.1

Similarities and Differences Between the Juvenile and Adult Justice Systems

Similarities	**Differences**
• Police officers use discretion with both juvenile and adult offenders. • Juvenile and adult offenders receive *Miranda* and other constitutional rights at time of arrest. • Juveniles and adults can be placed in pretrial facilities. • The juvenile court and the adult court use proof beyond a reasonable doubt as the standard for evidence. • Plea bargaining may be used with both juvenile and adult offenders. • Convicted juvenile and adult offenders may be sentenced to probation services, residential programs, or institutional facilities. • Boot camps are used with juvenile and adult offenders. • Released institutional juvenile and adult offenders may be assigned to supervision in the community.	• Juveniles can be arrested for acts that would not be criminal if they were adults (status offenders). • Police must take into account a child's age when he or she is questioned. • Age determines the jurisdiction of the juvenile court; age does not affect the jurisdiction of the adult court. • Parents are deeply involved in the juvenile process but not in the adult process. • Juvenile court proceedings are more informal, while adult court proceedings are formal and open to the public. • Juvenile court proceedings, unlike adult proceedings, are not considered criminal; juvenile records are generally sealed when the age of majority is reached. Adult records are permanent. • Juvenile courts cannot sentence juveniles to jail or prison; only adult courts can issue such sentences. • Juveniles are not eligible for the death penalty or a mandatory life sentence (if waived to adult court).

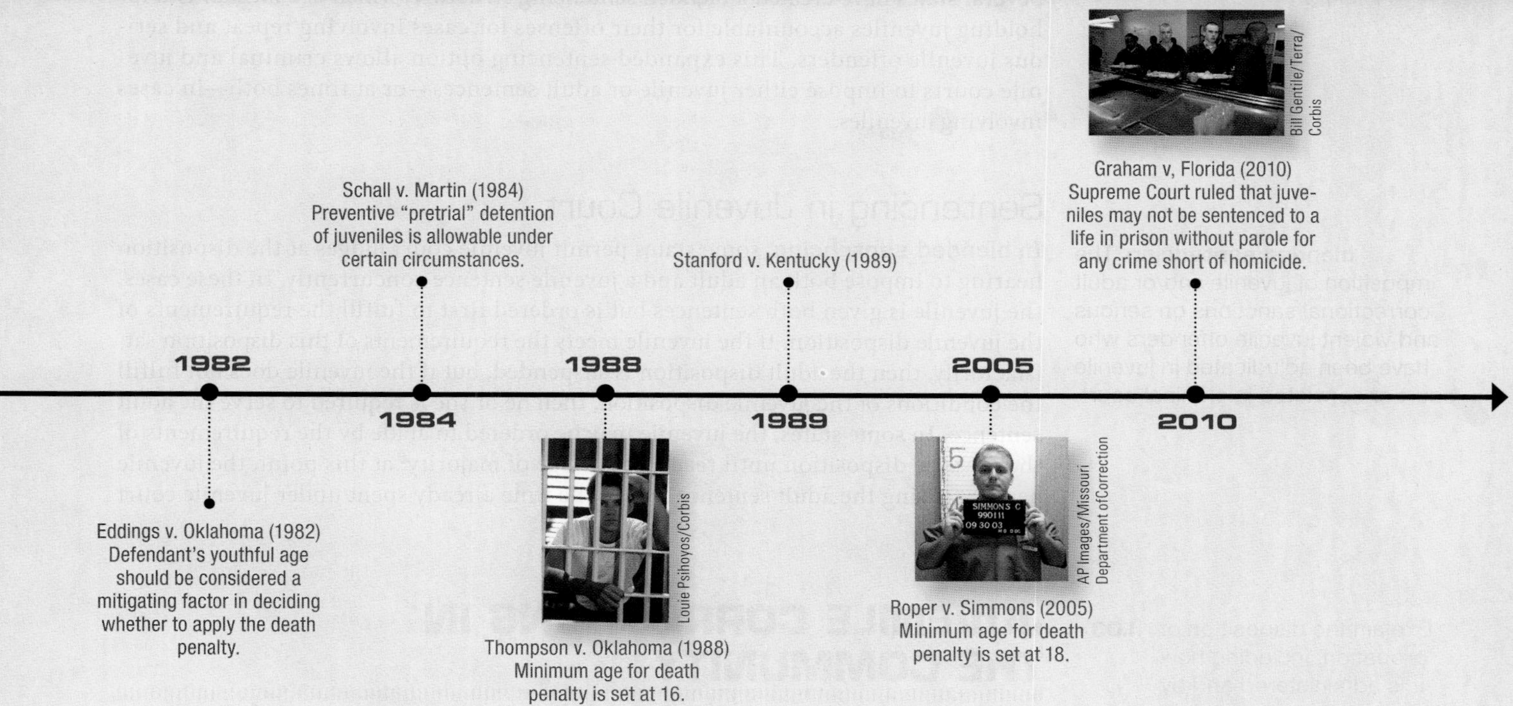

Schall v. Martin (1984)
Preventive "pretrial" detention of juveniles is allowable under certain circumstances.
Stanford v. Kentucky (1989)
Graham v, Florida (2010)
Supreme Court ruled that juveniles may not be sentenced to a life in prison without parole for any crime short of homicide.
Bill Gentile/Terra/Corbis
1982
1984
1988
1989
2005
2010
Eddings v. Oklahoma (1982)
Defendant's youthful age should be considered a mitigating factor in deciding whether to apply the death penalty.
Louie Psihoyos/Corbis
Thompson v. Oklahoma (1988)
Minimum age for death penalty is set at 16.
AP Images/Missouri Department ofCorrection
Roper v. Simmons (2005)
Minimum age for death penalty is set at 18.

The remainder of this chapter is divided into four parts: juvenile sentencing structures, juvenile corrections in the community, institutionalized juveniles, and juveniles in the adult system. The first two parts, juveniles in community-based treatments and juveniles in long-term juvenile institutions, will attempt to identify what is different about the juvenile and adult justice processes, rather than discuss what is similar about the juvenile and adult justice system processing of offenders.

Juvenile Sentencing Structures

LO2 Identify how sentencing structures in juvenile justice have changed in recent years

Determinate sentencing (fixed sentencing for specified offenses) is a new form of sentencing structure in juvenile justice and, in some jurisdictions, it is replacing the traditional form of indeterminate sentencing (sentencing at the judge's discretion). In addition, increasing numbers of juvenile courts are using a blended form of sentencing.

Criticism of the decision-making outcomes of juvenile justice has increased since the early 1970s. One of the first efforts at reform was the **Juvenile Justice Standards Project**, jointly sponsored by the Institute of Judicial Administration and the American Bar Association. Officially launched in 1971, the project proposed comprehensive guidelines for juvenile offenders that would base sentences on the seriousness of the crime rather than on the needs of the youth. Juvenile judges, not surprisingly, became quite critical about the proposed standards. Nevertheless, the states of Washington, Colorado, Kentucky, Idaho, Arizona, Georgia, Texas, and Missouri were influenced by the standards in their sentencing structures for juveniles.[10]

Juvenile Justice Standards Project A comprehensive set of guidelines for juvenile offenders, created by the Institute of Judicial Administration and the American Bar Association, that based sentencing on the seriousness of the crime rather than on the needs of the youth.

In the 1990s, nearly every state enacted mandatory minimum sentencing for violent and repetitive offenders. The development of graduated or accountability-based sanctions was another means that states used in the 1990s to ensure that juveniles who were adjudicated delinquent received an appropriate disposition by the juvenile court. Several states have created a blended sentencing structure, which is a mechanism for holding juveniles accountable for their offenses for cases involving repeat and serious juvenile offenders. This expanded sentencing option allows criminal and juvenile courts to impose either juvenile or adult sentences—or at times both—in cases involving juveniles.

Sentencing in Juvenile Court

blended sentencing The imposition of juvenile and/or adult correctional sanctions on serious and violent juvenile offenders who have been adjudicated in juvenile court or convicted in criminal court.

In **blended sentencing**, some states permit juvenile court judges at the disposition hearing to impose both an adult and a juvenile sentence concurrently. In these cases, the juvenile is given both sentences but is ordered first to fulfill the requirements of the juvenile disposition. If the juvenile meets the requirements of this disposition satisfactorily, then the adult disposition is suspended, but if the juvenile does not fulfill the conditions of the juvenile disposition, then he or she is required to serve the adult sentence. In some states, the juvenile may be ordered to abide by the requirements of the juvenile disposition until reaching the age of majority; at this point, the juvenile begins serving the adult sentence minus the time already spent under juvenile court supervision.[11]

Explain the disposition of probation, including how it is administered and by whom and recent trends in its use **LO3**

JUVENILE CORRECTIONS IN THE COMMUNITY

Probation and other forms of community treatment for juvenile offenders generally refer to nonpunitive legal disposition for delinquent youths, emphasizing treatment without incarceration.

Probation

Probation is the primary form of community treatment used by the juvenile justice system. A juvenile who is on probation is maintained in the community under the supervision of an officer of the court. Probation also encompasses a set of rules and conditions that must be met for the offender to remain in the community. Juveniles on probation may be placed in a wide variety of community-based treatment programs that provide services ranging from group counseling to drug treatment.

Traditional probation is still the backbone of community-based corrections. Probation continues to be a popular dispositional alternative for judges. Today, about 53 percent of all adjudicated delinquents, more than 500,000 per year, are given probationary sentences.[12]

It can be seen that a major difference between juvenile and adult probation officers is that the juvenile probation officers' duties are focused more on treatment, contact with families, and providing specialized services to juveniles. In contrast, the adult probation officer—while retaining responsibilities for treatment intervention—emphasizes more public safety and surveillance of offenders.

In the juvenile court, probation is often ordered for an indefinite period. Depending on the statutes of the jurisdiction, the seriousness of the offense, and the juvenile's adjustment on probation, youths can remain under supervision until the court no longer has jurisdiction over them (that is, when they reach the age of majority). State statutes determine whether a judge can specify how long a juvenile

FIGURE 14.1

Disposition of Delinquency Cases

Source: Office of Juvenile Justice and Delinquency Prevention, *Statistical Briefing Book*, April 2013, http://www.ojjdp.gov/ojstatbb/probation/qa07102.asp?qaDate=2011 (accessed July 2014).

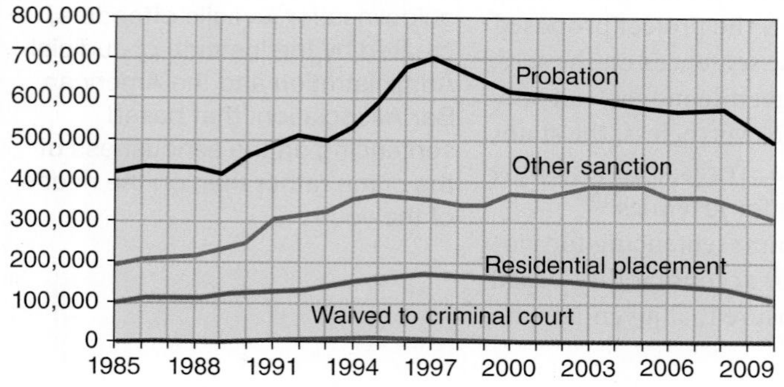

may be placed under an order of probation. In most jurisdictions, the status of probation is reviewed regularly to ensure that a juvenile is not kept on probation needlessly. Generally, discretion lies with the probation officer to discharge youths who are adjusting to the treatment plan.

Although juvenile probation services continue to be predominantly organized under the judiciary, recent legislative activity has been in the direction of transferring those services from the local juvenile court judge to a state court administrative office. Whether local juvenile courts or state agencies should administer juvenile probation services is debatable. In years past, the organization of probation services depended primarily on the size of the program and the number of juveniles under its supervision. Because of this momentum to develop unified court systems, many juvenile court services are being consolidated into state court systems.

Like the adult system, the juvenile justice system has developed intermediate probation/alternative sanction programs such as intensive supervision probation, electronic monitoring (EM), and house arrest.[13] A number of states, including Georgia, New Jersey, Oregon, and Pennsylvania, are experimenting with statewide intensive programs for juveniles. In addition, more and more juvenile court judges, especially in metropolitan juvenile courts, are placing high-risk juveniles on small caseloads and assigning them more frequent contact with a probation officer than would be true of traditional probation.

The use of EM in juvenile justice has been gradually gaining acceptance. Twenty years ago, only 11 juvenile programs used EM.[14] Today, EM programs are widely used in juvenile justice programs throughout the United States.

CRITICAL THINKING

Which juvenile crimes should receive a sentence of probation versus institutional treatment and confinement? Develop a list of criteria for each. **LO3**

Alternative Community Sanctions for Juveniles

LO4 Distinguish between community treatment and institutional treatment for juvenile offenders

Some juveniles need more intense confinement than can be provided by probation even if it is supplemented with intermediate sanctions such as house arrest and electronic monitoring. To meet the needs of these youth, the juvenile justice system has developed a set of community correctional programs. Some are residential, requiring that youth spend a period of time in a nonsecure facility while typically going to school and other activities during the day. Others are nonresidential programs that allow clients to live at home while receiving services in the community.

Residential programs are typically divided into four major categories: (1) group homes, (2) family group homes, (3) wilderness programs, and (4) boot camps. One residential program that would not be found in the adult system is **wilderness programs**, sometimes called "survival programs," which take place in settings such as the mountains, the woods, the beach, and the desert. The intent of these survival programs is to improve youths' self-confidence and sense of self-reliance.

Group homes are staffed by a small number of qualified persons, and generally house 12 to 15 youngsters. The institutional quality of the environment is minimized, and youths are given the opportunity to build a close relationship with the staff. Youths reside in the home, attend public schools, and participate in community activities in the area.

Family group homes combine elements of foster care and group home placements. Troubled youths have an opportunity to learn to get along in a family-like situation, and at the same time the state avoids the startup costs and neighborhood opposition often associated with establishing a public institution.

Boot camps for youthful offenders, like those for adult offenders, developed in the mid-1980s and 1990s. Emphasizing military discipline, physical training, and regimented activity for periods typically ranging from 30 to 120 days, these programs endeavor to shock juvenile delinquents out of committing further crimes. A fair assessment may be that the quality of boot camps depends largely on how much they tailor their programs to participants' maturity levels and how effective they are in implementing and sustaining effective aftercare services.[15] However, the follow-ups on

residential programs Programs conducted for the rehabilitation of youthful offenders within community-based and institutional settings.

wilderness programs Programs that occur in a wooded area, the mountains, desert, or a lake where adolescents are taught survival skills and cooperation with others.

group homes Nonsecure residences that provide counseling, education, job training, and family living.

family group homes Group homes that are run by a family rather than by a professional staff.

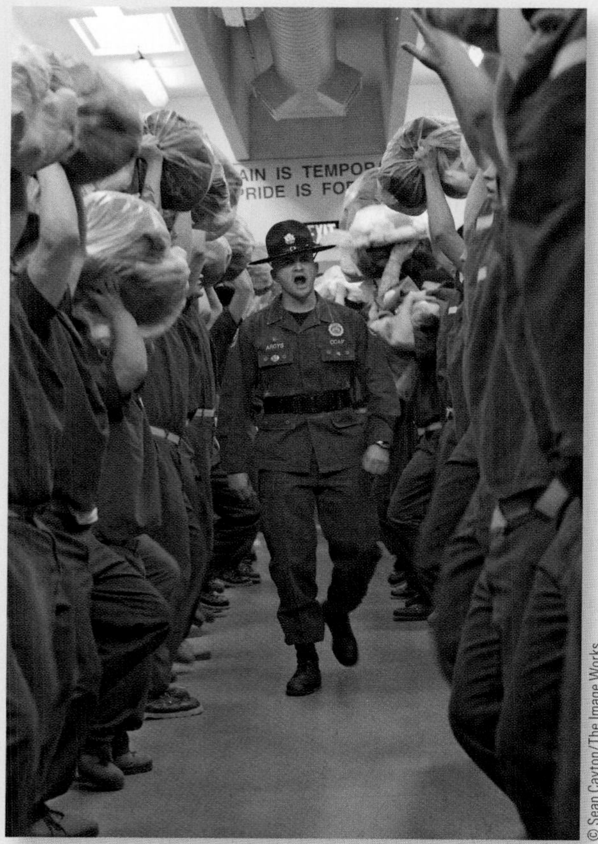

© Sean Cayton/The Image Works

Boot camps were once viewed as a correctional panacea. For example, the Colorado Corrections Alternative Program offered reduced prison sentences for men and women convicted of nonviolent crimes. The program was open to prisoners age 30 or younger. During the 90-day program, offenders also took addiction-recovery classes and worked on GEDs, if needed. A 2004 review of the program that showed 36 percent of those who completed the program 12 years earlier had gotten in more trouble with the law, compared with 52 percent of those who were qualified for the program but did not volunteer for it. The last class graduated in 2010 when rising recidivism rates cancelled out program benefits. But the deciding factor leading to the closure of the program was that it became too costly. As fewer inmates qualified or volunteered for the program, the cost per inmate rose from $78 a day to $110 in a single year (2010).

boot camps are mixed concerning their effectiveness.[16] The disappointing recidivism results, as well as charges of abuse, have prompted most states and the federal government to shut down this get-tough approach with juveniles.

In **nonresidential programs**, youths remain in their homes and receive counseling, education, employment, diagnostic, and casework services at a community-based center. A counselor or probation officer gives innovative and intensive support to help the youth remain at home. Family therapy, educational tutoring, and job placement may all be part of the program.

Is Community Treatment Effective?

Community-based programs continue to present a promising alternative for juvenile corrections:

- Some states have found that residential and nonresidential settings produce comparable or lower recidivism rates. There is evidence that youths in nonsecure settings are less likely to become recidivists than those placed in more secure settings.
- Community-based programs have lower costs and are especially appropriate for large numbers of nonviolent juveniles and those guilty of lesser offenses.
- Public opinion on community corrections remains positive. Many citizens prefer community-based programs for all but the most serious juvenile offenders.
- Many treatment programs have proven track records and seem to work. The research is strongest and most promising for school- and community-based interventions that can be used before the demands of public safety require a residential placement.[17]

As jurisdictions continue to face high rates of violent juvenile crime and ever-increasing costs for juvenile justice services, community-based programs will play an important role in providing rehabilitation of juvenile offenders and ensuring public safety. See Exhibit 14.2 for the comparison between community-based treatment in the juvenile and adult systems.

JUVENILE INSTITUTIONS TODAY: PUBLIC AND PRIVATE

Juveniles who are repeat offenders or commit very serious crimes may find themselves in secure facilities variously called training schools, reform schools, or locked facilities. These house the most dangerous, chronic juvenile offenders in institutions that can resemble adult facilities.

Most juveniles are housed in public institutions administered by state agencies: child and youth services, health and social services, corrections, or child welfare.[18] In some states these institutions fall under a centralized system that covers adults as well as juveniles. Recently, a number of states have removed juvenile corrections from an existing adult corrections department or mental health agency. However, the majority of states still place responsibility for the administration of juvenile corrections within social service departments.

Supplementing publicly funded institutions are private facilities that are maintained and operated by private agencies funded or chartered by state authorities. The majority

CRITICAL THINKING

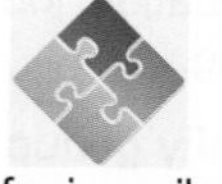

Many of the sanctions for juveniles involve removing juveniles from their homes in order to change a situation that may include violence and abuse. How might this affect them? LO4

EXHIBIT 14.2

Comparison Between Juvenile and Adult Justice Systems

Justice System	Role of the Courts	Community Treatment	Institutional Treatment
Juvenile system	Judicial court referral to proper placement. Appeals are rarely used.	Probation and various forms of residential and nonresidential treatment.	Short-term and long-term treatment. Some of the long-term training schools have violent residents' cultures.
Adult system	More complex court system and appeals are commonplace.	Also has probation and various forms of intermediate sanctions.	Large, much larger than juvenile facilities and inmates stay longer, sometimes for the remainder of their sentence, or are even executed.

of today's private institutions are relatively small facilities holding fewer than 30 youths. Many have a specific mission or focus (for example, treating females who display serious emotional problems). Although about 80 percent of public institutions can be characterized as secure, only 20 percent of private institutions are high-security facilities.

nonresidential programs Programs for youthful offenders that usually do not confine them overnight.

Population Trends in Juvenile Corrections

Whereas most delinquents are held in public facilities, most status offenders are held in private facilities. At last count, there were about 66,000 juvenile offenders being held in public (46,000) and private (19,000) facilities in the United States. There are a number of different types of facilities in use: large training schools tend to be state facilities and hold the most serious offenders; detention centers tend to be local facilities and hold youths pending disposition of their case; group homes tend to be private facilities and typically hold less serious criminal offenders and status offenders, children who are runaways and truants.

VOICES ACROSS THE PROFESSION

Jean Tomlinson
Correctional Officer

In the private versus the state, I did not like working for the for-profit operation very much. I was used to working with budgets in state operations. I was superintendent of this private facility and had been there 45 days or so when I was told, "You need to cut your budget by 10 percent." I asked them, "How do you want me to do this? Where do you want me to start?" They said, "Start with clothing." I looked outside, and there was a foot of snow. And my kids had not been issued jackets. I thought that guy was out of his mind.

The private operation was paying staff $7 an hour. With the state we pay better, and we have better insurance. With the high turnover, the kids would know when guards were green, and they would start playing all the tricks. They set them up for failure immediately. They get the guards to bring cigarettes, pop, drugs, and all sorts of stuff. [Private operation staff] are much easier to exploit than staff in state institutions. This is their second income. They would have the kids' parents send money [directly] to the officers' homes.

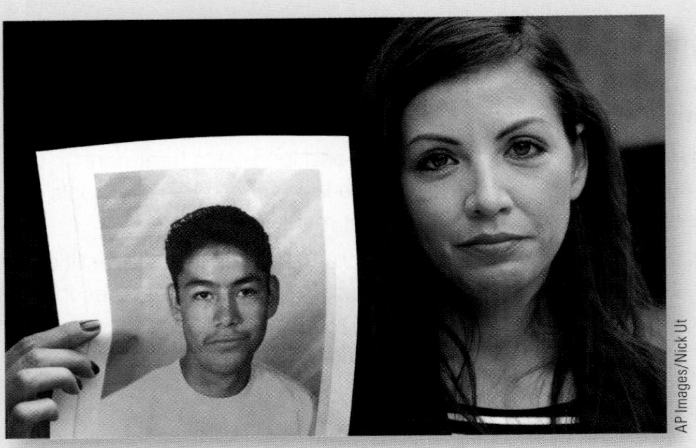

AP Images/Nick Ut

Lydra Espinoza Oregel holds a photo of her brother, Edel Gonzalez, taken when he was 16 years old. Gonzalez, now 38, was serving a life-without-parole prison term for a fatal carjacking that occurred more than 20 years ago before being resentenced under a new California law that allows him to become parole eligible in less than three years. Edel Gonzalez became the first inmate in California to have his life sentence for a crime committed as a youth reduced. The Supreme Court has ruled against mandatory life sentences for all youth under 18.

While the number of juveniles held in custody increased rapidly (41 percent) in the 1990s, it has been in decline since the year 1999, when 120,000 juveniles were being kept in secure confinement.[19] Between 2008 and 2012, the juvenile correctional population declined by about 18 percent, due to both a declining juvenile crime rate and greater reliance on less expensive and more effective community treatment programs.

In an important study, criminologist Daniel Mears found that there are three main explanations for why some states incarcerate juveniles at a much higher rate than others: (1) they have high rates of juvenile property crime and adult violent crime; (2) they have higher adult custody rates; and (3) there is a "cultural acceptance of punitive policies" in some parts of the country. Interestingly, Mears found that western and midwestern states were more likely to have higher juvenile incarceration rates than southern states, thus calling into question the widely held view that the South is disproportionately punitive.[20]

Institutionalized Juveniles

The typical resident of a juvenile facility is a 17-year-old male incarcerated for an average stay of 3.5 months in a public facility or 4 months in a private facility. Private facilities tend to house younger children, while public institutions provide custodial care for older children, including a small percentage of youths between 18 and 21 years of age. Most incarcerated youths are person, property, or drug offenders. In almost all facilities (92 percent) some or all residents attended some type of schooling. Most juvenile offenders are evaluated for substance use (70 percent), mental health needs (57 percent), and suicide risk (89 percent).

CRITICAL THINKING

Should status offenders be incarcerated for their own protection? Will this deter them from future status offenses such as underage drinking or truancy? What will deter this type of behavior? **LO4**

RACIAL INEQUALITY Racial disparity in juvenile disposition is a growing problem that demands immediate public scrutiny.[21] In October 2011, for every 100,000 non-Hispanic black juveniles living in the United States, 521 were in a residential placement facility; for Hispanics, the rate was 202, and for non-Hispanic whites it was 112.[22] Minority youths accused of delinquent acts are less likely than white youths to be diverted from the court system into informal sanctions and are more likely to receive sentences involving incarceration. Today, a disproportionate number of minority youth are still being held in locked facilities.

In response, many jurisdictions have initiated studies of racial disproportion in their juvenile justice systems, along with federal requirements to reduce disproportionate minority confinement (DMC), as contained in the Juvenile Justice and Delinquency Prevention Act of 2002.[23] While some progress has been made, many challenges remain, including the basic need to identify factors that contribute to DMC. There are success stories, such as those listed below:

- New Jersey, by implementing the Juvenile Detention Alternatives Initiative (JDAI) of the Annie E. Casey Foundation, is one of several localities that has produced significant reductions in DMC. Across five counties in New Jersey, the disparities dropped significantly between youth of color held in detention rather than being placed in community alternatives versus white youth similarly charged being detained rather than placed in the community.

Web App 14.1
Visit the Disproportionate Minority Contact (DMC) Resource Center at http://www.ojjdp.gov/dmc/ to understand more issues about DMC. **LO4**

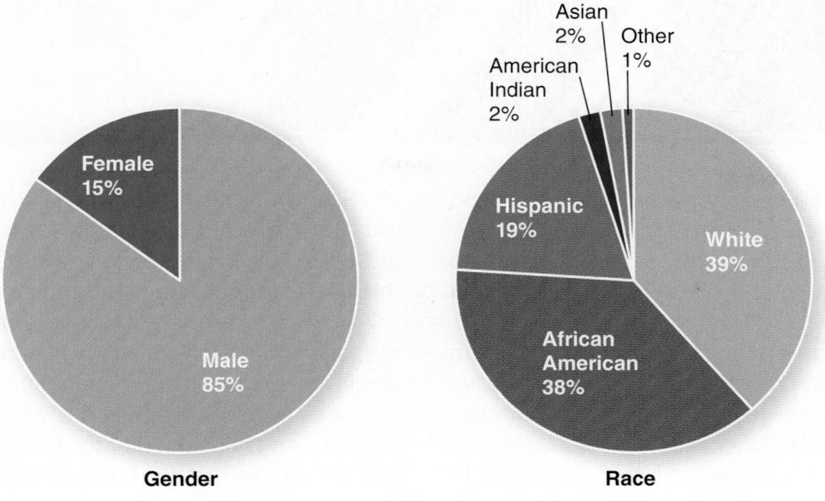

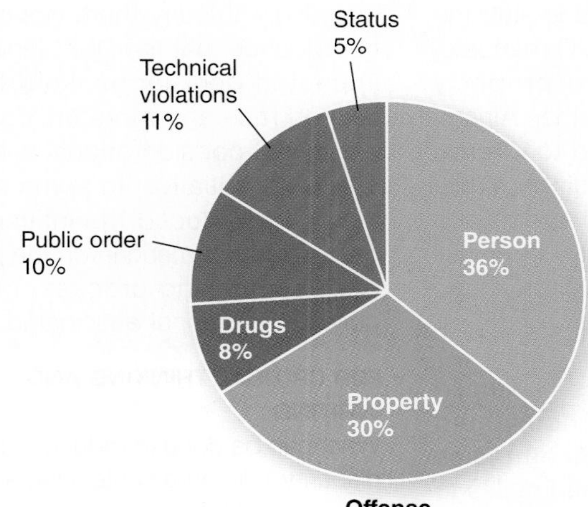

FIGURE 14.2

Institutionalized Juveniles

Source: Howard N. Snyder and Melissa Sickmund, *Juvenile Offenders and Victims 2006 National Report* (Pittsburgh: National Center for Juvenile Justice, 2006), Ch. 7.

- Peoria County, Illinois, has reduced disproportionate referrals of youth of color to the juvenile justice system by working with schools to strengthen school-based conflict resolution protocols and student retention/inclusion.
- Travis County, Texas, has reduced disproportionate incarceration of youth of color for technical probation violations with a sanction supervision program that instead offers intensive case management and probation services to youth and families.
- Baltimore County has reduced by 50 percent secure detention of African American youth resulting from bench warrants for failing to appear in court by instituting a reminder call program.[24]

While the DMC initiative was begun with great promise, the Evidence-Based Corrections feature shows that achieving racial justice can often be a difficult path.

GENDER DIFFERENCES: MALES Males make up the great bulk of institutionalized youth, and most treatment programs are directed toward their needs. In many ways their experiences mirror those of adult offenders. Research efforts confirm the notion that residents do in fact form cohesive groups and adhere to an informal inmate culture.[25] The more serious the youth's record and the more secure the institution, the greater the adherence to the inmate social code. Male delinquents are more likely

CRITICAL THINKING

Do you think that there is more disproportionate minority contact in areas where there are fewer opportunities for juveniles? Are these aspects related? LO4

EVIDENCE-BASED CORRECTIONS

Disproportionate Minority Confinement/ Contact (DMC)

The disproportionate minority confinement/contact (DMC) directive was designed to ensure that youthful offenders, regardless of their race or position in the social structure, receive equitable treatment within the juvenile justice system. Recently Michael Lieber and his associates examined the impact of the DMC on the processing of juvenile offenders within a state juvenile justice system. They chose Iowa for their study because it is one of the states that was selected to serve as a model for the implementation of strategies to reduce DMC. Their research focused on the extent that race influences decision makers, and whether the implementation of the DMC effort would result in the reduction or elimination of a race effect on decision-making outcomes. After controlling for a wide array of variables, they found that African Americans were more likely than whites to be referred at intake for further proceedings both before and after the implementation of the DMC initiative. The relative influence of race on intake decision making did not change following the implementation of the DMC initiative.

In some instances the researchers found that the DMC created an effect in opposition to what was intended. During the decade prior to the implementation of the DMC mandate, white adolescents who committed property offenses were less likely than African Americans to be referred to juvenile court for further proceedings. However, during the decade after the implementation of the DMC mandate, whites who committed property offenses were more likely than African Americans to be referred to juvenile court for further proceedings. While this change can be viewed as a movement toward equality, it actually was an overcorrection. Rather than helping African American youths, it penalized white offenders.

Decision making was influenced by gender and family household structure. African American males were more likely than white males to receive a court referral, and this racial disadvantage remained in the post-DMC period. After DMC was in place, African Americans who came from single-parent households were more likely to be referred to juvenile court than those who resided in two-parent households, although this was not the case for whites. Stated differently, after the DMC mandate, the effects of race became more covert and indirect, operating through family structure. One might conclude that this result reflects decision makers' reliance on stereotypes involving assessments of the African American single-parent family as dysfunctional and less able than either the white single-parent household or the African American two-parent household to supervise and socialize children effectively. In sum, there was little or no evidence that the DMC legislation impacted decision makers to rely less on race and more on legal and extralegal considerations at intake. The DMC initiative, to some extent, may have reduced the influence of being African American on the judicial decision-making process, but not quite in the manner anticipated.

FOR CRITICAL THINKING AND WRITING

What can be done to reduce racial disparity in juvenile sentencing and corrections? Is this sentencing differential a function of racism? Or does it simply reflect racial inequality in socioeconomic status and opportunity that exists in U.S. society?

Source: Michael Leiber, Donna Bishop, and Mitchell Chamlin, "Juvenile Justice Decision-Making Before and After the Implementation of the Disproportionate Minority Contact (DMC) Mandate," *Justice Quarterly* 28 (2011): 460–492.

to form allegiances with members of their own racial group and to attempt to exploit those outside the group. They also scheme to manipulate staff and take advantage of weaker peers. However, in institutions that are treatment oriented, and where staff–inmate relationships are more intimate, residents are less likely to adhere to a negativistic inmate code.

GENDER DIFFERENCES: FEMALES The number of females in juvenile institutions is far lower than males; nationally, females account for 13 percent of juvenile offenders in residential placement. For more than 40 years, feminists have pointed out that young women are still being forced to endure a double standard in the juvenile justice system because it is male-dominated and designed to "protect" young girls from their own sexuality. The double standard hits African American girls the hardest because they are more likely to be indigent and have less familial support than European American females.[26] Girls are still more likely than boys to be incarcerated for status offenses, such as running away or being sexually involved with older men and boys.[27]

The same double standard that brings a girl into an institution continues to exist once she is in custody. Females tend to be incarcerated for longer terms than males. In addition, institutional programs for girls tend to be oriented toward reinforcing traditional roles for females. Most of these programs also fail to take account of the different needs of African American and Caucasian females, as in the case of coping with past abuse.[28] Institutions for girls are generally more restrictive than those for boys, and they have fewer educational and vocational programs and fewer services. Institutions for girls also do a less-than-adequate job of rehabilitation.

Institutional Treatment for Juveniles

Nearly all juvenile institutions implement some form of treatment programs that are similar to what have been previously described for adult settings: counseling, vocational and educational training, recreational programs, and religious counseling. In addition, most institutions provide medical programs as well as occasional legal service programs. Generally, the larger the institution, the greater the number of programs and services offered. See Exhibit 14.3 for effectiveness of juvenile correctional care.

MYTH **All correctional clients have the right to treatment.**

FACT **Actually, while adults have no such right, juveniles do. The Supreme Court has ruled in a number of cases that juveniles cannot be held in secure treatment unless there is an effort to provide them with adequate care and rehabilitative services.**

The Legal Right to Treatment

The primary goal of placing juveniles in institutions is to help them reenter the community successfully. Therefore, lawyers claim that children in state-run institutions have a legal right to treatment. A number of cases—*Inmates of the Boys' Training School v. Affleck* in 1972, *Nelson v. Heyne, Morales v. Turman*—found that juveniles do have a right to treatment.[29] In *Pena v. New York State Division for Youth*, the court held that the use of isolation, hand restraints,

EXHIBIT 14.3
Effectiveness of Juvenile Institutions

- The purpose of these programs is to rehabilitate youths to become well-adjusted individuals and send them back into the community to be productive citizens.
- Despite good intentions, however, the goal of rehabilitation is rarely attained, due in large part to poor implementation of the programs.
- A significant number of juvenile offenders commit more crimes after release, and some experts believe that correctional treatment has little effect on recidivism.
- However, a large-scale empirical review of institutional treatment programs found that serious juvenile offenders who receive treatment have recidivism rates about 10 percent lower than similar untreated juveniles, and that the best programs reduced recidivism by as much as 40 percent.
- The most successful of these institutional treatment programs provide training to improve interpersonal skills and family-style teaching to improve behavioral skills.

Sources: Kristi Holsinger and Alexander M. Holsinger, "Differential Pathways to Violence and Self-Injurious Behavior: African American and White Girls in the Juvenile Justice System," *Journal of Research in Crime and Delinquency* 42 (2005): 211–242; Robert Barnes, "Supreme Court Restricts Life Without Parole for Juveniles," *Washington Post*, May 18, 2010, http://www.washingtonpost.com/wp-dyn/content/article/2010/05/17/AR2010051701355.html (accessed July 2014); Gary Fleming and Gerald Winkler, "Sending Them to Prison: Washington State Learns to Accommodate Female Youthful Offenders in Prison," *Corrections Today* 61 (April 1999): 132–133.

THINKING LIKE A CORRECTIONS PROFESSIONAL

As a local juvenile court judge, you have been assigned the case of Jamar, a 13-year-old juvenile so short he can barely see over the bench. On trial for armed robbery, the boy has been accused of threatening a woman with a knife and stealing her purse. Barely a teenager, he already has a long history of involvement with the law. At age 11 he was arrested for drug possession and placed on probation; soon after, he stole a car. At age 12 he was arrested for shoplifting. Jamar is accompanied by his legal guardian, his maternal grandmother. His parents are unavailable because his father abandoned the family years ago and his mother is currently undergoing inpatient treatment at a local drug clinic. After talking with his attorney, Jamar decides to admit to the armed robbery. At a dispositional hearing, his court-appointed attorney tells you of the tough life Jamar has been forced to endure. His grandmother states that, although she loves the boy, her advanced age makes it impossible for her to provide the care he needs to stay out of trouble. She says that Jamar is a good boy who has developed a set of bad companions; his current scrape was precipitated by his friends. A representative of the school system testifies that Jamar has above-average intelligence and is actually respectful of teachers. He has potential, but his life circumstances have short-circuited his academic success. Jamar himself shows remorse and appears to be a sensitive youngster who is easily led astray by older youths.

You must now make a decision. You can place Jamar on probation and allow him to live with his grandmother while being monitored by county probation staff. You can place him in a secure incarceration facility for up to three years. You can also put him into an intermediate program such as a community-based facility, which would allow him to attend school during the day while residing in a halfway house and receiving group treatment in the evenings. Although Jamar appears salvageable, his crime was serious and involved the use of a weapon. If he remains in the community, he may offend again; if he is sent to a correctional facility, he will interact with older, tougher kids. What mode of correctional treatment would you choose?

and tranquilizing drugs at Goshen Annex Center violated the Fourteenth Amendment right to due process and the Eighth Amendment right to protection against cruel and unusual punishment.[30]

The right to treatment has also been limited. For example, in *Ralston v. Robinson*, the Supreme Court rejected a youth's claim that he should continue to be given treatment after he was sentenced to a consecutive term in an adult prison for crimes committed while in a juvenile institution.[31] In the *Ralston* case, the offender's proven dangerousness outweighed the possible effects of rehabilitation. Similarly, in *Santana v. Callazo*, the U.S. First Circuit Court of Appeals rejected a suit brought by residents at the Maricao Juvenile Camp in Puerto Rico on the grounds that the administration had failed to provide them with an individualized rehabilitation plan or adequate treatment. The circuit court concluded that it was a legitimate exercise of state authority to incarcerate juveniles solely to protect society if they are dangerous.

JUVENILE AFTERCARE AND REENTRY

Aftercare in the juvenile justice system is the equivalent of parole in the adult criminal justice system. When juveniles are released from an institution, they are placed in an aftercare program of some kind, so that youths who have been institutionalized are not simply returned to the community without some transitional assistance. Whether individuals who are in aftercare as part of an indeterminate sentence remain in the community or return to the institution for further rehabilitation depends on their actions during the aftercare period. Aftercare is an extremely important stage in the juvenile justice process because few juveniles age out of custody.[32]

The Washington Post/Getty Images

Gary Durant, third from the left, speaks to high school youth during a grape juice toast as part of Free Minds, an at-risk youth outreach program at Anacostia High School in Washington, D.C. Durant, 23, was released from prison after being a juvenile convicted as an adult for accessory to a killing at the age of 16. Now, he is making the transition to life outside incarceration and is on a path of guiding youth away from lives of negativity.

CAREERS
IN CORRECTIONS

Jim Redmond
Primary Therapist, Juvenile Correctional Facility in Minnetonka, Minnesota

"I assess residents' needs and develop a treatment plan for them. In addition, I facilitate a corrective thinking group, an anger management group, a family skills group, provide individual therapy, and fulfill case management services. On an average day, I read staff logs, write reports for the courts, attend meetings, write treatment plans, monitor treatment plans, and meet for individual therapy. One of my challenges is that residents don't come willingly and are not receptive of forced changes."

"The job is extremely rewarding. Most residents struggle not because they are bad people, but because they received little direction in bad environments. When they come to our facility most of them do very well. Watching the transformation from being resistant to practicing new skills is inspiring."

See Chapter 15 for more detailed information on careers in corrections.

Postinstitutional Supervision of Juveniles

LO5 Discuss the nature of aftercare for juvenile offenders, including recent innovations in juvenile aftercare and reentry programs

aftercare The supervision of juveniles who are released from correctional institutions so that they can make an optimal adjustment to community living. Also, the status of a juvenile conditionally released from a treatment or confinement facility and placed under supervision in the community.

Juveniles in aftercare programs are supervised by parole caseworkers or counselors whose job is to maintain contact with the juvenile, make sure that a corrections plan is followed, and show interest and caring. The counselor also keeps the youth informed of services that may assist in reintegration and counsels the youth and his or her family. Unfortunately, aftercare caseworkers, like probation officers, often carry such large caseloads that their jobs are next to impossible to do adequately. New models of aftercare and reentry have been aimed at the chronic and/or violent offender. The Intensive Aftercare Program (IAP) model developed by David Altschuler and Troy Armstrong offers a continuum of intervention for serious juvenile offenders returning to the community following placement.[33]

© Jennifer Zdon/Landov Media

August Collins (left), a caseworker with the Youth Empowerment Project (YEP), guides King Sanchez IV, 19, through paperwork at the GED offices in New Orleans. YEP, a re-entry program for teenagers coming home from the state's juvenile facilities, has a waiting list for its services. Post-release care is a significant element of a successful return to the community, and recent funding cutbacks have endangered these important programs.

Aftercare Revocation Procedures

Juvenile parolees are required to meet established standards of behavior, which are similar to those of adults on parole. If these rules are violated, the juvenile may have his or her parole revoked and be returned to the institution. Most states have extended the same legal rights enjoyed by adults at parole revocation hearings to juveniles who are in danger of losing their aftercare privileges.

Explain how the juvenile is transferred and tried in adult court **LO6**

WAIVER TO THE ADULT COURT

One of the first actions taken during the juvenile court process is determining whether a case should be processed in the criminal justice system rather than in juvenile court. In most states, cases referred to juvenile court that meet certain criteria may be transferred to criminal court upon the authorization of the juvenile court judge. In such cases, the judge may waive the juvenile court's jurisdiction over the case, thus referring it to criminal court for prosecution. This mechanism is known as *judicial waiver.*

Because of concern over violent juvenile offenders and the threat they pose to the community, state legislatures have passed laws permitting juveniles to be transferred or waived to adult court, where they can be tried and punished as adults. Waiver is a very serious issue because it means that a minor child can be sent to an adult prison institution where they will interact with and be influenced by experienced criminals. See Exhibit 14.4 for the relationship between juvenile behavior and a life of crime.

States vary widely in the criteria they use in making this waiver decision. Some states focus on the age of the offender, and others consider both age and offense. Vermont (age 10), Georgia, Illinois, and Mississippi (age 13) transfer children at very

EXHIBIT 14.4

The Youthful Offender and a Future Life of Crime

One of the areas that has received vast examination is the relationship between juvenile behavior and adult crime. The following findings receive support:

- Adolescent gang involvement contributes to a likelihood of involvement in street crime and arrests in adulthood.
- Some evidence exists that delinquents who become adult offenders are somewhat more likely than other delinquents to have had more seriously offensive delinquent careers.
- Cumulate disadvantage of some delinquents (individual and parental deficits) make drug use and gang involvement more attractive, leading to dropping out of school and unemployment into their adult years. In turn, these antisocial behaviors continue from childhood delinquency into adult crime.
- For females, childhood victimization, especially sexual victimization, can contribute to adult involvement with drugs and prostitution.
- Being institutionalized as a juvenile seriously compromises adult adjustment.
- Some studies have found a relationship between such factors as poor parental supervision, parental rejection, parental criminality, or delinquent siblings and late adult criminality.

Sources: Marvin D. Krohn, Jeffrey T. Ward, Terence P. Thornberry, Alan J. Lizotte, and Rebekah Chu, "The Cascading Effects of Adolescent Gang Involvement Across the Life Course," *Criminology* 49 (November 2011): 991–1025; Nadine Lanctot, Stephen A. Cernkovich, and Peggy C. Giordano, "Delinquent Behavior, Official Delinquency, and Gender: Consequences for Adult Functioning and Well-Being," *Criminology* 45 (2007): 191–222; Brian Francis, Keith Soohill, and Alex R. Piquero, "Estimation Issues and Generational Changes in Modeling Criminal Career Length," *Crime and Delinquency* 53 (January 2007): 3–37.

young ages. More states transfer juveniles at 14 than at any other age; seven states transfer juveniles at either 15 or 16 years of age.

As Figure 14.3 shows, the number of delinquency cases judicially waived to criminal court more than doubled between 1985 and 1994 and then declined 55 percent through 2010. However, trends varied across offense categories.

The offenses juveniles commit are also important in the waiver decision. Some states permit waiver for any criminal offense, whereas others waive only those offenses specifically mentioned in the state's statutes. Many states permit waiver to the adult court if the juvenile previously has been adjudicated delinquent or has a prior criminal conviction. Depending on the state, three major mechanisms are used to waive juveniles: judicial waiver, prosecutorial waiver, and statutorial exclusion (see Exhibit 14.5).

FIGURE 14.3

Delinquency Cases Judicially Waived to Criminal Court

Source: Office of Juvenile Justice and Delinquency Prevention, *Statistical Briefing Book*, http://www.ojjdp.gov/ojstatbb/corrections/qa08201.asp?qaDate=2011 (accessed July 2014).

Delinquency cases judicially waived to criminal court, 1985–2010

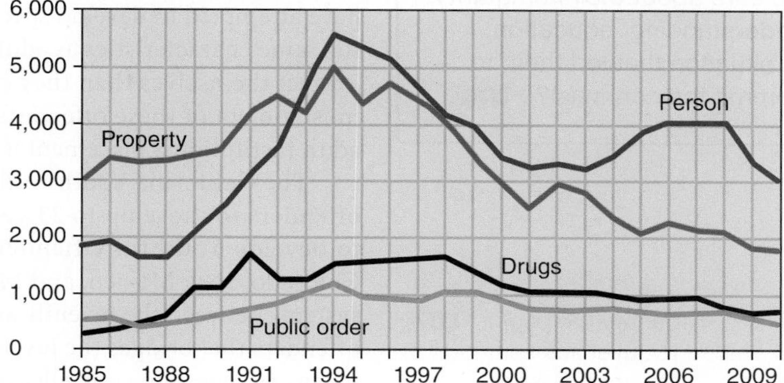

Methods of Waiver

Except where state laws mandate that a youth be tried in adult court, someone has to make the decision to waive a youth. **Judicial waiver**, the most widely used transfer mechanism, involves the actual decision-making process that begins when the juvenile is brought to intake. Predictably, the mechanisms used vary by state. In some states, intake personnel, juvenile prosecutors, or judges make the decision, based in part on the age or offense criteria.

judicial waiver The procedure of relinquishing the processing of a particular juvenile case in adult criminal court, also known as certifying or binding over to the adult court.

In other states, the prosecutor or judge in the adult court may decide where a juvenile is to be tried. The decision is determined by the requirements of the state and the way the intake officer, prosecutor, or judge interprets the youth's background. Typically, the criteria used include the age and maturity of the child; the child's relationship with parents, school, and community; whether the child is considered dangerous; and whether court officials believe that the child may be helped by juvenile court services.

Other state jurisdictions give prosecutors the authority to decide whether to try juveniles in either juvenile or adult courts. Nevada, Vermont, and Wyoming permit charges to be filed in either juvenile or adult court for any criminal offense, but most states specifically mention in their juvenile codes precisely which offenses may be tried in either court.

Some states have a **statutorial exclusion** of certain offenses from juvenile court, thereby automatically transferring perpetrators of those offenses to adult court. The statutes also, however, spell out the minimum age that youths must reach before they may be transferred to adult court.

statutorial exclusion Certain juvenile offenses in some states are automatically transferred to adult court.

Treating Juveniles as Adults

Although waivers are still relatively infrequent and have recently decreased in number, they are an important issue in juvenile justice. Significantly, juveniles waived to adult court are not always the most serious and violent offenders. With adult courts' massive caseload and their limited judicial experience with sentencing youths, little evidence exists that adult court judges know what to do with juveniles appearing before them.

EXHIBIT 14.5

Types of Waiver to Adult Court

- *Judicial waiver.* The juvenile court makes the decision to waive a juvenile to the adult court.
- *Prosecutorial waiver.* Some states give prosecutors the authority to decide whether to try juveniles in either juvenile or adult court.
- *Statutorial exclusion.* Certain offenses are excluded from juvenile court, thereby automatically transferring juveniles to adult court.

CRITICAL THINKING

Should more juveniles be treated as adults when they commit adult crimes? Should we care about their immaturity, understanding, education, or situation that led them to commit their crime(s)? LO6

Juveniles sentenced in adult courts are subject to the same range of dispositions as are adults. Cases may be dismissed or offenders may be found guilty. If found guilty, youths may be released to the care of their parents, placed on probation, fined, ordered to pay restitution, or referred to a social agency qualified to deal with their problem. But a very controversial disposition is the placement of youths in adult correctional facilities.

The crowding, violence, and exploitative relationships found in adult prisons make this disposition extremely questionable. Furthermore, although some states have attempted to develop special institutions for juveniles, even these appear to have the same characteristics as adult prisons. Youths who are placed in them can no better protect themselves than they can in adult facilities. Given the young age of even the most violent of these offenders, society has the task of deciding whether any type of adult institutional placement is appropriate for these youths.

The California Youth Authority has long extended its jurisdiction over youthful offenders to those up to 23 years of age. North Carolina was one of the first states to develop Youthful Offender Camps for 16- to 18-year-old males. In the 1990s, Colorado, New Mexico, and Minnesota also developed transitional, or intermediate, systems between the juvenile and adult systems. Intermediate sentencing for youthful offenders that bridges the juvenile and adult systems certainly appears to be a positive means to keep some juveniles out of adult correctional facilities.

Identify the plight faced by juveniles sent to adult prisons LO7

Youths in Adult Prisons

Adult prisons are a world apart from most training schools. Prisons are much larger, sometimes containing several thousand inmates and covering many acres of ground. Life on the inside is usually austere, crowded, and dangerous, and institutionalized youths are particularly subject to sexual victimization and sexual assault. Richard E. Redding concluded from his review of the programming that juveniles receive in adult correctional facilities: "Once incarcerated in adult facilities, juveniles typically receive fewer age-appropriate rehabilitative, medical, mental health and educational services, and are at greater risk of physical and sexual abuse and suicide."[34]

Despite efforts to reduce the number of juveniles in adult prisons, thousands are admitted each year. Providing for the care and special needs of juvenile offenders in adult facilities is proving to be a real problem. The youthful offenders may be as young as 13 and feel overwhelmed by older and more aggressive offenders. With their need to be part of something, youthful offenders tend to be highly impressionable and easily used or manipulated.[35] Some may be pressured into joining prison gangs and violent groups.

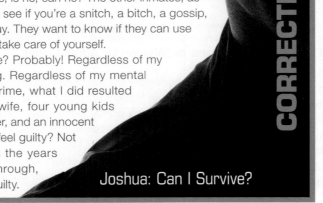

CORRECTIONAL LIFE

Joshua: Can I Survive?

At 17, for me at least, prison was many things. There is the fear. We've all seen the movies where the young kid (it's always the young kid) comes into prison and is quickly fed upon by the predators. He's raped or beaten, made a punk or killed, sometimes all of the above. I have a very active imagination, so I could foresee every possible bad outcome, played out in vivid detail inside my head. You tell yourself, "I'll be strong! I'll do whatever it takes to survive," but the fear is still there. Everything is so uncertain. You have no idea what to expect. It's a feeling of flux, and for a time your life simply doesn't belong to you. It's like you were a caterpillar sealed away inside your cocoon. You're constantly changing. You have to learn to adapt to your new environment. You're not sure what you'll have to become to come out okay.

It's a proving ground also. You're constantly tested, by yourself and others. Will he, won't he, is he, can he? The other inmates, as well as staff, feel you out to see if you're a snitch, a bitch, a gossip, or a "stand up" or "solid" guy. They want to know if they can use you, or if you're strong and take care of yourself.

Do I deserve to be here? Probably! Regardless of my age, what I did was wrong. Regardless of my mental status at the time of the crime, what I did resulted in a spouse who lost his wife, four young kids growing up without a mother, and an innocent person losing her life. Do I feel guilty? Not as much as I used to. As the years pass and the more I go through, it's harder to feel sorry or guilty.

In the Correctional Life feature, a 17-year-old sentenced to life without parole tells what prison initially was like for him.

Punishing Juveniles: The Death Penalty and Life in Prison

The execution of minor children has not been uncommon in our nation's history; at least 366 juvenile offenders have been executed since 1642.[36] However, on March 1, 2005, the U.S. Supreme Court, in the case of *Roper v. Simmons*, put an end to the practice of the death penalty for juveniles in the United States. At issue was the minimum age that juveniles who were under the age of 18 when they committed their crimes could be eligible for the death penalty.[37] At the time, 16- and 17-year-olds were eligible for the death penalty; 21 states permitted the death penalty for juveniles.[38] A total of 72 juvenile offenders were on death row at the time. In a 5–4 decision, the Court ruled that the juvenile death penalty was in violation of the Eighth Amendment's ban on cruel and unusual punishment. In its decision, the Court found that juveniles lack the maturity and sense of responsibility found in adults.

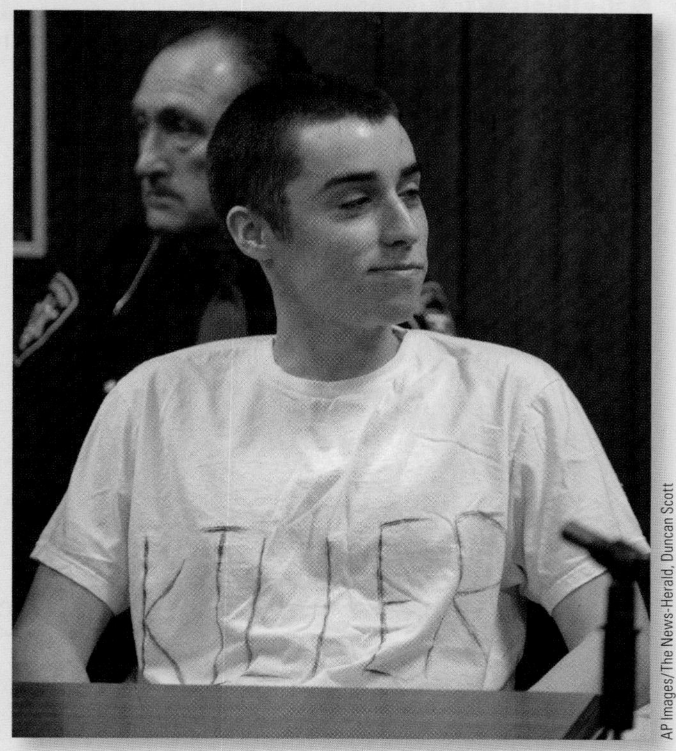

Thomas "T.J." Lane smirks as he listens to the judge during his sentencing hearing on March 19, 2013, in Chardon, Ohio. Lane was given three life sentences without the possibility of parole for opening fire in a high school cafeteria in a rampage that left three students dead and three others wounded at Chardon High School, east of Cleveland. Before the case went to adult court, a juvenile court judge ruled that Lane was mentally competent to stand trial despite evidence he suffers from hallucinations, psychosis, and fantasies. Should someone like Lane ever be released from prison? Can killers be rehabilitated?

What about a life sentence? Barry Feld, an opponent of life sentences for kids, argues that the Supreme Court's reasoning in *Roper v. Simmons* should also be applicable to cases in which juvenile offenders receive life sentences without the possibility of parole.[39] Feld proposes that "states formally recognize youthfulness as a mitigating factor by applying a 'youth discount' to adult sentence lengths."[40] On May 17, 2010, the Court agreed with Feld. It ruled on two Florida cases involving youths sentenced to life in prison for non-homicide crimes. One (*Sullivan v. Florida*) was convicted of raping a 72-year-old woman when he was 13; the other (*Graham v. Florida*) involved a home invasion robbery by a 17-year-old.[41] In its decision, the Court stated:

> The Constitution prohibits the imposition of a life without parole sentence on a juvenile offender who did not commit homicide.... A state need not guarantee the offender eventual release, but if it imposes a sentence of life it must provide him or her with some realistic opportunity to obtain release before the end of that term.

Then in 2012, the Supreme Court ruled in *Miller v. Alabama* that mandatory life without parole sentences for juveniles under 18 violate the Eighth Amendment even if the youth committed murder. Justice Elena Kagan, writing for the majority, stated:

> Mandatory life without parole for a juvenile precludes consideration of his chronological age and its hallmark features—among them, immaturity, impetuosity, and failure to appreciate risks and consequences.... It prevents taking into account the family and home environment that surrounds him—and from which he cannot usually extricate himself—no matter how brutal or dysfunctional.[42]

But juveniles who commit murder can still die in prison for crimes they committed when they were minors as long as the court takes their age and maturity into account during the sentencing deliberation. They can be sentenced in adult court to

FIGURE 14.4

State-by-State Map of Juveniles Serving Life without Parole

Source: Frontline, "When Kids Get Life," May 21, 2009.

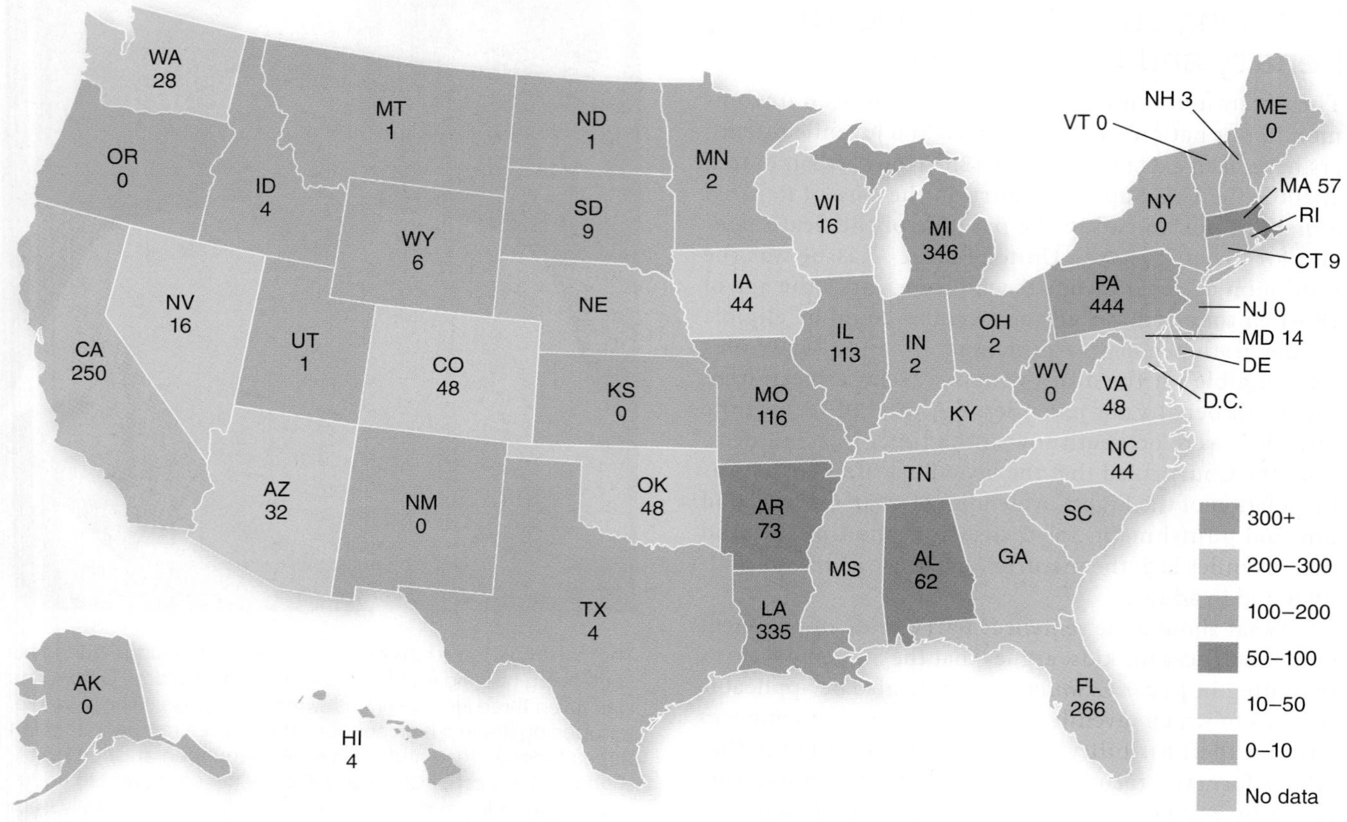

remain in prison for the duration of their natural lives without the possibility of parole (LWOP) if they commit murder and the sentencing judge considers their age. Only mandatory life sentences have been abolished. Locking up a juvenile for the rest of his or her life may be cruel punishment, but it is not unusual. There are currently more than 2,500 inmates who are serving life sentences for crimes they committed as juveniles, some as young as 13 and 14. More than half of those serving life sentences had no prior criminal convictions before being placed in prison.[43]

Helping Children in Custody

The state of Washington has attempted to manage imprisoned youthful offenders more effectively. In 1997, the state enacted Senate Bill 3900 defining the jurisdiction, custody, and management requirement for juvenile offenders. This legislation requires juvenile offenders to be placed in adult prisons for serious offenses such as aggravated murder. In addition, it dictates the housing and educational requirements for youthful offenders within the department of corrections (DOC) as follows:

- An offender under the age of 18 who is convicted in adult criminal court and sentenced to the DOC must be placed in a housing unit, or a portion of a housing unit, separated from adult inmates.
- The offenders may be housed in an intensive management unit or administrative segregation unit, if necessary, for the safety or security of the offender or the staff.

- The DOC must provide an educational program to an offender under the age of 18 who is incarcerated at a DOC facility. The program must enable the offender to obtain a high school diploma or general equivalency diploma (GED).[44]

Female youthful offenders are placed at the Washington Corrections Center for Women (WCCW), and males are confined at the Clallam Bay Corrections Center. A multidisciplinary team was formed in September 1997 in order to meet the challenge of accommodating juveniles in adult prisons. This team has been concerned with providing a safe and secure environment; an environment distant from adult offenders' contact and influences; programs and services similar to those available to the general population; and an educational program offering credit for a high school diploma or GED.[45]

Some variations on the practice of confining a juvenile in an adult institution do exist among the states. In some jurisdictions, states have no alternative but to place juveniles in adult institutions if the courts require incarceration. Some states can, under special circumstances, place youths in either juvenile or adult institutions, yet other states can refer juveniles back to juvenile court for their disposition. In some instances, very young offenders are sent to juvenile facilities but then are transferred to adult institutions when they come of age. Recognizing the dangers and inadequacies of placing juveniles with adults, some jurisdictions have developed special institutions for these younger adult offenders.

SUMMARY

LO1 Identify the early development of juvenile justice

Juvenile justice in the United States began in the colonial period. It changed in the twentieth century with a number of significant U.S. Supreme Court cases, in which juveniles were given more due process rights.

LO2 Identify how sentencing structures in juvenile justice have changed in recent years

Determinate sentencing (fixed sentencing for specified offenses) is a new form of sentencing structure in juvenile justice and, in some jurisdictions, it is replacing the traditional form of indeterminate sentencing (sentencing at the judge's discretion). In addition, increasing numbers of juvenile courts are using a blended form of sentencing.

LO3 Explain the disposition of probation, including how it is administered and by whom and recent trends in its use

Probation is the most widely used method of community treatment. Youths on probation must obey rules given to them by the court and participate in some form of treatment program. If rules are violated, youths may have their probation revoked. Behavior is monitored by probation officers. Formal probation accounts for more than 60 percent of all juvenile dispositions, and its use has increased significantly in the last decade.

LO4 Distinguish between community treatment and institutional treatment for juvenile offenders

Community treatment for juveniles consists of probation, residential programs, house arrest, and electronic monitoring. The secure juvenile institution was developed in the mid-nineteenth century as an alternative to placing youths in adult prisons. Youth institutions evolved from large, closed institutions to cottage-based education- and rehabilitation-oriented institutions.

LO5 Discuss the nature of aftercare for juvenile offenders, including recent innovations in juvenile aftercare and reentry programs

Aftercare in the juvenile justice system is the equivalent of parole in the adult criminal justice system. Juveniles released from institutions are placed in an aftercare program, so that they are not simply returned to the community without some transitional assistance. New types of programs include the Intensive Aftercare Program (IAP), which offers a continuum of intervention for serious juvenile offenders returning to the community following placement.

LO6 Explain how the juvenile is transferred and tried in adult court

Juveniles can be transferred to adult court through a judicial waiver by a juvenile court judge; by prosecutorial discretion in jurisdictions that give prosecutors the authority to try juveniles in either juvenile or adult courts; or by statutorial exclusion in those states that automatically transfer juveniles who commit certain offenses to adult court.

LO7 Identify the plight faced by juveniles sent to adult prisons

Thousands of juveniles are sent to adult prison each year. Providing for the special needs of juveniles in adult prisons poses a serious problem. Youthful offenders often feel overwhelmed by older and more aggressive offenders.

CRITICAL THINKING QUESTIONS

1. Would you want a community treatment program for juvenile offenders in your neighborhood? Why or why not?
2. If youths violate the rules of probation, should they be placed in a secure institution?
3. What are the most important advantages of community treatment for juvenile offenders?
4. What is the purpose of juvenile probation? Identify some conditions of probation and discuss the responsibilities of the juvenile probation officer.
5. Has community treatment generally proven successful?
6. Why have juvenile boot camps not been effective in reducing recidivism?

NOTES

1. Ralph Blumenthal, "Texas, Addressing Sexual Abuse Scandal, May Free Thousands of Its Jailed Youths," *New York Times*, March 24, 2007.
2. David W. Springer, *Transforming Juvenile Justice in Texas: A Framework for Action* (Austin, TX: Blue Ribbon Task Force Report, 2007).
3. Cited in John Prezas, "Rise in Violence Inside Secure Juvenile Correctional Institutions: Concerns of a Texas Juvenile Defense Attorney," February 15, 2012, http://www.texasappleseed.net/ (accessed July 2014).
4. Allen J. Beck, Paige M. Harrison, and Paul Guerino, *Sexual Victimization in Juvenile Facilities Reported by Youth, 2008–09* (Washington, DC: U.S. Government Printing Office; Bureau of Justice Statistics, 2010), p. 1.
5. Brandi Grissom and Becca Aaronson, "Violence at Texas' Youth Lockups Has Risen Since Overhaul," *Star-Tribune*, February 14, 2012, http://www.star-telegram.com/2012/02/13/3732336/violence-at-texas-youth-lockups.html (accessed July 2014).
6. Douglas Besharov, *Juvenile Justice Advocacy—Practice in a Unique Court* (New York: Practicing Law Institute, 1974), p. 2.
7. D. R. Rendleman, "*Parens Patriae*: From Chancery to the Juvenile Court," *South Carolina Law Review* (1971), p. 209.
8. Gustav L. Schramm, "The Judge Meets the Boy and His Family," *National Probation Association 1945 Yearbook*, pp. 182–194.
9. Anthony M. Platt, *The Child Savers: The Invention of Delinquency* (Chicago: University of Chicago Press, 1969).
10. Martin L. Forst, Bruce A. Fisher, and Robert B. Coates, "Indeterminate and Determinate Sentencing of Juvenile Delinquents: A National Survey of Approaches to Commitment and Release Decision Making," *Juvenile and Family Court Journal* 36 (1985): 1–12.
11. Larry Siegel and Brandon Welsh, *Juvenile Delinquency: Theory, Practice and Law* (Belmont, CA: Cengage Publishing, 2014).
12. Office of Juvenile Justice and Delinquency Prevention, *Statistical Briefing Book*, April 2013, http://www.ojjdp.gov/ojstatbb/probation/qa07102.asp?qaDate=2011 (accessed July 2014).
13. TDCJ-Community Justice Assistance Division, *Electronic Monitoring: Agency Brief* (n.d.), p. 1.
14. Joseph B. Vaughn, "A Survey of Juvenile Electronic Monitoring and Home Confinement Programs," *Juvenile and Family Court Journal* 40 (1989): 4, 22.
15. Howard N. Snyder and Melissa Sickmund, *Juvenile Offenders and Victims: 2006 National Report* (Pittsburgh: National Center for Juvenile Justice, 2006), p. 187.
16. Doris Layton MacKenzie, David B. Wilson, Gaylene Styve Armstrong, and Angela R. Gover, "The Impact of Boot Camps and Traditional Institutions on Juvenile Residents: Perceptions, Adjustment, and Change," *Journal of Research in Crime and Delinquency* 38 (August 2000): 279–313; Jean Bottcher and Michaele Ezell, "Examining the Effectiveness of Boot Camps: A Randomized Experiment with a Long-Term Follow-Up," *Journal of Research in Crime and Delinquency* 42 (2005): 309–320; Jerry Tyler, Ray Darville, and Kathi Stalnaker, "Juvenile Boot Camps: A Descriptive Analysis of Program Diversity and Effectiveness," *Social Sciences Journal* 38 (2001): 445–460.
17. Peter W. Greenwood, "Prevention and Intervention Programs for Juvenile Offenders," *Juvenile Justice* 18 (2008).
18. Data used in this section come from Sarah Hockenberry, Melissa Sickmund, and Arthur Sladky, *Juvenile Residential Facility Census, 2010* (Washington, DC: Office of Juvenile Justice and Delinquency Prevention, September 2013), p. 2 http://www.ojjdp.gov/pubs/241134.pdf (accessed July 2014).
19. Ibid.
20. Daniel P. Mears, "Exploring State-Level Variation in Juvenile Incarceration Rates: Symbolic Threats and Competing Explanations," *Prison Journal* 86 (2006): 470–490.
21. John F. Chapman, Rani A. Desai, Paul R. Falzer, and Randy Borum, "Violence Risk and Race in a Sample of Youth in Juvenile Detention: The Potential to Reduce Disproportionate Minority Confinement," *Youth Violence and Juvenile Justice* 4 (2006): 170–184.
22. Office of Juvenile Justice and Delinquency Prevention, "Juveniles in Corrections."
23. Heidi M. Hsia, George S. Bridges, and Rosalie McHale, *Disproportionate Minority Confinement: 2002 Update: Summary* (Washington, DC: Office of Juvenile Justice and Delinquency Prevention, 2004).
24. Coalition for Juvenile Justice, *Disproportionate Minority Contact (DMC), Facts and Resources*, http://www.juvjustice.org/ (accessed July 2014).
25. Christopher Sieverdes and Clemens Bartollas, "Security Level and Adjustment Patterns in Juvenile Institutions," *Journal of Criminal Justice* 14 (1986): 135–145.
26. Randall G. Shelden, *Delinquency and Juvenile Justice in American Society* (Long Grove, IL: Waveland Press, 2011).
27. Meda Chesney-Lind and Randall G. Shelden, *Girls, Delinquency, and the Juvenile Justice System* (Malden, MA: Wiley Blackwell, 2014).
28. Kristi Holsinger and Alexander M. Holsinger, "Differential Pathways to Violence and Self-Injurious Behavior: African American and White Girls in the Juvenile Justice System," *Journal of Research in Crime and Delinquency* 42 (2005): 211–242.
29. *Inmates of the Boys' Training School v. Affeck*, 346 F. Supp. 1354 (D.R.I. 1972); *Nelson v. Heyne*, 491 F.2d 353 (1974); *Morales v. Turman*, 383 F.Supp. 53 (E.D. Texas 1974).
30. *Pena v. New York State Division for Youth*, 419 F. Supp. 203 (S.D.N.Y. 1976).
31. *Ralston v. Robinson*, 102 S.Ct. 233 (1981).
32. Joan McCord, Cathy Spatz Widom, and Nancy A. Crowell, *Juvenile Crime, Juvenile Justice*, Panel on Juvenile Crime: Prevention, Treatment, and Control (Washington, DC: National Academy Press, 2001), p. 194.

33. David M. Altschuler and Troy L. Armstrong, "Juvenile Corrections and Continuity of Care in a Community Context—The Evidence and Promising Directions," *Federal Probation* 66 (2002): 72–77.
34. Richard E. Redding, "Juvenile Offenders in Criminal Court and Adult Prison: Legal, Psychological, and Behavioral Outcomes," *Juvenile and Family Court Journal* 50 (1999): 1–20.
35. Salvador A. Godinez, "Managing Juveniles in Prison," *Corrections Today* 61 (April 1999): 132–133.
36. Victor L. Streib, *The Juvenile Death Penalty Today: Death Sentences and Executions for Juvenile Crimes, January 1, 1973–September 30, 2003* (Ada, OH: Claude W. Pettit College of Law, Ohio Northern University, October 6, 2003), p. 3.
37. *Roper v. Simmons*, 125 S.Ct. 1183 (2005).
38. Erica Goode, "Young Killer: Bad Seed or Work in Progress?" *New York Times*, November 25, 2003.
39. Barry C. Feld, "A Slower Form of Death: Implications of *Roper v. Simmons* for Juveniles Sentenced to Life Without Parole," *Notre Dame Journal of Law, Ethics and Public Policy* 22 (2008): 9–65.
40. Ibid., P. 10.
41. *Graham v. Florida*, 560 U.S. ___ (2010) (decided May 17, 2010).
42. *Miller v. Alabama*, 567 U.S. ___ (2012).
43. American Civil Liberties Union, "Juvenile Life Without Parole," https://www.aclu.org/blog/tag/juvenile-life-without-parole (accessed July 2014).
44. Gary Fleming and Gerald Winkler, "Sending Them to Prison: Washington State Learns to Accommodate Female Youthful Offenders in Prison," *Corrections Today* 61 (April 1999): 132–133.
45. Ibid., P. 133.

Paws-training-academy

The story of Cece Miller shows that given the proper help and encouragement an inmate can turn his or her life around and actually become a corrections professional. This heartwarming story reveals the positive impact corrections can have on inmates' lives and also shows that a career in corrections can be open to anyone with the proper skills and motivation.

Cece Miller had a love of dogs that led her to work in one of the largest animal shelters in South Carolina.[1] In 2007, she found herself in the Federal Secure Female Facility at Hazelton, West Virginia. Shortly after arriving in the prison, and with the support of her correctional counselor, Miller started training to become a dog handler at the institution. Within months she was training her first dog, Solomon, who eventually went to a young girl who needed a canine companion. Miller became a senior trainer in the prison program where she was responsible for ensuring the dogs received effective, safe training. She mentored all other inmate dog trainers, and she remained in that role until she was released in 2010.

Three weeks after her release from prison, the Society for the Prevention of Cruelty to Animals (SPCA) hired Miller as a dog trainer; she built a training program and began to learn more about dog breeds, diseases, and medications. She volunteered for the paws4people organization, a nonprofit pet therapy organization that recruits, trains, certifies, and places therapy teams in more than 150 sites in Delaware, Maryland, Pennsylvania, and New Jersey. Miller led a mentoring program for ex-offenders who wish to continue their dog training services after release. Subsequently, she was elected to their board of directors, earned a master's degree, and in 2013 became a full-time employee at paws4people. Three years after her release, Cece Miller returned to prison as the director of paws4prisons and the PAWS Training Academy. Paws4prisons is a service-dog training program dedicated to helping adolescent children with disabilities and veterans suffering from posttraumatic stress disorder.[2] "It is different being on this side," says Miller of her return to Hazelton. "But I understand what they are going through. I can be empathetic but also authoritative." Cece Miller provides inmates with the academic and skills training necessary to train service dogs. In addition, she teaches inmates leadership skills, responsibility, and teamwork: "We don't just train a dog—we train a person at the same time."

Miller admits she does not know what she would have done had she not been introduced to dog training while she was an inmate with the Federal Bureau of Prisons. She credits the program at Hazelton with changing her life. She found a career and found herself. Miller believes the program made her a better mother to her children and helped mend her relationship with her own mother. Now when she visits prisons she brings her positive message of change and service for both dogs and people.[3]

15

Professionalism and Careers in Corrections

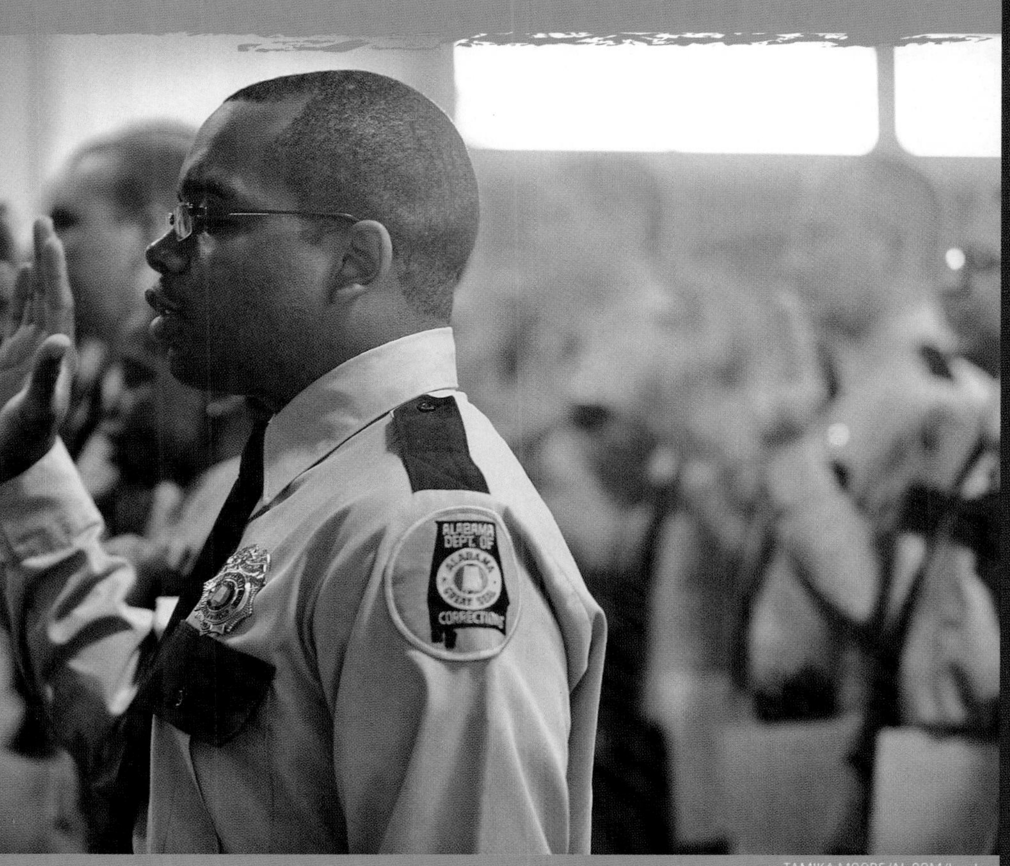

TAMIKA MOORE/AL.COM/Landov

LEARNING OBJECTIVES

 LO1 Discuss how far professionalism has brought corrections

 LO2 Define professionalism and the need for it in corrections

 LO3 Identify why corrections is a promising career

 LO4 Describe the various career paths in corrections

 LO5 Articulate why an internship in corrections makes sense to the student who is interested in a corrections career

PREVIEW OF KEY CONCEPTS

- pretrial officer
- treatment specialist
- parole officer
- jail officer
- jail administrator
- correctional counselor
- internal affairs investigator
- corrections ombudsman
- prison captain
- assistant warden for programming
- prison warden
- director or commissioner of corrections

One of the underlying themes of this book is that the committed corrections professional can have an exciting and fulfilling career and, at the same time, can make a difference in inmates' lives. The Voices Across the Profession features in the book have echoed this theme over and over. Yet there are challenges to the job. Overcrowded and sometimes violent prisons, lengthy sentences, and high rates of recidivism, to name a few, can impede inmate rehabilitation efforts and make the corrections professional's job a difficult task. The hope is that with this changing landscape corrections will become more humane in the treatment of offenders, more respectful of human rights, and more effective in preparing those who have violated society's laws for responsible community living.

We begin this chapter with a discussion of professionalism in the field of corrections, and then talk about the variety of careers in corrections.

© Ray Stanelle

VOICES ACROSS THE PROFESSION

Corrections is in my blood, and I am quite passionate about it. It is a great career.

Ray Stanelle
Senior Investigator for Drug Interdiction and Intelligence

I joined the Georgia Department of Corrections as a correction officer in June of 1994 when I was 45 years old. I attended Georgia College and State University and earned my B.S., with a major in criminal justice. During this time, I also completed a course in comparative law and corrections in England and Spain, next earning my M.P.A. with criminal justice as my discipline of concentration.

I must say I learned more about inmates and prisons and policy and procedures as a correction officer than I could have ever learned in a classroom. As a correction officer, I supervised inmates in the dormitory and also on inside details. The atmosphere of a dormitory changes with each shift, and each shift is a world unto itself. I was later assigned the position of disciplinary investigator where I remained until leaving to become a probation officer in 1997. I loved my probation officer job, which was very demanding and challenging. I ran a tight ship and expected all probationers to adhere to the terms and conditions of their probation. For all the tough talk, I discovered that by being consistent and fair, and by setting high standards, I had probationers completing probation who had never completed anything in their lives. I learned that if you expected excellence, their chance of success improved greatly.

I left probation when I was chosen to become an internal affairs investigator for the Georgia Department of Corrections. I left this position after four years to become a chief counselor, then became an acting deputy warden. I missed working in the field and jumped at an opportunity to return to internal affairs, where I investigated everything from excessive force to assaults, rapes, suicides, and inmate deaths. I have found this to be meaningful work. For example, I worked with one of my investigators for eight months and finally solved how a death row inmate was getting Internet pagers smuggled to him. The investigation took us from Georgia to Italy and then on to Singapore. The reward was the day we arrested the culprit who had been smuggling the pagers into the prison. I became a senior investigator for drug interdiction and intelligence, a job I still hold today.

Corrections is in my blood, and I am quite passionate about it. It is a great career. I would recommend it to students reading this book.

PROFESSIONALISM IN CORRECTIONS

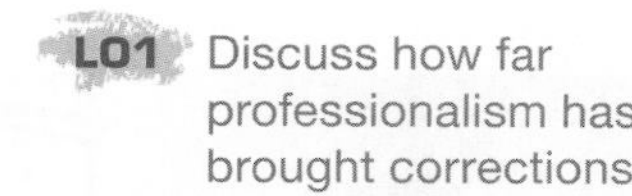

LO1 Discuss how far professionalism has brought corrections

As suggested in Chapter 1, professionalism brought corrections into the modern age and will guide it into the future. However, reaching this standard did not occur overnight. In this section, we discuss a few of the steps taken in the past to reach the current standard of corrections professionalism.

AP Images/David Goldman

Highly professional juvenile correctional officers are always in demand. Here, Sgt. Sharie McKevie embraces a classmate following their graduation from the Sergeants Academy at a training facility in Forsyth, Georgia.

Emerging Professionalism

Those who view corrections through the lens of reform conclude that the government must strike a balance between individual rights and the collective needs of the staff and inmate population. This balance, reflecting a long history of court involvement in correctional administration, is weighted on the side of individual rights. The courts have outlawed such practices as physical punishment and withholding proper medical care.

Reformers have advanced corrections and moved it toward professionalism. One early reformer, Richard A. McGee, changed the nature of corrections in California by upgrading the physical plants and staffing patterns, by institutional research, and by developing alternatives to imprisonment. Another, Kenneth Stoneman, closed Vermont's only maximum-security prison in the 1970s. Lloyd McCorkle, instead of building more prisons, developed a network of satellites in New Jersey at other human services institutions. Kenneth F. Schoen was instrumental in laying out the principles of Minnesota's groundbreaking Community Corrections Act. James V. Bennett closed Alcatraz, opened Marion, planned Morgantown, and created a professional bureaucracy at the Federal Bureau of Prisons. Elayn Hunt, before her death, was leading the Louisiana corrections system out of its dark ages.

STAFF TRAINING AND DEVELOPMENT The Federal Bureau of Prisons and a number of states began to emphasize staff training in the early 1970s. It was not long before state corrections training academies were established across the nation. In the late 1970s, the American Correctional Association (ACA) Commission on Accreditation established its training standards, which had wide influence on the field of corrections. One of its standards was to require 120 hours for preservice and 40 hours for annual in-service training. The National Institute of Corrections (NIC) and the Association of State Correctional Administrators (ASCA) were other agencies that began to offer training for correctional staff. Correctional officers, similar to law enforcement officers in training academies, and various levels of management staff soon had programs established for them as well. One of the advantages of staff training is that it ensures uniformity in administration. Staff training was one of the most important impetuses toward professionalism of American corrections.

IMPLEMENTING GENDER AND RACIAL INTEGRATION The acceptance of women in corrections took a long time, and it was not until midway through the twentieth century that women were widely accepted in positions of correctional leadership. Since that time, women have been directors or commissioners of corrections, many have been superintendents of women's prisons, and an increasing number have been wardens of men's prisons, even maximum-security ones. In addition to Elayn Hunt, who was Louisiana corrections commissioner between 1972 and 1976, women such as Ward Murphy in Maine, Ali Klein in New Jersey, and Ruth L. Rushen in California in the 1980s became the heads of adult corrections. In 1992,

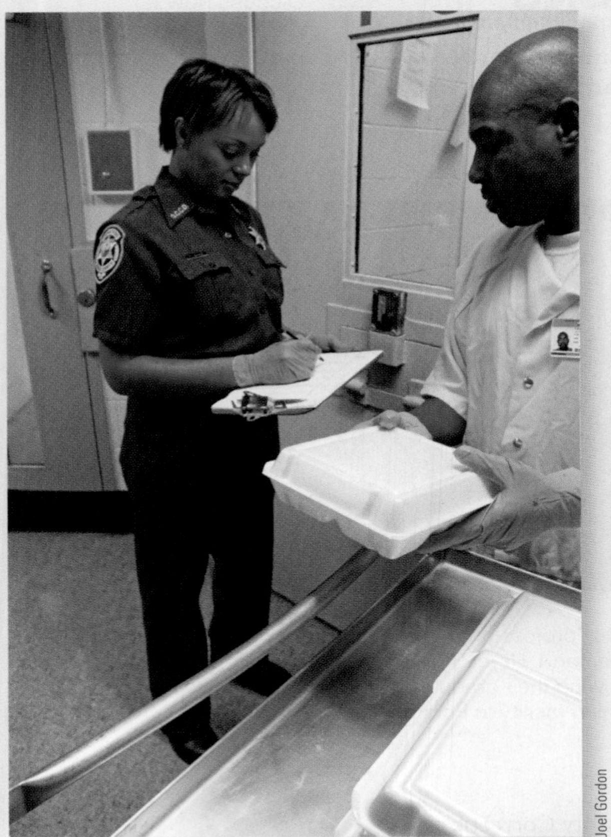

This correctional officer is taking a head count at the Orange County Jail in Orlando, Florida, during a lunch break. It is common to find female officers in male institutions.

Kathleen M. Hawk was appointed director of the Federal Bureau of Prisons, and in 2009, Collette S. Peters became the first female director of the Oregon Department of Corrections. By the end of the twentieth century, women represented about 10 percent of wardens and superintendents of the 900 statewide correctional facilities for men.

EMPHASIS ON ETHICS AND INTEGRITY Both corrections and law enforcement agencies realized in the late twentieth century that an emphasis on integrity was critically important in being recognized as professional entities. Persons of integrity demonstrate over a period of time that they are honest. They also show that there are no contradictions between what they say and what they do. Thus, "standing tall" is not something that can be earned in a day or a week. It occurs over a substantial period of time during which this integrity is tested on a regular basis. The credibility and honesty of these people are reflected in everything they say and do.

Corrections staff with integrity seem to have the ability to maintain their composure, regardless of the circumstances taking place around them. No matter how volatile an incident may be or how much they are upset by the behavior of other staff members or inmates, they are able to keep their cool. This calmness is reassuring to others because they know that even in the worst conditions, you can count on these people to keep their wits about them and stay focused on what has to be done to resolve the situation.

The American Correctional Association's Code of Ethics has contributed to this emphasis on ethics and integrity (see Exhibit 15.1). The code has statements regarding respecting the civil rights of others; treating every situation with concern for the welfare of those involved; refraining from using one's position to secure personal privileges or advantages; and respecting, promoting, and contributing to a workplace that is healthy, safe, and free of harassment in any form.[4] Implementation of standards and accreditation, spearheaded by the American Correctional Association, has developed across the nation. As of 2012, there were 1,289 correctional services across the United States that received accreditation from the ACA accreditation program.[5]

EXHIBIT 15.1

American Correctional Association's Code of Ethics

Preamble

The American Correctional Association expects of its members unfailing honesty, respect for the dignity and individuality of human beings and a commitment to professional and compassionate service. To that this end we subscribe to the following principles.

1. Member shall respect and protect the civil and legal rights of all individuals.
2. Member shall treat every professional situation with concern for the welfare of the individuals involved and with no intent to personal gain.
3. Member shall maintain relationships with colleagues to promote mutual respect within the profession and improve the quality of service.
4. Members shall make public criticism of their colleagues or their agencies only when warranted, verifiable, and constructive.

(continued)

5. Members shall respect the importance of all disciplines within the criminal justice system and work to improve cooperation with each segment.
6. Members shall honor the public's right to information and share information with the public to the extent permitted by law but subject to individuals' right to privacy.
7. Members shall respect and protect the right of the public to be safeguarded from criminal activity.
8. Members shall refrain from using their position to secure personal privileges or advantages.
9. Members shall refrain from allowing personal interest to impair objectivity in the performance of duty while acting in an official capacity.
10. Members shall refrain from entering into any formal or informal activity or agreement which presents a conflict of interest or is inconsistent with the conscientious performance of duties.
11. Members shall refrain from accepting any gifts, services, or favors that is or appears to be improper or implies an obligation inconsistent with the free and objective exercise of professional duties.
12. Members shall clearly differentiate between personal views/statements and views/statements/positions made on behalf of the agency or Association.
13. Members shall report to appropriate authorities any corrupt or unethical behavior in which there is sufficient evidence to justify review.
14. Members shall refrain from discriminating against any individual because of race, gender, creed, national origin, religious affiliation, age, disability, or any other type of prohibited discrimination.
15. Members shall preserve the integrity of private information; they shall refrain from seeking information on individuals beyond that which is necessary to implement responsibilities and perform their duties; members shall refrain from revealing nonpublic information unless expressively authorized to do so.
16. Members shall make all appointments, promotions, and dismissals in accordance with established civil service rules, applicable contract agreements, and individual merit, rather than furtherance of personal interest.
17. Members shall respect, promote, and contribute to a workplace that is safe, healthy, and free of harassment in any form.

Source: Adopted by the Board of Governors and Delegate Assembly in August 1994 and updated in 2009. Reprinted by permission of the ACA. Available online at http://www.aca.org/pastpresentfuture/ethics.asp (accessed July 2014).

Professionalism in Corrections Today

LO2 Define professionalism and the need for it in corrections

Corrections professionals, rather than following a script or providing minimum service, undertake a specialized set of tasks and complete them, believing passionately in what they do, never compromising their standards or values, and caring about clients even if they happen to be criminal offenders. Corrections professionals, as is true of other types of professionals, are experts at their work. They see their commitment to the organization as having the objective of obtaining the highest standards of excellence. As we briefly touched on at the beginning of this book, becoming a corrections professional means:

- Seeing oneself as a person of integrity
- Treating offenders with dignity and respect
- Modeling positive behaviors to both inmates and staff
- Refusing to accept unethical behavior from fellow staff members
- Doing what is possible to create a positive workplace
- Being committed to making a difference
- Being a proactive leader, anticipating and preventing problems before they occur

- Remembering that institutional security must always come first
- Maintaining a clean institution; cleanliness and orderliness of the institution are absolute necessities in correctional leadership
- Remembering the importance of accountability, attention to detail, and following the schedule
- Being a person who listens
- Keeping your personal stuff from getting in the way and refusing to permit your personal problems or issues keep you from doing an effective job
- Going the second mile for offenders, especially in community supervision, if it is the right thing to do

THE NEED FOR PROFESSIONALISM IN CORRECTIONS The encouraging changes that have taken place in recent decades are an indication of the influence of professionalism. Professionalism is affected by how staff dress, how they speak, and how they behave. Workplace attitudes also tell a lot about the level of professionalism in an organization. Professional employees maintain positive, can-do attitudes, even when faced with stressful situations. Professionalism and commitment to the organization are demonstrated by limiting absences, possessing high productivity, and effectively communicating with others.[6] There is still progress to be made, but the commitment of the professionals within the ranks of corrections has brought it a long way, and it is this same commitment that will ensure an even more positive day for corrections in the future.

PROFESSIONAL AND NONPROFESSIONAL To the professional, the job represents a career, a career in which he or she can grow and contribute. To the nonprofessional, the job represents merely a job, a paycheck. There is no commitment to the organization. He or she puts in the time and sees no reason to give any more of self than is absolutely necessary.

Unprofessional workplace conduct includes frequent tardiness, poor contact with inmates, and low employee morale. Nonprofessional behavior is also involved in participating in workplace gossip, turning on mobile devices, and using the institution for personal issues. For example, a nonprofessional staff member who has the reputation of sharing all the rumors and "lowdowns" on staff and inmates throughout the institution—much of which information may be unverified, offensive, and of a personal nature—can be very destructive to the quality of institutional life. A nonprofessional staff member who is reported as falling asleep or nodding off while on duty assignment can threaten the security of the institution and the safety of other staff. Finally, it can be argued that almost every major correctional crisis is preceded by systematic failure to perform the job.[7]

Norman Carlson, former director of the Federal Bureau of Prisons, defines a professional as a person who has a long-term commitment to a field of endeavor, which generally includes some preparation for his or her job. The nature of professionalism, according to Carlson, is such that a professional is one who is committed to the agency and is constantly learning and growing, and who seeks to learn from others. This person does whatever is necessary to stay current and up to date. The professional, emphasizes Carlson, has a high standard of personal ethics, both on and off the job. This person treats others with respect, including subordinates and inmates. Part of the commitment of the professional is to make the organization better. You foster professionalism, according to Carlson, by articulating the need for and justification of professionalism in a correctional context. The professional is aware that it is absolutely necessary for an organization to pursue professional behavior if it wants to move forward.[8]

With the issues that may arise in a prison setting, how would you increase and foster professionalism in corrections? LO1

FOSTERING PROFESSIONALISM Unquestionably, professionalism in corrections depends on the leadership of top administrators, including directors or commissioners of state or federal systems as well as wardens and superintendents of correctional institutions. What is encouraging is the number of outstanding correctional leaders who are advocating professional leadership today.

WHAT REMAINS TO BE DONE Professional ideals are sometimes hard to achieve, but the following are important processes in terms of attaining greater professionalism:

- Corrections staff cannot control overcrowded prisons, but they must do everything possible to reduce the violence and drug trafficking of prison life.
- It is necessary to suspend or terminate staff who abuse inmates and violate their rights.
- It is difficult to talk about professionalism when the no-frills and get-tough approaches with inmates result in taking needed programs and services away from them.
- Professionalism is further challenged by the fiscal constraints that currently exist in corrections; correctional administrators are expected to do more with less.
- It is important that correctional organizations develop greater clarity on their purpose—why the organization exists, what their mission is, what resources are needed to support the purpose and mission, and what the future direction of the organization should be.
- There needs to be a national set of principles and philosophy on what is acceptable behavior toward residents in community-based programs and inmates in prisons. Accreditation provides the broad map of what is expected in correctional care, but the subtle things expected from staff need further clarity and explanation.
- The quality of prisons has improved from the past, but there continue to be too many inhumane new prisons. New construction does not always result in a prison conducive to humane incarceration.
- The level of professionalism is very much affected by the ability to recruit the right staff and, once they are recruited, to explain the principles and behaviors that are expected from them.
- The continuation of correctional officers' commitment to a culture that sanctions abuse and mistreatment of prisoners must be eradicated. One way this can be done is to videotape any disciplinary interaction between correctional officers and inmates and to remind officers that charges will be brought in court if they violate the rights of inmates.
- The salaries of correctional personnel in the community and institutional contexts need to be continually increased. The salaries of these staff in some jurisdictions are still far too low. One advantage of increased salaries is that college-educated applicants are more frequently attracted to these positions.
- Administrative correctional staff must be willing to step forth when colleagues are out of line. This may come to the point of termination if that should be necessary.
- Private correctional facilities too frequently pay inadequate salaries to staff, have inferior construction, and fail to provide needed services for inmates. Private companies, if they intend to be in the corrections business, must maintain the standards of federal and state corrections.

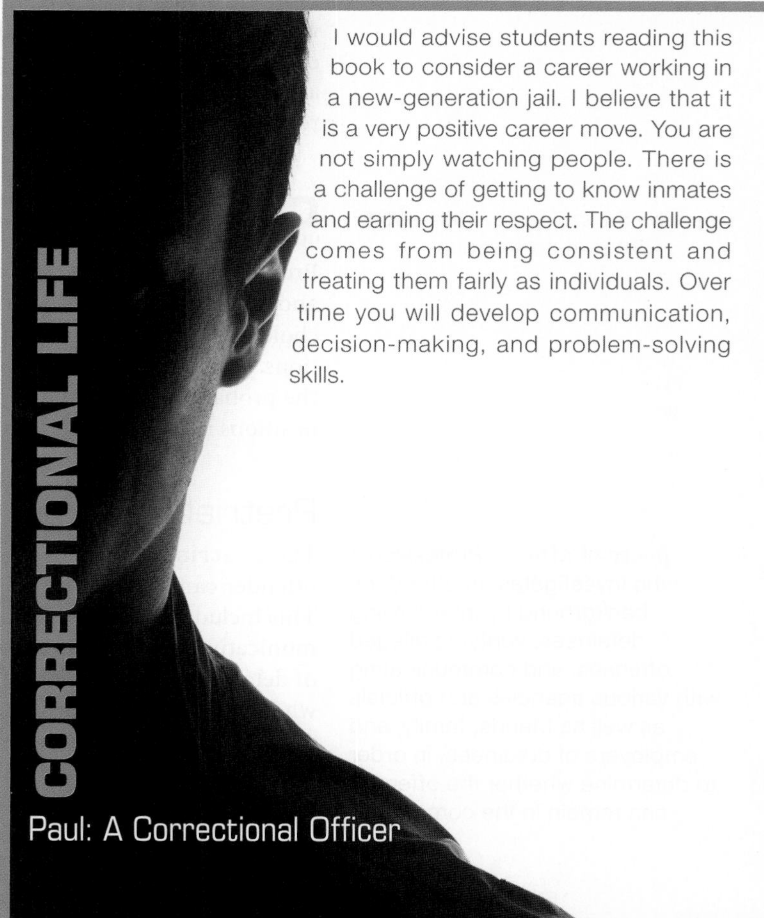

I would advise students reading this book to consider a career working in a new-generation jail. I believe that it is a very positive career move. You are not simply watching people. There is a challenge of getting to know inmates and earning their respect. The challenge comes from being consistent and treating them fairly as individuals. Over time you will develop communication, decision-making, and problem-solving skills.

Paul: A Correctional Officer

"Corrections is not for the faint of heart," was an expression that the late John P. Conrad, noted corrections practitioner, author, and consultant, used to make.[9] And it is true! Corrections is not an easy job, either in the community or in correctional institutional settings. However, as you read the many Voices Across the Profession features found in this text, a common theme emerges time after time, and it is that individuals find corrections to be a very rewarding career.

Identify why corrections is a promising career **LO3**

WHY A CAREER IN CORRECTIONS?

As many of the individuals we quote in the Voices Across the Profession features in this text have expressed, a career in corrections is a meaningful one in which you can have a positive impact on the lives of others and make a difference in your community. There are many jobs in corrections where opportunities for advancement are great. These vary from community programs to those in institutions, from juvenile to adult corrections, from privately administered agencies to state and federal agencies. Most states and the federal jurisdiction offer a good salary package for working in corrections. The health insurance and pension plans are further inducements for corrections employment. For example, the director of the California Department of Corrections earns more than $220,000 a year. And, as discussed in the previous section of this chapter, there is an encouraging movement of professionalism in the field. With a combination of academic study and employment experience, a corrections professional today can commit himself or herself to a long-term contribution to corrections that focuses on providing the highest quality service to others in the workplace, both colleagues and clients.

A career in corrections, although demanding and challenging, can be extremely rewarding and an ideal fit for those wanting to make society safer. Furthermore, the trend toward new generation jails and direct supervision gives correctional officers more involvement with inmates and more control over the populations they supervise, which translates into enhanced professionalism and greater job satisfaction. Once considered "just a guard," as professionalism in this career continues to be recognized and expected, so do opportunities to make a difference. Because most inmates will be released, the impact correctional officers have on those serving their time is significant.

Describe the various career paths in corrections **LO4**

CAREERS IN COMMUNITY CORRECTIONS

Probation officers and treatment specialists, parole officers, staff of pretrial release and diversion programs, staff of residential programs, drug counselors, forensic psychologists, and other nonprofessional and volunteer staff make up community corrections. This section examines a few of these careers. There is greater attention given to the probation officer and treatment specialists because there are generally the entre positions in adult corrections.

Pretrial Release and Pretrial Services Officers

pretrial officer Professional who investigates an offender's background by interviewing detainees, verifying alleged offenses, and communicating with various agencies and officials as well as friends, family, and employers of detainees, in order to determine whether the offender can remain in the community.

The **pretrial officer** investigates an offender's background to determine if the offender can be safely allowed back into the community before his or her trial date. This includes interviewing detainees, verifying alleged offenses committed, and communicating with various agencies and officials as well as friends, family, and employers of detainees. Officers must assess the risk and make a recommendation to the judge who decides on the appropriate sentencing or bond amount. They prepare a variety of related documents, maintain files, serve as officers in various hearings, and testify in court. They interact with judges, defense attorneys and public defenders, prosecutors, victim witnesses, law enforcement agencies, and the general public.

When offenders are allowed back into the community, pretrial officers supervise them to make sure that they stay within the terms of their release and appear at their trials, and recommend services and programs that can help the individual, such as substance abuse, anger management, educational and work services, and GED programs.

Probation Officers, Community Supervision Officers, and Treatment Specialists

Probation officers supervise people placed on probation by the courts, and many jurisdictions also supervise offenders released on parole. They can be federal probation officers, state probation officers, or county probation officers, working to ensure that offenders are not a danger to the community and helping in their rehabilitation. Most work exclusively with either adult or juvenile offenders. The **treatment specialist** has specific skills and education and can work with line staff to determine proper treatment placements in the community.

treatment specialist A probation officer with specific skills and education who works with line staff to determine proper treatment placements for clients in the community.

The three basic functions of a probation officer are to manage a caseload, to supervise probationers, and to make presentence investigation and other reports to the courts. Probation officers rely upon personal interactions to supervise the offender, including asking for assistance from family members, community organizations, religious institutions, and neighbors. They will help the offender obtain substance abuse services and job training if necessary. Probation officers are also involved in the sentencing process by investigating the offender's background, writing presentence reports, and even recommending sentences. Probation officers generally work a standard 40-hour week, which may include working evenings and/or weekends to supervise their caseload.

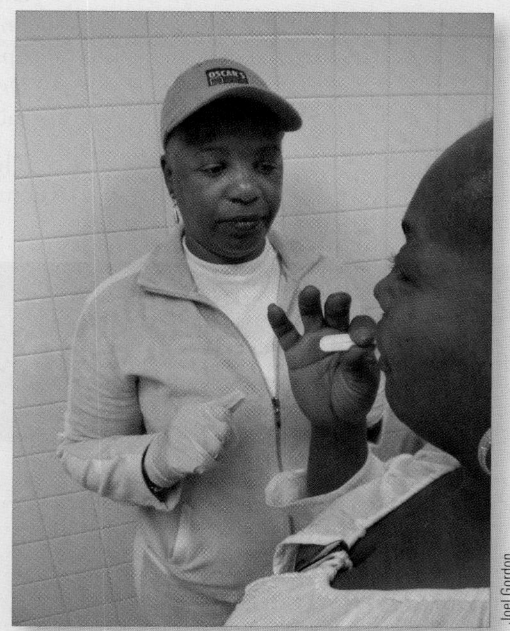

Joel Gordon

In addition to supervision and treatment, probation officers perform a number of tasks to support court orders. Here, a probation officer watches as an offender takes drug and DNA tests at the City of New York Department of Probation.

The Nature of the Job

There are now about 90,000 probation officers and correctional treatment specialists. Nearly all work for state or local governments. While supervising offenders, they may interact with others, such as family members and friends of their clients, who may be upset or suspicious of authority figured. Workers may be assigned to fieldwork in high-crime areas or in institutions where there is a risk of violence or communicable disease.

Probation officers and correctional treatment specialists must meet many court-imposed deadlines, which contributes to heavy workloads and extensive paperwork. Many officers travel to perform home and employment checks and property searches. Because of the hostile environments probation officers may encounter, some may carry a firearm or pepper spray for protection.

All of these factors, as well as the frustration some officers experience in dealing with offenders who violate the terms of their release, contribute to a stressful work environment. Although the high stress levels can make the job difficult at times, this work can also be rewarding. Many officers and specialists receive personal satisfaction from counseling members of their community and helping them become productive citizens.

The demands of the job often lead to working long hours. For example, many agencies rotate an on-call officer position. When these workers are on call, they must respond to any issues with offenders or law enforcement 24 hours a day. Extensive travel and paperwork can also contribute to more hours of work.

Most probation officers and correctional treatment specialists must complete a training program sponsored by their state government or the federal government, after which they may have to take and pass a certification test. In addition, they may be required to work as trainees for up to one year before being offered a permanent position. Some probation officers specialize in a certain type of casework. For example, an officer may work only with domestic violence offenders or deal only with substance-abuse cases. Officers receive training specific to the group they are working with so that they are better prepared to help that type of offender.

Most agencies require applicants to be at least 21 years old and, for federal employment, not older than 37 at the time of employment. In addition, most departments require candidates to have a record free of felony convictions and to submit to drug testing. A valid driver's license is often required. Although job requirements vary, previous work experience in probation, pretrial services, parole, corrections, criminal investigations, substance abuse treatment, social work, or counseling can be helpful in the hiring process. Previous experience working in courthouses or with offenders in the criminal justice field can also be useful for some positions. Advancement to supervisory positions is primarily based on experience and performance. A master's degree in criminal justice, social work, or psychology may be required for advancement.

Some important qualities that a probation officer or correctional treatment specialist should possess include:

- *Communication skills.* Probation officers and correctional treatment specialists must be able to effectively interact with many different people.
- *Critical thinking skills.* Workers must be able to assess the needs of individual offenders before determining the best resources for helping them.
- *Decision-making skills.* Probation officers and correctional treatment specialists must consider the relative costs and benefits of potential actions and be able to choose appropriately.
- *Emotional stability.* Workers must cope with hostile individuals or otherwise upsetting circumstances on the job.
- *Organizational skills.* Probation officers and correctional treatment specialists must be able to manage multiple cases at the same time.

The Evidence-Based Corrections feature reviews the application and success of a structured training program for probation officers.

EVIDENCE-BASED CORRECTIONS

Strategic Training Initiative in Community Supervision (STICS)

Strategic Training Initiative in Community Supervision (STICS) is a job-training program for probation officers to help them apply the risk–need–responsivity (RNR) model with probationers to reduce recidivism. The RNR model, first proposed by Donald Andrews, James Bonta, and Robert Hoge, has three core principles:

- *Risk principle.* The level of services should be matched to the level of offender. High-risk offenders should receive more intensive services; low-risk offenders should receive minimal services.
- *Need principle.* Target criminogenic needs with services—that is, target those factors that are associated with criminal behavior. Such factors might include substance abuse, procriminal attitudes, criminal associates, and the like. Do not target other, non-criminogenic factors (such as emotional distress, self-esteem issues) unless they act as a barrier to changing criminogenic factors.
- *Responsivity principle.* The ability and learning style of the offender should determine the style and mode of intervention. Research has shown the general effectiveness of using social learning and cognitive-behavioral style interventions.

Implementing STICS

The STICS-based training program was implemented in three Canadian provinces: British Columbia, Prince Edward Island, and Saskatchewan. The objectives of the training include changing how probation officers interact with offenders and adjusting the focus of sessions with clients. Research shows that probation officers often focus on non-criminogenic needs and infrequently use prosocial modeling, role playing, or other cognitive-behavioral techniques with probationers. By training probation officers to implement RNR principles into their interactions with probationers, they may reduce recidivism rates in their probationers. There was also recognition of General Personality and Cognitive Social Learning theoretical perspectives, which address how learning and risk/need factors affect criminal behavior. The theory suggests that criminal behavior is learned, that this learning occurs within a particular environment, and that some risk/need factors are more important in predicting criminal behavior than others. This theory then implies that offender behavior can change (as opposed, for instance, to a medical model that sees an offender as "sick").

Program Activities

The training program includes a 3-day training based on 10 modules. These modules are designed to explain the overview and rationale for STICS; introduce RNR model principles; teach how to implement those principles when working with probationers; encourage the use of prosocial modeling, reinforcement, and other cognitive-behavioral techniques; and explain the benefits of using a strategic supervision structure in individual sessions.

The training is followed by monthly meetings designed for skill maintenance. In these meetings, groups of 3 to 12 officers are encouraged to discuss and practice their skills. Prior to the meetings, officers receive themed exercises with audiotaped examples. Trainers are present via teleconference to guide the sessions and provide feedback. Also, formal clinical feedback is given to the officers based on their officer–client sessions, which are audiotaped and submitted for review. A one-day refresher course is delivered approximately a year after the initial training.

Evaluation Outcomes

The program was evaluated by James Bonta and colleagues and revealed significant changes in the officer population, but insignificant, though positive, differences regarding offenders' subsequent recidivism. Compared to control group officers, officers in the experimental group who received the RNR training spent significantly more session time focusing on criminogenic needs and procriminal attitudes. Likewise, they demonstrated higher-quality RNR-based skills and interventions with the exception of behavioral techniques, where there were no statistically significant differences between groups.

The results for offender survival rates and recidivism rates were encouraging. The offenders recruited by the officers assigned to the experimental group had the longest survival rate compared to both the control offenders and the "retrospective" probationer samples. Similarly, the offenders recruited by the officers assigned to the experimental group had lower recidivism rates than the offenders recruited by the officers assigned to the control group. Though the difference was statistically insignificant, it represented a 15 percent reduction (40.5 percent for the control clients; 25.3 percent for the experimental clients).

FOR CRITICAL THINKING AND WRITING

Does the STICS program suggest that careful training of probation officers and other correctional staff will eventually pay off in lower recidivism rates? Do you believe that treatment is a better approach than trying to reduce repeat offending through the threat of punishment?

Sources: National Institute of Justice, Program Profile, Strategic Training Initiative in Community Supervision (STICS), 2014, https://www.crimesolutions.gov/ProgramDetails.aspx?ID=47 (accessed July 2014); Donald Andrews, James Bonta, and Robert D. Hoge, "Classification for Effective Rehabilitation: Rediscovering Psychology," *Criminal Justice and Behavior* 17 (1990): 19–52; James Bonta, Tanya Rugge, Bill Sedo, and Ron Coles, *Case Management in Manitoba Probation* (Ottawa, Canada: Public Safety Canada, 2004), http://www.publicsafety.gc.ca/cnt/rsrcs/pblctns/cs-mngmnt-mntb/cs-mngmnt-mntb-eng.pdf (accessed July 2014); James Bonta, Tanya Rugge, Terri-Lynne Scott, Guy Bourgon, and Annie K. Yessine, "Exploring the Black Box of Community Supervision," *Journal of Offender Rehabilitation* 47 (2008): 248–70; Guy Bourgon, James Bonta, Tanya Rugge, Terri-Lynne Scott, and Annie K. Yessine, "Program Design, Implementation, and Evaluation in 'Real World' Community Supervision," *Federal Probation* 74 (2010): 2–15, http://www.uscourts.gov/viewer.aspx?doc=/uscourts/FederalCourts/PPS/Fedprob/2010-06/index.html (accessed July 2014); James Bonta, Guy Bourgon, Tanya Rugge, Terri-Lynne Scott, Annie K. Yessine, Leticia Gutierrez, and Jobina Li, *The Strategic Training Initiative in Community Supervision: Risk–Need–Responsivity in the Real World* (Ottawa, Canada: Public Safety Canada, 2010).

Becoming a Community Correctional Treatment Specialist

In most states, at least a four-year degree is required, which can often be in any area of study associated with the work (criminal justice, psychology, social work, etc.). Different agencies may prefer certain levels of experience or specific training or education. In addition, most employers require candidates to pass oral, written, and psychological exams. Typical requirements are the following:

- Monitor them through contacting others, including family members, employers, and treatment providers
- Direct them to services to help them—such as substance abuse or mental health treatment, medical care, training, or employment assistance—as ordered by the court
- Manage any risk they pose to individuals or the community by verifying their employment, monitoring their associates, restricting their travel, and taking other actions to make sure they're obeying the law

VOICES ACROSS THE PROFESSION

I see my job as both helping keep the community safe and providing an opportunity for offenders to get their lives back together for those who want. For those who don't, I'm the one who holds them accountable.

Gene Arvidson
Probation Officer

The work of a probation officer changes throughout every day. It's never the same thing twice, and a variety of skills are required. You have to know how to treat people with respect but not let them take advantage of you. A working knowledge of the Constitution, as well as of federal and state laws, is a requirement, as is knowing the variety of policies and procedures within the organization you work for. You have to know how to appear in court and develop professional relationships with the judges and the police. Of course, our job like all others is becoming increasingly dependent on technology, so computer skills are necessary.

The job of a probation officer can be even more varied depending on special opportunities one may pursue. I've been in community corrections for over 20 years. My present role working specifically with adult gang members is especially satisfying. I'm often out of the office interviewing clients, testifying in court, or executing search and arrest warrants along with the police. I see my job as both helping keep the community safe and providing an opportunity for offenders to get their lives back together for those who want. For those who don't, I'm the one who holds them accountable.

Earnings and Future Potential

According to the Federal Bureau of Labor Statistics, the median annual wage for probation officers and correctional treatment specialists is about $48,000 per year. The lowest 10 percent earn about $32,000, and the top 10 percent earn more than $83,000.[10] Employment of probation officers and correctional treatment specialists is projected to grow 11 percent between 2006 and 2016, as fast as the average for all occupations. In addition to openings due to growth, many jobs must be filled because of replacement needs, openings due to the large number of these workers who are expected to retire.

The fact is, no one works in the criminal justice field to become wealthy, but job satisfaction and what one can do to contribute to the community are the rewards those finding a satisfying career in this area receive.

Parole Officers

parole officer Parole officers help identify offenders who are eligible for conditional release from prison and, once they are released, work with offenders and monitor their postrelease activities.

The **parole officer** helps identify and supervise offenders who are eligible for conditional release from prison before they have completed their sentences, and—once they are released—helps them to reenter society. Some parole officers work inside correctional facilities, preparing reports for parole boards. They assess inmates' lives before and during incarceration, how prisoners' families will affect their community adjustment, and what job prospects an inmate might have if released. Based on officers' reports and interviews with inmates and their families, the board chooses certain inmates for release. In the community, officers monitor postrelease offenders and provide them with information about various resources, such as substance abuse counseling or job training, to aid in their rehabilitation. The officer helps parolees find jobs, schools, or treatment programs to try to change the offenders' behaviors and reduce the risk of reoffending and returning to prison.

Both probation and parole officers supervise offenders through personal contact with the offenders and their families. Probation and parole officers require regularly scheduled contact with offenders by telephone or through office visits, and they also may check on offenders at their homes or places of work. Probation and parole officers also oversee drug testing and electronic monitoring of offenders. In some states, officers do the jobs of both probation and parole officers.

Staff in Community-Based Residential Facilities

Line staff in residential programs face problems comparable to those of line staff in correctional institutions. They also are charged with providing services to residents. The "cream of the crop" offenders tend to remain on regular probation or receive parole; those placed in residential programs often have few resources and little or no employment history. Yet residential staff do not have the physical control over offenders as institutional staff have over their inmates. Residents usually have the freedom to leave the halfway house for part of the day, sometimes leading to problems for them when exposed to the temptations of the community. In probation referrals, the family and friends of residents are still in the immediate area, and they are at times the source of problems.

Other Career Opportunities in Community-Based Corrections

Because of factors such as increasing jail and prison populations, decreasing funding, aging facilities with limited housing, and ever-changing societal demands and expectations, both the adult and juvenile systems are considering alternatives to incarceration. Some options are residential facilities such as halfway houses, prerelease

CAREERS IN CORRECTIONS

Shirley Addison
Halfway House Program Director

"The average day is spent fulfilling these responsibilities:

- Administrative duties include preparing monthly and quarterly reports on program performance.
- Monthly billing reports must be submitted to various funding agencies; these reports are frequently sent to the executive office for agency-wide billing by the business manager.
- Other administrative duties include liaison work with other criminal justice and mental health agencies and speaking engagements outside the facility.
- Budget planning and review are also important.
- Staff supervision can be a frustrating task and may cause more problems for the director than any other.
- Decision making concerning disciplinary action toward residents is another major responsibility of top-level staff. These decisions will often affect a resident's freedom.
- One of the personal satisfactions is that the director can assume 'ownership' of the program."

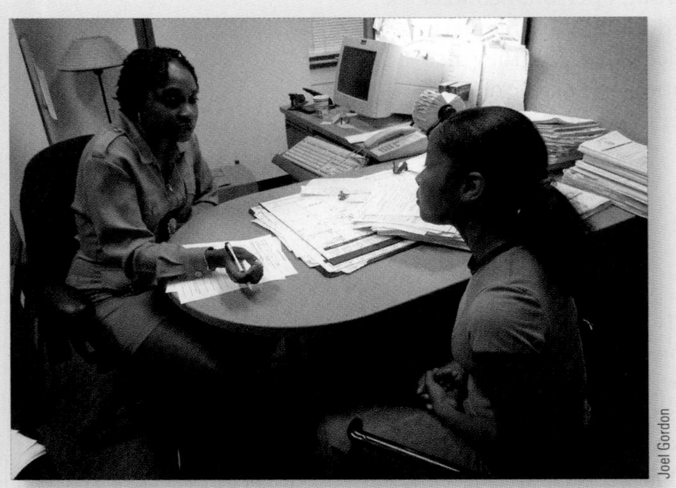

Joel Gordon

In New York, the day reporting center combines educational and vocational training with individual counseling in a highly structured program setting. Individual treatment and supervision plans (ITSPs) are created for each participant.

centers, transition centers, work furlough and community work centers, community treatment centers, and restitution centers. These facilities employ a wide range of staff, including probation/parole officers, counselors, caseworkers, educators, health care workers, and numerous administrative, management, and support/clerical personnel. Nonresidential correctional alternatives, such as day reporting centers, require similar personnel. Other options include less costly but often very effective alternatives, such as bringing offenders, victims, and community members together to confront the issues and support change by the offender.

CAREERS IN JAILS AND DETENTION FACILITIES

Jailors can be called correctional officers or detention officers, and their basic job is the security and control of the inmates. In larger jails, there are usually administrators who train staff, design programs, and develop strategy for the jail.

Jail Officer

jail officers Corrections professionals who have the responsibility of overseeing detainees and those who have been convicted of a crime and are sentenced to serve time in jail. They maintain security and inmate accountability to prevent assaults, disturbances, and escapes.

Jail officers have the responsibility of overseeing individuals who have been arrested or are awaiting trial or who have been convicted of a crime and are sentenced to serve time in jail. They maintain security and inmate accountability to prevent assaults, disturbances, and escapes. Sheriff's departments typically place newly appointed deputies in the jail for a period of time until they are transferred to law enforcement responsibility on the streets. Some sheriff's departments will employ jail officers in permanent positions in the jail; they may be known as detention officers. In jail facilities with direct supervision cellblocks, officers work unarmed. They are equipped with communication devices so they can summon help if necessary. Jailors need to be stable and mature individuals who can handle job responsibilities and the stress of working in a jail context. They need to have good communication skills and have the ability to defuse situations. Most jails require correctional officers to be at least 18 to 21 years of age and a U.S. citizen, have a minimum high school education, demonstrate job stability, usually by accumulating two years of work experience, and have no felony convictions. Employment and promotion opportunities are greatly enhanced by a college education.

Jail Administrator

jail administrator Corrections professional who is responsible for managing staff and generating programs within the local jail.

The **jail administrator** is responsible for managing staff, generating programs, and creating a vision for the jail in years to come. They need to have the skills to plan, organize, and implement the operations and programs in the jail. In smaller jails, it still might be possible to be employed as an administrator with an associate degree and law enforcement experience. Most jails, though, require at least a bachelor's degree as well as significant supervisory experience within the corrections field. Some jails require a graduate degree for this position in public administration, criminal justice, or a related field.

These administrators are known as commanding officer, assistant superintendent/warden of human services, and assistant jail administrator. They generally prepare work schedules, determine work assignments, conduct staff training, review employee performance, resolve problems, guarantee medical care for inmates, and address inmate grievances. Administrators must keep accurate records detailing general inmate population demographics and the personal histories of individual prisoners. They also must maintain financial records, including budgets, inventory and payroll documents, accounts receivable and accounts payable. Disciplinary incidents and injuries also must be reported.

CAREERS IN PRISONS AND INSTITUTIONS

Correctional officers, correctional counselors, internal affairs investigators, corrections ombudsman, captain, associate warden for programming, warden, and director of corrections make up those who work in prisons and correctional institutions. There is greater attention given to the correctional officer in this section because it is the entrée position for most students who go into adult corrections.

Correctional Officers

According to research by the Federal Bureau of Labor Statistics, correctional officers must be at least 18 to 21 years of age, must be a U.S. citizen or permanent resident, and must have no felony convictions. New applicants for federal corrections positions must be appointed before they are 37 years old.

Like many other jobs in criminal justice, working in correctional institutions likely involves shift work, including working nights, weekends, and holidays, with an element of danger always present. Also similar to other criminal justice jobs, stress can result from working in corrections. Thus, this job isn't for everyone. It takes a unique combination of being able to maintain calm but spring to immediate action when necessary.

Correctional officers usually work eight hours per day, five days per week, on rotating shifts. Jail and prison security must be provided around the clock. Some correctional facilities have longer shifts and more days off between scheduled workweeks. Many officers are required to work overtime.[11]

Officers carry out their duties in several ways. They may be housing unit officers, work detail supervisors, industrial shop and school officers, or perimeter security officers. Officers primarily enforce regulations through communication skills and moral authority and attempt to avoid conflict at all costs. Most officers attend to their duties unarmed, but a few officers hold positions in lookout towers with the use of high-powered rifles. In addition to the custodial duties demanded of them in prisons, correctional officers in federal facilities and some minimum-security state facilities are also responsible for providing rehabilitation services.

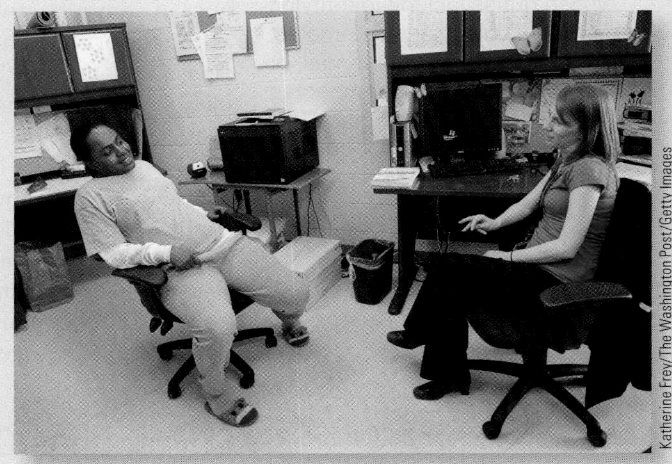
Katherine Frey/The Washington Post/Getty Images

Counseling and treatment are routine duties of corrections professionals. Here, inmate Stephanie Harris talks with her counselor at the Maryland Correctional Institute in Jessup.

How Does the Future Look for Career Correctional Officers?

According to the Federal Bureau of Labor statistics, correctional officers and jailers today make about $39,000 per year. The lowest 10 percent earn less than $27,000, and the top 10 percent earn more than $69,610. Median annual earnings of first-line supervisors/managers of correctional officers are $58,000, with a range from less than $38,000 to more than $92,000.[12]

Although some demand for correctional officers will occur over the coming decade, anticipated budget constraints and a general downward trend in crime rates in recent years will likely mitigate employment growth. Employment of correctional officers is projected to grow 5 percent from 2012 to 2022, slower than the average for all occupations. Faced with growing costs for keeping people in prison, many state governments have moved toward laws requiring shorter prison terms and alternatives to prison. Community-based programs designed to rehabilitate offenders and limit their risk of repeated offenses, while keeping the public safe, may also reduce prison rates.

Job prospects should be good in the private sector as public authorities contract with private companies to provide and staff corrections facilities. A growing number of state and federal corrections agencies are using private prison services. Some local and state corrections agencies experience high job turnover because of job-related stress and shift work. The need to replace correctional officers who transfer to other occupations, retire, or leave the labor force—coupled with rising employment demand—should also generate some job openings.[13]

Correctional Counselor

correctional counselors The chief treatment officer in many correctional institutions, both male and female.

Correctional counselors serve several functions in men's and women's prisons. They are treatment agents who are responsible for providing casework to inmates, interviewing inmates, and providing necessary paperwork. They have the responsibility to be advocates who make certain that inmates receive proper medical care and are assigned to desired programs upon availability. They are resource developers who provide the link between the prisoner and the outside world, as they help inmates plan for their return to the community. Furthermore, they are advocates who ensure to the greatest possible extent that inmates are not deprived of their constitutional rights.

A college education with an emphasis on criminology, social work, or counseling would be adequate preparation for the job. An M.A. in counseling or an M.S.W. in social work would be even greater preparation, and would help secure employment in the Federal Bureau of Prisons. Counselors are expected to have knowledge of individual and group counseling techniques; knowledge of the goals and objectives of correctional treatment services; and knowledge of the operations of a corrections facility.

Internal Affairs Investigator

internal affairs investigator A corrections professional whose duties include identifying individual involvement by inmates, correctional personnel, or public citizens that is suspected of criminal infractions of an administrative, civil, or criminal nature.

Few jobs within a correctional facility offer the variety of daily challenges that face the **internal affairs investigator**. The job consists of identifying individual involvement, whether by inmates, personnel, or public citizens, that is suspected of criminal infractions of administrative, civil, or criminal nature. This includes anything that occurs within the prison—things like theft, prostitution, assaults, blackmail, robbery, suicide, rape, and homicide. One case may involve allegations of physical abuse of inmates by staff, or perhaps an inmate-on-inmate assault, sometimes resulting in a homicide. Yet another case may involve staff or public involvement in smuggling contraband such as drugs over the guard line and into the facility.

This is one of the most valued careers in corrections, but it requires becoming familiar with correctional facilities, and it takes considerable experience to accomplish this. A career path for becoming an internal affairs investigator begins with a college degree. Strong written and oral communication skills are required. There is comparatively little turnover of internal affairs investigators. The challenging nature of the job, along with its prestige, makes this position highly sought after.

Corrections Ombudsman

corrections ombudsman An ombudsman (a Swedish word that means "representative") is a person or body that protects citizens against governmental abuses.

The **corrections ombudsman**, in those states that have such a position, investigates complaints that are alleged to be contrary or inconsistent with the law or department of corrections practices. These may be based on mistaken facts or irrelevant considerations, inadequately explained when reasons should have been revealed, inefficiently performed, unreasonable, unfair, or otherwise objectionable. The corrections ombudsman does not investigate when the complainant could reasonably be expected to use a different remedy or action, or if the complaint is trivial, frivolous, or not made in good faith. Ombudsman programs can serve such functions as investigating allegations, monitoring facilities, conducting research, educating the community, providing recommendations for improvement, or, if needed, bringing litigation. The ombudsman must have a familiarity with the world of corrections. This means that a person has worked in corrections, especially in institutional contexts. It is helpful if the person appointed to a corrections ombudsman is widely respected and is considered a person of good judgment. States that have such officers vary in their qualification and education requirements. A college degree is typically required. Some ombudsmen are attorneys, while in other states a law degree is not required, but the ombudsman must be particularly skilled and experienced in handling complaints. An increasing number of states are developing an office of corrections ombudsman, and, accordingly, the outlook is good for employment in this area. The salaries vary from one state to another. According to the Bureau of Labor Statistics, ombudsmen earn salaries ranging from $40,000 to $90,000.

Prison Captain

The **prison captain** is in charge of the security of most prisons. As the highest ranking uniformed officer (unless the prison has the office of a major), the role of the captain is to see that the warden's directives are being enforced in the prison and that staff are complying with these directives. The captain is also responsible to take whatever measures are necessary to prevent major incidents, such as offender physical altercations, assaults on staff, and contraband in the prison. If they occur, the job of the captain is to ensure that they are handled appropriately and to minimize the negative impact. The prison captain is responsible for developing emergency plans and to routinely conduct drills on these plans.

prison captain The corrections professional in charge of prison security.

This person has been in corrections for a number of years, has been promoted from correctional officer to sergeant, to lieutenant, and finally to captain. He or she knows the institution, is highly respected, is trusted by the warden as well as other staff, and has showed time after time that he or she is able to manage the security of the facility. The main quality desired is leadership as well as knowledge of the security of the facility.

Applicants start out as correctional officers and work through the ranks. Salaries and earnings vary from state to state but may be in the range of $100,000 per year.

Assistant Warden for Programming

The **assistant warden for programming** is responsible for all the services and programs afforded to inmates, such as recreation, chaplaincy, education, vocational programs, visitation, and pre-release. This person may be responsible for establishing programming. For example, Cathy Fontenot, the assistant warden for programming for the Louisiana State Penitentiary, is responsible for hospice, the on-site accredited branch of the New Orleans Baptist Theological Seminary college degree program, and the world-famous Angola Prison Rodeo and Art and Craft Festival. In addition, she was responsible for providing emergency housing for thousands of inmates evacuated from historic hurricanes and floods.

assistant warden for programming The corrections professional responsible for all the services and programs afforded to inmates, such as recreation, chaplaincy, education, vocational programs, visitation, and prerelease.

The assistant warden for programming is typically someone who has promoted through the ranks, beginning perhaps as a caseworker. He or she has earned the respect of other corrections staff, as well as the trust of the warden. Communication skills must be strong, and the assistant warden must be interested in providing helpful services to inmates.

The position generally requires a college degree, most likely in the areas of social work, sociology, criminology, or psychology. This job classification, along with the assistant warden for custody, reports to the warden and is expected to support the warden's mission and directives.

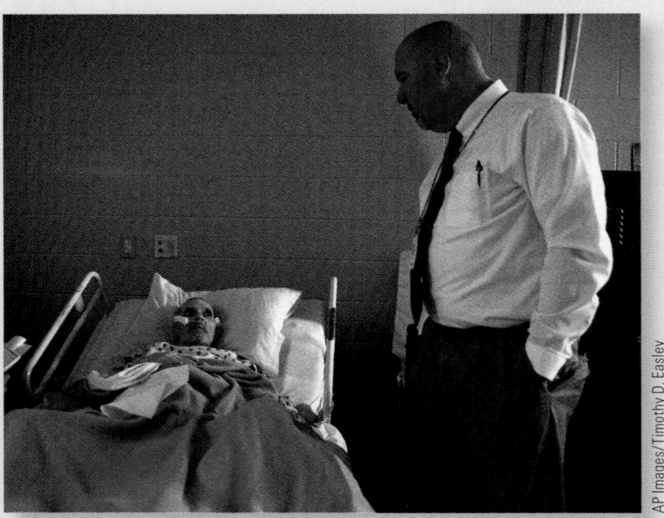

A warden's job involves keeping institutions within budgetary parameters. On April 17, 2014, Warden Clark Taylor speaks with Patrick O'Hara, an inmate at the Kentucky State Reformatory in LaGrange. It costs Kentucky $3.3 million a year to care for 50 elderly inmates who can't take care of themselves, a burden the state is preparing to shift to the federal government.

Warden

The **prison warden** is in charge of operating federal, state, or private prisons, hiring staff, managing the budget, and maintaining a secure institution. The warden exercises direct supervisory authority over immediate subordinates so that applicable plans are administered. The effective warden provides opportunities for inmates to improve themselves and to earn reasonable compensation for their participation in constructive programs and assignments. The warden organizes, plans, and implements a full range of structured institution systems of inmate accountability and discipline consistent with established law, policies, and regulations. The superintendent of a correctional facility has the same job description, although the size of the institution may be smaller and it may be a women's facility or a minimum-security prison.

prison warden The warden is in charge of operating a federal, state, or private prison, hiring staff, managing the budget, and maintaining a secure institution.

In addition to a college education, prison wardens need exposure to all levels of prison operations. As a person is promoted to increasing levels of responsibility, it is also important to observe and learn from other corrections staff. The majority of wardens across the nation have completed some college, and many possess an advanced degree. The warden, like other correctional staff, generally begins service as a correctional officer or a correctional counselor and with effective performance is promoted through various positions, including associate or assistant wardens of operations and programs. Those who aspire to be warden in the Federal Bureau of Prisons must be willing to undergo several transfers in the process. Sometimes, wardens from one state are given positions as wardens in other states.

Salaries of prison wardens tend to vary from state to state, but wardens tend to be paid very well and the job usually comes with a number of perks. For example, in California, a prison warden's compensation package is $123,624. The Bureau of Prisons salaries for wardens are generally $100,000 or more. In Florida, prison wardens are paid salaries between $80,000 and $90,000. A salary around $80,000 seems to be the average compensation of many state systems. Moreover, the job of the warden sometimes includes a residence and a vehicle.

Director of Corrections

director or commission of corrections The corrections professional who is responsible for directing the implementation of the agency's mission and all aspects of adult corrections in that state.

The **director or commission of corrections** is responsible for directing the implementation of the agency's mission and all aspects of adult corrections in that state. The director of the Federal Bureau of Prisons is responsible for the mission of the agency in community-based facilities, federal jails, and federal correctional institutions. The director's job, whether in a state or federal agency or department, is to provide vision and leadership, direct internal and external communication, develop and direct the agency's budgets, manage policies and procedures, and direct the agency's human resources. This involves performing a number of tasks, including using management policies that encourage staff innovation, educating others regarding agency mission and services, presenting budgets, establishing priorities to direct resources, and promote and ensure delivery of staff training programs. Good writing and speaking skills as well as the ability to handle complex managerial decisions are compulsory. In addition to these personal attributes, the observations of others who are performing well in their respective correctional jobs are helpful.

The director or commissioner of corrections is appointed by the governor. Usually, he or she has had responsible positions in correctional agencies before being appointed director. It is not unusual for someone in this position to have served as assistant or associate director. The person appointed to this position today almost always has a B.A. and many have gone on to earn an M.A.

There are only 50 of these jobs across the nation (one per state), and the director's job is not secure, as he or she serves at the appointment of the governor. If the department has problems that would embarrass the governor, this could put the director's job in jeopardy. If members of the legislature have problems with the director, this could persuade the director that it is time for a change. Or if a new governor is elected, he or she may appoint another director. For these and other reasons, directors usually stay only two or three years at the job. Yet this is a highly desired corrections position. Directors are well paid. Many earn more than $100,000 a year and salaries can range up to $200,000 in some states. In addition, the Federal Bureau of Prisons director who has completed 20 years of service can retire at age 50.

THINKING
LIKE A CORRECTIONS PROFESSIONAL

You have been appointed head of the correctional academy. At the opening exercise of the academy, you reveal what you feel are important themes for a corrections career. The head of corrections wants you to write a position paper on how you would approach training professional executives. Here are your themes! In your paper, address why each is important.

- Treat inmates with dignity and respect.
- Walk in integrity, both on and off the job.
- Pursue excellence in the facility.
- Maintain cleanliness and orderliness in the facility.
- Ensure as much as possible safety for both inmates and staff.
- Pursue proactive leadership in all that you do.
- Hold up the goal of professionalism in all that you do.

INTERNSHIPS IN CORRECTIONS

LO5 Articulate why an internship in corrections makes sense to the student who is interested in a corrections career

Internships are an excellent way to discover if a specific area of criminal justice is a good fit for you.[14] An internship is an opportunity to receive supervised, practical, on-the-job training in a specific area. Many correctional agencies and institutions offer internships, usually without pay, for those interested in learning about a specific area of employment while acquiring skills that make them more employable in that area. Often, individuals who complete an internship with a specific agency or institution might be hired after their formal education is complete. Or, conversely, the intern or the department may find that the fit is not good, and both are spared a difficult situation.

In *Internships for Dummies*, Craig Donovan and Jim Garnett describe two general kinds of interns: passive and active. Passive interns are those who "wait for opportunities to come to them … wait until an internship falls into their lap," whereas active interns take responsibility for their own internship—for their own work and learning and, ultimately, for their own future.[15]

Just as there are two basic types of interns, so too are there two types of internships. One is a *survey internship*; the other is a *practical internship*. Although intended for different people at different times of their careers, both become exceptionally important.

The survey internship is a relatively short-term experience during which the intern, most often a student, is permitted to observe work being done and ask questions pertinent to the profession and requisite tasks. It is a passive experience, as the intern does not actually participate in any work activities but merely watches them being done. Nonetheless, this kind of internship provides an excellent opportunity to learn about a job through observation and inquiry.

In criminal justice, a survey internship involves visiting the various divisions of a particular agency to observe others completing their jobs. For example, a student might sit in the dispatch center and see how incoming calls are handled and personnel dispatched. Later the student may observe jail operations, watch evidence technicians, sit with the administrative division, and even take a ride-along with a patrol unit. The result of such an experience is to see firsthand what really occurs in such an agency and how it differs from any preconceived notions the student may have.

The practical internship differs from the survey experience because, as the name implies, actual experience is the goal. The practical internship allows students to learn through hands-on involvement. These experiences tend to be longer than survey internships and can last months or more. Practical internships in correction can involve any number of activities, from entry-level tasks to actually working side by side with officers or other personnel. These experiences are not just for people exploring a career path or new to the field. It is not uncommon for more senior practitioners to participate in a practical internship with another agency that does things differently or specializes in something their home agency does not. It is also a way to cross-train employees and keep superiors in touch with the daily functions of their subordinates.

Locating Internship Opportunities

Although internships may be advertised, they are usually not advertised the way job listings are posted. You need a strategy to know where to find these opportunities. Resources are available that compile tens of thousands of internship sites along with general information about them. Princeton Review's *The Internship Bible* claims to offer "100,000 opportunities to launch your career," and *Peterson's Internships* provides almost 50,000 paid and unpaid internships.[16] A quick Internet search for internships in corrections will also provide a wealth of resources, such as the American Correctional Association (ACA), which offers many student internship opportunities, as well as a number of state correctional agencies.

One corrections professional who knows the value of internships is Laura E. Bedard, currently warden at Graceville Correctional Facility in Florida. She began her work in corrections as a jail administrator in 1984. She has served on

VOICES ACROSS THE PROFESSION

Laura E. Bedard
Warden, Graceville Correctional Facility, Florida

We all know that internships are an important part of a college education. Some fields, like nursing and education, require internships in order to complete a degree. I have been involved with student interns for most of my professional career. Heck, I was an intern way back when.

The field of corrections, however, has been slow to come around. Traditionally, corrections has been a closed career field. You got into the business because it was a family tradition or you knew someone in the field. Student internships are a way for the field of corrections to expand.

One common misconception is that interns are just volunteers who happen to be in college. This is far from the truth. The difference between student interns and civilian volunteers is well defined. Student interns are sponsored by a college or university, earn college credit for their experiences, are time limited (generally a semester in length), and have a faculty sponsor to help guide them through the process. Volunteers are just that—volunteers.

Internships are important for a number of reasons. First, they provide learning opportunities for the student. But they also provide opportunities for us in the field. Interns bring the newest, most innovative information to the field placement. Since they are active in their studies, the students are exposed to information that we as professionals might not have readily available. At the department, we established a "think tank" of the brightest graduate students. Their job was to think of ideas to implement and to review and develop different methods to utilize.

Internships allow us to prescreen potential employees. Generally, an intern works full time for 12 to 15 weeks. This gives us in the field the opportunity to observe their work ethic and get to know them prior to hiring.

Internships also allow us to get certain jobs or projects done that we might not otherwise be able to do. I know it sounds ironic, but when I was with the Department of Corrections, we had interns design and develop the professional internship program for the agency. I have used interns to work with inmates on mural projects, develop and implement family reading programs, and provide supervised mental health groups for inmates. If you think about the operation of a prison, interns can be used in a variety of settings. Interns from the business field could assist in our business office; nursing interns could be utilized in the medical department, hospitality interns could be used in food service, and social work interns can be utilized to assist with reentry initiatives. The possibilities are limited only by your imagination! Open your minds and open your facilities to allow interns into our field. I know we'll be better for it.

the administrative faculty for the College of Criminology at Florida State University for 17 years. In 2005, she became the first female deputy secretary of the Florida Department of Corrections. There she was responsible for 27,000 state employees and over 200,000 offenders in the third largest correctional system in the country. She also served as the warden at the Eden Detention Center in Texas. Bedard has published and lectured worldwide on a number of corrections-related topics, including women in prison, mental health issues, and correctional leadership. In the Voices Across the Profession feature, Warden Bedard discusses the value of correctional internships.[17]

School-Related Internships

Many, if not most, schools have relationships with agencies that provide internships. Some programs are formally structured, with internships taking the format of actual courses for which the student receives credit. Other programs offer rather informal or unstructured internship opportunities where students receive no credit but are afforded an invaluable "inside look" at a career they are considering. Some school-coordinated internships are optional, most likely providing elective credits, whereas other internships are required. An example of this is a criminal justice program that requires students to complete 115 hours of interning at a social service agency, the primary purpose being to learn about resources available to criminal justice practitioners.

In addition to speaking with an instructor or program director, be sure you know when agencies may have recruiters on campus to engage potential interns. These people are often asked to speak to classes, attend criminal justice/law enforcement club meetings, and staff display tables at job fairs. If these individuals offer you their card or provide their contact information, *keep it and follow up.* And never forget networking with other students who may currently be interning, working, or otherwise know of opportunities. It *always* pays to ask.

Credit versus Compensation

Some interns receive college credit and some actually get paid. And some are fortunate enough to get both. In some instances it can be the student's choice. Be clear what a particular internship offers and realize that interns are seldom afforded the opportunity to negotiate placement terms.

Start Early and Stay Organized

Internships, especially in the criminal justice field, require that you begin your search well before you are actually interested in beginning. The best internships require long-range planning, sometimes at least a year or more in advance. Many agencies require some sort of background check, so give yourself plenty of lead time when exploring internship options.

Because many people will be looking for a limited number of internships, keep a file of contacts, just as you should as part of your job-seeking strategy, so you have a ready networking list to use now and in the future. In addition to the obvious benefits of internships, the process of seeking such an experience is great, too, because of the similarities to job seeking. It is all about developing a strategy to achieve what you want ... and part of that strategy is to recognize the necessary time constraints.

Begin compiling a list of the types of work you are interested in. These can be general positions, such as probation officer, correctional officer, etc. Next, consider which jurisdictional level(s) are most appealing to you right now (federal, state, local) and explore the reasons you feel this way.

CRITICAL THINKING

Recognizing that an internship provides many opportunities to network, how would you go about taking full advantage of this? LO5

Making the Most of the Experience

Whether a survey or practical internship, for credit or not, you want to make the most of the experience. Not only do you want to gain as much information as possible, but you want to take full advantage of the networking opportunities to develop contacts that may serve your future job-search efforts. You will be meeting people actively engaged in the profession of interest, many of whom may be potential points of contact when you are ready to seek employment. Furthermore, if you participate in an internship long enough, some individuals will likely readily allow you to list them as a reference. You may even find a mentor, someone who will be supportive of and helpful to you throughout your job-seeking efforts, or even your career.

It is generally helpful, when embarking on a new experience, to know a little of what to expect. A criminal justice internship is:

- An opportunity to get real exposure to a variety of agencies in the local criminal justice community
- A chance to meet professionals in the field who can advocate for your future employment
- An opportunity to explore a specific profession prior to committing yourself to it in a full-time capacity
- An appointment as a representative and ambassador of your academic institution
- A privilege
- An opportunity to broaden your educational experience with some real practical experience
- A huge responsibility—the vast majority of which falls upon the student
- Unpaid (usually)
- To be set up far in advance of starting, usually five to ten weeks before the internship semester begins
- To be completed by individuals who have declared criminal justice as their major and are of junior or senior standing
- To be granted at the complete and mutual discretion of the internship coordinator and the participating agency
- For students who have demonstrated adequate academic performance, and are in good academic standing with the department, any faculty committees, and the college/university

A criminal justice internship is not:

- To be taken for granted
- A filler because you can't find a class that you like
- Something to do because you can't think of anything else to do
- A "fast-track" to guaranteed post-graduation employment
- A blow-off course
- A right as a student (see "privilege" above)
- Required
- A guaranteed "A"—students are assessed as stringently as in most other courses in the department
- To be done at an agency or business where you already work or have worked in the past
- For students who have any type of criminal history in their past (or present)—this would include outstanding traffic violations and other minor infractions that have turned into warrants

Some may think the worst thing to have happen with an internship is to select one that doesn't produce the anticipated results, whether that is a good grade, a strong letter of recommendation, or a solid job offer. Wrong. The worst thing is to leave on a bad note—one that could haunt you during your future job-seeking efforts.

SUMMARY

LO1 Discuss how far professionalism has brought corrections

It was not that long ago that corrections was considered to still be in the "dark ages," but corrections has come a long way in terms of professionalism in the past ten years or so. Staff development and training, an emphasis on ethics and integrity, and the implementation of standards and accreditation have contributed to the professionalism of corrections.

LO2 Define professionalism and the need for it in corrections

Corrections professionals undertake a specialized set of tasks and complete them, behave passionately in what they do, never compromise their standards or values, and care about clients, even if they happen to be criminal clients. Professionals are committed to the organization and have the objective of obtaining the highest standard of excellence.

LO3 Identify why corrections is a promising career

In corrections it is possible to make a difference in offenders' lives. The opportunities for advancement are great. In most jurisdictions, corrections jobs offer a good salary package, including salary, health insurance, and pension plan. Corrections further has an encouraging movement of professionalism.

LO4 Describe the various career paths in corrections

There are several career paths in corrections. The first is one in community-based corrections. This involves such jobs as probation officer, treatment specialist, parole officer, residential counselor, drug counselor, forensic psychologist, and administrators in probation, parole, and residential facilities. The second career path is jails and detention facilities. The jail correctional officer and the jail administrator are the two main jobs in the jail. The third career path is made up of those who work in institutional corrections, including the correctional officer, correctional counselor, corrections ombudsman, corrections captain, assistant warden for programming, warden, and director or commissioner of corrections. Other corrections paths include juvenile corrections and other jobs in corrections, such as recreation, school and vocational shops, and business office support staff.

LO5 Articulate why an internship in corrections makes sense to the student who is interested in a corrections career

A corrections internship is an excellent way to accomplish several goals. It helps you decide if corrections is a good career choice for you and provides hands-on experience on the job. It enables you to become known by those who work in the agency, which might be helpful when a job search is pursued, and it makes a positive impression on your résumé. The internship can be particularly helpful for the networking experience it provides. While internships vary from college credit to no credit, from compensation to no compensation, from the length of time they last—a summer, one semester, two semesters, or even longer—they all provide a positive experience for the student.

CRITICAL THINKING QUESTIONS

1. Is it important where you start out in corrections (e.g., minimum security or maximum security prison, or treatment or security staff)?
2. What advantages would community-based corrections have over working in a prison? What disadvantages?
3. How will you know when it is time to move to a new position?
4. How do you decide whether to work for the Federal Bureau of Prisons, state corrections, or a private agency?
5. How it possible to make a difference as a probation officer, a parole officer, or an administrator in a correctional institution?

NOTES

1. PAWS Training Academy, http://pawstrainingcenters.com/paws-training-academy/about/faculty/instructors/cece-miller/ (accessed August 2014).
2. Federal Bureau of Prisons press release, "Cece Miller Finds Purpose in Training Dogs and Helping People," April 17, 2014, http://www.legistorm.com/stormfeed/view_rss/402972/organization/95552.html (accessed August 2014).
3. paws4people, http://paws4people.org/cece-miller/ (accessed August 2014).
4. American Correctional Association, http://www.aca.org (accessed July 2014).
5. Spokesperson for the American Correctional Association reported this information in 2012.
6. Rose Johnson, "Topics of Professionalism in the Workplace," http://smallbusiness.chron.com/topics-professionalism-workplace-25820.html (accessed July 2014).
7. Gene Atherton, "The Professionalism and Safety Connection," Corrections.com, http://www.corrections.com/news/article/18532 (accessed July 2014).
8. Interviewed in 2012.

9. Conrad said this to one of the authors on a number of occasions; it can also be found throughout his publications.
10. Bureau of Labor Statistics, Occupational Outlook Handbook, "Correctional Officers," http://www.bls.gov/ooh/protective-service/mobile/correctional-officers.htm (accessed July 2014).
11. Ibid.
12. Ibid.
13. Ibid.
14. This section was adapted from J. Scott Harr and Kären M. Hess, *Careers in Criminal Justice and Related Fields* (Belmont, CA: Wadsworth, Cengage Learning, 2010). The authors appreciate their willingness to let us use their material.
15. Craig P. Donovan and Jim Garnett, *Internships for Dummies* (New York: Lifestyle Paperbacks, 2001).
16. Princeton Review, *The Internship Bible*, 10th ed. (Princeton, NJ: Princeton University Press, 2005).
17. Laura E. Bedard, "Internships in Corrections: Why You Need a Summer Intern," CorrectionsOne.com, July 11, 2011, http://www.correctionsone.com/corrections-jobs/articles/3952892-Internships-in-corrections-Why-you-need-a-summer-intern/ (accessed August 2014).

GLOSSARY

abolitionist arguments Those who oppose the death penalty base their arguments on several positions, including the moral issue, the constitutional issue, and the pragmatic issues.

administrative-control model A model that contends that the management style of the prison has influence over what takes place in inmate culture.

aftercare The supervision of juveniles who are released from correctional institutions so that they can make an optimal adjustment to community living. Also, the status of a juvenile conditionally released from a treatment or confinement facility and placed under supervision in the community.

aggravation When a jury finds a first-degree murder conviction on a defendant at the end of the trial phase, the defendant is then tried in a second phase, referred to as the penalty phase. The task of the prosecution is to establish that the sentence should be death because the aggravating causes in the case exceed mitigating causes.

anger management programs Programs designed to help inmates manage their anger, especially in interpersonal relations.

argot A form of slang inmates use in prison settings to express how they feel.

Ashurst-Sumners Act The 1935 Ashurst-Sumners Act was the product of cooperation between organized labor and business, and stemmed from the competition between the prisons and the free market.

assistant warden for programming The corrections professional responsible for all the services and programs afforded to inmates, such as recreation, chaplaincy, education, vocational programs, visitation, and prerelease.

Auburn cellblock An austere prison setting in Auburn, New York, in which inmates were made to endure great suffering.

Auburn silent system A system first used in the prison in Auburn, New York, that demanded silence from all prisoners at all times, even when they were eating or working together.

bail bond The means, financial or property, used to release a defendant from jail.

bail bondsman Bonding agents lend money for a fee to people who cannot make bail. They normally charge a percentage of the bail amount.

Bail Reform Act of 1966 Federal legislation that further spurred the bail reform movement by urging pretrial release for all noncapital cases unless the defendant appeared unlikely to return to court.

Bail Reform Act of 1984 This federal act formalized preventive detention provisions for those considered dangerous or unlikely to return to court.

Beccaria, Cesare Bonesana One of the founders of the classical school of criminology, who advocated that punishment should be public, immediate, and necessary.

behavior modification A technique in which rewards or punishments are used to alter or change a person's behavior.

bench, or unsupervised, probation A type of probation in which probationers are not subject to supervision.

Bentham, Jeremy One of the founders of the classical school of criminology, who believed that the law should accomplish the utilitarian purpose of the protection of society.

Big House A type of large fortress-like prison that dominated corrections in the early part of the twentieth century.

Bill of Rights The name given to the first 10 amendments to the U.S. Constitution, which are looked upon as fundamentally important in the processing of criminal defendants.

blameworthy The law defines that a person is criminally liable for his or her behavior.

blended sentencing The imposition of juvenile and/or adult correctional sanctions on serious and violent juvenile offenders who have been adjudicated in juvenile court or convicted in criminal court.

booking The process of admitting an arrestee or sentenced misdemeanant to jail.

boot camp A military-style facility used as an alternative to prison in order to deal with prison crowding and public demands for severe treatment.

bridewells Houses of corrections run by local authorities to teach habits of industry to vagrants and idlers.

Brockway, Zebulon Superintendent of the Elmira Reformatory in New York.

butch The dominant, or male, role in a homosexual relationship in the prison society.

campus design Open prison design that allows some freedom of movement; the units of the prison are housed in a complex of buildings surrounded by a fence.

case law The body of judicial precedent that is built on legal reasoning and previous interpretations of statutory laws.

civil forfeiture To confiscate property used in law violations and remove the illegally gained profits from violators.

Clemmer, Donald Known for his research at Southern Illinois Penitentiary; coined the term *prisonization*, which defines how inmates learn to adapt to prison while taking on the prison culture.

Code of Hammurabi Law code issued during the reign of Hammurabi of Babylon. The law of *lex talionis* makes its appearance in this code, one of the first comprehensive views of the law.

cognitive-behavior therapy (CBT) Therapy based on the assumption that the foundations for criminal behavior are dysfunctional patterns of thinking.

Cognitive Thinking Skills Program (CTSP) A cognitive-behavioral intervention, developed by Ross and Fabiano, designed to improve offenders' thinking processes.

community corrections act (CCA) State-based acts through which local governments that participate receive subsidies for diverting minor offenders from state prisons.

community service order A court order that requires an offender to perform a certain number of work hours at a private nonprofit or government agency.

community treatment Treatment provided to juveniles in the community versus an institutional context.

concurrent sentences Two or more sentences imposed at the same time and served simultaneously.

conjugal visits A visit lasting one or two days during which prisoners can enjoy private visitation with their families.

consecutive sentences Two or more sentences imposed at the same time and served one after the other.

contraband Unauthorized materials possessed by prisoners.

correctional counselor The chief treatment officer in many correctional institutions, both male and female.

Correctional Services Corp. v. Malesko Defines the protections and rights of inmates in private corporations' facilities.

corrections The institutions and methods that society uses to correct, control, and change the behavior of convicted offenders.

corrections ombudsman An ombudsman (a Swedish word that means "representative") is a person or body that protects citizens against governmental abuses.

courtyard design A prison design in which corridors surround a courtyard. Housing, educational, vocational, recreational, prison industry, and dining areas face the courtyard.

criminal forfeiture Following conviction, offenders must relinquish assets related to the offense.

Crofton, Walter Prison reformer who developed the Irish mark system, which eventually spread to the United States and influenced the development of parole.

cruel and unusual punishment Punishment that involves torture or the infliction of unnecessary and wanton pain.

day fine A fine that represents one day of income for the defendant.

day reporting center (DRC) A facility where an offender, usually on probation, must report every day to participate in counseling, social skills training, and other rehabilitative activities.

death-qualified jury During *voir dire*, any person opposed to capital punishment may be dropped from the jury pool.

deathwatch The period, generally 24 to 48 hours, before the execution; usually supervised by a team of correctional officers.

deferred prosecution programs Those referred to these programs benefit from having their charges dropped upon their successful completion.

deferred sentence A sentence that delays conviction on a guilty plea until the sentenced offender has successfully served his or her probation term.

deprivation model A model that views the losses experienced by an inmate during incarceration as one of the costs of imprisonment.

de Secondat, Charles-Louis, Baron de Montesquieu One of the founders of the classical school of criminology, who advocated the moderation of punishment.

determinate sentence Sentencing that imposes a sentence for a definite term. Its main forms are flat-time sentences, mandatory sentences, and presumptive sentences.

director or commissioner of corrections The corrections professional who is responsible for directing the implementation of the agency's mission and all aspects of adult corrections in that state.

direct-supervision jail In the new-generation jail, direct supervision is when the corrections officers' station is placed within the inmates' living area or pod and, as a result, the officer can see and speak with inmates.

discretionary parole The decision to release inmates is made by a parole board.

disenfranchisement laws Civil disabilities facing parolees when they return to the community.

drug courts Courts designed for nonviolent offenders with substance abuse problems who require integrated sanctions and services such as mandatory drug testing, substance abuse treatment, supervised release, and parole.

Eastern State Penitentiary A fortress-like prison in Philadelphia consisting of seven wings radiating from a control hub. Prisoners were kept in solitary confinement. It became a model for prisoners in several European countries.

Eighth Amendment Excessive bail shall not be required, nor excessive fines imposed, nor cruel and unusual punishments inflicted.

electronic monitoring (EM) The use of electronic equipment to verify that an offender is at home or in a community correctional center during specified hours.

equity goal of punishment That offenders usually gain from criminal violations makes it seem just and right that they repay society and victims for losses, expenses, and damages that result from their crimes.

evidence-based programs This approach is an analysis of programs with scientifically approved methods to discover what works with which offenders.

execution team Those who carry out the execution.

external classification system Determines the level of security and control needed for the incoming prison population.

family detention centers Minimum-security residential facilities that provide schooling for children, recreational activities, and access to religious services.

family group homes Group homes that are run by a family rather than by a professional staff.

federal sentencing guidelines These guidelines were adopted by Congress and until the U.S. Supreme Court ruled otherwise were to be binding on federal judges.

femme The docile, or female, role in a homosexual relationship in the prison society.

fictive families A grouping of unrelated individuals who have assumed the traditional family roles of mother, father, grandparents, and so on.

financial restitution Payment of a sum of money by an offender either to the victim or to a public fund for victims of crime.

fine A sanction that requires convicted offenders to pay a specified sum of money.

First Amendment Congress shall make no law respecting an establishment of religion, or prohibiting the free exercise thereof; or abridging the freedom of speech, or of the press; or the right of the people peaceably to assemble, and to petition the government for a redress of grievances.

First Correctional Congress A congress held in Cincinnati in 1870 to present progressive ideas about corrections, which resulted in the formulation of the Declaration of Principles.

first-generation jail Focuses on staff providing linear/intermittent surveillance of inmates, which they do by patrolling the corridors and observing inmates in their cells.

forfeiture Involves the government seizing property that was derived from or used in criminal activity.

Fourteenth Amendment [*Section 1*] All persons born or naturalized in the United States, and subject to the jurisdiction thereof, are citizens of the United States and of the State wherein they reside. No State shall make or enforce any law which shall abridge the privileges or immunities of citizens of the United States; nor shall any State deprive any person of life, liberty, or property, without due process of law; nor deny to any person within its jurisdiction the equal protection of the laws.

Fourth Amendment The right of the people to be secure in their persons, houses, papers, and effects, against unreasonable searches and seizures, shall not be violated, and no warrants shall issue but upon probable cause, supported by oath and affirmation, and particularly describing the place to be searched, and the persons or things to be seized.

Fry, Elizabeth Quaker who brought reform to women confined in prison.

Furman v. Georgia U.S. Supreme Court decision that declared the death penalty unconstitutional.

general deterrent effect The idea that punishing one person for his or her criminal acts will discourage others from committing similar acts.

Giallombardo Classic study that identified that women were involved in fictive families in adapting to imprisonment.

Gill, Howard B. Developed the "scamp" system at the Norfolk Prison colony in Virginia.

global positioning system (GPS) technology This has affected EM technology by the transmitter making continuous calls to a reporting station that updates the offender's location.

good time A deduction of time awarded to inmates for good behavior.

Gregg v. Georgia U.S. Supreme Court decision that superseded *Furman v. Georgia* and declared the death penalty constitutional if certain conditions are met.

grievance process A formalized arrangement in which inmates can register their complaints about the conditions of their confinement.

group homes Nonsecure residences that provide counseling, education, job training, and family living.

guilt/innocence phase In a capital trial, the phase in which the jury determines whether the accused is guilty or not guilty of the capital offense for which he or she is charged.

habeas corpus A Latin expression meaning "you have the body." A writ of *habeas corpus* brings a person before a court or judge to determine the legality of his or her restraint in custody.

halfway house Prerelease centers for inmates and intermediate sanctions for probationers, they include probation centers, restitution centers, county work-release centers, and therapeutic communities.

hands-off doctrine The idea that persons sentenced to prison are not entitled to the same constitutional protections they enjoyed before conviction.

Hawes-Cooper Act The Hawes-Cooper Act was passed on January 19, 1929, and mandated that prison-made goods and merchandise transported from one state to another were to be subject to the existing laws of the importing state.

Hefferman Classic study that found the presence of fictive families in women's adaptation to prison life.

home confinement program The federal courts use this program with both postsentence offenders and with pretrial defenders.

house arrest A court-imposed sentence that orders an offender to remain confined in his or her residence for the duration or remainder of the sentence.

houses of corrections Workhouses where vagrants were forced to work to achieve the purposes of discipline and punishment.

Howard, John English sheriff who advocated jail reform.

Human Rights Watch An international nongovernmental organization that is concerned with the rights of individuals, such as prisoners.

importation model A model that suggests that the influences prisoners bring into the prison affect their process of imprisonment.

incapacitation Isolating offenders to protect society.

indeterminate sentence Sentence that permits early release from a correctional institution after the offender has served a required minimum portion of his or her sentence.

inmate code An unwritten but powerful code regulating inmates' behavior; inmates codes are functional to both inmates and prison administrators because they tend to promote order within the walls.

inmate disturbance A disturbance, either violent or nonviolent, that brings disruption or even closes down the prison.

Innocence Projects These projects, found in a number of states, provide free legal assistance for those cases in which question remains regarding the legality of their convictions.

insight-based therapy Typically involves treatment designed to encourage communication of conflicts and insight into problems, with the goal being relief of symptoms, changes in behavior, and personality growth.

institutional treatment facility A correctional institution that provides long-term treatment for juveniles.

intensive probation Supervision that is far stricter than standard probationary supervision.

intensive supervision parole (ISP) More extensive supervision than is given for most parolees.

intermediate sanctions These forms of community sentencing include probation plus a variety of add-ons that range from fines to boot camps.

internal affairs investigator A corrections professional whose duties include identifying individual involvement by inmates, correctional personnel, or public citizens that is suspected of criminal infractions of an administrative, civil, or criminal nature.

internal classification system Determines the cell or housing unit where inmates will be housed as well as facility programs to which they are assigned.

Irish mark system A system in which prisoners received "marks of commendation" for completing assigned tasks. They could use the marks to buy food and clothing. Prisoners who accumulated enough marks received a ticket-of-leave.

jail A facility that is authorized to hold pretrial detainees and sentenced misdemeanants for periods longer than 48 hours.

jail administrator Corrections professional who is responsible for managing staff and generating programs within the local jail.

jailhouse lawyers Name given to inmates who develop an expertise in criminal law and help other inmates in preparing their cases.

jail officer Corrections professionals who have the responsibility of overseeing detainees and those who have been convicted of a crime and are sentenced to serve time in jail. They maintain security and inmate accountability to prevent assaults, disturbances, and escapes.

judicial reprieve Permitted judges to suspend judgment until offenders could seek a pardon or gather new evidence.

judicial waiver The procedure of relinquishing the processing of a particular juvenile case in adult criminal court, also known as certifying or binding over to the adult court.

just deserts Punishment that is commensurate with the seriousness of the offense or the harm done.

juvenile delinquent An underage minor who engages in antisocial activities that are defined as criminal behavior by the state's legal code.

Juvenile Justice Standards Project A comprehensive set of guidelines for juvenile offenders, created by the Institute of Judicial Administration and the American Bar Association, that based sentencing on the seriousness of the crime rather than on the needs of the youth.

juvenile justice system A system established over 100 years ago to provide for the care of law-violating youth.

kinship networks A type of prison socialization in which women deal with incarceration by becoming part of make-believe families.

landmark decision When a precedent establishes an important principle, or represents a change or new law.

lethal injection The predominant method of execution, used in 35 states and by the federal government.

Maconochie, Alexander Served as director of the prison colony in Australia and set up the "mark" system.

Madrid v. Gomez The judge in this case found that staff at the Pelican Bay Prison in California had used excessive and unnecessary force on inmates.

mandatory minimum sentence The imposition of sentences required by statute for those convicted of a particular crime with specific circumstances, such as selling drugs to a minor close to a school or robbery with a firearm.

mandatory parole release Inmate is released on parole when the unserved portion of the maximum prison term equals good time.

Manhattan Bail Project A Vera Institute of Justice program that provided ROR release for eligible defendants, which influenced later bail reform movements.

mass incarceration A term given to the high rates of incarceration in the United States.

maximum-security prison A prison in which complete control of any and all prisoners can be applied at any time.

McCleskey v. Kemp The Supreme Court ruled that race did not enter into the decision of the Georgia court and that there was no evidence of racial bias.

medical model The idea that criminality is a sickness that can be cured through psychological intervention.

medium-security prison A prison with single or double fencing, guarded towers or closed-circuit television monitoring, sallyport entrances, and zonal security systems to control inmate movement within the institution.

Megan's Law Named for Megan Kanka, a seven-year-old girl from New Jersey who was sexually assaulted and murdered in 1994 by a neighbor who, unknown to the victim's family, had been previously convicted for sex offenses against children. Megan's Laws are state and federal statutes that require convicted sex offenders to register with local police and to notify law enforcement authorities whenever they move to a new location. The statutes establish a notification process to provide information about sex offenders to law enforcement agencies and, when appropriate, to the public. The type of notification is based on an evaluation of the risk to the community from a particular offender.

minimization of system penetration A diversion whose purpose is to minimize the offender's contact with the justice process as much as possible.

minimum-security prison A prison with relaxed perimeter security, sometimes without fences or any other means of external security.

mitigation During the penalty phase of the jury proceedings, the defense attempts to establish that there are greater mitigating causes than aggravating causes and the jury should bring in a recommendation for less than death (usually for life imprisonment without the possibility of parole).

the mix Owen's term for women's involvement in problematic prison behaviors and activities.

monastic confinement Prisons established by the Church in the Middle Ages for those laity involved in offensive acts, such as incest and magic.

Morrissey v. Brewer Supreme Court ruled on procedures for revocation of parole.

needs assessment Attempts to offer treatment-relevant information, such as social adjustment, hygiene, and level of family support.

new-generation jail A facility with a podular architectural design that emphasizes the interaction of inmates and staff.

new penology A new approach in probation and other community-based corrections that focuses more on administrative control and regulation than on treatment and offering services.

no-frills policy Inmates will receive the bare minimum of food, services and programs, and medical care required by law.

nolle prosequi A formal entry in the record of the court indicating that the prosecutor does not intend to proceed any further in this case.

nonlegal factors in sentencing These include contextual factors, social class, gender, race, age, and victim characteristics.

nonresidential programs Programs for youthful offenders that usually do not confine them overnight.

OmniView Total Supervision (OVTS) An incarceration facility that has a centrally placed, high-strength mirrored glass control center with a panoramic view that provides 100 percent surveillance of the entire facility.

parens patriae A medieval English doctrine that sanctioned the right of the Crown to intervene in natural family relations whenever a child's welfare was threatened.

parole The conditional release from confinement of an offender serving an indeterminate sentence.

parole board An official panel that determines whether an inmate serving an indeterminate sentence is ready for parole.

parole guidelines Actuarial devices predicting the risk of recidivism based on information about the offender and the crime.

parole officer Parole officers help identify offenders who are eligible for conditional release from prison and, once they are released, work with offenders and monitor their postrelease activities.

penal harm A current movement that believes the purpose of corrections is to punish offenders as severely as possible.

penitentiary A prison in which persons found guilty of a felony are isolated from normal society.

Pennsylvania model A penal system based on the belief that most prisoners would benefit from the experience of incarceration.

percentage bail Defendants deposit about 10 percent of the bail amount with the court clerk.

presentence investigation (PSI) An investigation whose main purposes are to help the court decide whether to grant probation, to determine the conditions of probation, to determine the length of the sentence, and to decide on community-based or institutional placement for the defendant.

presumptive sentencing Sentencing in which the legislature sets penalties for criminal acts.

pretrial officer Professional who investigates an offender's background by interviewing detainees, verifying alleged offenses, and communicating with various agencies and officials as well as friends, family, and employers of detainees, in order to determine whether the offender can remain in the community.

pretrial release Release from jail or a pretrial detention center pending adjudication of the case.

preventive detention Retaining in jail defendants who are deemed dangerous or likely to commit crimes while awaiting trial.

principle of least eligibility States that prisoners should receive no better services than the general public receives. It means that the least advantaged in society should have a better life than do prisoners.

prison captain The corrections professional in charge of prison security.

prison classification A method of assessing inmate risks and needs that balances the security concerns of the institution with treatment needs of the individual.

prison culture The values, norms, and attitudes that inmates form in terms of institutional survival.

prison gang A group of inmates who are bound together by mutual interests, have identifiable leadership, and act in concert to achieve a specific purpose that generally includes the conduct of illegal activity.

prison-industrial complex A term given to describe the multimillion-dollar prison-building boom in which powerful corporate interest groups, large businesses, and politicians join together to profit from the burgeoning corrections industry.

prisonization The process by which inmates learn and internalize the customs and culture of prison.

Prison Litigation Reform Act (PLRA) Passed by Congress in 1996, this act limits the ability of inmates to complain about conditions of confinement and to allege violations of their constitutional rights.

Prison Rape Elimination Act (PREA) A program dedicated to collecting national prison rape statistics, data, and conducting research; a program dedicated to the dissemination of information and procedures for combating prison rape; a program to assist in funding state programs.

prison riot Collective response of inmates that is violent, in which they strike out against what they consider unfair prison conditions.

prison violence Can vary from riots to staff assaults, inmate assaults, staff assaults of inmates, or self-inflicted violence.

prison warden The warden is in charge of operating a federal, state, or private prison, hiring staff, managing the budget, and maintaining a secure institution.

proactive warden An approach to prison management that is focused on anticipating problems before they occur.

probation A form of punishment that permits a convicted offender to remain in the community, under the supervision of a probation officer and subject to certain conditions set by the court.

professionalism The conduct, aims, or qualities that characterize or make a profession or professional person.

protective custody A form of segregation, not for punishment but intended to isolate potential victims from predators.

punishment phase In a capital trial, the phase in which the jury determines whether the person will be sentenced to death or life in prison.

racial disparity in sentencing An actual pattern of racial discrimination in sentencing.

radial design In this wheel-shaped configuration, corridors radiate like spokes from a control center at the hub.

recognizance Permitted offenders to remain free if they promised to pay their debts to the state.

reformatory model A penal system for youthful offenders featuring indeterminate sentencing and parole, classification of prisoners, educational and vocational training, and increased privileges for positive behavior.

rehabilitation Changing an offender's character, attitudes, or behavior patterns so as to diminish his or her criminal propensities.

reintegrative philosophy A correctional approach aimed at returning offenders to the community as soon as possible.

release on own recognizance (ROR) The release without bail of defendants who appear to have stable ties in the community and are a good risk to appear for trial.

residential community corrections centers Residential centers for offenders that frequently offer a last chance before an offender is sent to prison or a last chance for parole violators.

residential programs Programs conducted for the rehabilitation of youthful offenders within community-based and institutional settings.

responsivity principle Maintains that programs should consider offenders' situations as well as characteristics that may become barriers to success in a correctional program.

restorative justice Making amends to the victim or to society for the harm resulting from a criminal offense.

restraining hands doctrine Supreme Court doctrine that gave correctional administrators freedom from excessive lower court interference.

retentionist arguments Defenders of the death penalty make several arguments supporting their positions, including its deterrent value, fairness, and the idea that life imprisonment does not sufficiently protect society.

retribution Something given or demanded as repayment for wrongdoing; "getting even" for violating the social contract on which the law is based.

revocation of parole A formal procedure that takes place when a parole board, after listening to the parolee and his or her parole officer and their witnesses, decides that parole must end because the offender committed a new crime or violated the conditions of parole.

revocation of probation A violation of the rules or terms of probation or the commitment of a new crime, which may result in the offender being placed in an institution.

Richardson v. McKnight Supreme Court held that correctional officers employed by a private firm are not entitled to a qualified immunity from suit by prisoners, charging a section 1983 violation.

risk assessment Designed to predict new offenses or prison misconduct.

risk management system A correctional system that is focused more on regulating and controlling offenders than on providing treatment or services for them.

Roper v. Simmons U.S. Supreme Court decision that disallows the execution of juveniles who committed a capital crime under the age of 18.

second-generation jail Staff use remote supervision as they remain in a secure control booth surrounded by inmate pods or living areas.

Section 1983 Provides for civil action for the deprivation of their rights by an agent of government in which the plaintiff can receive punitive damages as well as the costs of the litigation.

security threat groups (STGs) The name that law enforcement and corrections officials give to groups that exhibit ganglike activity.

segregation A punishment unit in which inmates are separated from other inmates and are fed in their cells. Unlike the past, inmates must be adequately fed and permitted some time out of their cells to exercise.

selective incapacitation Identifying high-rate offenders and providing for their long-term incarceration.

self-help programs Programs from which inmates seek self-improvement, such as anger management, or express ethnic or cultural goals.

sentencing guidelines Federal and state guidelines were created to limit judicial discretion so that persons committing similar crimes received similar terms of incarceration. They created structured punishments: the more severe the crime, the longer the sentence.

sentencing sanctions The various types of sentences that can be awarded by the courts.

SENTRY This system tracks and provides appropriate staff with access to critical inmate information, such as assignments, program completions, and inmate movement in every Federal Bureau of Prisons facility or while an inmate is in transit.

service project A worthy cause, such as disaster relief or peer counseling, in which inmates willingly participate.

sex offenders A variety of offenders including pedophiles and rapists.

sexual victimization Forcing an inmate to submit sexually to one or more inmates.

shock probation The offender, his or her attorney, or the sentencing judge can submit a motion to suspend the remainder of a sentence after a felon has served a period of time in prison

signature bond Generally given for minor offenses and based on the defendant's written promise to appear in court.

situational model A model that suggests that prison culture is influenced by situations rather than remaining constant and can vary over time and place.

special needs inmates These include HIV inmates and inmates with chronic mental health issues.

special offense inmates Inmates who are involved in substance abuse, are sex offenders, or are terrorists.

special population inmates These include the elderly prisoner and the illegal immigrant inmate.

specific deterrence The idea that an individual offender will decide against repeating an offense after experiencing the painfulness of punishment for that offense.

split sentence A sentence requiring an offender to spend a period of time in jail before being placed on probation in the community.

Stanford v. Kentucky U.S. Supreme Court decision allowing the execution of juveniles who were age 17 at the time of the crime.

status offender A juvenile who engages in an act that is considered illegal because of his or her age, such as running away, disobedience, or truancy.

statutes States may award rights to prisoners beyond those granted by the U.S. Constitution or state constitution.

statutorial exclusion Certain juvenile offenses in some states are automatically transferred to adult court.

substantive rights A right, such as life, liberty, or property, that is held to exist for its own sake and to constitute part of the legal order of society.

supermax prison Most secure of all prison systems, in which there is typically a 23-hour lockdown.

supervised release Requires more frequent contact with pretrial officers, phone calls, and officer interviews.

sureties Individuals who would agree to make themselves responsible for offenders who had been released from custody.

Sykes, Gresham Developed a typology of prison social roles and inmate culture.

technical violation A probationer violates one of the rules of probation, such as leaving the district without permission, drinking in a tavern, or losing employment.

telephone-pole design This prison has a long central corridor serving as the means for prisoners to go from one part of the prison to another. Extending out from the corridor are cross-arms containing housing, school, shops, and recreation areas.

terrorist One who acts with premeditated and politically directed violence directed against noncombatants.

therapeutic community (TC) A community treatment group designed to divert drug users from the criminal justice system; therapeutic communities vary in how much control they are given in prison settings.

third-party custody Takes place when the court assigns custody of the defendant to an individual or agency that promises to ensure his or her appearance in court.

Thompson v. Oklahoma U.S. Supreme Court decision that prohibits execution of juveniles under age 16 at the time of the offense.

three-strikes laws Rules for repeat offenders that require long sentences without parole for conviction of a third or higher-order felony.

ticket of leave In Maconochie's system of graduated release, this was the final stage.

ticking bomb scenario This scenario proposes that a dangerous explosive device is set to go off and kill thousands of people and, therefore, it might be necessary to take extreme measures, such as torture, on a subject to extract information from him or her.

total institution Term coined by Irving Goffman to describe an institution that has total control over all aspects of those confined there.

Treatment Alternatives to Street Crime (TASC) A treatment program designed to divert minor drug abusers away from the criminal justice system.

treatment specialist A probation officer with specific skills and education who works with line staff to determine proper treatment placements for clients in the community.

true diversion A diversion program where the offender has his or her criminal prosecution dropped upon successful completion of this program.

truth-in-sentencing A close connection between the imposed sentence and the actual time served in prison. The time that offenders actually serve on their sentence.

UNICOR The trade name used by Federal Prison Industries.

unsecured bail Allows defendants' release without a deposit or bail arranged through a bondsman.

Ward and Kassebaum Classic study that claimed women adapted to imprisonment by forming homosexual alliances.

wilderness programs Programs that occur in a wooded area, the mountains, desert, or a lake where adolescents are taught survival skills and cooperation with others.

NAME INDEX

In this index *n* or *nn* following a page reference indicates one or more note numbers on a page. Also, *f* indicates figures, *p* indicates photograph, and *t* indicates table.

D

E

F

G

H

SUBJECT INDEX

In this index *f* represents figures, *p* represents photographs, and *t* represents tables

D

E

H

I

J

S

T

U

V

W

Y